国家出版基金项目
NATIONAL PUBLICATION FOUNDATION

| 李顿调查团档案文献集 |

主编 张 生

国联调查团报告书

编者 张 生 陈海懿 杨 骏

南京大学出版社

本书由

国家社会科学基金"抗日战争研究"专项工程
"国外有关中国抗日战争史料整理与研究之一:李顿调查团档案翻译与研究"(16KZD017)

教育部人文社会科学重点研究基地"南京大学中华民国史研究中心"
重大项目"战时中国社会"(19JJD770006)

南京大学人文基金

江苏省优势学科基金第三期

资助

编译委员会

常国栋　南京大学历史学院博士研究生

苏　凯　南京大学历史学院博士研究生

马　瑞　南京大学历史学院博士研究生

菅先锋　南京大学历史学院博士研究生

吴佳佳　南京大学历史学院博士研究生

张圣东　日本明治大学文学研究科博士研究生

张一闻　日本明治大学文学研究科博士研究生

叶　磊　中山大学历史学系博士研究生

史鑫鑫　南京大学历史学院硕士研究生

李剑星　南京大学历史学院硕士研究生

马海天　南京大学历史学院硕士研究生

张雅婷　南京大学历史学院硕士研究生

杨师琪　南京大学历史学院硕士研究生

潘　健　南京大学历史学院硕士研究生

唐　杨　南京师范大学马克思主义学院硕士研究生

郝宝平　江苏科技大学马克思主义学院硕士研究生

陈梦玲　江苏科技大学马克思主义学院硕士研究生

张　任　江南大学马克思主义学院硕士研究生

黎纹丹　西南大学外国语学院硕士研究生

朱心怡　西南大学外国语学院硕士研究生

杨　溢　西南大学外国语学院硕士研究生

孙学良　西南大学外国语学院硕士研究生

孙　莹　西南大学外国语学院硕士研究生

费　凡　浙江师范大学人文学院硕士研究生

竺丽妮　浙江师范大学外国语学院硕士研究生

戴瑶瑶　浙江师范大学外国语学院硕士研究生

杨　越　西安电子科技大学

曹文博　浙江工业大学外国语学院

余松琦　西南大学含宏学院

序　言

中国历史的奥秘，深藏于大兴安岭两侧的广袤原野。

明治维新以来，日本企图步老牌帝国主义后尘，争夺所谓"生存空间"；俄国自彼得大帝新政，不断东进，寻找阳光地带和不冻港。日俄竞争于中国东北，流血漂杵；日本逐步占得上风，九一八事变发生，中国面临亡国灭种的新危机。

日本侵华之际，世界已进入全球化的新时代，民族国家成为国际社会的主体，以国际条约体系规范各国的行为，以政治和外交手段解决彼此的分歧，是国际社会付出重大代价以后得出的共识。而法西斯、军国主义国家如德、意、日，昧于世界大势，穷兵黩武，以求一逞。以故意制造的借口，发动侵华战争，霸占中国东北百余万平方公里土地、数千万人民，是日本昭显于世的侵略事实。

国际联盟（League of Nations）应中国方面之吁请，派出国联调查团处理此事。1932 年 1 月 21 日，国联调查团正式成立。调查团团长由英国人李顿爵士（The Rt. Hon. The Earl of Lytton）担任，故亦称李顿调查团（Lytton Commission）。除李顿外，美国代表为麦考益将军（Gen. McCoy），法国代表为亨利·克劳德将军（Gen. Claudel），德国代表为希尼博士（Dr. Schnee），意大利代表为马柯迪伯爵（H. E. Count Aldrovandi）。为显示在中日间不做左右祖，国联理事会还决定顾维钧作为顾问代表中国参加工作，吉田伊三郎代表日方。代表团秘书长为国联秘书处哈斯（Mr. Robert Haas）。代表团另有翻译、辅助人员。1932 年 9 月 4 日，代表团完成报告书，签署于中国北平。报告书确认：第一，九一八事变之责任，完全在于日本，而不在中国；第二，伪满洲国政权非由真正及自然之独立运动所产生；第三，申明东三省为中国领土。日本为此恼羞成怒，退出国联，自

绝于国际社会。

《李顿调查团档案文献集》就是反映李顿调查团组建、调查过程、调查结论、各方反应和影响的中、日等国相关资料的汇编,对于研究九一八事变和李顿调查团,具有重要的参考价值。

如何看待李顿调查团来东亚调查的来龙去脉?笔者认为应有三个维度的观照:

其一,在中国发现历史。

美国历史学家柯文提出的这一范式,相比"冲击—反应"模式,即从外部冲击观察中国历史的旧范式,自有其意义。近代以来,由条约体系加持的列强,对中国社会产生了巨大的影响。中国沿海通商口岸是中国最早接触西方世界的部分,在资本主义全球化的过程中得风气之先,所谓"西风东渐",对中国旧有典章制度的影响无远弗届。近代中国在西方裹挟下步履踉跄,蹒跚竭蹶,自为事实。但如果把中国近代历史仅仅看成西方列强冲击之结果,在理论、方法和事实上,均为重大缺陷。

主要从中国内部,探寻历史演进的机制和规律,是柯文提出的范式的意义所在。

事实上,九一八事变发生、国联调查团来华前后,中国社会内部对此作出了剧烈的反应。在瑞士日内瓦所藏国联巨量档案文献中,中国各界通过电报、快邮代电、信函等形式具名或匿名送达代表团的呈文引人注目,集中表达了国难当头之时中华民族谴责日本侵略、要求国际社会主持公道、收回东北主权、确保永久和平的诉求,对代表团、国联和整个国际社会形成了巨大影响,显示了近代中国社会演进的内在动力。

东北各界身受亡国之痛,电函尤多。基层民众虽文化程度不高,所怀民族国家大义却毫不含糊。东北某兵工厂机器匠张光明致信代表团称:"我是中华民国的公民,我不是'满洲国'人,我不拥护这国的伪组织。"高超尘说:"不少日子以前,'满洲国家'即已成立了,但那完全是日本人的主使,强迫我辽地居民承认。街上的行人,日人随便问'您是哪国人',你如说是'满洲人'便罢,如说是中国人,便行暴打以至死。"辽宁城西北大橡村国民小学校致函称:"逐出日本军,打到[倒]'满洲国',宁做战死鬼,不做亡国民。"陈子耕揭露说:"自事变

以后,日本恶势力已伸张入全东北,如每县的政事皆由日人权势下所掌握,复又收买警察、军人、政客等,以假托民意来欺骗世界人的耳目,硬说建设'满洲国'是中华人民的意思,强迫人民全出去游行,打着欢迎建设'新国家'的旗号……我誓死不忘我的中华祖国,敢说华人莫非至心不跳时、血停时,不然一定于[与]他们周旋。"小学生何子明来信说:"我小学生告诉您们'满洲国'成立我不赞成……有一天我在学校,日本人去了,教我们大家一齐说'大日本万岁',我们要不说他就杀我们,把我迫不得已的就说了。其中有一位七岁的小孩,他说'大中华万岁!打倒小日本!'日本人听了就立刻把那个小同学杀了,真叫我想起来就愁啊。"

经济地位和文化水平较高者,则向代表团分析日本侵占中国东北的深远危害。哈尔滨商民代表函称:"虽然,满洲吞并,恐不惟中国之不利。即各国之经济,亦将受其影响。世界二次大战,迫于眉睫矣。"中国国民党青年团哈尔滨市支部分析说:"查日本军阀向有一贯之对外积极侵略政策,吾人细玩以前田中义一之满蒙大陆政策,及最近本庄繁等上日本天皇之奏折,可以看出其对外一贯之积极侵略政策,即第一步占领满蒙,第二步并吞中国,第三步征服世界是也。……以今日之日本蕞尔岛国,世界各国尚且畏之如虎,而况并有三省之后版图增大数倍,恐不数年后,即将向世界各国进攻,有孰敢撄其锋镝乎?……勿徒视为亚洲人之事,无关痛痒,失国联之威信,而贻噬脐之后悔也。"

不惟东北民众,民族危亡激起了全中国人的爱国心。清华大学自治会1932年4月12日用英文致函代表团指出:中国面临巨大的困难,好似1806年的德国和1871年的法国,但就像"青年意大利"党人一样,青年人对国家的重建充满信心。日本的侵略,不仅危害了中国,也对世界和平形成严重威胁,青年人愿意为国家流尽"最后一滴血"。而国联也面临着建立以来最大的危机,对九一八事变的处理,将考验它处理全球问题的能力。公平和正义能否实现,将影响到人类的命运。他们向代表团严正提出"五点要求":1. 日本从中国撤军;2. 上海问题与东北问题一起解决;3. 不承认日本侵略和用武力改变的现状;4. 任何解决不得损害中国的领土和主权完整;5. 日本必须对此事件的后果负责。南京海外华侨协会1932年3月16日致电代表团:日本进兵东三省和淞沪地区,"违反了国联盟约和《凯洛格—白里安公约》",扰乱了远东地区和世界的和平。

同时,日本一直在做虚假的宣传,竭力蒙蔽整个世界。我们诚挚地请求你们到现场来,亲眼看看日军对中国人民的生命财产进行怎样的恣意破坏。希望你们按照国际法及司法原则,对其进行制裁。如果你们不能完成这一使命,那么世界上将无任何公平正义可言。在这种情况下,为了民族的生存,我们将采取一切手段自卫,决不会向武力屈服。"

除了档案,中国当时的杂志、报纸,大量地报道了九一八事变和国联调查团相关情况,其关切的细致程度,说明了各界的高度投入。那些浸透着时人忧虑、带着鲜明时代特色的文字表明:九一八事变的发生,对当时的中国社会是一场精神洗礼,每个人都从东北沦陷中感受到切肤之痛。这种舆论和思想的汇合,极大地改变了此后中国社会各界的主要诉求,抗日图存成为压倒性的任务,每一种政治力量都必须对此作出回应。

其二,在世界发现中国历史。

以中国为本位,探讨中国历史的内生力量,是题中应有之义。但全球化以来,中国历史已经成为世界历史的一部分。仅仅依靠中国方面的资料,不利于我们以更加广阔的视野看待中国历史和"九一八"的历史。

事实上,奔赴世界各地"动手动脚找东西",已经成为中国学者深化中国近现代史,特别是抗战史研究的不二法门。比如,在中日历史问题中占据核心地位的南京大屠杀问题。除中国各地档案馆、图书馆外,中国学者深入美、德、英、日、俄、法、西、意、丹等国相关机构,系统全面地整理了加害者日方、受害者中方和第三方档案文献,发现了大量珍贵文献、图像资料,出版《南京大屠杀史料集》72卷。不仅证明了日军进行大屠杀的残酷性、蓄意性和计划性,也证明南京大屠杀早在发生之时,就引起了各国政府和社会舆论的关注;南京和东京两场审判,进行了繁复的质证,确保了程序和判决的正义;日方细致的粉饰,在中国人民和全世界正义人士的揭露下真相毕露。全球性的资料,不仅深化了历史研究,也为文学、社会学、心理学、新闻传播学、艺术学等跨学科方法进入相关研究提供基础;不仅摧毁了右翼的各种谬论,也迫使日本政府不敢公然否认南京大屠杀的发生和战争犯罪性质。

国际抗战资料,展现了中国抗战史的丰富侧面。如美国驻中国各地使领馆的报告,具体生动地记录了战时中国各区域的社会、政治、军事等各方面情

形,对战时国共关系亦有颇有见地的分析;俄、美、日等国档案馆的细菌战资料,揭示了战时日本违反国际法研制细菌武器的规模和使用情况,记录了中国各地民众遭遇的重大伤亡和中国军民在当时条件下的应对,以及暗示了战后美国掩饰"死亡工厂"实情的目的;英美等国档案所反映的重庆大轰炸和日军对中国大中小城市的普遍的无差别轰炸,不仅记录了日本战争犯罪的普遍性,也彰显了战时中国全国军民同仇敌忾、不畏强暴的英勇气概。哈佛大学所藏费吴生档案、得克萨斯州州立大学奥斯汀分校所藏辛德贝格档案、曼彻斯特档案馆所藏田伯烈档案等则从个人角度凸显了中国抗战在"第三方"眼中的图景。

对于李顿调查团的研究,自莫能外。比如,除了前述中国各界给国联的呈文,最近在日内瓦"国联和联合国档案馆"中发现:调查团在日本与日本政要的谈话记录,在中国各地特别是在北平和九一八事变直接相关人士如张学良、王以哲、荣臻等人的谈话记录,调查团在东北实地调查、询问日军高层的记录,中共在"九一八"前后的活动,中国各界的陈情书,日本官方和东北伪组织人员、汉奸的表态,世界各国、各界的反应等。特别是张学良等人反复向代表团说明的九一八事变前夕东北军高层力避冲突的态度,王以哲、荣臻在"九一八"当晚与张学良的联系,北大营遭受日军进攻以后东北军的反应等情况,对于厘清九一八事变真相,有着不可取代的意义。

我们通过初步努力发现,李顿调查团成立前后,中方向国联提交了论证东北主权属于中国的篇幅巨大的系统性说帖,顾维钧、孟治、徐道邻等还用英文、德文进行著述。日方相应地提交了由日本旅美"学者"起草的说帖,其主攻点是中国的抗日运动、东北在张氏父子治下的惨淡、东北的"匪患",避而不谈柳条沟事件的蓄意性。日方资料表明,即使在九一八事变发生数月后,其关于"九一八"当晚情形的说辞仍然漏洞百出、逻辑混乱,在李顿询问时不能自圆其说。而欧美学者则向国联提供了第三方意见,如 *The Verdict of the League: China and Japan in Manchuria*(《国联的裁决:中日在满洲》),哈佛大学法学院教授曼利·哈德森(Manley O. Hudson)著;*Manchuria: Cradle of Conflict*(《满洲:冲突的策源地》),欧文·拉铁摩尔(Owen Lattimore)著;*The Manchuria Arena: An Australian View of the Far Eastern Conflict*(《满洲竞技场:远东冲突的澳洲视

角》),卡特拉克(F.M. Cutlack)著;*The Tinder Box of Asia*(《亚洲的火药桶》),乔治·索科尔斯基(George E. Sokolsky,中文名索克斯)著;*The World's Danger Zone*(《世界的危险地带》),舍伍德·艾迪(Sherwood Eddy)著;等等,为国联理解中国东北问题提供了有益的视角。另外,收藏在美国斯坦福大学胡佛研究所的蒋介石日记等也反映了当时国民政府高层的态度和举措。

这次出版的资料中,收集了中国台湾地区的"国史馆"藏档,日本外务省藏档,国联和联合国档案馆 S 系列藏档等多卷档案。丰沛的资料说明,即使是李顿调查团这样过去在大学教材中只是以一两段话提出的问题,其实仍有海量的各种海外文献可资研究。

可以说,世界各地抗日档案和各种资料,不仅补充了中国方面的抗日资料,也弥补了"在中国发现历史"范式的不足,体现了历史唯物主义对历史研究全面性、客观性的要求,自然地延伸推导出"在世界发现中国历史"的新命题。把"中国的"和"世界的"结合起来,才能更深广、入微地揭示抗日战争史的内涵。

其三,在中国发现世界历史。

中国历史,是世界历史的重要组成部分;中国抗战,构成了第二次世界大战的东亚主战场。离开中国历史谈世界历史注定是不周全的。只有充分发掘中国历史的世界意义,世界史才能获得真正的全球史意义。

过往的抗战史国际化,说明了中国抗战的世界意义。研究发现,东北抗联资料不仅呈现了十四年抗战的艰苦过程,也说明了战时东北亚复杂的国际关系。日方资料中的"华北治安战""清乡作战"资料,从反面反映了八路军、新四军的顽强,其牵制大量日军的事实,从另一面说明中共敌后游击战所发挥的中流砥柱作用。1937 年 12 月 12 日在南京江面制造"巴纳号事件"的日军航空兵官兵,后来是制造"珍珠港事件"的主力之一,说明了中国抗战与太平洋战争的联系。参与制造九一八事变、华北事变和南京大屠杀的许多日军部队,后来在太平洋战场上被美澳等盟国军队消灭,说明了太平洋战场和中国战场的相互支持。中国军队在滇缅战场的作战和在越南等地的受降,中国对朝鲜、马来亚、越南等地游击战和抗日斗争的介入和帮助,说明了中国抗战对东亚、东南亚解放的意义和价值。对大后方英美军人、"工合"人士、新闻界和其他各界人

士的研究,彰显了抗日统一战线的多重维度,等等。这对我们的研究富有启发性意义。

李顿调查团的相关资料表明,九一八事变及其后续发展,具有深刻的世界史含义。

麦金德1902年在英国皇家地理学会发表文章,提出"世界岛"的概念。麦金德认为,地球由两部分构成:由欧洲、亚洲、非洲组成的世界岛,是世界上面积最大、人口最多、最富饶的陆地组合。在"世界岛"的中央,是自伏尔加河到长江,自喜马拉雅山脉到北极的心脏地带,在世界史的发展中具有重要意义。其实,就世界近现代史而言,中国东北具有极其重要的地缘战略意义,堪称"世界之砧"——美国、俄罗斯、日本等这些当今世界的顶级力量,无不在中国东北及其周边地区倾注心力,影响世界大局。

今天看来,李顿调查团的组建,是国际社会运用国际规约积极调解大国冲突、维护当时既存的凡尔赛—华盛顿体系的一次尝试。参与各国均为当时世界强国,即为明证。

英国作为列强中在华条约利益最丰的国家,积极投入国联调查团的建立。张伯伦、麦克米伦等知名政治家均极愿加入代表团,甚至跟外交部官员暗通款曲,询问排名情况。李顿在中日间多地奔波,主导调查和报告书的起草,正是这一背景的反映。

美国作为国联非成员国,积极介入调查团,说明了美国对远东局势的关切,其态度和不承认日本用武力改变当时中国领土主权现状的"史汀生主义"是一致的。日美之间的紧张关系,一直延续到珍珠港事变发生。在日美最终谈判中,中国的领土和主权,仍然是美方的先决条件。可以说,九一八事变,从大历史的角度看,是改变日本和美国国运的大事。

苏联在国联未能采取强力措施制止日本侵略后,默认了伪满洲国的存在,后甚至通过对日条约加以承认,其对日本的忍让和妥协,延续到它对日本宣战。但日本关东军主力在苏联牵制下不敢贸然南下,影响了中国抗日战争的形态。

日本侵占中国东北,却始终得不到中国和国际主流社会的承认,乃不断扩大侵略,不仅影响了对苏备战,也使得其在"重庆政权之所以不投降,是因为有

英美支持"的判断下,不断南进,最终自取灭亡。2015年8月14日,日本首相安倍晋三在战后70年讲话中承认:"日本迷失了世界大局。满洲事变以及退出国际联盟——日本逐渐变成国际社会经过巨大灾难而建立起来的新的国际秩序的挑战者,前进的方向有错误,而走上了战争的道路。其结果,70年前,日本战败了。"从这个意义上说,九一八事变—李顿调查—退出国联,成为日本近代史的转折点。

亚马孙雨林的蝴蝶振动翅膀,可能在西太平洋引发一场风暴。发生在沈阳一个小地方的九一八事变,成为今天国际秩序的肇因。其故焉在?马克思和恩格斯在《德意志意识形态》中指出:在历史演进的过程中,人的"普遍交往"逐步发展起来,"狭隘地域性的个人为世界历史性的、真正普遍的个人所代替"。近代以来中国人民的历史,与世界历史共构而存续。

回望李顿调查团的历史,我仿佛感受到了太平洋洋底的咆哮呼啸前来,如同雷鸣。

是为序。

张　生
2019年10月

出版凡例

一、本文献集所选资料，原文中的人名、地名、别字、错字及不规范用字等，为尊重历史和文献原貌，均原文照录。因此而影响读者判断、引用之处，除个别需说明情况以脚注"译者按"或"编者按"形式标出外，别字、错字在其后以"[ ]"注明正字；增补的字，以"【 】"标明之；因原文献漫漶不清而缺字处，用"□"标识。

二、凡采用民国纪年或日本天皇年号纪年者等，为尊重历史和文献原貌，均原文照录。台湾地区的文献中涉及政治人物头衔和机构名称者，按有关规定处理，在页下一并说明。

三、所选资料均在起始处说明来源，或在文后标注其详细来源信息。

四、外文文献译文中，日本人名从西文文献译出者，保留其西文拼法，以便核对；其余外国人名，均在某专题或文件中第一次出现时标其西文拼法。不同时期形成的中文文献中涉及的外国人名、地名翻译差异较大，为尊重历史和文献原貌，一般不作改动。

五、所选文献经过前人编辑而加脚注注释者，以"原编辑者注"保留在页下。

六、所选资料中原有污蔑中国人民、美化日本侵略之词，或基于立场表达其看法之处，为尊重历史和文献原貌，不改动原文，或在页下特别说明，请读者加以鉴别。

本册说明

本册文献集呈现了英文、中文和日文三种文字版本的《国联调查团报告书》，希望本册多语种《国联调查团报告书》可以方便使用者进行比对和研究。

根据国际联盟的决议，1932 年 1 月 21 日，国联调查团正式宣告成立，该调查团由英、美、法、德、意五个国家的代表组成，由于团长是英国人李顿爵士，故又被称为李顿调查团。经过多种途径的调查，调查团于 1932 年 8 月开始草拟报告书，并于 10 月 2 日在东京、南京和日内瓦同时发表《国联调查团报告书》，共 10 章正文内容和 14 幅地图。

《国联调查团报告书》肯定了东北是中国领土一部分，主权属于中国，并且对事变经过和伪满洲国也有公正和客观的叙述，但报告书认为中国抵制日货运动是"中日冲突的重要原因"，苏联的"共产主义传播"是造成九一八事变的最重要因素。对于九一八事变的解决，该报告书的主张是既不应该维持伪满洲国的现状，也不应恢复到九一八事变以前的状态，而是中日两国都应该从中国东北撤出武装力量，中国东北由西方列强共管。报告书还具体提出了解决中日冲突的十条原则，即（一）适合中日双方之利益；（二）考虑苏俄利益；（三）遵守现行之多方面条约；（四）承认日本在满洲之利益；（五）树立中日间之新条约关系；（六）切实规定解决将来纠纷之办法；（七）满洲自治；（八）内部之秩序与免于外来侵略之安全；（九）奖励中日间之经济协调；（十）以国际合作促进中国之建设。

总之，国际联盟根据《国联调查团报告书》得出一个结论：日本是侵略国，满洲应由国联共管。因对国联不满，日本政府决定放弃与国联合作。1933 年 2 月 24 日，国联大会以 42 票赞成，日本 1 票反对，通过了十九国委员会关于接受《国联调查团报告书》的决议。在此之后，日本发出了退出国联的通告，并进一步实施侵华政策。《国联调查团报告书》对日本、中国和东亚秩序产生了深远影响。

本册所编纂的三种文字《国联调查团报告书》的来源分别是：1. 英文版《国联调查团报告书》(*Report of the Commission of Enquiry*)，录自日内瓦当地时间 1932 年 10 月 1 日公布的官方版本，现藏日内瓦国联图书馆；2. 中文版《国联调查团报告书》，录自国民政府外交部翻译的《国际联盟调查团报告书》，并由上海明社出版部于 1932 年 10 月 15 日公开出版；3. 日文版《国联调查团报告书》(リットン報告書)录自日本外务省翻译的《国联调查团报告书》，并于 1932 年 10 月 6 日由东治书院印刷发行。

目　录

国联调查团报告书(英文版)
Report of the Commission of Enquiry[①]

LIST OF MAPS[②]
(The fourteen Maps are inserted in the pocket of the cover.)

1. China and Japan.
2. Political Map of Manchuria.
3. Railway Map of Manchuria.
4. Relief Map of Manchuria.
5. Military Situation in Manchuria before September 18th, 1931.
6. Chart of the Mukden Incident (September 18th—19th, 1931).
7. Military Situation in Manchuria about September 30th, 1931.
8. Military Situation in Manchuria about December 10th, 1931.
9. Military Situation in Manchuria about May 1st, 1932.
10. Military Situation in Manchuria about August 20th, 1932.
11. Shanghai Area.
12. City of Shanghai.
13. Principal Route Map Showing Itineraries of the Commission in the Far East.

---

① 编者按:《国联调查团报告书》(英文版)录自日内瓦 1932 年 10 月 1 日公布的官方版本,该版本现藏于日内瓦国联图书馆。

② 编者按:《国联调查团报告书》的地图有清晰版本,研究者若有需要,可以联系编者获取,此处从略。

14. Supplementary Route Map showing Itineraries of the Commission in the Far East.

INTRODUCTION

Formal appeal by China, September 21st, 1931.

On September 21st, 1931, the representative of the Chinese Government at Geneva wrote to the Secretary-General of the League of Nations asking him to bring to the attention of the Council the dispute between China and Japan which had arisen from the events which took place at Mukden on the night of September 18th—19th, and appealed to the Council, under Article 11 of the Covenant, to "take immediate steps to prevent the further development of a situation endangering the peace of nations".

Resolution of the Council, September 30th.

On September 30th, the Council passed the following resolution:

"The Council:

"(1) Notes the replies of the Chinese and Japanese Governments to the urgent appeal addressed to them by its President and the steps that have already been taken in response to that appeal;

"(2) Recognizes the importance of the Japanese Government's statement that it has no territorial designs in Manchuria;

"(3) Notes the Japanese representative's statement that his Government will continue, as rapidly as possible, the withdrawal of its troops, which has already been begun, into the railway zone in proportion as the safety of the lives and property of Japanese nationals is effectively assured and that it hopes to carry out this intention in full as speedily as may be;

"(4) Notes the Chinese representative's statement that his Government will assume responsibility for the safety of the lives and property of Japanese nationals outside that zone as the withdrawal of the Japanese troops continues and the Chinese local authorities and police forces are re-established;

"(5) Being convinced that both Governments are anxious to avoid taking any action which might disturb the peace and good understanding between the two nations, notes that the Chinese and Japanese representatives have given assurances that their respective Governments will take all necessary steps to prevent any extension of the scope of the incident or any aggravation of the situation;

"(6) Requests both Parties to do all in their power to hasten the restoration of normal relations between them and for that purpose to continue and speedily complete the execution of the above-mentioned undertakings;

"(7) Requests both Parties to furnish the Council at frequent intervals with full information as to the development of the situation;

"(8) Decides, in the absence of any unforeseen occurrence which might render an immediate meeting essential, to meet again at Geneva on Wednesday, October 14th, 1931, to consider the situation as it then stands;

"(9) Authorizes its President to cancel the meeting of the Council fixed for October 14th, should he decide, after consulting his colleagues, and more particularly the representatives of the two Parties, that in view of such information as he may have received from the Parties or from other Members of the Council as to the development of the situation, the meeting is no longer necessary. "

In the course of the discussions that preceded the adoption of this resolution, the Chinese representative expressed the view of his Government that "the best method that may be devised by the Council for securing the prompt and complete withdrawal of the Japanese troops and police and the full re-establishment of the *status quo ante* is the sending of a neutral commission to Manchuria".

Session of the Council, October 13th—24th.

The Council held a further session for the consideration of dispute from October 13th to the 24th. In consequence of the opposition of the Japanese representative, unanimity could not be obtained for resolution proposed at thus session.

Session of the Council at Paris, November 16th—December 10th.

The Council met again on November 16th in Paris and devoted nearly four weeks to a study of the situation. On November 21st, the Japanese representative, after stating that his Government was anxious that the resolution of September 30th should be observed in the spirit and letter, proposed that a Commission of Enquiry should be sent to the spot. This proposal was subsequently welcomed by all the other Members of the Council and, on December 10th, 1931, the following resolution was unanimously adopted:

Resolution of December 10th.

"The Council:

"(1) Reaffirms the resolution passed unanimously by it on September 30th, 1931, by which the two Parties declare that they are solemnly bound; it therefore calls upon the Chinese and Japanese Governments to take all steps necessary to assure its execution so that the withdrawal of the Japanese troops within the railway zone may be effected as speedily as possible under the conditions set forth in the said resolution;

"(2) Considering that events have assumed an even more serious aspect since the Council meeting of October 24th, notes that the two Parties undertake to adopt all measures necessary to avoid any further aggravation of the situation and to refrain from any initiative which may lead to further fighting and loss of life;

"(3) Invites the two Parties to continue to keep the Council informed as to the development of the situation;

"(4) Invites the other Members of the Council to furnish the Council with any information received from their representatives on the spot;

"(5) Without prejudice to the carrying out of the above-mentioned measures;

"Desiring, in view of the special circumstances of the case, to contribute towards a final and fundamental solution by the two Government of the questions at issue between them:

"Decides to appoint a Commission of five members to study on the spot and to report to the Council on any circumstance which, affecting international relations, threatens to disturb peace between China and Japan, or the good understanding between them upon which peace depends;

"The Governments of China and of Japan will each have the right to nominate one Assessor to assist the Commission;

"The two Governments will afford the Commission all facilities to obtain on the spot whatever information it may require;

"It is understood that, should the two Parties initiate any negotiations, these would not fall within the scope of the terms of reference of the Commission, nor would it be within the competence of the Commission to interfere with the military arrangements of either Party;

"The appointment and deliberation of the Commission shall not prejudice in any way the undertaking given by the Japanese Government in the resolution of September 30th as regards the withdrawal of the Japanese troops within the railway zone;

"(6) Between now and its next ordinary session, which will be held on January 25th, 1932, the Council, which remains seized of the matter, invites its President to follow the question and to summon it afresh if necessary."

Declaration of the President.

In introducing this resolution, the President, M. Briand, made the following declaration:

"It will be observed that the resolution which is before you provides for action on two separate lines: (1) to put an end to the immediate threat to peace; (2) to facilitate the final solution of existing causes of dispute between the two countries.

"The Council was glad to find during its present sittings that an enquiry into the circumstances which tend to disturb the relations between China and Japan, in itself desirable, would be acceptable to the Parties. The Council therefore welcomed the proposal to establish a Commission which was brought before it on November 21st. The final paragraph of the resolution provides for the appointment and functioning of such a Commission.

"I shall now make certain comments on the resolution, paragraph by paragraph.

"Paragraph 1. —This paragraph reaffirms the resolution unanimously adopted by the Council on September 30th, laying particular stress on the withdrawal of the Japanese troops within the railway zone on the conditions described therein as speedily as possible.

"The Council attaches the utmost importance to this resolution and is persuaded that the two Governments will set themselves to the complete fulfilment of the engagements which they assumed on September 30th.

"Paragraph 2. —It is an unfortunate fact that, since the last meeting of the Council, events have occurred which have seriously aggravated the situation and have given rise to legitimate apprehension. It is indispensable and urgent to abstain from any initiative which may lead to further fighting, and from all other action likely to aggravate the situation.

"Paragraph 4. —Under paragraph 4, the Members of the Council other than the Parties are requested to continue to furnish the Council with information received from their representatives on the spot.

"Such information having proved of high value in the past, the Powers which have the possibility of sending such representatives to various localities have agreed to do all that is possible to continue and improve the present system.

"For this purpose, these Powers will keep in touch with the two Parties, so that the latter may, should they so desire, indicate to them the localities to which they would desire the despatch of such representatives.

"Paragraph 5 provides for the institution of a Commission of Enquiry. Subject to its purely advisory character, the terms of reference of the Commission are wide. In principle, no question which it feels called upon to study will be excluded, provided that the question relates to any circumstances which, affecting international relations, threaten to disturb peace between China and Japan, or the good understanding between them upon which peace depends. Each of the two Governments will have the right to request the Commission to consider any question the examination of which it particularly desires. The Commission will have full discretion to determine the questions upon which it will report to the Council, and will have power to make interim reports when desirable.

"If the undertakings given by the two Parties according to the resolution of September 30th have not been carried out by the time of the arrival of the Commission, the Commission should as speedily as possible report to the Council on the situation.

"It is specially provided that, 'should the two Parties initiate any negotiations, these would not fall within the scope of the terms of reference of the Commission, nor would it be within the competence of the Commission to interfere with the military arrangements of either Party'. This latter provision does not limit in any way its faculty of investigation. It is also clear that the Commission will enjoy full liberty of movement in order to obtain the information it may require for its reports."

Reservations and comments of the two Parties.

The Japanese representative, in accepting the resolution, made a reservation concerning paragraph 2 of the resolution, stating that he accepted it on behalf of his Government, "on the understanding that this paragraph was not intended to preclude the Japanese forces from taking such action as might be rendered necessary to provide directly for the protection of the lives and property of Japanese subjects against the activities of bandits and lawless elements rampant in various parts of Manchuria".

The Chinese representative, on his part, accepted the resolution, but asked that certain of his observations and reservations on points of principle should be placed on record as follows:

"Ⅰ. China must and does fully reserve any and all rights, remedies and juridical positions to which she is or may be entitled under and by virtue of all the provisions of the Covenant, under all the existing treaties to which China is a party, and under the accepted principles of international law and practice.

"Ⅱ. The present arrangement evidenced by the resolution and the statement made by the President of the Council is regarded by China as a practical measure embodying four essential and interdependent elements:

"(a) Immediate cessation of hostilities;

"(b) Liquidation of the Japanese occupation of Manchuria within the shortest possible period of time;

"(c) Neutral observation and reporting upon all developments from now on;

"(d) A comprehensive enquiry into the entire Manchurian situation on the spot by a Commission appointed by the Council.

"The said arrangement being in effect and in spirit predicated upon these fundamental factors, its integrity would be manifestly destroyed by the failure of any one of them to materialise and be effectively realised as contemplated.

"Ⅲ. China understands and expects that the Commission provided for in the resolution will make it its first duty to enquire into and report, with its recommendations, on the withdrawal of the Japanese forces, if such withdrawal has not been completed when the Commission arrives on the spot.

"Ⅳ. China assumes that the said arrangement neither directly nor by implication affects the question of reparations and damages to China and her nationals growing out of the recent events in Manchuria, and makes a specific reservation in that respect.

"Ⅴ. In accepting the resolution laid before us, China appreciates the efforts of the Council to prevent further fighting and bloodshed by enjoining both China and Japan to avoid any initiative which may lead to further fighting or any other action likely to aggravate the situation. It must be clearly pointed out that this injunction should not be violated under the pretext of the existence of lawlessness caused by a state of affairs which it is the very purpose of the resolution to do away with. It is to be observed that much of the lawlessness now prevalent in Manchuria is due to the interruption of normal life caused by the invasion of the Japanese forces. The only sure way of restoring the normal peaceful life is to hasten the withdrawal of the Japanese troops and allow the Chinese authorities to assume the responsibility for the maintenance of peace and order. China cannot tolerate the invasion and occupation of her territory by the troops of any foreign country; far less can she permit these troops to usurp the police functions of the Chinese authorities.

"Ⅵ. China notes with satisfaction the purpose to continue and improve the present system of neutral observation and reporting through representatives of other Powers, and China will from time to time, as occasion requires, indicate the localities to which it seems desirable to dispatch such representatives.

"Ⅶ. It should be understood that, in agreeing to this resolution which provides for the withdrawal of the Japanese forces to the railway zone, China in no way recedes from the position she has always taken with respect to the maintenance of military forces in the said railway zone.

"Ⅷ. China would regard any attempt by Japan to bring about complications of a political character affecting China's territorial or administrative integrity (such as promoting so-called independence movements or utilising disorderly elements for such purposes) as an obvious violation of the undertaking to avoid any further aggravation of the situation. "

Appointment of the Commission of Enquiry.

The Members of the Commission were subsequently selected by the President of the Council, and, after the approval of the two parties had been obtained, the membership was finally approved by the Council on January 14th, 1932, as follows:

H. E. Count ALDROVANDI (Italian),

Général de Division Henri CLAUDEL (French),

The Rt. Hon. The Earl of LYTTON, P. C. , G. C. S. I. , G. C. I. E. (British),

Major-General Frank Ross McCoy (American),

H. E. Dr. Heinrich SCHNEE (German).

Organisation of the Commission.

The European members, with a representative of the American member, held two sittings in Geneva on January 21st, at which Lord Lytton was unanimously elected Chairman and a provisional programme of work was approved. The Governments of Japan and China, each of which had, by virtue of the resolution of December 10th, "the right to nominate one Assessor to assist the Commission", subsequently appointed as their Assessors H. E. Mr. Isaburo Yoshida, Ambassador of Japan in Turkey, and H. E. Dr. Wellington Koo, a former Prime Minister and former Minister for Foreign Affairs of China.

The Secretary-General of the League designated M. Robert Haas,

Director in the Secretariat of the League, to act as Secretary-General of the Commission. ①

In the course of its work, the Commission was assisted by the technical advice of Professor G. H. Blakeslee, Professor at the Clark University, U. S. A. , Ph. D. , L. L. D. ; M. Dennery, Agrégé de l'Université de France; Mr. Ben Dorfman, B. A. , M. A. , William Harrison Mills Fellow, University of California, U. S. A. ; Dr. A. D. A. de Kat Angelino, Colonel T. A. Hiam, assistant to the Chairman of the Canadian National Railways; G. S. Moss, Esq. , C. B. E. , H. B. M. Consul in Weihaiwei; Dr. C. Walter Young, M. A. , Ph. D. , Far Eastern Representative of the Institute of Current World Affairs, New York City.

The European members of the Commission sailed from Le Havre and Plymouth on February 3rd, and were joined by the American member at New York on February 9th.

---

① 原编辑者注:The Secretary-General had put at the disposal of the Secretariat of the Commission:

Mr. Pelt, member of the Information Section; Mr. von Kotze, assistant to the Under-Secretary-General in charge of International Bureaux; Mr. Pastuhov, member of the Political Section; the Hon. W. W. Astor, temporary member of the Secretariat acting as Secretary of the Chairman of the Commission; and M. Charrère, of the Information Section.

Major P. Jouvelet, Army Medical Corps, French Army, acted as personal assistant to General Claudel, and Lieut. Biddle as personal assistant to General McCoy, and collaborated also in the general work of the Secretariat.

M. Depeyre, French Vice-Consul at Yokohama, acted as interpreter in the Japanese language.

Mr. Aoki and Mr. Wou Sao-fong, members of the Information Section, collaborated with the Secretariat of the Commission.

* Note by the Secretariat: For the itineraries of the Commission, see the Appendix, page 140, and Map Nos. 13 and 14.

Chinese Appeal to the League of Nations under Articles 10, 11 and 15 of the Covenant.

Meanwhile, the development of the situation in the Far East caused the Chinese Government, on January 29th, to submit a further appeal to the League of Nations under Articles 10, 11 and 15 of the Covenant. On February 12th, 1932, the Chinese representative requested the Council to submit the dispute to the Assembly in accordance with paragraph 9 of Article 15 of the Covenant. Since no further instructions were received from the Council, the Commission continued to interpret its mandate according to the resolution of the Council of December 10th. This included:

(1) An examination of the issues between China and Japan, which were referred to the Council, including their causes, development and status at the time of the enquiry;

(2) A consideration of a possible solution of the Sino-Japanese dispute which would reconcile the fundamental interests of the two countries.

This conception of its mission determined the programme of its work.

Arrival of the Commission at Tokyo, February 29th, 1932.

Before reaching Manchuria, the main theatre of the conflict, contact was established with the Governments of Japan and China and with representatives of various shades of opinion, in order to ascertain the nature of the interests of the two countries. The Commission arrived in Tokyo on February 29th, where it was joined by the Japanese Assessor. It had the honour of being received by His Majesty the Emperor. Eight days were spent in Tokyo, and daily conferences were held with members of the Government and others, including the Prime Minister, Mr. Inukai, the Minister for Foreign Affairs, Mr. Yoshizawa, the Minister of War, Lieutenant-General Araki, the Minister of Navy, Admiral Osumi. Interviews were also held with leading bankers, business-men, representatives of various organisations and others. From all of these we received information regarding the rights and interests of Japan in Manchuria and her historical associations with that country. The Shanghai situation was also discussed. After leaving Tokyo, we learned while in Kyoto of the establishment of a new " State " in Manchuria, under the name of "Manchukuo" (the Manchu State). In Osaka, conferences were arranged with representatives of the business community.

Shanghai, March 14th—26th.

The Commission reached Shanghai on March 14th and was joined there by the Chinese Assessor. Here a fortnight was occupied, in addition to our general enquiry, in learning as much as possible about the facts of the recent fighting and the possibility of an armistice, which we had previously discussed with Mr. Yoshizawa in Tokyo. We paid a visit to the devastated areas, and heard statements from the Japanese naval and military authorities regarding recent operations. We also interviewed some of the members of the Chinese Government and leaders of business, educational and other circles, including Canton.

Nanking, March 26th—April 1st.

On March 26th, the Commission proceeded to Nanking, some of its members visiting Hangchow on the way. During the following week, it had the honour of being received by the President of the National Government. Interviews were held with Mr. Wang Ching-wei, President of the Executive Yuan; General Chiang Kai-shek, Chairman of the Military Council; Dr. Lo Wen-kan, Minister for Foreign Affairs; Mr. T. V. Soong, Minister of Finance; General Cheng Ming-chu, Minister of Communications; Mr. Chu Chia-hua, Minister of Education; and other members of the Government.

Yangtze Valley, April 1st—7th.

In order to acquaint ourselves more fully with representative opinion and with conditions existing in various parts of China, we proceeded on April 1st to Hankow, stopping *en route* at Kiukiang. Some representatives of the Commission visited Ichang, Wanhsien and Chungking in the province of Hupeh and Szechuan.

Peiping, April 9th—19th.

On April 9th, the Commission arrived at Peiping (as Peking is now called), where several conferences were held with Marshal Chang Hsueh-liang and with officials who had been members of the administration in Manchuria until September 18th. Evidence was also given by the Chinese Generals who had been in command of the troops at the barracks at Mukden on the night of September 18th.

Our stay in Peiping was prolonged owing to a difficulty which arose regarding the entry into Manchuria of Dr. Wellington Koo, the Chinese Assessor.

In proceeding to Manchuria, the Commission divided into two groups, some of the party travelling to Mukden by rail via Shanhaikwan, and the remainder, including Dr. Koo, by sea via Dairen, thus remaining within the Japanese railway area. The objection to Dr. Koo's entry into "Manchukuo" territory was finally withdrawn after the arrival of the Commission in Changchun, the northern terminus of the Japanese railway area.

Manchuria, April 20th—June 4th.

We remained in Manchuria for about six weeks, visiting Mukden, Changchun, Kirin, Harbin, Dairen, Port Arthur, Anshan, Fushun and Chinchow. We had intended to visit Tsitsihar as well, but, while we were in Harbin, there was continuous fighting in the surrounding districts, and the Japanese military authorities stated that they were unable at that moment to guarantee the safety of the Commission by rail on the western branch of the Chinese Eastern Railway. Accordingly, some members of our staff visited Tsitsihar by air. From there they travelled by the Taonan-Angangchi and Ssupingkai-Taonan Railways and rejoined the main body in Mukden.

During our stay in Manchuria we wrote a Preliminary Report, which we despatched to Geneva on April 29th. ①

We had numerous conferences with Lieutenant-General Honjo, Commander of the Kwantung Army, other military officers, and Japanese consular officials. At Changchun we visited the Chief Executive of "Manchukuo", the former Emperor, Hsuan Tung, now known by his personal name of Henry Pu-yi. We also had interviews with members of the "Manchukuo" Government, including officials and advisers of Japanese nationality, and Governors of Provinces. Delegations were received from the local population, most of which were presented by the Japanese or "Manchukuo" authorities. In addition to our public meetings, we were able to arrange interviews with a great number of individuals, both Chinese and foreign.

Peiping, June 5th—28th.

The Commission returned to Peiping on June 5th, where an analysis of the voluminous documentary material collected was begun. Two more conferences were also held with Mr. Wang Ching-wei, President of the Executive Yuan; Dr. Lo Wen-kan, Minister for Foreign Affairs; and Mr. T. V. Soong, Minister of Finance.

Tokyo, July 4th—15th.

On June 28th the Commission proceeded to Tokyo via Chosen (Korea). Its departure for Japan was delayed by the fact that no Foreign Minister had yet been appointed in the Cabinet of Admiral Viscount Saito. After their arrival in Tokyo on July 4th, conferences were held with leaders of the new Government, including the Prime Minister, Admiral Viscount Saito; the Minister for Foreign Affairs, Count Uchida; and the Minister of War, Lieutenant-General Araki. From these we learned the present views and policy of the Government regarding the development of the situation in

---

① 原编辑者注：See Appendix I (separate volume).

Manchuria and Sino-Japanese relations.

Peiping, July 20th.

Having thus renewed contact with both the Chinese and the Japanese Governments, the Commission returned to Peiping, where the drafting of the Report was undertaken.

Assessors.

The two Assessors, who throughout spared no effort to assist the work of the Commission, presented a great amount of valuable documentary evidence. The material received from each Assessor was shown to the other, and an opportunity given for subsequent comment. These documents will be published.

The large number of persons and organisations interviewed, as listed in the Appendix, will illustrate the amount of evidence examined. Further, in the course of our travels, we have been presented with a great quantity of printed pamphlets, petitions, appeals, and letters. In Manchuria alone, we received approximately 1,550 letters in Chinese and 400 letters in Russian, without mentioning those written in English, French or Japanese. The arrangement, translation and study of these documents involved a considerable labour, which was carried out in spite of our continual movement from place to place. It was finally completed on our return to Peiping in July and before our last visit to Japan.

The conception of its mission under resolution of December 10th, determined the plan of the Commission's Report.

The Commission's conception of its mission, which determined the programme of its work and itinerary, has equally guided the plan of its Report.

First, we have tried to provide an historical background by describing the rights and interests of the two countries in Manchuria, which provide the fundamental causes of the dispute; the more recent specific issues which immediately preceded the actual outbreak were then examined, and the course of events since September 18th, 1931, described.

Throughout this review of the issues, we have insisted less on the responsibility for past actions than on the necessity of finding means to avoid their repetition in the future.

Finally, the Report concludes with some reflections and considerations which we have desired to submit to the Council upon the various issues with which it is confronted, and with some suggestions on the lines on which it seemed to us possible to effect a durable solution of the conflict and the re-establishment of a good understanding between China and Japan.

CHAPTER Ⅰ   OUTLINE OF RECENT DEVELOPMENTS IN CHINA

A knowledge of antecedent conditions necessary to a complete understanding of the present conflict.

The events of September 18th, 1931, which first brought the present conflict to the notice of the League of Nations, were but the outcome of a long chain of minor occasions of friction, indicating a growing tension in the relations between China and Japan. A knowledge of the essential factors in the recent relations of these two countries is necessary, to a complete understanding of the present conflict. It has been necessary, therefore, to extend our study of the issues beyond the limits of Manchuria itself and to consider in their widest aspect all the factors which determine present Sino-Japanese relations. The national aspirations of the Republic of China, the expansionist policy of the Japanese Empire and of the former Russian Empire, the present dissemination of Communism from the U. S. S. R. , the economic and strategic needs of these three countries: such matters as these, for example, are factors of fundamental importance in any study of the Manchurian problem.

Situated as this part of China is geographically between the territories of Japan and Russia, Manchuria has become politically a centre of conflict, and wars between all three countries have been fought upon its soil. Manchuria is in fact the meeting-ground of conflicting needs and policies, which themselves require investigation before the concrete facts of the present conflict can be fully appreciated. We shall therefore begin by reviewing these essential factors *seriatim*.

China, a nation in evolution.

The dominating factor in China is the modernisation of the nation itself which is slowly taking place. China to-day is a nation in evolution, showing evidence of transition in all aspects of its national life. Political upheavals, civil wars, social and economic unrest, with the resulting weakness of the Central Government, have been the characteristics of China since the revolution of 1911. Those conditions have adversely affected all the nations with which China has been brought into contact and, until remedied, will continue a menace to world peace and a contributory cause of world economic depression.

China first opened to foreigners in 1842.

Of the stages by which the preset conditions have been reached only a brief summary can here be given, which in no sense aims at being a comprehensive history. Throughout the first centuries of her intercourse with individual Occidentals, China remained, as far as Western influence is concerned, practically an isolated country. This condition of isolation was bound to come to an end when, at the beginning of the 19th century, the improvement of modern communication diminished distance and brought the Far East within easy reach of other nations, but in fact the country was not ready for the new contact when it came. As a result of the Treaty of Nanking, which ended the war of 1842, some ports were opened to foreign trade and residence. Foreign influences were introduced into a country whose Government had made no preparations to assimilate them. Foreign traders began to settle in her ports before she could provide for their administrative, legal, judicial, intellectual and sanitary requirements. The former therefore brought with them conditions and standards to which they were accustomed. Foreign cities sprang up in the Treaty Ports. Foreign methods of organisation, of administration and business asserted themselves. Any efforts there may have been on either side to mitigate the contrast were not effective, and a long period of friction and misunderstanding followed.

The efficacy of foreign arms having been demonstrated in a series of armed conflicts, China hoped, by building arsenals and by military training according to Western methods, to meet force with force. Her efforts in this direction, restricted as they were in scope, were doomed to failure. Much more fundamental reforms were needed to enable the country to hold its own against the foreigner, but China did not desire such reforms. On the contrary, she wanted to protect her culture and dominion against them.

Japanese comparison.

Japan had to face similar problems when that country was first opened to Western influences: new contacts with disturbing ideas, the conflict of different standards, leading to the establishment of foreign settlements, one-sided tariff conventions and extra-territorial claims. But Japan solved these problems by internal reforms, by raising her standards of modern requirements to those of the West and by diplomatic negotiations. Her assimilation of Western thought may not yet be complete, and friction may sometimes be seen between the old and the new ideas of different generations, but the rapidity and the thoroughness with which Japan has assimilated Western science and technique and adopted Western standards without diminishing the value of her old traditions have aroused general admiration.

China's problem vastly more difficult.

However difficult Japan's problems of assimilation and transformation may have been, those faced by China were much more difficult, owing to the vastness of her territory, the lack of national unity of her people, and her traditional financial system, under which the whole of the revenue collected did not reach the central Treasury. Although the complexity of the problem which China has to solve may be so much greater than that which confronted Japan as to make unjust any comparison between the two, yet the solution required for China must ultimately follow lines similar to those adopted by Japan. The reluctance of China to receive foreigners and her attitude towards those who were in the country was bound to have serious consequences. It concentrated the attention of her rulers on resistance to and restriction of foreign influence, and prevented her from profiting by the experience of more modern conditions in the foreign settlements. As a result, the constructive reform necessary to enable the country to cope with the new conditions was almost completely neglected.

China's losses from conflict with foreign Powers.

The inevitable conflict of two irreconcilable conceptions of respective rights and international relations led to wars and disputes resulting in the progressive surrender of sovereign rights and the loss of territory, either temporary or permanent. China lost a huge area on the north bank of the Amur River[①], and the Maritime Province; the Luchu Islands; Hong-Kong; Burma; Annam; Tongking; Laos; Cochin-China (provinces of Indo-China); Formosa[②]; Korea; and several other tributary States; she also granted long leases of other territories. Foreign courts, administration, police and military establishments were admitted on Chinese soil. The right to regulate at will her tariff on imports and exports was lost for the time being. China

---

① 编者按:即黑龙江,为俄语 Amur 的音译。
② 编者按:即台湾。

had to pay damages for injuries to foreign lives and property and heavy war indemnities which have been a burden to her finance sever since. Her very existence was even threatened by the division of her territory into spheres of interest of foreign Powers.

Reform movement starts after Boxer uprising in 1900.

Her defeat in the Sino-Japanese war of 1894—95, and the disastrous consequences of the Boxer uprising of 1900, opened the eyes of some thoughtful leaders to the necessity for fundamental reform. The reform movement was willing at first to accept the leadership of the Manchu House, but turned away from this dynasty after its cause and its leaders had been betrayed to the Empress Dowager, and the Emperor Kwang Hsu was made to expiate his hundred days of reform in virtual imprisonment to the end of his life in 1908.

Fall of the Manchu Dynasty.

The Manchu Dynasty had ruled China for 250 years. In its later years it was weakened by a series of rebellions: the Taiping rebellion (1850—1865), the Mohammedan risings in Yunnan (1856—1875), and the risings in Chinese Turkestan (1864—1877). The Taiping rebellion especially shook the Empire to its foundation and dealt a blow to the prestige of the dynasty, from which it never recovered. Finally, after the death of the then Empress Dowager in 1908, it collapsed through its own inherent weakness.

After some minor attempts at insurrection, the revolutionaries were successful in South China. A brief period followed during which a Republican Government was established at Nanking, with Dr. Sun Yat-sen, the leading figure of the Revolution, as provisional President. On February 12th, 1912, the then Empress Dowager, in the name of the child Emperor, signed a decree of abdication, and a provisional constitutional regime, with Yuan Shih-kai as President, was then inaugurated. With the abdication of the Emperor, his representatives in the provinces, prefectures and districts lost the influence and moral prestige which they had derived from his authority. They became ordinary men, to be obeyed only in so far as they were able to enforce their decisions. The gradual substitution of military for civil governors in the provinces was an inevitable consequence. The post of central executive could, likewise, be held only by the military leader who had the strongest army or was supported by the strongest group of provincial or local military chiefs.

Tendency towards military dictatorship in the North.

This tendency toward military dictatorship, which was more apparent in the North, was facilitated by the fact that the army had gained some popularity by the support it had given in many instances to the Revolution. Military leaders did not hesitate to lay claim to the merit of having made the Revolution a success. Most of them were Northern leaders, to a certain extent grouped together in the so-called Peiyang Party—men who had risen from a low status to higher commands in the model army trained by Yuan Shih-kai after the Sino-Japanese war. They could more or less be trusted by him because of the tie of personal allegiance which, in China, has not yet given place to the corporate loyalty which characterises organisations in the West. These men were appointed military governors by Yuan Shih-kai in the provinces under his control. There the power rested in their hands and provincial revenues could accordingly be taken at will by them to be used for their personal armies and adherents.

Position in the South.

In the Southern provinces, the situation was different, partly as a result of intercourse with foreign countries and partly on account of the different social customs of the population. The people of South China have always been averse to military autocracy and official interference from outside. Dr. Sun Yat-sen and their other leaders remained faithful to the idea of constitutionalism. They had, however, little military force behind them, because the re-organisation of the army had not yet progressed very far in the provinces south of the Yangtze, and they had no well-equipped arsenals.

Revolt against Yuan Shih-kai, 1913.

When, after much procrastination, the first Parliament was convened in Peking in 1913, Yuan Shih-kai had consolidated his military position, and lacked only sufficient financial resources to ensure the loyalty of the provincial armies. A huge foreign loan, the so-called Re-organisation Loan, provided him with the necessary financial means. But his action in concluding that loan without the consent of Parliament brought his political opponents of the Kuomintang or Nationalist Party, under Dr. Sun's leadership, into open revolt. In a military sense the South was weaker than the North, and was still more weakened when the victorious Northern commanders, after conquering a number of Southern provinces, placed the latter under Northern generals.

Civil war and political unrest, 1914—1928.

There were several attempts to reinstate the 1913 Parliament, which had been introduced by Yuan Shih-kai, or to convene bogus Parliaments, two attempts to establish monarchical rule, many changes of Presidents and Cabinets, continuous shifting of allegiance among military leaders, and many declarations of temporary independence of one or more provinces. In Canton, the Kuomintang Government, headed by Dr. Sun, succeeded in maintaining itself from 1917 onwards, with occasional intervals during which it ceased to function. During these years China was ravaged by warring factions; and the ever-present bandits grew into veritable armies by the enlistment of ruined farmers, desperate inhabitants of famine-stricken districts, or unpaid soldiers. Even the constitutionalists, who were fighting in the South, were repeatedly exposed to the danger of militarist feuds arising in their midst.

Re-organisation of the Kuomintang.

In 1923, convinced by Russian revolutionists that a definite programme, strict party discipline, and systematic propaganda were necessary to ensure the victory of his cause, Dr. Sun Yat-sen re-organised the Kuomintang with a programme which he outlined in his "Manifesto" and "Three Principles of the People[①]". Systematic organisation ensured party discipline and unity of action through the intermediary of a Central Executive Committee. A political training institute instructed propagandists and organisers of local branches, while a military training institute at Whampoo, with the help of Russian officers, was instrumental in providing the party with an efficient army, the leaders of which were permeated with the idea of the party. Thus equipped, the Kuomintang was soon ready to establish contacts with the people at large. Sympathisers were organised in local branches or in peasant and labour unions affiliated to the party. This preliminary conquest of the people's mind was, after the death of Dr. Sun in 1925, followed up by the successful Northern Expedition of the Kuomintang Army, which, by the end of 1928, succeeded in producing a nominal unity for the first time in many years, and a measure of actual unity which lasted for a time.

The first, or military, phase of Dr. Sun's programme had thus been brought to a successful end.

The second period of political tutelage under party dictatorship could begin. It was to be devoted to the education of the people in the art of self-government and to the reconstruction of the country.

A Central Government established.

In 1927, a Central Government was established at Nanking. It was controlled by the party — it was, in fact, merely one important organ of the party. It consisted of five Yuans or Boards (the Executive, the Legislative,

---

① 原编辑者注: National Independence, Democratic Government and Social Re-organisation.

the Judicial, the Control, and the Examination Boards). The Government had been modelled as closely as possible on the lines of Dr. Sun's "Five-Power Constitution"—the Trias Politica of Montesquieu with the addition of two old Chinese institutions, the Censorate and the Public Services Examination Board—in order to facilitate the transition to the final or constitutional stage, when the people, partly directly and partly through its elected representatives, would itself take charge of the direction of its government.

In the provinces, similarly, a committee system was adopted for the organisation of provincial governments, while in villages, towns and districts, the people were to be trained in the handling of local self-government. The party was now ready to put into operation its schemes of political and economic reconstruction, but was prevented from doing so by internal dissensions, the periodical revolt of various Generals with personal armies, and the menace of Communism. In fact, the Central Government had repeatedly to fight for its very existence.

The authority of the Central Government challenged from without and weakened by dissensions within.

For a time unity was maintained on the surface. But not even the semblance of unity could be preserved when powerful war lords concluded alliances amongst themselves and marched their armies against Nanking. Though they never succeeded in their object, they remained, even after defeat, potential forces to be reckoned with. Moreover, they never took the position that war against the Central Government was an act of rebellion. It was in their eyes simply a struggle for supremacy between their faction and another one which happened to reside in the national capital and to be recognised as the Central Government by foreign Powers. This lack of hierarchical relations is all the more dangerous because serious dissensions in the Party itself have weakened the title of the Central Government to be the unquestioned successors of Dr. Sun. The new schism has led to the estrangement of influential Southern leaders, who retired to Canton, where the local authorities and the local branch of the Kuomintang frequently act independently of the Central Government.

From this summary description it appears that disruptive forces in China are still powerful. The cause of this lack of cohesion is the tendency of the mass of the people to think in terms of family and locality, rather than in terms of the nation, except in periods of acute tension between their own country and foreign Powers. Although there are, nowadays, a number of leaders who have risen above particularist sentiments, it is evident that a national outlook must be attained by a far greater number of citizens before real national unity can result.

Present condition of China compared with that at the time of the Washington Conference.

Although the spectacle of China's transitional period, with its unavoidable political, social, intellectual and moral disorder, is disappointing to her impatient friends and has created enmities which have become a danger to peace, it is nevertheless true that, in spite of difficulties, delays and failures, considerable progress has in fact been made. An argument which constantly reappears in the polemics of the present controversy is that China is "not an organised State" or "is in a condition of complete chaos and incredible anarchy", and that her present-day conditions should disqualify her from membership of the League of Nations and deprive her of the protective clauses of the Covenant. In this connection, it may be useful to remember that an altogether different attitude was taken at the time of the Washington Conference by all the participating powers. Yet, even at that time, China had two completely separate Governments, one at Peking and one at Canton, and was disturbed by large bandit forces which frequently interfered with communications in the interior, while preparations were being made for a civil war involving all China. As a result of this war, which was preceded by an ultimatum sent to the Central Government on

January 13th, 1922, when the Washington Conference was still in session, the Central Government was overthrown in May, and the independence of Manchuria from the Government installed at Peking in its place was declared in July by Marshal Chang Tso-lin. Thus, there existed no fewer than three Governments professing to be independent, not to mention the virtually autonomous status of a number of provinces or parts of provinces. Although, at present, the Central Government's authority is still weak in a number of provinces, the central authority is not, at least openly, repudiated, and there is reason to hope that, if the Central Government as such can be maintained, provincial administration, military forces and finance will acquire an increasingly national character. Those, among others, were doubtless the reasons which induced the Assembly of the League of Nations last September to elect China to the Council.

Efforts for Chinese reconstruction.

The present Government has tried to balance its current receipts and expenditure and to adhere to sound financial principles. Various taxes have been consolidated and simplified. In default of a proper budgetary system, an annual statement has been issued by the Ministry of Finance. A Central Bank has been established. A National Financial Committee has been appointed, which includes among its members influential representatives of banking and commercial interests. The Ministry of Finance is also trying to supervise the finances of the provinces, where the methods of raising taxes are often still highly unsatisfactory. For all these measures the Government is entitled to credit. It has, however, been forced by recurrent civil wars to increase its domestic indebtedness by about a billion dollars (silver) since 1927. Lack of funds has prevented it from executing its ambitious plans of reconstruction, or completing the improvement of communications which is so vitally necessary for the solution of most of the country's problems. In many things, no doubt, the Government has failed, but it has already accomplished much.

Nationalism.

The nationalism of modern China is a normal aspect of the period of political transition through which the country is passing. National sentiments and aspirations of a similar kind would be found in any country placed in the same position. But, in addition to the natural desire to be free from any outside control in a people that has become conscious of national unity, the influence of the Kuomintang has introduced into the nationalism of China an additional and abnormal tinge of bitterness against all foreign influences, and has expanded its aims so as to include the liberation of all Asiatic people still subject to "imperialistic oppression". This is partly due to the slogans of its early communistic connection. Chinese nationalism to-day is also permeated by memories of former greatness, which it desires to revive. It demands the return of leased territories, of administrative and other not purely commercial rights exercised by a foreign agency in railway areas, of administrative rights in concessions and settlements, and of extra-territorial rights which imply that foreigners are not amenable to Chinese laws, law courts and taxation. Public opinion is strongly opposed to the continuance of these rights, which are regarded as a national humiliation.

Attitude of foreign Powers on the subject of extra-territoriality.

Foreign Powers have in general taken a sympathetic attitude towards these desires. At the Washington Conference, 1921—22, they were admitted to be acceptable in principle, though there was divergence of opinion as to the best time and method of giving effect to them. It was felt that an immediate surrender of such rights would impose upon China the obligation to provide administration, police and justice of a standard which, owing to financial and other internal difficulties, she could not at present attain. The present single issue of extra-territoriality might lead to a number of separate issues with foreign Powers if the former were abolished prematurely. It was also felt that international relations would not improve but would deteriorate if foreign nationals were to be exposed to the same unjust treatment and extortionate taxation as Chinese citizens were subjected to in so many parts of the country. In spite of these reservations, much was actually accomplished, especially at Washington, or as a result of that Conference. China has recovered two out of five leased territories, many concessions, administrative rights in the area of the Chinese Eastern Railway, Customs autonomy, and postal rights. Many treaties on the basis of equality have also been negotiated.

Having started upon the road of international co-operation for the purpose of solving her difficulties, as was done at Washington, China might have made more substantial progress in the ten years that have since elapsed had she continued to follow that road. She has only been hampered by the virulence of the anti-foreign propaganda which has been pursued. In two particulars has this been carried so far as to contribute to the creation of the atmosphere in which the present conflict arose—namely, the use made of the economic boycott, to which reference is made in CHAPTER Ⅶ, and the introduction of anti-foreign propaganda into the schools.

Nationalism in the schools.

It is provided in the Provisional Constitution of China promulgated on June 1st, 1931[1] that "the Three Principles of the People shall be the basic principles of education in the Republic of China". The ideas of Dr. Sun Yat-sen are now taught in the schools as if they had the same authority as that of the Classics in former centuries. The sayings of the master receive the same veneration as the sayings of Confucius received in the days before the Revolution. Unfortunately, however, more attention has been given to the negative than to the constructive side of nationalism in the education of the young. A perusal of the text-books used in the schools leaves the impression on the mind of a reader that their authors have sought to kindle patriotism with the flame of hatred, and to build up manliness upon a sense of injury.

---

① 原编辑者注：Article 47 of the Chapter on "Education of the Citizens".

As a result of this virulent anti-foreign propaganda, begun in the schools and carried through every phase of public life, the students have been induced to engage in political activities which sometimes have culminated in attacks on the persons, homes or offices of Ministers and other authorities, and in attempts to overthrow the Government. Unaccompanied by effective internal reforms or improvements in national standards, this attitude tended to alarm the foreign Powers and to increase their reluctance to surrender the rights which are at the moment their only protection.

Problems of law and order: Necessity of adequate communications.

In connection with the problems of maintaining law and order, the present inadequate means of communication in China is a serious handicap. Unless communications are sufficient to ensure prompt transportation of national forces, the safeguarding of law and order must largely, if not completely, be entrusted to provincial authorities, who, on account of the distance of the Central Government, must be allowed to use their own judgment in handling provincial affairs. Under such conditions, independence of mind and action may easily cross the boundary of law, with the result that the province gradually takes on the aspect of a private estate. Its armed forces are also identified with their commander, not with the nation.

Local armies.

The transfer of a commander from one army to another by order of the Central Government is, in many cases, impossible. The danger of civil war must continue to exist so long as the Central Government lacks the material means to make its authority swiftly and permanently felt all over the country.

Banditry.

The problem of banditry, which may be traced throughout the history of China, and which exists to-day in all parts of the country, is subject to the same considerations. Banditry has always existed in China and the administration has never been able to suppress it thoroughly. Lack of proper communications was one of the reasons which prevented the administration from getting rid of this evil, which increased or decreased according to changing circumstances. Another contributing cause is to be found in the local uprisings and rebellions which have often occurred in China, especially as a result of maladministration. Even after the successful suppression of such rebellions, bandit gangs recruited from the ranks of the rebels often remained active in parts of the country. This was specially the case in the period following the suppression of the Taiping rebellion (1850—1865). In more recent times, bandits have also originated from the ranks of unpaid soldiers who were not able to find other means of living and had been accustomed to looting during the civil wars in which they had taken part.

Other causes which have given rise to an increase of banditry in parts of China were floods and droughts. These are more or less regular occurrences, and they have always brought famine and banditry in their wake. The problem has been further aggravated by the pressure of a rapidly increasing population. In congested areas, normal economic difficulties were still further increased and, amongst people living on a bare subsistence level with no margin to meet times of crisis, the slightest deterioration in the conditions of life might bring large numbers to the point of destitution. Banditry, therefore, has been largely influenced by the prevailing economic conditions. In prosperous periods or districts it has diminished, but where for any of the reasons mentioned the struggle for existence was intensified or the political conditions were disturbed it was sure to increase.

When once banditry had become well established in any area, its suppression by force was rendered difficult because of the defective communications in the interior of the country. It is in regions which are difficult of access, where a few miles may involve days of travel, that large armed bandits can move freely, appearing and disappearing suddenly, without their abodes and movements being known. When bandit suppression has been long neglected, and when the soldiers even co-operate with bandits secretly, as has happened often enough, traffic along highways and waterways is interfered with. Such occurrences can only be stopped by adequate police forces. In the districts of the interior, bandit suppression is much more difficult, because guerilla warfare inevitably develops.

Communism① a challenge to the authority of the Central Government.

But, though the personal armies of local Generals and the prevalence of bandit hordes throughout the country may disturb the internal peace of the country, they are no longer a menace to the authority of the Central Government as such. There is, however, a menace of this kind from another source—namely, Communism.

Origin of Communism in China, 1921.

The communist movement in China, during the first years of its existence, remained restricted within intellectual and labour circles, where the doctrine gained considerable influence in the period 1919—1924. Rural China was, at that time, scarcely touched by this movement. The manifesto of the Soviet Government of July 25th, 1919, declaring its willingness to renounce all privileges "extorted" from China by the former Tsarist Government, created a favourable impression throughout China, especially amongst the intelligentsia. In May 1921, the Chinese Communist Party was formally constituted. Propaganda was especially conducted in labour circles at Shanghai, where "red" syndicates were organised. In June 1922, at its second congress, the Communist Party, which did not then number more than three hundred members, decided to ally itself with the Kuomintang. Dr. Sun Yat-sen, although opposed to the Communist doctrine, was

---

① 编者按:《国联调查团报告书》(英文版)中对共产主义、中国共产党及其革命事业存在错误描述。请读者注意鉴别。下同。

prepared to admit individual Chinese Communists into the party. In the autumn of 1922, the Soviet Government sent a Mission to China, headed by Mr. Joffe. Important interviews, which took place between him and Dr. Sun resulted in the joint declaration of January 26th, 1923, by which assurance was given of Soviet sympathy and support to the cause of the national unification and independence of China. It was explicitly stated, on the other hand, that the Communist organisation and the Soviet system of government could not be introduced at that time under the conditions prevailing in China. Following this agreement, a number of military and civil advisers were sent from Moscow by the end of 1923, and "undertook, under the control of Dr. Sun, the modification of the internal organisation of the Kuomintang and of the Cantonese Army".

At the first National Congress of the Kuomintang, convened in March 1924, the admission of Chinese Communists into the party was formally agreed to, on condition that such members should not take any further part in the preparation of the proletarian revolution. The period of tolerance with regard to Communism thus began.

Period of tolerance with regard to Communism, 1924—1927.

This period lasted from 1924 until 1927. Early in 1924 the Communists counted about 2,000 adherents, and "red" syndicates approximately 60,000 members. But the Communists soon acquired enough influence inside the Kuomintang to raise anxiety amongst the orthodox members of the party. They presented to the Central Committee, at the end of 1926, a proposal going so far as to include the nationalisation of all landed properties except those belonging to workmen, peasants or soldiers; the re-organisation of the Kuomintang; the elimination of all military leaders hostile to Communism; and the arming of 20,000 Communists and 50,000 workmen and peasants. This proposal, however, was defeated, and the Communists ceased to support the intended campaign of the Kuomintang against the Northern militarists, although they had previously been most active in the organisation of the Nationalist forces. Nevertheless, at a later stage, they joined in it, and when the Northern Expedition reached Central China and established a Nationalist Government at Wu-Han in 1927, the Communists succeeded in obtaining a controlling position in it, as the Nationalist leaders were not prepared to join issue with them until their own forces had occupied Nanking and Shanghai. The Wu-Han Government put into operation in the provinces of Hunan and Hupeh a series of purely communistic measures. The Nationalist Revolution was almost on the point of being transformed into a Communist Revolution.

Break between Kuomintang and Communism, 1927.

The Nationalist leaders at last decided that Communism had become too serious a menace to be tolerated any longer. As soon as they were firmly established at Nanking, where another National Government was constituted on April 10th, 1927, a proclamation was issued in which the Nanking Government ordered the immediate purification of the Army and the Civil Service from Communism. On July 15th, the majority of the Central Executive of the Kuomintang at Wu-Han, who had so far refused to join the Nationalist leaders at Nanking, adopted a resolution excluding Communists from the Kuomintang and ordering the Soviet advisers to leave China. As a result of this decision, the Kuomintang regained its unity and the Government at Nanking became generally recognised by the party.

Affairs of Nanchang and Canton.

During the period of tolerance, several military units had been gained to the Communist cause. These had been left in the rear, mostly in Kiangsi Province, when the Nationalist Army was marching to the North. Communist agents were sent to co-ordinate these units and to persuade them to take action against the National Government. On July 30th, 1927, the garrison at Nanchang, the capital of Kiangsi Province, together with some other military units, revolted and subjected the population to numerous excesses. However, on August 5th, they were defeated by the Government forces and withdrew to the South. On December 11th, a Communist rising at Canton delivered control of the city for two days into their hands. The Nanking Government considered that official Soviet agents had actively participated in these uprisings. An order of December 14th, 1927, withdrew the exequatur of all the consuls of the U. S. S. R. residing in China.

Continuation of armed struggle with the Communist armies.

The recrudescence of civil war favoured the growth of Communist influence in the period between 1928 and 1931. A "Red army" was organised, and extensive areas in Kiangsi and Fukien were sovietised. Only in November 1930, shortly after the defeat of a powerful coalition of Northern militarists, was the Central Government able to take up the suppression of Communism in earnest. The Communist forces had operated in parts of Kiangsi and Hunan Provinces and were then reported to have caused in two or three months the loss of 200,000 lives and of property valued at about one billion dollars (silver). [1] They had now become so strong that they were able to defeat the first and frustrate the second expedition sent against them by the Government. The third expedition, directed by the Commander-in-Chief, General Chiang Kai-shek, defeated the Communist armies in several encounters. By the middle of July 1931, the most important Communist strongholds had been taken, and their forces were in full retreat towards Fukien.

Whilst constituting a political commission to re-organise the areas which had been devastated, General Chiang Kai-shek pursued the "Red armies", and drove them into the mountainous region north-east of Kiangsi.

The Nanking Government was thus on the point of putting the principal "Red army" out of action, when events occurred in different parts of China

---

[1]　编者按:《国联调查团报告书》(英文版)存在对中国共产党及其事业的错误描述。请读者注意鉴别。下同。

which obliged them to suspend this offensive and to withdraw a large part of their troops. In the North had occurred the rebellion of General Shih Yu-san, supported by a hostile intervention on the part of the 19 Cantonese troops in the province of Hunan; simultaneously with this intervention came the events of September 18th at Mukden. Encouraged by these circumstances, the "Reds" resumed the offensive, and before long the fruits of the victorious campaign were almost completely lost.

Present extent of Communist organisations.

Large parts of the provinces of Fukien and Kiangsi, and parts of Kwangtung, are reliably reported to be completely "sovietised". Communist zones of influence are far more extensive. They cover a large part of China south of the Yangtze, and parts of the provinces of Hupeh, Anhwei, and Kiangsu north of that river. Shanghai has been the centre of Communist propaganda. Individual sympathisers with Communism may probably be found in every town in China. So far, two provincial Communist governments only have been organised in Kiangsi and Fukien, but the number of minor Soviets runs into hundreds. The Communist government itself is formed by a committee elected by a congress of local workers and peasants. It is, in reality, controlled by representatives of the Chinese Communist Party, which sends out trained men for that purpose, a large number of whom have been previously trained in the U. S. S. R. Regional Committees, under the control of the Central Committee of the Chinese Communist Party, in their turn control provincial Committees and these, again, district committees, and so on, down to the Communist cells organised in factories, schools, military barracks, etc.

Methods employed by the Communists.

When a district has been occupied by a "Red army", efforts are made to sovietise it, if the occupation appears to be of a more or less permanent nature. Any "opposition" from the population is "suppressed" by "terrorism". A

Communist government, as described above, is then established. The complete organisation of such governments comprises: Commissariats for Internal Affairs, for the struggle against the anti-revolutionaries (G. P. U.), for Financial Affairs, for Rural Economy, for Education, for Hygiene, for Post and Telegraph, for Communications; and Committees for Military Affairs and for the control of workmen and peasants. Such elaborate government organisations exist only in completely sovietised districts.

Elsewhere the organisation is much more modest.

The programme of action consists in the cancellation of debts, the distribution among landless proletarians and small farmers of land forcibly seized, either from large private owners or from religious institutions, such as temples, monasteries and churches. Taxation is simplified; the peasants have to contribute a certain part of the produce of their lands. With a view to the improvement of agriculture, steps are taken to develop irrigation, rural credit systems, and co-operatives. Public schools, hospitals and dispensaries may also be established.

Thus the poorest farmers derive considerable benefit from Communism, whereas the rich and middle-class landowners, merchants and local gentry are completely ruined, either by immediate expropriation or by levies and fines, and, in applying its agrarian programme, the Communist Party expects to gain the support of the masses. In this respect, its propaganda and action have met with considerable success, notwithstanding the fact that Communist theory conflicts with the Chinese social system. Existing grievances resulting from oppressive taxation, extortion, usury and pillage by soldiery or bandits were fully exploited. Special slogans were employed for farmers, workmen, soldiers and intellectuals, with variations specially adapted to women.

Special character of Communism in China.

Communism in China not only means, as in most countries other than the U. S. S. R., either a political doctrine held by certain members of existing parties, or the organisation of a special party to compete for power with other political parties. It has become an actual rival of the National Government. It possesses its own law, army and government, and its own territorial sphere of action. For this state of affairs there is no parallel in any other country. Moreover, in China, the disturbance created by the Communist war is made more serious by the fact that the country is going through a critical period of internal reconstruction, still further complicated during the last eleven months by an external crisis of exceptional gravity. The National Government seems to be determined to regain the control of the districts under Communist influence, and to pursue in those districts, once their recovery is achieved, a policy of economic rehabilitation; but in its military campaigns, apart from difficulties already mentioned, both internal and external, it is hampered by lack of funds and defective communications. The problem of Communism in China is thus linked up with the larger problem of national reconstruction.

In the summer of 1932, important military operations, having for their object a final suppression of the "Red" resistance, were announced by the Government of Nanking. They were commenced and, as stated above, were to have been accompanied by a thorough social and administrative reorganisation of the recaptured regions, but up to the present no important results have been announced.

Effect of these conditions upon Sino-Japanese relations.

So far as Japan is China's nearest neighbor and largest customer, she has suffered more than any other Power from the lawless conditions described in this chapter. Over two-thirds of the foreign residents in China are Japanese, and the number of Koreans in Manchuria is estimated at about 800,000. She has more nationals, therefore, than any other Power, who would suffer if they were made amenable to Chinese law, justice and taxation under present conditions.

Japan felt it impossible to satisfy Chinese aspirations so long as satisfactory safeguards to take the place of her Treaty rights could not be hoped for. Her interests in China, and more especially in Manchuria, began to be more prominently asserted as those of the other major Powers receded into the background. Japan's anxiety to safeguard the life and property of her subjects in China caused her to intervene repeatedly in times of civil war or of local disturbances. Such action was bitterly resented by China, especially when it resulted in an armed clash such as occurred in 1928 at Tsinan. In recent years, the claims of Japan have come to be regarded in China as constituting a more serious challenge to national aspirations than the rights of all the other Powers taken together.

International interest in the problems of Chinese reconstruction.

This issue, however, though affecting Japan to a greater extent than other Powers, is not a Sino-Japanese issue alone. China demands immediately the surrender of certain exceptional powers and privileges because they are felt to be derogatory to her national dignity and sovereignty. The foreign Powers have hesitated to meet these wishes as long as conditions in China did not ensure adequate protection of their nationals, whose interests depend on the security afforded by the enjoyment of special Treaty rights. The process of fermentation, inevitable in a period of transition, which this chapter has attempted to describe, has developed forces of public opinion which will probably continue to embarrass the Central Government in the conduct of its foreign policy, as long as it is weakened by failure to complete the unification and reconstruction of the country. The realisation of China's national aspirations in the field of foreign relations depends on her ability to discharge the functions of a modern Government in the sphere of domestic affairs, and until the discrepancy between these two has been removed the danger of international friction and of incidents, boycotts, and armed interventions will continue.

International co-operation offers the best hope of their solution.

The present extreme case of international friction having forced China once more to seek the intervention of the League of Nations should, if a satisfactory settlement can be effected, convince her of the advantages of the policy of international co-operation, which was inaugurated at Washington with such beneficial results in 1922. China has not at the moment the capital nor the trained specialists necessary for the unaided accomplishment of her national reconstruction. Dr. Sun Yat-sen himself realised this, and actually drew up an ambitious plan of international participation in the economic development of his country. The National Government, too, has in recent years sought and accepted international help in the solution of her problems—in financial matters since 1930, in matters relating to economic planning and development in liaison with the technical organisations of the League of Nations since the constitution of the National Economic Council in 1931, and in relief of the distress caused by the great flood of the same year. Along this road of international co-operation, China would make the surest and most rapid progress towards the attainment of her national ideals, and such a policy would make it easier for foreign Powers to give what support the Central Government may seek, and to help in the removal as rapidly and as effectively as possible of any causes of friction which may endanger her peaceful relations with the rest of the world.

CHAPTER Ⅱ   MANCHURIA

DESCRIPTION, RELATIONS WITH THE REST OF CHINA AND WITH RUSSIA.

1. Description

Introductory.

Manchuria, which is known in China as the Three Eastern Provinces, a large fertile region only forty years ago almost undeveloped and even now still under-populated, has assumed an increasingly important role in the solution of the surplus population problems of China and Japan. The provinces of Shantung and Hopei have poured millions of destitute farmers into Manchuria, while Japan has exported to that country her manufactured articles and capital, in exchange for food supplies and raw materials. In providing for the respective needs of China and Japan, Manchuria has proved the usefulness of their partnership. Without Japan's activity, Manchuria could not have attracted and absorbed such a large population. Without the influx of Chinese farmers and labourers, Manchuria could not have developed so rapidly, providing Japan thereby with a market and with supplies of food, fertilisers, and raw materials.

Manchuria a coveted region, first on account of its strategic advantages, subsequently on account of agricultural and mineral resources.

Yet, Manchuria, so largely dependent on co-operation, was destined, for reasons already indicated, to become a region of conflict: at first between Russia and Japan, later between China and her two powerful neighbours. At first, Manchuria entered into this great conflict of policies only as an area, the occupation of which was thought to imply domination of Far-Eastern politics. It became coveted for its own sake later, when it's agricultural, mineral and forestry resources had been discovered. Exceptional treaty rights were acquired in the first instance by Russia at the expense of China. Those which concerned South Manchuria were subsequently transferred to Japan. The use of the privileges so acquired became more and more instrumental in furthering the economic development of South Manchuria. Strategical considerations have remained paramount, but the extensive economic interests resulting from the active part taken by Russia and Japan in the development of Manchuria found an ever-increasing insistence in the foreign policy of these two countries.

Occupation of the soil by Chinese farmers.

China at first showed little activity in the field of development. She almost allowed Manchuria to pass from her control to that of Russia. Even after the Treaty of Portsmouth, which reaffirmed her sovereignty in Manchuria, the economic activities of Russia and Japan in developing those provinces figured more prominently than her own in the eyes of the world. Meanwhile the immigration of millions of Chinese farmers settled the future possession of the land. This immigration was in fact an occupation, peaceful, inconspicuous, but none the less real. While Russia and Japan were engaged in delimiting their respective spheres of interest in North and South Manchuria, Chinese farmers took possession of the soil and Manchuria is now unalterably Chinese. In such circumstances China could afford to wait for a favourable opportunity to reassert her sovereign rights. The Russian revolution of 1917 gave her that opportunity in North Manchuria. She began to take a more active part in the government and development of the country, which had been so long neglected. In recent years she has tried to diminish Japan's influence in South Manchuria. Growing friction resulted from that policy, the culminating point of which was reached on September 18th, 1931.

Population.

The total population is estimated at about 30,000,000, of whom 28,000,000 are said to be Chinese or assimilated Manchus. The number of Koreans is put at 800,000, of whom a large number are congregated in the so-called Chientao District on the Korean border, the remainder being widely scattered in Manchuria. Mongol tribes live in the pasture lands bordering Inner Mongolia, their number being small. There may be about 150,000 Russians in Manchuria, most of them living in the area along the Chinese Eastern Railway, especially at Harbin. About 230,000 Japanese are mainly concentrated in the settlements along the South Manchuria Railway and in the Kwantung Leased Territory (Liaotung Peninsula). The total number of

Japanese, Russians and other foreigners (excluding Koreans) in Manchuria does not exceed 400,000.

Area.

Manchuria is a vast country with an area as large as that of France and Germany taken together, estimated at about 380,000 square miles. In China it is always referred to as the "Three Eastern Provinces" because of its administrative division into the three provinces of Liaoning (or Fengtien) in the South, Kirin in the East, and Heilungkiang in the North. Liaoning is estimated to have an area of 70,000 square miles, Kirin of 100,000, Heilungkiang of over 200,000.

Geography.

Manchuria is continental in its characteristics. There are two mountain ranges, the Changpai Range in the south-east and the Great Khingan Range in the north-west. Between these two mountain ranges lies the great Manchurian plain, of which the northern part belongs to the basin of the Sungari River and the southern part to that of the Liao River. The watershed between them, which has some historical importance, is a range of hills dividing the Manchurian plain into a northern and a southern part.

Manchuria is bounded on the west by the province of Hopeh and by Outer and Inner Mongolia. Inner Mongolia was formerly divided into three special administrative areas—Jehol, Chahar and Suiyuan—which were given the full status of provinces by the National Government in 1928. Inner Mongolia, and more especially Jehol, has always had relations with Manchuria, and exercises some influence in Manchurian affairs. On the north-west, north-east, and east, Manchuria is bounded by the Siberian provinces of the U. S. S. R. , on the south-east by Korea, and on the south by the Yellow Sea. The southern end of the Liaotung Peninsula has been held by Japan since 1905. Its area is over 1,300 square miles, and it is administered as a Japanese leased territory. In addition, Japan exercises certain rights over a narrow strip of land, which extends beyond the Leased Territory, and which contains the lines of the South Manchuria Railway. The total area is only 108 square miles, whereas the length of the lines is 690 miles.

Economic resources.

The soil of Manchuria is generally fertile, but its development is dependent on transportation facilities. Many important towns flourish along its rivers and railways. Formerly, development was practically dependent on the river system, which is still of much importance, though the railways have now taken the first place as a means of transport. The production of important crops, such as soya beans, kaoliang, wheat, millet, barley, rice, oats, has doubled in fifteen years. In 1929, these crops were estimated at over 876,000,000 bushels. According to estimates given in the *Manchurian Year-Book*, 1931, only 12.6 per cent of the total area has been brought under cultivation in 1929, whereas 28.4 per cent was cultivable. A large increase of production may therefore be expected in the future if economic conditions improve. The total value of the agricultural products of Manchuria for the year 1928 was estimated at over £130,000,000 sterling. A large part of the agricultural produce is exported. Pongee or tussah silk is another important article of export from Manchuria.

Timber and minerals.

The mountainous regions are rich in timber and minerals, especially coal. Important deposits of iron and gold are also known to exist, while large quantities of oil shale, dolomite, magnesite, limestone, fireclay, steatite, and silica of excellent quality have been found. The mining industry may therefore be expected to become of great importance. [1]

---

[1] 原编辑者注: See also CHAPTER Ⅶ and the special studies No. 2 and No. 3 annexed to this Report.

2. Relations with the Rest of China

Early history of the fall of the Manchu Dynasty.

Manchuria has, since the dawn of history, been inhabited by various Tungus tribes, who mixed freely with Mongol Tartars. Under the influence of Chinese immigrants of superior civilisation they learned to organise themselves and established several kingdoms which sometimes dominated the greater part of Manchuria and some northern districts in China and Korea. The Liao, Chin, and Manchu Dynasties even conquered large parts or the whole of China over which they ruled for centuries. China, on the other hand, under strong emperors, was able to stem the tide from the North, and in her turn to establish sovereignty over large parts of Manchuria. Colonisation by Chinese settlers was practised at a very early date. Various Chinese towns which radiated the influence of Chinese culture through the surrounding districts date from the same early time. For two thousand years a permanent foothold has been maintained, and Chinese culture has always been active in the southernmost part of Manchuria. The influence of this culture had become very strong during the rule of the Ming Dynasty (1368—1644), whose authority extended over practically the whole of Manchuria. The Manchus were permeated by Chinese culture and had amalgamated to a great extent with the Chinese before they overthrew the Ming administration in Manchuria in 1616, and in 1628 passed the Great Wall to conquer China. In the Manchu Army were large numbers of Chinese who were organised in separate military units known as Chinese Banners.

After the conquest, the Manchus quartered their garrisons in the more important cities of China, forbade Manchus to engage in certain professions, prohibited intermarriage between Manchus and Chinese, and restricted the immigration of Chinese into Manchuria and Mongolia. These measures were inspired more by political than by racial discrimination, and aimed at safeguarding the permanent dominance of the dynasty. They did not affect the numerous Chinese Bannermen, who enjoyed practically the same privileged status as the Manchus themselves.

The exodus of the Manchus and their Chinese allies greatly reduced the population of Manchuria. However, in the South, Chinese communities continued to exist. From this foothold a few settlers spread across the central part of Fengtien province. Their number was increased by a continuous infiltration of immigrants from China, who succeeded in evading the exclusion laws or who had profited by their modifications from time to time. Manchus and Chinese became still more amalgamated, and even the Manchu language was virtually replaced by Chinese. The Mongols, however, were not assimilated but pushed back by the advancing immigrants. Finally, to stem the Russian advance from the North, the Manchu Government decided to encourage Chinese immigration. In 1878, various parts of Manchuria were accordingly opened and various forms of encouragement given to immigrants, with the result that, at the time of the Chinese Revolution in 1911, the population of Manchuria was estimated at 18,000,000.

In 1907, a few years only before its abdication, the Manchu Dynasty had decided to reform the administration in Manchuria. These provinces had hitherto been administered as a separate, extra-mural dominion, with its own form of government. The Chinese practice of entrusting the civil administration in the provinces to scholars who had passed the competitive examinations had not been followed in Manchuria, which had been placed under a purely military regime in which Manchu officials and traditions were maintained. In China, officials were not allowed to hold office in their native province. Each Manchurian province had a military governor, who exercised complete power in civil as well as in military matters. Later, attempts had been made to separate military and civil administration. The results were not satisfactory. The demarcation of the respective spheres of authority was not adequate; misunderstandings and intrigues were frequent and inefficiency resulted. In 1907, therefore, this attempt was given up. The three military governors were replaced by a Viceroy for all Manchuria, with the object of centralising authority, especially in the domain of foreign policy. Provincial civil governors under the control of the Viceroy were in charge of provincial administration. This reorganisation prepared the way for the later administrative reforms which introduced the Chinese system of provincial government. These last measures of the Manchus were very effective, thanks to the able administrators in charge of Manchurian affairs after 1907.

After the fall of the Manchu Dynasty.

When the Revolution broke out in 1911, the Manchurian authorities who were not in favour of the Republic succeeded in saving these provinces from the turmoil of civil war by ordering Chang Tso-lin, who was later to become the dictator of both Manchuria and North China, to resist the advance of the revolutionary troops. When the Republic had been established, the Manchurian authorities accepted the fait accompli and voluntarily followed the leadership of Yuan Shih-kai, who was chosen the first President of the Republic. To each province both civil and military governors were appointed. In Manchuria, as in the rest of China, the military governors soon succeeded in putting their civil colleagues into the background.

1916. Chang Tso-lin appointed Governor of Fengtien province.

In 1916, Chang Tso-lin was appointed military governor of Fengtien province, concurrently acting as civil governor. His personal influence extended much further. When the question arose of declaring war against Germany, be joined the military leaders in China in their request to dissolve the Parliament which had opposed that measure. When the request was rejected by the President, he declared his province independent from the Central Government at Peking. Later, he withdrew that declaration and in 1918, in recognition of his service to the Central Government, he was appointed Inspector-General of all Manchuria. In this way Manchuria again became an administrative unit with its own special regime.

1922. He severs allegiance to Central Government at Peking.

Chang Tso-lin accepted the honours accorded by the Central Government, but his attitude from time to time depended on the nature of his personal relations with the military leaders who controlled the changing central authorities. He seems to have looked upon his relations with the Government in the sense of a personal alliance. In July 1922, when he failed to establish his authority south of the Great Wall and saw his rivals taking control of the Peking Government, he renounced allegiance to the Central Government and maintained complete independence of action in Manchuria until he extended his authority south of the Wall and became master of Peking as well. He expressed his willingness to respect foreign rights, and accepted the obligations of China, but he requested foreign Powers to negotiate henceforth directly with his administration in all matters concerning Manchuria.

The Mukden Agreement with U. S. S. R. 1924.

Accordingly, he repudiated the Sino-Soviet Agreement of May 31st, 1921, though very advantageous to China, and persuaded the U. S. S. R. to conclude a separate agreement with him in September 1924. It was virtually identical with that of May 31st, 1924, with the Central Government. This fact emphasised Chang Tso-lin's insistence on the recognition of his complete independence of action, both in domestic and foreign policy.

Marshal Chang Tso-lin defeats General Wu Pei-fu.

In 1924, he invaded China again and was successful, because General (now Marshal) Feng Yu-hsiang abandoned his superior, General (now Marshal) Wu Pei-fu, at a critical moment in the campaign. The immediate result was the overthrow of the Central Government and the expansion of Marshal Chang's influence as far south as Shanghai.

Mutiny of Kuo Sung-lin, 1925.

In 1925, Marshal Chang had again to resort to arms, this time against his late ally, General Feng. In this campaign one of this commanders, Kuo Sung-lin, abandoned him at a most critical moment in favour of General Feng. The mutiny of Kuo Sung-lin in November 1925 was of more than passing interest, because it involved both the U. S. S. R. and Japan, the action of the former having been indirectly of advantage to General Feng and that of the latter to Marshal Chang. Kuo Sung-lin, though a subordinate of the Marshal, shared General Feng's views about social reform, and turned against his superior in the belief that his downfall was necessary to put an end to civil war. This defection put the Marshal in a most critical position. Kuo Sung-lin was in possession of the territory west of the railway and the Marshal was at Mukden with greatly reduced forces. At this moment, Japan, in her own interests in South Manchuria, declared a neutral zone of 20 li (7 miles) on each side of the South Manchuria Railway, across which she would allow no troops to pass. This prevented Kuo Sung-lin from advancing against the Marshal and allowed time for the reinforcements from Heilungkiang to reach him. They were delayed by the action of the Soviet railway authorities, who refused to allow them to travel over the railway without first paying their fares in cash, but they managed to travel by another route.

The arrival of these reinforcements and the more or less open help given by the Japanese settled the campaign in the Marshal's favour. Kuo Sung-lin was defeated and General Feng was forced to withdraw and to abandon Peking to Marshal Chang. Marshal Chang resented the action of the authorities of the Chinese Eastern Railway on this occasion and left no stone unturned to retaliate by continuous encroachments on the rights of this railway. The experience provided by this incident appears to have been an important factor in causing him to build an independent railway system connecting the three provincial capitals of Manchuria.

Meaning of Manchurian independence.

The independence declared by Marshal Chang Tso-lin at different times never meant that he or the people of Manchuria wished to be separated from China. His armies did not invade China as if it were a foreign country, but merely as participants in the civil war. Like the war lords of any other province, the Marshal alternately supported, attacked, or declared his territory independent of the Central Government, but never in such a way as to involve the partition of China into separate States. On the contrary, most Chinese civil wars were directly or indirectly connected with some ambitious scheme to unify the country under a really strong Government. Through all its wars and periods of "independence", therefore, Manchuria remained an integral part of China.

Chang Tso-lin and the Kuomintang.

Although Marshal Chang Tso-lin and the Kuomintang had been allies in the wars against Wu Pei-fu, the former did not himself accept the doctrines of the Kuomintang. He did not approve of the constitution as desired by Dr. Sun, as it did not seem to him to harmonise with the spirit of the Chinese people; but he desired the unification of China, and his policy with regard to the spheres of interest of the U. S. S. R. and Japan in Manchuria shows that he would have liquidated both if he could have done so. Indeed, he almost succeeded in accomplishing this in the case of the sphere of the U. S. S. R. and initiated the policy of railway construction already referred to, which was to cut off the South Manchuria Railway from some of its feeder districts. This attitude towards U. S. S. R. and Japanese interests in Manchuria may be attributed partly to impatience at the limitations of his authority in dealing with these countries and partly to the resentment which he shared with all shades of Chinese opinion regarding the privileged position of foreigners in China. In fact, in November 1924, he invited Dr. Sun to a re-organisation conference in the programme of which the latter wanted to include the improvement of the standard of living, the convening of a national convention, and the abolition of unequal treaties. Dr. Sun's fatal illness prevented this conference from taking place; but his proposals suggest a certain understanding with the Marshal and a possible basis of agreement between them with regard to the foreign policy of their country.

Last years of Chang Tso-lin.

In the last years of his life, Marshal Chang Tso-lin showed increasing unwillingness to allow Japan to profit by the privileges she derived from various treaties and agreements. Their relations at times became somewhat strained. Japanese advice that he should keep out of the factional strife in China and concentrate his energy on the development of Manchuria he resented and disregarded, as did his son after him. After the defeat of General Feng, Chang Tso-lin became the chief of the alliance of the Northern militarists, with the title of Great Marshal.

In 1928, he suffered defeat at the hands of the Kuomintang Army in their Northern Expedition referred to in CHAPTER I , and was advised by Japan to withdraw his armies into Manchuria before it was too late. The declared object of Japan was to save Manchuria from the evils of civil war which would have resulted from the entry of a defeated army pursued by its victors.

Death of Marshal Chang Tso-lin, June 4th, 1928.

The Marshal resented the advice, but was obliged to follow it. He left Peiping (formerly Peking) on June 3rd, 1928, for Mukden, but was killed the next day by an explosion which wrecked his train just outside the city at the spot where the Peiping-Mukden Railway passes underneath the bridge over which run the lines of the South Manchuria Railway.

The responsibility for this murder has never been established. The tragedy remains shrouded in mystery, but the suspicion of Japanese complicity to which it gave rise became an additional factor in the state of tension which Sino-Japanese relations had already reached by that time.

Succeeded by his son, Marshal Chang Hsueh-liang.

After the death of Marshal Chang Tso-lin, his son, Chang Hsueh-liang, became the ruler of Manchuria. He shared many of the national aspirations of the younger generation, and desired to stop civil warfare and assist the Kuomintang in its policy of unification. As Japan had already some experience of the policy and tendencies of the Kuomintang, she did not welcome the prospect of such influences penetrating into Manchuria. The young Marshal was advised accordingly. Like his father, he resented that advice and decided to follow his own counsel.

The young Marshal declares allegiance to the Central Government.

His relations with the Kuomintang and with Nanking became closer and, in December 1928, he accepted the national flag and declared his allegiance to the Central Government. He was made Commander-in-Chief of the North-Eastern Frontier Army and was also confirmed as chief of the administration of Manchuria, with the addition of Jehol, a part of Inner Mongolia with an area of about 60,000 square miles.

The union of Manchuria with Nationalist China necessitated some changes in the administrative organisation, which was made to approximate to that of the Central Government. The committee system was introduced and Kuomintang headquarters were established. In reality, the old system and its personnel continued to function as before.

Kuomintang connection more nominal than real.

The interference of party branches with the local administrations, such as continually occurred in China, was not tolerated in Manchuria. The provision which required all important military officers and civil officials to be members of the Kuomintang was treated as a mere formality. The relationship with the Central Government depended, in all affairs—military, civil, financial and foreign—on voluntary co-operation. Orders or instructions requiring unquestioning obedience would not have been tolerated. Appointments or dismissals against the wishes of the Manchurian authorities were unthinkable. In various other parts of China, a similar independence of action in government and party affairs existed. All important appointments are, in such cases, really made by the local authorities and only confirmed by the Central Government.

Effect of union with Nationalist Government on foreign policy in Manchuria.

In the domain of foreign policy, the union of Manchuria with the Nationalist Government was to have more important consequences, although, in this respect, the local authorities were also left much liberty of action. The persistent assaults of Marshal Chang Tso-lin on the position of the Chinese Eastern Railway in Manchuria and his disregard of certain rights claimed by Japan show that, in Manchuria, a "forward policy" had already been adopted before the union with the Nationalists. However, after the union, Manchuria was opened to well-organised and systematic Kuomintang propaganda. In its official party publications and numerous affiliated organs, it never ceased to insist on the primary importance of the recovery of lost sovereign rights, the abolition of unequal treaties, and the wickedness of imperialism. Such propaganda was bound to make a profound impression in Manchuria, where the reality of foreign interests, courts, police, guards or soldiers on Chinese soil, was apparent. Through the Nationalist school-books, party propaganda entered the schools. Associations such as the Liaoning Peoples' Foreign Policy Association made their appearance. They stimulated and intensified the nationalist sentiment and carried on an anti-Japanese agitation. Pressure was brought to bear on Chinese house-owners and landlords to raise the rents of Japanese and Korean tenants, or to refuse renewal of rent contracts[1]. The Japanese reported to the Commission many cases of this nature. Korean settlers were subjected to systematic

---

① 原编辑者注：See special study No. 9 annexed to this report.

persecution. Various orders and instructions of an anti-Japanese nature were issued. Cases of friction accumulated and dangerous tension developed. The Kuomintang Party headquarters in the provincial capitals were established in March 1931, and subsequently branch organisations were set up in the other towns and districts. Party propagandists from China came North in increasing numbers. The Japanese complained that the anti-Japanese agitation was intensified every day. In April 1931, a five-days' conference under the auspices of the People's Foreign Policy Association was held at Mukden, with over three hundred delegates from various parts of Manchuria in attendance. The possibility of liquidating the Japanese position in Manchuria was discussed, the recovery of the South Manchuria Railway being included in the resolutions adopted. At the same time, the U. S. S. R. and her citizens suffered from similar tendencies, while the White Russians, although they had no sovereign rights or exceptional privileges to surrender, were subjected to humiliation and ill-treatment.

Effect on domestic affairs.

As regards domestic affairs, the Manchurian authorities had retained all the power they wanted, and they had no objection to following administrative rules and methods adopted by the Central Government so long as the essentials of power were not affected.

The Political Committee of the North-Eastern Provinces.

Soon after the union, the Political Committee of the North-Eastern Provinces was established at Mukden. It was, under the nominal supervision of the Central Government, the highest administrative authority in the North-Eastern Provinces. It consisted of thirteen members, who elected one of their members as President. The Committee was responsible for the direction and supervision of the work of the Governments of the four provinces of Liaoning, Kirin, Heilungkiang and Jehol, and of the so-called Special District which, since 1922, had replaced the administrative sphere of the Chinese Eastern Railway. The Committee had authority to deal with all matters not specifically reserved to the Central Government and to take any action which did not conflict with their laws and orders. It was the duty of the Governments of the Provinces and of the Special District to carry out the decisions reached by the Committee.

The administrative system of the Provinces did not differ essentially from the organisation adopted in the rest of China. The concession made with regard to the preservation of Manchuria as an administrative unit was the most important difference. Without this concession, voluntary union would probably not have taken place. In fact, notwithstanding external changes, the old conditions continued to exist. The Manchurian authorities realized that, as before, their power derived much more from their armies than from Nanking.

The Army—Military expenditure 80 percent of total expenditure.

This fact explains the maintenance of large standing armies numbering about 250,000 men, and of the huge arsenal on which more than $ 200,000,000 (silver) are reported to have been spent. Military expenses are estimated to have amounted to 80 per cent of the total expenditure. The remainder was not sufficient to provide for the costs of administration, police, justice and education. The treasury was not capable of paying adequate salaries to the officials. As all power rested in the hands of a few military men; office could be owned only through them. Nepotism, corruption, and maladministration continued to be unavoidable consequences of this state of affairs. The Commission found grave complaints concerning this maladministration to be widely current. This state of affairs, however, was not peculiar to Manchuria, as similar or even worse conditions existed in other parts of China.

Heavy taxation was needed for the upkeep of the army. As ordinary revenues were still insufficient, the authorities further taxed the people by steadily depreciating the irredeemable provincial currencies①. This was often done, particularly of late, in connection with "official bean-buying" operations, which by 1930 had already assumed monopolistic proportions. By gaining control over Manchuria's staple products, the authorities had hoped to enhance their gains by compelling the foreign bean-buyers, particularly the Japanese, to pay higher prices. Such transactions show the extent to which the authorities controlled banks and commerce. Officials likewise engaged freely in all sorts of private enterprise, and used their power to gather wealth for themselves and their favourites.

Constructive efforts of the Chinese administration in Manchuria.

Whatever the shortcomings of the administration in Manchuria may have been in the period preceding the events of September 1931, efforts were made in some parts of the country to improve the administration, and certain achievements must be noted, particularly in the field of education, progress, of municipal administration, and of public utility work. It is necessary, in particular, to emphasize that, during this period, under the administration of Marshal Chang Tso-lin and Marshal Chang Hsueh-liang, the Chinese population and Chinese interests played a much greater part than formerly in the development and organisation of the economic resources of Manchuria. ②

The extensive settlement of Chinese immigrants, already mentioned, helped to develop the economic and social relations between Manchuria and the rest of China. But apart from this colonisation, it was during this period that Chinese railways, independent of Japanese capital, notably the Mukden-Hailung, the Tahushan-Tungliao (a branch of the Peiping-Mukden system), the Tsitsihar-Koshan, and the Hulun-Hailun railways, were built, and that

---

①　原编辑者注：See special studies No. 4 and No. 5 annexed to this Report.

②　原编辑者注：See also CHAPTER Ⅷ and special study No. 3 annexed to this Report.

the Hulutao Harbour project, the Liao River Conservancy work, and some navigation enterprises on various rivers were started. Official and private Chinese interests participated in many enterprises. In mining, they had an interest in the Penhsihu, Muting, Chalainoerh and Laotoukou coal-mines, and sole responsibility for the development of other mines, many of them under the direction of the official North-Eastern Mining Administration; they were also interested in gold-mining in Heilungkiang province. In forestry, they had a joint interest with Japanese in the Yalu Timber Company and were engaged in the timber industry in Heilungkiang and Kirin Provinces. Agricultural experimental stations were started in various places in Manchuria, and agricultural associations and irrigation projects were encouraged. Finally, Chinese interests were engaged in milling and textile industries, bean, oil and flour mills in Harbin, spinning and weaving mills for Pongee or Tussah silk, cotton and wool.

Commercial relations with the rest of China.

Commerce between Manchuria and the rest of China also increased[①]. This trade was partly financed by Chinese banks, notably the Bank of China, which had established branches in the leading towns in Manchuria. Chinese steamships and native junks plied between China Proper and Dairen, Yingkow (New-chwang) and Antung. They carried increasing amounts of cargo and occupied second place in Manchuria's shipping, being exceeded only by Japanese tonnage. Chinese insurance business was also on the increase, and the Chinese Maritime Customs derived an ever-increasing revenue from the trade of Manchuria.

Thus, during the period preceding the conflict between China and Japan, both the political and economic ties between Manchuria and the rest of China were gradually strengthened. This growing interdependence

----

① 原编辑者注: See also CHAPTER Ⅷ and special study No. 6 annexed to this Report.

contributed to induce Chinese leaders, both in Manchuria and in Nanking, to pursue an increasingly nationalist policy directed against the interests and rights acquired by Russia or Japan.

3. Relations with Russia

Russo-Chinese Relations.

The Sino-Japanese war of 1894—95 had given Russia an opportunity to intervene, ostensibly on behalf of China, but in fact in her own interest, as subsequent events proved. Japan was forced by diplomatic pressure to return to China the Liaotung Peninsula in South Manchuria, which had been ceded to Japan by the Treaty of Shimonoseki in 1895, and Russia assisted China to pay off the war indemnities which had been imposed by Japan. In 1896, a secret defensive alliance was concluded between the two countries and, in the same year, in consideration of the services above referred to, Russia was authorised by China to carry a branch of the Trans-Siberian Railway across Manchuria in a direct line from Chita to Vladivostok.

The Chinese Eastern Railway.

This line was said to be needed for the transportation of Russian forces to be sent to the East in case Japan should again attack China. The Russo-Chinese Bank (later the Russo-Asiatic Bank) was established to mask somewhat the official character of the enterprise. The Bank formed in its turn the Chinese Eastern Railway Company for the construction and operation of the railway.

Contract of September 8th, 1896.

By the terms of the contract of September 8th, 1896, between the Bank and the Chinese Government, the Company was to build the railway and operate it for eighty years, at the end of which it was to become the property of China free of charge, but China had the right of purchasing it at a price to be agreed upon at the end of thirty-six years. During the period of the contract, the company was to have the absolute and exclusive right of administration of its lands. This clause was interpreted by Russia in a much broader way than various other stipulations in the contract seem to warrant. China protested against the continuous Russian attempts to enlarge the scope of the contract, but was not able to prevent it. Russia gradually succeeded in exercising in the Chinese Eastern Railway area, with its rapidly developing railway towns, rights equivalent to rights of sovereignty. China had also consented to hand over free of charge all Government lands needed by the railway, while private lands might be expropriated at current prices. The Company had, furthermore, been permitted to construct and operate the telegraph lines necessary for its own use.

Lease of the Liaotung Peninsula to Russia, 1898.

In 1898, Russia secured a lease for twenty-five years of the southern part of the Liaotung Peninsula, which Japan had been forced to give up in 1895, and also secured the right to connect the Chinese Eastern Railway to Russia, at Harbin with Port Arthur and Dalny (now Dairen) in the leased territory. Authority was given for the construction of a naval port at Port Arthur. In the area traversed by this branch line, the Company was granted the right to cut timber and to mine coal for the use of the railway. All the stipulations of the contract of September 8th, 1896, were extended to the supplementary branches. Russia was authorised to make her own tariff arrangements inside the leased territory. In 1899, Dalny (now Dairen) was declared a free port and opened to foreign shipping and commerce. No railway privileges were to be given to the subjects of other Powers in the area traversed by the branch line. In the neutral ground north of the leased territory, no ports were to be opened to foreign trade and no concessions or privileges were to be granted without the consent of Russia.

Russian occupation of Manchuria, 1900.

In 1900, Russia occupied Manchuria on the ground that the Boxer rising had endangered her nationals. Other Powers protested and demanded the withdrawal of her forces, but Russia delayed taking action in this sense. In February 1901, the draft of a secret Sino-Russian treaty was discussed in St. Petersburg, by the terms of which China, in return for the restoration of her civil authority in Manchuria, was to sanction the maintenance of the railway guards which Russia had established under Clause 6 of the Fundamental Contract of 1896, and to engage not to transfer to other nations or their subjects, without the consent of Russia, mines or other interests in Manchuria, Mongolia, and Sinkiang. These and some other clauses in the draft treaty, when they became known, aroused opposition from public opinion in China and other countries and, on April 3rd, 1901, the Russian Government issued a circular note to the effect that the project had been withdrawn.

Japan resorted to war against Russia, February 10th, 1904.

Japan followed these manoeuvres with particular attention. On January 30th, 1902, she had concluded the Anglo-Japanese Treaty of Alliance and accordingly felt herself more secure. However, she was still concerned at the prospect of Russian encroachments into Korea and Manchuria. She therefore pressed with the other Powers for the evacuation of the Russian forces in Manchuria. Russia declared her willingness to withdraw on conditions which would have virtually closed Manchuria and Mongolia to other than Russian enterprise. In Korea, Russian pressure increased also. In July 1902, Russian troops appeared at the mouth of the Yalu River. Several other acts convinced Japan that Russia had decided upon a policy which was a menace to her interests, if not to her wry existence. In July 1903, she began negotiations with Russia concerning the maintenance of the policy of the Open Door and the territorial integrity of China, but, having met with no success whatever, she resorted to war on February 10th, 1904. China remained neutral.

Treaty of Portsmouth.

Russia was defeated. On September 5th, 1905, she concluded the Treaty of Portsmouth, whereby she relinquished her exceptional rights in South Manchuria in favour of Japan. The leased territory and all rights connected with the lease were transferred to Japan, and also the railway between Port Arthur and Changchun, with its branches, as well as all coalmines in that region belonging to or worked for the benefit of the railway. Both parties agreed to restore to the exclusive administration of China all portions of Manchuria occupied or under the control of their respective troops, with the exception of the leased territory. Both reserved the right to maintain (under certain specified conditions) guards to protect their respective railway lines in Manchuria, the number of such guards not to exceed fifteen per kilometre.

Russian influence restricted to North Manchuria.

Russia had lost half of her sphere of influence, which was henceforth to be restricted to North Manchuria. She retained her position there and increased her influence in the following years, but, when the Russian Revolution broke out in 1917, China decided to reassert her sovereignty in this area.

Siberian expedition.

At first, her action was restricted to participation in the Allied intervention (1918—1920) which, in connection with the chaotic conditions rapidly developing, after the Russian Revolution, in Siberia and North Manchuria, had been proposed by the United States of America for the double purpose of protecting the vast stores of war material and supplies accumulated at Vladivostok and of assisting the evacuation of some 50,000 Czechoslovak troops, who were retreating from the eastern front across Siberia. This proposal was accepted and it was arranged that each country should send an expeditionary force of 7,000 mean to be assigned to its own special section of the Trans-Siberian line, the Chinese Eastern Railway being confided to the sole charge of the Chinese. To ensure the working of the railways in co-operation with the Allied forces, a special Inter-Allied Railway Committee was formed in 1919 with technical and transportation boards under it. In 1920, the intervention came to an end and the Allied forces were withdrawn from Siberia except the Japanese, who had become involved in open hostilities with the Bolsheviks. The fighting dragged on for nearly two years. In 1922, after the Washington Conference, the Japanese troops were also withdrawn and, simultaneously, the Inter-Allied Committee, with its technical board, ceased to exist.

After outbreak of Russian Revolution in 1917, China revokes privileges granted to Russia in 1896.

Meanwhile, China, after an abortive attempt of General Horvath, the head of the Chinese Eastern Railway, to set up an independent regime in the railway area, assumed responsibility for the preservation of order in that area (1920). In the same year, she concluded an agreement with the re-organised Russo-Asiatic Bank and announced her intention of assuming temporarily supreme control of an agreement with a new Russian Government. China also announced her intention of resuming the advantages conferred on her by the contract of 1896 and the original statutes of the Company. Thenceforth, the President and four members of the Board of Directors of the Company and two members of the Audit Committee were to be nominated by the Chinese Government. Russian predominance was also weakened by other measures which followed. The Russian armed forces in the railway area were disarmed and replaced by Chinese soldiers. The extra-territorial status of Russians was abolished. The courts were forcibly entered and closed. Russians were made amenable to Chinese law, justice and laxation. They could be arrested by the Chinese police and held by them indefinitely, as the police had large powers and were insufficiently controlled.

Special Administrative Districts joined.

In 1922, the railway area which so far had been under the administration of the Company was transformed into a Special District of the Three Eastern Provinces under a Chief Administrator directly responsible to Mukden. The administration of the lands belonging to the railway was also interfered with Marshal Chang Tso-lin had practically liquidated the Russian sphere before Russia's new Government had been recognised, and private interests had suffered heavily in the process. When the Soviet Government succeeded to the Manchurian inheritance of its predecessor, the railway had been shorn of most of its privileges.

Sino-Soviet agreement.

The declarations of policy made in 1919 and 1920 by the Soviet Government with regard to China implied a complete relinquishment of the special rights which the Imperial Government had acquired in China, notably those acquired in North Manchuria.

Agreement of 1924.

In accordance with this policy, the Soviet Government agreed to the regularisation of the fait accompli by a new agreement. By the Sino-Russian Agreement of May 31st, 1924, the Chinese Eastern Railway became a purely commercial concern under joint management, in which China also acquired a financial interest. The Government of the U. S. S. R. had, however, the right of appointing the General Manager (who exercises extensive and ill-defined powers) and, under the Agreement, the Government of the U. S. S. R. exercised a preponderant influence in the affairs of the railway and was able to retain the essential parts of its economic interests in North Manchuria. As mentioned above, the Agreement of May 1924, concluded with the Chinese Government at Peking, was not accepted by Marshal Chang Tso-lin, who insisted on a separate Agreement being concluded with himself. This Agreement, signed in September 1924, was almost identical in its terms, but by it the lease of the railway was shortened from eighty to sixty years.

Chang Tso-lin's aggressive policy against the interests of the U. S. S. R.

This Agreement did not inaugurate a period of friendly relations between the U. S. S. R. and the administration of Marshal Chang Tso-lin in Manchuria. The convening of the conference which was to deal with the many questions left unsettled in the two Agreements of 1924 was postponed on various pretexts. On two occasions, in 1925 and 1926, the General Manager of the Chinese Eastern Railway refused to transport troops of the Marshal on the railway. The second incident led to the arrest of the General Manager and to an ultimatum from the U. S. S. R. (January 23rd, 1926). Nor were these isolated incidents. Nevertheless, the Chinese authorities persisted in a policy which was directed against Russian interests and which was resented both by the Government of the U. S. S. R. and by the White Russians.

Final efforts of China to liquidate Soviet influence in Manchuria, 1929.

After the adherence of Manchuria to the Nanking Government, nationalist spirit increased in strength, and the efforts of the U. S. S. R. to maintain predominating control over the railway were, more than ever before, resented. In May 1929, an attempt was made to liquidate the last remnants of the Russian sphere of interest. The attack started with a raid on the Soviet consulates at various places by the Chinese police, who made many arrests and claimed to have found evidence proving that a Communist revolution was being plotted by employees of the Soviet Government and of the Chinese Eastern Railway. In July, the telegraph and telephone systems of the railway were seized, and many important Soviet organisations and enterprises were forcibly closed down. Finally, the Soviet Manager of the railway was requested to hand over the management to a Chinese appointee. He refused to do so and was thereupon forbidden to carry on his duties. The Chinese authorities replaced freely members of the Soviet staff by their own nominees, many Soviet citizens were arrested, and some were deported. The Chinese justified the violent action taken on the ground that the Soviet Government had broken its pledge not to engage in propaganda directed against the political and social systems of China. The Soviet Government, in its note of May 30th, denied the charge.

Action of the U. S. S. R.

In consequence of the forcible liquidation of the remaining Russian rights and interests, the Soviet Government decided to take action. After the exchange of several notes, it recalled from China its diplomatic and commercial representatives, and all its nominees to posts in the Chinese Eastern Railway, and severed all railway communications between its territory and China. China, likewise, broke off relations with the U. S. S. R. and withdrew all Chinese diplomatic officers from Soviet territory. Raids by Soviet troops across the Manchurian border began and developed into a military invasion in November 1929. After having suffered defeat and severe loss of prestige, the Manchurian authorities, to whom the Nanking Government entrusted the settlement of the dispute, were forced to accept the demands of the U. S. S. R.

Protocol of Habarovsk, December 22nd, 1929.

On December 22nd, 1929, a Protocol was signed at Habarovsk whereby the status quo was re-established. During the dispute, the Soviet Government had always taken the position, in answer to various memoranda from third-Power signatories to the Pact of Paris, that her action had been taken in legitimate self-defence and could in no way be interpreted as a breach of that agreement.

Russo-Japanese relations regarding Manchuria since 1905.

Before describing the interests of Japan in Manchuria, which are dealt with at length in the next chapter, a brief reference must be made, in this account of the position of Russia in Manchuria, to the relations between that country and Japan since 1905.

Policy of co-operation, 1907—1917.

It is an interesting fact that the war between Russia and Japan was followed almost immediately by a policy of close co-operation, and when peace was concluded they were able to strike a satisfactory balance between their respective spheres of interest in North and South Manchuria. Such traces of the conflict as might have remained behind were rapidly effaced by controversies with other Powers which wanted to engage actively in the development of Manchuria. The fear of other rivals hastened the process which was reconciling the two countries. The Treaties of 1907, 1910, 1912 and 1916 brought the two countries progressively closer together.

Effect of the Russian Revolution on Japan.

The Russian Revolution of 1917, followed by the declarations of the Soviet Government of July 25th, 1919, and of October 27th, 1920, regarding its policy towards the Chinese people and, later, by the Sino-Soviet Agreements of May 31st, 1924, and September 20, 1924, shattered the basis of Russo-Japanese understanding and co-operation in Manchuria. This fundamental reversal of policy radically changed the relations of the three Powers in the Far East. Moreover, the Allied intervention (1918—1920) with its aftermath of friction between the Japanese and Soviet forces in Siberia (1920—1922), had accentuated the change in the relations between Japan and Russia. The attitude of the Soviet Government gave a strong impetus to China's nationalistic aspirations. As the Soviet Government and the Third international had adopted a policy opposed to all imperialist Powers which maintained relations with China on the basis of the existing treaties, it seemed probable that they would support China in the struggle for the recovery of sovereign rights. This development revived all the old anxieties and suspicions of Japan towards her Russian neighbour. This country, with which she had once been at war, had, during the years which followed that war, become a friend and ally. Now this relationship was changed, and the possibility of a danger from across the North-Manchurian border again became a matter of concern to Japan. The likelihood of an alliance between the Communist doctrines in the North and the anti-Japanese propaganda of the Kuomintang in the South made the desire to impose between the two a Manchuria which should be free from both increasingly felt in Japan. Japanese misgivings have been still further increased in the last few years by the predominant influence acquired by the U. S. S. R. in Outer Mongolia and the growth of Communism in China.

The Convention concluded between Japan and the U. S. S. R. in January 1925 served to establish regular relations, but did not revive the close co-operation of the pre-revolution period.

CHAPTER Ⅲ   MANCHURIAN ISSUES BETWEEN JAPAN AND CHINA
(Before September 18th, 1931)

1. Japan's Interest in China

During the quarter of a century before September 1931, the ties which bound Manchuria to the rest of China were growing stronger and, at the same time, the interests of Japan in Manchuria were increasing. Manchuria was admittedly a part of China, but it was a part in which Japan had acquired or claimed such exceptional rights, so restricting the exercise of China's sovereign rights, that a conflict between the two countries was a natural result.

Japan's Treaty Rights of 1905.

By the Treaty of Peking of December 1905, China gave her consent to the transfer to Japan of the Kwantung Leased Territory, which was formerly leased to Russia, and of the southern branch of the Russian-controlled Chinese Eastern Railway as far north as Changchun. In an additional agreement, China granted to Japan a concession to improve the military railway line between Antung and Mukden and to operate it for fifteen years.

South Manchuria Railway Company was organised in August 1906.

In August 1906, the South Manchuria Railway Company was organised by Imperial Decree to take over and administer the former Russian Railway, as well as the Antung-Mukden Railway. The Japanese Government acquired control of the company by taking half of the shares in exchange for the railway, its properties, and the valuable coal-mines at Fushun and Yentai. The company was entrusted, in the railway area, with the functions of administration and was allowed to levy taxes; it was also authorised to engage in mining, electrical enterprises, warehousing, and many other branches of business.

Annexation of Korea.

In 1910, Japan annexed Korea. This annexation indirectly increased Japanese rights in Manchuria, since Korean settlers became Japanese subjects over whom Japanese officials exercised jurisdiction.

The Treaty and Notes of 1915.

In 1915, as a result of the group of exceptional demands made by the Japanese and generally known as the "Twenty-one Demands", Japan and China signed a Treaty and exchanged Notes on May 25th regarding South Manchuria and Eastern Inner Mongolia. By those agreements, the lease of the Kwantung Territory, including Port Arthur and Dalny (now Dairen), which was originally for a period of twenty-five years, and the concessions for the South Manchuria and the Antung-Mukden Railways, were all extended to ninety-nine years. Furthermore, Japanese subjects in South Manchuria acquired the right to travel and reside, to engage in business of any kind, and to lease land necessary for trade, industry and agriculture. Japan also obtained rights of priority for railway and certain other loans in South Manchuria and Eastern Inner Mongolia, and preferential rights regarding the appointment of advisers in South Manchuria. At the Washington Conference, 1921—22, however, Japan relinquished her rights regarding the loans and the advisers.

These treaties and other agreements gave to Japan an important and unusual position in Manchuria. She governed the leased territory with practically full rights of sovereignty. Through the South Manchuria Railway she administered the railway areas, including several towns and large sections of such populous cities as Mukden and Changchun; and in these areas she controlled the police, taxation, education and public utilities. She maintained armed forces in many parts of the country: the Kwantung Army in the Leased Territory. Railway Guards in the railway areas, and Consular Police throughout the various districts.

Exceptional character of the political, economic and legal relations between Japan and China in Manchuria.

This summary of the long list of Japan's rights in Manchuria shows clearly the exceptional character of the political, economic and legal relations created between that country and China in Manchuria. There is probably nowhere in the world an exact parallel to this situation, no example of a country enjoying in the territory of a neighbouring state such extensive economic and administrative privileges. A situation of this kind could possibly be maintained without leading to incessant complications and disputes if it were freely desired or accepted on both sides, and if it were the sign and embodiment of a well-considered policy of close collaboration in the economic and in the political sphere. But in the absence of those conditions, it could only lead to friction and conflict.

2. Conflict between the Fundamental Interests of Japan and China in Manchuria

Chinese attitude towards Manchuria.

The Chinese people regard Manchuria as an integral part of China and deeply resent any attempt to separate it from the rest of their country. Hitherto, these Three Eastern Provinces have always been considered both by China and by foreign Powers as a part of China, and the de jure authority of the Chinese Government there has been unquestioned. This is evidenced in many Sino-Japanese treaties and agreements, as well as in other international conventions, and has been reiterated in numerous statements issued officially by Foreign Offices, including that of Japan.

Manchuria, China's first line of defence.

The Chinese regard Manchuria as their "first line of defence". As Chinese territory, it is looked upon as a sort of buffer against the adjoining territories of Japan and Russia, a region which constitutes an outpost against the penetration of Japanese and Russian influences from those regions into the other parts of China. The facility with which China, south of the Great Wall, including the city of Peiping, can be invaded from Manchuria has been demonstrated to the Chinese from historical experience. This fear of foreign invasion from the north-east has been increased in recent years by the development of railway communication, and has been intensified during the events of the past year.

China's economic interest in Manchuria.

Manchuria is also regarded by the Chinese as important to them for economic reasons. For decades they have called it the "granary of China", and more recently have regarded it as a region which furnishes seasonal employment to Chinese farmers and labourers from neighbouring Chinese provinces.

Whether China as a whole can be said to be over-populated may be open to question, but that certain regions and provinces—as, for example, Shantung—are now peopled in such numbers as to require emigration is generally accepted by the most competent authorities on this subject[①]. The Chinese, therefore, regard Manchuria as a frontier region, capable of affording relief for the present and future population problems of other parts of China. They deny the statement that the Japanese are principally responsible for the economic development of Manchuria, and point to their own colonisation enterprises, especially since 1925, to their railway development, and other enterprises, in refutation of these claims.

Japanese Interests in Manchuria: sentiment resulting from the Russo-Japanese War.

Japanese interests in Manchuria differ both in character and degree from those of any other foreign country. Deep in the mind of every Japanese is the memory of their country's great struggle with Russia in 1901—05, fought on the plains of Manchuria, at Mukden and Liaoyang, along the line of the South Manchuria Railway, at the Yalu River, and in the Liaotung Peninsula. To the Japanese the war with Russia will ever be remembered as a life-and-death struggle fought in self-defence against the menace of Russian encroachments. The facts that a hundred thousand Japanese soldiers died in this war and that two billon gold yen were expended have created in Japanese minds a determination that these sacrifices shall not have been made in vain.

Japanese interest in Manchuria, however, began ten years before that war. The war with China, in 1894—95, principally over Korea, was largely fought at Port Arthur and on the plains of Manchuria; and the Treaty of Peace signed at Shimonoseki ceded to Japan in full sovereignty the Liaotung Peninsula. To the Japanese, the fact that Russia, France and Germany forced them to renounce this cession does not affect their conviction that

---

① 原编辑者注：See also special study No. 3 annexed to this Report.

Japan obtained this part of Manchuria as the result of a successful war and thereby acquired a moral right to it which still exists.

Japan's strategic interest in Manchuria.

Manchuria has been frequently referred to as the "life-line" of Japan. Manchuria adjoins Korea, now Japanese territory. The vision of a China, unified, strong and hostile, a nation of four hundred millions, dominant in Manchuria and in Eastern Asia, is disturbing to many Japanese. But to the greater number, when they speak of menace to their national existence and of the necessity for self-defence, they have in mind Russia rather than China. Fundamental, therefore, among the interests of Japan in Manchuria is the strategic importance of this territory.

There are those in Japan who think that she should entrench herself firmly in Manchuria against the possibility of attack from the U. S. S. R. They have an ever-present anxiety lest Korean malcontents in league with Russian Communists in the nearby Maritime Province might in future invite, or co-operate with, some new military advance from the North. They regard Manchuria as a buffer region against both the U. S. S. R, and the rest of China. Especially in the minds of Japanese military men, the right claimed, under agreements with Russia and China, to station a few thousand railway guards along the South Manchuria Railway is small recompense for the enormous sacrifices of their country in the Russo-Japanese War, and a meagre security against the possibility of attack from that direction.

Japan's "special position" in Manchuria.

Patriotic sentiment, the paramount need for military defence, and the exceptional treaty rights all combine to create the claim to a "special position" in Manchuria. The Japanese conception of this "special position" is not limited to what is legally defined in treaties and agreements either with China or with other States. Feelings and historical association, which are the heritage of the Russo-Japanese War, and pride in the achievements of

Japanese enterprise in Manchuria for the last quarter century, are an indefinable but real part of the Japanese claim to a "special position", it is only natural, therefore, that the Japanese use of this expression in diplomatic language should be obscure, and that other States should have found it difficult, if not impossible, to recognise it by international instruments.

The Japanese Government, since the Russo-Japanese War, has at various times sought to obtain from Russia, France, the United Kingdom and the United States of America recognition of their country's "special position", "special influence and interest", or "paramount interest" in Manchuria. These efforts have only met with partial success, and, where recognition of such claims has been accorded, in more or less definite terms, the international agreements or understandings containing them have largely disappeared with the passage of time, either by formal abrogation or otherwise—as, for example: the Russo-Japanese secret Conventions of 1907, 1910, 1912 and 1916, made with the former Tsarist Government of Russia; the Anglo-Japanese Conventions of Alliance, Guarantee and Declaration of Policies; and the Lansing-Ishii Exchange of Notes of 1917. The signatories of the Nine-Power Treaty of the Washington Conference of February 6th, 1922[①], by agreeing "to respect the sovereignty, the independence, and the territorial and administrative integrity" of China, to maintain "equality of opportunity in China for the trade and industry of all nations", by refraining from taking advantage of conditions in China "in order to seek special rights or privileges" there, and by providing "the fullest and most unembarrassed opportunity to China to develop and maintain for herself an effective and stable government", challenged to a large extent the claims of any signatory State to a "special position" or to "special rights and interests" in any part of China, including Manchuria.

---

① 原编辑者注: The nine Powers were: the United States of America, Belgium, the British Empire, China, France, Italy, Japan, the Netherlands, Portugal.

But the provisions of the Nine-Power Treaty and the abandonment, by abrogation or otherwise, of such agreements as those mentioned above have led to no change in the attitude of the Japanese. Viscount Ishii doubtlessly well expressed the general view of his countrymen in his recent Memoirs (Gaiko Yoruku), when he said:

"Even if the Lansing-Ishii agreement is abolished, Japan's special interests unshakenly exist there. The special interests which Japan possesses in China neither were created by an international agreement, nor can they become the objects of abolition."

Japan's claims to a "special position" in Manchuria in conflict with China's sovereign rights and policies.

This Japanese claim with respect to Manchuria conflicts with the sovereign rights of China and is irreconcilable with the aspirations of the National Government, which seeks to curtail existing exceptional rights and privileges of foreign States throughout China and to prevent their further extension in the future. The development of this conflict will be clearer from a consideration of the respective policies pursued by Japan and China in Manchuria.

Japan's general policy towards Manchuria.

Until the events of September 1931, the various Japanese Cabinets, since 1905, appeared to have the same general aims in Manchuria, but they differed as to the policies best suited to achieve these aims. They also differed somewhat as to the extent of the responsibility which Japan should assume for the maintenance of peace and order.

The general aims for which they worked in Manchuria were to maintain and develop Japan's vested interests, to foster the expansion of Japanese enterprise, and to obtain adequate protection for Japanese lives and property. In the policies adopted for realising these aims there was one cardinal feature which may be said to have been common to them all. This feature has been the tendency to regard Manchuria and Eastern Inner Mongolia as distinct from the rest of China. It resulted naturally from the Japanese conception of their country's " special position " in Manchuria. Whatever differences may have been observable between the specific policies advocated by the various Cabinets in Japan—as, for example, between the so-called "friendship policy" of Baron Shidehara and the so-called "positive policy" of the late General Baron Tanaka, they have always had this feature in common.

The " friendship policy " developed from about the time of the Washington Conference and was maintained until April 1927; it was then supplanted by the "positive policy", which was followed until July 1929; finally, the "friendship policy" was again adopted and continued the official policy of the Foreign Office until September 1931. In the spirit which actuated the two policies there was a marked difference: the "friendship policy" rested, in Baron Shidehara's words, "on the basis of good will and neighbourliness"; the "positive policy" rested upon military force. But, in regard to the concrete measures which should be adopted in Manchuria, these two polices differed largely on the question as to the lengths to which Japan should go to maintain peace and order in Manchuria and to protect Japanese interests.

The "positive policy" of the Tanaka Ministry placed greater emphasis upon the necessity for regarding Manchuria as distinct from the rest of China; its positive character was made clear by the frank declaration that, "if disturbances spread to Manchuria and Mongolia, and, as a result, peace and order are disrupted, thereby menacing our special position and rights and interests in these regions", Japan would "defend them, no matter whence the menace comes". The Tanaka policy definitely asserted that Japan would take upon herself the task of preserving "peace and order" in Manchuria—in contrast to previous policies which limited their objectives to protecting Japanese interests there.

The Japanese Government has generally pursued a firmer policy in

Manchuria than elsewhere in China, in order to preserve and develop those vested interests which are peculiar to that region. Certain of the Cabinets have tended to place great reliance on the use of interventionist methods, accompanied by a threat of force. This was true especially at the time of the presentation of the "Twenty-one Demands" on China in 1915, but as to the wisdom of the "Twenty-one Demands", as well as to other methods of intervention and force, there has always been a marked difference of opinion in Japan.

The effect of the Washington Conference upon Japan's position and policy in Manchuria.

The Washington Conference, although it had a marked effect upon the situation in the rest of China, made little actual change in Manchuria. The Nine-Power Treaty of February 6th, 1922, in spite of its provisions with respect to the integrity of China and the policy of the "Open Door", has had but qualified application to Manchuria in view of the character and extent of Japan's vested interests there, although textually the Treaty is applicable to that region. The Nine-Power Treaty did not materially diminish the claims based on these vested interests, although, as already stated, Japan formally relinquished her special rights regarding loans and advisers which had been granted in the Treaty of 1915.

Japan's relations with Chang Tso-lin.

During the period from the Washington Conference until the death of Marshal Chang Tso-lin in 1928, the policy of Japan in Manchuria was chiefly concerned with its relations with the de facto ruler of the Three Eastern Provinces. Japan gave him a measure of support, notably during the Kuo Sung-lin mutiny mentioned in the last chapter. Marshal Chang Tso-lin, in return, although opposed to many of the Japanese demands, felt it necessary to give due recognition to Japan's desires, since these might at any time be enforced by superior military power. He also wished to be able, upon occasion, to obtain Japanese support against Russian opposition in the North. Upon the whole, Japanese relations with Marshal Chang Tso-lin were reasonably satisfactory from her point of view, although they became increasingly disturbed towards the end of his life in consequence of his failure to fulfil some of his alleged promises and agreements. Some evidence even of a revulsion of Japanese feeling against him became apparent in the months preceding his defeat and final retreat to Mukden in June 1928.

Japan's claim to maintain peace and order in Manchuria.

In the spring of 1928, when the Nationalist armies of China were marching on Peking in an effort to drive out the forces of Chang Tso-lin, the Japanese Government, under the premiership of Baron Tanaka, issued a declaration that, on account of her "special position" in Manchuria, Japan would maintain peace and order in that region. When it seemed possible that the Nationalist armies might carry the civil war north of the Great Wall, the Japanese Government, on May 28th, sent to the leading Chinese generals a communication which said:

"The Japanese Government attaches the utmost importance to the maintenance of peace and order in Manchuria, and is prepared to do all it can to prevent the occurrence of any such state of affairs as may disturb that peace and order, or constitute the probable cause of such a disturbance.

In these circumstances, should disturbances develop further in the direction of Peking and Tientsin, and the situation become so menacing as to threaten the peace and order of Manchuria, Japan may possibly be constrained to take appropriate effective steps for the maintenance of peace and order in Manchuria. "

At the same time, Baron Tanaka issued a more definite statement, that the Japanese Government would prevent "defeated troops or those in pursuit of them" from entering Manchuria.

The announcement of this far-reaching policy brought protests from both the Peking and the Nanking Governments, the Nanking note stating that such measures as Japan proposed would be not only "an interference with Chinese domestic affairs, but also a flagrant violation of the principle of mutual respect for territorial sovereignty".

In Japan itself, this "positive policy" of the Tanaka Government, while it received strong support from one party, was vigorously criticised by another, especially by the Shidehara group, on the ground that the preservation of peace and order over all Manchuria was not the responsibility of Japan.

Strained relations between Japan and Chang Hsueh-liang.

Japan's relations with Marshal Chang Hsueh-liang, who succeeded his father in 1928, were increasingly strained from the outset. Japan wished Manchuria to remain separate from the newly established National Government at Nanking, while Marshal Chang Hsueh-Jiang was in favour of recognising the authority of that Government. Reference has already been made to the urgent advice given by Japanese officials that allegiance should not be pledged to the Central Government. When, however, the Mukden Government raised the Nationalist flag over Government buildings in Mukden in December 1928, the Japanese Government made no attempt to interfere.

Japanese relations with Marshal Chang Hsueh-liang continued to be strained and acute friction developed in the months immediately preceding September 1931.

3. Sino-Japanese Railway Issues in Manchuria

Manchurian international politics largely railway politics.

The international politics of Manchuria for a quarter of a century have been largely railway politics. Considerations of a purely economic and railway-operating character have been overshadowed by the dictates of State policies, with the result that Manchurian railways cannot be said to have contributed their maximum to the economic development of the region. Our study of Manchurian railway questions has revealed that in Manchuria there has been little or no co-operation between the Chinese and Japanese railway builders and authorities directed to achieving a comprehensive and mutually beneficial railway plan. In contrast with railway development in such regions as western Canada and Argentina, where economic considerations have in large measure determined railway expansion, railway development in Manchuria has been largely a matter of rivalry between China and Japan. No railway of any importance has ever been constructed in Manchuria without causing an interchange of notes between China and Japan or other interested foreign States.

The South Manchuria Railway served Japan's "Special Mission" in Manchuria.

Manchurian railway construction began with the Russian-financed-and-directed Chinese Eastern Railway which, after the Russo-Japanese War, was replaced in the South by a Japanese-controlled system, the South Manchuria Railway, thus making inevitable future rivalry between China and Japan. The South Manchuria Railway Company, although nominally a private corporation, is, in fact, a Japanese Government enterprise. Its functions include, not only the management of its railway lines, but also exceptional rights of political administration. From the time of its incorporation, the Japanese have never regarded it as a purely economic enterprise. The late Viscount Goto, first President of the Company, laid down a fundamental principle that the South Manchuria Railway should serve Japan's "special mission" in Manchuria.

The South Manchuria Railway system has developed into an efficient and well-managed railway enterprise and has contributed much to the economic development of Manchuria, serving at the same time as an example for the Chinese in its numerous services of a non-railway character, such as its schools, laboratories, libraries and agricultural experiment stations. But this has been accompanied by limitations and positive hindrances arising out of the political character of the Company, its connection with party politics in Japan, and certain large expenditures from which no commensurate financial returns can have been expected. Since its formation, the policy of the Railway Company has been to finance the construction of only such Chinese lines as would be connected with its own system; thus, by means of through-traffic agreements, to divert the major part of the freight to the South Manchuria Railway for seaboard export at Dairen in the Japanese leased territory. Very large sums have been expended in financing these lines and it is doubtful if their construction, in certain cases, was justified on purely economic grounds, especially in view of the large capital advances made and the loan considerations involved.

The very existence of such a foreign-controlled institution as the South Manchuria Railway on Chinese soil was naturally looked upon with disfavour by the Chinese authorities, and questions concerning its rights and privileges under treaties and agreements have constantly arisen since the Russo-Japanese War. More particularly, after 1924, when the Chinese authorities in Manchuria, having come to recognise the importance of railway development, sought to develop their own railways independent of Japanese capital, did these problems become more critical. Both economic and strategic considerations were involved.

Chinese efforts to build their own railways anteceded Manchuria's allegiance to Nanking.

The Tahushan-Tungliao line, for example, was projected to develop new territory and to increase the revenues of the Peking-Mukden Railway, while, on the other hand, the Kuo Sung-lin mutiny in December 1925 demonstrated the possible strategic and political value of independently owned and operated Chinese lines. The Chinese declaration of attempt to overcome the Japanese monopoly, and to place obstacles in the way of its future development, anteceded the period of political influence of the Nationalist Government in Manchuria, the Tahushan-Tungliao, Mukden-Hailungcheng and Hulan-Hailun Railways, for example, having been constructed while Marshal Chang Tso-lin was in power. The policy of Marshal Chang Hsueh-liang, after his assumption of authority in 1928, re-enforced by the widespread movement for "rights recovery" sponsored by the Central Government and the Kuomintang, came into collision with Japan's monopolistic and expansionist policies, centred, as they were, around the South Manchuria Railway Company.

The conflict over "parallel lines".

In the Japanese justification of their resort to forceful means in Manchuria, on and after September 18th, 1931, they have alleged violation of Japan's "treaty rights" and have emphasised China's failure to carry out an engagement made by the Chinese Government during the Sino-Japanese Conference held at Peking in November-December 1905, which was to the following effect:

"The Chinese Government engages, for the purpose of protecting the interests of the South Manchuria Railway, not to construct, prior to the recovery by it of the said railway, any main line in the neighbourhood of and parallel to that railway, or any branch line which might be prejudicial to the interests of the above-mentioned railway."

This dispute over the question of so-called "parallel railways" in Manchuria is of long-standing importance. The issue first arose in 1907—08, when the Japanese Government, asserting this claim of right, presented the Chinese from constructing, under contract with a British firm, the Hsinmintun-Fakumen Railway. Since 1924, when the Chinese in Manchuria undertook with renewed vigour to develop their own railways independent of Japanese financial interest, the Japanese Government has protested against the construction by the Chinese of the Tahushan-Tungliao and the Kirin-Hailungcheng lines, although both these lines were completed and opened to traffic in spite of Japanese protests.

The question as to the existence of a "treaty right" or a "secret protocol".

Prior to the arrival of the Commission in the Far East, there had been much doubt as to the actual existence of any such engagement as was claimed by Japan. In view of the longstanding importance of this dispute, the Commission took special pains to obtain information on the essential facts. In Tokyo, Nanking and Peiping, all the relevant documents were examined, and we are now able to state that the alleged engagement of the Chinese plenipotentiaries of the Peking Conference of November-December 1905 regarding so-called "parallel railways" is not contained in any formal treaty; that the alleged engagement in question is to be found in the minutes of the eleventh day of the Peking Conference, December 4th, 1905. We have obtained agreement from the Japanese and Chinese Assessors that no other document containing such alleged engagement exists beyond this entry in the minutes of the Peking Conference.

The real question at issue.

The real question at issue, therefore, is not whether there exists a "treaty right" whereby Japan is entitled to claim that certain railways in Manchuria have been constructed by the Chinese in violation of such an engagement, but whether this entry in the minutes of the Peking Conference of 1905, whether called a "protocol" or not, is a binding commitment on the part of China, having the force of a formal agreement and without limitations as to the period of circumstances of its application.

The determination of the question whether this entry into the minutes of the Peking Conference constituted, from an international legal point of view, a binding agreement, and whether, if so, there is but one interpretation which may reasonably be placed upon it, was properly a matter for judgment by an impartial judicial tribunal.

The Chinese and Japanese official translations of this entry into the minutes of the Conference leave no doubt that the disputed passage concerning "parallel railways" is a declaration or statement of intention on the part of the Chinese plenipotentiaries.

That there was a statement of intention has not been disputed by the Chinese, but there has, throughout the controversy, been a difference of opinion between the two parties as to the nature of the intention expressed. Japan has claimed that the words employed preclude China from building or allowing to be built any railway which, in the opinion of the South Manchuria Railway Company, was in competition with its system. The Chinese, on the other hand, contend that the only commitment involved in the disputed passage was a statement of intention not to build lines with the deliberate object of unduly impairing the commercial usefulness and value of the South Manchuria Railway. During the exchange of notes of 1907 concerning the Hsinmintun-Fakumen-Railway project, Prince Ching, representing the Chinese Government, stated to Baron Hayashi, the Japanese Minister, in a communication dated April 7th, 1907, that the Japanese plenipotentiaries in the Peking Conference, while refusing to agree to a definition of the term "parallel line" in terms of specific mileage from the South Manchuria Railway, declared that Japan "would do nothing to prevent China from any steps she might take in the future for the development of Manchuria". It would seem, therefore, that the Chinese Government during this period admitted in practice that there was, on their part, an obligation not to construct railways patently and unreasonably prejudicial to the interests of the South Manchuria Railway, though they have always denied that Japan had any valid claim to a right to monopolise railway construction in Southern Manchuria.

There has never been a definition as to what would constitute a parallel railway, although the Chinese desired one. When the Japanese Government opposed the construction of the Hsinmintun-Fakumen Railway in 1906— 1908, the impression was created that Japan considered a "parallel" railway one within approximately thirty-five miles of the South Manchuria Railway, but, in 1926, the Japanese Government protested against the construction of the Tahushan-Tungliao Railway as a "competitive parallel line", noting that the distance between the proposed railway and the South Manchuria Railway would be "no more than seventy miles on the average". It would be difficult to make a thoroughly satisfactory definition.

Difficulties in interpretation of a clause phrased so broadly and non-technically.

From a railway-operating point of view, a "parallel" line can be considered a "competing line": one which deprives another railway of some part of the traffic which naturally would have gravitated to it. Competitive traffic includes both local and through traffic and, especially when the latter is considered, it is not difficult to see how a stipulation against the construction of "parallel" lines is capable of very broad interpretation. Nor is there any agreement between China and Japan as to what constitutes a "main line" or a "branch line". These terms, from a railway-operating point of view, are subject to change. The Peiping-Mukden Railway line from Tahushan extending north was originally considered by that administration as a "branch line", but, after the line had been completed from Tahushan to Tungliao, it was possible to regard this as a "main line".

It was only natural that the interpretation of the undertaking in regard to parallel railways should lead to bitter controversy between China and Japan. The Chinese attempted to build their own railways in South Manchuria, but in almost every case met with a protest from Japan.

Issues caused by Japanese loans for construction of Chinese railways in Manchuria.

A second group of railway issues which increased the tension between China and Japan before the events of September last were those which arose from the agreement under which the Japanese advanced money for the construction of various Chinese Government Railways in Manchuria. Japanese capital to the present value, including arrears and interests, of 150,000,000 yen had been expended in the building of the following Chinese lines: the Kirin-Changchun, the Kirin-Tunhua, the Ssupingkai-Taonan, and the Taonan-Angangchi Railways, and certain narrow-gauge lines.

The Japanese complained that the Chinese would not pay these loans, nor make adequate provision for them, nor carry out various stipulations in the agreements, such as those respecting the appointment of Japanese railway advisers. They made repeated demands that the Chinese should fulfil the alleged promises made by their Government that Japanese interests should be permitted to participate in the construction of the Kirin-Kwainei Railway. This projected line would extend the Kirin-Tunhua Railway to the Korean border, and would make available for Japan a new short sea-and-rail route from her seaports to the centre of Manchuria, and, in conjunction with the other railways, shorten the communications with the interior.

The Chinese defence.

In defence of the failure to repay their loans, the Chinese pointed out that these were not normal financial transactions. They claimed that the loans were made largely by the South Manchuria Railway in order to monopolise railway construction in South Manchuria; that the object was primarily strategic and political; and that, in any case, the new lines had been so heavily over-capitalised that they were, at least for the time being, financially unable to earn the necessary money to repay the construction expenses and loans. They contended that in each instance of alleged failure to fulfil obligations, an impartial examination would show adequate justification for their conduct. As for the Kirin-Kwainei Railway, they denied the moral, and even the legal, validity of the alleged agreements.

The South Manchuria Railway desired a system of branch lines.

There were certain conditions which existed in connection with those railway agreements which made it natural for the loan controversy to arise. The South Manchuria Railway had practically no branches and wished to develop a system of feeder lines in order to increase its freight and passenger traffic. The Company was therefore willing to advance money for the building of such new lines, even though there was little likelihood that the loans would be repaid in the near future; it was also willing to continue to make further advances when earlier loans were still outstanding.

In these circumstances, and so long as the newly constructed Chinese lines functioned as feeders to the South Manchuria system and were operated in some measure under its influence, the South Manchuria Railway Company appeared to make no special effort to force payment of the loans, and the Chinese lines operated with ever-increasing debt obligations. But when certain of these lines were connected with a new Chinese railway system, and in 1930—31 started a serious competition with the South Manchuria Railway, the non-payment of the loans at once became a subject of complaint.

The Nishihara loans.

Another complicating factor, in the case of certain of these loan agreements, was their political character. It was as a result of the "Twenty-one Demands" that the Kirin-Changchun Railway was placed under the direction of the South Manchuria Railway Company, and the outstanding indebtedness of the line converted into a long-term loan, maturing in 1947. The advance of 20,000,000 yen made in 1918 in consequence of the so-called "Four Manchuria-Mongolia Railways Agreement" was one of the so-called "Nishihara loans", made to the military Government of the "Anfu clique", without any restriction as to the purpose for which it might be used. Similarly, it was from a Nishihara loan that an advance was made of 10,000,000 yen to this clique in connection with the preliminary loan contract agreement of 1918 for the construction of the Kirin-Kwainei Railway. Chinese national sentiment has been greatly aroused over the subject of the "Nishihara loans" ever since their negotiation; but, in spite of this, the Chinese Government has never repudiated them. In these circumstances, the Chinese felt little moral obligation to fulfil the conditions of the loan contracts.

The Kirin-Kwainei Railway project.

Especially important in Sino-Japanese relations were the issues over the Kirin-Kwainei Railway project. The first act of issues related to the section of the line from Kirin to Tunhua, the construction of which was completed in 1928. From that time on, the Japanese complained because the Chinese would not convert the Japanese advances for construction purposes into a formal loan secured by the earnings of the railway, and maintained that the Chinese were violating the contract by their refusal to appoint a Japanese accountant for the line.

The Chinese in turn claimed that the construction costs submitted were not only much higher than the estimates of the Japanese engineers, but were greatly in excess of the amount for which vouchers were presented. They refused to take over the line formally until the construction costs should be settled; and contended that, until they should do so, they were under no obligation to appoint a Japanese accountant.

These issues, definite and technical, involving no problems of principle or policy, were obviously suited for arbitration or judicial discrimination, but they remained unsettled and served to intensify the mutual resentment of Chinese and Japanese.

The projected Tunhua-Kwainei line.

Of much greater importance, and far more complicated, was the issue over the construction of the railway from Tunhua to Kwainei. This section would complete the railway from Changchun to the Korean border, where it would connect with a Japanese railway running to a nearby Korean port. Such a line, giving direct entrance to Central Manchuria and opening a region rich in timber and mineral resources, would be of economic value as well as of great strategic importance to Japan.

The Japanese were insistent that this line should be built and that they should participate in its financing. They claimed that China had given treaty assurances to this effect. The Chinese Government had promised, they pointed out, in the Chientao Agreement of September 4th, 1909, to build the line "upon consultation with the Government of Japan", the promise being given in part as a consideration for Japan's relinquishing the old claims of Korea to the Chientao region in Manchuria. Later, in 1918, the Chinese Government and the Japanese banks signed a preliminary agreement for a loan for the construction of this line and, in accordance with the agreement, the banks advanced to the Chinese Government the sum of 10,000,000 yen. This, however, was one of the Nishihara loans, a fact which, in the view of the Chinese, affected the validity of the engagement.

Neither of them, however, was a definitive loan contract agreement, obliging China, without condition and before a specific date, to permit Japanese financiers to participate in the construction of such a line.

The contracts of May 1928.

It was alleged that formal, definitive contracts for the construction of this line were signed in Peking in May 1928, but there was much uncertainty regarding their validity. Such contracts were doubtless signed, under very irregular circumstances, on May 13th—15th by a representative of the Ministry of Communications of the Government at Peking, then under Marshal Chang Tso-lin. But the Chinese contend that the Marshal, who was then hard-pressed by the Nationalist Armies and was about to evacuate Peking, gave his consent that this official should sign, under "a duress of compulsion", due to threats of the Japanese that, if he should not sanction the contracts, his retreat to Mukden would be endangered. Whether Marshal Chang Tso-lin himself also signed the contracts has been a matter of dispute. After the death of the Marshal, the North-Eastern Political Council at Mukden and Marshal Chang Hsueh-liang both refused to approve the contracts on the ground that they were faulty in form and negotiated under duress and had never been ratified by the Peking Cabinet or the North-Eastern Political Council.

The underlying reason for the opposition of the Chinese to the construction of the Tunhua-Kwainei line was their fear of Japan's military and strategic purposes and their belief that their sovereign rights and interests would be threatened by this new Japanese approach to Manchuria from the Japan Sea.

This particular railway issue was not primarily a financial or commercial problem, but involved a conflict between the State policies of Japan and China.

Through-traffic controversies.

There were additional issues over through-traffic arrangements between the Chinese and Japanese lines, rate questions and rivalries between the seaport of Dairen and such Chinese ports as Yingkow (Newchwang).

By September 1931, the Chinese had built unaided and were owning and operating railways with a total length of nearly a thousand kilometres, of which the most important were: the Mukden-Hailung, the Hailung-Kirin, the Tsitsihar-Koshan, the Hulan-Hailun and the Tahushan-Tungliao (a branch of the Peiping-Mukden system) lines; and they owned the Peiping-Mukden Railway and the following Japanese-financed lines: the Kirin-Changchun, the Kirin-Tunhua, Ssupingkai-Taonan and Taonan-Angangchi lines. During the two years preceding the outbreak of the present conflict, the Chinese attempted to operate these various lines as a great Chinese railway system and made efforts to route all freight, if possible, exclusively over the Chinese-operated lines, with a seaboard exit at the Chinese port of Yingkow (Kewchwang)—potentially at Hulutao. As a result, the Chinese made through-traffic arrangements for all ports of their railway system and refused in important sections to make similar traffic agreements between their lines and the South Manchuria system. The Japanese claimed that this discrimination deprived the South Manchuria Railway of much freight from North Manchuria which would normally pass over at least a part of its line and would find an outlet at Dairen.

A war of railway rates.

Associated with these through-traffic controversies, a bitter rate war sprang up between the Japanese and Chinese lines, which began in 1929—30, when the Chinese reduced their rates after the opening of the Tahushan-Tungliao and the Kirin-Hailung lines. The Chinese lines appeared to have a natural advantage at that time due to the fall in the value of the Chinese silver currency, which made the silver rates on these lines cheaper than the gold-yen rates on the South Manchuria Railway. The Japanese claimed that the Chinese rates were so low that they constituted unfair competition, but the Chinese replied that their aim was not primarily to make profits, as was the case with the South Manchuria, but to develop the country and to enable the rural population to reach the markets as cheaply as possible.

Allegations of national discrimination in favour of native-manufactured goods.

Incidental to this rivalry in rate-cutting, allegations were made by each side that the other indulged in rate discrimination or secret rebates in favour of its own nationals. The Japanese complained that the Chinese made railway classifications which enabled Chinese products to be carried over Chinese lines more cheaply than foreign goods, and that they gave lower rates than normal for native goods and for freight shipped over Chinese lines to a Chinese-controlled seaport. The Chinese, on their side, charged the South Manchuria Railway with granting secret rebates, pointing out particularly that a Japanese forwarding agency was quoting rates for freight consigned through them which were lower than the regular scheduled rates of the South Manchuria line.

These issues were highly technical and involved, and it was difficult to determine the justice of the charges which each side was making against the other. It is obvious that such questions as these should normally be settled by a Railroad Commission or by regular judicial determination[①].

Port controversies.

The railway policies of the Chinese authorities in Manchuria were focused upon the new port development at Hulutao. Yingkow was to be the secondary port and, pending the completion of Hulutao, the principal one. Many new railways were projected which would serve practically all parts of Manchuria. The Japanese claimed that the through-traffic arrangements and the low rates put into effect by the Chinese deprived the port of Dairen of much cargo that would normally have moved to it and that this situation was particularly evident in 1930. They stated that the export freight carried to Dairen by the South Manchuria Railway fell off over a million metric tons in 1930, while the port of Yingkow actually showed an increase over the previous year. The Chinese, however, pointed out that the falling-off in freight at Dairen was due principally to the general depression and to the especially severe slump in soya beans, which constituted a large part of the freight normally carried over the South Manchuria line. They claimed also that the increase at Yingkow was the result of traffic from regions recently opened by the new Chinese railway lines.

The Japanese appeared to be especially concerned over the potential competition of the Chinese lines and the port of Hulutao, and complained that the purpose of the Chinese in planning to construct many new railways and in developing Hulutao Harbour was to make "the port of Dairen as well as the South Manchuria Railway itself as good as valueless".

Viewing these many railroad issues as a whole, it is evident that a number of them were technical in character and were quite capable of settlement by ordinary arbitral or judicial process, but that others of them were due to intense rivalry between China and Japan which resulted from a deep-seated conflict in national policies.

---

① 原编辑者注：See special study No. 1 annexed to this Report.

The Sino-Japanese railway negotiations of 1931.

Practically all these railway questions were still outstanding at the opening of the year 1931. Beginning in January and continuing sporadically into the summer, a final but futile effort was made by both Japan and China to hold a conference in order to reconcile their policies with respect to these outstanding railway questions. These Kimura-Kao negotiations, as they were called, achieved no result. There was evidence of sincerity on both sides when the negotiations began in January, but various delays occurred for which both Chinese and Japanese were responsible, with the result that the formal conference, for which extended preparations had been made, had not yet met when the present conflict started.

4. The Sino-Japanese Treaty and Notes of 1915 and Related Issues

The Twenty-one Demands and the Treaty and Notes of 1915.

With the exception of their railway controversies, the Sino-Japanese issues of greatest importance which were outstanding in September 1931 were those which arose from the Sino-Japanese Treaties and Notes of 1915, which in turn were a result of the so-called "Twenty-one Demands". These issues mainly concerned South Manchuria and Eastern Inner Mongolia, since, with the exception of the question of the Hanyohping Mine (near Hankow), the other agreements negotiated in 1915 had either been replaced by new ones or had been voluntarily given up by Japan. The controversies in Manchuria were over the following provisions:

(1) The extension of the term of Japanese possession of the Kwantung Leased Territory to ninety-nine years (1997);

(2) The prolongation of the period of Japanese possession of the South Manchuria Railway and the Antung-Mukden Railway to ninety-nine years (2002 and 2007 respectively);

(3) The grant to Japanese subjects of the right to lease land in the interior of "South Manchuria"—i. e. , outside those areas opened by treaty or otherwise to foreign residence and trade;

(4) The grant to Japanese subjects of the right to travel, reside and conduct business in the interior of South Manchuria and to participate in joint Sino-Japanese agricultural enterprises in Eastern Inner Mongolia.

The legal right of the Japanese to enjoy these grants and concessions depended entirely upon the validity of the Treaty and Notes of 1915, and the Chinese continuously denied that these were binding upon them. No amount of technical explanation or argument could divest the minds of the Chinese people, officials or laymen, of their conviction that the term "Twenty-one Demands" was practically synonymous with the "Treaties and Notes of 1915" and that China's aim should be to free herself from them. At the Paris Conference, 1919, China demanded their abrogation on the ground that they had been concluded "under coercion of a Japanese ultimatum threatening war". At the Washington Conference, 1921—22, the Chinese delegation raised the question "as to the equity and justice of these agreements and therefore as to their fundamental validity", and, in March 1923, shortly before the expiration of the original twenty-five-year lease of the Liaotung (Kwantung) Territory which China granted in 1898 to Russia, the Chinese Government communicated to Japan a further request for the abrogation of the provisions of 1915, and stated that "the Treaties and Notes of 1915 have been consistently condemned by public opinion in China". Since the Chinese maintained that the agreements of 1915 lacked "fundamental validity", they declined to carry out the provisions relating to Manchuria except in so far as circumstances made it expedient to do so.

The Japanese complained bitterly of the consequent violations of their treaty rights by the Chinese. They contended that the Treaties and Notes of 1915 were duly signed and ratified and were in full force. To be sure, there was a considerable body of public opinion in Japan which from the first did not agree with the "Twenty-one Demands"; and, more recently, it has been common for Japanese speakers and publicists to criticise this policy. But the Japanese Government and people appeared unanimous in insisting upon the validity of those provisions which related to Manchuria.

The extension of the lease of the Liaotung Territory and of the concessions for the South Manchuria and Antung-Mukden Railway.

Two important provisions in the Treaty and Notes of 1915 were those for the extension of the lease of the Kwantung Territory from twenty-five to ninety-nine years, and of the concessions of the South Manchuria and the Antung-Mukden Railways to a similar period of ninety-nine years. For the dual reasons that these extensions were a result of the 1915 agreements and that recovery of the territories originally leased by former Governments was included in the Nationalist "Rights Recovery" movement directed against foreign interests in China, the Kwantung Leased Territory and the South Manchuria Railway were made objects, at various times, of agitation and even diplomatic representation on the part of the Chinese. The policy of Marshal Chang Hsueh-liang of declaring Manchuria's allegiance to the Central Government and of permitting the spread of Kuomintang influence in Manchuria made these issues acute after 1928, although they remained in the background of practical politics.

Associated also with the Treaty and Notes of 1915 was the agitation for the recovery of the South Manchuria Railway, or for stripping that institution of its political character in order to reduce it to a purely economic enterprise. As the earliest date fixed for the recovery of this railway on repayment of the capital and interest outlay was 1939, the mere abrogation of the 1915 Treaties would not in itself have recovered the South Manchuria Railway for China. It was extremely doubtful whether China, in any case, would have been able to obtain the capital for this purpose. The occasional utterances of Chinese Nationalist spokesmen, urging recovery of the South Manchuria Railway, served as an irritant to the Japanese, whose legitimate rights and interests were thereby threatened.

The disagreement between the Japanese and Chinese as to the proper functions of the South Manchuria Railway continued from the time of the railway company's organisation in 1906. Technically, of course, the railway company is organised under Japanese law as a private joint-stock enterprise and is quite beyond the pale of Chinese jurisdiction in practice. Particularly since 1927, there had been an agitation among Chinese groups in Manchuria for divesting the South Manchuria Railway of its political and administrative functions and converting it into a "purely commercial enterprise". No concrete plan for achieving this end seems to have been proposed by the Chinese. The railway company was in fact a political enterprise. It was a Japanese Government agency, the Government controlling a majority of its shares; its administrative policy was so closely controlled by the Government that the company's higher officials were almost invariably changed when a new Cabinet came into power in Japan. Moreover, the company had always been charged, under Japanese law, with broad political administrative functions, including police, taxation and education. To have divested the company of these functions would have been to abandon the entire "special mission" of the South Manchuria Railway, as originally conceived and subsequently developed.

The railway area.

Numerous issues arose in regard to the administrative rights of the Japanese within the South Manchuria Railway area, especially as to the acquisition of land, the levying of taxes, and the maintenance of railway guards.

The railway area includes, in addition to a few yards on each side of the railway tracks, fifteen municipalities, termed Japanese "railway towns", situated along the entire system of the South Manchuria Railway from Dairen to Changchun and from Antung to Mukden. Some of these railway towns, such as these at Mukden, Changchun and Antung, comprise large sections of populous Chinese cities.

The right of the South Manchuria Railway to maintain practically complete municipal governments in the railway area rested legally upon a clause in the original Russo-Chinese Railway Agreement of 1896, which gave the railway company "absolute and exclusive administration of its lands".

The Russian Government, until the Sino-Soviet Agreement of 1924, and later the Japanese Government, which acquired the original rights of the Chinese Eastern Railway so far as concerned the South Manchuria Railway, interpreted this provision as granting political control of the railway area. The Chinese always denied this interpretation, insisting that other provisions in the treaty of 1896 made it clear that this clause was not intended to grant such broad administrative rights as control of police, taxation, education, and public utilities.

Land disputes.

Disputes regarding the acquisition of land by the railway company were common. By virtue of one clauses of the original agreement of 1896, the railway company had the right to acquire by purchase or lease private lands "actually necessary for the construction, operation and protection of the line." But the Chinese contended that the Japanese attempted to make improper use of this right, in order to obtain additional territory. The result was almost continuous controversy between the South Manchuria Railway Company and the Chinese local authorities.

Controversies over the tight of taxation in the railway areas.

Conflicting claims as to the right to levy taxes within the railway area led to frequent controversy. The Japanese based their claim upon the original grant to the railway company of the "absolute and exclusive administration of its land"; the Chinese, upon the rights of the sovereign State. Speaking generally, the de facto situation was that the railway company levied and collected taxes from Japanese, Chinese and foreigners residing in the railway areas, and that the Chinese authorities did not exercise such authority, although they claimed the legal right to do so.

A type of controversy which was frequently arising was where the Chinese attempted to tax produce, (such as soya-bean shipments), which was being carted to the South Manchuria Railway towns for transport by rail to Dairen over the Japanese line. This was described by the Chinese as a uniform tax, necessarily to be collected at the boundaries of the Japanese "railway towns", since to refrain from doing so would have been to discriminate in favour of produce carried by the South Manchuria Railway.

The question of Japan's right to maintain "railway guards" along the South Manchuria Railway.

The issues as to Japanese railway guards led to almost continuous difficulty. They were also indicative of a fundamental conflict of State policies in Manchuria already referred to and were the cause of a series of incidents, resulting in considerable loss of life. The legal basis of Japan's alleged right to maintain these guards was the oft-quoted clause in the original Agreement of 1896, which granted to the Chinese Eastern Railway "the absolute and exclusive right of administration of its land." Russia maintained, and China denied, that this gave the right to guard the railway line by Russian troops. In the Portsmouth Treaty, 1905, Russia and Japan, as between themselves, reserved the right to maintain railway guards "not to exceed 15 men per kilometre." But in the subsequent Treaty of Peking, signed by China and Japan later in the same year, the Chinese Government did not give its assent to this particular provision of the agreement between Japan and Russia. China and Japan, however, did include the following provision in Article Ⅱ of the Additional Agreement of December 22, 1905, which is an annex to the Sino-Japanese Treaty of Peking of that date:

"In view of the earnest desire expressed by the Imperial Chinese Government to have the Japanese and Russian troops and railway guards in Manchuria withdrawn as soon as possible, and in order to meet this desire, the Imperial Japanese Government, in the event of Russia agreeing to the withdrawal of her railway guards, or in case other proper measures are agreed to between China and Russia, consent to take similar steps accordingly. When tranquility shall have been re-established in Manchuria and China shall have become herself capable of affording full protection to the lives and property of foreigners, Japan will withdraw her railway guards simultaneously with Russia. "

Japanese contention.

It is this article upon which Japan based her treaty right. Russia, however, long since withdrew her guards and she relinquished her rights to keep them by the Sino-Soviet Agreements of 1924. But Japan contended that tranquility had not been established in Manchuria, and that China was not herself capable of affording full protection to foreigners; therefore she claimed that she still retained a valid treaty right to maintain railway guards.

Japan has appeared increasingly inclined to defend her use of these guards less upon treaty right than upon the ground of "absolute necessity under the existing state of affairs in Manchuria. "

Chinese contention.

The Chinese Government consistently controverted the contention of Japan. It insisted that the stationing of Japanese railway guards in Manchuria was not justified either in law or in fact, and that it impaired the territorial and administrative integrity of China. As to the stipulation in the Sino-Japanese Treaty of Peking, already quoted, the Chinese Government contended that this was merely declaratory of a de facto situation of a provisional character, and that it could not be said to confer a right, especially of a permanent character. Moreover, it claimed that Japan was legally obligated to withdraw her guards, since Russia had withdrawn hers, tranquility had been re-established in Manchuria, and the Chinese authorities were able to give adequate protection to the South Manchuria Railway, as they were doing for other railway lines in Manchuria, provided the Japanese guards would permit them to do so.

Activities of the Japanese railway guards outside of the railway area.

The controversies which arose regarding the Japanese railway guards were not limited to their presence and activities within the railway area. These guards were regular Japanese soldiers, and they frequently carried their police function into adjoining districts or conducted manoeuvres outside the railway areas, with or without the permission of, and with or without notification to, the Chinese authorities. These acts were particularly obnoxious to the Chinese, officials and public alike, and were regarded as unjustifiable in law and provocative of unfortunate incidents.

Frequent misunderstandings and considerable damage to Chinese farm crops resulted from the manoeuvres, and material remuneration failed to alleviate the hostile feelings thus aroused.

Japanese Consular Police.

Closely associated with the question of the Japanese railway guards was that of the Japanese Consular Police. Such police were attached to the Japanese consulates and branch consulates in all the Japanese consular districts in Manchuria, not only along the South Manchuria Railway, but in such cities as Harbin, Tsitsihar and Manchouli, as well as in the so-called "Chientao District", the area in which lived a large number of the Koreans resident in Manchuria.

The Japanese justification for stationing Consular Police in Manchuria.

The Japanese claimed that the right to maintain consular police was a corollary to the right of extra-territoriality; that it was merely an extension of the judicial functions of the consular courts, these police being necessary to protect and discipline Japanese subjects. In fact, Japanese consular police, in smaller numbers, have also been attached to Japanese consulates in other parts of China, contrary to the general practice of countries having extraterritorial treaties.

As a practical matter, the Japanese Government apparently believed that the stationing of consular police in Manchuria was a necessity under the conditions which prevailed there, especially in view of the importance of the

Japanese interests involved, and the large number of resident Japanese subjects, including Koreans.

The Chinese denied the Japanese claims.

The Chinese Government, however, always contested this position advanced by Japan as justification for stationing Japanese consular police in Manchuria, and sent frequent protests to Japan on the subject. She claimed that there was no necessity to station Japanese police officers anywhere in Manchuria, that the question of police could not be associated with extra-territoriality, and that their presence was without treaty basis and a violation of China's sovereignty.

Whether justified or not, the presence of consular police led in a number of cases to serious conflicts between members of their force and those of the local Chinese authorities.

The right of the Japanese to travel, reside and conduct commercial enterprises in interior places in South Manchuria.

The Sino-Japanese Treaty of 1915, provided that "Japanese subjects shall be free to reside and travel in South Manchuria and to engage an business and manufacture of any kind whatsoever. " This was an important right, but one which was objectionable to the Chinese since in no other part of China were foreigners as a class permitted to reside and to engage in business outside the treaty ports. It was the policy of the Chinese Government to withhold this privilege until extra-territoriality should be abolished and foreigners should be subject to Chinese laws and jurisdiction.

In South Manchuria, however, this right had certain limitations: the Japanese were required to carry passports and observe Chinese laws and regulations while in the interior of South Manchuria; but the Chinese regulations applicable to Japanese were not to be enforced until the Chinese authorities had first "come to an understanding with the Japanese Consul".

On many occasions the action of the Chinese authorities was

inconsistent with the terms of this agreement, the validity of which they always contested. The fact that restrictions were placed upon the residence, travel and business activities of Japanese subjects in the interior of South Manchuria, and that orders and regulations were issued by various Chinese officials prohibiting Japanese or other foreigners from residing outside the treaty ports or from renewing leases of buildings is not contested in the documents officially presented to the Commission by the Chinese Assessor. Official pressure, sometimes supported by severe police measures, was exerted upon the Japanese to force them to withdraw from many cities and towns in South Manchuria and Eastern Inner Mongolia, and upon Chinese property owners to prevent them from renting houses to Japanese. It was stated by the Japanese that the Chinese authorities also refused to issue passports to Japanese, harassed them by illegal taxes, and for some years before September, 1931, failed to carry out the stipulation in the agreement by which they had undertaken to submit to the Japanese Consul the regulations which were to be binding upon the Japanese.

The defence and the explanation of the Chinese.

The object of the Chinese was the execution of their national policy of restricting the exceptional privileges of Japanese in Manchuria and thus strengthening the control of China over these Three Eastern Provinces. They justified their actions on the ground that they regarded the Treaty of 1915 as without "fundamental validity". They pointed out, moreover, that the Japanese attempted to reside and conduct business in all parts of Manchuria, although the treaty provision was limited to South Manchuria.

This controversy was a constant irritant until the events of September, 1931.

In view of the conflicting national policies and aims of China and Japan it was almost inevitable that continuous and bitter controversies should arise over this treaty provision. Both countries admit that the situation was a growing irritant in their mutual relations up to the events of September, 1931.

The Land Lease issue.

Closely associated with the right to reside and to do business in the interior of South Manchuria was the right to lease land, which was granted to Japanese by the Treaty of 1915 in the following terms: "Japanese subjects in South Manchuria may, by negotiations, lease land necessary for erecting suitable buildings for trade and manufacture or for prosecuting agricultural enterprises." An exchange of notes between the two Governments at the time of the Treaty defined the expression "lease by negotiation" to imply, according to the Chinese version, "a long-term lease of not more than thirty years and also the possibility of its unconditional renewal"; the Japanese version simply provided for "leases for a long term up to thirty years and unconditionally renewable." Disputes naturally arose over the question whether the Japanese land leases were, at the sole option of the Japanese, "unconditionally renewable."

The Chinese interpreted the desire of the Japanese to obtain lands in Manchuria, whether by lease, purchase, or mortgage as evidence of a Japanese national policy to "buy Manchuria." Their authorities therefore very generally attempted to obstruct efforts of the Japanese to this end, and became increasingly active in the three or four years preceding September, 1931, a period during which the Chinese "Rights-Recovery Movement" was at its height.

In making strict regulations against the purchase of land by the Japanese, their ownership of it in freehold, or their acquisition of a lien through mortgage, the Chinese authorities appeared to be within their legal rights since the Treaty granted only the privilege of leasing land. The Japanese, however, complained that it was not in conformity with the spirit of the Treaty to forbid mortgages upon land.

Chinese officials, however, did not accept the validity of the Treaty and consequently put every obstacle in the way of Japanese leasing land, by orders, provincial and local, calculated to make the leasing of lands to Japanese punishable under the criminal laws; by imposition of special fees and taxes payable in advance on such leases; and by instructions to local officials prohibiting them under threat of punishment, from approving such transfers to Japanese.

The Japanese have acquired land by lease, mortgage and purchase in "North Manchuria" as well as in "South Manchuria".

In spite of these obstacles, great tracts of land have, as a matter of fact, not only been leased by the Japanese, but actually obtained in freehold—although the titles might not be recognised in a Chinese court—through outright purchase, or by the more usual means of foreclosing a mortgage. These mortgages on land have been obtained by Japanese loan operators, especially large loan associations, certain of which have been organised especially for the purpose of acquiring land tracts. The total area of lands leased to Japanese in the whole of Manchuria, and in Jehol, according to Japanese official sources, increased from about 80,000 acres in 1922—1923 to over 500,000 acres in 1931. A small proportion of this total was in North Manchuria where the Japanese had no legal right under Chinese law and international treaty to acquire land leases.

Sino-Japanese negotiations on the issue of land lease.

Due to the importance of this land lease issue there were at least three attempts during the decade preceding 1931, to reach some agreement by direct Sino-Japanese negotiation. A possible solution which there is reason to believe was under consideration, would have treated together the two subjects of land leasing and the abolition of extra-territoriality; in Manchuria, the Japanese were to surrender extra-territoriality and the Chinese were to permit the Japanese to lease land freely. But the negotiations were unsuccessful.

This long-standing Sino-Japanese controversy over the right of Japanese to lease land arose, like the other issues already mentioned, out of the fundamental conflict between rival State policies, the allegations and counter statements concerning violation of international agreements being less consequential in themselves than the underlying objectives of each policy.

5. The Korean Problem in Manchuria

The presence of about 800,000 Koreans in Manchuria, who possess Japanese nationality under the Japanese law, served to accentuate the conflict of policies of China and of Japan. Out of this situation there arose various controversies, in consequence of which the Koreans themselves were victimized, being subjected to suffering and brutalities. [1]

Chinese opposition to Korean acquisition, by purchase or lease, of land in Manchuria was resented by the Japanese, who claimed that the Koreans were entitled, as Japanese subjects, to the privileges of land leasing acquired by Japan in the Treaty and Notes of 1915. The problem of dual nationality also arose, as the Japanese refused to recognize the naturalization of Koreans as Chinese subjects. The use of Japanese consular police to invigilate and protect the Koreans was resented by the Chinese and resulted in innumerable clashes between Chinese and Japanese police. Special problems arose in the Chientao District, just north of the Korean border, where the 400,000 Korean residents outnumber the Chinese by three to one. By 1927, these questions led the Chinese to pursue a policy of restricting the free residence of Koreans in Manchuria, a policy which the Japanese characterized as one of unjustifiable oppression.

Sino-Japanese agreements governing the status of Koreans in Manchuria.

The status and rights of Koreans in Manchuria are determined largely in three Sino-Japanese agreements, viz., the Agreement relating to the Chientao Region, September 4th, 1909; the Treaty and Notes of May 25th,

---

[1]　原编辑者注：See special study No. 9 annexed to this Report.

1915, concerning South Manchuria and Eastern Inner Mongolia; and the so-called "Mitsuya Agreement" of July 8th, 1925. The delicate question of dual nationality in the case of the Koreans has never been regularized by Sino-Japanese agreement.

By 1927, the Chinese authorities in Manchuria generally came to believe that the Koreans had become, in fact, "a vanguard of Japanese penetration and absorption" of Manchuria. In this view, so long as the Japanese refused to recognize the naturalization of Koreans as Chinese subjects, and especially since the Japanese consular police constantly exercised surveillance over Koreans, the acquisition of land by Koreans, whether by purchase or lease, was an economic and political danger "which threatened the very existence of Chinese people in Manchuria".

Chinese contentions.

The view was prevalent among the Chinese that the Koreans were being compelled to migrate from their homeland in consequence of the studied policy of the Japanese Government to displace Koreans with Japanese immigrants from Japan, or to make life so miserable for them, politically and economically, especially by forcing them to dispose of their land holdings, that emigration to Manchuria would naturally follow. According to the Chinese view, the Koreans, being an "oppressed race" ruled by an alien Government in their own land, where the Japanese monopolised all the important official posts, were forced to migrate to Manchuria to seek political freedom and an economic livelihood. The Korean immigrants, 90 per cent of whom are farmers, and almost all of whom cultivators of rice-fields, were thus at first welcomed by the Chinese as an economic asset and favoured out of a natural sympathy for their supposed oppression. They contended that, but for the Japanese refusal to permit Koreans to become naturalized Chinese subjects and the Japanese policy of pursuing them into Manchuria on the pretext of offering them necessary police protection, this Korean colonisation in Manchuria would have created no major political and economic problems. The Chinese deny that the efforts admittedly made by their officials in Manchuria, especially after 1927, to restrict the free settlement of Koreans on the land in Manchuria except as mere tenants or labourers, can be regarded as instances of "oppression".

Japanese denial of those Chinese accusations.

The Japanese admit that the Chinese suspicion was the principal cause of Chinese "oppression" of the Koreans, but vigorously deny the allegation that they pursued any definite policy of encouraging Korean migration to Manchuria, stating that "Japan having neither encouraged nor restricted it, the Korean emigration to Manchuria must be regarded as the outcome of a natural tendency," a phenomenon uninfluenced by any political or diplomatic motives. They therefore declare that "the fear on the part of China that Japan is plotting the absorption of the two regions by making use of Korean immigrants is entirely groundless."

The Korean problem intensified the Sino-Japanese hostilities, victimising the Koreans themselves.

These irreconcilable views intensified such problems as those related to the leasing of land, questions of jurisdiction and the Japanese consular police, these having created a most unfortunate situation for the Koreans and embittered Sino-Japanese relations. ①

The Koreans and the land lease question.

There exist no Sino-Japanese agreements which specifically grant or deny the right of Koreans to settle, reside, and conduct occupations outside the Treaty Ports, or to lease or otherwise acquire land in Manchuria, except in the so-called Chientao District. Probably, however, over 400,000 Koreans do live in Manchuria outside Chientao. They are widely distributed,

---

① 原编辑者注：see special study No. 9 annexed to this Report.

especially in the eastern half of Manchuria, and are numerous in the regions lying north of Korea, in Kirin Province, and have penetrated in large numbers into the region of the eastern section of the Chinese Eastern Railway, the lower Sungari valley and along the Sino-Russian border from north-eastern Korea to the Ussuri and the Amur river valleys, their migration and settlement having overflown into the adjoining territories of the U. S. S. R. Moreover, partly because a very considerable group of the Koreans are natives of Manchuria, their ancestors having immigrated generations ago, and partly because others have renounced their allegiance to Japan and have become naturalised Chinese subjects, a great many Koreans today actually possess agricultural lands in Manchuria, outside of Chientao, both by virtue of free-hold title and lease-hold. The vast majority, however, cultivate paddy fields simply as tenant farmers under rental contracts, on a crop division basis, with the Chinese landlords, these contracts usually being limited to periods from one to three years, renewable at the discretion of the landlord.

Conflict over the Sino-Japanese agreements concerning the right of Koreans to lease land.

The Chinese deny that the Koreans have the right to purchase or lease agricultural lands in Manchuria outside the Chientao District, since the only Sino-Japanese agreement on the point is the Chientao Agreement of 1909, which is restricted in its application to that area. Only Koreans, who are Chinese subjects, therefore, are entitled to purchase land, or, for that matter, to reside and lease land in the interior of Manchuria. In denying the claim of right of the Koreans to lease land freely in Manchuria, the Chinese Government has contended that the Chientao Agreement of 1909, which granted Koreans the right of residence with special landholding privileges in the Chientao District alone, and specified that the Koreans were to be subject to Chinese jurisdiction is in itself a self-contained instrument "purporting to settle, by mutual concessions, local issues then pending between China and Japan in that area. " The Chientao Agreement contained a quid pro quo, Japan waiving the claim of jurisdiction over the Koreans, China granting them the special privilege of possessing agricultural lands.

The Chinese contention.

Both countries continued to observe the agreement after the annexation of Korea by Japan in 1910, China contending that the Treaty and Notes of 1915 could not alter the stipulations of the Chientao Agreement, especially as the new Treaty contained a clause specifying that "all existing treaties between China and Japan, relating to Manchuria, shall, except as otherwise provided for, by this treaty, remain in force. " No exception was made for the Chientao Agreement. The Chinese Government further contends that the Treaty and Notes of 1915 do not apply to the Chientao District, since the latter is not geographically a part of "South Manchuria"—a term which is ill-defined both geographically and politically.

The Japanese contention.

This Chinese contention has been contested by the Japanese since 1915, their position being that, inasmuch as the Koreans became Japanese subjects by virtue of the annexation of Korea in 1910, the provisions of the Sino-Japanese Treaty and Notes of 1915 concerning South Manchuria and Eastern Inner Mongolia, which grant Japanese subjects the right to reside and lease lands in South Manchuria and to participate in joint agricultural enterprises in Eastern Inner Mongolia, apply equally to the Koreans. The Japanese Government has contended that the Chientao Agreement was superseded by these provisions of the 1915 agreements in conflict therewith, that the Chinese contention that the Chientao Agreement is a self-contained instrument is untenable, since the right secured by the Koreans in Chientao was actually in consequence of Japan's agreement to recognise that region as a part of Chinese territory. They assert that it would be discriminatory on their part to refrain from seeking for the Koreans in Manchuria rights and privileges granted to other Japanese subjects.

The effect of these rival contentions on the conditions of the Koreans.

The Japanese reason for favouring the acquisition of land by Koreans in Manchuria is partly due to their desire to obtain rice exports for Japan, a desire which, so far, has been but partly satisfied, since probably half of the rice production of over seven million bushels in 1930 is consumed locally, and the export of the balance has been restricted. The Japanese assert that the Koreans tenants, after having reclaimed waste lands and making them profitable for the Chinese owners, have been unjustly ejected. The Chinese, on the other hand, while equally desirous of having the cultivable lowlands producing rice, have generally employed the Koreans as tenants or labourers to prevent the land itself from falling into Japanese hands. Many Koreans have therefore become naturalised Chinese subjects in order to possess land, some of them, however, having acquired such titles, transferring them to Japanese land mortgage associations. This suggests one reason why there has been a difference of opinion among the Japanese themselves as to whether naturalisation of Koreans as Chinese subjects should be recognised by the Japanese Government.

The problem of dual nationality of Koreans in Manchuria.

Under a Chinese Nationality Law of 1914 only aliens who, under the law of their own country, were permitted to become naturalised in another were capable of being naturalised Chinese subjects. The Chinese revised Nationality Law of February 5th, 1929, however, contained no provision by which an alien was required to lose his original nationality in order to acquire Chinese nationality. Koreans were, therefore, naturalised as Chinese regardless of the Japanese insistence that such naturalisation could not be recognized under Japanese law. The Japanese nationality laws have never permitted Koreans to lose their Japanese nationality, and although a revised Nationality Law of 1924 contained an article to the effect that "a person who acquires foreign nationality voluntarily loses Japanese nationality", this general law has never been made applicable to the Koreans by special Imperial Ordinance. Nevertheless, many Koreans in Manchuria, varying from 5 to 20 percent of the total Korean population in certain districts, especially where they are relatively inaccessible by the Japanese consular officials, have become naturalised as Chinese. Others, incidentally, when migrating beyond the Manchurian borders into Soviet territory, have become citizens of the U. S. S. R.

Effect of dural nationality of the Koreans on Chinese policy.

This problem of dual nationality of the Koreans influenced the National Government of China and the provincial authorities in Manchuria generally to look with disfavour upon indiscriminate naturalisation of Koreans, fearing that they might, by temporarily acquiring Chinese nationality, become potential instruments of a Japanese policy of acquiring agricultural lands. In regulations issued by the Kirin Provincial Government, September 1930, governing the purchase and sale of land throughout the province, it was provided that "when a naturalised Korean purchases land, investigation must be made in order to discover whether he wants to purchase it as a means of residing as a permanently naturalised citizens, or on behalf of some Japanese. " The local district officials, however, seem to have wavered in their attitude, at times enforcing the orders of the higher authorities but frequently issuing temporary naturalisation certificates in lieu of formal certificates requiring the approval of the provincial government and the Ministry of Interior at Nanking. These local officials, especially in areas far removed from Japanese consulates, often readily consented to the issuing of such certificates to the Koreans who applied for them, and, on occasion, no doubt actually compelled the Koreans to become naturalised or leave the country, their actions being influenced both by the policy of the Japanese and by the revenue derivable from the naturalization fees. The Chinese have asserted, moreover, that some Japanese themselves actually connived at this business of naturalizing Koreans in order to use them as dummy landowners or to acquire lands by transfer from such naturalised Koreans. Generally speaking, however, the Japanese authorities discountenanced naturalisation of Koreans and assumed jurisdiction over them wherever possible.

Problems arising from conflicting claims to police jurisdiction peculiarly serious, involving the Koreans.

The Japanese claim of right to maintain consular police in Manchuria as a corollary of extra-territoriality became a source of constant conflict where the Koreans were involved. Whether the Koreans desired such Japanese interference, ostensibly in their behalf, or not, the Japanese consular police, especially in the Chientao District, undertook not only protective functions but freely assumed the right to conduct searches and seizures of Korean premises, especially where the Koreans were suspected of being involved in the Independence Movement, or in Communist or anti-Japanese activities. The Chinese police, for their part, frequently came into collision with the Japanese police in their efforts to enforce Chinese laws, preserve the peace, or suppress the activities of "undesirable" Koreans. Although the Chinese and Japanese police did cooperate on many occasions, as provided for in the so-called "Mitsuya Agreement" of 1925, which it was agreed that in eastern Fengtien Province the Chinese would suppress "the Korean societies" and turn over "Koreans of bad character" to the Japanese on the letter's request, the actual state of affairs was really one of constant controversy and friction. Such a situation was bound to cause trouble.

The special problem of Chientao.

The Korean problems and the resulting Sino-Japanese relations over the Chientao District had attained a peculiarly complicated and serious character. Chientao (called "Kanto" in Japanese and "Kando" in Korean) comprises the three districts of Yenchi, Holung and Wangching in Liaoning (Hengtien) Province, and, in practice, as evidenced by the attitude of the Japanese

Government, includes also the district of Hunchun, which four districts adjoin the northeast corner of Korea just across the Tumen River.

The Japanese attitude and policy towards Chientao.

The Japanese, describing the traditional attitude of the Koreans towards the Chientao area, have been disinclined to admit that the Chientao Agreement of 1909 closed once and for all the issue whether this territory should belong to China or to Korea, the idea being that, since the district is predominantly Korean, over half of the arable land being cultivated by them, "they have so firmly established themselves in the locality that it may practically be regarded as a Korean sphere". In Chientao, more than elsewhere in Manchuria, the Japanese Government has been insistent on exercising jurisdiction and surveillance over the Koreans, over 400 Japanese consular police having been maintained there for years. The Japanese Consular Service, in co-operation with Japanese functionaries assigned by the Government-General of Chosen, exercise broad powers of an administrative character in the region, their functions including maintenance of Japanese schools, hospitals and government-subsidised financing media for the Koreans. The area is regarded as a natural outlet for Korean emigrants who cultivate rice-fields, while politically it has special importance since Chientao has long been a refuge of Korean independence advocates, communist groups and other disaffected anti-Japanese partisans, a region where, as evidenced by the Hunchun Rising of Koreans against the Japanese in 1920, after the Independence Outbreak in Korea, the Japanese have had serious political problems intimately associated with the general problem of governance of Korea. The military importance of this region is obvious from the fact that the lower reaches of the Tumen River form the boundary between Japanese, Chinese and Soviet territory.

Conflicts of the Chinese and Japanese interpretations of the Chientao Agreement.

The Chientao Agreement provided that "the residence of Korean subjects, as heretofore, agricultural lands lying north of the River Tumen", should be permitted by China; that Korean subjects residing on such lands should henceforth "be amenable to the jurisdiction of the Chinese local officials"; that they should be given equal treatment with the Chinese; and that, although all civil and criminal cases involving such Koreans should be "heard and decided by the Chinese authorities", a Japanese consular official should be permitted to attend the court, especially in capital cases, with the right to "apply to the Chinese authorities for a new trial" under special Chinese judicial procedure.

The Japanese, however, have taken the position that the Sino-Japanese Treaty and Notes of 1915 override the Chientao Agreement in so far as jurisdictional questions are concerned, and that, since 1915, Koreans, as Japanese subjects, are entitled to all the rights and privileges of extraterritorial status under the Japanese treaties with China. This contention has never been admitted by the Chinese Government, the Chinese insisting that the Chientao Agreement, if applicable in so far as the right granted to Koreans to reside on agricultural lands is concerned, is also applicable in those articles where it is provided that the Koreans should submit to Chinese jurisdiction. The Japanese have interpreted the article permitting Korean residence on agricultural lands to mean the right to purchase and lease such lands in Chientao; the Chinese, contesting this interpretation, take the position that the article must be interpreted literally and that only Koreans who have become naturalised Chinese subjects are entitled to purchase land there.

The actual situation as to Korean land ownership is anomalous.

The actual situation is, therefore, anomalous, since, as a matter of fact, there are non-naturalised Koreans in Chientao who have acquired lands in freehold title, with the connivance of the local Chinese officials, although as a general rule the Koreans themselves recognise the acquisition of Chinese nationality as a necessary condition of obtaining the right to purchase land in Chientao. Japanese official figures represent over half the arable land of Chientao (including Hunchun) as "owned" by Koreans, their figures admitting that over 15 percent of the Koreans there have become naturalised as Chinese subjects. Whether it is these naturalised Koreans who "own" these lands is impossible to say. Such a situation naturally gave rise to numerous irregularities and constant differences, often manifested by open clashes between the Chinese and Japanese police.

Japanese allegations of Chinese oppression of the Koreans.

The Japanese assert that, about the end of 1927, a movement for persecuting Korean immigrants in Manchuria broke out, under Chinese official instigation, as an aftermath of a general anti-Japanese agitation, and state that this oppression was intensified after the Manchurian provinces declared their allegiance to the National Government at Nanking. Numerous translations of orders issued by the central and local Chinese authorities in Manchuria have been submitted as evidence to the Commission of a definite Chinese policy of oppressing the Koreans by forcing them to become naturalised as Chinese, driving them from their rice-fields, compelling them to re-migrate, subjecting them to arbitrary levies and exorbitant taxation, preventing them from entering into contracts of lease or rental for houses and lands, and inflicting upon them many brutalities. It is stated that this campaign of cruelty was particularly directed against the "pro-Japanese" Koreans, that Korean Residents' Associations, which are subsidised by the Japanese Government, were the objects of persecution, that non-Chinese schools maintained by or for the Koreans were closed, that "undesirable Koreans" were permitted to levy blackmail and perpetrate atrocities upon Korean farmers, and that Koreans were compelled to wear Chinese clothing and renounce any claim of reliance upon Japanese protection or assistance in their miserable plight.

The fact that the Manchurian authorities did issue orders discriminatory against non-naturalised Koreans is not denied by the Chinese, the number and character of these orders and instructions, especially since 1927, establishing beyond a doubt that the Chinese authorities in Manchuria generally regarded the Korean infiltration, in so far as it was accompanied by Japanese jurisdiction, as a menace which deserved to be opposed.

Special attention given to the Korean problem by the Commission.

Because of the seriousness of the Japanese allegations and the pitiable plight of the Korean population of Manchuria, the Commission gave special attention to this subject and, without accepting all these accusations as adequately descriptive of the facts, or concluding that certain of these restrictive measures applied to the Koreans were entirely unjustified, is in a position to confirm this general description of the Chinese actions towards the Koreans in certain parts of Manchuria. While in Manchuria, numerous delegations, who represented themselves as spokesmen of Korean communities, were received by the Commission.

It is obvious that the presence of this large minority of Koreans in Manchuria served to complicate the Sino-Japanese controversies over land leasing, jurisdiction and police, and the economic rivalries which formed a prelude to the events of September 1931. While the great majority of the Koreans only wanted to be left alone to earn their livelihood, there were among them groups which were branded by the Chinese or Japanese, or both, as "undesirable Koreans", including the advocates and partisans of the independence of Korea from Japanese rule, Communists, professional law breakers, including smugglers and drug traders, and those who, in league with Chinese bandits, levied blackmail or extorted money from those of their own blood. Even the Korean farmer himself frequently invited oppression by his ignorance, improvidence and willingness to incur indebtedness to his more agile-minded landlord.

The Chinese explanation of their treatment of the Koreans.

Aside from the involvement of the Koreans, however unwittingly, in the controversies which, in the Chinese view, were the inevitable results of the general Japanese policies with respect to Manchuria, the Chinese submit that much of what has been termed "oppression" of the Koreans should not properly be so called, and that certain of the measures taken against the Koreans by the Chinese were actually either approved or connived at by the Japanese authorities themselves. They assert that it should not be forgotten that the great majority of the Koreans are bitterly anti-Japanese and unreconciled to the Japanese annexation of their native land, and that the Korean emigrants, who would never have left their homeland but for the political and economic difficulties under which they have suffered, generally desire to be free from Japanese surveillance in Manchuria.

So-called "Mitsuya Agreement", 1925.

The Chinese, while admitting a certain sympathy with the Koreans, draw attention to the existence of the "Mitsuya Agreement" of June—July 1925 as evidence both of a willingness on the part of the Chinese authorities to curb the activities of Koreans whom the Japanese consider "bad characters" and a menace to their position in Korea, and of official sanction on the part of the Japanese themselves for certain of those very acts which the Japanese would have others believe are instances of Chinese "oppression" of the Koreans. This agreement, which has never been widely known abroad, was negotiated by the Japanese Police Commissioner of the Government-General of Chosen and the Chinese Police Commissioner of Fengtien Province. It provided for co-operation between the Chinese and Japanese police in suppressing "Korean societies" (presumably of an anti-Japanese character) in Eastern Fengtien Province, stipulating that "the Chinese authorities shall immediately arrest and extradite those leaders of the Korean societies whose names had been designated by the authorities of Korea", and that Koreans of "bad character" should be arrested by the

Chinese police and turned over to the Japanese for trial and punishment. The Chinese assert, therefore, that "it is largely for the purpose of giving practical effect to this agreement that certain restrictive measures have been put into force governing the treatment of Koreans. If they are taken as evidence proving the oppression of Koreans by Chinese authorities, then such measures of oppression, if indeed they are, have been resorted to principally in the interest of Japan". Furthermore, the Chinese submit that, "in view of the keen economic competition with native farmers, it is but natural that the Chinese authorities should exercise their inherent right to take measures to protect the interests of their own countrymen".

6. The Wanpaoshan Affair and the Anti-Chinese Riots in Korea

The relations of the Wanpaoshan affair to the events of September 1931.

The Wanpaoshan affair, together with the case of Captain Nakamura, have been widely regarded as the causes immediately contributing to the Sino-Japanese crisis in Manchuria. The intrinsic importance of the former, however, was greatly exaggerated. The sensational accounts of what occurred at Wanpaoshan, where there were no casualties, led to a feeling of bitterness between Chinese and Japanese and in Korea, to the serious attacks by Koreans upon Chinese residents. These anti-Chinese riots, in turn, revived the anti-Japanese boycott in China. Judged by itself, the Wanpaoshan affair was no more serious than several other incidents involving clashes between Chinese and Japanese troops or police which had occurred during the past few years in Manchuria.

A lease contract for rice-land between the Chinese landowners and the Chinese broker required the official approval of the Chinese authorities.

Wanpaoshan is a small village located some 18 miles (30 kilometres) north of Changchun, adjoining a low marshy area alongside the Itung River. It was here that one Hao Young-teh, a Chinese broker, leased on behalf of the Chang Nung Agricultural Company, from the Chinese owners, a large tract of land by a contract dated April 16th, 1931. It was stipulated in the contract that it should be null and void in case the District Magistrate refused to approve its terms.

This land was sub-leased by the Chinese broker to the Korean tenants.

Shortly after this, the lessee sub-leased this entire plot of land to a group of Koreans. This second contract contained no provision requiring official approval for enforcement and took for granted that the Koreans would construct an irrigation canal with tributary ditches. Hao Young-teh had sub-leased this land to the Korean farmers without first having obtained Chinese formal approval of the original lease contract with the Chinese owners.

The digging of an irrigation ditch by the Koreans across land owned by Chinese farmers was the principal cause of local Chinese opposition.

Immediately after the conclusion of the second lease the Koreans, began digging an irrigation ditch or canal, several miles long, in order to divert the water of the Itung River and distribute it over this low marshy area for the purpose of making it suitable for paddy cultivation. This ditch traversed large areas of land cultivated by Chinese who were not parties to either lease transaction, since their lands lay between the river and that leased by the Koreans. In order to provide ample water supply to be deflected through this ditch to their holdings, the Koreans undertook to construct a dam across the Itung River.

The Chinese farmers demanded the cessation of work on the irrigation ditch and the evacuation of the Koreans.

After a considerable length of the irrigation ditch had been completed, the Chinese farmers whose lands were cut by the canal rose up en masse and protested to the Wanpaoshan authorities, begging them to intervene in their behalf. As a result, the Chinese local authorities despatched police to the spot and ordered the Koreans to stop excavation work at once and to vacate the area. At the same time, the Japanese Consul at Changchun sent consular police to protect the Koreans. Local negotiations between the Japanese and Chinese representatives failed to solve the problem. Somewhat later both sides sent additional police, with resulting protests, counter-statements and attempted negotiations.

The Chinese and Japanese authorities at Changchun agreed upon a joint investigation.

On June 8th, both sides agreed to withdraw their police forces and to conduct a joint investigation of the situation at Wanpaoshan. This investigation revealed the fact that the original lease contained a clause providing that the entire contract would be "null and void" if it should not be approved by the Chinese District Magistrate, and that this approval was never given.

Inclusive investigation.

The joint investigators, however, apparently failed to agree upon their findings, the Chinese maintaining that the digging of the irrigation ditch could not fail to violate the rights of the Chinese farmers whose lands were cut by it and the Japanese insisting that the Koreans should be permitted to continue their work, since it would be unfair to eject them on account of the error in the lease procedure for which they were in no way at fault. Shortly thereafter, the Koreans, assisted by Japanese consular police, continued to dig the ditch.

The incident of July 1st.

Out of this train of circumstances came the incident of July 1st, when a party of 400 Chinese farmers whose lands were cut by the irrigation ditch, armed with agricultural implements and pikes, drove the Koreans away and filled in much of the ditch. The Japanese consular police thereupon opened rifle fire to disperse the mob and to protect the Koreans, but there were no casualties. The Chinese farmers withdrew and the Japanese police remained on the spot until the Koreans completed the ditch and the dam across the Itung River.

After the incident of July 1st, the Chinese municipal authorities continued to protest to the Japanese Consul at Changchun against the action of the Japanese consular police and of the Koreans.

The anti-Chinese riots in Korea.

Far more serious than the Wanpaoshan affair was the reaction to this dispute in Chosen (Korea). In consequence of sensational accounts of the situation at Wanpaoshan, especially of the events of July 1st, which were printed in the Japanese and Korean Press, a series of anti-Chinese riots occurred throughout Korea. These riots began at Jinsen on July 3rd, and spread rapidly to other cities.

Heavy loss of life and property among the Chinese residents.

The Chinese state, on the basis of their official reports, that 127 Chinese were massacred and 393 wounded, and that Chinese property to the value of 2,500,000 Yen was destroyed. They claim, moreover, that the Japanese authorities in Korea were in large measure responsible for the results of these riots, since, it was alleged, they took no adequate steps to prevent them and did not suppress them until great loss of Chinese life and property had resulted.

Alleged responsibility of the Japanese authorities in Korea.

The Japanese and Korean newspapers were not prevented from publishing sensational and incorrect accounts of the Wanpaoshan incident of July 1st, which were of a character to amuse the hatred of the Korean populace against the Chinese residents.

The Japanese claim, however, that these riots were due to the spontaneous outburst of racial feeling, and that the Japanese authorities suppressed them as soon as possible.

The riots in Korea intensified the anti-Japanese boycott in China.

A result of importance was the fact that these outbreaks in Korea served directly to revive the anti-Japanese boycott throughout China.

The Japanese Government expressed regret for the anti-Chinese riots and offered compensation for the families of the dead.

Shortly after the anti-Chinese riots in Korea and while the Wanpaoshan affair was still unsettled, the Chinese Government made a protest to Japan, on account of the riots, charging Japan with full responsibility for failure to suppress them. The Japanese Government, in reply, on July 15th, expressed regret at the occurrence of these riots and offered compensation for the families of the dead.

The grounds for Chinese protests concerning the Wanpaoshan affair.

From July 22nd until September 15th, there were negotiations and exchanges of notes between the Chinese and Japanese local and central authorities over the Wanpaoshan affair. The Chinese maintained that the difficulties at Wanpaoshan were due to the fact that the Koreans were living where they had no right to be, since their privileges of residing and leasing of land did not extend outside the Chientao District, in accordance with the Chientao Agreement of September 4th, 1909.

The Chinese Government protested against the stationing of Japanese consular police in China and asserted that the despatch of a large force of these police to Wanpaoshan was responsible for the incident of July 1st.

The Japanese position.

The Japanese, on the other hand, insisted that the Koreans had a treaty right to reside and lease land at Wanpaoshan, since their privileges were not limited to those specified in the Chientao Agreement, but included the rights granted to Japanese subjects in general, of residing and leasing land throughout South Manchuria. The status of the Koreans, it was claimed, was identical with that of other Japanese subjects. The Japanese also urged that the Koreans had undertaken their rice cultivation project in good faith and that the Japanese authorities could not assume responsibility for the irregularities of the Chinese broker who arranged the lease. The Japanese Government consented to the withdrawal of the consular police from Wanpaoshan, but the Korean tenants remained and continued to cultivate their rice-lands.

A complete solution of the Wanpaoshan affair had not been reached by September 1931.

7. The Case of Captain Nakamura

Importance of the Nakamura case.

The case of Captain Nakamura was viewed by the Japanese as the culminating incident of a long series of events which showed the utter disregard of the Chinese for Japanese rights and interests in Manchuria. Captain Nakamura was killed by Chinese soldiers in an out-of-the-way region in Manchuria during the mid-summer of 1931.

Captain Nakamura was on a military mission in interior Manchuria.

Captain Shintaro Nakamura was a Japanese military officer on active duty and, as was admitted by the Japanese Government, was on a mission under the orders of the Japanese Army. While passing through Harbin, where his passport was examined by the Chinese authorities, he represented himself as an agricultural expert. He was at that time warned that the region in which he intended to travel was a bandit-ridden area, and this fact was noted on his passport. He was armed, and carried patent medicine which, according to the Chinese, included narcotic drugs for non-medical purposes.

Captain Nakamura and companions were killed by Chinese soldiers.

On June 9th, accompanied by three interpreters and assistants, Captain Nakamura left Ilikotu Station on the western section of the Chinese Eastern Railway. When he had reached a point some distance in the interior, in the direction of Taonan, he and the other members of his party were placed under detention by Chinese soldiers under Kuan Yuheng, the Commander of the Third Regiment of the Reclamation Army. Several days later, about June 27th, he and his companions were shot by Chinese soldiers and their bodies were cremated to conceal the evidence of the deed.

The Japanese contention.

The Japanese insisted that the killing of Captain Nakamura and his companions was unjustified and showed arrogant disrespect for the Japanese Army and nation; they asserted that the Chinese authorities in Manchuria delayed to institute official enquiries into the circumstances, were reluctant to assume responsibility for the occurrence, and were insincere in their claim that they were making every effort to ascertain the facts in the case.

The Chinese contention.

The Chinese declared, at first, that Captain Nakamura and his party were detained pending an examination of their permits, which, according to custom, were required of foreigners travelling in the interior; that they had been treated well; and that Captain Nakamura was shot by a sentry while endeavoring to make his escape. Documents, including a Japanese military map and two diaries, they stated, were found on his person, which proved that he was either a military spy or an officer on special military mission.

Investigations.

On July 17th, a report of the death of Captain Nakamura reached the Japanese Consul-General at Tsitsihar and, at the end of the month, Japanese officials in Mukden informed the local Chinese authorities that they had definite evidence that Captain Nakamura had been killed by Chinese soldiers. On August 17th, the Japanese military authorities in Mukden released for publication the first account of his death (see *Manchuria Daily News*, August 17th, 1931). On the same day, Consul-General Hayashi, and also Major Mori, who had been sent by the Japanese General Staff from Tokyo to Manchuria to investigate the circumstances, had interviews with Governor Tsang Shih-yi, of Liaoning Province. Governor Tsang promised to investigate it at once.

Immediately thereafter, Governor Tsang Shih-yi communicated with Marshal Chang Hsueh-liang (who was then ill in a hospital in Peiping) and with the Minister for Foreign Affairs in Nanking and, also, appointed two Chinese investigators, who proceeded at once to the scene of the alleged murder. These two men returned to Mukden on September 3rd. Major Mori, who had been conducting an independent investigation on behalf of the Japanese General Staff, returned to Mukden on September 4th. On that day Consul-General Hayashi called on General Yung Chen, the Chinese Chief of Staff, and was informed that the findings of the Chinese investigators were indecisive and unsatisfactory, and that it would therefore be necessary to conduct a second enquiry. General Yung Chen left for Peiping on September 4th to consult with Marshal Chang Hsueh-liang on the new developments in the Manchurian situation, returning to Mukden on September 7th.

Efforts of Chinese to reach a settlement.

Having been informed of the seriousness of the situation in Manchuria, Marshal Chang Hsueh-liang instructed Governor Tsang Shih-yi and General Yung Chen to conduct, without delay and on the spot, a second enquiry into the Nakamura case. Learning from his Japanese military advisers of the deep concern of the Japanese military over this affair, he sent Major Shibayama to Tokyo to make it clear that he wished to settle the case amicably. Major Shibayama arrived in Tokyo on September 12th, and stated, according to subsequent Press reports, that Marshal Chang Hsueh-liang was sincerely desirous of securing an early and equitable termination of the Nakamura issue. In the meantime, Marshal Chang had sent Mr. Tang Er-ho, a high official, on a special mission to Tokyo to consult with the Minister for Foreign Affairs, Baron Shidehara, in order to ascertain what common ground might be found for a solution of various pending Sino-Japanese questions concerning Manchuria. Mr. Tang Er-ho had conversations with Baron Shidehara, General Minami and other high military officials. On September 16th, Marshal Chang Hsueh-liang gave out an interview to the Press which reported him as saying that the Nakamura case, in accordance with the wish of the Japanese, would be handled by Governor Tsang Shih-yi and the Manchurian authorities, and not by the Foreign Office at Nanking.

The second Chinese commission of investigation, after visiting the scene of the killing of Captain Nakamura, returned to Mukden on the morning of September 16th. On the afternoon of the 18th, the Japanese Consul called upon General Yung Chen, when the latter stated that Commander Kuan Yu-heng had been brought to Mukden on September 16th charged with responsibility for the murder of Captain Nakamura and would be immediately tried by a military court-martial. Later, it was made known by the Japanese, after their occupation of Mukden, that Commander Kuan had been detained by the Chinese in a military prison.

Consul-General Hayashi, Mukden, was reported on September 12th—13th to have reported to the Japanese Foreign Office that "an amicable settlement would probably be made after the return of the investigators to Mukden", especially as General Yung Chen had definitely admitted that Chinese soldiers had been responsible for the death of Captain Nakamura. The Mukden correspondent of the Nippon Dempo Service telegraphed a dispatch on September 12th stating that "an amicable settlement of the alleged murder case of Captain Shintaro Nakamura of the Japanese General Staff Office by soldiers of the Chinese Reclamation Army Corps is in sight". Numerous statements of Japanese military officers, however, especially those of Colonel K. Doihara, continued to question the sincerity of the

Chinese efforts to arrive at a satisfactory solution of the Nakamura case, in view of the fact that Commander Kuan, alleged to have been responsible for the death of Captain Nakamura, had been taken into custody in Mukden by the Chinese authorities, the date of his court-martial having been announced as to occur within a week. Since the Chinese authorities admitted to Japanese consular officials in Mukden, in a formal conference held on the afternoon of September 18th, that Chinese soldiers were responsible for the death of Captain Nakamura, expressing also a desire to secure a settlement of the case diplomatically without delay, it would seem that diplomatic negotiations for attaining a solution of the Nakamura case were actually progressing favourably up to the night of September 18th.

The results of the Nakamura case.

The Nakamura case, more than any other single incident, greatly aggravated the resentment of the Japanese and their agitation in favour of forceful means to effect a solution of outstanding Sino-Japanese difficulties in regard to Manchuria. The inherent seriousness of the case was aggravated by the fact that Sino-Japanese relations just at this time were strained on account of the Wanpaoshan affair, the anti-Chinese riots in Korea, the Japanese military manœuvres across the Tumen River on the Manchurian-Korean frontier, and the Chinese mob violence committed at Tsingtao, in protest against the activities of the local Japanese patriotic societies.

Captain Nakamura was an army officer on active service, a fact which was pointed to by the Japanese as a justification for strong and swift military action. Mass meetings were held in Manchuria and in Japan for the purpose of crystallising public sentiment in favour of such action. During the first two weeks of September, the Japanese Press repeatedly declared that the army had decided that the "solution ought to be by force", since there was no other alternative.

The Chinese claimed that the importance of the case was greatly exaggerated and that it was made a pretext for the Japanese military occupation of Manchuria. They denied the contention of the Japanese that there was insincerity or delay on the part of the Chinese officials in dealing with the case.

By the end of August 1931, therefore, Sino-Japanese relations over Manchuria were severely strained in consequence of the many controversies and incidents described in this chapter. The claim that there were 300 cases outstanding between the two countries and that peaceful methods for settling each of them had been progressively exhausted by one of the parties cannot be substantiated. These so-called "cases" were rather situations arising out of broader issues, which were rooted in fundamentally irreconcilable policies. Each side accuses the other of having violated, unilaterally interpreted, or ignored the stipulations of the Sino-Japanese agreements. Each side had legitimate grievances against the other.

The account here given of the efforts made by one side or the other to secure a settlement of these questions at issue between them shows that some efforts were being made to dispose of these questions by the normal procedure of diplomatic negotiation and peaceful means, and these means had not yet been exhausted. But the long delays put a severe strain on the patience of the Japanese. Army circles in particular were insisting on the immediate settlement of the Nakamura case and demanded satisfactory reparation. The Imperial Ex-Soldiers' Association, amongst others, was instrumental in rousing public opinion.

In the course of September, public sentiment regarding the Chinese questions, with the Nakamura case as the focal point, became very strong. Time and again the opinion was expressed that the policy of leaving so many issues in Manchuria unsettled had caused the Chinese authorities to make light of Japan. Settlement of all pending issues, if necessary by force, became a popular slogan. Reference was freely made in the Press to a decision to resort to armed force, to conferences between the Ministry of War, the General Staff and other authorities for the discussion of a plan with this object, to definite instructions regarding the execution, in case of necessity, of that plan to the Commander-in-Chief of the Kwantung Army and to Colonel Doihara, Resident Officer at Mukden, who had been summoned to Tokyo early in September and who was quoted by the Press as the advocate of a solution of all pending issues, if necessary by force and as soon as possible. The reports of the Press regarding the sentiments expressed by these circles and some other groups point to a growing and dangerous tension.

CHAPTER Ⅳ   NARRATIVE OF EVENTS IN MANCHURIA ON AND SUBSEQUENT TO SEPTEMBER 18th, 1931

Situation immediately preceding the outbreak.

In the preceding chapter the growing tension between the Japanese and Chinese interests in Manchuria was discussed and its effect on the attitudes of the military forces of the two nations described. Certain internal, economic and political factors had undoubtedly for some time been preparing the Japanese people for a resumption of the "positive policy" in Manchuria. The dissatisfaction of the army; the financial policy of the Government; the appearance of a new political force emanating from the army, the country districts and the nationalist youth, which expressed dissatisfaction with all political parties, which despised the compromise methods of western civilisation and relied on the virtues of Old Japan and which included in its condemnation the self-seeking methods whether of financiers or politicians; the fall in commodity prices which inclined the primary producer to look to an adventurous foreign policy for the alleviation of his lot; the trade depression which caused the industrial and commercial community to believe that better business would result from a more vigorous foreign policy: all these factors were preparing the way for the abandonment of the Shidehara "policy of conciliation" with China which seemed to have achieved such meager results. This impatience in Japan was even greater among the Japanese in Manchuria, where the tension throughout the summer was increasing. As September wore on, this tension reached such a point that it was apparent to all careful observers that a breaking point must soon be reached. The public press of both countries tended rather to inflame than to calm public opinion. Vigorous speeches of the Japanese War Minister in Tokyo, counseling direct action by their army in Manchuria were reported. Protracted delay by the Chinese authorities in making satisfactory investigation of and redress for the murder of Captain Nakamura had particularly incensed the young officers of the Japanese army in Manchuria, who clearly showed their sensitiveness to irresponsible remarks and slurs made by equally irresponsible Chinese officers on the streets or in restaurants and other places of close contact. And so the stage was set for the events which followed.

The night of September 18th—19th.

On the morning of Saturday, September 19th, the population of Mukden woke to find their city in the hands of Japanese troops. During the night sounds of firing had been heard, but there was nothing unusual in this; it had been a nightly experience throughout the week, as the Japanese had been carrying out night manoeuvres involving vigorous rifle and machine gun firing. True, that on the night of September 18th, the booming of guns and the sound of shells caused some alarm to the few that distinguished them, but the majority of the population considered the firing to be merely another repetition of Japanese manoeuvres, perhaps rather noisier than usual.

Appreciating the great importance of this occurrence which, as will be shown, was the first step of a movement which resulted in the military occupation of practically the whole of Manchuria, the Commission conducted an extensive inquiry into the events of that night. Of great value and interest, of course, were the official accounts of the Japanese and Chinese military leaders involved. The Japanese case was presented by Lieutenant Kawamoto, who is the earliest witness in the story, by Lieutenant-Colonel Shimamoto, the Commanding Officer of the battalion which carried out the attack on the North Barracks at Peitaying, and by Colonel Hirata, who captured the walled city. We also heard evidence from Lieutenant-General Honjo, the Commander-in-Chief of the Kwantung Army, and from several members of his staff. The Chinese case was presented by General Wang I-Cheh, the officer in command of the Chinese troops in the North Barracks, supplemented by the personal narratives of his Chief of Staff and of other officers who were present during the operations. We also heard the evidence of Marshal Chang Hsueh-liang and of his Chief of Staff, General Yung Chen.

The Japanese version.

According to the Japanese versions, Lieutenant Kawamoto, with six men under his command, was on patrol duty on the night of September 18th, practising defence exercises along the track of the South Manchuria Railway to the north of Mukden. They were proceeding southwards in the direction of Mukden. The night was dark but clear, and the field of vision was not wide. When they reached a point at which a small road crosses the line, they heard the noise of a loud explosion a little way behind them. They turned and ran back, and after going about 200 yards they discovered that a portion of one of the rails on the down track had been blown out. The explosion took place at the point of junction of two rails; the end of each rail had been cleanly severed, creating a gap in the line of 31 inches. On arrival at the site of the explosion, the patrol was fired upon from the fields on the east side of the line. Lieutenant Kawamoto immediately ordered his men to deploy and return the fire. The attacking body, estimated at about five or six, then stopped firing and retreated northwards. The Japanese patrol at once started in pursuit, and, having gone about 200 yards, they were again fired upon by a larger body, estimated at between three and four hundred.

Finding himself in danger of being surrounded by this large force, Lieutenant Kawamoto then ordered one of his men to report to the Commander of No. 3 Company, who was also engaged in night manoeuvres some 1,500 yards to the north; at the same time he ordered another of his men to telephone (by means of a box telephone near the spot) to Battalion Headquarters at Mukden for reinforcements.

At this moment the south-bound train from Changchun was heard approaching. Fearing that the train might be wrecked when it reached the damaged line, the Japanese patrol interrupted their engagement and placed detonators on the line in the hope of warning the train in time. The train, however, proceeded at full speed. When it reached the site of the explosion it was seen to sway and heel over to one side, but it recovered and passed on without stopping. As the train was due at Mukden at 10:30 p. m. , where it arrived punctually, it must have been about 10 o'clock p. m. , according to Lieutenant Kawamoto, when he first heard the explosion.

Fighting was then resumed. Captain Kawashima, with No. 3 Company, having heard the explosion, was already proceeding southwards when he met Lieutenant Kawamoto's messenger, who guided them to the spot. They arrived at about 10:50 p. m. Meanwhile, Lieutenant-Colonel Shimamoto, the Battalion Commander, on receipt of a telephone message, at once ordered the 1st and 4th Companies that were with him at Mukden to proceed to the spot. He also sent orders to the 2nd Company, which was at Fushun—an hour and a half away—to join them as soon as possible. The two Companies proceeded by rail from Mukden to Liutiaohu, and then on foot to the scene of action, where they arrived a little after midnight.

Lieutenant Kawamoto's patrol, reinforced by Captain Kawashima's Company, was still sustaining the Area of the Chinese troops concealed in the tall kaoliang grass, when the two Companies arrived from Mukden. Although his force was then only 500, and he believed the Chinese army in the North Barracks numbered 10,000, Lieutenant-Colonel Shimamoto at once ordered an attack on the Barracks, believing, as he told us, that "offence is the best defence". The ground between the railway and the North Barracks—a distance of about 250 yards—was difficult to cross in mass formation because of patches, of water, and while the Chinese troops were being driven back over this ground Lieutenant Noda was sent up the railway with a section of the 3rd Company to intercept their retreat. When the Japanese reached the North Barracks, which were described as glittering with electric light, an attack was made by the 3rd Company, which succeeded in occupying a corner of the left wing. The attack was vigorously contested by the Chinese troops within, and there was fierce fighting for some hours. The 1st Company attacked on the right, and the 4th Company in the centre. At 5:00 a. m. the south gate of the Barracks was blown in by two shells from a small cannon left in an outhouse immediately opposite to it by the Chinese, and by 6:00 o'clock a. m. the entire barracks were captured at the cost of two Japanese privates killed and twenty-two wounded. Some of the barracks caught area during the fighting; the remainder were burned out by the Japanese on the morning of the 19th. The Japanese stated that they buried 320 Chinese but only found about 20 wounded.

In the meantime operations in other places were being carried out with equal rapidity and thoroughness. Colonel Hirata received a telephone message from Lieutenant-Colonel Shimamoto about 10:40 p. m. to the effect that the South Manchuria Railway track had been destroyed by Chinese troops and that he was about to start to attack the enemy. Colonel Hirata approved his action, and himself decided to attack the walled city. The concentration of his troops was complete by 11:30 p. m. and his attack commenced. No resistance was offered, only occasional fighting on the streets, mostly with the Chinese police of whom 75 were killed. At 2:15 a. m. , the wall of the city was scaled. By 3:40 a. m. , He had captured it. At 4:50 a. m. he received information that the staff of the 2nd Division and a part of the 16th Regiment had left Liaoyang at 3:30 a. m. These troops arrived shortly after 5 a. m. At 6 a. m. the occupation of the eastern wall was completed; the Arsenal and aerodrome were captured at 7:30. The East

Barracks were then attacked only by 1 p. m. were occupied without fighting. The total casualties in those operations were seven Japanese wounded and 30 Chinese killed.

Lieutenant-General Honjo, who had only returned from his tour of inspection that very day, received the first news of what was happening at Mukden by telephone from a newspaper agent at about 11 o'clock. The Chief of Staff received a telegraphic report at 11:46 a. m. from the Special Service Station at Mukden, giving details of the attack, and orders were immediately sent to the troops at Liaoyang, Yingkow and Fengsheng to proceed to Mukden. The fleet was ordered to leave Port Arthur and proceed to Yingkow and the Commander-in-Chief of the Japanese Garrison Army in Korea was asked to send reinforcements. Lieutenant-General Honjo left Port Arthur at 3:30 a. m. and arrived at Mukden at noon.

The Chinese version.

According to the Chinese version, the Japanese attack on the Barracks at Peitaying was entirely unprovoked and came as a complete surprise. On the night of September 18th all the soldiers of the 7th Brigade, numbering about 10,000, were in the North Barracks. As instructions had been received from Marshall Chang Hsueh-liang on September 6th[①] that special care was to be taken to avoid any clash with the Japanese troops in the tense state of feeling existing at the time, the Sentries at the walls of the Barracks were only armed with dummy rifles. For the same reason the west gate in the mud wall surrounding the camp which gave access to the railway had been closed. The Japanese had been carrying out night manoeuvres around

---

① 原编辑者注:The text of the telegram shown to the Commission at Peiping was as follows:"Our relations with Japan have become very delicate. We must be particularly cautious in our intercourse with them. No matter how they may challenge us, we must be extremely patient and never resort to force, so as to avoid any conflict whatever. You are instructed to issue, secretly and immediately, orders to all the officers, calling their attention to this point. "

the barracks on the nights of September 14th, 15th, 16th, and 17th. At 7:00 p. m. on the evening of the 18th, they were manoeuvring at a village called Wenkuantun. At 9 p. m. officer Liu reported that a train composed of three or four coaches, but without the usual type of locomotive, had stopped there. At 10 p. m. the sound of a loud explosion was heard, immediately followed by rifle fire. This was reported over the telephone by the Chief of Staff to the Commanding Officer, General Wang I-Cheh, who was at his private house situated near the railway, about six or seven miles from the barracks, to the south. While the Chief of Staff was still at the telephone, news was brought to him that the Japanese were attacking the barracks and that two sentries had been wounded. At about 11 o'clock p. m. a general attack on the southwest corner of the barracks began, and at 11:30 p. m. the Japanese had effected an entry through a hole in the wall. As soon as the attack began the Chief of Staff gave orders for the lights to be extinguished, and again reported to General Wang I-Cheh by telephone. The latter replied that no resistance was to be offered. Distant artillery fire was heard at 10:30 o'clock p. m. from the southwest and northwest. At midnight live shells began to fall inside the Barracks. On reaching the south gate, the retreating troops of the 621st Regiment found that the Japanese were attacking that gate, and that the guard was withdrawing. They accordingly took shelter in some trenches and earthworks until after the Japanese soldiers had passed through into the interior, when they were able to make their escape through the south gate and reached the village of Erhtaitze, to the north-east of the barracks, about 2 a. m. Other troops made their escape through the east gate and the empty barracks just outside the east wall, finally reaching the same village between 3 and 4 a. m.

The only resistance was offered by the 620th Regiment, quartered in the northeast corner building and the second building south of it. The commander of this Regiment stated that when the Japanese troops entered through the south gate at 1 a. m. the Chinese troops withdrew from one building to another, leaving the Japanese to attack empty buildings. After the main body of the Chinese troops had withdrawn, the Japanese turned eastwards and occupied the eastern exit. The 620th Regiment thus found themselves cut off, and had no option but to fight their way through. They started to break through at 5 a. m. , but did not get completely clear until 7 a. m. This was the only actual fighting that took place in the barracks, and was responsible for most of the casualties. This regiment was the last to reach the village of Erhtaitze.

As soon as they were all assembled, the Chinese troops left the village in the early morning of the 19th for Tungling Station. From here they made their way to a village near Kirin, where they obtained a supply of winter clothing. Colonel Wang was sent to obtain permission from General Hsi Hsia for the troops to enter Kirin city. The Japanese residents at Kirin were so alarmed at the approach of the Chinese soldiers that reinforcements were at once sent from Changchun, Ssupingkai and Mukden to Kirin. Consequently the Chinese turned back towards Mukden. They left their trains thirteen miles outside Mukden, separated into nine groups, and marched round Mukden by night. To escape detection by the Japanese, General Wang I-Cheh himself rode through the town disguised as a peasant. In the morning the Japanese obtained news of their presence and sent aeroplanes to bomb them. They were obliged to lie hidden by day, but continued their march at night. Eventually they reached a station on the Peiping-Mukden Railway, and here they were able to order seven trains, which brought them to Shanhaikwan by October 4th.

Opinion of the Commission.

Such are the two stories of the so-called incident of September 18th as they were told to the Commission by the participants on both sides. Clearly, and not unnaturally in the circumstances, they are different and contradictory.

Appreciating the tense situation and high feeling which had preceded this incident, and realising the discrepancies which are bound to occur in accounts of interested persons, especially with regard to an event which took place at night, we, during our stay in the Far East, interviewed as many as possible of the representative foreigners who had been in Mukden at the time of the occurrences or soon after, including newspaper correspondents and other persons who had visited the scene of conflict shortly after the event, and to whom the first official Japanese account had been given. After a thorough consideration of such opinions, as well as of the accounts of the interested parties, and after a mature study of the considerable quantity of written material and a careful weighing of the great mass of evidence which was presented or collected, the Commission has come to the following conclusions:

Tense feeling undoubtedly existed between the Japanese and Chinese military forces. The Japanese, as was explained to the Commission in evidence, had a carefully prepared plan to meet the case of possible hostilities between themselves and the Chinese. On the night of September 18th—19th, this plan was put into operation with swiftness and precision. The Chinese in accordance with the instructions referred to on page 69[①], had no plan of attacking the Japanese troops, or of endangering the lives or property of Japanese nationals at this particular time or place. They made no concerted or authorised attack on the Japanese forces, and were surprised by the Japanese attack and subsequent operations. An explosion undoubtedly occurred on or near the railroad between 10 and 10:30 p. m. on September 18th, but the damage, if any, to the railroad did not in fact prevent the punctual arrival of the south-bound train from Changchun, and was not in itself sufficient to justify military action. The military operations of the Japanese troops during this night, which have been described above, cannot be regarded as measures of legitimate self-defence. In saying this the Commission does not exclude the hypothesis that the officers on the spot

---

① 编者按:见本书第133页。

may have thought they were acting in self-defence. The narrative of the subsequent events must now be resumed.

Movements of Japanese troops.

On the night of September 18th the Japanese troops in Manchuria were distributed as follows: In addition to the four Companies of the Battalion of Railway Guards which took part in the attack on the North Barracks, and the 29th Regiment of the 2nd Division under Colonel Hirata which captured the Walled City of Mukden, already described, the rest of the 2nd Division was distributed in various places; the Headquarters of the 4th Regiment was at Changchun, of the 16th at Liaoyang, of the 30th at Port Arthur; other parts of these regiments were stationed at Antung, Yingkow, and at many smaller places on the Changchun-Mukden branch and the Mukden-Antung branch of the South Manchuria Railway. Another battalion of Railway Guards was at Changchun, and units of the Railway Guards and Gendarmerie were distributed with the 2nd Division in the smaller places already mentioned. Lastly, there were the Garrison troops of Korea.

All the forces in Manchuria, and some of those in Korea, were brought into action almost simultaneously on the night of September 18th over the whole area of the South Manchuria Railway from Changchun to Port Arthur. Their total strength was as follows: 2nd Division, 5,400 men and 16 field guns, Railway Guards about 5,000 men, Gendarmerie about 500. The Chinese troops at Antung, Yingkow, Liaoyang and other smaller towns were overcome and disarmed without resistance. The Railway Guards and Gendarmerie remained in those places while the units of the 2nd Division at once concentrated at Mukden to take part in the more serious operations. The 16th and 30th Regiments arrived in time to join Colonel Hirata and assisted in the capture of the East Barracks. The 39th Mixed Brigade of the 20th Division (4,000 men and artillery) concentrated at 10 a.m. on the 19th at Shingishu on the Korean frontier, crossed the Yalu River on the 21st, and arrived at Mukden at midnight. From here detachments were sent to

Chengchiatun and Hsinmin, which they occupied on the 22nd.

Occupation of Changchun September 18—19, and Kirin September 21st.

The Chinese Garrisons of Kuanchengtze and Nanling at Changchun, with an estimated strength of 10,000 men and 40 guns, were attacked on the night of the 18th of September by the 4th Regiment of the 2nd Division and 1st Railway Guard Battalion stationed there (under Major-General Hasebe). Here, however, some resistance was shown by the Chinese. Fighting began at midnight. Nanling barracks were captured by 11 a. m. on the 19th, those of Kuanchengtze by 3 p. m. that day. The total Japanese casualties involved were 3 officers and 64 men killed and 3 officers and 85 men wounded. As soon as the fighting at Mukden was over the Regiments of the 2nd Division were concentrated at Changchun, the staff, with General Tamon, the 30th Regiment and one Battalion of Field Artillery arriving on the 20th, and the 15th Brigade under General Amano arriving on the 22nd. Kirin was occupied on the 21st without the firing of a shot, and the Chinese troops were removed to a distance of about eight miles.

The Herald of Asia, a semi-official Japanese publication of that time, states that all military operations were then regarded as completed, and that no further movements of troops were anticipated. The military operations which in fact ensued are attributed to Chinese provocation; an anti-Japanese demonstration at Chientao on the 20th; the destruction of a railway station at Lungsingtsun; and the explosion of some bombs which did no damage on Japanese premises at Harbin on September 23rd, are mentioned as examples of such provocation. Complaint is also made of growing banditry and of the activities of disbanded soldiers. All of these things, it is claimed, finally forced the Japanese to new military operations against their will.

Bombing of Chinchow.

The first of these operations was the bombing, on October 8th, of Chinchow, to which place the Provincial Government of Liaoning Province

had been transferred by Marshal Chang Hsueh-liang at the end of
September. According to the Japanese account, the bombing was chiefly
directed against the military barracks and the Communications University,
where the offices of the Civil Government had been established. The
bombing of a civil administration by military forces cannot be justified and
there is some doubt whether the area bombed was in fact as restricted as the
Japanese allege. Mr. Lewis, an American honorary Adviser of the Chinese
Government, arrived at Chinchow on October 12th and wrote on account of
what he found there to Dr. Koo, Who passed on the information later to the
Commission in his capacity of Assessor. According to Mr. Lewis, the
military barracks were in fact not touched at all and a multitude of bombs fell
everywhere in the town, even on the Hospital, as well as on the University
buildings. The Commander of the bombing planes informed a Japanese
newspaper shortly afterwards that four planes from Changchun were ordered
to Mukden at 8:30 a. m. on the 8th. There they joined other planes and a
squad of six scouting and five bombing planes were immediately despatched
to Chinchow heavily loaded with bombs and fuel. They arrived at about
1 p.m. , within ten to fifteen minutes dropped eighty bombs, and
immediately returned to Mukden. The Chinese, according to Mr. Lewis, did
not return the fire.

Nonni Bridge operations.

The next operation was that of the Nonni River Bridges, which started
in the middle of October and ended on the 19th of November with the
occupation of Tsitsihar by the Japanese troops. The justification for this
given by the Japanese was that they were attacked while repairing the bridge
over the Nonni River which had been destroyed by General Ma Chan-shan.
But the story must be begun earlier and an explanation given of the
destruction of the bridges.

At the beginning of October General Chang Hai-peng, the Garrison
Commander at Taonan, who in former times had held the same rank as Ma

Chan-shan and Wang Fu-lin, and had tried to become Governor of Heilungkiang in their place, started an advance movement along the Taonan-Angangchi Railway with the obvious object of seizing the Provincial Government by force. It is alleged in the Chinese Assessor's document No. 3, and this view is supported by information from neutral sources, that this offensive was instigated by the Japanese. In order to prevent the advance of Chang Haipeng's troops, General Ma Chan-shan ordered the destruction of the bridges over the Nonni River and both armies faced each other across the large and swampy valley of that River.

The Taonan-Angangchi Railway had been built with capital supplied by the South Manchuria Railway and the line was pledged as security for the loan. Accordingly, the South Manchuria Railway authorities felt that the interruption to the traffic on this line could not be allowed to continue at a season when the transportation of crops from the North of Manchuria was particularly needed. The Japanese Consul-General at Tsitsihar, on instructions from his Government, requested General Ma Chan-shan, who had arrived at Tsitsihar on October 20th, to have the bridges repaired as soon as possible, but no time limit accompanied this request. The Japanese authorities believed that General Ma Chan-shan would delay as long as possible the repairing of the bridges, as this interruption helped him to keep General Chang Haipeng's troops at a distance. On October 20th a small party of employees of the Taonan-Angangchi Railway and the South Manchuria Railway, without military escort, attempted to inspect the damage to the bridges, and was fired upon by Chinese troops in spite of explanations previously given to an officer of the Heilungkiang Provincial forces. This aggravated the situation, and accordingly on October 28th Major Hayashi, the representative of General Honjo at Tsitsihar, demanded the completion of the repairs by noon of November 3rd, stating that if they were not carried out by that date, engineers of the South Manchuria Railway, under the protection of Japanese troops, would take over the work. The Chinese authorities asked for an extension of the time limit but no answer was returned to this request and Japanese troops were despatched from Ssupingkai for the purpose of protecting the execution of the repair work.

By November 2nd the negotiations had not progressed and no decision had been reached. On that day Major Hayashi delivered an ultimatum to Generals Ma Chan-shan and Chang Haipeng, demanding that neither of them should use the railway for tactical purposes and that both should withdraw their forces to a distance of 10 kilometres from each side of the river. It was intimated that if the troops of either of these Generals obstructed the repair of the bridges by the engineers of the South Manchuria Railway, the Japanese would regard them as enemies. The ultimatum was to take effect as from noon of November 3rd, and the Japanese protective detachment was under orders to advance to Tahsing, on the north side of the valley, by noon of November 4th. The Chinese Assessor (document No. 3), the Japanese Consul-General at Tsitsihar and various officers of the 2nd Division all concur that General Ma Chan-shan replied that pending instructions from the Central Government he provisionally accepted, on his own authority, the Japanese demands. But the Japanese witnesses, on the other hand, added that they did not believe in the sincerity of General Ma, who obviously did not intend to permit the damaged bridges to be quickly or effectively repaired. Twice on the November 4th a joint Commission, including Major Hayashi, a representative of the Japanese Consul-General, and Chinese officers and civil officials, went to the bridges in order to avoid an outbreak of hostilities, and the Chinese delegates asked for a postponement of the Japanese advance. The demand was not complied with, and Colonel Hamamoto, the Commander of the 16th Infantry Regiment, in compliance with his orders, advanced to the bridges with one battalion of his regiment, two companies of field artillery and one company of engineers, to begin the repair work in accordance with the terms of the Japanese ultimatum. The engineers, under the command of Captain Hanai, started work on the morning of November 4th, and one infantry company, with two Japanese flags, began its advance to Tahsing Station by noon of that day.

Hostilities actually began during the second attempt of the above-mentioned mixed commission which went to the spot early in the afternoon of the 4th in order to make a last attempt to secure the withdrawal of the Chinese troops. As soon as firing began Colonel Hamamoto realised that his men were in a very difficult position and went immediately to their support with whatever troops he had available. A rapid reconnaissance convinced him that a frontal attack was impossible on account of the swampy ground, and that nothing but an encircling movement against the left wing of the opposing force would help him out of this difficult situation. Accordingly he despatched his reserve companies to attack the hill on which the left wing of the opposing forces rested, but the small number of his forces and the impossibility of bringing his guns near enough for action prevented him from gaining the position before nightfall. The hill was captured by 8:30 p. m., but no further advance was possible on that day.

The Kwantung Army Headquarters, on receiving a report of the position, immediately despatched strong reinforcements, and another battalion of infantry arrived during the night, enabling the Colonel to reopen his attack at dawn of November 5th. Even then, after a couple of hours and reaching the first Chinese position, he found himself confronted with a strong line of trenches defended, according to his own statement to the Commission, with about seventy automatic and machine guns. His attack was held up, and his troops suffered heavy losses, as a result of a Chinese encircling counter-attack executed by infantry and cavalry men. The Japanese troops were forced to retire, and for the second time they could do nothing but hold their position until nightfall. During the night of the 5th—6th November, two fresh battalions arrived. This relieved the situation, and a renewed attack on the morning of the 6th rolled up the entire Chinese front, and brought Tahsing Station into the hands of the Japanese troops by noon. As Colonel Hamamoto's mission was only to occupy Tahsing Station, in order to cover the repair work of the bridges, no pursuit of the retreating

Chinese troops was made, but the Japanese troops remained in the vicinity of the station.

The Chinese Assessor, in the same document No. 3, alleges that Major Hayashi, on November 6th, made a new request to the Heilungkiang Government, asking (1) that General Ma Chan-shan should resign from the Governorship in favour of General Chang Hai-peng, and (2) that a public safety committee should be organised. A photograph of Major Hayashi's letter containing these requests was shown to the Commission. This document further states that on the following day, without waiting for a reply, the Japanese troops began a new attack on the provincial forces now stationed at Sanchienfang, about 20 miles north of Tahsing, and that on November 8th Major Hayashi sent another letter repeating the demand for General Ma Chan-shan's retirement from the Governorship of the Province in favour of General Chang Hai-peng, and for a reply before midnight of that day. On November 11th, the Chinese account continues, General Honjo himself asked by telegram for General Ma Chan-shan's retirement, the evacuation of Tsitsihar, and the right for the Japanese troops to advance to Angangchi Station, again requiring a reply before nightfall of that day. On November 13th Major Hayashi increased the third demand to one for the Japanese troops to occupy not only Angangchi Station but Tsitsihar Station as well. General Ma Chan-shan pointed out in reply that Tsitsihar Station had nothing to do with the Taonan-Angangchi Railway.

On November 14th and 15th the Japanese combined forces renewed their attack with the support of four aeroplanes. On November 16th General Honjo demanded the retreat of General Ma Chan-shan to the north of Tsitsihar, the withdrawal of Chinese troops to the north of the Chinese Eastern Railway, and an undertaking not to interfere in any way with the traffic and operation of the Taonan-Angangchi Railway, these demands to be carried out within ten days from November 15th, and a reply to be sent to the Japanese Special Bureau at Harbin. When General Ma Chan-shan declined to accept these terms, General Tamon began a new general attack on November 18th. General Ma Chan-shan's troops retreated, first to Tsitsihar, which was taken by the Japanese on November 19th, and then to Hailun, to which place the administrative offices of the Government were removed.

According to the evidence of Japanese Generals commanding on the spot, the new operations did not begin before November 12th. General Ma Chan-shan at that time had gathered about 20,000 of his troops to the west of Sanchienfang, and even sent for the land colonisation troops in Heilungkiang Province and the forces of General Ting Chao. Against these large forces, which showed an increasingly threatening attitude, the Japanese could oppose only the new concentrated division of General Tamon, consisting of two brigades under Generals Amano and Hasebe. In order to relieve this tense situation General Honjo demanded, on November 12th, that all Heilungkiang troops should retire to the north of Tsitsihar, and that his troops should be allowed to proceed northward for the protection of the Taonan-Angangchi Railway. The advance did not begin before November 17th, when the Chinese sent cavalry troops around the right flank of the Japanese and attacked them. General Tamon informed the Commission that in spite of his small strength of 3,000 infantrymen and 24 field guns he ventured to attack the Chinese forces, and completely defeated them on November 18th, with the result that Tsitsihar was occupied on the morning of the 19th. One week later the 2nd Division returned to its original quarters, leaving General Amano with one infantry regiment and one battery of artillery at Tsitsihar to hold the place against General Ma Chan-shan's troops. This small Japanese force was subsequently reinforced by the newly-formed "Manchukuo" troops, but these new troops at the time of our visit to Tsitsihar in May, 1932, were not yet considered capable of fighting the forces of General Ma Chan-shan.

The attached Military Situation Chart No. 2 on page shows the distribution of regular troops of both sides at the time of the first resolution of the Council. No account is taken of disbanded soldiers and bandit groups which, at that time, specially infested the areas east and west of the Liao River and the Chientao district. Both the parties have accused each other of purposely instigating banditry—the Japanese attributing to the Chinese the motive of wishing to create disorder in the lost parts of Manchuria, and the Chinese suspecting the Japanese of wishing to find pretexts for occupying the country and still further extending their military operations. The strength and military value of these gangs is so vague and changeable that it would not be possible to insert an accurate estimate of their significance into the picture of the military situation. The chart shows that the Command of the North-Eastern troops had succeeded in organising a force of considerable strength in the south-western part of Liaoning Province. These troops had been able to construct a strongly entrenched position on the right bank of the Taling River very close to the foremost Japanese outposts. Such a situation may well have caused the Japanese military authorities some anxiety as they estimated the total strength of these regular troops at 35,000 men, or about double the total admitted strength of their own forces in Manchuria at that moment.

The Tientsin incident.

This situation was relieved by action taken in consequence of certain events which occurred at Tientsin during the month of November. Reports as to the origin of the trouble differ widely. There were two outbreaks, on the 8th, and the 26th, of November respectively, but the whole affair is extremely obscure.

Outbreak of November 8th: Japanese version.

According to the Japanese account in the *Herald of Asia*, the Chinese population at Tientsin was divided between those who supported and those who opposed Marshal Chang Hsueh-liang, and the latter organised forces to create a political demonstration in the Chinese city by attacking the guardians of public order on the 8th of November. In this dispute between two Chinese factions the Commander of the Japanese garrison observed strict neutrality from the beginning, but was forced to open fire when Chinese guards in the vicinity of the Japanese Concession began to shoot indiscriminately into his district. His demand that the combating Chinese forces should keep at 300 yards' distance, the border of the Concession, did not relieve the situation which grew so tense that on November 11th or 12th, all foreign garrisons mounted guard.

The Chinese version.

The account given by the Municipal Government of Tientsin is very different. They assert that the Japanese employed Chinese ruffians and Japanese plain clothes men, who were formed into operating gangs within the Japanese Concession in order to start trouble in the Chinese city. Their police authorities being timely informed by agents of this situation, were able to repulse the disorderly bands emerging from the Japanese Concession. They say that from the confession of arrested members of these gangs they are able to prove that the riot was organised by the Japanese, and that the men were armed with guns and ammunition of Japanese make. They admit that the Japanese garrison Commander complained on the morning of the 9th that some of his men had been wounded by stray bullets, and that he had asked for a withdrawal to a distance of 300 yards, but they assert that in spite of their acceptance of these conditions the Japanese regular troops attacked the Chinese city with armoured cars and shelled it.

The account of the Municipal Government further states that on November 17th, an agreement was reached which fixed the details for the withdrawal to a distance of 300 yards, but it asserts that the Japanese did not carry out their part of the agreement, and that consequently the situation grew worse.

On November 26th a terrific explosion was heard, immediately followed by firing of cannons, machine guns and rifles. The electric lights in the Japanese Concession were put out, and plain clothes men emerged from it, attacking the police stations in the vicinity.

Outbreak of November 26th: Conflicting accounts.

The Japanese account of this later disturbance as given in the *"Herald of Asia"* is to the effect that on the 26th the situation had become so much better that their volunteer corps was disbanded, and that on the same evening the Chinese opened fire on the Japanese barracks, and as the fire, in spite of their protests, did not stop until noon of the 27th, they had no choice but to accept the challenge and to fight the Chinese. The battle went on until the afternoon of the 27th, when a peace conference was held. On that occasion the Japanese demanded the immediate cessation of hostilities and the withdrawal of Chinese troops and police forces to a distance of 20 Chinese li from all places where foreign troops were stationed. The Chinese agreed to withdraw their soldiers but not their police forces, which were alone responsible for the safety of foreigners in that district. The Japanese say that on November 29th the Chinese offered their withdrawal from the neighbourhood of the Concession: their offer was accepted; the Chinese armed police withdrew on the morning of the 29th, and the defence work was removed on the 30th.

Effect of the Tientsin disturbances on the situation in Manchuria.

The threatening situation at Tientsin on the 26th caused the staff officers of the Kwantung Army to propose to the Commander an immediate expedition of troops via Chinchow and Shanhaikwan to reinforce the endangered small force at Tientsin. As a mere transport problem it would have been easier and quicker to despatch reinforcements by sea via Dairen. But considered strategically, the suggested route had this advantage, that it would enable the advancing troops to dispose en route of the very inconvenient Chinese concentration around Chinchow. It was assumed that the delay in taking this route would not be long as little or no resistance from the Chinese was anticipated. The suggestion was approved, and one armoured train, one troop train, and a couple of aeroplanes crossed the Liao River on November 27th, and their attack on the first Chinese outposts was sufficient to initiate a retreat of the Chinese troops from their entrenched position. The armoured car corps also changed its position. A shade of resistance led the Japanese to reinforce their strength by more armoured trains, infantry trains, and artillery. They also repeatedly threw bombs on Chinchow, but news of the improved situation at Tientsin soon deprived the expedition of its original objective and on November 29th, to the great surprise of the Chinese, the Japanese forces were withdrawn to Hsinmin.

Another consequence of the earlier disturbances at Tientsin was that the former Emperor, who had been living in the Japanese Concession there, sought a safer refuge at Port Arthur on November 13th, after a talk with Colonel Doihara.

The occupation of Chinchow.

The districts evacuated by the Japanese were re-occupied by the Chinese troops, and this fact was widely advertised. Chinese morale was slightly raised; and the activities of irregular forces and bandits increased. Profiting by the winter season, they crossed the frozen Liao River at many points and raided the country round Mukden. The Japanese military authorities realised that even to maintain their existing positions reinforcements would be necessary, and with these reinforcements they hoped to be able to get rid of the menace of the Chinese concentration at Chinchow.

Japanese reservation when accepting the resolution of the Council on December 10th.

Meanwhile the situation in Manchuria was a subject of further discussion in Geneva. When accepting the resolution on December 10th the Japanese delegate stated that his acceptance "was based on the understanding that this paragraph (No. 2) was not intended to preclude the Japanese forces from taking such action as might be necessary 'to provide directly for the protection of the lives and property of Japanese subjects against the activity of bandits and lawless elements rampant in various parts of Manchuria'. Such action was admittedly 'an exceptional measure called for by the special situation prevailing in Manchuria', and its necessity would end when normal conditions should be restored there". To that the Chinese representative replied "that the injunction to the parties not to aggravate the situation should not be violated under the pretext of the existence of lawlessness caused by the state of affairs in Manchuria", and several Council members taking part in the discussion admitted that "circumstances might arise there causing danger to Japanese lives and property and in such an emergency it might be inevitable that Japanese forces in the neighbourhood should take action". When this matter has been referred to by Japanese officers who have given evidence before the Commission it is usually asserted that the resolution of December 10th, "gave Japan the right to maintain her troops" in Manchuria, or made the Japanese army responsible for the suppression of banditry there. In describing the subsequent operations they assert that while executing this right against the bandit forces near the Liao River, they incidentally came in conflict with the remaining Chinese forces near Chinchow which were in consequence withdraw within the Great Wall. The fact remains that having made their reservation at Geneva the Japanese continued to deal with the situation in Manchuria according to their plans.

Arrival of reinforcements.

The 2nd Division, with the exception of its garrison at Tsitsihar, was concentrated west of Mukden. Reinforcements soon began to arrive; the 4th Brigade of the 8th Division[①] between the 10th and 15th of December. On December 27th Imperial sanction was obtained for the despatch of the Staff of the 20th Division and another brigade from Korea. Changchun and Kirin

---

① 原编辑者注：All the statements here given concerning numbers of units and strength of the Japanese forces are based on official Japanese information.

were for the time being only protected by Independent Railway Guards.

Abortive negotiations for the withdrawal of Chinese troops.

As a Japanese advance on Chinchow was imminent, the Chinese Minister of Foreign Affairs made an attempt to prevent further fighting by offering to withdraw the Chinese troops to within the Great Wall provided that three or four foreign Powers were willing to guarantee the maintenance of a neutral zone north and south of Chinchow. Nothing came of the proposal. Meanwhile, conversations were initiated between Marshal Chan Hsueh-liang and the Japanese Charge d'Affaires at Peiping, but these too were abortive for different reasons. The Chinese allege in their document No. 3, Annex "E", that, at each successive visit, on December 7th, 25th, and 29th, the Japanese delegate increased his demands concerning the Chinese retreat and his promises with regard to the restraint of the Japanese troops became more and more vague. The Japanese, on the other hand, claim that the Chinese promises to withdraw were never sincere.

Attack on Chinchow.

The concentrated attack of the Japanese forces began on December 23rd when the 19th Chinese Brigade was forced to give up its position. From that day the advance continued with perfect regularity and hardly met with any resistance at all, the Chinese Commander having given out a general order to retreat. Chinchow was occupied on the morning of January 3rd and the Japanese forces continued their advance right up to the Great Wall at Shanhaikwan, where they established a permanent contact with the Japanese garrison in that place. The complete evacuation of Manchuria by the troops of Marshal Chan Hsueh-liang, practically—without striking a blow, was not unconnected with the internal conditions of China south of the Wall. Reference has been made in an earlier chapter to the feuds between rival Generals and it must be remembered these feuds had not ceased.

The occupation of Harbin.

The comparatively ease with which the offensive down to Shanhaikwan was carried out enabled the Japanese to release some of their troops from their original positions and make them available for advances in other directions. The main force of the 2nd Division, which had done nearly all the fighting so far, returned to their quarters at Liaoyang, Mukden, and Changchun for a rest. On the other hand, the increased length of railway line to be protected against possible bandit raids at any point necessitated the use of a large number of troops the fighting strength of which was diminished by their distribution over such wide areas. The two brigades under the command of the Staff of the 20th Division were left for this purpose in the newly occupied zone, and the 4th Brigade of the 8th Division joined them more to the north. The Japanese military authorities assured us that within these well guarded areas a state of law and order was soon established and that banditry was practically extinguished on both sides of the Liao River during the following weeks. This statement was made to us in the month of June, but at the moment of writing this Report we read of vigorous raids from Volunteer troops on Yingkow and Haicheng, with threats even to Mukden and Chinchow.

The district which at the beginning of this year gave more trouble than any other was that north and east of Harbin, to which the remaining followers of the two former Provincial Governments of Kirin and Heilungkiang had withdrawn. The Chinese Generals in this northern section seemed to have maintained some contact with Headquarters at Peiping, whence they received some support from time to time. The advance on Harbin began, as that on Tsitsihar had done, by an encounter between two Chinese forces. General Hsi Hsia at the beginning of January prepared for an expedition to the North with the view to occupying Harbin. Between him and that city were Generals Ting Chao and Li Tu, with what are described as anti-Kirin forces. According to information provided by the Japanese Assessor, when our preliminary report was under consideration, satisfactory terms would have been arranged by negotiation between the parties had it not been for the influence of the authorities at Peiping. Negotiations were in fact initiated and while they were being carried on General Hsi Hsia advanced with his troops as far as Shuangcheng, which they reached on January 25th, but when it came to serious fighting on the following morning in the immediate neighbourhood south of the city, the advance was at once checked. The situation thus created was felt by the Japanese to be full of danger for the large Japanese and Korean colonies at Harbin. Fighting between two more or less irregular Chinese forces in the immediate neighbourhood would have resulted in the retreat on the town of a defeated army, the horrors of which the recent history of China provides so many examples. Urgent appeals were therefore sent to the Kwantung Army, even Chinese merchants, so the Japanese assert, joining in the appeal from fear that their property might be looted.

Colonel Doihara, now General, who, in this emergency, was sent to Harbin on the 26th in order to take over the office of the special Japanese service there, told the Commission that the fighting between the two Chinese forces around Harbin continued for about ten days, and that there was great anxiety for the 4,000 Japanese residents, who mostly lived in a menaced area, together with 1,600 Koreans in the Chinese suburb of Fuchiatien, who were exposed to the danger of massacre. In spite of the fact that the anti-Kirin forces held the town during ten days of continual fighting, the casualties among the Korean and Japanese residents were comparatively few. The latter organised themselves into armed volunteer bands and helped their nationals to escape from the Chinese suburb. One Japanese and three Koreans are said to have been killed while trying to escape. In addition, one of the Japanese aeroplanes, sent to reconnoitre the threatening situation, was forced to land owing to engine trouble, and its occupants are said to have been killed by Ting Chao's troops.

These two incidents decided the Japanese military authorities to intervene. Again the 2nd Division was called upon to help its endangered countrymen. But this time the problem was not so much one of lighting as of transportation, the railway north of Changchun being a joint Sino-Russian undertaking. As the rolling stock of the southern branch of the Chinese Eastern Railway was greatly depleted, the Commander of the 2nd Division decided to send, in the first instance, only General Hasebe and two infantry battalions. Negotiations with the railway authorities were started, but when these seemed likely to be long drawn out, the Japanese officers decided to enforce the transport of their troops. The railway authorities protested and refused to work the trains, but in spite of their opposition the Japanese military authorities succeeded on the night of January 28th in forming three military trains, which went as far north as the second Sungari bridge, which they found damaged by the Chinese forces. As the repairs were made on the 29th, Shuangcheng was reached on the afternoon of January 30th. Early on the following morning, and still under cover of darkness, the small Japanese force was attacked by Ting Chao's troops, and severe fighting took place, resulting in the repulse of the Chinese, but no further progress was possible that day. By that time the Soviet and Chinese railway authorities had agreed that the transport of Japanese troops on the Chinese Eastern Railway would be allowed, on the understanding that they were proceeding with the sole object of giving protection to the Japanese residents at Harbin. The fares of the troops were paid for in cash. On February 1st the Japanese troops began to arrive and the main force of the 2nd Division was concentrated near Shuangcheng on the morning of February 3rd. Reinforcements were even called upon from Tsitsihar, where, as will be remembered, a part of the 2nd Division had remained since November 19th. But many difficulties had still to be overcome, as the line between Harbin and Tsitsihar was cut by the Chinese who at the same time attacked detachments of the Independent Railway Guards on the southern branch of the Chinese Eastern Railway at different places.

On February 3rd the anti-Kirin troops, now estimated to have a total strength of about 13,000 to 14,000 soldiers with 16 guns, had taken up an entrenched position along the southern boundary of the city. The 2nd Division began to advance against this position on the same day, reaching the Nanchengtze River, about 20 miles north of Shuangcheng, on the night of February 3rd—4th. Fighting commenced on the following morning. On the evening of the 4th the Chinese position was partly taken by the Japanese troops and by noon of the 5th a final decision was reached. Harbin was occupied on the afternoon of the same day, and the Chinese withdrew in the direction of Sanhsing.

Further Japanese Military operations up to the end of August 1932.

The successful attack of the 2nd Division brought the town of Harbin into the hands of the Japanese authorities, but, as it was not immediately followed by any pursuit of the retiring Chinese forces, little change was produced on the situation in northern Manchuria as a whole. The railways, north and east of Harbin and the important waterway of the Sungari River still remained under the control of the anti-Kirin troops and those of Ma Chan-shan. The arrival of further reinforcements, repeated expeditions to the east and north and six months of fighting took place before the occupied area was extended as far as Hailun in the north and the districts of Fangcheng and Hailin in the east. According to Japanese official statements, the anti-Kirin troops with those of General Ma Chan-shan were completely routed, but according to official Chinese sources, they are still in existence. Although reduced in their fighting strength they continually hamper the Japanese forces, at the same time avoiding actual encounters in the open field. According to newspaper information, both the eastern and western branch of the Chinese Eastern Railway is still being attacked and damaged at different places between Harbin and Hailin.

The Japanese operations since the beginning of February may be summarised as follows:

Towards the end of March the main part of the 2nd Division left Harbin in the direction of Fangcheng in order to suppress the anti-Kirin troops of

General Ting Chao and Li Tu. The Division advanced as far as the region of Sanhsing and returned to Harbin in the earlier part of April. By that time, the 10th Division had arrived at Harbin and took over the sector from the 2nd Division. This unit was engaged for about a month in constant fighting against the anti-Kirin troops with the greater part of its forces in the district near Sanhsing and with a minor detachment along the eastern branch of the Chinese Eastern Railway, in the direction of Hailin.

In the earlier part of May, the Japanese forces in the north of Manchuria were further reinforced by the 14th Division. A detachment of this unit took part in the fighting against the anti-Kirin forces and advanced as far as the valley of Mutan River, south of Sanhsing, forcing the opposing troops to withdraw to the most eastern corner of Kirin Province. But the main operations of the 14th Division, which began in the latter part of May, took place in the region north of Harbin and were directed against the troops of General Ma Chan-shan. The 14th Division carried out its main attack to the north of Harbin, along the Hulan-Hailun Railway, and, with minor forces to the east from Keshan, the proposed terminus of the Tsitsihar-Keshan Railway. The Japanese claim that during the earlier part of August the troops of General Ma Chan-shan were again effectively routed, and that they have strong evidence that the General himself was killed. The Chinese assert that the General is still alive. In this action cavalry, newly arrived from Japan, likewise took part.

During the month of August, several minor engagements took place on the borders of Fengtien and Jehol Provinces, mainly near the Chinchow-Peipiao branch line (of the Peiping-Mukden Railway), which is the only means of access to Jehol by railway. There are widespread fears in China that these events are only a prelude to larger military operations at an early date, aimed at the occupation of Jehol by the Japanese. The main lines of communication which still exist between China Proper and the Chinese forces in Manchuria run through Jehol, and the fear of a Japanese attack in this Province, which is already claimed as part of the territory of "Manchukuo", is not unreasonable. Its imminence is freely discussed in the Japanese press.

The Japanese version of the recent events submitted to the Commission by the Japanese Assessor is as follows:

An official attached to the Kwantung Army Headquarters named Ishimoto was kidnapped by Chinese "Volunteers" on July 17th from a train traveling between Peipiao and Chinchow, within the boundaries of the Province of Jehol. A small detachment of Japanese infantry with light artillery made an immediate attempt to rescue him but failed in their purpose, and the result was the occupation of a village on the frontier of Jehol by Japanese troops.

During the latter part of July and in August, Japanese aeroplanes demonstrated several times over this part of Jehol and dropped some bombs, but "uninhabited areas outside the villages" were carefully selected. On August 19th, a Japanese staff officer was sent to Nanling, a small town situated between Peipiao and the provincial boundary, to negotiate for the release of Mr. Ishimoto. On his return journey with a small infantry detachment he was fired upon. In self-defence the area was returned, and on the arrival of another infantry detachment, Nanling was occupied but evacuated on the following day.

Through the Chinese Assessor extracts were submitted to the Commission from the reports of General Tang Yu-ling, the Governor of the Province of Jehol. These reports claim that fighting on a much larger scale took place, and that a Chinese battalion of railway guards was in action against a superior number of Japanese infantry, supported by two armoured trains. They claim that the bombing referred to by the Japanese was directed against Chaoyang, one of the larger towns in that region, and that as a result 30 casualties were caused among both military and civilians. The Japanese offensive was resumed on August 10th when an armoured train attacked Nanling.

The information given by the Japanese Assessor concludes by stating that, although the maintenance of order in Jehol is "a matter of internal policy for Manchukuo, Japan cannot be indifferent to the situation in that region in view of the important role played by Japan in the maintenance of peace and order in Manchuria and Mongolia, and that any disorders in Jehol would immediately produce very serious repercussions throughout Manchuria and Mongolia. "

General Tang Yu-ling concludes his report by stating that all possible measures were being taken to offer effective resistance should the Japanese attacks be renewed.

From these communications it seems that an extension of the area of conflict in this region is a contingency which must be reckoned with.

Nature of resistance offered by the Chinese.

Although the main Chinese army was withdrawn within the Great Wall at the end of 1931, the Japanese continued to meet with opposition of an irregular kind in different parts of Manchuria. There have been no further battles such as occurred on the Nonni River but fighting has been constant and widely dispersed. It has been the practice of the Japanese to describe indiscriminately as "bandits" all the forces now opposed to them. There are, in fact, apart from bandits, two distinct categories of organised resistance to the Japanese troops or to those of "Manchukuo"; namely, the regular and irregular Chinese troops. It is extremely difficult to estimate the number of these two, and, as the Commission was not able to meet any of the Chinese generals still in the field, it is necessary to make reservations with regard to the reliability of the information given below. Chinese authorities are naturally reluctant to give away exact information about such troops as are still offering resistance to the Japanese in Manchuria. Japanese authorities, on the other hand, are disposed to minimize the numbers and fighting value of the forces still opposed to them.

Remnant of the original North-Eastern armies.

The remnants of the Original Northeastern armies are to be found exclusively in the Provinces of Kirin and Heilungkiang. The reorganisation of troops which took place around Chinchow late in 1931 was not of long duration, because all those units were subsequently withdrawn inside the Great Wall. But the regular Chinese troops, which, before September 1931, were stationed in the Sungari region and along the Chinese Eastern Railway, have never been seriously engaged with the Japanese troops, and continue to carry on a guerilla warfare which has given, and still gives, much trouble to the Japanese and "Manchukuo" forces. The Generals Ma Chan-shan, Ting Chao and Li Tu have acquired great fame throughout China as leaders of these troops. All three are former brigade-generals in command of railway guards or garrison troops in north Manchuria. Probably the greater part of the troops under their command remained faithful to their respective leaders and the cause of China after the destruction of the Young Marshal's regime. The strength of General Ma's troops cannot easily be determined, because, as will be remembered, this General changed his allegiance.

As Governor of Heilungkiang Province, he was in command of all the provincial troops, the number of which was given to us as seven brigades in all. Since the month of April he has definitely taken up a position against Japan and "Manchukuo". The number of troops at his disposal between Holan River, Hailun and Taheiho is estimated by Japanese authorities as six regiments, or between 7,000 and 8,000 men. Generals Ting Chao and Li Tu control six old brigades of Chang Hsueh-liang's army, and have since raised in the country three additional brigades. Their total strength at the time of our Preliminary Report was estimated by Japanese authorities as about 30,000. But it is very probable that the troops of General Ma Chan-shan as well as those of Generals Ting Chao and Li Tu have considerably diminished in number since the month of April and are now below the estimated figure. Both units, as will be seen later on, have suffered a great deal from concentrated attacks of regular Japanese troops since the occupation of Harbin. At present they seem unable to hinder any operation by the Japanese troops and carefully avoid meeting them in the open field. The use of aeroplanes by the Japanese and the complete absence of this weapon on the other side, accounts for the greater part of such losses as they have sustained.

Irregular forces Volunteers.

When considering the irregular forces it is necessary to distinguish between the different volunteer forces in Kirin Province cooperating with the armies of Generals Chao and Li Tu. In our Preliminary Report of April 29, 1932, we mentioned, on page 5, under the heading "Volunteers", three different volunteer armies and several minor corps, one of the latter between Tunhua and Tienpaoshan remaining in touch with these regular troops of Generals Ting Chao and Li Tu. Owing to the absence of railways and other means of communication in those districts this corps still keeps the same position. Its Chief, Wang Tey-ling, united different "anti-Manchukuo" forces and kept them firmly under his command. Though this force may be of small significance compared with Japanese troops (which hardly exhibit any activity to the east of Tunhua), it seems well able to hold its own against the "Manchukuo" troops and maintains its position in a considerable part of Kirin Province. No evidence is available concerning the present activity of the "Big Sword Society" which, while keeping in touch with Wang Teh-ling, created considerable disturbance in the Chientao district. On the other hand, no action of importance has been undertaken against it by Japanese troops.

An official Japanese document has been submitted to the Commission enumerating a large number of so-called route armies and other Chinese units, each containing not more than 200 to 400 men, which form the subdivisions of the volunteer armies. Their field of activity extends to the areas around Mukden and the Mukden-Antung Railway, to Chinchow and the boundary between Jehol and Fengtien Provinces, to the western branch of the Chinese Eastern Railway and to the district between Hsinmin and Mukden. Thus the area covered by these volunteers and the anti-Kirin forces combined comprises the greater part of Manchuria.

In the middle of August, fighting broke out in the immediate neighbourhood of Mukden, at different places of the southern part of the South Manchuria Railway, especially at Haicheng and at Yingkow. On several occasions the Japanese troops have found themselves in a difficult position, but nowhere have the volunteers succeeded in attaining a victory of any importance. It seems doubtful whether any change in the general situation in Manchuria is to be anticipated in the near future, but at the time of the completion of our Report, fighting continues over a wide area.

Bandits.

As in China, banditry has always existed in Manchuria. Increasing or diminishing in numbers in relation to the activity or the weakness of the Government, professional bandits are to be found in all parts of the Three Provinces and their services were often employed by different parties for political purposes. The Chinese Government has presented to the Commission a document stating that during the last 20 or 30 years Japanese agents to a great extent instigated bandits to serve their political interests. A passage from the "Second Report of Progress of Manchuria in 1930", published by the South Manchuria Railway, is quoted in this document to the effect that within the railway area alone the number of cases of banditry had increased from 9 cases in 1906 to 368 in 1929. According to the Chinese document quoted above, banditry has been encouraged by the smuggling of arms and munitions on a large scale from Dairen and the Kwantung, Leased Territory. It is asserted, for instance, that the notorious bandit chief, Lin Yin-shin, was provided in November last with arms, munitions and other means in order to establish the so-called Independent Self-Defence Army which was organised with the help of three Japanese agents and destined to attack Chinchow. After the failure of this attempt another bandit chief got Japanese help for the same purpose but fell into the hands of the Chinese authorities with all his material of Japanese origin.

Japanese authorities, of course, see the state of banditry in Manchuria in quite a different light. According to them, its existence is due exclusively to the inefficiency of the Chinese Government. They allege also that Chang Tso-lin to a certain extent favoured the existence of bandit gangs in his territory, because he thought that in time of need they could easily be converted into soldiers. The Japanese authorities, while admitting the fact that the complete overthrow of Chang Hsueh-liang's government and army greatly added to the number of bandits in the country, claim that the presence of their troops in the country will enable them to wipe out the principal bandit units within from two to three years. They hope that the organisation of "Manchukuo" police and of self-defence corps in each community will help to put an end to banditry. Many of the present bandits are believed to have been peaceful citizens who on account of the complete loss of their property were induced to take up their present occupation. Given the opportunity of resuming the occupation of farming, it is hoped that they will return to their former peaceful mode of life.

CHAPTER Ⅴ SHANGHAI

The Shanghai affair.

(*See Map No. 11.*) At the end of January, fighting broke out at Shanghai. The story of that affair has already been told in its broad outlines down to February 20th by the Consular Committee appointed by the League. The fighting was still in progress when the Commission arrived at Tokyo on the 29th, and several discussions took place with members of the Japanese Government on the origin, motives and consequences of their armed intervention in this place. When we reached Shanghai, on March 14th, the fighting was over, but the negotiations for an armistice were proving difficult. The arrival of the Commission at this moment was opportune, and may have helped to create a propitious atmosphere. We were able to appreciate the tense feeling which had been created by the recent hostilities and to obtain an immediate and vivid impression both of the difficulties and of the issues involved in this controversy. The Commission was not instructed to continue the work of the Consular Committee or to make a special study of the recent events there. In fact, we were informed by the Secretary-General of the League of Nations that the Chinese Government had expressed themselves as opposed to any suggestion that the Commission should delay its journey to Manchuria for the purpose of studying the situation at Shanghai.

We heard the views of both the Chinese and the Japanese Governments on the Shanghai affair, and were the recipients of a large amount of literature from both sides on the subject. We also visited the devastated area and heard statements from Japanese naval and military officers on the recent operations. In an individual capacity, too, we had conversations with the representatives of many shades of opinion on matters which were fresh in the memory of everyone living in Shanghai. But we did not, as a Commission, officially investigate the Shanghai affair and therefore express no opinion upon the disputed points connected with it. We shall, however, for purposes of record, complete the story of the operations from February 20th until the final withdrawal of the Japanese troops.

Narrative of events at Shanghai from February 20th onwards. (*See Map No. 12.*)

The last report of the Consular Committee ended, it will be remembered, by stating that the Japanese, on February 20th, opened a new attack in the Kiangwan and Woosung areas. This attack brought no marked success to the Japanese troops, despite the fact that it was continued on the following days, but it enabled them to learn that parts of the so-called Chinese Bodyguard Army—viz., the 87th and 88th Divisions—were now fighting against them as well as the 19th Route Army. This fact, together with the difficulties which the nature of the country presented, decided the Japanese to reinforce their troops by two more divisions—namely, the 11th and 14th.

On February 28th, the Japanese troops occupied the western part of Kiangwan, which had been evacuated by the Chinese. On the same day, the Woosung fort and fortifications along the Yangtse River were again bombed from the air and from the sea, and bombing-planes operated over the whole front, including the aerodrome at Hungjao and the Nanking Railway. General Shirakawa, who was appointed to the supreme command of the Army, arrived in Shanghai on February 29th. From this date onwards the Japanese Headquarters announced substantial progress. In the district of Kiangwan they advanced slowly, and the Naval Headquarters stated that the opposing forces at Chapei showed signs of giving way as a consequence of the daily bombardment. On the same day, the aerodrome at Hangchow, which is 100 miles distant from Shanghai, was bombed from the air.

On March 1st, as the frontal attack had advanced but slowly, the Japanese Army Commander initiated a wide enveloping movement by landing the main force of the 11th Division at some distance on the right bank of the Yangtze River, in the vicinity of Tsiyakow, for the purpose of making a surprise attack on the left flank of the Chinese Army. The manœuvre was successful in compelling an immediate retreat of the Chinese forces beyond the 20-kilometre limit originally asked for in the Japanese Commander's ultimatum of February 20th. Woosung fort had been evacuated by the Chinese troops when, on March 3rd, it was entered by the Japanese troops after many aerial and naval bombardments. On the previous day, bombing operations had been extended as far as 7 kilometres east of Quinsan Station on the Shanghai-Nanking Railway, with the alleged object of preventing the transportation of reinforcements to the Chinese front.

On the afternoon of March 3rd, the Japanese Commander gave the order to stop fighting. The Chinese Commander issued a similar order on March 4th. A strong complaint was made by the Chinese that the 14th Japanese Division was landed at Shanghai between March 7th and 17th, after the cessation of hostilities, and about a month later was transported to

Manchuria in order to reinforce the Japanese troops there.

In the meantime, attempts to secure a cessation of hostilities through the good offices of friendly Powers and of the League of Nations had been continued. On February 28th, the British Admiral, Sir Howard Kelly, received on his flagship the delegates of both parties. An agreement on the basis of mutual and simultaneous withdrawal and of a temporary character was proposed. The conference was not successful, owing to the differing opinions of the two parties as to the basis of the negotiations.

On February 29th, the President of the Council of the League of Nations made recommendations which contemplated, amongst other things, "a mixed conference in the presence of other interested Powers in view of the final conclusion of the fighting and for a definite cessation of hostilities, subject to local arrangements". Both parties accepted, but a successful outcome of the negotiations was rendered impossible by the conditions of the Japanese delegates, who demanded that: (1) the Chinese troops should first begin to withdraw, and (2) the Japanese, having ascertained that the withdrawal was taking place, should then retire, not, as formerly stated, to the International Settlement and the extra-Settlement streets, but to an area extending from Shanghai to Woosung.

On March 4th, the Assembly of the League, recalling the suggestions of the Council, (1) called on both Governments to make the cessation of hostilities effective; (2) requested other interested Powers to inform the Assembly on the execution of the previous paragraph; and (3) recommended negotiations, with the assistance of other Powers, for the conclusion of the arrangements in order to render definite the cessation of hostilities and to regulate the withdrawal of the Japanese troops, wishing to be informed by the Powers on the development of these negotiations.

On March 9th, the Japanese sent a memorandum to the Chinese through the intermediary of the British Minister, in which their readiness to negotiate on the basis of the points laid down by the Assembly was expressed.

On March 10th, the Chinese replied through the same channel that they too were ready to negotiate on this basis, but on condition that the conference should be limited to matters pertaining to the definite cessation of hostilities and the complete and unconditional withdrawal of the Japanese troops. On March 13th, the Japanese intimated that they were not disposed to regard the Chinese reservations as modifying the sense of the resolutions of the League of Nations or in any way binding on themselves. They thought that both parties should meet on the basis of the resolutions.

On March 24th, the Sino-Japanese Conference on the cessation of hostilities was opened. In the meantime, the withdrawal of Japanese military and naval forces had actually begun. On March 20th naval and air contingents left Shanghai, reducing the remaining strength to something not far above normal. The Japanese Headquarters announced on March 27th, on the occasion of further withdrawal, that this had nothing to do with the above-mentioned Conference or with the League of Nations, but was simply the outcome of the independent decision of the Headquarters of the Imperial Japanese Army to recall units no longer required at Shanghai.

On March 30th, the Conference announced that, on the preceding day, an agreement relative to a definite cessation of hostilities had been reached, but further difficulties supervened and it was not till May 5th that a complete armistice agreement was ready for signature. It provided for a definite cessation of hostilities, fixed a line to the west of Shanghai as a temporary limit for the advance of Chinese troops, pending further arrangements upon the re-establishment of normal conditions, and provided for the withdrawal of the Japanese troops to the International Settlement and the extra-Settlement roads (streets) as previous to January 28th. Certain areas outside the Settlement had to be temporarily included, because the number of Japanese troops was too large to be quartered within the Settlement alone, but these do not require to be mentioned as they have since been evacuated. A Joint Commission, in which the assistant friendly Powers—the United States of America, Great Britain, France and Italy and the two parties were represented, was established to certify the mutual withdrawal. This Commission was also to collaborate in arranging for the transfer from the Japanese forces to the Chinese Police.

The Chinese added two qualifications to the agreement. The first declared that nothing in the agreement was to imply permanent restriction of the movement of Chinese troops in Chinese territory, and the second that it was to be understood that, even in areas temporarily provided for the stationing of the Japanese troops, all municipal functions, including that of policing, would remain with the Chinese authorities.

The terms of this agreement as a whole have in the main since been carried out. The evacuated areas were turned over to the Chinese Special Police Force between May 9th and 30th. The turning-over, however, of these four areas has been somewhat delayed. It was but natural that, when the Chinese owners of houses and factories, officials of railways and companies, and others began to re-enter the evacuated areas, numerous complaints concerning looting, willful destruction and carrying away of property should have been addressed to the Japanese military authorities. In the opinion of the Chinese, the whole question of reparations remains for further negotiations. They estimate the casualties in killed, wounded and missing as 24,000 officers, men and civilians, and the total material loss at approximately 1,500,000,000 Mexican dollars. A draft agreement dealing with the extra-Settlement road areas bas been initialled by representatives of the Shanghai Municipal Council and of the Chinese Municipality of Greater Shanghai, but it has not yet received the approval of either the Municipal Council or of the City Government. The Municipal Council has referred it to the Senior Consul for the observations of the Consular Body.

Effect on the Manchurian situation of the Chinese resistance at Shanghai.

The Shanghai affair undoubtedly exercised considerable influence upon the situation in Manchuria. The ease with which the Japanese had been able to occupy the greater part of Manchuria, and the absence of any resistance by the Chinese troops, not only led to a belief in Japanese naval and military circles that the fighting quality of the Chinese Army was negligible, but also caused profound depression throughout China. The stout resistance put up from the first by the Chinese 19th Route Army, with the assistance later of the 87th and 88th Guard Divisions, was hailed throughout China with the greatest enthusiasm, and the fact that the original 3,000 marines had to be supplanted by three divisions and a mixed brigade of the Japanese Army before the Chinese forces were finally dislodged and driven back after six weeks of fighting created a profound impression upon the Chinese morale. The feeling prevailed that China must be saved by her own efforts. The Sino-Japanese conflict was brought home to the people throughout China. Everywhere opinion hardened and the spirit of resistance increased. Former pessimism gave place to equally exaggerated optimism. In Manchuria, the news from Shanghai put fresh heart into the scattered forces still opposing the Japanese troops. It encouraged the subsequent resistance of General Ma Chan-shan and stimulated the patriotism of the Chinese all over the world. The resistance of the Volunteer Armies increased. Expeditions to suppress them met with indifferent success, and in some areas the Japanese stood on the defensive, taking up positions along certain railway lines, which were frequently attacked.

The incident of Nanking, February 1st, 1932.

The hostilities at Shanghai were followed by several other incidents, one of which was the short bombardment of Nanking. This incident created much excitement and alarm, even outside China. It happened on the late evening of February 1st, but did not last for more than an hour. The incident was probably caused by a misunderstanding, but had the important consequence of a temporary removal of the Chinese Government from Nanking to Loyang.

Chinese and Japanese versions both of the origin and of the facts are widely divergent. Two justifications were given to us from Japanese sources. The first was that, since the outbreak of hostilities at Shanghai, the Chinese had extended the Lion Hill Forts, constructed trenches and established artillery positions at the gates near the river and on the opposite side of it, thus making military preparations on a scale sufficient to arouse concern amongst the Japanese, who had warships on the river. The second was that the vernacular papers had spread untruthful stories of Chinese victories at Shanghai, which had caused great excitement among the Chinese population of Nanking. In consequence, Chinese employed by Japanese were, it is alleged, forced by threats to give up their situations, and Chinese merchants refused to sell even the necessary food supplies to Japanese residents, including the Consular staff and the crews of warships.

The Chinese did not comment on these complaints. They assert that the general uneasiness and tense atmosphere prevailing were caused by the fact that the Japanese, after the Shanghai outbreak, increased the number of their warships from two to five, and subsequently to seven (the Japanese authorities give the number as six, these being three old gunboats and three destroyers); that the Commander of the warships landed a certain number of sailors and put them on guard duty before the wharf of the Nisshin Kisen Kaisha, where the Japanese Consular staff and all the Japanese residents had taken refuge on a hulk. With the events of Shanghai fresh in their memories, such measures may well have filled the minds of the already-excited population at Nanking with fears of a similar experience.

We know from a report of the Police Commissioner of Nanking to the Ministry of Foreign Affairs that the authorities at Nanking who were solely responsible for the protection of their own subjects and of foreign nationals at that place greatly resented the landing of Japanese naval forces. They addressed representations to the Japanese Vice-Consul, who replied that he was unable to do anything in the matter. At the same time, special instructions were given to the local police station at Hsiakwan, where the warships were anchored and the above-mentioned wharf was situated, to prevent, if possible, any contact between Chinese and Japanese in this area, especially at night-time. According to the Japanese official reports, their refugees were taken on board a steamer of the name *Nisshin Kisen Kaisha* during the days following January 29th, and a considerable number were transported to Shanghai. On the late evening of February 1st, the Japanese assert that three gunshots were suddenly fired, apparently from the Lion Hill Forts. At the same time, Chinese regulars fired on the Japanese naval guards on the river banks, causing two casualties, of which one was fatal. The fire was returned, but directed only at the immediate neighbourhood of their landing-place and stopped as soon as the firing from the shore bad ceased. Such is the Japanese version. The Chinese, on the other hand, stoutly deny that any firing at all took place, but allege that eight shells in all were fired at the forts, at Hsiakwan station and at other places, accompanied by machine-gun and rifle firing, and that during this time searchlights were directed at the shore. This caused considerable panic amongst the inhabitants, who rushed into the interior of the city; but no casualties were reported and the material damage was not great.

It is also possible that the incident was first started by the firing of crackers by the excited Chinese population, celebrating a supposed victory at Shanghai.

CHAPTER VI   "MANCHUKUO"

PART I   Stages in the formation of the new "State"

Chaotic conditions resulting from Japanese occupation of Mukden.

As a result of the events of September 18th, 1931, as described in the last Chapter, the civil administration of Mukden city and of the Province of Liaoning (Fengtien) was completely disorganised and even that of the other two provinces was affected to a lesser extent. The suddenness of the attack on Mukden, which was not only the political centre of all Manchuria but, next to Dairen, the most important commercial centre of South Manchuria, created a panic among the Chinese population. Most of the prominent officials, and the leading members of the educational and commercial communities, who could afford to do so, left immediately with their families. During the days following September 19th, over 100,000 Chinese residents left Mukden by the Peiping-Mukden railway, and many who could not get away went into hiding. The police, and even the prison warders, disappeared. The municipal, district and provincial administrations at Mukden completely broke down, the public utility companies for the supply of electric light, water, etc. , the buses and tramways, and the telephone and telegraph services, ceased to function. Banks and shops kept their doors closed.

Restoration of order and civil administration in Mukden city.

The immediate necessity was the organisation of a municipal government and the restoration of the ordinary civic life of the city. This was undertaken by the Japanese and carried through quickly and efficiently. Colonel Doihara was installed as Mayor of Mukden and within three days normal civil administration was restored. Several hundred police and most of the prison warders were brought back with the help of General Tsang Shih-yi, the Civil Governor of the Province, and the public utility services were restored. An Emergency Committee with a majority of Japanese members helped Colonel Doihara, who held his post for one month. On October 20th, the reins of municipal government were restored to a qualified Chinese body, with Dr. Chao Hsin-po (a lawyer who had studied for eleven years in Japan and was a Doctor of Law of Tokyo University) as Mayor.

The reorganisation of Provincial Government: (1) Liaoning Province.

The next problem was to reorganise the provincial administration in each of the Three Provinces. This task was more difficult in Liaoning than in either of the other two, because Mukden was the centre of this provincial administration; most of the influential men had fled, and for a time a

Chinese provincial administration continued to be carried on at Chinchow. It was three months, therefore, before the reorganisation was completely accomplished.

General Tsang Shih-yi refuses to organise an independent Provincial Government.

Lieutenant General Tsang Shih-yi, the existing President of the Liaoning Provincial Government, was first approached on September 20th and invited to organize a Provincial Government, independent of the Chinese Central Government. This he refused to do. He was then put under arrest and released on December 15th.

Formation of a "Peace and Order Maintenance Committee" under the chairmanship of Mr. Yuan Chin-kai, September 25th.

After General Tsang Shih-yi had refused to help in the establishment of an independent Government, another influential Chinese official, Mr. Yuan Chin-kai, was approached. He was a former provincial governor and a Vice-President of the Northeastern Political Committee. The Japanese military authorities invited him and eight other Chinese residents to form a "Committee for the maintenance of Peace and Order". This Committee was declared to have been formed on September 24th. The Japanese Press at once acclaimed it as the first step in a separatist movement, but Mr. Yuan Chin-kai publicly disclaimed any such intention on October 5th. The Committee, he said, had "been brought into being to preserve peace and order after the breakdown of the former administration. It assisted, moreover, in relieving refugees, in restoring the money market, and it attended to some other matters, solely for the sake of preventing unnecessary hardship. It had, however, no intention of organising a Provincial Government or declaring independence".

Board of Finance opened, October 19th.

On October 19th the Committee opened the Board of Finance, and Japanese advisers were appointed to assist the Chinese functionaries. The Director of the Board of Finance had to obtain the approval of the military authorities before giving effect to the Board's decisions. In the districts, the tax collectors' offices were controlled by the Japanese gendarmerie or other agencies. In some cases they had to submit their books daily for inspection to the gendarmerie, whose approval had to be obtained for the disbursement of any moneys on public objects, such as police, justice, education, etc. Any case of remittance of taxes to the "hostile party" at Chinchow was to be at once reported to the Japanese authorities. At the same time à Financial Readjustment Committee was organised, the chief business of which was to reorganise the taxation system. Japanese representatives and the representatives of Chinese guilds were allowed to take part in discussions on taxation. According to a statement in the "History of the Independence of Manchukuo", dated May 30th, 1932, and submitted to the Commission by the "Department of Foreign Affairs" at Changchun, these discussions led to the abolition on November 16th, 1931, of six taxes, the reduction of four others by half, the transfer of eight others to local governments, and the prohibition of all levies, without a legal basis.

Board of Industry established, October 21st.

On October 21st the Board of Industry was opened by the Committee whose name was now changed to that of "Liaoning Province Self-Government Office". The consent of the Japanese military authorities was sought and obtained and a number of Japanese advisers were appointed. Before issuing any orders the Director was required to obtain the approval of the Japanese military authorities.

Northeastern Communications Committee.

Lastly, the Liaoning Self-Government Office organised a new North-

Eastern Communications Committee, which gradually assumed control of various railways, not only in Liaoning Province, but also in Kirin and Heilungkiang. This Committee was separated from the Liaoning Self-Government Office on November 1st.

Declaration of November 7th, and establishment of a Provincial Government on November 10th.

On November 7th the Liaoning Province Self-Government Office transformed itself into the Liaoning Provincial Government *ad interim*, which issued a declaration by which it severed its relations with the former Northeastern Government and with the Central Government at Nanking. It requested the local governments in Liaoning to abide by the decrees it had issued, and announced that henceforth it would exercise the authority of a Provincial Government. On November 10th a public opening ceremony took place.

Appointment of Supreme Advisory Board.

Simultaneously with the transformation of the Self-Government Office into the Liaoning Provincial Government *ad interim*, a Supreme Advisory Board was inaugurated under the chairmanship of Mr. Yu Chung-han, who had been Vice Director of the Peace and Order Maintenance Committee. Mr. Yu announced the objects of this Board as: the maintenance of order, the improvement of administration by the suppression of bad taxes, the reduction of taxation, and the improvement of the organisation of production and sale. The Board was, furthermore, to direct and supervise the acting Provincial Government, and to foster the development of local self-government in accordance with the traditions of local communities and with modern needs. It comprised sections dealing with general affairs, investigation, protocol, guidance, supervision, and an Institute for Training in Self-Government. Nearly all the important functionaries were Japanese.

Name of Province changed to Fengtien on November 20th and General Tsang Shih-yi installed as Governor on December 15th.

On November 20th, the name of the Province was changed to that of Fengtien, which had been its name before its union with Nationalist China in 1928, and on December 15th Mr. Yuan Chin-kai was replaced by General Tsang Shih-yi, who was released from his confinement and installed as Governor of Fengtien Province.

(2) Kirin Province.

The task of establishing a provincial Government in the province of Kirin was far easier. On the 23rd, the Commander of the 2nd Division, Major-General Tamon, had an interview with Lieutenant-General Hsi Hsia, the acting head of the provincial administration in the absence of General Chang Tso-hsiang, and invited him to assume the chairmanship of the Provincial Government. After this interview General Hsi Hsia summoned the various Government organisations and public associations to a meeting on September 25th, which was also attended by Japanese military officers. No opposition was expressed to the idea of establishing a new provisional government, and a proclamation to that effect was published on September 30th. The Organic Law of the new Provincial Government of Kirin was subsequently announced. The Committee system of government was abolished, and Governor Hsi Hsia took full responsibility for the conduct of government. Some days later the principal officials of the new Government were appointed by him and some Japanese functionaries were added later. The chief of the Bureau of General Affairs was a Japanese. In the districts also some administrative reorganisation and change of personnel took place. Out of 43 districts 15 were reorganised, which involved the dismissal of the Chinese District Officers. In 10 others the District Officers were retained after declaring their allegiance to General Hsi Hsia. The others still remained under Chinese military leaders loyal to the old regime, or kept aloof from the contending factions.

(3) The Special Administrative District of the Chinese Eastern Railway.

The Chief Administrator of the Special District, Lieutenant-General Chang Ching-hui, was friendly to the Japanese. He had no military force behind him, whereas the old regime could still dispose of considerable forces both in Kirin and Heilungkiang, as well as the railway guards in the Special District itself. On September 27th, he summoned a conference in his office at Harbin to discuss the organisation of the Emergency Committee of the Special District. This Committee was formed with General Chang as Chairman and eight other members, amongst whom were General Wang Juihwa and General Ting Chao, who later, in January 1932, became the leader of the "anti-Kirin" forces, in opposition to General Hsi Hsia. On November 5th the anti-Kirin army under the command of the Generals of Chang Tso-hsiang, established a new Kirin Provincial Government at Harbin. After General Chang Ching-hui had been appointed, on January 1st, 1932, Governor of Heilungkiang, he declared in that capacity the independence of the Province on January 7th. On January 29th General Ting Chao took possession of the office of the Chief Administrator and placed General Chang under restraint in his own house. The latter regained his liberty when the Japanese forces came north and occupied Harbin on February 5th after defeating General Ting Chao. From that time onwards the Japanese influence made itself increasingly felt in the Special District.

(4) Heilungkiang.

In Heilungkiang Province a more complicated situation had arisen owing to the conflict between General Chang Haipeng and General Ma Chan-shan, which was described in the last chapter. After the occupation of Tsitsihar by the Japanese on November 19th, a Self-Government Association of the usual type was established, and this Association, which was said to represent the will of the people, invited General Chang Ching-hui, of the Special District, to act concurrently as Governor of Heilungkiang. As the situation around Harbin was still unsettled, and no definite agreement with General Ma had been reached, this invitation was not accepted until early in January, 1932. Even then General Ma's attitude was ambiguous for some time. He co-operated with General Ting Chao until the latter's defeat in February, and then came to terms with the Japanese accepting the Governorship of Heilungkiang out of General Chang's hands, and subsequently cooperated with the other Governors in the establishment of the new "State". A Self-Government Guiding Committee was established at Tsitsihar on January 25th and the same form of Provincial Government as in the other Provinces was gradually established.

(5) Jehol.

The Province of Jehol has hitherto kept aloof from the political changes which have taken place in Manchuria. Jehol is part of Inner Mongolia. Over 3,000,000 Chinese settlers now live in the Province and they are gradually pushing out to the north the nomadic Mongols, who still live under their traditional tribal or Banner system. These Mongols, who are said to number about one million, have maintained some relations with the Mongol Banners settled in the west of Fengtien Province. The Mongols in Fengtien and Jehol have formed "Leagues" the most influential of which is the Cherim League. The Cherim League joined the Independence movement, as did also the Mongols in the Barga District, or Hulunbuir, in the west of Heilungkiang, who have often attempted to free themselves from Chinese rule. The Mongols do not easily assimilate with the Chinese. They are a proud race, and every Mongol remembers the exploits of Genghis Khan and the conquest of China by Mongol warriors. They resent Chinese overlordship and they resent particularly the immigration of Chinese settlers, by which they are being gradually extruded from their territory. The Leagues of Chaota and Chosatu in Jehol are keeping in touch with the Banners in Fengtien, which are now ruled by committees. General Tang Ju-lin, the Governor of the Province, is reported to have assumed full responsibility for his Province on September 29th, and to have kept in touch with his colleagues in Manchuria.

At the inauguration of "Manchukuo" on March 9th, Jehol was included in the new "State". In fact, however, no decisive step was taken by the Government of the Province. The latest events in this Province were referred to at the end of CHAPTER Ⅳ.

The creation of an independent "State".

The local self-governing administrations thus established in all the Provinces were subsequently combined into a separate and independent "State". To understand the ease with which this was accomplished and the amount of evidence which it has been possible to bring forward of Chinese support for it when it was accomplished, it is necessary to consider a peculiar feature of Chinese organised life which in some circumstances is a strength and in others a weakness. As has been already stated in CHAPTER Ⅰ, the community obligations recognised by the Chinese are rather to the family, to a locality, or to persons, than to the State. Patriotism as it is understood in the West is only beginning to be felt. Guilds, associations, leagues, armies, are all accustomed to follow certain individual leaders. If, therefore, the support of a particular leader can be secured by persuasion or coercion, the support of his adherents over the whole area of his influence follows as a matter of course. The foregoing narrative of events shows how successfully this Chinese characteristic was utilised in the organisation of the Provincial Governments, and the agency of the same few individuals was used to complete the final stage.

The Self-Government Guiding Board.

The chief agency in bringing about independence was the Self-Government Guiding Board, which had its central office in Mukden. By reliable witnesses, it was stated to the Commission to have been organised and in large part officered by Japanese, although its chief was a Chinese, and to have functioned as an organ of the Fourth Department of the Kwantung Army Headquarters. Its main purpose was to foster the independence movement. Under the direction and supervision of this Central Board, local Self-Government Executive Committees were formed in the districts of Fengtien Province. To those various districts, as occasion demanded, the Central Board sent out members from its large and experienced staff of inspectors, directors and lecturers, many of whom were Japanese. It utilised also a newspaper, which it edited and published.

The Proclamation of the Self-Government Guiding Board, Mukden, January 7th.

The nature of the instructions given by the Central Board is apparent from the proclamation which it issued as early as January 7th, under date of January 1st. The proclamation stated that the Northeast was faced with the need of developing, without delay, a great popular movement for the establishment of a new independent State in Manchuria and Mongolia. It described the development of its work in various districts in Fengtien Province, and outlined its plan for the extension of its activities to the remaining districts and even to the other Provinces. It then appealed to the people of the Northeast to overthrow Marshal Chang Hsueh-liang, to join the Self-Government Association, to co-operate in setting up a clean administration and improving the living conditions of the people, and it ended with the words: "Organisations of the North, East, Unite! Towards the new 'State'! Towards Independence!" Of this proclamation, fifty thousand copies were distributed.

Plans of the Chief of the Board in January.

As early as January, also, the Chief of the Self-Government Guiding Board, Mr. Yu Chung-han, was already making plans, together with Governor Tsang Chih-yi, for the new "State" which, it was reported, was to be established on February 10th. But the Harbin outbreak of January 29th, and General Ma's ambiguous attitude during the conflict with Ting Chao, appear to have been the main reasons for the temporary postponement of further preparations at that time.

The Mukden Conference, February 16th—17th.

Later, after Ting Chao's defeat, negotiations between Lieutenant-General Chang Ching-hui and General Ma had brought about, on February 14th, a settlement according to which General Ma was to become Governor of Heilungkiang. The meeting at which the foundation of the new "State" was to be arranged was held on February 16th and 17th at Mukden. The Governors of the Three Provinces and the Special District were present in person, as well as Dr. Chao Hsin-po, who had played a prominent part in all the preparatory work.

At a meeting of these five men it was decided that a new "State" should be established, that a Northeastern Administrative Council should be organised which would exercise temporarily the supreme authority over the Provinces and the Special District, and, finally, that this Supreme Council should, without delay, make all necessary preparations for the founding of the new "State". On the second day of the Conference, two Mongol Princes attended, one representing the Barga District (Hulunbuir) in western Heilungkiang, the other, Prince Chiwang of the Cherim Leagues, representing practically all Banners, who respect this Prince more than any other leader.

The Supreme Administrative Council, February 17th.

The Supreme Administrative Council was constituted the same day. Its members were Lieutenant-General Chang Ching-hui, Chairman of the Council, the Governors of Fengtien, Kirin, Heilungkiang and Jehol, and Prince Chiwang and Prince Ling Sheng for the Mongolian districts. The first decisions of the Council were: to adopt the republican system for the new "State"; to respect the autonomy of the constituting Provinces; to give the title of "Regent" to the Chief Executive, and to issue a Declaration of Independence, to be signed by the Governors of the four Provinces and the

Special District, by Prince Chiwang for all the Banners, and by Prince Kueifu for Hulunbuir in Heilungkiang. The Commander-in-Chief of the Kwantung Army gave that night an official dinner in honour of the "Heads of the new 'State'", whom he congratulated on their success and assured of his assistance in case of need.

The Declaration of Independence, February 18th.

The Declaration of Independence was published on February 18th. It referred to the ardent wishes of the people to have permanent peace and to the duty of the Governors, who were said to have been chosen by the people, to fulfill those wishes. The Declaration referred to the necessity of the establishment of a new "State", and claimed that the North-Eastern Administrative Council had been constituted for this purpose. Now that relations with the Kuomintang and the Government at Nanking had been severed, the people were promised the enjoyment of good government. This declaration was sent by circular wire to all places in Manchuria. Governor Ma and Governor Hsi Hsia then returned to their respective provincial capitals, but they designated representatives to meet Governor Tsang Shih-yi, Governor Chang Ching-hui, and Mayor Chao Hsin-po for the purpose of working out the details of the plan.

Plans for the new "State".

In a subsequent meeting held by this group, on February 19th, it was decided to establish a Republic, to lay down the principle of the separation of powers in the Constitution, and to ask the former Emperor Hsuan-Tung to become the Chief Executive. In the following days it was decided that the capital should be Changchun; the new era of government was to be styled "Tatung" (Great Harmony), and the design of the national flag was fixed. Notification of the decisions taken was sent, on February 25th, to all provincial governments, including Jehol, as well as to the Mongol administrative offices of Hulunbuir and of the Cherim, Chaota and Chosatu

Leagues. The last-named Leagues are established in Jehol. They could, therefore, as already stated, take no steps against the wishes of the Chairman of the Government of that Province.

The State Foundation Acceleration Movement.

After the Declaration of Independence and the announcement of the plans for the new "State", the Self-Government Guiding Board took the leading part in organising popular manifestations of support. It was instrumental in forming societies for the "Acceleration of the Foundation of the New State". It instructed its branches in the various districts throughout Fengtien, the Self-Government Executive Committees, to do everything possible to strengthen and hasten the independence movement. In consequence, the new "Acceleration Societies" sprang up rapidly centering around the Self-Government Executive Committees.

From February 20th onwards, these newly-formed "Acceleration Societies" became active. Posters were prepared, slogans printed, books and pamphlets issued, a "Northeastern Civilisation Half-Monthly" was edited and red scrolls were distributed. Leaflets were sent by post to various prominent citizens asking them to help the propaganda work. At Mukden the scrolls were distributed by the Chinese Chamber of Commerce, to be placed on the door-posts.

The organisation of popular approval of independence.

During the same time the Self-Government Executive Committees in the districts summoned meetings of popular representatives, such as members of the local gentry, and the Chairman and prominent members of commercial, agricultural, industrial and educational associations. In addition, mass meetings were organised and parades or processions were conducted through the principal streets of the district capitals. Resolutions expressing the wishes either of the people in general or of special groups were passed at conferences of prominent local men and at the mass meetings, in which it was claimed many thousands of persons took part. These resolutions were naturally sent to the Self-Government Guiding Board at Mukden.

The Mukden resolutions favouring a New "State", February 28th.

After the Association Societies and the Self-Government Executive Committees had been active in various districts of Fengtien, a provincial convention was organised at Mukden to give concrete evidence of the general desire of the people for the establishment of the "State". Accordingly, on February 28th, a meeting was held in which about 600 persons took part, including all the district officers of the Province and the representatives of nearly all classes and organisations. This meeting issued a declaration which stated that it expressed the joy of the 16,000,000 inhabitants of Fengtien Province at the downfall of the old oppressive military caste and the dawn of a new era. As far as Fengtien was concerned, the movement had thus been brought to a conclusion.

The Independence Movement in Kirin Province.

The movement in Kirin Province in favour of a new "State" was also organised and directed. While in the Conference at Mukden on February 16th, Governor Hsi Hsia sent a circular telegram to his District Officers asking them to enlighten him as to public opinion in regard to the policy to be followed by the new "State". The District Officers were enjoyed to give adequate guidance to the various guilds and associations in their districts. In direct response to the telegram, independence movements sprang up everywhere. On February 20th, the Kirin Provincial Government created the State Foundation Committee, which was to guide the various organisations in conducting their independence campaigns. On February 24th, The People's Association at Changchun held a mass meeting in which about 4,000 persons are reported to have taken part. They demanded the acceleration of the foundation of the new "State". Similar meetings were held in other districts and also in Harbin. On February 25th, the mass meeting for the whole Province was held at the city of Kirin. About ten thousand persons were reported to have been present. A declaration was duly issued similar to that passed at Mukden on February 28th.

In Heilungkiang Province.

In Heilungkiang Province, the Mukden Self-Government Guidance Board played an important part. On January 7th, after General Chang Ching-hui had accepted the governorship of Heilungkiang, he declared the Province to be independent.

The Board lent its assistance in conducting the acceleration movement in Heilungkiang. Four directing officers, two of whom were Japanese were despatched from Mukden to Tsitsihar. Two days after their arrival, on February 22nd, they convened a meeting in the reception hall of the Government House, in which a large number of associations were represented. It was a Pan-Heilungkiang Conference, which was to decide upon the methods of preparing for the establishing of the "State". It was resolved to hold a mass demonstration on February 24th.

Many thousands of persons took part in the mass demonstration at Tsitsihar, which was covered with posters, scrolls, streamers and pennants in commemoration of the event. The Japanese artillery fired 101 guns in honour of the day. Japanese planes circled overhead, dropping down leaflets. A declaration was promptly issued which favoured a republican form of government, with a responsible form of government, with a responsible cabinet and a president as the head of the "State". All powers were to be concentrated in the "Central Government", and the provincial governments were to be abolished, leaving districts and municipalities as the units of local government.

By the end of February, Fengtien, Kirin, Heilungkiang and the Special District had passed the stages of district and provincial declarations. The Mongol Banners had also given their allegiance to the new "State", since it was known that it would mark off special autonomous Mongol districts and would in other ways guarantee the rights of the Mongol inhabitants. The Mohammedans had already, at a meeting on February 15th, at Mukden, pledged their allegiance. The majority of the small number of unassimilated Manchus were also in favour of the new "State" as soon as it had become known that their former Emperor would probably be offered the post of Chief Executive.

The All-Manchuria Convention, Mukden, February 29th.

After the districts and provinces had given formal support to the plan of a new "State", the Self-Government Guiding Board took the lead in convening an All-Manchuria Convention which was held at Mukden on February 29th. There were present official delegates from the provinces, the districts of Fengtien Province and the Mongol territories, and, in addition, many others, including representatives of various groups, such as the Koreans in Kirin Province and the Special District, and the branches of the Youth League of Manchuria and Mongolia: altogether over 700 persons.

Speeches were delivered and a declaration and resolution were unanimously approved, the former denouncing the previous regime, the latter welcoming the new "State". A second resolution was also adopted designating as the provisional President of the new "State" the former Emperor Hsuan Tung, now known by his personal name as Mr. Henry Pu-yi.

Mr. Henry Pu-yi, the former Emperor, accepts the headship of "Manchukuo".

The North-Eastern Administrative Council met at once in urgent session and elected six delegates to proceed to Port Arthur, to convey their invitation to the former Emperor at Port Arthur, where he had been residing since he left Tientsin in the previous November. Mr. Pu-yi at first declined it, but on March 4th a second delegation comprising twenty-nine delegates, obtained his consent to accept the post for one year only. Then the Administrative Council elected its chairman, Lieutenant-General Chang

Ching-hui, and nine others, to be the Reception Committee. On March 5th, the Committee went to Port Arthur and was received in audience. In response to its request the former Emperor, on March 6th, left Port Arthur for Tangkangtze, and after two days began, on the 8th, to receive homage as the Regent of "Manchukuo".

The inauguration ceremonies, Changchun, March 9th.

The inauguration ceremonies were held at the new capital, Changchun, on March 9th. Mr. Pu-yi, as Regent, made a declaration in which he promised to found the policy of the new "State" upon the basis of "morality, benevolence and love". On the 10th, the principal members of the "Government" were appointed; the members of the Cabinet, the Presidents of the Board of Legislation and the Board of Control; the President and Vice-President and Councillors of the Privy Council, the Governors of the Provinces and of the Special District, the Commanders of the Defence Forces of the Provinces, and some other high officials. A notice regarding the establishment of "Manchukuo" was issued by telegram on March 12th to the Foreign Powers. The declared purpose of this notice was to communicate to the Foreign Powers the fundamental object of the formation of "Manchukuo"; and its principles of foreign policy; and the request that they recognise it as a new "State".

Prior to the arrival of the Regent, a number of laws and regulations, on which Dr. Chao Hsin-po had been working for some time, had been made ready for adoption and promulgation. They came into force on March 9th, simultaneously with the law regulating the organisation of the Government, while the laws which theretofore had been in effect, insofar as they were not in conflict with the new laws, or with the fundamental policy of the "State", were provisionally adopted by special ordinance of the same date.

Sources of Information.

This narrative of the stages by which the "State of Manchukuo" was created had been compiled from all the sources of information available. The events were reported at length, as they occurred, in Japanese newspapers, and most fully, perhaps, in the columns of the Japanese-edited *Manchuria Daily News*. The two documents entitled "Histoire de l'Indépendance du Mandchoukouo—Ministère des Affaires étrangères du Mandchoukouo" and "A General Outline of Manchukuo—Department of Foreign Affairs, Manchukuo", which were prepared at Changchun on May 30th by the present administration; and the "Memorandum on the so-called Independence Movement in the Three Eastern Provinces", prepared by the Chinese Assessor, have also been carefully studied. In addition, wherever possible, neutral sources of information were utilised.

Civil Administration since September 18th.

The measures of civil administration taken by the Japanese military authorities between September 18th and the establishment of the "Manchukuo Government", notably the control of the Banks, the administration of the public utility services and the management of the railways, indicated that from the commencement of the operations objects more permanent than the requirements of a temporary military occupation were being pursued. Immediately after the occupation of Mukden, on September 19th, guards were placed in or in front of all Chinese banks, railway offices, the administrative offices of public utility services, the office of the Mining. Administration, and similar premises. Investigations were then conducted into the financial and general situation of these enterprises. When they were allowed to reopen, Japanese were appointed as advisors, experts, or secretaries to officials, usually with administrative powers. Many business enterprises were owned by the former administration of the Three Eastern Provinces, as well as by the provincial administrations; and as the previous Government was regarded as are enemy Governments in time of war, no bank, no mining, agricultural or industrial enterprise, no railway offices, no public utility—in fact, no single source of revenue in: which they had been interested in either their public or private capacities—was left without supervision.

Railways.

As regards railways, the measures taken by the Japanese authorities from the outset of the period of military occupation were designed to settle definitely, in a manner favourable to Japanese interests some of the questions which had long been in dispute between the Chinese and Japanese railways, and which have been described in CHAPTER Ⅲ. The fallowing measures were promptly taken:

1. All the Chinese-owned railways north of the Great Wall, and the moneys standing to their credit in banks in Manchuria, were seized.

2. In order that the railways might be co-ordinated with the South Manchuria Railway, certain changes were made in the arrangement of tracks in and around Mukden, by cutting the tracks of the Peiping-Mukden Railway at the viaduct under the South Manchuria Railway, thus closing the Liaoning Central station, the Fengtien East station, the Fengtien North Gate station, and thus severing the connection with the Chinese Government railway to Kirin (later replaced).

3. At Kirin a physical connection was made between the Hailun-Kirin line and the Kirin-Tunhua and Kirin-Changchun railways.

4. A staff of Japanese technical advisers was installed in various departments of the railways.

5. The "special rates" adopted by the Chinese authorities were abolished and the original tariffs restored, thus bringing freight rates on Chinese railways more into conformity with those of the South Manchuria Railway.

During the period between September 18th, when the North Eastern Communications Committee ceased to function, and the date of the creation of the "Manchukuo Ministry of Communications", the Japanese authorities assumed entire responsibility for the administration of the railways.

Other public utilities.

Measures of a similar kind, which went beyond those which were necessary for the protection of the lives and property of their nationals, were taken by the Japanese in respect of the public electricity supplies at Mukden and Antung. Also, in the period between September 18th and the establishment of "Manchukuo", the Japanese authorities made changes in the administration and management of the Chinese Government telephone, telegraph and wireless services which would ensure their intimate co-ordination with the Japanese telephone and telegraph services in Manchuria.

Conclusions.

Since September 18th, 1931, the activities of the Japanese military authorities, in civil as well as in military matters, were marked by essentially political considerations. The progressive military occupation of the Three Eastern Provinces removed in succession from the control of the Chinese authorities the towns of Tsitsihar, Chinchow and Harbin, finally all the important towns of Manchuria; and following each occupation the civil administration was reorganised. It is clear that the Independence Movement which had never been heard of in Manchuria before September 1931, was only made possible by the presence of the Japanese troops.

A group of Japanese civil and military officials, both active and retired, who were in close touch with the new political movement in Japan to which reference was made in CHAPTER Ⅳ, conceived, organised and carried through this movement, as a solution to the situation in Manchuria as it existed after the events of September 18th.

With this object they made use of the names and actions of certain Chinese individuals, and took advantage of certain minorities among the inhabitants, who had grievances against the former administration.

It is also clear that the Japanese General Staff realised from the start, or at least in a short time, the use which could they provided assistance and gave direction to the organisers of the movement. The evidence received from all sources has satisfied the Commission that while there were a number of factors which contributed to the creation of "Manchukuo" the two which, in combination, were most effective, and without which, in our judgment, the new "State" could not have been formed, were the presence of Japanese troops and the activities of Japanese officials, both civil and military.

For this reason the present regime cannot be considered to have been called into existence by a genuine and spontaneous independence movement.

PART Ⅱ The Present Government of "Manchukuo"

The Organic Law.

"Manchukuo" is governed in accordance with an Organic Law and a Guarantee Law of Civil Rights. The Organic Law prescribes the fundamental organisation of the Governmental organs. It was-promulgated by Ordinance No. 1 issued on March 9th, the first year of Tatung (1932).

The Regent is head of the State. All executive power is vested in him, and he has also the authority to overrule the Legislative Council. He is assisted by a Privy Council, which is to advise him upon important affairs.

A characteristic feature of the Organic Law is the separation of governmental power into four divisions or departments: the Executive, the Legislative, the Judicial and the Supervisory.

The Executive Department.

The functions of the Executive Department are carried out, under the direction of the Regent, by the Premier and the Ministers of State, who together form a State Council or Cabinet. The Premier supervises the work of the Ministries, and, through the powerful Board of General Affairs, has direct charge of their confidential matters, personnel, accounting and supplies. Subordinate to the State Council are various bureaus, especially the important Advisory Bureau and the Legislative Bureau. Executive power is thus largely concentrated in the hands of the Premier and the Regent.

The Legislative Department.

The legislative power is vested in the Legislative Council. Its approval will be necessary for all laws and revenue acts. But should it reject any Bill, the Regent may ask the Council to reconsider its decision, and if it should again reject it, the Regent, after consulting the Privy Council, shall decide the matter. At present, however, no law has yet been passed for the organisation of the Council, with the result that laws are drafted by the State Council and become effective after the Privy Council has been consulted and the approval of the Regent has been obtained. So long as the Legislative Council is not organised, the Premier's position is predominant.

The Judicial Department.

The judiciary comprises a number of law courts, divided into three grades, the Supreme Court, Higher Courts, and District Courts.

The Supervisory Department.

The Supervisory Council supervises the conduct of officials, and audits their accounts. The members of the Council may not be dismissed except for a criminal offence or disciplinary punishment, and may not be subjected to suspension or, transfer of office, or reduction of salary, against their wishes.

Provinces and Special Districts.

For purposes of local government, "Manchukuo" is divided into five provinces and two special districts. The provinces are Fengtien, Kirin, Heilungkiang, Jehol, and Hsin-An or Hsingan. The last-named, which contains the Mongol districts, is subdivided into three areas or Sub-Provinces, so as to conform to the traditional Banner system and the union of Banners into Leagues. The special districts are the old Chinese Eastern Railway, or Harbin district, and the newly-established Chientao, or Korean district. By means of this administrative division the important minorities,

Mongols, Koreans and Russians, are to be guaranteed, as far as possible, special administration in conformity with their needs. Although the Commission made several requests to be shown a map of the area claimed to be included in the "State of Manchukuo", this was not provided, but a letter was received giving the boundaries of the "State" as follows:

"The new 'State' is bounded on the south by the Great Wall, and the Mongol Leagues and Banners in the same comprise Hulunbuir and the Leagues of Cherim, Chaota and Chosatu and their Banners."

At the head of the provinces are Civil Governors. But since it is desired to concentrate executive power in the Central Government, they are to be given no authority over either troops or finance. In the provinces, as well as in the Central Government, the General Affairs Department holds a controlling position. It is in charge of confidential matters, of personnel, accounting, correspondence, and matters which do not come under other departments.

Districts and Municipalities.

Provinces are divided into districts. These are administered largely by district Self-Government offices, which have under their direction various governmental departments, particularly that of General Affairs. Municipal governments exist at Mukden, Harbin, and Changchun. At Harbin, however, it is planned to create a Greater Harbin which will include both the Russian and the Chinese cities. The Special Railway District is to be abolished. Part of it will be included in Greater Harbin, and the remainder, stretching East and West along the Chinese Eastern Railway, is to be added to Heilungkiang and Kiring Provinces.

The "Government of Manchukuo" regards the provinces as administrative areas, and the districts and the municipalities as units of finance. It determines the amount of their taxes and passes upon the budget. All local revenues must be paid into the central treasury which will then supervise the proper disbursement. These revenues may not be retained, in whole or in part, by the local authorities, as was customary under the old regime. Naturally, this system has not as yet been brought into satisfactory operation.

Japanese officials and advisers.

In the "Government of Manchukuo" Japanese officials are prominent, and Japanese advisers are attached to all important Departments. Although the Premier and his Ministers are all Chinese, the heads of the various Boards of General Affairs, which in the organisation of the new "State" exercise the greatest measure of actual power, are Japanese. At first they were designated as advisers, but more recently those holding the most important posts have been made full Government officials on the same basis as the Chinese. In the central government alone, not including those in local governments or in the War Office and the military forces, or in government enterprises, nearly 200 Japanese are "Manchukuo" officials.

Japanese control the Board of General Affairs and the Legislative and Advisory Bureaus, which in practice constitute a Premier's offices, the General Affairs Department in the Ministries and in the Provincial Governments, and the Self-Government Directing Committees in the Districts, and the police departments in the Provinces of Fengtien, Kirin, and Heilungkiang. In most bureaus, moreover, there are Japanese advisors, counsellors and secretaries.

There are also many Japanese in the railway offices and in the Central Bank. In the Supervisory Council Japanese hold the posts of Chief of the Bureau of General Affairs, Chief of the Control Bureau, and Chief of the Auditing Board. In the Legislative Council the Chief Secretary is a Japanese. Finally, some of the most important officials of the Regent are Japanese, including the Chief of the Office of Internal Affairs, and the Commander of the Regent's bodyguard. ①

The aims of the Government.

The aim of the Government, as expressed in the proclamation of the Northeastern Administrative Committee of February 18th, and of the "Government of Manchukuo" of March 1st, is to rule in accordance with the fundamental principle of "Wang Tao". It is different to find an exact English equivalent for this phrase. The interpreters provided by the "Manchukuo" authorities translated it "love", but scholars give the meaning as the "kingly way" which may have many shades of meaning; which according to Chinese tradition, has been of the old basis of a good administration, sincerely concerned with the welfare of the people. Traditionally, the Chinese have used the expression "Wang Tao" as antithetical to "Pa Tao", which latter expression as discussed by Dr. Sun Yat-sen in his "San Min Chu Yi" (Three Peoples' Principles), connotes reliance upon physical force and compulsion. Sun Yat-sen explained that "Wang Tao", therefore, was the antithesis of "Might makes right".

The policy of the Self-Government Guiding Board, the chief agency in the creation of the new Government, was continued by the Advisory Bureau, which had superseded it. Military officers were not to be allowed to interfere in matters of administration. Regulations governing the qualifications for government service are to be enacted, and appointments are to be made on the basis of the ability of the candidates.

Taxation.

Taxation is to be reduced and placed on a legal basis, and reformed in accordance with sound principles of economies and administration. Direct taxes are to be transferred to the District and Municipal Governments, while

---

① 原编辑者注：The more important appointments have meanwhile been announced in the "Manchukuo Government Gazette".

the Central Government is to secure the income derived from indirect taxes.

The documents supplied by the Changchun authorities state that a number of taxes have already been abolished, while others have been reduced. Hopes are expressed that readjustment of Government enterprises and Government-owned resources will increase revenue, and that the eventual reduction of the military forces will lessen expenditure. However, for the time being, the financial position of the new "State" is unsatisfactory. Guerilla warfare has kept military expenditure high, while, at the same time, the Government is not receiving revenues from various normal sources. Expenditure for the first year is now roughly estimated at ＄85,000,000, against revenue ＄65,000,000, showing a deficit of ＄20,000,000, which it is intended to cover by a loan from the newly established Central Bank, as explained hereafter. ①

The Government declares its intentions, as financial conditions improve, to spend as much as possible of its revenue upon education, public warfare, and development of the country, including reclamation of waste land, exploitation of mineral and forestry resources, and extension of the system of communications. It states that it will welcome foreign financial assistance in the development of the country, and that it will adhere to the principles of Equal Opportunity and of the Open Door.

Education.

The Government has already begun to reopen primary and secondary schools, and it intends to train a large number of teachers who will thoroughly understand the spirit and policies of the new "State". A new curriculum is to be adopted, new textbooks compiled, and all anti-foreign education abolished. The new educational system will aim to improve primary schools and to stress vocational education, the training of the primary school teachers, and the teaching of sound ideas as to sanitary

---

① 原编辑者注：See special study No. 4 annexed to the Report.

living. The teaching of English and Japanese is to be compulsory in the middle schools and of Japanese is to be voluntary in the Primary Schools.

Justice and police.

The "Manchukuo" authorities have decided that in the domain of justice, the interference of administrative authorities should not be tolerated. The status of judicial officers is guaranteed by the law, and their salaries are to be adequate. The qualifications for judicial positions will be raised. Extraterritorial rights, for the time being, will be respected, but the Government intends to start negotiations with Foreign Powers for their abolition as soon as adequate reforms in the present system shall have been effected. The police are to be properly selected, trained and paid, and completely separated from the army, which is not to be allowed to usurp police functions.

The army.

Reorganisation of the army is planned, but since at present it consists largely of the old Manchurian soldiery, caution is felt to be necessary in order to avoid increasing discontent and mutiny.

"Manchukuo" Central Bank opened its head offices in Changchun and branches in many other Manchurian cities on July 1st, 1932.

The Central Bank of "Manchukuo" was established on June 14th, and officially opened its doors for business on July 1st. The Bank has its head offices in Changchun, the capital of "Manchukuo" and branches and sub-branches to the number of 170 in most of the cities of Manchuria.

The Bank was organised as a Joint-stock company with a charter to run for thirty years. Its first officers were Chinese and Japanese bankers and financiers. It was empowered to "regulate the circulation of the domestic currency, maintain its stability and control the financing service". The capital of the Bank was authorised at $30,000,000 (silver) and permission was given it to issue notes against a specie reserve of at least 30%.

The Central Bank absorbed all of the old provincial banks including the Frontier Bank.

The old provincial banks, including the Frontier Bank were amalgamated with the new Central Bank and their entire businesses, including affiliated enterprises, were turned over to it. Provision was further made for liquidating the non-Manchurian branches of the old provincial banks.

In addition to what it will be able to salvage from the old banks, the Central Bank has a Japanese loan reported at ￥20,000,000 Yen[1] and a subscription to its capital of ＄7,500,000 (silver) from the "Manchukuo" government on which to establish itself. [2] The Bank has planned to unify all the Manchurian currencies by redeeming them for new notes at rates which have been officially prescribed as from July 1st, 1932.

New currency to be based on the silver dollar but whether it will be convertible is not clear.

These notes are based on the silver dollar and are to be covered to the extent of at least 30% by silver, gold, foreign currency or deposits. Whether or not the new currency is to be convertible on demand and without limit into hard money is not made clear in official pronouncements. The old notes will be permitted to circulate for two years from the passage of the Conversion Act but will not be valid after that time.

Present Manchurian currencies essentially what they were prior to September 18th, 1931.

The order for the new Central Bank notes has been placed with the Japanese Government but thus far neither the notes nor the new hard money

---

① 原编辑者注：It is quite possible that this was intended to be "yuan".

② 原编辑者注：According to the preliminary budget furnished the Commission by the "Manchukuo" Finance Minister on May 5th, 1932.

are in circulation. The present currencies of Manchuria remain what they were prior to September 18th, 1931, with the exception that the notes are being surcharged with the signature of Mr. Yung-hou, (the president of the new Central Bank) as they pass through the various banks.

"Manchukuo's" unification programme based on inadequate supply of hard money.

It is not clear how the new "Manchukuo" Bank can hope to accomplish its ambitious programme of unifying and stabilising all Manchurian currencies with the limited amount of capital at its disposal. The resources inherited from the old provincial banking institutions with the addition of a loan from Japanese banks and a subscription to its capital from the "Manchukuo" Government, seem entirely inadequate for the purpose. Moreover, it is not clear on what basis the financial relations between the Bank and the "Manchukuo Government" will be established. According to the preliminary "Manchukuo" budget supplied to the Commission by the Finance Minister, "Manchukuo" expects to face a deficit of over 20,000,000 Yuan[①] during its first year of existence. According to the Minister, this was to be covered by a loan from the Central Bank (not then in existence). A government which subscribes 7,500,000 Yuan to its bank and then borrows over 20,000,000 Yuan from it to balance its budget is not establishing either its central bank or its budget on a sound financial basis.

---

① 原编辑者注：This and the following items in the budget were given as Yen in an interview by the "Manchukuo" Finance Minister with a Commissioner but in the English translation of "A General Outline of Manchukuo" presented by the "Department of Foreign Affairs, Manchukuo", they are given in terms of Yuan. The Commission therefore takes the liberty of using Yuan rather than Yen in its reference to this and the following budgetary items.

The fact that the Chinese symbol for Yuan is the same as the one which the Japanese employ for the Yen has been a constant source of difficulty in dealing with the English and French translations supplied the Commission by both the Chinese and Japanese.

Central Bank more likely to unify the currencies than to make them convertible.

Unless the Central Bank can obtain more actual hard money than it now appears to possess, it can hardly hope to unify and stabilize all Manchurian currencies on a convertible silver dollar basis. Even if it were to succeed in creating a currency which was uniform though not convertible it would possibly have accomplished something, but even a uniform currency, the stability of which is not guaranteed by conversion, falls short of the requirements of a sound monetary system. [1]

The Japanese extend their control over the Chinese Public Utility System.

In regard to various public utilities, as well as in regard to the railways, arrangements have been made which have tended to link up the Chinese and Japanese systems. Before the outbreak at Mukden the Japanese were anxious to bring this about, but the Chinese consistently refused to give their consent. Between September 18th, however, and the formation of "Manchukuo", steps were at once taken to realise the wishes of the Japanese, as already mentioned in the first section of this chapter. Since the formation of the new "State" the policy of the "Manchukuo Ministry of Communication," seems to be to enter into agreements with the South Manchuria Railway Company for the exploitation of at least some of the main railway lines under its authority.

The Chinese Telephone, Telegraph and Radio Systems.

The Chinese telephone, telegraph and radio systems in Manchuria, being entirely Government-owned, had their own executives, and, in addition were subject to a unified control by the Northeastern Telephone, Telegraph and Radio Administration. Since September 18th, all three of these systems have been brought into closer co-operation with existing

---

[1] 原编辑者注:See special study NO. 5 annexed to this Report.

Japanese systems throughout Manchuria. Moreover, arrangements have been made between the Japanese and the North-Eastern Telegraph Administration for through telegrams from or to any place in Manchuria and to or from any place in Kwantung Leased Territory, Japan, Korea, Formosa, and the South Sea Islands. Between the principal centres in North Manchuria and the Japanese post-offices at Dairen, Mukden and Changchun, direct circuit lines have been constructed to ensure the quick transmission of messages.

Japanese "kana"[1] messages have been given especially low rates. To learn to handle Japanese "kana" syllables, special training is being given to the Chinese staff, and it is planned to have Japanese clerks gradually join the Chinese telegraph workers at the chief centres. Thus, every facility has been given to favour telegraphic intercourse between Manchuria and the whole Japanese Empire. Naturally, the commercial connections between the countries are thereby greatly strengthened.

The Salt Gabelle. The Japanese military authorities took control, in September 1931, of the Salt Gabelle.

After the events of September 18th—19th, the Japanese authorities issued orders to the offices and banks in which the revenue of the Salt Gabelle was retained, that no payment from these funds was to be made without their consent.

Supervision over the Salt Gabelle was insisted upon on the ground that the greater part of the revenue from this source, though nominally national, had in fact been retained by Marshal Chang Hsueh-liang's Government. Income from this source, in 1930, had amounted to about $25,000,000, silver, of which $24,000,000 had been retained in Manchuria. Only $1,000,000 had been remitted to the Inspectorate-General of the Salt Gabelle in Shanghai.

---

[1] 原编辑者注:A Japanese phonetic script.

Marshal Chang Hsueh-liang agreed in 1928 to pay the Manchurian quota.

After Marshal Chang Hsueh-liang had joined the National Government in December, 1928, he agreed to pay the monthly quota of $86,600 silver which had been fixed as the amount due from Manchuria towards the loans secured on the Salt Gabelle. Somewhat later, in April, 1930, a revised table was announced in which the Manchurian monthly quota was raised to $217,800. Because of local pressure upon the Manchurian finances, however, Marshal Chang requested a postponement of the new assignment. At the time of the Mukden Incident, his arrears amounted to $576,200. The first remittance at the new rate of $217,800 was actually made on September 29, 1931, by consent of the Japanese army officers. Since then, to March, 1932, inclusive, the newly-established authorities in Manchuria have remitted to the Central Government not only these monthly quotas but also the quota arrears left unpaid by Marshal Chang Hsueh-liang. The surplus from the Salt revenue, however, they regarded as Manchurian, and not National, income, and therefore considered that they were justified in retaining it for local purposes.

The Seizure of Salt funds at Newchwang in October and November, 1931.

After the Mukden Committee for the Maintenance of Peace and Order had been transformed into the Provincial Government ad interim, it ordered the District Salt Inspectorate at Newchwang to transfer all its funds to the Provincial Bank for disbursement by the Board of Finance. According to Chinese official reports the Bank of China at Newchwang was, likewise, on October 30th, forced to give up the Salt funds on deposits, amounting to $672,709.56 silver without authority from the original depositors. A receipt was given in the name of the Liaoning Finance Board, which was signed only by the Japanese adviser to that Board.

The new Kirin Provincial Government also seized the Salt Revenue.

The new Kirin Provincial Government took similar steps with regard to the Salt Transportation Office of Kirin and Heilungkiang. According to Chinese official report it demanded the transfer of the Salt revenue to its provincial treasury. When the Chief of the office refused, he was detained for some days and replaced by a nominee of Governor Hsi Hsia, who, on October 22nd, forcibly took possession of the Office, while the Auditorate Office was closed under Governor Hsi Hsia's orders. In this case, too, the Salt funds deposited in the Bank of China and the Bank of Communications were claimed by the new Kirin authorities, and on November 6th, were transferred to the Provincial Bank. Since then Salt funds have from time to time been withdrawn and expended by the local authorities, while the monthly quotas have been sent regularly to Shanghai. From October 30th, 1931, to August 25th, 1932, for which period Chinese official figures are available, Salt revenue amounting to $14,000,000, silver, was retained in Manchuria.

The Salt Administration throughout Manchuria continued to function, although under the restrictions described and under supervision until March 28th, when the Minister of Finance of the "Manchukuo Government" ordered that the deposits, accounts, documents, and other properties belonging to the Inspectorate should be handed over on the following day to the Salt Comptroller of "Manchukuo", and that the collection of Salt revenue, which was originally undertaken by the Bank of China, should be transferred to the Bank of the Three Eastern Provinces. He stated that those officials who wished to continue their service in the Salt Gabelle Administration of the "Manchukuo" should report their names to the Salt Comptroller's office, and promised that their applications would receive serious consideration provided they first renounced allegiance to the Government of the Republic of China.

The "Government of Manchukuo" took over the administration of Salt Gabelle.

On April 15th, the District Inspectorate at Newchwang was dissolved by force. The Director and Deputy-Director were put out of office. The premises were occupied, and safes and documents, and seals, were seized. The remaining officials were requested to continue their service, but they are all reported to have refused. A number of those who had been in the Salt Administration followed the Director to Tientsin and waited for further instructions from Shanghai. The work of the former Salt Inspectorate in the Three Eastern Provinces was thus completely taken over by the new Comptroller's Office of "Manchukuo". The new "Government", however, has stated that it is prepared to continue to pay its equitable proportion of the sums required for the service of the foreign loans secured on the Salt revenue.

The Customs.

Since the Customs funds collected in Manchuria had always been remitted to the Central Government, the Japanese military authorities did not interfere with the Customs administration nor with the remittance of funds to Shanghai. Interference with this revenue was first made by the "Manchukuo Government" on the ground that their State was independent.

Customs revenue in Manchuria.

One of the first acts of the North-Eastern Administrative Committee, which was established on February 17th as the Provincial "Government of Manchukuo", was to instruct the Superintendents of Customs at the Manchurian Treaty ports that although the Customs revenue belonged of right to "Manchukuo" and would, in the future, be under the control of the Committee, for the time being the Superintendents and Commissioners of Customs should carry on their duties as usual. They were informed that a Japanese Customs Adviser had been appointed at each Manchurian port for the purpose of supervising the general Customs administration. The ports concerned were Lungchingtsun, Antung, Newchwang and Harbin, together with some sub-stations, at which the revenue collected in 1931 amounted respectively to HK. Tls. 574,000, 3,682,000, 3,792,000, and 5,272,000. The port of Aigun, which is still outside the sphere of control of the "Manchukuo Government", is functioning under the Chinese Customs Service. The port of Dairen, in the Kwantung Leased Territory, has a distinct status. The fact that the Customs revenue collected in the Manchurian ports, including Dairen, amounted in 1930 to 14.7% and in 1931 to 13.5% of the total for all China, shows the importance of Manchuria in the Chinese Customs Administration.

The "Government of Manchukuo" took over the Customs Administration and Revenue, March-June, 1932.

The procedure by which the "Manchukuo" authorities took over the entire Customs administration in Manchuria, is well illustrated by the action taken at Antung, which has been described as follows by the Inspectorate-General of Customs:

A Japanese Customs Adviser was appointed to the Antung Customs Office in March, but he took no active steps until the middle of June, when he sent definite orders from the "Manchukuo" Ministry of Finance to the Bank of China that Customs funds were no longer to be remitted to Shanghai. On June 16th, four armed "Manchukuo" Police, accompanied by the Assistant Superintendent of Police, a Japanese, visited the Bank of China and informed the Manager that they had come to guard the revenue. On June 19th the Bank of China handed over to the Bank of the Three Eastern Provinces Tls. 783,000, and informed the Commissioner that this action was taken as a result of *force majeure*.

On June 26th and 27th a Japanese Adviser of the "Manchukuo Government" demanded that the Customs House at Antung should be handed over to him. The Commissioner refused, but "Manchukuo" police, all Japanese subjects, forced the Commissioner to leave the Customs House. The Commissioner, however, still attempted to carry on the Customs work in his home, since eighty per cent, of the Antung Customs revenue is collected in the railway area, hoping that the Japanese authorities would not permit interference within this area. But the "Manchukuo" police entered the Japanese railway area, arrested a number of Customs staff, intimidated the others, and forced the Commissioner to suspend the Chinese Customs Service.

The Customs situation at Dairen.

Until June 7th, the Dairen Customs revenue was remitted to Shanghai at intervals of three or four days, but, under date of June 9th, the "Manchukuo Government" gave notice that these remittances should no longer be made. When no further funds reached Shanghai, the Inspector-General of Customs took up the matter by telegraph with the Japanese Commissioner at Dairen. As a result the Commissioner refused to send on the Customs receipts on the ground that the Chief of the Foreign Section of the Government of the Japanese Leased Territory had advised him that the remittance of the Customs revenue might severely affect Japanese interests. The Inspector-General therefore, on June 24th, dismissed the Dairen Commissioner for insubordination.

The "Manchukuo Government", on June 27th, appointed the dismissed Commissioner and the members of his staff as "Manchukuo" officials, to serve in their former positions. It had threatened to establish a new Custom House at Wafangtine, on the frontier of the Leased Territory, if the Japanese authorities should prevent them from taking charge of the Dairen Customs. The Japanese authorities of the Leased Territory did not oppose the passing of the Customs administration into the hands of the newly-appointed "Manchukuo" officials. They maintained that the problem did not concern Japan, but was an issue solely between "Manchukuo" on the one hand the Government of China and its Dairen Commissioner on the other.

The view of the "Manchukuo Government" regarding the Customs.

The "Manchukuo Government" maintains that, since "Manchukuo" is an independent state, it exercises of right, complete jurisdiction over the Customs Administration of its territory. But it has stated that, in view of the fact that various foreign loans and indemnities were based upon the Chinese Customs revenue, it is prepared to pay its equitable proportion of the annual sums necessary to meet these obligations. It hopes that, after depositing this amount in the Yokohama Specie Bank, there will be a Customs surplus for 1932—1933 available for local use of about $19,000,000 silver.

The Postal Administration in Manchuria.

The Japanese military authorities in Manchuria after September 18th did not greatly interfere with the Post Office, apart from exercising a certain censorship of newspapers and letters. After the establishment of "Manchukuo" the "Government" desired to take over the postal services of the territory, and appointed, on April 14th, special officers to take charge of the transfer of the postal administration. On April 24th, it applied for permission to join the International Post Union for which they have not yet qualified.

As the Postal Commissioners refused to surrender their offices, the status quo was for some time respected, although "Manchukuo" supervisors were placed in certain offices with a view to exercising a measure of control. The "Manchukuo Government", however, finally decided to issue its own stamps and to discontinue the use of the Chinese stamps. By ordinance of the Ministry of Communications of July 9th, in formed the public that the new stamps and cards would be offered for sale on August 1st. At this stage the Chinese Government ordered the Postal Commissioners to close the office in Manchuria, and to give the staff the choice of receiving three months' pay or of returning to designated bases in China for service at other places. The "Manchukuo" authorities, in turn offered to take into their service all the postal employees who wished to remain, and promised to guarantee their financial and other rights acquired under the Chinese Administration. On

July 26th the "Manchukuo Government" took over completely the postal service throughout Manchuria.

The treatment of private property.

The "Manchukuo Government" has stated that it will respect private property and all concessions awarded by either the Central Government of China or by the former Government of Manchuria, provided the concessions were legally granted in accordance with the laws and regulations previously in force. It has also promised to pay the lawful debts and obligations of the former administration and has appointed a Commission to pass upon claims of indebtedness. In regard to the properties belonging to Marshal Chang Hsueh-liang and some of the other prominent leaders of the former regime, it is yet too early to state what action will be taken. According to Chinese official reports, all the personal property of Marshal Chang Hsueh-liang, General Wan Fu-lin, General Pao Yu-lin, and certain others, has been confiscated. The "Manchukuo" authorities, however, take the view that since the former Government officials used their power to amass wealth for themselves, they are not yet prepared to recognise property thus acquired as properly "private property". A careful investigation is being made of the possessions of the former officials. This is reported to have been finished as far as Bank deposits are concerned.

Comments.

Having thus described the organisation of the "Manchukuo Government", its programme, and some of the measures it has taken to affirm its independence from China, we must state our conclusions regarding its operations and its principal characteristics.

The programme of this "Government" contains a number of liberal reforms, the application of which would be desirable not only in Manchuria but in the rest of China; in fact, many of these reforms figure equally in the programme of the Chinese Government. In their interviews with the

Commission the representatives of this "Government" claimed that with the help of the Japanese they would be able to establish peace and order within a reasonable time, and would thereafter be able to maintain it permanently. They expressed the belief that they would be able to secure the support of the people in time by assuring them an honest and efficient administration, security from bandit raids, lower taxation as the result of reduced military expenditure, currency reform, improved communications and popular political representation.

But after making every allowance for the short time which has hitherto been at the disposal of the "Manchukuo Government" for carrying out its policy, and after paying due regard to the steps already taken, there is no indication that this "Government" will in fact be able to carry out many of its reforms. To mention but one example[①], there seem to be serious obstacles in the way of the realisation of their budgetary and currency reforms. A thorough programme of reforms, orderly conditions and economic prosperity, could not be realised in the conditions of insecurity and disturbance which existed in 1932.

As regards the "Government" and the public services, although the titular heads of the Departments are Chinese residents in Manchuria, the main political and administrative power rests in the hands of Japanese officials and advisers. The political and administrative organisation of the "Government" is such as to give to these officials and advisers opportunities not merely of giving technical advice but of actually controlling and directing the administration. They are doubtless not under the orders of the Tokyo Government, and their policy has not always coincided with the official policy either of the Japanese Government or of the Headquarters of the Kwantung Army. But in the case of all important problems these officials and advisers, some of whom were able to act more or less independently in the first days of the new organisation, have been constrained more and more

---

① 原编辑者注:See special studies No. 4 and No. 5 annexed to this Report.

to follow the direction of Japanese official authority. This authority, in fact, by reason of the occupation of the country by its troops, by the dependence of the "Manchukuo Government" on those troops for the maintenance of its authority both internally and externally, in consequence, too, of the more and more important role entrusted to the South Manchuria Railway Company in the management of the railways under the jurisdiction of the "Manchukuo Government", and finally by the presence of its consuls, as liaison agents, in the most important urban centres, possesses in every contingency the means of exercising an irresistible pressure. The liaison between the "Manchukuo Government" and Japanese official authority is still further emphasised by the recent appointment of a special ambassador, not officially accredited, but resident in the capital of Manchuria, exercising in his capacity of Governor-General of the Kwantung Leased Territory a control over the South Manchuria Railway Company and concentrating in the same office the authority of a diplomatic representative, the head of the consular service, and Commander-in-chief of the Army of Occupation.

The relations between "Manchukuo" and Japan have hitherto been somewhat difficult to define, but the latest information in the possession of the Commission indicates that it is the intention of the Japanese Government to define them before long. A letter dated August 27th, 1932, addressed to the Commission by the Japanese Assessor states that the Special Ambassador, General Muto, "left Tokyo on August 20th for Manchuria. On arrival he will commence negotiations for the conclusion of a fundamental treaty concerning the establishment of friendly relations between Japan and Manchuria. The Government of Japan regards the conclusion of this treaty as a formal recognition of 'Manchukuo'".

PART Ⅲ The opinions of the inhabitants of Manchuria

Attitude of the inhabitants of Manchuria.

It was one of the objects of the Commission to ascertain the attitude of the inhabitants of Manchuria towards the new "State". Owing to the circumstances in which the enquiry had to be made, however, the obtaining of evidence presented some difficulty. The danger, real or supposed, to the Commission from bandits, Korean Communists, or supporters of the new "Government" who might be angered by the presence of the Chinese Assessor on account of his criticism of that regime, provided a reason for exceptional measures of protection. There were no doubt occasional real dangers in the unsettled conditions of the country, and we are grateful for the efficient protection with which we were provided throughout our tour. But the effect of the police measures adopted was to keep away witnesses; and many Chinese were frankly afraid of even meeting members of our staff. We were informed at one place that before our arrival it had been announced that no one would be allowed to see the Commission without official permission. Interviews were therefore usually arranged with considerable difficulty and in secrecy, and many informed us that it was too dangerous for them to meet us even in this way.

In spite of these difficulties we were able to arrange private interviews with business men, bankers, teachers, doctors, police, tradesmen and others, in addition to our public interviews with "Manchukuo" officials, Japanese consuls and military officers. We also received over 1,500 written communications, some delivered by hand, the majority sent by post to different addresses. The information so received was checked as far as possible from neutral sources.

Deputations and prepared statements.

Many delegations representing public bodies and associations were received, and usually presented to us written statements. Most of the delegations were introduced by the Japanese or "Manchukuo" authorities and we had strong grounds for believing that the statements left with us had previously obtained Japanese approval. In fact, in some cases persons who had presented them informed us afterwards that they had been written or substantially revised by the Japanese, and were not to be taken as the expression of their real feelings. These documents were remarkable for the studied neglect to comment either favourably or otherwise upon Japanese participation in the establishment or maintenance of the "Manchukuo" administration. In the main these statements were concerned with the relations of grievances against the former Chinese administration, and contained expressions of hope and confidence in the future of the new "State".

Letters.

The letters received came from farmers, small tradesmen, town workers and students, and related the feelings and experiences of the writers. After the return of the Commission to Peiping in June this mass of correspondence was translated, analysed and arranged by an expert staff specially selected for the purpose. All these 1,550 letters, except two, were bitterly hostile to the new "Manchukuo Government" and to the Japanese. They appeared to be sincere and spontaneous expressions of opinion.

Officials of the "Manchukuo".

The higher Chinese officials of the "Manchukuo Government" are in office for various reasons. Many of them were previously in the former regime and have been retained either by inducements or by intimidation of one kind or another. Some of them conveyed messages to the Commission to the effect that they had been forced to remain in office under duress, that all power was in Japanese hands, that they were loyal to China, and that what they had said at their interviews with the Commission in the presence of the Japanese was not necessarily to be believed. Some officials have remained in office to prevent their property from being confiscated, as has happened in the case of some of those who had fled into China. Others, men of good repute, joined in the hope that they would have the power to improve the administration, and under promise of the Japanese that they would have a free hand. Some Manchus joined in the hope of getting benefits for persons of Manchu race. Some of these have been disappointed, and complained that no real authority was conceded to them. Lastly, a few men are in office because they had personal grievances against the former regime or for reasons of profit.

Minor and local officials.

The minor and local officials have in the main retained their offices under the new regime, partly because of the necessity of earning a living and supporting their families, and partly because they feel that if they go, worse men might be put in their place. Most of the local magistrates have also remained in office, partly from a sense of duty to the people under their charge, and partly under pressure. While it was often difficult to fill the higher posts with reputable Chinese, it was an easy matter to get Chinese for service in minor posts and local offices, though the loyalty of the service rendered in such circumstances is at least questionable.

Police.

The "Manchukuo" police are partly composed of members of the former Chinese police, partly of new recruits. In the larger towns there are actually Japanese officers in the police, and in many other places there are Japanese advisers. Some individual members of the police who spoke to us expressed their dislike of the new regime, but said they must continue to serve to make a living.

Army.

The "Manchukuo Army" also consists in the main of the former Manchurian soldiers reorganised under Japanese supervision. Such troops were at first content to take service under the new regime provided they were merely required to maintain local order. But since they have on occasions been called upon to engage in serious warfare against Chinese forces, and to fight under Japanese orders side by side with Japanese troops, the

"Manchukuo Army" has become increasingly unreliable. Japanese sources report the frequent defection of "Manchukuo" forces to the Chinese side, while the Chinese claim that one of their most reliable and fruitful sources of warlike supplies is the "Manchukuo Army".

Business-men and bankers.

The Chinese business-men and bankers who were interviewed by us were hostile to "Manchukuo". They dislike the Japanese; they feared for their lives and property, and frequently remarked: "We do not want to become like the Koreans." After September 18th, there was a large exodus of business-men to China, but some of the less rich ones are now returning. Generally speaking, the smaller shopkeepers expect to suffer less from Japanese competition than do the larger merchants and manufacturers, who often had profitable relations with the former officials. Many shops were still closed at the time of our visit. The increase in banditry adversely affected business in the countryside, and the machinery of credit has largely broken down. The announced Japanese intention to exploit Manchuria economically, and the numerous visits of Japanese economic missions to Manchuria in the last few months have caused apprehension among Chinese business-men, in spite of the fact that many of these missions are reported to have returned to Japan disappointed.

Professional classes: doctors, teachers, students.

The professional classes, teachers and doctors, are hostile to "Manchukuo". They allege that they are spied upon and intimidated. The interference with education, the closing of universities and some schools, and the alterations in the school text books, have added to their hostility, already great on patriotic grounds. The censorship of the press, post, and opinion is resented, as is also the prohibition of the entry into "Manchukuo" of newspapers published in China. There are, of course, Chinese who have been educated in Japan who are not included in this generalisation. Many letters were received from students and young people directed against "Manchukuo".

Farmers and town workers.

Evidence regarding the attitude of farmers and town workers is divergent and naturally difficult to obtain. Opinion among foreigners and educated Chinese was to the effect that they were either hostile or indifferent to "Manchukuo". The farmer and worker are politically uneducated, usually illiterate, and normally takes little interest in the Government. The following reasons were advanced by witnesses for the agricultural population being hostile to "Manchukuo", and were confirmed in some of the letters received from this class of person. The farmers have good grounds for believing that the new regime will lead to an increased immigration of Koreans, and possibly of Japanese. The Korean immigrants do not assimilate with the Chinese, and their methods of agriculture are different. While the Chinese farmer mainly grows beans, kaoliang and wheat, the Korean farmer cultivates rice. This means digging canals and dykes and flooding the fields. If there are heavy rains, the dykes built by the Koreans are liable to burst and flood neighbouring Chinese land, ruining the crops. There have also been constant quarrels in the past with Koreans over land ownership and rents. Since the establishment of "Manchukuo" the Chinese allege that the Koreans have often ceased to pay rent, that they have seized lands from the Chinese, and that the Japanese have forced the Chinese to sell their lands at an unfavourable price. The farmers near the railways and towns have suffered from orders forbidding the planting of kaoliang,—a crop which grows to ten feet in height and favours the operations of bandits— within five hundred metres of railway lines and towns. The falling off of the seasonal migration of labourers from China Proper, due to the economic depression and accentuated to some extent by the political disturbances, continues. The public lands, usually available on terms to immigrants from China, have now been taken over by "Manchukuo".

Since September 18th, 1931, there has been an unparalleled growth of banditry and lawlessness in the countryside, partly due to disbanded soldiery and partly due to farmers who, having been ruined by bandits, have to take to banditry themselves for a living. Organised warfare, from which Manchuria, compared to the rest of China, had been free for many years, is now being waged in many parts of the Three Provinces between Japanese and "Manchukuo" troops and the scattered forces still loyal to China. This warfare naturally inflicts great hardships on the farmers, especially as the Japanese aeroplanes have been bombing villages suspected of harbouring anti-"Manchukuo" forces. One result has been that large areas have not been planted and next year the farmer will find it harder than ever to pay his taxes. Since the outbreak of disorders, large numbers of the more recently established immigrants from China have fled back inside the Wall. These material reasons, when added to a certain ingrained dislike of the Japanese, caused many witnesses to tell us that the Chinese farmers, who constitute the overwhelming mass of the population of Manchuria, suffer from and dislike the new regime, and that their attitude is one of passive hostility.

As regards the towns people, in certain places they have suffered from the attitude of Japanese soldiers, gendarmes and police. Generally speaking the behaviour of the Japanese troops has been good, there being no widespread lootings or massacres, though we have received in our letters complaints of individual brutality. On the other hand, the Japanese have been vigorous in suppressing elements that they believed to be hostile. The Chinese allege that many executions have taken place, and also that prisoners have been threatened and tortured in Japanese gendarmerie stations.

It was, we were told, impossible to stimulate in the towns a show of popular enthusiasm for the inauguration ceremonies of "Manchukuo". Generally speaking, the attitude of the town population is a mixture of passive acquiescence and hostility.

Minorities.

While we found the Chinese majority either hostile or indifferent to the "Manchukuo", the new "Government" receives some support from among various minority racial groups in Manchuria, such as the Mongols, Koreans, White Russians and Manchus. They have in varying degrees suffered oppression from the former administration, or economic disadvantage from the large immigration of Chinese in the last few decades, and while no section is entirely enthusiastic, they hope for better treatment from the new regime, whose policy in turn is to encourage these minority groups.

Mongols.

The Mongols have remained a race apart from the Chinese, and, as already stated, have preserved a strong race-consciousness, as well as their tribal system, aristocracy, language, dress, special modes of life, manners, customs and religion. Though still mainly a pastoral people, they are increasingly engaged in agriculture, and in the transportation of products by carts and animals. The Mongols bordering Manchuria have suffered increasingly from Chinese immigrants who obtain possession of and cultivate their lands from which they are being gradually extruded. This leads to chronic and unavoidable ill-feeling. Mongol delegations we received complained also of past sufferings from the rapaciousness of Chinese officials and tax-gatherers. The Mongols of Inner Mongolia have seen Outer Mongolia pass under the influence of the U. S. S. R. , whose extension to Inner Mongolia they dread. They wish to preserve their separate national existence against the encroachments of the Chinese on the one hand, and the U. S. S. R. on the other. Placed in this precarious position, they have greater hope of preserving their separate existence under the new regime. It must be observed, moreover, that the Princes are mainly dependent for their wealth on fixed property and on their special privileges, and that they therefore tend to become amenable to de facto authorities. A deputation, however, of Mongol Princes was received by the Commission in Peiping, and stated their opposition to the new regime. At present the connection between the Mongols bordering on Manchuria and the "Manchukuo Government" is undefined and the "Manchukuo Government" has so far refrained from interfering in their administration. While the support of certain of these Mongol elements at present is genuine, if cautious, they are quite prepared to withdraw it should the Japanese prove a menace to their independence or economic interests at some future date.

Manchus.

The Manchus have been almost completely assimilated with the Chinese, although in Kirin and Heilungkiang there still exist small and politically unimportant colonies of Manchus who, though bilingual, remain distinctly Manchu. Since the establishment of the Republic the remnants of the Manchu race lost their privileged position; although the Republic promised to continue the payment of their subsidies, they were paid in depreciated currency, and were therefore forced to take up farming and trade in which they had no experience. The few distinct Manchu groups that remain may cherish hopes that with establishment of "Manchukuo", whose backers spoke so often about the inhabitants of Manchuria being distinct in race from those of the rest of China, and in which the last of the Manchu Emperors is the Chief Executive, they may once more get privileged treatment. Persons of Manchu race have entered the "Government" with such hopes, but Chinese witnesses in Manchuria alleged that these office-holders have been disillusioned by finding all the power in Japanese hands and their own proposals ignored. Although there may still exist some sentimental loyalty to the ex-Emperor among persons of Manchu blood, there does not exist any race-conscious Manchu movement of any significance. They have been so largely assimilated with the Chinese that although efforts have been made to recruit Manchus for the administration and to stimulate Manchu race-consciousness, this source of support for the new "Government" is not sufficient to give it any title to represent the people.

Koreans.

In the past there has been much friction between Korean farmers backed by the Japanese authorities on the one hand, and Chinese officials, landowners and farmers, on the other. There is no doubt that in the past Korean farmers suffered from violence and extortion. The Korean deputation which appeared before the Commission generally welcomes the new regime, but we cannot say to what extent they were representative of their community. In any case, these Koreans who are political refugees, having emigrated to escape Japanese domination, might not be expected to welcome an extension of that domination. These refugees have proved a fertile ground for communist propaganda, and maintain contact with the revolutionary groups inside Korea. [1]

White Russians.

Of all the minority communities in Manchuria, the small colony of White Russian—at least 100,000 in number—in and around Harbin has suffered the most in recent years. Because they are a minority community with no national Government to protect them, they have been subjected to every kind of humiliation by the Chinese officials and police. They are in conflict with the Government of their own country and are, even in Manchuria, in constant anxiety on that account. The richer and more educated members of their community can earn a livelihood, but they have been liable to suffer whenever the Chinese authorities have thought some advantage was to be gained from the U. S. S. R. at their expense. The poorer members find it very hard to make a living, and have suffered continually at the hands of the police and the Chinese courts. In a province where taxes are assessed by a process of bargaining, they have been made to pay a higher

---

[1]　原编辑者注：See also CHAPTER Ⅲ and special study No. 9.

portion of their assessed taxes than their Chinese neighbours. They have experienced many restrictions on their trade and movements, and have had to pay bribes to the officials to have their passports examined, their contracts approved or their land transferred. It is not to be wondered at that many members of this community, whose condition could not well be made worse, should have welcomed the Japanese and now entertain hopes that their lot may be improved under the new administration.

We received a deputation of White Russians when we were in Harbin, as well as many letters, and we gathered from them that they would support any regime which would guarantee to them:

(1) The right of asylum;

(2) An honest and efficient police administration;

(3) Justice in the law courts;

(4) An equitable system of taxation;

(5) Rights of trade and settlement, not dependent on the payment of bribes;

(6) Facilities for educating their children;

Their requirements in this respect were chiefly efficient teaching of foreign languages to enable them to emigrate, and good technical education to enable them to obtain business employment in China;

(7) Some assistance regarding land settlement and emigration.

Conclusions of the Commission.

Such are the opinions of the local population conveyed to us during our tour in Manchuria. After careful study of the evidence presented to us in public and private interviews, in letters and written statements, we have come to the conclusion that there is no general Chinese support for the "Manchukuo Government", which is regarded by the local Chinese as an instrument of the Japanese.

CHAPTER Ⅶ   JAPAN'S ECONOMIC INTERESTS AND THE CHINESE BOYCOTT①②

Chinese boycott of Japanese goods an important factor in Sino-Japanese struggle.

The three preceding chapters have been chiefly confined to a description of military and political events since September 18th, 1931. No survey of the Sino-Japanese conflict would be accurate or complete without some account of another important factor in the struggle, namely the Chinese boycott of Japanese goods. To understand the methods employed in this boycott movement and their effect on Japanese trade, some indication must be given of the general economic position of Japan, of her economic and financial interests in China, and of the foreign trade of China. This is also necessary to understand the extent and character of the economic interests of both China and Japan in Manchuria, which will be discussed in the next chapter.

Japan's over-population.

During the Meiji Restoration period in the sixties of the last century, Japan emerged from her isolation of over two centuries, and within less than fifty years developed into a world power of the first rank. A population formerly almost stationary started to grow rapidly from 33,000,000 in 1872 until it reached a figure of 65,000,000 in 1930; and this tremendous growth

---

① 原编辑者注：BOYCOTT：The word was first used in Ireland and was derived from the name of Captain Charles Cunningham Boycott (1832—97), agent for the estates of the Earl of Erne in County Mayo. For refusing in 1880 to receive rents at figures fixed by the tenants, Captain Boycott's life was threatened, his servants were compelled to leave him, his fences torn down, his letters intercepted and his food supplies interfered with. The term soon came into common English use, and was speedily adopted into many foreign languages.

Encyclopedia Britannica, 14th. edition, 1929.

② 原编辑者注：See special study No. 8 on this subject annexed to this Report.

still continues at the rate of about 900,000 per year.

The population of Japan compared with its total surface is approximately 437 persons per square mile, as against about 41 in the United States, 330 in Germany, 349 in Italy, 468 in Great Britain, 670 in Belgium and 254 in China.

Comparing the population of Japan per square mile of arable land with that of other countries, the ratio for Japan is exceptionally high, due to the particular geographical formation of the Island Empire:

Japan·················2,774

Great Britain·········2,170

Belgium··············1,709

Italy···············819

Germany·············806

France·············467

United States of America·················229

Due to a highly concentrated population on agricultural land, the individual holdings are exceedingly small, 35% of the farmers tilling less than one acre and 34% less than two and one half acres. The expansion limit of tillable land has been reached, as has also the limit of cultivation intensity—in short, the soil of Japan cannot be expected to produce much more than it does today, nor can it provide much additional employment.

Agrarian difficulties.

Moreover, as a result of intensive cultivation and the widespread use of fertilisers the cost of production is high.

The price of land is far higher than in any other part of Asia, and even in the most overcrowded parts of Europe. Much discontent seems to exist amongst the heavily indebted population, and conflicts between tenants and landowners are on the increase. Emigration has been considered a possible remedy, but for reasons dealt with in the next chapter it has not, up to the present time, proved to be a solution.

Japan at first turned to industrialism to foster the growth of an urban population which would both provide a home market for agricultural products and turn labour to the production of goods for domestic and foreign use. Several changes have occurred since that time. Where, formerly, Japan was more than self-sufficing from the point of view of good supply, of recent years from 8% to 15% of its total imports have been foodstuffs, the fluctuation being due to the varying conditions of the home crops, principally rice. The importation of foodstuffs, and the probable increasing need of these imports necessitate an attempt to offset the country's already unfavourable trade balance by an increase in exports of industrial products.

Need for further industrialization.

If Japan is to find employment for her increasing population through the process of further industrialisation the development of her export trade and of foreign markets capable of absorbing an increasing amount of her manufactured and semi-manufactured goods becomes more and more essential. Such markets would, at the same time, serve as a source of supply of raw materials and of foodstuffs.

China a market for Japanese export trade.

Japanese export trade, as hitherto developed, has two main directions: her luxury product, raw silk, goes to the United States; and her staple manufactures, chiefly cotton textiles, go to the countries of Asia, the United States taking 42.5% of her exports and the Asia market as a whole taking 42.6%. Of this latter trade China, the Kwantung Leased Territory, and Hong Kong take 24.7%, and a large share of the remainder is handled by Chinese merchants in other parts of Asia. [①]

During 1930, the last year for which complete figures are available, the total exports of Japan amounted to 1,469,852,000 Yen, and her imports to

---

① 原编辑者注:Figures for 1929—*Japan Year Book of 1931*.

1,546,071,000 Yen. Of the exports, Yen 260,826,000 or 17.7%, went to China (excluding the Kwantung Leased Territory and Hong Kong), while of the imports 161,667,000 Yen, or 10.4%, came from China (excluding the Kwantung Leased Territory and Hong Kong).

Analysing the principal commodities exported by Japan to China, it will be found that China takes 32.8% of all aquatic products exported by Japan; 84.6% or refined sugar; 75.1% of coal, and 31.9%, of cotton tissues, or an average of 51.6%.

The same analysis applied to the commodities imported from China shows that 24.5% of the total amount of beans and peas imported by Japan comes from China; 53% of the oil cake; and 25% of vegetable fibres; or an average of 34.5%.

As these figures are for China only, excluding Hong Kong and the Kwantung Leased Territory, they do not indicate the extent of Japanese trade with Manchuria, which passes mainly through the port of Dairen.

Importance of Sino-Japanese trade relations.

The facts and figures just given clearly show the importance to Japan of her trade with China. Nor is Japan's interest in China limited to trade alone; she has a considerable amount of capital invested in industrial enterprises, as well as in railways, shipping and banking, and in all of these branches of financial and economic activity the general trend of development has been increasing considerably during the last three decades.

Japanese investments in China.

In 1898 the only Japanese investment of any consequence was a small cotton gin in Shanghai owned jointly with Chinese, representing a value of about 100,000 taels. By 1913 the estimated total of Japanese investments in China and Manchuria amounted to 435,000,000 Yen, out of a total of Yen 535,000,000 estimated investments abroad. By the end of the World War, Japan had more than doubled her investments in China and Manchuria over those of 1913, a considerable part of this increase being due to the famous "Nishihara loans," which had been partially granted for political considerations. Notwithstanding this setback, Japan's investments in China and Manchuria[①] in 1929 were estimated at almost 2,000,000,000 Yen[②] out of her total investments abroad of 2,100,000,000 Yen, showing that Japan's China and Manchuria, the latter having absorbed by far the greater part of this investment (particularly in railways).

Apart from these investments, China has been indebted to Japan for various state, provincial and municipal loans which in 1925 were estimated at a total of 304,458,000 Yen(the greater part unsecured), plus 18,037,000 Yen interest.

Although the bulk of Japan's investments are in Manchuria, a considerable amount is invested in industries, shipping and banking in China proper. Nearly 50 per cent of the total number of spindles operated in the spinning and weaving industry in China in 1929 were owned by Japanese. Japan was second in the carrying trade of China, and the number of Japanese banks in China in 1932 is put at thirty, a few of which are joint Sino-Japanese enterprises.

China's interest in the development of trade with Japan.

Although the foregoing figures are stated from the standpoint of Japan, it is easy to see their relative importance from the standpoint of China. Foreign trade with Japan has held first place in the total foreign trade of China up to 1932. In 1930, 24.1% of her exports went to Japan, while in the same year 24.9% of her imports came from Japan. This, in comparison with the figures from Japan's standpoint, shows that the trade of China with Japan is a greater percentage of her total foreign trade than is the trade of

---

① 编者按:即中国和中国东北地区。下同。

② 原编辑者注:According to another estimate, Japan's investments in China, including Manchuria, total approximately ¥1,800,000,000.

Japan with China of the total foreign trade of Japan. But China has no investments, banking or shipping interests in Japan. China requires, above all else, to be able to export her products in increasing quantities to enable her to pay for the many finished products she needs and in order to establish a sound basis of credit on which to borrow the capital required for further development.

Sino-Japanese economic and financial relations easily affected by many disturbing factor.

From the foregoing, it is evident that Sino-Japanese economic and financial relations are both extensive and varied, and, consequently, easily affected and disorganised by any disturbing factor. It also appears that, in its entirety, Japanese dependence on China is greater than China's dependence on Japan. Hence Japan is the more vulnerable and has more to lose in case of disturbed relations.

It is therefore clear that the many political disputes which have arisen between the two countries since the Sino-Japanese war of 1895 have in turn affected their mutual economic relations, and the fact that in spite of these disturbances the trade between them has continued to increase proves that there is an underlying economic tie that no political antagonism has been able to sever.

Origin of boycott.

For centuries the Chinese have been familiar with boycott methods in the organisation of their merchants, bankers, and craft guilds. These guilds, although they are being modified to meet modern conditions, still exist in large numbers and exercise great power over their members in the defence of their common professional interest. The training and attitude acquired in the course of this century old guild life has been combined, in the present-day boycott movement, with the recent fervent nationalism, of which the Kuomintang is the organised expression.

Modern anti-foreign boycotts.

The era of modern anti-foreign boycotts employed on a national basis as a political weapon against a foreign power (as distinct from a professional instrument used by Chinese traders against each other) can be said to have started in 1905 with a boycott directed against the United States because of a stipulation in the Sino-American Commercial Treaty, as renewed and revised in that year, restricting more severely than before the entry of Chinese into America. From that moment onward until today there have been ten distinct boycotts which can be considered as national in scope (besides anti-foreign movements of a local character), nine of which were directed against Japan[①] and one only against the United Kingdom.

Causes of these boycott movements.

If these boycotts are studied in detail, it will be found that each of them can be traced back to a definite fact, event or incident, generally of a political nature and interpreted by China as directed against her material interests or detrimental to her national prestige. Thus, the boycott of 1931 was started as a direct sequel to the massacre of Koreans in July, following the Wanpaoshan incident in June of that year, and has been accentuated by the events at Mukden in September and at Shanghai in January, 1932. Each boycott has its own immediately traceable cause, but none of the causes in themselves would have initiated economic retaliation on so extensive a scale

---

① 原编辑者注:The date and immediate cause of each of these boycotts is:

1908　The *Tatsu Maru* incident.
1909　The Antung-Mukden Railway question.
1915　The "21 Demands".
1919　The Shantung question.
1923　Port Arthur and Dairen recovery question.
1925　May 30th incident.
1927　Despatch of troops to Shantung.
1928　Tsinan incident.
1931　The Manchurian affair (Wanpaoshan and Mukden events).

had it not been for the mass psychology described in CHAPTER Ⅰ. The factors contributing to the creation of this psychology are: a conviction of injustice (rightly or wrongly considered as such), an inherited faith in Chinese cultural superiority over foreigners, and a fervent nationalism of a western type, mainly defensive in aims but in which certain aggressive tendencies are not lacking.

Boycott movements before 1925.

Although a Society for the Regeneration of China (Hsing Chung Hui), which may be considered the progenitor of the Kuomintang, was founded as far back as 1893, and although there can be no doubt that all the boycotts from 1905 to 1925 were launched with the war-cry of Nationalism, there is no concrete evidence that the original nationalist associations, and later the Kuomintang, had a direct hand in their organisation. Inspired by Dr. Sun Yat-sen's new creed, Chambers of Commerce and Student Unions were fully capable of such a task, guided as they were by century-old secret societies, guild experience and guild mentality. The merchants furnished the technical knowledge, means of organisation and rules of procedure, while the students inspired the movements with the enthusiasm of their newly acquired conviction and their spirit of determination in the national cause, and helped to put them into operation. While the students were generally moved by nationalistic feelings alone, the Chambers of Commerce, though sharing these feelings, thought it wise to participate from a desire to control the operation of the boycott. The actual rules of the earlier boycotts were designed to prevent the purchase of the goods of the country against which the boycott was directed. Gradually, however, the field of action was extended to a refusal to export Chinese goods to the country concerned, or to sell or render services to its nationals in China. Finally, the avowed purpose of the more recent boycotts has become to sever completely all economic relations with the "enemy country".

It should be pointed out that the rules thus established were never carried out to the fullest extent, for reasons which have been fully dealt with in the special study annexed to this report. Generally speaking, the boycotts have always had more impetus in the South, where nationalistic feelings found their first and most fervent adherents, than in the North, Shantung especially having withheld support.

Boycott movement since 1925. Action of the Kuomintang Party.

From 1925 onward a definite change took place in the boycott organisation. The Kuomintang, having from its creation supported the movement, increased its control with each successive boycott until today it is the real organising, driving, co-ordinating and supervising factor in these demonstrations.

In doing this, the Kuomintang, as indicated by evidence in the possession of the Commission, did not dismiss the associations which had hitherto been responsible for the direction of boycott movements. It rather co-ordinated their efforts, systematised and made uniform their methods, and put unreservedly behind the movement the moral and material weight of its powerful party organisation. Having branches all over the country, possessing vast propaganda and information services, and inspired by a strong nationalistic sentiment, it rapidly succeeded in organising and stimulating a movement which had, up to that time, been somewhat sporadic, as a consequence, the coercive authority of the organisers of the boycotts over the merchants and the general public became stronger than ever before, although at the same time a fair margin of autonomy and initiative was left to the individual boycott associations.

Methods employed.

The boycott rules continued to vary according to local conditions but parallel with the strengthening of the organisation, the methods employed by the Boycott Societies became more uniform, more strict and effective. At the same time the Kuomintang Party issued instructions prohibiting the destruction of commercial houses belonging to Japanese or the infliction of physical harm. This does not mean that the lives of Japanese in China have never been threatened in the course of a boycott, but as a whole it may be stated that during the more recent boycotts, acts of violence against Japanese subjects have been less numerous and serious than in earlier days.

An examination of the technique of the methods employed shows that the atmosphere of popular sentiment without which no boycott could succeed is created by a formidable propaganda uniformly carried out all over the country, using slogans well chosen to incite the popular mind against the "enemy" country.

Anti-Japanese propaganda.

In the present boycott directed against Japan which the Commission has seen in operation, every available means was employed to impress upon the people the patriotic duty of not buying Japanese goods. The columns of the Chinese press were filled with propaganda of this kind, the walls of buildings in the towns were covered with posters, often of an extremely violent character[①]; anti-Japanese slogans were printed on currency notes, on letters and telegram-forms; chain letters went from hand to hand, etc. These examples were by no means exhaustive, but serve to show the nature of the methods employed. The fact that this propaganda does not differ essentially from that used in certain countries of Europe and America during the World War 1914—1918 only proves the degree of hostility towards Japan which the Chinese have come to feel as a result of the political tension between the two countries.

---

① 原编辑者注：In most cities visited, by the Commission these posters had been removed beforehand but declarations from reliable local witnesses who often possessed samples of these posters bore out the fact mentioned above. Moreover, samples are to be found in the archives of the Commission.

Boycott rules adopted by Anti-Japanese Associations.

Essential as the political atmosphere of a boycott may be to its ultimate success, nevertheless no such movement could be effective if the boycott associations had not secured a certain uniformity in their rules of procedure. The four general principles adopt at the first meeting of the Shanghai Anti-Japanese Association held on July 17th, 1931, may serve as an illustration of the main objects aimed at by these rules. They were:

a. To withdraw the orders for Japanese goods already ordered;

b. To stop shipment of Japanese goods already ordered but not yet consigned;

c. To refuse to accept Japanese goods already in the godowns but not yet paid for;

d. To register with the Anti-Japanese Association, Japanese goods already purchased and to suspend temporarily the selling of these goods. The procedure of registration will be separately decided upon.

Subsequent resolutions adopted by the same Association are much more detailed and contain provisions for all possible cases and eventualities.

A powerful means of enforcing the boycotts is the compulsory registration of Japanese goods held in stock by Chinese merchants. Inspectors of the Anti-Japanese societies watch the movement of Japanese goods, examine those of doubtful origin in order to ascertain whether or not they are Japanese, undertake raids on stores and godowns where they suspect the presence of non-registered Japanese goods, and bring to the attention of their principals any case of the violation of the rules they may discover. Merchants who are found to be guilty of such a breach of the rules are fined by the Boycott Associations themselves and publicly exposed to popular disapproval, while the goods in their possession are confiscated and sold at public auction, the proceeds going into the funds of the Anti-Japanese organisation.

The boycott is not limited to trade alone. Chinese are warned not to travel on Japanese ships, to use Japanese banks or to serve Japanese in any capacity, either in business or in domestic service. Those who disregard these instructions are subjected to various forms of disapproval and intimidation.

Another feature of this boycott, as of previous ones, is the wish not only to injure Japanese industries, but to further Chinese industries by stimulating the production of certain articles which have hitherto been imported from Japan. The principal result has been an extension of the Chinese textile industry at the expense of the Japanese-owned mills in the Shanghai area.

Fluctuations of the Boycott movement in 1931—32.

The boycott of 1931, organised on the lines just described, continued until about December of that year, 1932, when a certain relaxation became apparent. In January, 1932, in the course of the negotiations then proceeding between the Mayor of Greater Shanghai and the Japanese Consul-General in that city, the Chinese even undertook to dissolve voluntarily the local anti-Japanese association.

Material effects of boycott movement.

During the hostilities in Shanghai, and the months immediately following the evacuation of the Japanese troops, the boycott, although never completely abandoned, was moderated, and during late spring and early summer it even looked as if Japanese trade in different parts of the country might resume. Then, quite suddenly, at the end of July and beginning August, coinciding with the reported military activity on the borders of Jehol, there was a marked revival of the boycott movement. Articles urging the people not to buy Japanese goods appeared anew in the Chinese press, the Shanghai Chamber of Commerce published a letter suggesting the resumption of the boycott, and the Coal Merchants' Guild in the same city decided to restrict to the minimum the importation of Japanese coal. At the same time more violent methods were employed, such as the throwing of a bomb into the compound of a coal dealer suspected of having handled

Japanese coal, and the sending of letters to storekeepers threatening to destroy their property unless they stopped selling Japanese commodities. Some of the letters reproduced in the newspapers were signed the "Blood and Iron Group"—or the "Blood and Soul Group for the punishment of traitors".

Such is the situation at the time of writing this Report. This recrudescence of the boycott activity caused the Japanese Consul-General in Shanghai to lodge a formal protest with the local authorities.

The various boycott movements, and the present one in particular, have seriously affected Sino-Japanese relations, both in a material and in a psychological sense.

As far as the material effects are concerned—that is, the loss of trade—the Chinese have a tendency to understate them in their desire to present the boycott as rather a moral protest than as an act of economic injury, while the Japanese attach too absolute a value to certain trade statistics. The arguments used in this connection by the two parties are examined in the annexed Study already referred to. In that Study will also be found full particulars of the extent of the damage done to Japanese trade, which has certainly been considerable.

Another aspect of the subject should also be mentioned. The Chinese themselves suffer losses from goods already paid for, not registered with the Boycott Associations, and seized for public auction; from lines paid to the associations for violation of the boycott rules; from revenue not received by the Chinese Maritime Customs; and generally speaking, from loss of trade. These losses are considerable.

The psychological effect on Sino-Japanese relations.

The psychological effect of the boycott on Sino-Japanese relations, although even more difficult to estimate than the material effect, is certainly not less serious in that it has had a disastrous repercussion on the feelings of large sections of Japanese public opinion towards China. During the visit of the Commission to Japan, both the Tokyo and the Osaka Chambers of

Commerce stressed this subject.

The knowledge that Japan is suffering injuries against which she cannot protect herself has exasperated Japanese public opinion. The merchants whom we interviewed at Osaka were inclined to exaggerate certain abuses of boycott methods, such as racketeering and blackmailing, and to under-estimate or even to deny completely the close relationship between Japan's recent policy towards China and the use of the boycott as a defensive weapon against that policy. On the contrary, instead of regarding the boycott as China's weapon of defence, these Japanese merchants insisted that it was an act of aggression against which the Japanese military measures were a retaliation. Anyway there is no doubt that the boycott has been amongst the causes which have profoundly embittered the relations between China and Japan in recent years.

Controversial issues in connection with the boycott.

There are three controversial issues involved in the policy and methods of the boycott.

(1) Whether the movement is spontaneous or organized.

The first is the question whether the movement is purely spontaneous, as the Chinese themselves claim, or whether, as the Japanese allege, it is an organised movement imposed upon the people by the Kuomintang, by methods which at times amount to terrorism. On this subject much may be said on both sides. On the one hand it would appear to be impossible for a nation to exhibit the degree of co-operation and sacrifice involved in the maintenance of a boycott over a wide area and for a long period if there did not exist a foundation of strong popular feeling. On the other hand, it has been clearly shown to what extent the Kuomintang, using the mentality and the methods which the Chinese people have inherited from their old guilds and secret societies, has taken control of the recent boycotts, and particularly of the present one. The rules, the discipline, and the sanctions used against the "traitors", which form such an essential part of the present boycott, show that however spontaneous, the movement is certainly strongly organised.

All popular movements require some measure of organisation to be effective. The loyalty of all adherents to a common cause is never uniformly strong, and discipline is required to enforce unity of purpose and action. Our conclusion is that the Chinese boycotts are both popular and organised; that though they originate in and are supported by strong national sentiment, they are controlled and directed by organisations which can start or call them off, and that they are enforced by methods which certainly amount to intimidation. While many separate bodies are involved in the organisation, the main controlling authority is the Kuomintang.

(2) Legality or otherwise of boycott methods.

The second issue is whether or not in the conduct of the boycott movement the methods employed have always been legal. From the evidence collected by the Commission it is difficult to draw any other conclusion than that illegal acts have been constantly committed, and that they have not been sufficiently suppressed by the authorities and the courts. The fact that these methods are mainly the same as those used in China in olden days may be an explanation but not a justification. When in former days a Guild elected to declare a boycott, searched the houses of suspected members, brought them before the Guild Court, punished them for a breach of rules, imposed fines and sold the goods seized, it acted in conformity with the customs of that time. Moreover, it was an internal affair of a Chinese community, and no foreigner was involved. The present situation is different. China has adopted a code of modern laws, and these are incompatible with the traditional methods of trade boycotts in China. The memorandum in which the Chinese Assessor has defended his country's point of view with regard to the boycott does not contest this statement but argues that "the boycott... is pursued, generally speaking, in a legitimate manner". The evidence at the disposal of the Commission does not bear out this contention.

In this connection a distinction should be made between the illegal acts committed directly against foreign residents, in casu Japanese, and those committed against Chinese with the avowed intention, however, of causing damage to Japanese interests. As far as the former are concerned, they are clearly not only illegal under the laws of China but also incompatible with treaty obligations to protect life and property, and to maintain liberty of trade, residence, movement and action. This is not contested by the Chinese, and the boycott associations, as well as the Kuomintang authorities, have tried, although they may not always have been successful, to prevent offences of this kind. As already stated they have occurred less frequently during the present boycott than on previous occasions. ①

With regard to illegal acts committed against the Chinese, the Chinese Assessor observed on page 17 of his memorandum on the boycott:

"We would like to observe in the first place that a foreign nation is not authorised to raise a question of internal law. In fact, we find ourselves confronted with acts denounced as unlawful but committed by Chinese nationals in prejudice to other Chinese nationals. Their suppression is a matter for the Chinese authorities, and it seems to us that no one has the right of calling into account the manner in which the Chinese penal law is applied in matters where both offenders and sufferers belong to our own nationality. No state has the right of intervention in the administration of exclusively domestic affairs of another state. This is what the principle of mutual respect for each others' sovereignty and independence means."

So stated, the argument is incontestable, but it overlooks the fact that the ground of the Japanese complaint is not that one Chinese national has been illegally injured by another, but that the injury has been done to

---

① 原编辑者注：According to recent Japanese information, there were 35 instances in which goods belonging to Japanese merchants were seized and kept in detention by members of the Anti-Japanese Associations in Shanghai during the period from July, 1931 to the end of December, 1931. The value of the goods involved was estimated approximately at 287,000 dollars. Of these instances, in August, 1932, five were reported as still remaining unsolved.

Japanese interests by the employment of methods which are illegal under Chinese law, and that failure to enforce the law in such circumstances implies the responsibility of the Chinese Government for the injury done to Japan.

(3) Responsibility of the Chinese Government for the boycott.

This leads to a consideration of the last controversial point involved in the policy of the boycott—namely the extent of the responsibility of the Chinese Government. The Chinese official attitude is that "the liberty of choice in making purchases is a personal right which no government can interfere with; while the governments are responsible for the protection of lives and property, they are not required by any commonly-recognised regulations and principles to prohibit and punish the exercise of an elemental right of every citizen."

The Commission has been supplied with documentary evidence which is reproduced in the Study No. 8 annexed to this Report, and which indicates that the part taken by the Chinese Government in the present boycott has been somewhat more direct than the quotation above would tend to indicate. We do not suggest that there is anything improper in the fact that Government Departments should support the boycott movement: we only wish to point out that official encouragement involves a measure of Government responsibility. In this connection the question of relations between the Government and the Kuomintang must be considered. Of the responsibility of the latter there can be no question. It is the controlling and co-ordinating organ behind the whole boycott movement. The Kuomintang may be the maker and the master of the Government, but to determine at what point the responsibility of the Party ends and that of the Government begins is a complicated problem of constitutional law on which the Commission does not feel it proper to pronounce.

Comments.

The claim of the Government that the boycott is a legitimate weapon of defence against military aggression by a stronger country, especially in cases where methods of arbitration have not previously been utilised, raises a question of a much wider character. No one can deny the right of the individual Chinese to refuse to buy Japanese goods, use Japanese banks, or ships, or to work for Japanese employers, to sell commodities to Japanese, or to maintain social relations with Japanese. Nor is it possible to deny that the Chinese, acting individually or even in organised bodies, are entitled to make propaganda on behalf of these ideas, always subject to the condition, of course, that the methods do not infringe the laws of the land. Whether, however, the organised application of the boycott to the trade of one particular country is consistent with friendly relations or in conformity with treaty obligation is rather a problem of international law than a subject for our Enquiry. We would express the hope, however, that in the interest of all States this problem should be considered at an early date and regulated by international agreement.

In the course of the present chapter it has been shown first that Japan, in connection with her population problem, is seeking to increase her industrial output and to secure for this purpose reliable oversea markets; secondly, that, apart from the export of raw silk to the United States, China constitutes the principal market for Japanese exports and at the same time supplies the Island Empire with an important amount of raw materials and food-stuffs. Further, China has attracted nearly the whole of Japan's foreign investments, and even in her present disturbed and undeveloped condition, offers a profitable field to Japanese economic and financial activities of various types. Finally, an analysis of the injury caused to Japanese interests in China by the various boycotts which have succeeded one another from 1908 until today has drawn attention to the vulnerable character of these interests.

The dependence of Japan on the Chinese market is fully recognised by the Japanese themselves. On the other hand, China is a country which stands in the most urgent need of development in all fields of economic life, and Japan, which in 1931, notwithstanding the boycott, occupied the first place in her total foreign trade, seems more than any other foreign Power indicated as an ally in economic matters.

The interdependence of the trade of these two neighbouring countries and the interests of both call for an economic rapprochement, but there can be no such rapprochement so long as the political relations between them are so unsatisfactory as to call forth the use of military force by one and the economic force of the boycott by the other.

CHAPTER VIII ECONOMIC INTERESTS IN MANCHURIA[①]

It has been shown in the preceding chapter that the economic requirements of Japan and China, unless disturbed by political considerations, would lead to mutual understanding and co-operation, and not to conflict. The study of the inter-relation between Japanese and Chinese economic interests in Manchuria, taken in themselves and apart from the political events of recent years leads to the same conclusion. The economic interests of both countries in Manchuria are not irreconcilable; indeed, their reconciliation is necessary if the existing resources and future economic possibilities of Manchuria are to be developed to the fullest extent.

In CHAPTER III the claim of Japanese public opinion that the resources, both actual and potential, of Manchuria are essential to the economic life of their country has been fully examined. The object of this chapter is to consider how far this claim is in conformity with economic facts.

Investments.

It is a fact that in South Manchuria, Japan is the largest foreign

---

① 原编辑者注:See for this chapter special studies No. 2, 3, 6, 7.

investor, whereas in North Manchuria the same is true of the U. S. S. R. Taking the Three Provinces as a whole, the Japanese investments are more important than those of the U. S. S. R. although it is difficult to say to what extent because of the impossibility of obtaining reliable comparative figures. As the subject of investments is examined in detail in an annex to this Report, a few essential figures will be sufficient to illustrate the relative importance of Japan, the U. S. S. R. , and other countries as participating factors in the economic development of Manchuria.

According to a Japanese source of information, Japanese investments were estimated in 1928 at about 1,500,000,000 Yen, a figure which, if correct, must have grown today to approximately 1,700,000,000 Yen. [1] A Russian source puts Japanese investments at the present time at about 1,500,000,000 Yen, for the whole of Manchuria inclusive of the Kwantung Leased Territory, and at about 1,300,000,000 Yen for the Three Provinces, the bulk of Japanese capital being invested in Liaoning Province.

With regard to the nature of these investments it will be found that the majority of the capital has been devoted to transportation enterprises (mainly railways), agriculture, mining, and forestry coming next. As a matter of fact, the Japanese investments in South Manchuria centre mainly round the South Manchuria Railway while the investments of the U. S. S. R. in the North are to a great extent, directly or indirectly, linked up with the Chinese Eastern Railway.

Foreign investments other than Japanese are more difficult to estimate, and in spite of the helpful assistance of those immediately interested, the information obtained by the Commission has been meagre. Most of the figures given by the Japanese are prior to 1917, and consequently out of date. For the U. S. S. R. , as has been stated, no definite estimate is possible. With regard to other countries, a recent Russian estimate for

---

① 原编辑者注：Another Japanese authority put the total of Japanese investments in China, including Manchuria, in 1929 at a figure of approximately 1,500,000,000 Yen.

North Manchuria only, which it has not been possible to verify, indicates Great Britain as the next largest investor with G. $11,185,000[1], followed by Japan with G. $9,229,400, the United States with G. $8,220,000, Poland with G. $5,025,000, France with G. $1,760,000, Germany with G. $1,235,000, and miscellaneous investments G. $1,129,600, making a total of G. $37,784,400. For South Manchuria similar figures are not available.

Japan's economic relations with Manchuria.

It is now necessary to analyse the part Manchuria plays in the economic life of Japan. A detailed study on this subject will be found in an Annex to this Report from which it will be seen that although this part is an important one, it is at the same time limited by circumstances which must not be overlooked.

It does not seem from past experience that Manchuria is a region suitable for Japanese emigration on a large scale. As already stated in CHAPTER II, the farmers and coolies from Shantung and Shihli (now Hopei) have in the last few decades taken possession of the soil. Japanese settlers are, and for many years will mostly be, business men, officials, salaried employees who have come to manage the investments of capital, the development of various enterprises, and the utilisation of natural resources.

Agriculture.

As regards her supplies of agricultural produce, Japan to-day depends on Manchuria mainly for the soya bean and its derivatives, the use of which as food stuff and as forage may even increase in the future. (As a fertiliser, which is today one of its chief uses, its importance is likely to decrease with the growth of chemical industries in Japan.) But the question of food supply is not at the moment acute for Japan, the acquisition of Korea and Formosa

---

① 原编辑者注:G. $ = gold dollar.

having helped to solve, at least for the time, her rice problem. If at some future date the need of this commodity becomes urgent for the Japanese Empire, Manchuria may be able to provide an additional source of supply. But in that case a large amount of capital would have to be spent in the development of a sufficient irrigation system.

Heavy industries.

Larger still, it seems, will be the amount of capital necessary for the creation of Japanese heavy industries, if these are destined to become independent of foreign countries, as a result of the utilisation of the resources of Manchuria. Japan seeks above all to develop in the Three Eastern Provinces the production of those raw materials which are indispensable to her national defence. Manchuria can supply her with coal, oil, and iron. The economic advantage, however, of such supplies are uncertain. For coal, only a comparatively small part of the production is utilised in Japan; oil is extracted from shale only in very limited quantities; while it would appear that iron is definitely produced at a loss. But economic considerations are not the only ones which influence the Japanese Government. The resources of Manchuria are intended to assist the development of an independent metallurgic system. In any case Japan must seek abroad a great part of her coke and certain non-siliceous ores. The Three Eastern Provinces may ensure greater security in the supplies of certain products which are indispensable for her national defence but heavy financial sacrifices may be involved in obtaining them. The strategic interests of Japan in Manchuria involved in this question have been mentioned elsewhere.

Further, Manchuria is not likely to supply Japan with those raw materials which she needs most for her textile industries.

Manchuria as a market for Japanese products.

The Three North-Eastern Provinces provide a regular market for

Japanese manufactured goods; and the importance of this market may even increase with their growth in prosperity. But Osaka in the past has always depended more on Shanghai than on Dairen. The Manchurian market may perhaps offer more security, but it is more restricted than the Chinese market.

The idea of economic "blocs" has penetrated to Japan from the West. The possibility of such a bloc comprising the Japanese Empire and Manchuria is often found in the writings of Japanese statesmen, professors and journalists. In an article written shortly before he took office, the present Minister of Commerce and Industry pointed to the formation in the world of such economic blocs American, Soviet, European and British, and stated that Japan should also create with Manchuria such a bloc.

There is nothing at present to show that such a system is practicable. Some voices have recently been raised in Japan to warn their compatriots against dangerous illusions. Japan depends for the bulk of her commerce far less on Manchuria than she does on the United States, China proper and British India.

Manchuria may become in the future of great assistance to an overpopulated Japan but it is as dangerous not to discern the limitations of its possibilities as it is to underestimate their value.

China's economic relations with Manchuria[①].

When studying the economic relations of the rest of China with her Three Eastern Provinces, it will be apparent that, contrary to what we have seen in the case of Japan, her chief earlier contribution to their development consisted in the sending of seasonal workers and permanent settlers to whom the great agricultural development of the country is due. More recently, however, particularly in the last decade, her participation in railway construction and in the development of mineral and forestry resources and in

---

① 编者按:意指中国关内地区与中国东北地区的经济关系。

industry, trade and banking, has also shown a marked progress, the extent of which cannot be adequately shown due to-lack of date. On the whole it may be said that the principal ties between Manchuria and the rest of China are racial and social rather than economic. It has been recalled in CHAPTER Ⅱ that the present population of Manchuria is, in the main, drawn from recent immigrations. The Spontaneous character of these immigrations show clearly how they have fulfilled a real need. They have been a consequence of famine, although they were encouraged to some extent by both the Japanese and Chinese.

The Japanese have for a number of years recruited Chinese labour for the Fushun mines, for the Dairen harbour works and for the construction of railway lines. But the number of Chinese thus recruited has always been very limited and this recruitment ceased in 1927, when it appeared that the local supplies of labour were sufficient.

The Provincial authorities in Manchuria have also on several occasions assisted the settlement of Chinese immigrants, although in practice these activities of the authorities of the Three Eastern Provinces have only had a limited influence on immigration. The authorities in North China, and the charitable societies, have also in certain periods endeavoured to encourage the settlement of families in Manchuria.

The principal assistance received by the immigrants has been the reduced rates offered by the South Manchuria Railway, the Chinese lines, and the Chinese Eastern Railway. These encouragements given to newcomers showed that at least until the end of 1931, the South Manchuria Railway, the Manchurian provincial authorities and the Chinese Government regarded this exodus with favour all of them profited by the peopling of the Three Eastern Provinces, although their interests in the movement were not always identical.

Emigrants, once settled in Manchuria, maintain their relations with their province of origin in China proper. This is best shown by a study of the remittances that the emigrants sent back to their families in the villages of their birth. It is impossible to estimate the total of these remittances, which are effected through banks, through the post and through money taken back by returning emigrants. It is believed that twenty million dollars are so taken annually into Shantung and Hopei, while the Post Office statistics showed in 1928 that the Provinces of Liaoning and Kirin remitted to the Province of Shantung by money orders a sum equal to the amount remitted to that province by all the other provinces in China. There is no doubt that these remittances form an important economic link between Manchuria and China Proper. They are the index of the contact maintained between the emigrants and their families in the provinces of their origin. This contact is all the easier because conditions on either side of the Great Wall do not greatly differ. The produce of the soil is in the main the same and the agricultural methods identical. The most pronounced variations between caused by differences of climate, varying density of population and different states of economic development. These factors do not prevent the agriculture of the Three Eastern Provinces from tending to resemble more and more the agricultural conditions in Shantung. In Liaoning, a long settled territory, rural conditions resemble more closely those in Shantung than do those in Heilungkiang, a territory more recently opened up.

The organisation of direct trade with the agriculturalists in Manchuria resembles also the conditions in China Proper. In the Three Provinces such commerce is in the hands of Chinese, who alone buy directly from the farmers. Similarly in the Three Provinces as in China Proper, credit performs an important function in such local trade. One can even say that the resemblance in commercial organisation in Manchuria and China Proper is found not only in local countryside trade but also in trade in the towns.

In fact, the social and economic Chinese organisation in Manchuria is a transplanted society which has kept the customs, dialect and activities of its home. The only changes necessary are those required to meet the conditions of a land more vast, less inhabited and more open to outside influences.

The question arises whether this mass migration has been merely an episode or whether it will continue in the future. When account is taken of the areas in South Manchuria and certain valleys in the south and east, such as the Sungari, Liao and Mutanchiang Valleys, it is clear that from the purely agricultural point of view, Manchuria can still absorb numerous colonists. According to one of the best experts on the staff of the Chinese Eastern Railway, the population of Manchuria could reach in forty years a figure of 75,000,000.

But economic conditions may in the future limit the rapid growth of the population of Manchuria. Economic conditions in fact alone render the future of soya bean farming uncertain. On the other hand, crops recently introduced into Manchuria, some Japanese have placed in the development of cotton growing seem to be subject to certain limitations. Consequently economic and technical factors may to some extent limit the entry of newcomers into the Three Provinces.

The recent political events are not the only cause of the decline of Chinese migration into Manchuria. The economic crisis had already in the first six months of the year 1931, diminished the importance of the seasonal migration. The world depression added to the effect of an unavoidable local crisis. Once this economic crisis is over and order has been re-established, Manchuria may once more serve as an outlet for the population of China proper. The Chinese are the people best adapted for the colonisation of Manchuria. An artificial restriction of this migration by arbitrary political measures would be prejudicial to the interests of Manchuria as it would be to the interests of Shantung and Hopei.

The ties between Manchuria and the rest of China remain chiefly racial and social. At the same time economic ties are continuously becoming stronger, which is shown by the growing commercial relations between Manchuria and the rest of China. Nevertheless, according to Customs returns, Japan remains the best customer and chief supplies of Manchuria, China proper occupying the second place.

The chief imports from Manchuria into the rest of China are the soya bean and its derivatives, coal and small amounts of groundnuts, raw silk , miscellaneous cereals and a very limited amount of iron, maize, wool, and timber. The chief exports to Manchuria from China proper are cotton piece goods, tobacco preparations, silken and other textiles, tea, cereals and seeds, raw cotton, paper and wheat flour.

Consequently China Proper relies on Manchuria for certain foodstuffs, most important of which is the soya bean and its derivatives, but her imports of minerals with the exception of coal and her imports of timber, animal products and raw materials for manufacturing purposes have in the past been slight. Furthermore, China Proper is able to use only a portion of Manchuria's favourable balance to offset its own unfavourable balance. It is able to do this not by virtue of its political affiliation as such, as is generally thought, but chiefly because the Manchurian Post Offices and Customs have been highly profitable institutions and because of the substantial remittances of Chinese settlers to their families in Shanghai and Hopei.

Comments.

The resources of Manchuria are great and as yet not fully ascertained. For their development they require population, capital, technical skill, organisation and internal security. The population is almost entirely supplied by China. Large numbers of the existing population were born in provinces of North China where their family ties are still very close. Capital, technical still and organisation have hitherto chiefly been provided by Japan in South Manchuria and by Russia north of Changchun. Other foreign countries to a much smaller degree have interests throughout the Three Provinces but principally in the large cities. Their representatives have exercised a conciliatory influence in the recent years of political tension, and will continue to do so, provided that Japan, as the dominating economic Power, does not attempt to monopolise the field. The all-important problem at the present time is the establishment of an administration, acceptable to the population and capable of supplying the last need—namely the maintenance of law and order.

No foreign Power could develop Manchuria or reap any benefit from an attempt to control it without the good-will and wholehearted co-operation of the Chinese masses which form the bulk of the population, tilling its soil, and supplying the labour for practically every enterprise in the country. Neither will China ever be free from anxiety and danger unless these northern Provinces cease to afford a battle ground for the conflicting ambitions of neighbouring Powers. It is as necessary therefore for China to satisfy the economic interests of Japan in this territory as for Japan to recognise the unalterably Chinese character of its population.

Maintenance of the Open Door.

Parallel to an understanding of this kind and in order to allow all interested Powers to co-operate in the development of Manchuria it seems essential that the principle of the Open Door should be maintained not only from the legal point of view but also in the actual practice of trade, industry and banking. Amongst foreign business-men in Manchuria other than Japanese there is a fear that Japanese business concerns will try to reap benefit from the present political position by other means than those of free competition. If this fear came to be justified, foreign interests would be discouraged and the population of Manchuria might be the first to suffer. The maintenance of a real Open Door manifested by free competition in the field of trade, investment, and finance, would be in the interest of both Japan and China. [1]

---

[1]　原编辑者注: In this connection it is necessary to mention the extraordinary extent to which goods are being smuggled into Manchuria, especially over the Korean border and through Dairen. Not only is this practice detrimental to the Customs revenue but it disorganises trade, and rightly or wrongly gives rise to the belief that the Power which has virtual control over the Customs Administration might discriminate against the trade of other Powers.

CHAPTER Ⅸ PRINCIPLES AND CONDITIONS OF SETTLEMENT

Review of previous chapters.

In the previous chapters of this Report, it has been shown that, though the issues between China and Japan were not in themselves incapable of solution by arbitral procedure, yet the handling of them by their respective Governments, especially those relating to Manchuria, had so embittered their relations as sooner or later to make a conflict inevitable. A sketch has been given of China as a nation in evolution with all the political upheavals, social disorders and disruptive tendencies inseparable from such a period of transition. It has been shown how seriously the rights and interests claimed by Japan have been affected by the weakness of the authority of the Central Government in China, and how anxious Japan has shown herself to keep Manchuria apart from the government of the rest of China. A brief survey of the respective policies of the Chinese, Russian and Japanese Governments in Manchuria has revealed the fact that the administration of these Provinces has more than once been declared by their rulers to be independent of the Central Government of China, yet no wish to be separated from the rest of China has ever been expressed by their population, which is overwhelmingly Chinese. Finally, we have examined carefully and thoroughly the actual events which took place on and subsequent to September 18th, 1931, and have expressed our opinion upon them.

Complexity of the problem.

A point has now been reached when attention can be concentrated on the future, and we would dismiss the past with this final reflection. It must be apparent to every reader of the preceding chapters that the issues involved in this conflict are not as simple as they are often represented to be. They are, on the contrary, exceedingly complicated, and only an intimate knowledge of all the facts, as well as of their historical background, should entitle anyone to express a definite opinion upon them. This is not a case in which one country has declared war on another country without previously exhausting the opportunities for conciliation provided in the Covenant of the League of Nations. Neither is it a simple case of the violation of the frontier of one country by the armed forces of a neighbouring country, because in Manchuria there are many features without an exact parallel in other parts of the world.

The dispute has arisen between two States, both Members of the League, concerning a territory the size of France and Germany combined, in which both claim to have rights and interests, only some of which are clearly defined by international law; a territory which, although legally an integral part of China, had a sufficiently autonomous character to carry on direct negotiations with Japan on the matters which lay at the root of this conflict.

Conditions in Manchuria unparalleled elsewhere.

Japan controls a railway and a strip of territory running from the sea right up into the heart of Manchuria, and she maintains for the protection of that property a force of about 10,000 soldiers, which she claims the right by treaty to increase, if necessary, up to 15,000. She also exercises the rights of jurisdiction over all her subjects in Manchuria and maintains consular police throughout the country.

Diversity of interpretations.

These facts must be considered by those who debate the issues. It is a fact that, without declaration of war, a large area of what was indisputably the Chinese territory has been forcibly seized and occupied by the armed forces of Japan and has, in consequence of this operation, been separated from and declared independent of the rest of China. The steps by which this was accomplished are claimed by Japan to have been consistent with the obligations of the Covenant of the League of Nations, the Kellogg Pact and the Nine-Power Treaty of Washington, all of which were designed to prevent action of this kind. Moreover, the operation which had only just begun when the matter was first brought to the notice of the League was completed during the following months and is held by the Japanese Government to be consistent with the assurances given by their representative at Geneva on September 30th and December 10th. The justification in this case has been that all the military operations have been legitimate acts of self-defence, the right of which is implicit in all the multilateral treaties mentioned above, and was not taken away by any of the resolutions of the Council of the League. Further, the administration which has been substituted for that of China in the Three Provinces is justified on the ground that its establishment was the act of the local population, who, by a spontaneous assertion of their independence, have severed all connection with China and established their own Government. Such a genuine independence movement, it is claimed, is not prohibited by any international treaty or by any of the resolutions of the Council of the League of Nations, and the fact of its having taken place has profoundly modified the application of the Nine-Power Treaty and entirely altered the whole character of the problem being investigated by the League.

It is this plea of justification which makes this particular conflict at once so complicated and so serious. It is not the function of our Commission to argue the issue, but we have tried to provide sufficient material to enable the League of Nations to settle the dispute consistently with the honour, dignity and national interest of both the contending parties. Criticism alone will not accomplish this: there must also be practical efforts at conciliation. We have been at pains to find out the truth regarding past events in Manchuria and to state it frankly; we recognise that this is only part, and by no means the most important part, of our work. We have throughout our mission offered to the Governments of both countries the help of the League of Nations in composing their differences, and we conclude it by offering to the League our suggestions for securing, consistently with justice and with peace, the permanent interest of China and Japan in Manchuria.

Unsatisfactory suggestions of settlement:

(1) Restoration of the *status quo ante*.

It must be clear from everything that we have already said that a mere restoration of the *status quo ante* would be no solution. Since the present conflict arose out of the conditions prevailing before last September, to restore these conditions would merely be to invite a repetition of the trouble. It would be to treat the whole question theoretically and to leave out of account the realities of the situation.

(2) The Maintenance of "Manchukuo"

From what we have said in the two preceding chapters, the maintenance and recognition of the present regime in Manchuria would be equally unsatisfactory. Such a solution does not appeal to us compatible with the fundamental principle of existing international obligations, nor with the good understanding between the two countries upon which peace in the Far East depends. It is opposed to the interests of China. It disregards the wishes of the people of Manchuria, and it is at least questionable whether it would ultimately serve the permanent interests of Japan.

About the feelings of the people of Manchuria towards the present regime there can really be no doubt; and China would not voluntarily accept as a lasting solution the complete separation of her Three Eastern Provinces. The analogy of the distant province of Outer Mongolia is not an entirely pertinent one, as Outer Mongolia is bound to China by no strong economic or social ties, and is sparsely inhabited by a population which is mainly non-Chinese. The situation in Manchuria is radically different from that in Outer Mongolia. The millions of Chinese farmers now settled permanently on the land have made Manchuria in many respects a simple extension of China south of the Wall. The Three Eastern Provinces have become almost as Chinese in race, culture and national sentiment as the neighbouring Provinces of Hopei and Shantung, from which most of the immigrants came.

Apart from this, past experience has shown that those who control Manchuria have exercised a considerable influence on the affairs of the rest of China—at least of North China—and possess unquestionable strategic and political advantages. To cut off these provinces from the rest of China, either legally or actually, would be to create for the future a serious irredentist problem which would endanger peace by keeping alive the hostility of China and rendering probable the continued boycott of Japanese goods.

The Commission received from the Japanese Government a clear and valuable statement of the vital interests of their country in Manchuria. Without exaggerating the economic dependence of Japan on Manchuria beyond the limits ascribed to it in a previous chapter, and certainly without suggesting that economic relationship entitles Japan to control the economic, still less the political, development of those provinces, we recognise the great importance of Manchuria in the economic development of Japan. Nor do we consider unreasonable her demand for the establishment of a stable Government which would be capable of maintaining the order necessary for the economic development of the country. But such conditions can only be securely and effectively guaranteed by an administration which is in conformity with the wishes of the population and which takes full account of their feelings and aspirations. And equally is it only in an atmosphere of external confidence and internal peace, very different from that now existing in the Far East, that the capital which is necessary for the rapid economic development of Manchuria will be forthcoming.

In spite of the pressure of increasing over-population, the Japanese have not as yet fully utilised their existing facilities for emigration, and the Japanese Government has not hitherto contemplated a large emigration of their people to Manchuria. But the Japanese do look to further industrialisation as a means to cope with the agrarian crisis and with the population problem. Such industrialisation would require further economic outlets and the only large and relatively sure markets that Japan can find are in Asia and particularly in China. Japan requires, not only the Manchurian, but the whole Chinese market, and the rise in the standard of living which will certainly follow the consolidation and modernisation of China should stimulate trade and raise the purchasing power of the Chinese market.

This economic *rapprochement* between Japan and China, which is of vital interest to Japan, is of equal interest to China, for China would find that a closer economic and technical collaboration with Japan would assist her in her primary task of national reconstruction. China could assist this *rapprochement* by restraining the more intolerant tendencies of her nationalism and by giving effective guarantees that, as soon as cordial relations were re-established, the practice of organised boycotts would not be revived. Japan, on her side, could facilitate this *rapprochement* by renouncing any attempt to solve the Manchurian problem by isolating it from the problem of her relations with China as a whole, in such a way as to make impossible the friendship and collaboration of China.

It may, however, be less economic considerations than anxiety for her own security which has determined the actions and policy of Japan in Manchuria. It is especially in this connection that her statesmen and military authorities are accustomed to speak of Manchuria as "the life-line of Japan". One can sympathise with such anxieties and try to appreciate the actions and motives of those who have to bear the heavy responsibility of securing the defence of their country against all eventualities. While acknowledging the interest of Japan in preventing Manchuria from serving as a base of operations directed against her own territory, and even her wish to be able to take all appropriate military measures if in certain circumstances the frontiers of Manchuria should be crossed by the forces of a foreign Power, it may still be questioned whether the military occupation of Manchuria for an indefinite period, involving, as it must, a heavy financial burden, is really the most effective way of insuring against this external danger; and whether, in the event of aggression having to be resisted in this way, the Japanese troops in Manchuria would not be seriously embarrassed if they were surrounded by a restive or rebellious population backed by a hostile China. It is surely in the interest of Japan to consider also other possible solutions of the problem of security, which would be more in keeping with the principles on which rests the present peace organisation of the world, and analogous to arrangements concluded by other great Powers in various parts of the world. She might even find it possible, with the sympathy and good-will of the rest of the world, and at no cost to herself, to obtain better security than she will obtain by the costly method she is at present adopting.

International interests.

Apart from China and Japan, other Powers of the world have also important interests to defend in this Sino-Japanese conflict. We have already referred to existing multilateral treaties, and any real and lasting solution by agreement must be compatible with the stipulations of these fundamental agreements, on which is based the peace organisation of the world. The considerations which actuated the representatives of the Powers at the Washington Conference are still valid. It is quite as much in the interests of the Powers now as it was in 1922 to assist the reconstruction of China and to maintain her sovereignty and her territorial and administrative integrity as indispensable to the maintenance of peace. Any disintegration of China might lead, perhaps rapidly, to serious international rivalries, which would become all the more bitter if they should happen to coincide with rivalries between divergent social systems. Finally, the interests of peace are the same the world over. Any loss of confidence in the application of the principles of the Covenant and of the Pact of Paris in any part of the world diminishes the value and efficacy of those principles everywhere.

Interests of U. S. S. R.

The Commission has not been able to obtain direct information as to the extent of the interests of the U. S. S. R. in Manchuria, nor to ascertain the views of the Government of the U. S. S. R. on the Manchurian question.

But, even without sources of direct information, it cannot overlook the part played by Russia in Manchuria nor the important interests which the U. S. S. R. have in that region as owners of the Chinese Eastern Railway and of the territory beyond its north and north-east frontiers. It is clear that any solution of the problem of Manchuria which ignored the important interests of the U. S. S. R. would risk a future breach of the peace and would not be permanent.

Conclusions.

These considerations are sufficient to indicate the lines on which a solution might be reached if the Governments of China and Japan could recognise the identity of their chief interests and were willing to make them include the maintenance of peace and the establishment of cordial relations with each other. As already stated, there is no question of returning to the conditions before September 1931. A satisfactory regime for the future might be evolved out of the present one without any violent change. In the next chapter, we offer certain suggestions for doing this, but we would first define the general principles to which any satisfactory solution should conform. They are the following:

Conditions of a satisfactory solution.

1. *Compatibility with the interests of both China and Japan.*

Both countries are Members of the League and each is entitled to claim the same consideration from the League. A solution from which both did not derive benefit would not be a gain to the cause of peace.

2. *Consideration for the interests of the U. S. S. R.*

To make peace between two of the neighbouring countries without regard for the interests of the third would be neither just nor wise, nor in the interests of peace.

3. *Conformity with existing multilateral treaties.*

Any solution should conform to the provisions of the Covenant of the

League of Nations, the Pact of Paris, and the Nine-Power Treaty of Washington.

4. *Recognition of Japan's interests in Manchuria.*

The rights and interests of Japan in Manchuria are facts which cannot be ignored, and any solution which failed to recognise them and to take into account also the historical associations of Japan with that country would not be satisfactory.

5. *The establishment of new treaty relations between China and Japan.*

A re-statement of the respective rights, interests and responsibilities of both countries in Manchuria in new treaties, which shall be part of the settlement by agreement, is desirable if future friction is to be avoided and mutual confidence and co-operation are to be restored.

6. *Effective provision for the settlement of future disputes.*

As a corollary to the above, it is necessary that provision should be made for facilitating the prompt settlement of minor disputes as they arise.

7. *Manchurian autonomy.*

The government in Manchuria should be modified in such a way as to secure, consistently with the sovereignty and administrative integrity of China, a large measure of autonomy designed to meet the local conditions and special characteristics of the Three Provinces. The new civil regime must be so constituted and conducted as to satisfy the essential requirements of good government.

8. *Internal order and security against external aggression.*

The internal order of the country should be secured by an effective local gendarmerie force, and security against external aggression should be provided by the withdrawal of all armed forces other than gendarmerie, and by the conclusion of a treaty of non-aggression between the countries interested.

9. *Encouragement of an economic rapprochement between China and Japan.*

For this purpose, a new commercial treaty between the two countries is desirable. Such a treaty should aim at placing on an equitable basis the commercial relations between the two countries and bringing them into conformity with their improved political relations.

10. *International co-operation in Chinese reconstruction.*

Since the present political instability in China is an obstacle to friendship with Japan and an anxiety to the rest of the world (as the maintenance of peace in the Far East is a matter of international concern), and since the conditions enumerated above cannot be fulfilled without a strong Central Government in China, the final requisite for a satisfactory solution is temporary international co-operation in the internal reconstruction of China, as suggested by the late Dr. Sun Yat-sen.

Results which would follow from the fulfilment of these conditions.

If the present situation could be modified in such a way as to satisfy these conditions and embody these ideas, China and Japan would have achieved a solution of their difficulties which might be made the starting-point of a new era of close understanding and political co-operation between them. If such a *rapprochement* is not secured, no solution, whatever its terms, can really be fruitful. Is it really impossible to contemplate a new relationship even in this hour of crisis Young Japan is clamorous for strong measures in China and a policy of thoroughness in Manchuria. Those who make these demands are tired of the delays and pin-pricks of the pre-September period; they are impetuous and impatient to gain their end. But, even in Japan, appropriate means must be found for the attainment of every end. After making the acquaintance of some of the more ardent exponents of this "positive" policy, and those especially who, with undoubted idealism and great personal devotion, have constituted themselves the pioneers of a delicate undertaking in the "Manchukuo" regime, it is impossible not to realise that, at the heart of the problem for Japan, lies her anxiety concerning the political development of modern China, and the future to which it is tending. This anxiety has led to action with the object of controlling that development and steering its course in directions which will secure the economic interests of Japan and satisfy strategic requirements for the defence of her Empire.

Japanese opinion is nevertheless vaguely conscious that it is no longer practicable to have two separate policies, one for Manchuria and one for the rest of China. Even with her Manchurian interests as a goal, therefore, Japan might recognise and welcome sympathetically the renaissance of Chinese national sentiment, might make friends with it, guide it in her direction and offer it support, if only to ensure that it does not seek support elsewhere.

In China, too, as thoughtful men have come to recognise that the vital problem, the real national problem, for their country is the reconstruction and modernisation of the State, they cannot fail to realise that this policy of reconstruction and modernisation, already initiated with so much promise of success, necessitates for its fulfilment the cultivation of friendly relations with all countries, and above all with that great nation which is their nearest neighbour. China needs, in political and economic matters, the co-operation of all the leading Powers, but especially valuable to her would be the friendly attitude of the Japanese Government and the economic co-operation of Japan in Manchuria. All the other claims of her newly awakened nationalism—legitimate and urgent though they may be—should be subordinated to this one dominating need for the effective internal reconstruction of the State.

CHAPTER X   CONSIDERATIONS AND SUGGESTIONS TO THE COUNCIL

Suggestions to facilitate a final solution.

It is not the function of the Commission to submit directly to the Governments of China and Japan recommendations for the solution of the present dispute. But, in order "to facilitate the final solution of existing causes of dispute between the two countries", to quote the words used by M. Briand when explaining to the Council the text of the resolution which originated the Commission, we now offer to the League of Nations, as the result of our studies, suggestions designed to help the appropriate organ of the League to draw up definite proposals for submission to the parties to the dispute. It should be understood that these suggestions are intended as an illustration of one way in which the conditions we have laid down in the preceding chapter might be met. They are mainly concerned with broad principles; they leave many details to be filled in and are susceptible of considerable modification by the parties to the dispute if they are willing to accept some solution on these lines.

Even if the formal recognition of "Manchukuo" by Japan should take place before our Report is considered in Geneva—an eventuality which we cannot ignore—we do not think that our work will have been rendered valueless. We believe that, in any case, the Council would find that our Report contains suggestions which would be helpful for its decisions or for its recommendations to the two great Powers concerned, with the object of satisfying their vital interests in Manchuria.

It is with this object that, whilst bearing in mind the principles of the League of Nations, the spirit and letter of the Treaties concerning China and the general interests of peace, we have not overlooked existing realities, and have taken account of the administrative machinery existing and in process of evolution in the Three Eastern Provinces. It would be the function of the Council, in the paramount interest of world peace, whatever may be the eventuality, to decide how the suggestions made in our Report may be extended and applied to events which are still developing from day to day, always with the object of securing a durable understanding between China and Japan by utilising all the sound forces, whether in ideals or persons, whether in thought or action, which are at present fermenting in Manchuria.

Invitation to the parties to discuss settlement.

We suggest, in the first place, that the Council of the League should invite the Governments of China and Japan to discuss a solution of their dispute on the lines indicated in the last chapter.

An Advisory Conference.

If the invitation is accepted, the next step would be the summoning as soon as possible of an Advisory Conference, to discuss and to recommend detailed proposals for the constitution of a special regime for the administration of the Three Eastern Provinces.

Such conference, it is suggested, might be composed of representatives of the Chinese and Japanese Governments and of two delegations representing the local population, one selected in a manner to be prescribed by the Chinese Government and one selected in a manner to be prescribed by the Japanese Government. If agreed by the parties, the assistance of neutral observers might be secured.

If the conference were unable to reach agreement on any particular point, it would submit to the Council the point of difference, and the Council would then attempt to secure an agreed settlement on these points.

Simultaneously with the sitting of the Advisory Conference, the matters at issue between Japan and China relating to respective rights and interests should be discussed separately, in this case also, if so agreed, with the help of neutral observers.

Finally, we suggest that the results of these discussions and negotiations should be embodied in four separate instruments:

1. A Declaration by the Government of China constituting a special administration for the Three Eastern Provinces, in the terms recommended by the Advisory Conference;

2. A Sino-Japanese Treaty dealing with Japanese interests;

3. A Sino-Japanese Treaty of Conciliation and Arbitration, Non-Aggression and Mutual Assistance.

4. A Sino-Japanese Commercial Treaty.

It is suggested that, before the meeting of the Advisory Conference, the broad outlines of the form of administration to be considered by that body should be agreed upon between the parties, with the assistance of the Council. Among the matters to be considered at that stage are the following:

The place of meeting of the Advisory Conference, the nature of the representation, and whether or not neutral observers are desired;

The principle of the maintenance of the territorial and administrative integrity of China and the grant of a large measure of autonomy to Manchuria;

The policy of creating a special gendarmerie as the sole method of maintaining internal order;

The principle of settling the various matters in dispute by means of the separate treaties suggested;

The grant of an amnesty to all those who have taken part in the recent political developments in Manchuria.

When once these broad principles have been agreed upon beforehand the fullest possible discretion as regards the details would be left to the representatives of the parties at the Advisory Conference or when negotiating the treaties. Further reference to the Council of the League of Nations would only take place in the event of failure to agree.

Advantages claimed for the procedure.

Among the advantages of this procedure, it is claimed that, while it is consistent with the sovereignty of China, it will enable effective and practical measures to be taken to meet the situation in Manchuria as it exists to-day and, at the same time, allow for such modifications hereafter as the changes in the internal situation in China may warrant. Notice, for instance, has been taken in this Report of certain administrative and fiscal changes which have either been proposed or actually carried out in Manchuria recently, such as the re-organisation of provincial governments, the creation of a central bank, the employment of foreign advisers. These features might be retained with advantage by the Advisory Conference. The presence at the conference of representatives of the inhabitants of Manchuria, selected in some such way as we have suggested, should also facilitate the passage from the present to the new regime.

The autonomous regime contemplated for Manchuria is intended to apply to the three provinces of Liaoning (Fengtien), Kirin and Heilungkiang only. The rights at present enjoyed by Japan in the province of Jehol (Eastern Inner Mongolia) would be dealt with in the treaty on the subject of Japanese interests.

The four Instruments can now be considered seriatim:

1. The Declaration.

The final proposals of the Advisory Conference would be submitted to the Chinese Government, and the Chinese Government would embody them in a Declaration, which would be transmitted to the League of Nations and to the signatory Powers of the Nine-Power Treaty. The Members of the League and the signatory Powers of the Nine-Power Treaty would take note of this Declaration, which would be stated to have for the Chinese Government the binding character of an international engagement.

The conditions under which subsequent revision of the Declaration, if required, might take place would be laid down in the Declaration itself, as agreed to in accordance with the procedure suggested hereabove.

The Declaration would distinguish between the powers of the Central Government of China in the Three Eastern Provinces and those of the autonomous local Government.

It is suggested that the powers to be reserved to the Central Government should be the following:

Powers to be reserved to the Central Government.

1. The control of general treaty and foreign relations not otherwise

provided for; it being understood that the Central Government would not enter into any international engagements inconsistent with the terms of the Declaration.

2. The control of the Customs, the post office, and the salt Gabelle, and possibly of the administration of the stamp duty and the tobacco and wine taxes. The equitable division, between the Central Government and the Three Eastern Provinces, of the net income from these revenues would be determined by the Advisory Conference.

3. The power of appointment, at least in the first instance, of the Chief Executive of the Government of the Three Eastern Provinces in accordance with the procedure to be laid down in the Declaration. Vacancies would be filled in the same way, or by some system of selection in the Three Eastern Provinces, to be agreed upon by the Advisory Conference and inserted in the Declaration.

4. The power of issuing to the Chief Executive the carrying out of the international engagements entered into by the Central Government of China in matters under the administration of the autonomous Government of the Three Eastern Provinces.

5. Any additional powers agreed upon by the Conference.

Powers of the local government.

All other powers would be vested in the autonomous Government of the Three Eastern Provinces.

Expression of local opinion.

Some practical system might be devised to secure an expression of the opinion of the people on the policy of the Government, possibly through the traditional agency of the Chambers of Commerce, Guilds and other civil organisations.

Minorities.

Some provision should also be made to safeguard the interests of White Russians and other minorities.

Gendarmerie.

It is suggested that a special gendarmerie should be organised, with the collaboration of foreign instructors, which would be the only armed force within the Three Eastern Provinces. The organisation of the gendarmerie should either be completed within a period to be specified in advance, or the time of its completion should be determined in accordance with a procedure to be laid down in the Declaration. As this special corps would be the only armed force in the territory of the Three Eastern Provinces, its organisation, when completed, should be followed by the retirement from this territory of all other armed forces, including any special bodies of police or railway guards, whether Chinese or Japanese.

Foreign advisers.

An adequate number of foreign advisers would be appointed by the Chief Executive of the autonomous Government, of whom a substantial proportion should be Japanese. The details would be worked out by the procedure described above and would be stated in the Declaration. Nationals of small States, as well as of the Great Powers, would be eligible.

The appointment of two foreigners of different nationalities to have supervision of (1) the constabulary and (2) the fiscal administration would be made by the Chief Executive from a panel submitted by the Council of the League. These two officials would have extensive powers during the period of organization and trial of the new regime. The powers of the advisers would be defined in the Declaration.

The appointment of one foreigner as a general adviser to the Central Bank of the Three Eastern Provinces would be made by the Chief Executive from a panel submitted by the Board of Directors of the Bank for

International Settlements.

The employment of foreign advisers and officials is in conformity with the policy of the founder of the Chinese Nationalist Party and with that of the present National Government. It will not, we hope, be difficult for Chinese opinion to recognize that the actual situation and the complexity of the foreign interests, rights and influences in those provinces require special measures in the interests of peace and good government. But it cannot be too strongly emphasised that the presence of the foreign advisers and officials here suggested, including those who, during the period of the organisation of the new regime, must exercise exceptionally wide powers, merely represents a form of international co-operation. They must be selected in a manner acceptable to the Chinese Government and one which is consistent with the sovereignty of China. When appointed, they must regard themselves as the servants of the Government employing them, as has always been the case in the past with the foreigners employed in the Customs and Postal administration or with the technical organisations of the League that have collaborated with China. In this connection, the following passage in the speech of Count Uchida in the Japanese Diet on August 25th, 1932, is of interest:

"Our own Government, since the Meiji Restoration, has employed many foreigners as advisers or as regular officials; their number, for instance, in the year 1875 or thereabout exceeded 500. "

The point must also be stressed that the appointment of a relatively large number of Japanese advisers, in an atmosphere of Sino-Japanese co-operation, would enable such officials to contribute the training and knowledge specially suited to local conditions. The goal to be kept in view throughout the period of transition is the creation of a civil service composed of Chinese, who will ultimately make the employment of foreigners unnecessary.

2. The Sino-Japanese Treaty dealing with Japanese Interests.

Full discretion would of course be left to those who will negotiate the three suggested treaties between China and Japan, but it may be useful to indicate the matters with which it is suggested they should deal.

The treaty dealing with Japanese interests in the Three Eastern Provinces and with some Japanese interests in the Province of Jehol would have to deal principally with certain economic rights of Japanese nationals and with railway questions. The aims of this treaty should be:

(1) The free participation of Japan in the economic development of Manchuria, which would not carry with it a right to control the country either economically or politically;

(2) The continuance in the Province of Jehol of such rights as Japan now enjoys there;

(3) An extension to the whole of Manchuria of the right to settle and lease land, coupled with some modification of the principle of extra-territoriality;

(4) An agreement regarding the operation of the railways.

Japanese rights of settlement.

Hitherto, the rights of settlement of Japanese nationals have been confined to South Manchuria, though no definite boundary line between North and South Manchuria has ever been fixed, and to Jehol. These rights have been exercised under conditions which China found unacceptable and this caused continued friction and conflicts. Extra-territorial status as regards taxation and justice was claimed both for the Japanese and the Koreans, and in the case of the latter there were special stipulations which were ill-defined and the subject of disputes. From evidence given before the Commission, we have reason to believe that China would be willing to extend to the whole of Manchuria the present limited right of settlement, provided it was not accompanied by extra-territorial status, the effect of which, it was claimed, would be to create a Japanese State in the heart of a

Chinese territory.

It is obvious that the right of settlement and extra-territoriality are closely associated. It is, however, equally clear that the Japanese would not consent to abandon their extra-territorial status until the administration of justice and finance had reached a very much higher standard than has hitherto prevailed in Manchuria.

Two methods of compromise have suggested themselves. One is that the existing rights of settlement, accompanied by extra-territorial status, should be maintained, and that such rights should be extended both to Japanese and Koreans in North Manchuria and Jehol without extra-territorial status. The other is that the Japanese should be granted the right to settle anywhere in Manchuria and Jehol with extra-territorial status, and that the Koreans should have the same rights without extra-territorial status. Both proposals have some advantages to recommend them and both have rather serious objections. It is obvious that the most satisfactory solution of the problem is to make the administration of these Provinces so efficient that extra-territorial status will no longer be desired. It is with this object that we recommend that at least two foreign advisers, one of whom should be of Japanese nationality, should be attached to the Supreme Court, and other advisers might with advantage be attached to other Courts. The opinions of these advisers might be made public in all cases in which the Courts were called upon to adjudicate on matters in which foreign nationals were involved. We also think that, in the period of re-organisation, some foreign supervision of the administration of finance is desirable and, in dealing with the Declaration, we have presented some suggestions to that effect.

A further safeguard would be provided by the establishment, under the treaty of conciliation, of an arbitration tribunal to deal with any complaints which the Chinese or Japanese Governments might bring in their own names or in those of their nationals.

The decision of this complicated and difficult question must rest with the parties negotiating the treaty, but the present system of foreign protection, when applied to a minority group as numerous as the Koreans, who are, moreover, increasing in number and who live in such close touch with the Chinese population, is bound to produce many occasions of irritation, leading to local incidents and foreign intervention. In the interests of peace, it is desirable that this fruitful source of friction should be removed.

Any extension of the rights of settlement in the case of Japanese would apply on the same conditions to the nationals of all other Powers which enjoy the benefits of a "most-favoured-nation" clause, provided that those Powers whose nationals enjoy extra-territorial rights enter into a similar treaty with China.

Railways.

As regards railways, it has been pointed out in CHAPTER Ⅲ that there has been little or no co-operation in the past between the Chinese and Japanese railway builders and authorities directed to achieving a comprehensive and mutually beneficial railway plan. It is obvious that, if future friction is to be avoided, provisions must be made in the treaty at present under discussion for bringing to an end the competitive system of the past, and substituting a common understanding as regards freights and tariffs on the various systems. The subject is discussed in the special study No. 1 annexed to this Report. In the opinion of the Commission, there are two possible solutions, which could be considered either as alternatives or as stages to one final solution. The first, which is the more limited in scope, is a working agreement between the Chinese and Japanese railway administrations, which would facilitate their co-operation. China and Japan might agree to manage their respective railway systems in Manchuria on the principle of co-operation, and a joint Sino-Japanese Railway Commission, with at least one foreign adviser, might exercise functions analogous to those of boards which exist in some other countries. A more thorough remedy would be provided by an amalgamation of the Chinese and Japanese railway interests. Such an amalgamation, if it could be agreed upon, would be the true mark of that Sino-Japanese economic collaboration to secure which is one of the objects of this Report. While safeguarding the interests of China, it would place at the disposal of all the railways in Manchuria the benefit of the great technical experience of the South Manchuria Railway and could be evolved without difficulty from the system which has been applied to the railways of Manchuria in the last few months. It might even pave the way in the future to some wider international agreement which might include the Chinese Eastern Railway. Though a fairly detailed description of such an amalgamation is to be found in the annex as an example of the sort of thing that might be done, only direct negotiations between the parties could evolve a detailed scheme. Such a solution of the railway question would make the South Manchuria Railway a purely commercial enterprise, and the security provided by the special corps of gendarmerie, when once this body was fully organised, would enable the Railway Guards to be withdrawn, thus saving a considerable item of expense. If this is done, it would be well that special land regulations and a special municipal administration should previously be instituted in the railway area in order to safeguard the vested interests of the South Manchuria Railway and of Japanese nationals.

If a treaty on these lines could be agreed upon, a legal basis for Japanese rights in the Three Eastern Provinces and in Jehol would have been found which would be at least as beneficial to Japan as the present treaties and agreements, and one which would be more acceptable to China. China might then find no difficulty in recognising all the definite grants made to Japan by such treaties and agreements as those of 1915, unless abrogated or modified by the new treaty. All minor rights claimed by Japan, the validity of which may be open to dispute, should be the subject of agreement. In case of disagreement, resort should be made to the procedure outlined in the treaty of conciliation.

3. **The Sino-Japanese Treaty of Conciliation and Arbitration, Non-Aggression and Mutual Assistance.**

It is not necessary to describe in any detail the subject-matter of this treaty, of which there are many precedents and existing examples.

Such a treaty would provide for a board of conciliation, whose functions would be to assist in the solution of any difficulties as they arise between the Governments of China and Japan. It would also establish an arbitration tribunal composed of persons with judicial experience and the necessary knowledge of the Far East. This tribunal would deal with any disputes between the Chinese and Japanese Governments regarding the interpretation of the declaration or of the new treaties, and with such other categories of disputes as might be specified in the treaty of conciliation.

Finally, in conformity with the provisions for non-aggression and mutual assistance inserted in the treaty, the contracting parties should agree that Manchuria should gradually become a demilitarized area. With this object, it would be provided that, after the organisation of the gendarmerie had been effected, any violation of the demilitarized territory by either of the parties or by a third party would constitute an act of aggression entitling the other party, or both parties in the case of a third-party attack, to take whatever measures might be deemed advisable to defend the demilitarised territory, without prejudice to the right of the Council of the League to take action under the Covenant.

If the Government of the U. S. S. R. desired to participate in the non-aggression and mutual assistance section of such a treaty, the appropriate clauses could be embodied in a separate tripartite agreement.

4. **The Sino-Japanese Commercial Treaty.**

The commercial treaty would naturally have as its object the establishment of conditions which would encourage as much as possible the exchange of goods between China and Japan, while safeguarding the existing treaty rights of other countries. This treaty should also contain an undertaking by the Chinese Government to take all measures within its power to forbid and repress organised boycott movements against Japanese trade, without prejudice to the individual rights of Chinese consumers.

Comments.

The above suggestions and considerations regarding the objects of the proposed Declaration and treaties are submitted for the consideration of the Council of the League. Whatever may be the details of future agreements, the essential point is that negotiations should be begun as soon as possible and should be conducted in a spirit of mutual confidence.

Our work is finished.

Manchuria for a year past has been given over to strife and turmoil.

The population of a large, fertile and rich country has been subjected to conditions of distress such as it has probably never experienced before.

The relations between China and Japan are those of war in disguise, and the future is full of anxiety.

We have reported the circumstances which have created these conditions.

Everyone is fully aware of the gravity of the problem which confronts the League of Nations and of the difficulties of the solution.

At the moment of concluding our Report, we read in the Press two statements by the Foreign Ministers of China and Japan, from each of which we would extract one point of the utmost importance.

On August 28th, Mr. Lo Wen Kan declared at Nanking:

"China is confident that any reasonable proposal for the settlement of the present situation will necessarily be compatible with the letter and spirit of the Covenant of the League of Nations and the anti-war Pact, and the Nine-Power Treaty, as well as with China's sovereign power, and will also effectively secure a durable peace in the Far East."

On August 30th, Count Uchida is reported to have declared at Tokyo:

"The Government considers the question of Sino-Japanese relations as more important than the question of Manchuria and Mongolia. "

We cannot close our Report more appropriately than by reproducing here the thought underlying these two statements: as exactly does it correspond with the evidence we have collected, with our own study of the problem, and consequently with our own convictions, so confident are we that the policy indicated by these declarations, if promptly and effectively applied, could not fail to lead to a satisfactory solution of the Manchurian question in the best interests of the two great countries of the Far East and of humanity in general.

Signed at Peiping, September 4th, 1932.

LYTTON.

ALDROVANDI.

H. CLAUDEL.

Frank McCOY.

SCHNEE.

APPENDIX. [①]

ITINERARY IN THE FAR EAST OF THE LEAGUE OF NATIONS COMMISSION OF ENQUIRY.

(*Council Resolution of December 10th, 1931.*)

(See also Maps Nos. 13 and 14.)

Date	Arrived or departed	Place	Means of travel	Remarks	Map symbol	Personnel
February 29th	Arr.	**Yokohama**	Water	S. S. *President Coolidge*	1	Commissioners, Pelt, von Kotze, Pastuhov, Astor, Jouvelet, Biddle. Joined by Haas (arrived February 25th, from Shanghai).
	Left	**Yokohama**	Rail			
	Arr.	**Tokyo**				
February 29th to March 8th		**Tokyo**			1	Joined by Aoki (February 29th). Dropped Haas (March 8th, followed party to Osaka, March 9th).
March 8th	Left	**Tokyo**	Rail		1	
9th	Arr.	**Kyoto**				
10th	Left	"[②]				
	Arr.	**Nara**				
	Left	"				

---

① 编者按：英文版本的《国联调查团报告书》里面有关于国联调查团远东调查的行程，但在中文和日文版本里面没有相应内容。

② 编者按：此符号为原文所有，意思是指：同上，此处即指代上列中的 Kyoto。下同。

(续表)

Date	Arrived or departed	Place	Means of travel	Remarks	Map symbol	Personnel
	Arr.	**Osaka**				Rejoined by Haas (from Tokyo).
11th	Left	**Osaka**	Motor and cable car	Via Mt. Rokko		
	Arr.	**Kobe**				
	Left	"	Water	S. S. *President Adams*		
14th	Arr.	**Shanghai**				
14th to 26th		**Shanghai**			1	Joined by Charrère, Wou (March 14th) and Young (March 18th, from Peiping). Dropped Aoki (March 25th, returned to Tokyo) and Haas (March 26th; followed party to blanking, March 28th).
March 26th	Left	**Shanghai**	Rail		1	Claudel, McCoy, Schnee, Young, Blakeslee, von Kotze, Jouvelet, Biddle.
27th	Arr.	**Hangchow**	Motor			
	Left	"				
	Arr.	**Ihsing**				
	Left	"				
	Arr.	**Nanking**				

（续表）

Date	Arrived or departed	Place	Means of travel	Remarks	Map symbol	Personnel
26th	Left	**Shanghai**	Water	S. S. *Toongwo*	1	Lytton, Aldrovandi, Pelt, Pastuhov, Astor, Charrère, Wou.
27th	Arr.	**Nanking**				
March 27th to April 1st		**Nanking**			1	Rejoined by Haas (March 29th, form Shanghai). Dropped Young and Astor (April 1st; see A, below).
April 1st	Left	**Nanking**	Air		A	Young, Astor.
	Arr.	**Hankow**				
2nd	Left	”				
	Arr.	**Chungking**				
3rd	Left	”				
	Arr.	**Ichang**				
4th	Left	”				
	Arr.	**Hankow**				Rejoined main party
1st	Left	**Nanking**	Water	S. S. *Loongwoo*	1	Commissioners, Haas, Blakeslee, Pelt, von Kotze, Pastuhov, Jouvelet, Charrère, Wou, Biddle.
3rd	Arr.	**Kiukiang**				
	Left	”				
4th	Arr.	**Hankow**				Rejoined by Young and Astor (See A, above).

（续表）

Date	Arrived or departed	Place	Means of travel	Remarks	Map symbol	Personnel
5th	Left	**Hankow**				
6th	Arr.	**Kiuliang**				
	Left	"				
7th	Arr.	**Pukow**				
	Left	"	Rail			
8th	Arr.	**Tsinan**				
	Left	"				
9th	Arr.	**Tientsin**				
	Left	"				
	Arr.	**Peiping**				
9th to 19th		**Peiping**			1	Joined by Angelino (April 14th, from Java).
19th	Left	**Peiping**				
20th	Arr.	**Chinwangtao**				
20th	Left	**Chinwangtao**	Water	Chinese and Japanese warships	2	Lytton, Claudel, Schnee, Pelt, Pastuhov, Astor, Jouvelet, Wou.
	Arr.	**Dairen**				
21st	Left	"	Rail			
	Arr.	**Mukden**				
April 20th	Left	**Chinwangtao**	Rail		2	Aldrovandi, McCoy, Haas, Angelino, Young, Blakeslee, von Kotze, Charrère, Biddle.
21st	Arr.	**Shanhaikwan**				
	Left	"				

（续表）

Date	Arrived or departed	Place	Means of travel	Remarks	Map symbol	Personnel
	Arr.	**Chinwangtao**				
	Left	"				
	Arr.	**Shanhaikwan**				
	Left	"				
	Arr.	**Mukden**				
April 21st to May 2nd		**Mukden**			2	Joined by Haim (April 21st; arrived April 16th, from Canada), Moss (May 1st, form Weihaiwei) and de Peyre (May 1st, from Kobe).
May 2nd	Left	**Mukden**	Rail		2	Commissioners, Haas, Angelino, Hiam, Young, Blakeslee, Pelt, von Kotze, Pastuhov, Astor, Jouvelet, Moss, de Peyre, Charrère, Wou, Biddle.
	Arr.	**Kungchuling**				
	Left	**Kungchuling**				
	Arr.	**Changchun**				
2nd to 7th		**Changchun**				
7th	Left	**Changchun**				
	Arr.	**Kirin**				
	Left	"				
	Arr.	**Changchun**				
7th to 9th		**Changchun**				
9th	Left	**Changchun**				

（续表）

Date	Arrived or departed	Place	Means of travel	Remarks	Map symbol	Personnel
	Arr.	**Harbin**				
9th to 21st		**Harbin**			2	Joined by Dennery（May 9th；arrived May 6th,from Paris），Dorfman（May 10th；arrived May 9th, from Tokyo）. Dropped: von Kotze, Hiam, Astor, Moss, Biddle,（May 21st；see B below）; Young（May 21st：followed to Mukden, May 23rd）；Pelt, Dennery, Dorfman（May 21st；followed to Changchun and Mukden（May 23rd）.
May 21st	Left	**Harbin**	Rail		2	Commissioners, Haas, Angelino, Blakeslee, Pastuhov, Jouvelet, Charrère, Wou, de Peyre.
	Arr.	**Changchun**				
	Left	”				
	Arr.	**Mukden**				
22nd	Left	**Harbin**	Air		B	Von Kotze, Hiam, Astor, Moss, Biddle.
22nd to 24th		**Tsitsihar**				
24th	Left	**Tsitsihar**	Rail			
	Arr.	**Taonan**				

（续表）

Date	Arrived or departed	Place	Means of travel	Remarks	Map symbol	Personnel
	Left	"				
25th	Arr.	**Mukden**				
21st to 25th		**Mukden**			2	Departed: de Peyre (May 21st, for Kobe). Rejoined by: Young (May 24th, from Harbin); Pelt, Dennery, Dorfman (May 25th, from Harbin and Changchun); von Kotze, Hiam, Astor, Moss, Biddle (May 25th; see B, above).
25th	Left	**Mukden**	Rail		2	Commissioners, Haas, Angelino, Hiam, Young, Blakeslee, Pelt, Dennery, Dorfman, von Kotze, Pastuhov, Astor, Jouvelet, Moss, Charrère, Wou, Biddle.
26th	Arr.	**Dairen**				
27th	Left	"	Motor			
	Arr.	**Port Arthur**				
	Left	"				
	Arr.	**Dairen**				
26th to 30th		**Dairen**				Dropped: Angelino, Young, Pastuhov (May 30th; preceded party to Peiping, via Tangku).

Date	Arrived or departed	Place	Means of travel	Remarks	Map symbol	Personnel
30th	Left	**Dairen**	Rail		2	Commissioners, Haas, Blakeslee, Pelt, Dennery, Dorfman, von Kotze, Astor, Jouvelet, Moss, Charrère, Wou, Biddle.
31st	Arr.	**Anshan**				Dropped Dennnery (followed to Mukden, May 31st).
	Left	"				
	Arr,	**Mukden**				
May 30th to June 4th		**Mukden**			2	Rejoined by Dennery (May 31st, from Anshan). Dropped; Dennery (June 1st, preceded party to Fushun); Haas, Hiam(June 1st; preceded party to Peiping, via Shanhaikwan); Pelt, Dorfman (June 2nd; see C, below).
June 1st	Left	**Mukden**	Rail		2	Commissioners, von Kotze, Blakeslee, Pelt, Dennery, Dorfman, Astor, Jouvelet, Moss, Charrère, Wou, Biddle.

(续表)

Date	Arrived or departed	Place	Means of travel	Remarks	Map symbol	Personnel
	Arr.	**Fushun**				Rejoined by Dennery (preceded party from Mukden).
	Left	"				Dropped Dennnery (proceeded to Dairen).
	Arr.	**Mukden**				
2nd	Left	**Mukden**	Rail		C	Pelt, Dorfman.
3rd	Arr.	**Dairen**				Rejoined by Dennery (arrived June 2nd, from Fushun).
3rd to 6th		**Dairen**				
6th	Left	**Dairen**	Water	S. S. *Saiisu Maru*		
7th	Arr.	**Tangku**				
	Left	"	Rail			
	Arr.	**Peiping**				
4th	Left	**Mukden**	Rail		2	Commissioners, von Kotze, Blakeslee, Astor, Jouvelet, Moss, Charrère, Wou, Biddle.
	Arr.	**Chinchow**				
	Left	"				
	Arr.	**Shanhaikwan**				
	Left	"				

（续表）

Date	Arrived or departed	Place	Means of travel	Remarks	Map symbol	Personnel
	Arr.	**Peitaiho Beach**				
5th	Left	"				
	Arr.	**Peiping**				
5th to 28th		**Peiping**			3	Departed: Moss (June 26th, for Weihaiwei). Dropped: Dennery (June 25th, preceded party to Tientsin); Dorfman (June 27th; see D, below).
June 8th	Left	**Peiping**	Rail		3	Lytton, Aldrovandi, Schnee, Charrère, Biddle.
9th	Arr.	**Tsingtao**				
10th	Left	"				
11th	Arr.	**Taian**				
	Left	"				
12th	Arr.	**Peiping**				
27th	Left	**Peiping**	Rail		D	Dorfman
29th	Arr.	**Nanking**				
	Left	"				
30th	Arr.	**Shanghai**				
June 30th to July 15th		**Shanghai**				
July 15th	Left	**Shanghai**				
17th	Arr.	**Peiping**				

Date	Arrived or departed	Place	Means of travel	Remarks	Map symbol	Personnel
June 28th	Left	**Peiping**	Rail		4	Commissioners, Haas, Young, Blakeslee, Pelt, Astor, Jouvelet, Charrère, Biddle.
	Arr.	**Tientsin**				Rejoined by Dennery (arrived June 25th, from Peiping).
	Left	”				
29th	Arr.	**Shanhaikwan**				
	Left	”				
	Arr.	**Mukden**				
30th	Left	”				Dropped Pelt (see G, below).
	Arr.	**Antung**				
	Left	”				
July 1st	Arr.	**Keijo**				
2nd	Left	”				
	Arr.	**Fushun**				
	Left	”	Water	S. S. *Shokei Maru*		
3rd	Arr.	**Shimonoseki**				
	Left	”	Rail			
4th	Arr.	**Tokyo**				
June 28th to July 20th		Peiping			E	Angelino, Hiam, Dorfman, von Kotze, Pastuhov, Wou. Dropped Hiam (June 29th; see F, below), von

（续表）

Date	Arrived or departed	Place	Means of travel	Remarks	Map symbol	Personnel
						Kotze (July 2nd, see H, below), Pastuhov (July 4th, followed main party to Tokyo). Rejoined by Pelt (July 10th; see G, below). Dropped Pelt (July 19th, proceeded to Tsinan by air).
June 29th	Left	**Peiping**	Rail		F	Hiam.
July 1st	Arr.	**Shanghai**				
4th	Left	"	Water	S. S. *Empress of Japan*		
6th	Arr.	**Kobe**				
	Left	"	Rail			
	Arr.	**Tokyo**				Rejoined main party
June 30th	Left	**Mukden**	Rail		G	Pelt
July 1st	Arr.	**Changchun**				
	Left	"				
2nd	Arr.	**Harbin**				
2nd to 7th		**Harbin**				
7th	Left	**Harbin**				
8th	Arr.	**Mukden**				
9th	Left	"				
10th	Arr.	**Peiping**				

（续表）

Date	Arrived or departed	Place	Means of travel	Remarks	Map symbol	Personnel
2nd	Left	**Peiping**	Air		H	von Kotze
	Arr.	**Shanghai**				
2nd to 6th		**Shanghai**				
6th	Left	**Shanghai**				
	Arr.	**Peiping**				
4th to 16th		**Tokyo**			4	Rejoined by Aoki (July 4th; arrived March30tth, from Shanghai), Hiam (July 6th; see F, above), Pastuhov (July 8th, from Peiping). Departed: Hiam (July 8th, for Canada). Dropped Lytton (July 15th, preceded party to Kobe, by water from Yokohama), Haas (July 15th, preceded party to Kyoto), Young (July 15th; see I, below).
9th	Left	**Tokyo**	Rail and motor			Aldrovandi, Claudel, McCoy, Schnee, Young, Blakeslee, Pastuhov, Jouvelet, Biddle.
	Arr.	**Miyanoshita**				
9th to11th		**Miyanoshita**				
11th	Left	**Miyanoshita**				

Date	Arrived or departed	Place	Means of travel	Remarks	Map symbol	Personnel
	Arr.	**Tokyo**				
July 14th	Left	**Tokyo**				
	Arr.	**Nikko**	Rail and motor			Aldrovandi, McCoy, Schnee, Biddle.
15th	Left	**Nikko**				
	Arr.	**Tokyo**				
15th	Left	**Tokyo**	Rail		I	Young
16th	Arr.	**Shimonoseki**				
	Left	"	Water	S. S.		
17th	Arr.	**Fushun**				
	Left	"	Rail			
	Arr.	**Keijo**				
17th to 20th		**Keijo**				
20th	Left	**Keijo**	Rail			
21st	Arr.	**Kwainei**				
	Left	"				
	Arr.	**Lungchingtsun**				
21st to 23rd		**Lungchingstun**				
23rd	Left	**Lungchingtsun**	Air			
	Arr.	**Kirin**				
	Left	"				
	Arr.	**Changchun**				
	Left	"	Rail			
24th	Arr.	**Dairen**				

（续表）

Date	Arrived or departed	Place	Means of travel	Remarks	Map symbol	Personnel
25th	Left	"	Water	S. S. *Chohei Maru*		
26th	Arr.	**Tangku**				
	Left	"	Rail			
	Arr.	**Peiping**				Rejoined party.
16th	Left	**Tokyo**	Rail		4	Aldrovandi, Claudel, McCoy, Schnee, Dennery, Pastuhov, Astor, Jouvelet, Charrère, Aoki, Biddle.
17th	Arr.	**Kyoto**				Rejoined by Haas (arrived July 16th, from Tokyo).
	Left	"				
	Arr.	**Kobe**				Rejoined by Lytton (arrived July 16th, from Tokyo).
	Left	"	Water	S. S. *Chichibu Maru*		
19th	Arr.	**Tsingtao**				
	Left	"	Rail			
20th	Arr.	**Tainan**				Rejoined by Pelt (arrived July 19th; by air, from Peiping).
20th	Left	**Tsinan**	Rail			Aldrovandi, McCoy, Schnee, Haas, Pelt, Pastuhov, Charrère, Biddle.

（续表）

Date	Arrived or departed	Place	Means of travel	Remarks	Map symbol	Personnel
	Arr.	**Peiping**				
July 20th	Left	**Tsinan**	Air		4	Lytton, Claudel, Dennery, Astor, Jouvelet.
July 20th to September 4th		**Peiping**			4	Rejoined by: Angelino, Dorfman, von Kotze, Wou. (July 20th, see E, above); Young (July 26th; see I, above). Departed: Dennnery (August 26th, for Paris via U. S. A.). Blakeslee (August 31st, for U. S. A.); Lytton, Aldrovandi, McCoy, von Kotze, Astor, Biddle (September 4th for Geneva, via Shanghai and Suez); Claudel, Schnee, Jouvelet (September 5th, for Geneva, via Siberia).

国际联盟调查团报告书(中文版)①

一九三二年九月四日在北平签字

绪　言

一九三一年九月二十一日,中国正式向国联申诉

一九三一年九月二十一日,中国政府代表在日内瓦致函国际联合会秘书长,请其促使国联行政院注意中日争端,该项争端,由于九月十八日夜沈阳事件而发生;并依照国联盟约第十一条,请求行政院"立即采取办法,使危害国际和平之局势不致扩大"。

国联行政院九月三十日之决议

九月三十日,国联行政院为下列之决议:

(一)行政院知悉中日政府对于行政院主席所谓紧急声请之答复,及为应付此种声请所取之步骤。

(二)行政院对于日本政府之声明,谓对于东三省并无图谋领土之意,认为重要。

(三)行政院知悉日本代表之声明,谓日本军队,业经开始撤退,日本政府当以日本人民生命财产之安全有切确之保证为比例,仍继续将其军队从速撤退至铁路区域以内;并希望从速完全实行此项旨愿。

(四)行政院知悉中国代表之声明,谓中国政府对于该区域以外日侨生命财产之安全,在日军继续撤退,中国地方官吏及警察再行恢复时,当负责任。

(五)行政院深信双方政府亟欲避免采取任何行动,足以扰乱两国间之和

---

① 　编者按:录自上海明社出版部编《国际联盟调查团报告书》,上海明社出版部,1932 年 10 月 15 日。该版本根据国民政府外交部翻译的文字进行整理后出版。

平及谅解者,并知悉中日代表已保证各该国政府采取一切必要步骤,以防止事变范围之扩大或情势之愈加严重。

（六）行政院请求当事两方尽力所能,速行恢复两国间通常之关系,并为求达到此项目的,继续并从速完成上述保证之实行。

（七）行政院请求当事两方随时将关于情势发展之消息,充分供给于行政院。

（八）行政院决定如无意外事件发生有即时开会之必要者,则于十月十四日在日内瓦再行开会,以考量彼时之情势。

（九）行政院授权于其主席,经向各同僚尤其两关系国代表咨询后,认为根据从当事国或从其他各会员方面,所得关于情势进展之消息,无须再行开会时,得取消本院十月十四日之会议。

当决议通过前,正辩论时,中国代表发表其本国政府意见,声称"对于确保日本军警之迅速的及完全的撤退,及原状之完全恢复,行政院所得采取之最妙方法,即为派遣中立委员会至满洲"。

十月十三日至二十四日行政院会议

行政院为考量中日争端起见,自十月十三日起至二十四日止,重开会议。该会议之决议,因日本代表之反对,未能全体通过。

十一月十六日至十二月十日行政院在巴黎开会

十一月十六日行政院在巴黎重行开会,专心研究当时之局势,几达四星期之久。十一月二十一日日本代表声称:日本政府,切望九月三十日决议,在精神上及字句上措诸实行;提议派遣调查团实地考察。该项提议,嗣为行政院其他一切会员所赞成。一九三一年十二月十日,全体通过下列决议:

十二月十日之决议

"（一）行政院重申九月三十日一致通过之决议,该决议经中日两方声明各受其庄严约束。故行政院要求中日政府采取必要步骤,实行该项决议,俾日军得依照该决议内所开条件,尽速撤退至铁路区域内。

（二）行政院认为自十一月二十四日会议后,事变更为严重,知悉两方担任采取必要办法,防止情势之再行扩大,并避免任何行动,致再令发生战争及丧失生命之事。

（三）行政院请两方继续将情势之发展,随时通知行政院。

（四）行政院请其他会员国将各该国代表就地所得之消息,随时供给行

政院。

（五）行政院鉴于本案之特殊情形,欲协力促进两国政府谋两国间各项问题之最后根本解决,故并不妨碍上述办法之实行,决定派遣一委员会,该委员会以五人组织之,就地研究任何情形影响国际关系而有扰乱中日两国和平或和平所维系之谅解之虞者,并报告于行政院。中日两国政府各得派参加委员一人襄助该委员会。两国政府对于该委员会应予以一切便利,俾该委员会所需之任何消息,均可得到。兹了解如两方开始任何商议,该项商议不在该委员会职务范围之内。又该委员会对于任何一方之军事办法,无干涉之权。该委员会之委派及其考量,对于日本政府在九月三十日决议内,所为日军撤退至铁路区域内之保证,并无任何妨碍。

（六）在现在及一月二十五日举行下次常会之间,行政院仍在受理本问题中,请主席注意本问题,并于必要时再行召集会议。"

主席之声明

主席白里安提出上述决议时,为下列之声明:

"兹应请注意者,现置于诸君前之决议案,就两种不同途径,规定办法:（一）停止对于和平之急迫危险,（二）促进两国争执现有原因最后之解决。

本院于此次集会时,欣悉当事双方对于调查足以扰乱中日关系之情形一节,可予接受。此项调查,本身颇属需要。故本院对于十一月二十一日会上所提出设立委员会之提议,表示欢迎。决议案末节规定委员会之委派及其职务。

余现就决议案逐节加以说明:

第一节　本节将九月三十日一致通过之决议,重予申明,特别注重日军应依照该决议规定之条件,尽速退至铁路区域内。

本院对于该项规定,极为重视,并深信两国政府,将着手完全履行各该政府九月三十日所担承之约言。

第二节　所不幸者,自上次本院会议后,即曾发生使情势益趋严重及引起正当忧惧之事件。故避免任何行动致再令发生战争,及其他一切足使情势扩大之举动,实为必要而急切。

第四节　依照第四节规定,本院会员国除当事两方外,应请其继续以各该国代表就地得到之消息,供给于行政院。

此项报告,在过去时间,已经证明甚有价值。凡能派代表赴东省各处之各国,均已同意尽量继行现在办法,并请求其改善。

因此各该国应常与当事两方接洽，俾当事两方，如愿意时，得以其所意欲此项代表派往之地点，向各该国表示。

第五节　此节规定设立调查委员会。此项委员会，虽系顾问性质，而其职务范围甚广。在原则上无论何项问题关系任何情形，足以影响国际关系而有扰乱中日两国和平及和平所维系之谅解之虞，经该委员会认为须加研究者，均不得除外。该委员会得用充分之裁量，以决定何项问题应报告于行政院，如认为适宜时，并得缮具临时报告。

如委员会达到时，双方依照九月三十日决议案所为之保证，尚未履行，委员会应将此情势尽速报告于行政院。

'如两方开始任何商议，该项商议不在该委员会职务范围之内。又该委员会对于任何一方之军事办法，无干涉之权'，已经特别规定。但此项规定并不限制委员会调查之权。至委员会应享有行动之完全自由，俾能获得所需报告之各种消息，此事亦甚为明显。"

当事国双方之保留及评论

日本代表接受决议时，对于决议第二节作一保留。声称彼代表其政府，接受决议："惟了解此节之用意，并非阻止日本军队得采取为直接保护日本人民生命财产势所必需之行动，以对抗满洲各地盗匪及不法份子之活动"。

中国代表亦接受决议，但要求将下列原则上所有数项观察及保留，载诸纪录中：

"（一）中国必须保留，并实行保留在国联盟约下，在中国为缔约国之一切现行条约下，及在国际公法国际惯例公认之原则下，中国所应行或可行享有之任何及一切权利，补救办法及法律地位。"

"（二）现经决议案及行政院主席宣言所证实之办法，中国认为系一种实际上之办法，包括四项互相关连之要点如下：

（甲）立即停止战事。

（乙）日本占领东省在最短期内终了。

（丙）中立人员对于今后一切发展作视察及报告。

（丁）行政院所派遣之委员会，对东省全局作实地详核之调查。

本办法在实际上及精神上均基于上述四要点而成立，此四要点中，若有一点不能如原来之期望而实现，则本办法之完整性，显将为之破坏无余。

（三）中国了解并期望决议案内所规定之委员会，如于其到达目的地时，

日本军队之撤退尚未完成,该委员会将以调查该项撤退情形并附具建议提出报告,为其首要之职责。

(四)中国推定本办法对于中国及中国人民因东省事件而发生之损害及赔偿问题,无论直接或间接,均不生影响;中国关于此点,特提出特别之保留。

(五)中国于接受本决议案时,对于行政院因防止再启战争及流血而努力告诫中日两方避免再启战争之任何举动,或足使情势愈形扩大之其他任何行为,表示感佩。然有须明白揭示者,行政院告诫一节,不得借口于现在事态所造成之无纪律情形,而予以破坏,盖决议案之目的,原在于解除该项事态也。尤应注意者,东省现有之无纪律情形,实因日军侵入,使生活失其常轨之所致。恢复寻常平安生活之唯一妥善办法,厥为迫促日军之撤退,而使中国当局得负维持治安与秩序之责任。中国不能容忍任何外国军队侵略并占领其领土,更不能容许此类军队,攫夺中国当局之警察职权。

(六)各国代表之中立视察及报告,其现行办法将行继续并改善,中国得悉此旨,颇为满意。中国并将就情势之需要,随时指示各该代表应行前往之地点。

(七)兹有应了解者,中国对于本决议案规定日本军队应向铁路区域内撤退一节,表示同意者,绝非对于在该铁路区域内驻扎外国武装队伍一事,退让其向来所取之态度。

(八)中国对于日本所有任何之图谋,足以引起政治性质之纠纷,影响中国领土及行政之完整者,(如唆使所谓独立运动或为此种目的而利用不法份子)认为显系违背避免再行扩大情势之承诺。"

调查团之委派

调查团委员,由行政院主席遴选,经两当事国同意后,其委员资格于一九三二年一月十四日复经行政院核准。其名单如下:

马柯迪伯爵(义国)[①]

亨利克劳德中将(法国)

李顿爵士(英国)

佛兰克洛斯麦考益少将(美国)

恩利克希尼博士(德国)

---

① 编者按:即意大利。下同。

调查团之组织

欧洲各国委员及美国委员之代表一人,于一月二十一日,在日内瓦开会两次,一致推举李顿为委员长;并通过工作暂行程序单。中日两国政府依照十二月十日之决议,各有"派参加委员一人襄助调查团之权"。嗣日本派驻土耳其大使吉田为代表,中国派前国务总理前外交部长顾维钧博士为代表。

国联秘书长委派国联秘书厅股长哈斯为调查团秘书长。(秘书长将下列人员,交由调查团秘书处任用:情报股股员派尔脱;掌理国际局事务之副秘书长之助理万考芝;政治股股员派斯塔柯夫;国联秘书厅临时职员爱斯托充调查团主席之秘书;情报股职员卡尔利等。法国军队医药组少校助佛兰,充克劳德将军私人助理;中尉皮特尔充麦考益将军私人助理,兼办秘书厅事务;法国驻横滨副领事迪藩勒,充日文译员;情报股职员青木及吴秀峰,在秘书处办事。)

调查团聘请专家多人协助其工作:即哲学博士文学博士美国克拉克大学教授勃来克斯雷氏,法兰西大学助教台纳雷氏,彭道夫门氏,学士硕士美国加利福尔尼大学威廉汉力申梅尔斯菲洛氏,开脱盎葛林诺博士,加拿大国有铁路助理上校希爱慕氏,威海卫领事莫思氏,纽约世界时事社远东代表硕士哲学博士渥尔脱杨格氏等。

调查团欧洲各国委员于二月三日由哈佛及泼莱冒斯登轮出发;美国委员于二月九日在纽约加入。

中国根据国联盟约第十条第十一条第十五条申诉

是时远东局势,益形扩大;中国政府于一月二十九日根据国联盟约第十条第十一条及第十五条,再向国联提出申诉。一九三二年二月十二日中国代表请求行政院依照国联盟约第十五条,将中日争端提交大会。自此以后,调查团未曾接到行政院新训令,故继续依照十二月十日行政院决议,履行其使命,即:

(一)考察业经提交行政院之中日争端,包括所有该项争端之原因,发展,及调查时之状况;

(二)考虑中日争端之可能的解决方法,该解决方法将使两国基本利益能相融洽者。对于调查团使命,既有上述观念,其工作程序亦遂依此而定。

一九三二年二月二十九日调查团抵东京

在到达纠纷主要舞台,即满洲之前,曾与中日政府及各界代表接洽一切,借以考察两国利益之性质。二月二十九日调查团抵东京,日本代表即在该处加入。调查团蒙日皇赐予接见。在东京勾留八日。连日与政府中人,即首相

犬养毅,外相芳泽,陆相荒木中将,海相大角上将等(及其他人员),开会讨论;并与银行界实业领袖及各项团体代表会晤。由上述人员中,吾等获得关于日本在满洲各种权利及利益之消息,及日本与满洲历史关系之报告。上海情形亦加以讨论,离东京后,吾等在西京得悉满洲已建立新"国家"名为"满洲国"。在大阪与实业界代表开会讨论。

上海三月十四日至二十六日

三月十四日调查团抵上海,中国代表即行加入。在此两星期,吾等除普通调查工作外,努力研究最近战争之事实及休战之可能性。此事在东京时,曾与芳泽讨论。吾等参观被战争破坏之区域,并接到日本陆海军当局关于最近作战之声明。吾等亦访晤中国政府要人及实业教育及其他各界领袖,包括广东方面在内。

南京三月二十六日至四月一日

三月二十六日调查团赴南京。其中数委员,乘便赴杭州一行。在次星期内,调查团蒙国民政府主席赐予接见;并与行政院长汪兆铭,军事委员会委员长蒋中正,外交部长罗文干,财政部长宋子文,交通部长陈铭枢,教育部长朱家骅,及其他政界中人,会晤谈话。

扬子江流域四月一日至七日

为欲对于舆论及中国各地情形益加明了起见,吾等于四月一日赴汉口,中途在九江略事勾留。调查团中数代表并赴湖北及四川之宜昌万县及重庆等处。

北平四月九日至十九日

四月九日调查团抵北平(外人现仍称北京),与张学良及九月十八日前东三省行政官吏等,屡开会议。九月十八夜在沈阳兵营中统辖军队之中国军官,亦提出证据。

因中国代表顾维钧博士入东三省问题,发生波折,故居留北平时间为之延长。

赴满洲时,调查团分为二部份;一部份由铁道经山海关至沈阳;其他部份包括顾维钧博士由海道经大连入日本铁路区域。调查团抵日本铁路区域北端之长春后,反对顾维钧博士入"满洲国"之声浪,卒归沉寂。

满洲四月二十日至六月四日

吾等居留满洲约六星期;观察沈阳,长春,吉林,哈尔滨,大连,旅顺,鞍山,

抚顺,及锦州等地。吾等本欲赴齐齐哈尔观察;但在哈尔滨时,该地周围区域在继续激战中。日本军事当局,声称不能在是时担保中东路西部支线上调查团之安全。乃由调查团中职员数人,乘飞机观察齐齐哈尔,复由该处经洮昂四洮两铁路,在沈阳与调查团全体再行会合。

我等在满洲时,作一初步报告书;于四月二十九日送至日内瓦。(见附录)

我等与关东司令本庄中将,其他军官,及日本领馆职员等,屡有会谈。在长春见"满洲国"执政,即前宣统帝名亨利溥仪者是。我等又与"满洲国"政府中人,包括日本籍之官吏及顾问,及省长等,互相会晤,并接见当地人民代表,大部份系由日本当局或"满洲国"当局所介绍。除公开会见外,我等又得与诸多中国及外国个人相会晤。

北平六月五日至二十八日

六月五日调查团回北平,所搜集之文书材料,卷帙浩繁,至是乃开始分析工作。又与行政院长汪兆铭外交部长罗文干财政部长宋子文等,开两次会议。

东京七月四日至十五日

六月二十六日,调查团由朝鲜赴东京。因斋藤内阁斯时尚未派定外相,故赴日之期,为之延迟。七月四日赴东京后,与新政府要人首相海军上将斋藤子爵,外相内田伯爵,陆相荒木中将,会晤讨论。由上述诸人中,我等得知日本政府对于满洲形势之发展及中日关系所抱之最近主张及政策。

北平七月二十日

调查团得重与中国及日本政府接洽后,回至北平,从事起草报告书。

两国代表

两国代表自始至终,努力襄助调查团工作;提出许多有价值之书面证据。凡由此方面接到材料,即提示于彼方面;并使其有加以评论之机会。此类文件,行将予以公布。

与调查团接洽之人员及团体,为数甚多,如附录上所纪载;此足以表现所有考查证据之数量。且在我等旅行中,接到印刷小册请愿书,申诉帖,及书函等甚多。仅在满洲方面,我等约接到中文信件一五五〇封,俄文信件四百封,英文法文或日文函件,尚不在内。该项文件之整理翻译及研究,极费功夫;虽我等迁移不定,但仍能不废所事。在七月回平后及重赴日本前该项工作幸得告竣。

依照十二月十日决议调查团使命之观念决定调查团报告书之计划

调查团对于其使命之观念,实所以决定该团之工作程序及其路程,亦所以

范型该团报告书之计划。

我等首欲说明两国在满洲之权利利益，借以明了历史背影；该项权利及利益，乃两国争议之基本原因也。次乃考查此次事变前之最近特定问题，并说明一九三一年九月十八日后之经过情形。当我等校阅各种问题时，我等对于已往行动之责任，注意较轻，而对于寻求方法以防止将来重生此类行动之必要，注意较重。

最后报告书结论中，载有关于各种问题之感想及考虑，为我等所欲提出于行政院者；并提议数项方法我等认为足使中日争端得一持久之解决，并足使中日间之善良谅解重行树立焉。

第一章 中国近年变迁之概况

欲了解现时冲突须明了过去情形

此次冲突之事件中，其最先诉诸国际联合会者，厥为一九三一年九月十八日之事变，而该项事变实由中日两国间年来外交紧张，时相轧轹所酿成。现欲明了此次之纷争，须先将该两国间迩来关系之原动力，加以研究。故吾人研究此问题之范围，宜扩大于满洲以外，并须将种种原动力，凡有足以影响目前中日间之关系者，澈底审量方可。例如中华民国国民之志愿，及日本帝国与前俄帝国之扩张政策，苏联传播之共产主义，暨此三国经济上及战略上之需要等，均为研究满洲问题者所应视为重要之原动力。

满洲为中国之一部，而在地理上，并处于日俄两国领土之间。故从政治上言，满洲已成为纷争之中心点，且并曾为三国之战场。而事实上，满洲亦为各该国彼此经济政治互相冲突之接触地，此种经济及政治之本身，必须加以研究，方能完全明了此次冲突之具体事实。吾人故先将此类原动力依次论之如下：

一、新中国之变迁

中华民族在进化中

现在中国之重要原动力，即为其民族自身之近代化。今日之中国，实为一正在进化中之民族。所有其国民之种种生活，均呈过渡现象。自一九一一年革命以来，中国之特点，乃为政变，内讧，及社会上暨经济上之恐慌。结果乃使

中央政府日就衰颓。此种现状,所有与中国有密切关系之国,无不受其不良影响。倘不设法补救,势必继续危及世界和平,且为世界上经济不景气之助因。

一八四二年中国开始开放

至造成此种现状之途径,现只能摘要叙述,殊非完备之纪载。中国与泰西人士接触,为时虽久,然以西方文明之影响而论,中国几乎格格不入,历数世纪而不渝。迨十九世纪初叶,交通设备日精,各国相距过程渐形短缩,远东与其他诸国间往来便捷,前此之孤立地位,不得不行打破。惟事实上交接伊始,中国尚无此项动作之准备。及一八四二年,南京条约成立,战事告终,乃开数口岸通商,并许外侨居留。因是外国风气输入中华。但其政府绝对不事变通,难为同化。外商散居通商口岸,中国政府又未能为其办理行政法律司法教育卫生等种种适宜之设备,以供其需要。外侨乃就其素所习惯之情形与标准,自为设备。在通商各口,次第建设西式城市,所有组织及行政暨营业均采西法。中西两方虽屡次设法减少异点,惟收效极微。因而发生冲突及误会情事,垂数十年。

后经战事数次,因受外国精锐军械之影响,中国乃创办军械局,并仿西法教练陆军,以期用武力相抵抗。惟中国此项设施,范围过狭,终归失败。其实中国须从根本上多方改良,方能保其固有地位而御外侮。乃中国计不出此,欲坚守其旧文化及领域,而与泰西相颉颃。

与日本比较

当日本与泰西通商之始,其难题与中国无异。因初与外邦人士理想接触,不胜烦扰。彼此所持之标准大异,时有抵触。亦遂设立外侨居留地,且订立单方关税协约,并予以领事裁判权之权利。惟日本之解决此种问题,其方法为由内部改良,并将其种种新设施提高,使与泰西并驾齐驱,复用外交协商方式以行之。日本之吸纳泰西思想,或尚非完全,故老幼间因新旧见解之不同,而生冲突,亦所常有。惟日本同化于泰西科学及艺术,既如此神速而透澈,且能一面采纳泰西标准,一面仍不使其世传之旧文化因而减损价值,实为世人所赞羡不置者也。

中国之问题较为困难

日本之变法及改革各问题,无论如何困难,要不及中国之困难也。缘中国领土广阔,人民乏团结之观念,且财政制度积弊甚深,各省所收税款,几全不汇解国库。夫中国所须解决之问题,其复杂容或远出日本之上,强与比较,似未

允当,然中国终须解决此项问题,实不能不沿与日本同样之途径。奈中国对于外国人士,不愿接纳,其已在华之外侨,亦加歧视,其不免造成不良之结果者势也。其政策徒知使全国当轴专心抵抗及防范外国思潮,甚至对于各租界之种种新建设,本可借镜者,亦横加阻止。其结果致足以令中国应付新环境所必须之种种建设上之改革,几完全忽略。

中国与列强抗争之损失

关于种种权利及国际关系,中国与列强各持成见,无法融洽,势必出于抵触,发生战事。经数次战争之结果,中国主权,逐渐损失,且割让领土,计有阿穆尔河①北岸之大地暨滨海全省,余为琉球群岛,香港,缅甸,安南,东京,老挝,交趾支那(越南诸省),台湾,朝鲜,暨其他藩属诸国,此外尚有长期租借地数处,且准在中国领土内设立外国法庭,行政公署,及军警各机关,至货物出入口税,当时亦失其自由规定之权。凡有伤害外侨之生命财产事件,中国均须赔偿,且战败赔款甚巨,自此中国财政负担日重。甚至全国领土,竟为列强分为若干势力范围,其本身之生存,亦曾遭危险。

一九〇〇年拳乱后之维新运动

一八九四年中国既败于日,一九〇〇年拳匪事变,中国又大受贻累,痛定思痛,有心人士乃认定非根本改革不可。当维新运动之始,固未尝不愿保存满洲皇朝。惟旋有人将该运动之目的及其首领泄漏于皇太后。光绪帝之百日维新,因而告终,且又身受监禁,直至一九〇八年光绪崩逝时乃止。故后之维新者,乃决意废除有清。

清之灭亡

满洲皇朝入主中国,垂二百五十年。清季叛变迭作,渐趋萎靡。计一八五〇年至一八六五年有太平天国之乱,一八五六至一八七三年云南回民叛变,一八六四年新疆叛变。最烈者莫如太平天国,清廷危如累卵,其威信已受一致命伤,终未恢复元气。一九〇八年,皇太后崩逝后,清朝本身衰弱,随乃倾颓。

中国革命运动,初曾起事数次,旋乃于华南获得凯报。即在南京建立共和政府,以革命首领孙中山博士为临时大总统。一九一二年二月十二日由当时之皇太后以幼帝名义,签署退位谕旨。临时立宪政体随即成立,而以袁世凯为总统,自幼帝退位后,所有前此由清朝所派之地方官吏,自督抚以至州县知事

---

① 编者按:即黑龙江,为俄语 Amur 的音译。

均同时失其威权，变为庶民。间有仍能使人民服从其意旨，则其本人尚有实力，足资执行耳，前此之封疆大吏，本属文员，渐假而替以武员，遂为势所必至之事，即中央之行政元首亦然，只有掌握最重之兵符，或为各省或地方最强之将领团所拥戴者，方能充任。

华北军阀独裁之趋势

军阀独裁之趋势，在华北尤为明显。而此种趋势之终能实现者，实因军队当时颇负时望。盖革命运动，屡次起事多赖军队之助力，方克平复，各将领遂以有功革命自居，毫无愧色，该将领等之多数，系北方军人领袖，互相结合，成为所谓北洋派，此种将领，本系出身寒微。自中日战役之后，袁世凯教练模范陆军，编入行伍，旋迁官佐，以至司令。袁世凯因彼辈有效忠于一己之关系，故信任之。盖在中国之内，此种效忠个人之旧习，今犹未能变其态度以效忠社会，而在泰西，则以效忠社会，为其种种组织之特性也。袁世凯任用此辈为各省督军，而归其统制。地方大权，握于督军之手，各省税收，因而由彼辈任意提用，以养其个人军队及附属之人员。

华南情形

在南方各省，情形迥异。一因与外国接触较深，一因南省人民之社会情形与北方不同。南省人民，向来厌恶军阀专制，且不喜官厅横加干预。孙中山博士及其他革命领袖始终抱定宪政宗旨。惟彼辈殊少军人援助，因清时改练陆军，在长江以南诸省，推行未广，且无完备之兵工厂也。

一九一三年倒袁运动

中华民国成立后，第一届国会迁延日久，方于一九一三年在北京召集。其时袁世凯已将其在武力上之地位布置巩固，所缺者唯须财政充足，方能保证各省陆军之确实效忠于己耳。于是订借一巨额外债，名为善后借款，以图其营私之活动。惟袁氏订借此债之办法，并未商得国会同意，故凡在孙中山博士指导下之国民党员，而为袁氏政敌者，均公然为倒袁之运动。若从军事上言之，南省本较北省为弱，迨北方军阀于征服南方诸省之余，将各该省置之北军将领管辖之下，南省之弱遂更甚矣。

一九一四至一九二八年间之内讧及政潮

一九一三年之国会，已为袁世凯解散，其后曾有数次运动恢复旧国会，或召集变相之国会，两次运动设立君主政体，总统阁员屡易其人，军阀则拥甲倒乙，朝秦暮楚，且有若干省屡屡宣布暂时独立。至国民党在广州建立政府，以

孙博士为首领,自一九一七年以后,竟能力自保持,惟中经事变数次,偶尔不能行使职权耳。在此变乱之数年内,中国屡遭军阀蹂躏,且土匪蔓延颇广,致失业农夫,荒区灾民,欠饷兵卒均被引诱入伙,遂成大帮股匪。甚至以拥护宪法自任在南省从事革命之人士,亦屡有自相挞伐之虞。

国民党之改组

一九二三年间,孙中山博士闻诸俄国革命家谓如欲使其革命要义能获最后胜利,务须有一定之程序,严厉政党之训练,及有统系之宣传方可。孙博士深然其说,故决将国民党改组,教国人依照其"宣言"及"三民主义"①所载之程序进行。但须有有系统之组织,方可期望有政党之训练,故设中央执行委员会,代为负责,以求步伐整齐。并设政治训练部,专司训育宣传人才,及组织各地支部之人才。又在黄埔设立军官学校,聘俄国军官教练,造就国民党之军事人才,以为将来陆军领袖,且使其在肄业期间服膺党义要旨。国民党之设备如此,不久当可与全民发生密切关系。凡与国民党表同情者,均可收纳于地方支部或党部所统属之农工团体,此种初步政策,殊可使国民心悦诚服。故自孙博士于一九二五年逝世后,国民党仍坚守不移。及北伐成功,于一九二八年促成名义上之南北统一,实为多年未有之事,且进而为一部分事实上之统一,延长至相当时期。

照孙博士之程序,第一时期为军事时期,至此乃告成功。

第二时期为在国民党统治下之训政时期,至此乃可开始。此时期专为训育全民自治,并进行国家建设事业也。

建设中央政府

一九二七年设立中央政府于南京,统治于国民党之下——实际上此政府不过系国民党之一重要机关耳。政府设五院(行政院,立法院,司法院,监察院,考试院),此项政府制度,系切遵孙博士之"五权宪法"——此为孟德斯鸠之三权分立,加以中国古制两种,即都察院之弹劾权,及吏礼两部之职掌也——而成立。其目的在使宪政时期急于实现,届时政府授政于人民,人民遂得直接,或间接由其所选出之代表,以执行政权焉。

在省区亦然,省政府之组织,用委员制至乡城县各部份之人民,现正受地方自治之训练。国民党深愿将其政治及经济上之建设计划即予施行。惟目前

———————————————

① 原编辑者注:民族主义,民权主义,民生主义。

未能如愿实施者,良以内争尚未完全消灭,各处将领间有率其统属军队,而为叛变之行动。且共产主义之传播,亦属堪虞。其实中央政府,尚须时时奋斗,以保其本身之生存也。

中央政府之权威内外受敌

中国政府,在表面上业已统一,但一旦强有力之军阀私自结合,率兵进攻南京,则统一之形式,立刻不保。自国民政府成立以来,虽尚无人能侵入南京,惟彼辈败退之后,尚拥有重兵,未可轻视。况向中央政府宣战等事,自彼辈观之,未尝认为叛逆行为。盖在彼辈目光中与中央政府交战,亦不过两军阀争衡,其一为其本人之党羽,其他则适居国都,为外国所承认,而名为中央政府耳。阶级关系既不存在,危险殊甚,尤因党内各派意见纷歧,致令中央政府为孙博士当然继任者之地位渐形衰弱,例如新近各分派别,致使有力之南方领袖,避处广州,而该处之地方长官,及当地国民党支部,往往任意作为,超立于中央政府之外。

综观上述情形,可见中国内部之分裂势力,尚属强盛。此种缺乏团结力之原因,实由大数之国民只知有家族乡土,而不知有国,仅在其本国与他国外交情势非常紧张时,乃稍有感觉耳。现时虽间有领袖人士,不为私人情感所系,而以国家为前提,惟仍须有多数国民,从国家上着想,方能有真正国民团结之可言也。

中国现状与华盛顿会议时之情形比较

中国过渡时代之景况,及其势所难免之政治社会文化道德各方面之紊乱,不免令其不耐烦之友人感觉失望,甚且引嫉恨之意,致为国际和平之危害。惟虽有此种种困难,迟延及失败,其进步之处,亦属不少。迨此次冲突事起,论者莫衷一是,屡有人提议,谓中国"并非有组织之国家",或谓中国内部"完全纷乱,陷于无政府状态",又谓中国现状如此,应取消其国际联合会会员国之资格,所有盟约中之保护各条款,均不适用于中国,关于此事,若将华盛顿会议时之情形,一为回溯,则颇有注意之价值。查当时所有参与会议之列强,所持之态度,与此种论调,完全不同。然当时中国内,实有完全分离之政府两处,一在北京,一在广州,且为大帮土匪所骚扰,内地交通时被阻碍。同时军阀方面,又急筹内战,以致恶氛弥漫,全国骚然。当一九二二年一月二十三日,华府会议,正值开会时期,其国内军阀,竟致通牒于中央政府挑战。其战争之结果,中央政府于五月间竟被推翻。尔后北京虽有新政府之设立,而满洲之军事领袖张

作霖又于七月间宣布满洲独立。则当时中国境内,不啻有三个政府存在,其他事实上独立之省分,更无论矣。若以现在中国之中央政府相比较,则又何如。现虽在数省内政府威力未免稍弱,惟并未有敢公然否认中央政权者,若能照此现象维持下去,则各省行政,军队,与财政等等,当能逐渐变为国家性。去年九月间国联大会,所以选举中国入行政院者,此类事实亦为其原因之一也。

中国建设之努力

中国政府,现在所采之政策,乃量入为出:务使其收支平衡,而适于财政上合理之原则。其中许多税收,均纳入于统税之内。采用化简税则。虽现在尚无正式决预算,但其收支数目,财政部均有年报。又设立中央银行,及组织财政委员会,其重要之银行及商业各界均有代表充任委员会委员。至各省税收制度,虽未良善,但财政部现已设法监督。凡此种种新政,皆为中国现政府之成绩。只因内讧未息,不能不从内债上着想,以为救济。查自一九二七年以来,中国所增内债,大约在十万万银元之谱,中国百事待举,惟以财政未裕之故,所有各种建设计划,均难实行。并不能完成其交通事业,而国内大多数问题,均待交通事业完成,方能解决也。中国政府,虽有种种失败之处,而其所成就者,亦已不少矣。

民族主义

新中国之民族主义,为中国在此过渡期中,所应有之现象。无论何国,若在同样地位,莫不有此国家思想与愿望也。凡一个民族既有国家统一之觉悟,自然愿欲脱离外界之束缚。但在此以外中国国民党,复欲以排除外国势力特殊色彩,引入于中国民族主义之中,并将其运动之目标扩大,期将所有亚洲之民族,尚受"帝国主义压迫"者,尽举而解放之。此种概念系受前与共产党接近时所贴标语之影响,今日中国民族主义复充满中国从前光荣伟大之记忆,而谋所以恢复之。故要求收回租界,及铁路区域内外国所享有之行政权及非纯粹商业性质之权,又租界及外侨居留地之行政权亦欲一并收回,尤欲取消有约国之领事裁判权,按照此项领事裁判权,中国法律不能适用于外侨,此种权利,若继续有效,当为中国一般舆论所极端反对,而视为国家之羞。

各国对领判权之态度

各国对于中国取消领事裁判权之愿望,大致均取同情态度,一九二一年至一九二二年,在华府会议,彼等均承认在原则上可以接受,惟对于最适宜之时期及实行之方法,意见颇有纷歧。有以为立时放弃此项权利,将使中国负筹备

合乎某一种标准之警察及司法行政之义务,而因财政及其他内部之难,中国现时尚未能办到。如时机未熟,先予废止,恐单纯之法权问题,或将引起对各国无数节外之问题。又有以为如外国人民须受与在许多地方之中国人民所受之同样不公平待遇及苛勒之税捐,则国际关系,匪特不能进步,抑将退化矣,然虽有此种种保留,而成就颇属不少,尤以华府会议,或该会议之结果,为最多。五处租借地之中,中国收回其二,并收回许多让与权,中东铁路之行政权,关税自主权,邮政权,复缔结多种基于平等原则之条约。

中国既已如在华府会议所为,采取国际联合作为解决自身困难之途径,苟能继续一贯,则在已往之十年中,当已有更具体之进步。奈因采取猛烈之排外宣传,致遭阻碍,并在两点特殊之处,肆意为之,以致助成发生现时冲突之形势。斯即利用经济抵制,及在学校内介入排外宣传是也。经济抵制在第七章中论之。

学校内之民族主义

一九三一年六月,中国所颁布之临时宪法内规定①,"三民主义为中华民国教育之基本原则"。各学校内均教授孙中山博士之主义。其权力一等于前世纪之经学。孙先生之言论其受人尊崇,无异于革命前之孔子。然不幸在教育青年上,民族主义之建设方面,似不如其破坏方面,能得较多之注意。试一翻阅各校课本,即使读者感觉著书之人,图以嫉恨之火焰燃烧爱国观念,又欲于仇害心理之上,建树人格。此种猛烈排外之宣传,初起于学校,继用之于社会生活上之各方面,其结果引诱学生参加政治活动,有时甚而发为攻击各部长及其他官吏之身体,家宅,或衙署之行动,与推翻政府之企图。此种态度,既乏有效之内政改革,或国家程度之增进,以为之陪衬,徒使各国惊骇,对于现时借为唯一保障之权利,更增不愿放弃之感。

法律与秩序问题充分交通之必要

关于维持法律及秩序问题,目前中国缺乏充分交通,实为一严重之障碍。在交通未能充足保证国家军队之迅捷运输时,则维持法律与秩序,虽不完全,亦不得不大多付托于各省官吏。而因其与中央相隔甚远,又不得不容许其自作主张,以解决省内之事。在此种情势之下,意思与行动之独立,颇易逾越范围。其结果,各省遂逐渐变而为私人之产业矣。其军队亦只认识长官,而不知

---

① 原编辑者注:《国民教育章》第四十七条。

有国家矣。

地方军队

中央政府不能调动军队长官，已数见不鲜，盖政府无切实办法，能使其权力迅速而永久及于全国，则内战之危险，势必继续存在。

土匪

土匪问题在中国历史上班班可考，今日仍存在于全国各地，其理由今古相同。中国向有土匪，政府曾未能澈底去之。缺乏适宜交通，致政府不能除去此害，此为理由之一。而其害乃得随时势之变迁，自为消长。尚有另一助成之原因，即系在中国常见之地方上变乱，尤其因失政而发生之变乱为甚。往往变乱敉平之后，叛徒加入匪群，仍复在地方上活动。此在太平变乱削平后由一八五〇至一八六五年间一段时期，尤为确切。在较近时期，土匪亦来自欠饷军队之行列中，盖兵士既无法维持生活，而在参加内战时，业已习于抢劫也。

其他增加土匪原因，厥为水旱灾祲，旱灾水灾，几为常有之事变。饥荒土匪亦随之来。而益以人口骤增之压迫，问题更加严重，在人烟稠密之区，通常经济困难愈见增加。而在仅足生存，毫无余力以应付不测之人民中，苟其生活稍有降落，则大多数必致流落无依。因此匪风大都受流行经济状况之影响。在经济繁荣时期，或经济繁荣地方，土匪必减。但因上述理由，而致生存竞争剧烈，或政治状况不定，则土匪定必增加。

当一朝土匪已在任何区域负固以后，以内地交通之不便，用兵剿办每感困难。难达之地，数里之遥，或须数日行程。而大帮土匪能行动自由，来去飘忽，令人不能捉摸其踪迹与行动。遇剿匪松懈，或兵匪秘密勾结时（此种情事常见不鲜），水陆大道之交通均受其扰害，此种事件只能以充分之警力制止之，在内地各县剿匪尤难，盖不规则之游击，在所不免也。

共产主义[①]对中央政府之权力挑战

各地军阀之私人军队及通国之土匪横行，虽足以扰乱国内治安，然不足为中央政府权力之患，但另有患源，即共产主义是也。

一九二一年中国共产主义之原始

在中国之共产运动，其发生之初，仅限于知识及劳工两界。在一九一九至一九二四年间，其主义甚为畅行。惟是时中国农村，尚少受其影响。一九一九

---

① 编者按：报告书对共产主义多有错误描述，读者需注意鉴别。下同。

年七月二十五日苏联政府之宣言表示愿意放弃所有前俄帝政府时代由中国强行取得之一切权利,使全中国发生好感,尤以知识阶级为最。一九二一年间,中国共产党乃正式成立,专在上海劳工界宣传,并组织"赤色"协会。一九二二年六月共产党第二次大会(其时会员不过三百人)与国民党联合。孙中山博士虽反对共产主义,然中国共产党员个人,则仍准其加入国民党。一九二二年秋间,苏联政府派代表团来华,以越飞为领袖,与孙博士作重要之晤谈,其结果为一九二三年一月二十六日之共同宣言。由此宣言苏联表示对中国之统一及独立予以同情及援助。在他一方面,则明白声明共产组织及苏维埃制度之政府,在彼时中国情状之下,不能介入中国。继此协定,莫斯科于一九二三年末派遣若干文武顾问来华。"并在孙博士管理之下,担任整理国民党及广东军队之内部组织。"

一九二四年三月召集之国民党第一次全国大会正式议决容纳中国共产党入党,但以入党后不得再参加于筹备无产阶级革命为条件。容共时期,于焉开始。

一九二四至二七年容共时期

此期自一九二四年开始,至一九二七年终止。一九二四年初间,共产党计有附和者约二千人,"赤色"协会会员约六万人,但不久即在国民党内,取得充分势力,使公正党员,咸怀疑虑。一九二六年末,彼等向中央委员会有所提议。其提议中竟列有:全国土地,除工人农人或兵士所有者外,一律收归公有;改组国民党,铲除敌视共产主义之军事领袖;二万共产"党徒"与五万农工之武装等条。但此项提议遭遇失败。而共产党遂不复赞助国民党之北伐。然以前彼等固为组织国民革命军之最活动者也。但彼等后又加入北伐,自北伐军已抵中国中部,并在武汉设立国民政府(一九二七年),共产党在政府中竟取得支配之权。盖国民党领袖,非俟自己军队已占领南京上海后,无暇与彼等较短长也。武汉政府在湖南湖北两省实施共产制度。国民革命,几变为共产革命矣。

一九二七年国共分裂

最后国民党领袖决定,共产主义为患过烈,不能再事优容。故一九二七年四月十日在南京确立政权成立国民政府之后,当即明令军队及各机关立即肃清共产。武汉国民党中央执行委员会,原与南京之国民党领袖拒绝携手,而于七月十五日以大多数通过决议案,将国民党中之共产党人开除党籍,并令苏联顾问离华。以此决议之结果,国民党遂重归统一,而在南京之政府,乃为全党

所公认。

南昌事件与广州事件

容共期间有若干军队为共党①所吸收。当国民军北上时，此项军队留存后方，大多数在江西。共党乃派员前往，加以整理，并诱劝反抗南京政府。一九二七年七月三十日，江西省会南昌警备队连同其他军队变叛，荼毒居民。但至八月五日，彼等即被政府军击败，乃退至南部。十二月十一日共产党在广州起事，据城二日，南京政府以正式苏联代表，曾经实行参加乱事，乃于一九二四年十二月十四日下令取消所有苏联共和国驻华领事之证书。

与共产军队继续战斗

一九二八至一九三一年之间，内战复炽，殊有利于共产势力之增长。"赤军"成立，江西福建被共化之地甚广。直至一九三○年十一月，斯时北方联合军新败，中央政府方能从事认真剿共。共产军队在江西湖南各部扰乱，据报在两三个月之间损失生命约二十万，财产约值一万万元。彼时共党势力之强，能将政府第一第二两次派往剿办之军队击败。第三次剿共，系蒋总司令中正亲自指挥。始将共产军屡次挫败。迄一九三一年七月中，共党所据之最重要"巢穴"，均被克复。共党军队全部向福建退却。

蒋中正将军将"赤军"追逐至江西西南山中，同时在曾被"赤匪"蹂躏之区，设立政治委员会以改组之。

南京政府正在将重要"赤军"渐次消灭之际，乃因他处事势，不得不停止攻势，将大部份军队撤回。斯时石友三在北方变叛，而湖南省之粤军亦起而乱，遥为声援。同时又有沈阳九月十八日之事发事。"赤军"受上述情形之鼓励，复取攻势。为时不久，而前此战胜之结果，均消失无遗矣。

福建江西之大部份，及广东之一部份，据确实报告，均已全被"赤化"，而"赤党"之势力范围，更为广大，远及扬子江以南之一大部份，及扬子江以北湖北安徽江苏各省之一部份。上海为共党宣传之中心。中国各市镇几无处不有与共产主义表同情之人。迄今在江西福建曾经组织两个共产省政府。但具体而微之苏维埃制度则不下数百之多。共产政府系以当地农工大会选举之委员会组织之。在实际上，受中国共产党代表之管理。由该党派出曾受训练人员

① 编者按：指代中国共产党。报告书对中国共产党多有误解，读者需注意鉴别。下同。

以管理之。被派之人大多数曾在苏俄国内受过训练者。共产党区委员会受中国共产党中央委员会之管辖。而区委员会复管辖省委员会,省委员会管辖县委员会,以次递推。下至各工厂学校军营中所组织之共产细胞。

共产所用之方法

共党军队,既占领一县后,如似有久占之可能时,即尽力使之"赤化",居民如有"反动",即以恐怖手段镇慑之①。上述之共产政府乃即设立。此种政府之全部组织含有:内政,办理反革命事务,财政,农村经济,教育,卫生,邮电,交通等委员会。又有军事委员会及管理农工委员会。此种完备之政府组织,仅见于全部苏维埃化之各县,在他处则组织当为较逊。

其行为计划包括取销欠债,没收大业主或宗教组织如庙宇庵寺及教堂等之地产,而分予无产阶级及小农民。征税则删繁就简。农民须献纳其地出产之一部。为改进农务起见,发展灌溉,办理农民借贷制度,及合作事业,并设立公共学校病院药房。

因此,极贫苦之农民得由共产主义而享受甚多之利益。惟富豪及中等之地主商人,及本地士绅,或遭直接没收,或被间接惩罚,均已摧毁糜遗。共产党以实施其农业政策,希望博得民众之赞助。关于此点,其宣传及行动颇有成效,固无间于共产主义与中国社会制度之互相凿枘也。因苛税,苛捐,重利,军,匪,肆劫所生之一切民生痛苦,尽为共产党利用之以为宣传之资料,并作成特别标语用于农民工人兵士及智识阶级。其对妇女则标语特予变更,以期适用。

中国共产主义之特性

共产主义之在一般国家(苏联除外),仅为一种政党党员所持之政治主义,或为一种特别党的组织,冀与其他政党竞夺政权。但在中国则否,其在中国现已成为国民政府之强敌,有自制之法律,及政府,以及其自身行动之土地范围,此种情况为他国所无。再则中国现正在建设内部之紧急关头,再加以过去十一月中之非常严重之外患,共党战事所造成之扰攘,因之更为严重。国民政府似已决心恢复共党支配下之各县,并于恢复之后在各该县实行经济善后办法。惟于其军事计划上,除前述之内外困难足以削弱中央政府之地位外,尚有缺乏款项及交通不便之障碍,故共产问题之在中国,实与较大之国家建设问题,具

---

① 编者按:报告书对当时中国共产党活动存有严重误解。读者需注意鉴别。下同。

有关联。

一九三二年夏间，南京政府宣布重要军事计划，以期消灭共党之抵抗力。并已开始进行，如上所述，同时并拟在克复区域之内，施行澈底的社会与行政之改组。但直至今日，尚无重要之效果宣布。

上述情形在中日关系上之影响

夫日本既为中国之比邻，又为最大之顾客，故因本章所述之扰乱情形而受之损失自较任何其他国家为大，侨华外人三分之二为日本人，而在满洲之朝鲜人约计有八十万之数，故日本人数，较任何他国为多。设若在现状之下，须受中国法律，司法及税政之支配，自必感受痛苦。日本既不能希望设有满意之安全保障以代替其条约上之权利，故自知无法可以满足中国之愿望。因其他各大国之权利渐形落后，遂使日本在华之权利尤其在满洲者日益彰著。日本对于在中国之人民生命财产上所抱之顾虑，曾使其迭次干涉中国内战或地方上乱事。此项行动，向为中国人所嫉恶而以其干涉之结果酿成武装冲突，如一九二八年济南事件者为尤甚。近数年中，日本之要求，在中国方面已认为对于中国国家愿望之一种严重挑衅，较之列强所主张之一切权利犹有甚焉。

中国建设中之国际利益

本问题影响日本之程度，虽较他国为多，然并非一单纯之中日问题，中国要求立即收回某种特别权利及利益，盖以其有损中国尊严与主权也。而列强则以中国情形既不能保证充分保护侨民，即对中国此种欲望，不能不抱迟疑，盖其侨民之利益，全恃享有特别条约权利而获得安全也。本章所述之变化程序，为过渡时期所不可免者，业已造成一种舆论上之势力。如政府因不能完全统一及改建国家而显示萎弱，则此种舆论势力必将对于其外交政策上继续予政府以难堪。中国在外交上之国家的愿望能否实现，全视中国在内政范围内有无履行现代政府职务之能力以为断。非俟外交与内政两者间之悬隔业经消除，则国际冲突，意外事件，排货，及武力干涉之种种危险，势将继续矣。

国际合作为最善之解决

目前极端之国际冲突事件业经迫中国再度求国联之干涉。如能得一圆满解决，则应使中国确知国际合作政策之有利。此种国际合作，开始于一九二二年之华府会议，而获有效果。现时中国缺乏资本与必要之专门人才，以完成其国家之建设。孙中山博士已见及此，并拟有国际参加发展中国经济之伟大计划。国民政府近来，对于解决中国各种问题均寻求及接受国际之援助，如自一

九三〇年以来之财政事宜，自一九三一年全国经济委员会成立以来，联络国联专门机关以办理经济之设计及发展事宜，又于同年办理水灾救济事宜等等皆是。中国遵循此国际合作之道，当能得最确定及最迅速之进步，以达到其国家之理想。而此种政策可使列强易于供应中央政府之需求，并迅速而有效的赞助中国移去足以危害中国与其余世界间之和平关系之任何原因。

第二章　满洲之状况及其与中国其他部份及俄国之关系

一、满洲之状况

绪言

满洲，在中国称为东三省，乃一广袤膏腴之区域，四十年前，几未开辟。即迄今人口仍形稀少，对于解决中日人口过剩问题，其所占地位日见重要。山东河北两省之贫苦农民，已经移殖于满洲者，以数百万计，日本则将其工业品及资本输入于满洲，以换取粮食暨原料，在供应中日两国之需要上满洲已证明两国合作之有益。若无日本之活动，满洲不能吸引如许巨额之人民；若无中国农民及工人之源源而往，满洲亦不能如此迅速发展，使日本因此得有市场，得有粮食，肥料，及原料。

满洲始因其形胜，继因其农矿富藏成为觊觎之区

夫满洲之发展，虽大多有赖于合作；然因有前述理由，已注定为一竞争之区域。初则为日俄竞争之区域，继则为中国与其两大强邻角逐之地方。其始也，满洲不过以其地位关系，被卷入逐角政策之大漩涡中，盖以占领该地，即含有操纵远东政治之意义。其继也，因其自身所蕴藏之农林矿山之富，发现于世，遂复成为群雄觊觎之区。初则俄国以中国之牺牲，取得特殊条约权利；其后所有关于南满之特殊权利，尽移转于日本。利用如此得来之特权，以促进南满之经济发展，自属更形便利。军事之计虑，固仍居首要；然因日俄采取积极步骤，开发满洲，结果得有广大之经济利益，此项广大之经济利益，在日俄两国之外交政策上已日益增加其重要性。

中国农民占有满洲土地

初，中国于开发满洲方面所表现之活动，微乎其微，几使满洲坐让俄国支

配。即在重行保证中国在满洲主权之朴资茅斯和约[1]以后,日俄于开发此数省之经济活动,在世界人士眼光中,较中国自身之经济活动为尤显著。彼时中国数百万农民之移殖,实决定斯土将来之占有权。此种移殖,实系占领[2],虽属和平而不显著,然其为实际占领则一也。当日俄彼此从事划分其南北利益范围之际,中国农民已占有其土地;而今日之满洲,遂为中国人之满洲,不可移易矣。在此种情势之下,中国固可坐待良机,重行主张其统治权。一九一七年之俄国革命,使中国在北满得此良机;中国于是对此久经忽视之国土,开始采取较为积极之步骤,以从事治理与开发。最近数年间,中国亟欲减削日本在南满之势力,此种政策之结果,致使冲突扩大,至一九三一年九月十八日而达于顶点。

人口

人口总数,约计三千万;据称其中二千八百万为中国人或同化之满洲人;八十万为朝鲜人,鲜人大多数聚居于朝鲜边境地方,即所谓间岛区域者是;其余则散居于满洲各地。蒙古人部落则居于内蒙古边境之牧场,其人数甚少。俄人之在满洲者,或有十五万人之谱,大多数在中东路沿线区域,尤以哈尔滨为最多。日人约有二十三万,大概集居于南满铁路沿线之居留地及关东租借地(即辽东半岛)。日人俄人及其他外国人(鲜人除外)之居留于满洲者,总计不过四十万人。

面积

满洲地方广袤,其面积之大,与法德合并之幅员相等,约计三十八万方哩,中国向称之为东三省,以其行政区域划为三省,南为辽宁(或奉天),东为吉林,北为黑龙江。辽宁之面积,约计七万方哩,吉林十万方哩,黑龙江二十万方哩有奇。

地理

满洲具有大陆性之特征,其山脉计有两系,长白山位于东南,大兴安岭位于西北,在此两大山脉之间,为大满洲平原,其北部属于松花江流域。南部属于辽河流域。在此两流域之间,又有岗峦起伏之分水岭,将满洲平原分为南北二部;此分水岭自历史方面观之,殊为重要。

满洲西与河北省及内外蒙古相毗连。内蒙古昔划为三特别行政区,即热

---

    ①   编者按:又译朴茨茅斯条约。下同。

    ②   编者按:原文如此。中国农民移殖东北,不能称之为占领。读者需注意鉴别。

河察哈尔及绥远是也。一九二八年,国民政府予该三特别区以完全省区之地位。内蒙古,尤以热河为最,向与满洲发生关系,且不无运用势力,以干预满洲事务之处。满洲之西北东北暨东陲,与苏俄之西比利亚省①相毗连,其东南与朝鲜为邻,南以黄海为界。辽东半岛之南端,自一九〇五年即为日本所据,其面积计一千三百方哩有奇,日人视为其租借地而管理之,不宁惟是,日人并使行某种权利于租借地以外之一段狭长地带,将南满铁路包括在内,其面积总计不过一百零八方哩,而其长度竟延长至六百九十方哩。

经济富源

满洲之土壤,概称肥沃,然其发展,端赖运输便利。故河流沿岸及铁路沿线地方,重要城市繁兴。往昔之发展,实际全赖河运,今兹之运输方法,虽则首推铁路,然河运仍甚重要。十五年间,重要产物,如大豆,高粱,麦,黍,大麦,米,及雀麦等,收获倍增,一九二九年,此项收获,计有八万七千六百万蒲式耳(Bushel)有奇(按:每 Bushel 约合中国四斗)。据一九三一年满洲年鉴所载预计,一九二九年已经垦殖之田地仅占全面积百分之一二点六,而其可耕之地,则占全面积百分之二八点四。以是若经济情形有所改进,则将来生产可望大为增加。一九二八年满洲农产品之价值,总计一万三千万金镑有奇。大部农产品系运输出口,茧绸或野蚕丝亦为满洲重要出口货物之一。

木材及矿产

山地多森林,并富藏矿产,尤以煤为最多。重要矿产,如金如铁,亦以富藏见称。此外并曾发现多量之火油石,白云石,菱苦土矿,石灰石,火泥,蜡石,及品质极佳之二养化矽②。因此采矿事业,可望成为极重要之事业。③

二、与中国其他部份之关系

满清④灭亡前之历史

自有史以来,满洲即为与蒙古族鞑靼人自由混入之通古斯族各部落所居。继而受文化较高之中国人⑤移殖之影响,始知组织之道。于是建立若干王国,

---

① 编者按:即西伯利亚。
② 编者按:二养化矽为二氧化硅的旧称。
③ 原编辑者注:参阅第八章暨本报告书附件第二第三号专论。
④ 编者按:即指清朝。下同。
⑤ 编者按:指代关内的中国人,以汉人为主体。

间或控有满洲大部份地方及中国北部与朝鲜北部区域,辽金及满清三代,竟将中国大部份或中国全部征服而治理之,凡数百年。反之,中国遇有英武之主,辄能挽北来之狂澜,依次在满洲大部份地方,树立主权。查中国人向满洲移殖之事,为时极早;而各地中国城市之传播中国文化势力,于其四周邻近地区者,为期之早,亦正相同。盖中国人在满洲之地位,根深蒂固,迄今已二千年,中国文化在满洲极南部份亦早已活跃。当明代之时(一三六八年至一六四四年),此种文化之势力,已极强盛;明代之威权实际已遍及于满洲之全部。在一六一六年满人推翻明代在满洲之政治,暨在一六二八年满人越长城而征服中国之前,中国之文化,实已深入于满族之人心,而满人已多数与中国人互相同化。在往昔满清军队中,有由多数中国人组织特种军团,称之为汉军旗者。

满人于征服中国之后,派遣其守备队驻扎于中国较为重要之各城市,禁止满人从事某项职业,禁止满人与中国人互通婚媾,并制止中国人移殖于满蒙。促成此种办法者,政治原因实重于种族观念;其目的在保障满清之永久统治权。此种办法对于与满人实际享受同等优越地位之多数汉军旗人,并无影响。

满人及其同盟汉军旗人之外迁,致使满洲人口大为减少。然在满洲南部,中国人之市缠,继续存在。少数移殖之人,即自此策源地,越奉天省中部而散居焉。中国之人,或以善能规避移民禁令,或受移民禁令时时变易之利,遂自中国①源源渗人[入],人数有增无已。以是满洲人与中国人愈形混杂;甚至满族之言语,卒被淘汰,而代以汉文。至蒙人则未经同化,但进占之移民,喧宾夺主,逼使蒙人后退。卒之,满清政府,为阻止俄人自北方前进计,决计鼓励中国人之移殖。一八七八年间,满洲各地,遂尔开放。且对移往者,往往予以各种奖励。结果,当一九一一年中国革命之际,满洲之人口,计有一千八百万人。

满清政府,在一九〇七年间,时距清室退位前不过数年,曾决定改革满洲地方政府。中国前此视满洲三省为关外领地,另行设治,自具规模。所有在中国通行将各省民政交由科举出身之文人治理之制,并不施行于满洲。而将满洲置诸纯粹军治之下,以维持满族官吏及习俗。在中国,凡官吏均不得在本省服官。满洲各省,置将军一名,运用全权,以处理军民政事。嗣拟将军民政事划分,乃其结果未见满意,两种权力范围之划分,既不完备,于是误会滋多,诡

---

① 编者按:此处"中国"指代中国关内地区,后面的"中国人"亦指关内地区的中国人。下同。

谋叠出,卒无成效。以是于一九〇七年间,此种计划,遂尔放弃;乃将三省将军取消,以一总督管辖满洲全境。其目的在集中权力,尤其在外交政策方面。总督之下,置有巡抚,治理省政。后来种种行政改革,渐渐仿行中国之省政制度,实以上述之改组为其嚆矢。满人此项最后办法,卓著成效,则一九〇七年以后办理满洲事务之能员,有足多焉。

清朝灭亡以后

当一九一一年革命爆发时,满洲各官员之不赞成共和者,令张作霖抵抗革命军之前进,满洲各省运得免牵入内战漩涡。嗣张作霖独裁满洲及中国北部之政治,迨共和建立,袁世凯氏被选为民国第一任大总统,满洲各官员顺从已成之事实,自愿听袁氏之指挥。当时各省设有军事及民事长官,惟不久满洲及中国其他各部之民事长官,均为军事长官所排挤。

一九一六年张作霖被任为奉天省长

一九一六年张作霖被任为奉天省督军,同时代理省长。其个人威权,大见扩张,当对德宣战问题发生时,国会表示反对,张作霖加入中国督军团,请求解散国会。该项请求,未为总统所接受,张作霖遂向北京中央政府宣告奉天省独立,继复收回此种宣言。一九一八年时,张氏因有功中央,被任为满洲全境巡阅使,于是满洲虽仍保存其特殊制度,但在行政上归复统一。

一九二二年张作霖与北京中央政府断绝关系

张作霖接受中央政府之荣典,惟中央当局时见易人,而张氏之态度,则时视其与操纵中央政局之军人个人关系之性质而转移。张氏之视彼与政府间之关系,似与私人间之结合意义相同。一九二六年七月,张氏树立威权于长城以南之企图失败,并见监督北京政府之权,为对方所攫取,于是宣告与中央政府脱离关系。张氏维持其在满洲行动之完全独立,直至其势力达于长城以南,并为北京主人之日始止。张氏表示愿尊重外人权利,并承认中国所负义务,惟要求各国对于有关满洲之一切事件,此后应直接与彼所统辖之行政机关相洽商。

一九二四年奉天与苏联之协定

故一九二四年五月三十一日之中苏协定,于中国虽甚为有利,但张氏竟予否认,卒获与苏联于一九二四年九月另订协定。该协定与一九二四年五月三十一日苏联与中国中央政府所订之协定,实际上无甚出入。该项事实适足以表明张氏不问在内政或外交方面,均主张行动上之完全独立也。

张作霖上将击败吴佩孚将军

一九二四年张氏复侵入关内,并因冯玉祥将军(现称上将)在战事紧急时,背弃其长官吴佩孚将军(现称上将),张氏遂得胜利。直接之结果,为推翻中央政府,并扩张张作霖上将之势力而南达于上海。

一九二五年十一月郭松龄之变

一九二五年张上将对于其昔时同盟之冯玉祥将军,复以兵戎相见。是役也,张氏部属中有郭松龄者,在战事最紧急时,背弃张氏,归冯玉祥将军。一九二五年十一月郭松龄之叛乱,其意义之深不仅限于一时,盖此事牵涉俄日两方,俄方行动,间接利于冯玉祥将军,而日方行动,则利于张上将。郭松龄虽为张之僚属,但其对于社会之改革,实赞同冯之主张。其背叛长官也,以为张之去位,为中止内战所必要。郭氏之叛,实使张氏陷于极困难之地位。郭占有铁路以西之地面,张则驻节奉天,兵力单薄。是时日本为在南满自身之利益计,将南满铁路两旁各二十里之地带(七英里),宣布为中立区域,不许任何军队通过。该项举动,实所以阻止郭松龄进击张氏,而予黑龙江援军以时日,令其得以到达,黑龙江军队因苏联铁路人员要求先以现款缴付运价方许乘车,故设法另取他道,到达时期,遂致延缓。上述援军之到达,及日方若干明显之援助,遂使战事结束有利于张。郭松龄败北,冯氏亦迫而撤退,弃北京于张氏。张氏对于当时中东铁路人员之行为,不无遗恨,嗣后对于该路权利,时加侵蚀,用尽方法,以谋报复。其建筑一独立铁路系,联络满洲三省都城,似以此事件受之经验,为其主要原因。

满洲独立之意义

张作霖上将迭次宣布之独立,绝不含有渠个人或满洲人民情愿与中国分离之意义。其军队侵入中国[①],并不视中国为外国,不过仅为参加内战而已。张上将之于中央政府,时而拥护,时而攻击,时而将其所辖领土宣布独立,与其他各省军阀正复相同,绝未采用一种方法,足使中国分成数国者。实则所有中国内战大致均系一种建立真正强健政府,以图统一全国之野心计划。故满洲虽迭经战事及独立时期,但仍为中国完整之一部。

张作霖与国民党

当张作霖上将与吴佩孚作战时,张氏虽曾与国民党为同盟,但张氏本身并

---

① 编者按:指代中国关内地区。

不接受国民党之主义。张上将不赞成孙中山博士所期望之约法,以为该项约法,与中国人民之精神不相适合。但张上将愿望中国之统一。其对于苏联及日本在满利益范围所抱之政策,表示如果力能出此,渠不惮将上述二种利益范围,一概予以扫除。要知关于苏联之利益范围,张上将军之企图,几近成功。张氏倡始上文所已述之建筑铁路政策,其结果为断绝南满铁路与供应南满路诸区域中某某数区域之关系,张氏对于俄日在满利益之此项态度,半由于每逢与俄日交涉时其威权常受限制,张氏不复能忍受此项限制;而半亦由于渠及中国各方舆论,对于外人在中国之特殊地位,同抱愤恨故也。一九二四年十一月间,张上将曾经邀请孙中山博士开善后会议,当时孙博士欲在该会议程之中,列入改善生活程度,召集国民会议,及取消不平等条约诸端。旋孙博士因病逝世,上述会议,遂未果行。但从孙博士之建议,可以知孙博士已与张氏有某种谅解,并可知两人之间关于中国外交政策或可达到一种可能同意之基础也。

张作霖之末年

张氏末年时,尤表示不愿任日本坐享因各种条约协定所取之特殊利益。是以两方关系,有时颇为紧张。日本劝告张氏不宜加入中国各党派之纷争,应注其全力,以图满洲之发达,张氏对之,殊为愤怒,不愿听从,其子继之亦复如此。自冯玉祥氏失败后,张氏为北方各军人联盟之领袖,号称大元帅。

一九二八年,国民党军队北伐时,张氏遭遇失败,此在第一章中已言之矣。是时日本劝告张氏及时将军队退守满洲。日方标明之目的,为救满洲于内战祸害之中,此种祸害,为胜军追击,败军退入境内时必然之结果也。

张作霖之死亡——一九二八年六月四日

张氏对于此种劝告,颇为愤怒。然不能不予听从。一九二八年六月三日张氏离去北平(时称北京),遄返奉天,翌日达城外某一地点,为北宁线在桥下,南满线在桥上互相交叉通过之处,炸药爆发,所乘列车被炸,张氏竟尔殒命。

张氏遇害之责任,迄今尚未判明。惨案内幕仍在五里雾中;惟此事颇引起日方同谋之嫌疑,于是当时中日邦交,业已紧张之状态,至是复多一原因。

张学良将军继父之后

张上将死后,其子张学良继而统治满洲。张学良富于青年国家思想,愿望停止内战,并扶助国民党统一全国之政策。日本对于国民党之政策倾向,既有若干经验,故并不欢迎该项势力,侵入满洲。张学良氏曾接到此种劝告,对之殊为愤恨,与乃父相同。决意遵循一己意见,其与国民党及南京之关系,日趋

接近。

张学良宣告服从中央政府

一九二八年十二月,张学良氏承认易帜,宣告服从中央,受命任东北边防总司令,而其领袖满洲行政之地位,亦再经确定,并兼管热河。热河为内蒙之一部,面积约六万方哩。

满洲与国民党之关系:近名义而远事实

满洲既加入国民政府,行政组织,必须有若干之改变,以便与中央政府之行政组织相近似。委员会制度于以输入,并设立国民党总部。其实旧时制度及人员,仍然沿用,与昔无异。中国各处所习见之党部干涉地方行政,在满洲实所不许。然而一切重要文武官吏应为国民党员之规定,在满洲亦不过视同一种之具文。凡军事、民事、财政、外交,其与中央政府之关系,纯系乎一种自愿之合作。至必须严格服从之各项命令训令,不甚忍受于满洲。官吏之任免,苟违背满洲当局意愿者,亦不能见于实行。此种在政务上党务上行动之自由,中国其他各处,亦有如此者。在此类情形中,一切重要之任命,事实上均出自地方当局,中央政府则不过加以证实已耳。

加入国民政府对于满洲对外政策之影响

就对外政策范围而言,满洲地方当局虽仍保有高度之行动自由,但其加入国民政府,在对外政策上实具有比较重要之影响。试观张作霖上将对于在满洲中东路地位,时加侵犯,且不愿日本所主张之某某各种权利,可见满洲在未加入民国以前,已采取一种"迈进之政策"。惟既加入以后,国民党富有组织纪律之宣传,满洲对之已经开放,国民党利用正式党刊及多数附属之言论机关,一再声称恢复已失主权及取消不平等条约之重要,与夫帝国主义之险恶。此种宣传,在满洲自必有深切之影像,良以该处外人在中国领土内之利益,法院,警察,守备队,军队,真相尤为显著也。国民党之宣传,由国民主义教科书以输入于学校,各项会社,若辽宁人民外交协会等,亦见发生。彼辈激发并促进民族主义之思想,实行排日之煽动,并以压力施诸中国房主地主,迫其提高日本及朝鲜租户之租金,或拒绝日本及朝鲜租户重订租约。[①] 日方曾举出类此之若干事件,报告于本调查团。朝鲜移民曾受有一种有统系之虐待,并曾颁行各项排日性质之命令训令。纠纷案件愈多,形势紧张愈甚。一九三一年三月,国

---

① 原编辑者注:参阅本报告所附专论第九号。

民党干部,设立于各省会;嗣后各支部在其他城中或县份中成立。中国党义宣传员,赴北方者日众,日方声诉反日活动日益加剧。一九三一年四月,沈阳在人民外交协会指导之下召开会议五日,出席者有东省各地代表达三百余人。对于清除日本在东省地位是否可能,曾加以讨论;收回南满铁路问题,载在通过之决议中。同时苏俄及其人民,亦因同样之风气,感受痛苦;白俄虽无主权及特别权利可放弃,亦受凌辱与不良待遇。

内政之影响

在内政方面,东省当局,保持其所欲保持之一切权力,对于遵从中央政府之行政规则及办法,若不影响于其权力之最要成份者,则不表示反对。

东北政务委员会

统一未久,即设立东北政务委员会于沈阳。该委员会名义上受中央政府监督,实为东北各省之最高行政机关,内置委员十三人,由委员中推选一人为委员长。该委员会负责指导并监督辽宁吉林黑龙江热河四省,及自一九二二年称为特别区域即以前中东铁路区域之行政。该委员会亦有权处理凡一切未经中央政府特别保留之事项,并得采取不与中央法令相抵触之任何行动。各省政府及特别区政府,有执行该委员会决议案之义务。

东省行政制度,与中国其他部份所采用者,并无重要区别。容许保留满洲为一行政单位,乃为其最要异点。若无此项容许,则其自动与中央联合,大概不能实现。故就实际言之,在东省除外表稍有更变外,一切情形仍旧。东省当局亦深知其权力得之于其军队者,较之得之于南京政府者为多,此项情形,固与以往无异也。

军队——军事上费用达总支出百分之八十

上项事实,足以解释何以在东省方面有二十五万之巨额常备军,及据称消费二万万元(银币)之巨大兵工厂。军事上之费用,在总支出项下,依估计达百分之八十之谱。则其剩余数目,以之供给行政,警察,司法,教育等费,自感不足。省库方面,对于官员不能支付相当薪俸。一切权力,集于少数军人之手;而各种位置须经彼等之手,方能获得。故滥用私人,官吏腐化,行政窳败,乃为此种情形下不可避免之结果。关于此种普遍的不良政治,调查团获得重要的申诉。但此种情形,不为东省所独有;在中国其他各部,亦有同样状况,或且过之。

为维持其巨额军队计,不得不苛征重税。普通税收,既不敷应用,东省当

局乃复使不能兑现之劣钞,逐渐跌价,致人民负担,益形加重。[①] 此种情形,屡见不鲜;其尤著者,则为"大豆官营"之举。自一九三一年以来,已成为垄断状态。东省当局既得支配东省主要产品,希望强迫外国大豆主顾,支付较高价格,以增加其利得;其目标尤注重于日本顾客。此种处置,足以表现东省当局控制银行及商业之程度。东省官吏,同时又自由从事种种私人企业,并运用其权力,为其自己或为其私人从中牟利。

东省中国当局之努力建设

虽然,东省行政在一九三一年九月事变以前,无论有若何弊病,但在若干地方,未尝不努力改良行政,其成绩颇有可观。在教育市政公用事业方面,尤多进步。其更可特别留意者,即张作霖氏及张学良氏统治时代,关于东省中国人民及利益,其经济富源之发展及组织,较从前确有显著之进步。[②]

如前所述,中国方面之大规模移民垦殖,使东省及中国其他部份间经济上及社会上关系,日益扩充。在此时期中,除移垦外,更建筑与日本资本不发生关系之中国铁路,最著者有沈海铁路,打通铁路(北宁路之一支线),齐克铁路,及呼海铁路等;葫芦岛筑港计划,辽河疏浚工程,及各河流航行事业,亦均于该时期中开始。对于各种企业,官私利益均多参加。在矿务方面,对于本溪湖穆稜札兰诺尔及老头沟各煤矿,华人均有利益在内;其他矿产之发展,由华人单独负责;其中大多数,受东北矿务局之监督。华人更投资经营黑龙江省金矿。在森林方面,华人与日人合股经营鸭绿江采木公司,从事吉黑二省森林事业。农业试验场均在东省各地,开始建设。关于农会及灌溉计划,均予以奖励。华人更投资经营面粉及毛织厂;在哈尔滨设立豆油,面粉厂;并创茧丝或野蚕丝棉毛等纺织工厂等。

与中国其他部份商业关系

东省与中国其他部份之商业,亦有进步。[③] 该项商业一部份受中国各银行金融上之援助,最要者,为中国银行;其分行遍设于东省各重要城市。中国轮船及帆船,往来于中国内部与大连营口(牛庄)及安东间。在东省航运上,此项船舶所运货物之数量日有增加,其吨数仅次于日轮所载之数目。中国保险

---

① 原编辑者注:参阅报告书所附载一专论第四号及第五号。
② 原编辑者注:参阅报告书第八章及附载之专论第三号。
③ 原编辑者注:参阅报告书第八章及其纪载之专论第六号。

事业,亦有进步。中国海关,由东省商业上,征得日见增加之税收。

故在中日冲突发生以前,东省及中国其他部份,政治上与经济上的联络,渐臻巩固。此种逐渐滋长的相依状态,促使中国东省及南京方面领袖,采取一种民族思想日形发展之政策,以与日俄既得权利相对抗。

三、与俄国之关系

中俄关系

一八九四年至一八九五年中日战争,使俄国获得出面干涉之机会;其干涉自表面上观之,似为中国;究其实际,经以后事实之证明,乃为其本身利益。日方受外交上压迫,不得不交还由一八九五年马关条约所割让之南满辽东半岛于中国,俄国更援助中国清偿日方所要求之战事赔款。一八九六年,中俄两国间成立秘密防守同盟。

中东铁路

是年为酬报上文所述及之俄国援助起见,中国承认俄国建筑一经过满洲的西伯利亚铁路支线,由赤塔直达海参威[崴]。据称如日人再行攻击中国,此线实为俄方运兵至远东所必要。华俄道胜银行(后改为俄亚银行)即行创办,借以掩饰上述事业之官样性质。该银行即组织中东铁路公司,从事铁路之建筑经营。

一八九六年九月八日合同

依照一八九六年九月八日中国政府与该银行所述合同条款,该铁路公司建筑并经营该铁路,以八十年为期。期满后,无偿交给中国,成为中国财产;但中国政府于三十年后,有权以双方同意之价格,备资赎回。在合同期间,该铁路公司有管理其土地之绝对的及除外的权利。俄方解释该项条款异常宽泛,远过于合同中其他各项条款所能予以证明者。中国对于俄方不断的企图推广合同之范围,提出抗议,但不能制止之。沿路城市,迅速发展,俄方逐渐在中东路区域内,行使一种与统治权相等之权利。中国更允许无偿的交付铁路所需之一切公地。私人土地,须按照时价收用。该公司更得建筑并经营其本身应用上所必需之电线。

一八九八年俄国租借辽东半岛

一八九八年,俄国获得辽东半岛南部之二十五年租借权,该地即为日本于一八九五年被迫交还者;同时取得联络中东铁路由哈尔滨至租借地内旅顺,大

连之权。并得在旅顺建造军港。在该支线经过区域内,公司有采伐木材开掘煤矿以供铁路使用之权。一八九六年九月八日合同内规定,俱得推用于该附加的支线上。俄国得在租借地内,自订税则。一八九九年,宣布大连等自由港;开放外国船舶及贸易。在支线经过区域内,铁路上之特别权利,不得给与他国之人民。在租借地以北之中立地方,未经俄方同意,不得开放与外国贸易之商埠,亦不得为让与或特别权利之允许。

一九○○年俄国占领下之东省

一九○○年,俄国借口拳匪之乱,危及其侨民,出兵占领东省。各国提出抗议,要求其军队之撤退,但俄方延迟其行动。一九○一年二月,在圣彼得堡磋商起草中俄密约,其中有下列条件:若中国欲收回东省政权,须对基于一八九六年基本合同第六款而设立之护路警察准予存留,并约定对于东省蒙古新疆之矿产及其他利益,未经俄国同意,不得转让于他国或他国人民。草约中上述的及其他的条款,经发觉后,惹起中国及他国舆论之反对。一九○一年,俄政府发出通告,声明此项计划,业已撤销。

一九○四年二月十日日本对俄开战

日本对于俄国策略,特别注意。一九○二年一月三十日,订立英日同盟条约;故日本自觉其地位益形稳固。但逆料俄国将侵入朝鲜及东省,不免仍怀忧虑。故与他国督促撤退在东省之俄国军队。俄方声称愿意撤兵;但须附有条件,即除俄国企业外,对于他国采取封闭满蒙办法。在朝鲜方面,俄之压迫,亦日见增加。一九○二年七月,在鸭绿江口发现俄国军队。此外更有其他各项情形,使日方相信俄方已决定一种政策;该项政策,纵非威胁日本之生存,亦将威胁日本之利益。一九○三年七月,日本开始与俄国磋商维持门户开放,中国领土完整之政策,但毫无结果;遂于一九○四年二月十日向俄国开战。中国守中立。

扑资茅斯条约①

是役俄国战败。遂于一九○五年九月三日订立扑资茅斯条约,放弃其在南满之特殊权利。并将租借地及与租借权连带之一切权利,长春旅顺间之铁路及其支路,与在该区域内附属于铁路或为铁路利益起见所经营之一切煤矿,一并转让于日本。双方同意,除租借地外,将所有两国军队占领及管辖之满洲

---

① 编者按:即朴茨茅斯和约。

部份,交还中国单独管理。双方保留(在某种特定条件之下)置守备队保护满洲各该国铁路线之权。是项守备队之人数,每一公里不得超过十五名。

俄国势力限于北满

俄国之势力范围,至是已失其半,而限于北满一隅。其后数年,俄国保持其在北满之地位,且增长其势力。但至一九一七年,俄国革命爆发之时,中国乃决意在该地恢复其主权。

出兵西伯利亚

最初,中国之行动限于参加协约国干涉(一九一八至一九二○年)。其时,鉴于俄国革命后在西伯利亚与北满一带发生之纷乱情形,美国提议协约国出师干涉,原具有二重目的,一为保护储积于海参崴之大宗军用材料与粮物,一为援救由东线退却经过西伯利亚之五万余捷克军队。此项提议,经协约各国接受,并约定每国应各派遣远征军七千人,前往西伯利亚铁道沿线各该指定地段驻扎。而中东铁道,则委托中国完全负责。一九一九年,为保证铁道运用与协约国军队间取得联络起见,特别成立一协约国间铁道特别委员会,并于该委员会之下,设技术与运输二部。一九二○年干涉终局,协约国军队相继从西伯利亚撤退,惟日本军队逗留不去,且与布尔雪维克军[①]发生战斗。战事拖延经两年之久,至一九二二年华府会议后,日本军队始行撤退。而协约国间铁道委员会及其技术部亦于同时取消。

一九一七年俄国革命爆发后中国取消一八九六年所予俄国之特权

是时适际中东铁路长官霍尔瓦特将军在铁路区域企图创设独立政体失败之后,中国遂起而担负维持该区治安之责任(一九二○年)。同年中国与曾经改组之华俄道胜银行订立合同,并宣称欲于与俄国新政府缔结协约之前,暂时掌握该路之最高管辖权。中国并宣布欲恢复一八九六年合同及该公司原有章程所赋予中国之权利。此后公司理事会之理事长一人,理事四人,及监事会之监察二人,应由中国政府指派。俄国之优势,嗣复因其他办法,大受减削。铁路区内之俄军均经缴械解散,而代以中国军队。并封闭俄国法庭。取消俄人领判权地位,使服从中国法律,受中国法院制裁,负纳税义务。当时中国警察握有大权,加以管理欠当,俄人每遭逮捕及无期拘押。

[①]　编者按:即布尔什维克军。

特别行政区域之成立

一九二二年,向在该公司管理下之设铁路区域改为东三省特别区,设行政长官一人,直接对奉天负责,铁路所有土地之管理权亦同遭干预。在俄国新政府未被承认之前,张作霖上将事实上,已将俄国之势力范围实行清除,但于进行中,私人利益则蒙受重大之损失。及至苏联政府承受其旧俄政府在满洲之遗业时,铁路之特权业已剥削殆尽。

一九一九至一九二〇年之中俄协定

一九一九至一九二〇年苏俄政府对华政策之宣言,对于旧俄帝国政府在中国所获之特殊权利尤显著者,在北满所获之特殊权利——寓有完全放弃之意。

一九二四年之协定

苏俄政府,依照此项政策,同意订立一新协定,以规定既成之事实。中东铁路,因一九二四年五月三十一日之中俄协定,成为一共同管理之纯粹商营事业,其中中国亦获得一部份之经济利益。苏政府有指派局长之权,但局长所能行使之职权广泛而未经详细规定。且在该协定下,苏俄政府对于铁路事务,占有优越势力,并得保持北满经济利益之重要部份。一九二四年五月北京中国政府所缔结之协定,未得张作霖氏之接受。曾于上文提及张氏坚持应由彼个人另订协定。是项协定嗣于一九二四年九月签字,其条款,除将经营铁路期限,由八十年缩短为六十年外,几与前者完全相同。

张作霖对于苏俄利益之进取政策

此项协定并未克创立苏俄与满洲张氏行政间友好关系之新纪元。

解决一九二四年两协定中各种悬案之会议,以各种借口延未举行。中东铁路局长于一九二五年及一九二六年,两次拒绝该路运输张氏军队。因第二次拒绝之事,致有局长之被捕,与苏俄之最后通牒(一九二六年正月二十三日)。凡此种种并非不相关连之事变。然而中国当局始终采取一反对俄国利益之政策,极为苏俄政府与白俄所恚愤。

一九二九年中国清除苏俄满洲势力之最后努力

满洲归附南京政府之后,中国民族精神益见激昂,对于苏俄维持中东铁路优越管辖权之努力,民情愤慨,较前尤烈。一九二九年五月遂有清除俄国利益范围最后残余之尝试。着手之始,中国警察搜查苏俄领馆数处逮捕多人,并宣称获有证据,证明苏俄政府及中东铁路之雇员正在阴谋煽动共产革命。七月

间,进占铁路电报电话机关,并强行封闭苏俄之重要团体与企业多处。最后令该铁路俄局长将事务移交中国继任人员。该局长拒绝交卸,遂受禁止不得执行职务。中国当局复自由更动俄员,以自派人员替补。苏联人民被捕者多人,遣送出境者亦复有之。中国方面力自辩护其所取之暴力行动,责苏俄政府以破坏信约而从事反对中国政治及社会组织之宣传。苏俄政府于五月三十日通牒中,对此罪名,加以否认。

苏俄政府之行动

中国既对于剩余之俄国权利与利益强行清除,因是,苏俄政府决定采取行动,经几度换文之后,撤回驻华之外交商务代表,以及所派之中东铁路在职人员,并断绝所有中俄间铁路交通。中国亦自苏俄境内撤回所有外交官吏,而断绝与苏俄之关系,苏俄军队遂越满洲边界,开始袭击,继续进展。至一九二九年十一月,已成武力侵略之局势。满洲当局,受南京政府之委托,解决中俄争执于既遭败北复损威望之余,迫不得已接受苏俄之条件。

一九二九年十二月二十二日伯利议定书①

一九二九年十二月二十二日中俄议定书在伯利签字,原状因以恢复。当争议之时,苏俄政府,对于签订巴黎非战公约各第三国之通牒,所采取之态度,始终自认其所取行动为合法之自卫,不得视为违犯该约。

一九〇五年以来关于满洲之日俄关系

日本在满洲之利益,将于下章详细讨论。但于未叙述之前,势须于叙述俄国在满洲地位之中,简略提及一九〇五年来日俄两国间之关系。

一九〇七至一九一七年之合作政策

日俄两国能于战争后随即采取一密切合作之政策,而彼此在南北满之利益范围能于缔结和约时获得一满意之均势,实为一饶有兴趣之事实。因其他列强之欲积极从事于开发满洲而引起之争执,使是项战后遗留之创痕迅归消灭。两国修好之进行因恐惧其他竞争者之心而增速。一九〇七年,一九一〇年,一九一二年,与一九一六年之条约均能使两国关系日趋密切。

俄国革命对日本之影响

一九一七年之俄国革命,与其后一九一九年七月二十五日一九二〇年十月二十七日苏俄政府宣布对华政策之两次宣言,及一九二四年五月三十一日

---

① 编者按:又译伯力议定书。下同。

九月二十日之两次中俄协定,将日俄在满洲谅解与合作之基础,根本推翻。此种政策上之根本改革,使远东三国间之关系发生彻底之变化。加以,协约国干涉(一九一八年至一九二〇年),及日俄军队在西伯利亚冲突(一九二〇年至一九二二年)之结果,使日俄关系之变化,益形显著。苏俄政府之态度,实予中国民族之热望以有力之兴奋,盖苏俄政府至第三国际对于根据现存条约维持对华关系之一切帝国主义国家,既采取反对政策,则对于中国恢复主权之奋斗,似亦有予以赞助之可能情形。此种之进展,使昔时日本对俄之忧虑与猜疑完全复活。曾经一度与日本交战之俄国,于战后数年中,一变而为日本同盟之友。现在此种关系业经改变,而俄国势力越出北满范围之危险,竟成为日本关切之问题。在北有俄国之共产主义,在南有国民党之反日宣传,两者联合大有可能,日本于是益觉于两者间置一与两者无关之满洲之为得策。日本之疑惧,益因最近数年来苏俄政府在外蒙所得之优越势力,以及共产主义之滋长于中国而随以俱增。

一九二五年一月日本与苏俄缔结之协约,虽设立正式之邦交,但革命前之密切合作终未克因之恢复。

第三章 一九三一年九月十八日以前中日关于满洲之争执

一、日本在中国之利益

一九三一年九月以前二十五年间满洲与中国其余部份之连锁关系,日臻密切,而同时日本在满洲之利益亦逐渐增加,满洲之为中国一部无待证明,惟在此部份内日本业已取得或要求如彼之非常权利,以限中国主权之行使,则中日间之发生冲突,自属自然之事。

一九〇五年条约上之日本权利

根据一九〇五年十二月会议东三省事宜正约,中国同意将前此租予俄国之旅大租借地及长春以南中东路支线转让于日本。在附约内中国并允准日本改良安奉间之军用铁道,并准其经营十五年。

南满铁路株式会社组织于一九〇六年八月

一九〇六年八月南满株式会社奉日皇上谕正式成立,接收东清铁路之南

段及安奉铁路并管理之。日本政府以铁路及其财产暨沿线之抚顺烟台煤矿抵充该铁路株式会社股本之半数，遂取得管辖该株式会社之权；并委托该会社管理铁道地带，征收税捐，复准许其经煤业电气事业，堆栈事业，及其他商业。

日本并吞朝鲜

一九一〇年日本并吞朝鲜，日本在满洲之权益，以是间接增加，因居住满洲之朝鲜人，改隶于日本而受日本官吏之管辖也。

一九一五年之条约及换文

一九一五年以日本突然对中国提出非常要求即所谓"二十一条"者之结果，五月二十五日中日双方关于南满东内蒙当即签定条约，并互换条文。根据是项协定，关东租借地（包括旅顺大连在内）之租借年限原为二十五年者今则改订为九十九年，南满及安奉铁道之租用年限亦展为九十九年。在南满之日本人民且取得旅行，居住，从事各种营业，租地以经营商业工业及农业之种种权利。在南满东蒙，日本关于建筑铁道及供给借款有优先权。关于南满雇用顾问亦有优先权。惟日本在一九二一年至一九二二年之华盛顿会议席上曾声明放弃关于借款及顾问之权利。

由上述条约及其他协定遂使日本在南满享有重要及非常地位，其管理租借地几有完整之统治权。且用南满铁道名义以管理铁路地带，若干城镇及居民稠密奉安长春之大部，均在该地带之内。日本在是项铁路地带内管理警察，征税，教育，及公用事业。南满各处驻有日本军队，如租借地内之关东军，铁道地带内之守备队，以及其他各处之领馆警察均是。

满洲境内中日间政治经济法律关系之非常性质

上述日本在满洲之种种权利，足征［证］满洲境内中日间政治经济法律关系具有非常性质。如斯状况，举世殆无可比拟。一国在其邻国之领土内，享有范围如此广大之经济及行政权利，殊为罕见。如此状况只有在二种条件下，或可维持而不至于发生不断之纠纷及争执。此条件为：或出于双方之自由愿意与接受；或出于双方关于经济政治事项恳切合作之政策；非然者只有引起龃龉与冲突而已。

二、中日在满洲根本利益之冲突

中国对于满洲之态度

中国人民认满洲为整个中国之一部。使满洲脱离中国之任何阴谋，皆在

极端反对之列,东三省为中国之一部,此为中国及列国共认之事实。中国政府当地法律上之主权,亦从未发生疑问,在中日条约及协定上其他国际条约上均可证明,各国外交部之正式公牍上亦一再申述,日本外务省之公牍亦然。

满洲为中国之第一防线

中国人民认满洲为第一防线。满洲与日俄两国接壤,中国人民视为缓冲地,并视为斥候地,盖惧日俄两国势力由此侵入中国其他各部也。长城所以限南北,外寇由此侵入关内,危及北平,殷鉴不远,中国人之惴惴,盖有由也。近年以来,东北铁道纵横,交通发达,中国人民益虑外患之来自东北。此种忧惧以过去一年间之事变,尤觉为之锐增。

中国在满洲之经济利益

以经济理由言,中国人民亦重视满洲。近数十年来,中国人民常称满洲为"中国之粮食策源地"。近年来满洲邻近各省农工,相率出关,满洲盖关内人民按时令谋生之地也。

中国全部是否人口过剩,虽属问题,但某某区域与行省,例如山东,则确系人口过剩,必须移殖,此人口专家所公认者也①,以是中国人民认满洲为边陲旷地,足以调剂中国其他部份现在及将来之人口问题。日本人民常自诩满洲之经济发展,日人之力独多。中国人则列举中国历年来之殖民事业,尤其一九二五年后大规模之殖民事业。铁路之发展以及其他事业以为反证,而否认日本之誓言。

日本对于满洲之关系:日俄战争引起之情绪

日本对于满洲之关系,其性质与程度均与其他各国不同。一九○四至一九○五年之日俄战争以满洲平原为战场,奉天,辽阳,沿南满铁道一带,鸭绿江头,辽东半岛等处,曾经血战,日本人民心目中留有甚深之印象。缅怀往事,记忆犹新。日本人民盖永久不忘日俄之战为反抗俄人侵略之自卫战争。生死存亡,关系匪浅。日俄之役日本军人战死者十万人,战费至二十万万日元之巨。日本人民心目中以为如此巨大牺牲,不应无相当代价。

日本对于满洲,在日俄战争十年前即已发生关系。一八九四年至一八九五年中日因争朝鲜而开战,以旅顺及满洲平原为战场。迨中日议和,签订马关条约,中国割让辽东半岛,嗣后俄法德三国出而干涉,日本遂放弃此项割让。

---

① 原编辑者注:参阅本报告附件专论第三号。

日人迄今尚以为日本因战胜而取得满洲之一部,并不因三国干涉而受若何影响,精神上至今仍保持享有辽东半岛之权。

日本在战略上对满洲之关系

日本屡称满洲为日本之生命线,其地与日本之属地朝鲜接壤。日本人心目中以为中国一旦统一,国力强盛,以四万万人民之国雄据满洲及远东,而又对日仇视,当然于日本不利,故常感不安。但日本人口称"日本民族存在之威胁及自卫之心必要时,其心中盖重视苏俄甚于中国。故日本对于满洲之特别关怀,实因满洲在军事上为形势要地故也"。

日本国内人民以为日本应在满洲占据形胜,深沟高垒,预防苏俄之可能的攻击者颇不乏人。日人无时不忧虑朝鲜失意份子与海滨省境内之苏俄共产党徒勾结,将来或招致来自北方之武力进攻,或竟与之合作,因此视满洲为对俄与对中国之其他部份之缓冲地。日本军界以为依据日俄间中日间各种协定所得在南满铁道沿线地带驻扎数千铁道守备队之权利,较之日俄战争日方之绝大牺牲,殊为得不偿失。而欲借此以防来自北方的攻击之可能,尤非有力之保障。

日本在满洲之特殊地位

爱国情绪,国防需要,非常条约权利,三者合而造成日本对满洲境内"特殊地位"之要求。日本关于特殊地位之观念,并不为中国日本间或日本列国间各种条约及协定上法律规定者所限制。日人因日俄战争而发生之情感及属于历史的联想,与夫因最近二十五年来满洲日本事业之成功,而发生之自尊心理,皆构成日本"特殊地位"要求之成分。是项心理成分虽属言之凿凿,然实则无从加以定义,因此日本外交辞令上所用"特殊地位"一名词,遂致涵义不明,以致其他列国对于所谓"特殊地位"用国际文件加以承认一节,虽非不可能,但终觉不无困难。

日俄战争以后,日本政府屡向俄法英美等国要求承认日本在满洲之"特殊地位","特殊势力及利益"或"最要利益"。日本此项努力,只得一部份之成功,国际间协定或谅解,间有相当承认是项要求者,例如一九〇七年一九一〇年一九一二年一九一六年日本帝俄间之密约,英日同盟条约,及一九一七年蓝辛石井换文等皆是。然此等协定或谅解,大都时过境迁,因正式废止或其他手续,业已不复存在。一九二二年二月六日华盛顿会议,签订九国条约。各签字国[①]赞

---

① 原编辑者注:九国即美,比,英,中国,法,意,日本,荷兰,葡萄牙。

同"尊重中国之主权与独立暨领土与行政之完整"维持"各国在中国之商务实业机会之均等",不得因中国状况"乘机营谋特别权利",并给予中国"完全无碍之机会,以发展并维持一有力巩固之政府",皆予签字国对于在中国各部——满洲亦在内"特殊地位""特殊权益"之要求,以极大之打击。

惟九国公约之规定,及上述各种条约因废止及其他手续而失效一节,并未能使日人改变态度。石井子爵在其近著《外交余录》内发表其本国人之见解,极为明晰。其言曰:"蓝辛石井协定虽已取消,而日本之特殊利益并未摇动。日本在中国之利益既未因国际协定而造成,故亦不能成为取消之对象。"

日本在满洲"特殊地位"之要求与中国主权及政策之冲突

日本关于满洲之要求与中国之主权冲突,并与国民政府减少在华各国现有之非常权利及制止是项权利将来扩充之希望,亦不能相容。试将中日双方在满洲所取之政策加以考索,则双方冲突之日甚,即灼然可见。

日本对于满洲之一般政策

自一九〇五年迄一九三一年九月事变,日本历届内阁对满之一般目标始终相同,所不同者在达到此项目标之政策耳。日本对于维持治安应负责至若何程度一节,历届内阁对之亦不一致。

日本历届内阁关于满洲之一般目标,不外维持及发展日本之既得利益,促进日本各种事业之扩充,及取得日本人民,生命财产之充分保护。至用以实现此项目标之政策,则有一共同之主要特征,即倾向于一种趋势,谓满洲及东部内蒙古不得与中国其他部份一律看待,是盖由日本人在满洲之"特殊地位"之观念而来。历届内阁所采用之特别政策无论如何不同,例如所谓币原男爵之"亲善政策",已故陆军大将田中男爵之"积极政策"彼此互异。然其具有是项公共特征则一。

"亲善政策"发生于华盛顿会议之时,维持至一九二七年四月。继起之"积极政策"维持至一九二七年七月,嗣后又仍采"亲善政策",以继续日本外务省之正式政策,直至于一九三一年九月,以促成是二种政策之精神论,其间有极显著之区别。"亲善政策"币原男爵曾云系以"善意与睦邻之道为基础","积极政策"则以武力为基础。至就对满应采用之具体措置而论,则关于维持满洲治安,保护日本利益,日本究应进行至如何程度,两派政策亦自不同。

田中内阁之积极政策对于满洲与中国其他部份不得一律看待之必要一节,极为注重。日本曾坦白声明"万一纷乱波及于满蒙,治安因而蒙其影响,危

及吾人在该两区域内之特殊地位与权益时"，"无论其威胁从何处发动，日本将起而保障之"。积极之性质，至是而益形显著。田中政策切实声明日本负责维持满洲之治安，此即与前此仅以保护日本利益为目的之政策不同之处也。

日本对华政策以在满洲者尤为坚决，盖欲保护及发展在该地方之既得利益也。日本内阁亦有侧重于军用带有武力威吓之干涉方法者，一九一五年对华提出"二十一条"，即其尤著之一例。至于"二十一条"及其他干涉与威胁方法是否适当，则意见亦殊不一致。

华盛顿会议关于日本在满洲地位及政策之影响

华盛顿会议对于中国其他部份之景况虽曾发生显著之影响，而在满洲则实际上丝毫无变更。一九二二年二月六号签订九国条约关于中国领土完整及门户开放政策虽有规定，然从日本在满洲既得利益之性质与范围观点上立论，则九国公约对于满洲之适用，却受有限制，虽以该约之文字言，该约固可适用于满洲。日本虽已正式抛弃，如上文所言，一九一五年之条约给予日本关于外债及顾问之特别权利，然而九国条约的实质上并未减少日本以既得利益为根据之要求。

日本与张作霖之关系

自华盛顿会议至一九二八年张作霖总司令身故，日本在满洲之政策，多注意其与东三省事实上统治者之关系。日本对于张作霖曾予以相当之援助，当上章所述郭松龄倒戈事件发生时，尤然显著，张作霖总司令虽反对日本提出之许多要求，然亦觉日本之愿望不能不予以相当承认，盖深虑日本随时可用优越之武力强迫其承受其愿望也。且张氏亦而有意于利用日本奥援，以抵御北方苏俄之势力。就大体论，日本与张作霖总司令之关系，自日本立场言之，尚不失为相当圆满。惟张氏晚年不欲履行所谓允诺及协定，双方因而时生龃龉。在张氏于一九二八年六月间因失败而退回奉天之以前数月间，日本对张氏之感情突变而反对张氏，其事亦不无佐证。

日本主张维持满洲之治安与秩序

一九二八年春中国国民革命军逼近北京驱逐张作霖势力之际，日本田中首相以政府名义，发表声明，称为日本满洲有"特殊地位"，故欲维持该地方之治安。当战事有展及关外之势时，日本政府于五月二十八日致通牒于当时各军事领袖，其文曰：

"满洲之治安维持，为帝国所最重视，苟有紊乱该地方治安，或成为紊

乱该地方原因之事态发生,帝国政府将竭力阻止之。故战乱进展至京津地方其祸乱将及满洲之时,则帝国政府为维持满洲治安计,不得不取适当而且有效之措置。"

同时田中男爵发表宣言措辞尤为肯定,谓日本政府将阻止"战败之军队或追逐之军队"进入满洲。

是项关系远大之政策宣布后,北京政府及南京政府均有抗议。南京政府之照会内云日本议拟之措置,"不独干涉中国之内政,且与国际公法上列国相互尊重领土主权之原则显相违反"。

田中内阁之积极政策,日本国内政党赞成者有之,剧烈抨击者亦有之。币原派攻击尤力,其所持理由为维持满洲全部之治安,并非日本之责任。

日本张学良间关系之紧张

一九二八年张学良继乃父为总司令,对日关系自始即呈逐渐紧张之概。日本希望满洲始终脱离新成立之南京国民政府。而张学良总司令则赞成承认国民政府之权力。关于日本官吏紧急劝告不可服从中央政府一节,上文亦已述及矣。惟一九二八年十二月奉天各衙署易帜时,日本政府并未曾干涉。

日本张学良间之关系继续紧张。一九三一年九月以前之数月内,双方冲突,益形尖锐。

三、中日关于满洲铁道之争执

满洲国际之争大半为铁道之争

最近二十五年来满洲之国际政治,大半系关于铁路问题。国家政策上之需要,较之纯粹经济及铁道业务上之理由,更为重要。故满洲各铁道对于该地之经济发展,并未尽其最大之效用。中日铁道当局殊鲜合作,甚至毫无合作,以共图实现双方有益之铁道政策,此则吾人研究铁道问题所发现者也。试以西加拿大及阿根廷铁道事业为比例,其铁道之扩充皆以经济关系为前题,而在满洲铁道事业之发展,则竟成为中日双方之竞争。满洲建筑稍有关重要铁道不引起中日间或其他有关之列国交换照会互相抗议者,盖未之有也。

南满铁路在满洲对日负有"特殊使命"

满洲之有铁道,始于以俄资建造归俄人管理之东清铁路。日俄战争以后,东清路之南段归日本管理,是为南满铁路,以是中日间之竞争遂不可免。南满铁道株式会社名义上虽为财团法人,而实际则为日本政府之营业。该公司之

职权不独管理铁路,且兼有一般行政上之非常权利,议该公司组织成立以来,日人从未视为纯粹经济事业。该公司第一任总裁之已故后藤子爵以为南满铁道在满洲对日负有"特殊使命",是即该铁道业务之根本原则也。

南满铁路经营二十余年,管理极善,效率素著。对于满洲经济之发展,贡献殊多。该铁路株式会社除营业外,附设学校,实验所,图书馆,农事试验场,均可资中国人民之攻错。惟该株式会社之兼有政治性质,以及与日本政党政治之关系,亦颇足为其障碍;而该会社之大宗支出,往往不能获得相等之利。该株式会社成立以还,定策借款与华方建筑可与南满铁路衔接之路线,以便用联运办法将大宗货物移向南满铁路转运至日本租借地内之大连港出口。该公司对于建造此类铁路之投资,为数甚巨,然从纯粹经济理由着想,此类路线之建造,是否合算,则殊为疑问。且从大宗资本之垫付及借款条件上之观点着想,其理由之是否充分,尤属可疑。

中国领土上有外人掌管之机关如南满铁路者,中国当局当然不表赞同,日俄战争以后,中国方面对于该铁路条约及协定上之权利时时发生疑问。一九二四年以后,满洲之中国当局,认识铁道事业之重要,决定不借日资自行建造铁路,于是此项问题益呈严重之象。筑路计划不免与经济军事两种关系,相提并论矣。

满洲宣布服从南京政府以前华方自筑铁路之努力

打通线原为达展垦区及增加京奉线之收入而建筑,然因一九二五年郭松龄倒戈之役,中国独有并自营铁路之军事及政治的价值,亦同时表现。华方之开始打破日本之铁路垄断,并阻止其将来之发展,其事在国民政府政治影响及于满洲之前。张作霖总司令当权时代,打通线,奉海线,呼海线业已筑成。一九二八年张学良总司令继承政权,当时中央政府及国民党提倡"恢复利权"运动,声势甚盛。张学良总司令之政策得此项运动之声援,遂与日本以南满铁路株式会社为中心之垄断政策及拓大政策,发生冲突矣。

关于"并行线"之冲突

日本于一九三一年九月十八日以还,在满洲采用军事手段,其所持理由,则借口于中国方面破坏日本之"条约权利",且声称华方未履行一九〇五年十一月至十二月间中日北京会议时中国政府之承诺。此项承诺,约略如下:

"中国政府为维持东省铁路利益起见,于未收回该路之前,允于该路附近不筑并行干路,及有损于该路利益之枝路。"

关于满洲地方"并行铁路"问题之争执,迁延已久,关系重要。一九〇七至一九〇八年间,日本政府第一次要求此项权利,阻止中国政府建筑业经与英国公司订定合同之新法铁路。一九二四年后在满华人重振精神,自行建造铁路,且不借重日资,日本政府因提出抗议,反对华人自行建造打通线及吉海线。然虽经日本之抗议,两路工程仍告竣通车。

关于"条约权利"或"秘密议定书"之存在问题

在本调查团未到远东以前,关于日本所称此项承诺是否实有其事一节,疑窦滋多。本调查团鉴于此项争执之悠久重要性,竭力收集有关之主要事实,抵东京南京北平时,曾详阅有关之文卷。吾人现可声明所谓一九〇五年十一月至十二月间中国出席于北京会议之全权代表关于"并行铁路"之允诺,并未载于任何正式条约;惟一九〇五年十一月四号北京会议第十一日之会议纪录中载有此项所谓承诺。吾等并已获得参与本调查团之日本代表及中国代表之同意,承认除北京会议纪录所载者外,并无其他文件载有此项承诺。

真正问题之所在

由此可知有关系之真正问题,不在日本抗争中国政府爽约在满洲建筑某某铁路之"条约权利"是否存在,而在一九〇五年会议录上之纪录,无论其为"议定书"与否,华方有无履行之义务,是否有正式条约之效力,且在适用上并不受时间及事态之限制。

此项北京会议录上之纪录就国际法律观点论,是否为有效之承诺,如系有效,是否只有一种解释,此项问题之解决,久应取决于公正法庭之判断矣。

此项会议录上之记录,中日双方均有正式译文。以是项译文论,则此段关于"并行铁道"彼此争辩之文字,实为中国全权代表之一种声明意旨之语,是则毫无疑义者也。

中国方面并未否认声明意旨之语之存在。惟对于此项声明之语其性质究竟如何,自有争执以来,双方意见殊不一致。日方主张所用以文字论,确已不许中国建筑南满铁路株式会社认为与南满铁路竞争之任何路线;而中国方面则谓此项声明语含有之效力,仅限制中国不得建筑以故意妨害南满铁道之商务功用及价值为目的之任何铁路。一九〇七年新法铁道案发生,中日双方交换照会。庆亲王代表中国政府于一九〇七年四月七日照会日本驻华公使林男爵,声称出席北京会议之日本全权代表虽曾拒绝承认以距离南满铁路之里数确定"并行线"一名词之定义,但亦曾声明"中国将来凡有开发满洲地方之举,

日本决不拦阻"。准是则中国政府当时实际上似已承认不建筑显然无理损害南满铁道利益之铁道为华方之义务,但始终未承认日本有在南满垄断敷设铁道之权。

究竟何者为并行铁道,迄无定义,而中国方面极愿得一定义。一九〇六年至一九〇八年间,日本政府反对建筑新法铁路时,时人有凡在南满铁道约三十五英里以内之铁道日本均视为"并行"铁道之印象。但一九二六年日本又以打通路线距离南满铁路"平均七十哩以下",视为"竞争并行线",而反对其建筑,故十分满意之定义,颇不易确定也。

广泛通俗辞句解释之困难

就铁路业务观点论,"并行线"即可视为竞争线,凡夺取某铁路能自然吸收之运输之一部份者,谓为竞争路线。竞争运输包括区间运输及联运输二者而言,故限制建筑"并行线"之规定,有时可作极广泛之解释。何为干路何为枝路,中日间亦未经双方共同认定。从铁路业务观点言,此项名词亦随时改变。京奉路线之自打虎山展向北方者原称为枝线。但打通线完工以后,该段铁路亦可认为干线。

情形如斯,无怪关于并行线之承诺之解释问题,引起中日间之剧烈争执。华方欲在南满自行建筑铁路,几于无次不招致日本之抗议也。

因在满洲建筑铁路之日本借款而发生之争执

第二种铁路争执,使在九月十八日事变前,中日邦交益趋紧张者,发生于在满洲为建筑各种中国政府铁路而垫款之各项协定。日本资本,依照现在价格,包括到期未付之款及利息,共一五〇,〇〇〇,〇〇〇日金,业已耗用于建筑下列中国铁路:即吉长吉敦四洮洮昂等铁路,及其他狭轨铁路。

日本申诉中国不付上述债款,不为相当准备,又不履行协定上各项条款,例如任命日本铁路顾问是。日方屡次要求,中国应履行其所谓中国政府之承诺,即允许日本利益得以参加吉会铁路之建筑。该项在计划中路线,将延长吉敦铁路至朝鲜边境,使日本取得由其口岸达于满洲腹地之新海陆短路线,而与其他铁路联络后,又可缩短与内地交通之路程。

中国之辩护

中国为辩护其不付债款起见,指明该项债款,与寻常金融交易不同。并称此项债款,系南满铁路株式会社为垄断南满之铁路建筑权而出贷者,其重要目的属于军事及政治;且无论如何,新铁路之资本,估价过高,故至少在目前营业

上,不能获得相当款项,以偿付其建筑费及债款。又称日方所称任何不履行义务之情形,经公平研究后,即能发现中国方面之行动,完全合理。至于吉会铁路,中国方面否认在道德或即在法律方面,日方所称之协定有效。

南满铁路希望成立一支线系统

有数项情形,与铁路线定相牵连者,使之不得不发生关于债款纠纷。南满铁路实际上无支线,故欲开拓一培养的支线系统,以加增其运费及旅客运输。因而南满铁路株式会社,愿意垫款,建筑此等新路。虽该项借款,未必能于短时期内偿还,亦弗顾也。且于旧借款未清理时,亦愿意继续垫款。

在上述情形中,只须中国新筑各路能为南满之培养线,且其经营上,在某种范围内,受南满势力之支配时,则该路对于债务,似即不汲汲于强迫偿还,而中国铁路之债务,遂日益加增。但至此种铁路中之某某线与中国新铁路系统相联络,于一九三〇年至一九三一年,竟开始与南满铁路为严重的竞争时,则不付借款之声诉,立即随之以起。

西原借款

数种借款协定,含有政治性质,亦为发生纠纷之一种原因。因受"二十一条"之影响,吉长铁路,始置于南满铁路株式会社管理之下。而将该路未还债务,改换为一九四七年期满之长期借款。因"满蒙四铁道协定"而订立之一九一八年日金二千万元垫款,即为"西原借款"之一种;"西原借款"者乃系借给于"安福系"之军事政府,其用途毫无限制者也。又在同样情形之上,向安福系垫付日金一千万元,与建筑吉会路之一九一八年预备借款合同协定相牵连者,亦为一种西原借款。中国国民心理,自商议西原借款后,甚为激昂。但中国政府则从未否认该项借款。因此种种情形,中国方面,遂感觉对于履行各借款契约上之条件,并不负何种道德上之义务。

吉会铁路计划

在中日关系中,吉会铁路计划之争端,特别重要。起初在吉林至敦化一段上,发生种种争论。该段业于一九二八年建筑完成。自此以后,因中国不愿将建筑该路之日本垫款,改为以该路收入作为担保之正式借款,日本表示不满意;且称中国拒绝任命铁路上日本会计员,系违反合同之规定。

中国方面,则声称提出之建筑价值,不特较日本工程师之估计为高,且超过单据上之数目甚巨。中国在建筑价值确定以前,拒绝正式接收路线;且称在接收以前,并无任命日本会计员之义务。

此种种争端,具有确定的及技术性质;并不包含原则或政策问题;宜适用公断或司法上之判断,甚为明显。但迄今尚未解决;使中日双方怨恨,益形强烈。

敦化会宁线之计划

其更为重要且更为复杂者则为敦化会宁线建筑之问题。该段建筑后,即将使长春至朝鲜边境之铁路,一气呵成,而在朝鲜边境,复可与开至邻近的朝鲜口岸之日本铁路相联络。该段铁路之完成,得直接进入满洲腹地;并开放富于材木及矿产之区域,于日本经济上及战略上,均极重要。

日本坚持该段铁路,必须建筑;且要求建筑时,必须加入日资,声称关于此点,中国已为条约上之担保。且谓中国政府在一九〇九年九月四日中日图们江中韩界务条款中曾允许"与日政府商定"建筑该段铁路。中国所以肯为该项允许者,半由日本放弃在间岛区域关于朝鲜方面之旧有要求之故。至一九一八年,中国政府与日本银行签订建筑该路之借款预备合同。日本银行,依照协定,垫款日金一千万于中国政府。但此为西原借款之一种,而所谓西原借款者,由中国方面视之,即为影响约定效力事实。

但两者皆非确定的借款合同协定,中国并无无条件的及在一定日期前,允许日本银行家参加建筑该路之义务。

一九二八年五月之各合同

据云建筑此线之正式确定的各合同,系于一九二八年五月在北京签字,但其究属有效与否,则甚难决定。各该合同,系于不规则之情势下,于五月十三—十五日间,由张作霖时代北京政府交通部之代表签字,固属无有疑义。但中国方面,则主张,彼等时张作霖,正受国民军之压迫,将由北京退出,不获已允许该代表签字,实系在一种胁迫之下,缘当时日方曾向张氏威吓,谓彼如不批准各该合同,则彼之退出关外,将有危险也。究竟张氏自身,曾否亦签字于各该合同,至今尚属聚讼。张氏去世后,奉天之东北政务委员会,及张学良,则均谓各该合同,形式错误,且系于胁迫之情形下交涉,复从未经北京内阁或东北政务委员会批准,因对于各该合同,拒绝认可。

中国反对敦化会宁线之建筑,其根本原因,即在于中国方面,深惧日本将利用此线,以达其军事上战略上之目的。并深信中国之主权与利益,将因日本取此新道由日本海以前往满洲,而受有威胁。

要之此路问题,非财政与商务之问题,乃中日双方国家政策冲突之问

题也。

通运之争议

此外又有中日各路线联运问题，运费问题，大连与中国营口（即牛庄）等港口竞争之问题。

在一九三一年九月时，中国自力建筑，享有所有权，并经营其业务之各铁路，计长约一千启罗米突①。其重者为：奉天海龙线，海龙吉林线，齐齐哈尔克山线，呼兰海伦线及打虎山通辽线（此线系北平辽宁线之一支路），中国并有北平辽宁线，及以下由日资建筑之各线，即吉林长春线，吉林敦化线，四平街洮南线，及洮南昂溪线。在东省事件未爆发以前之两年间，中国方面，颇企图将各该线之业务联络，成为一伟大之中国铁路系统。且努力使一切货傤，于可能范围内，均一律由中国经营之铁路转运，而以营口（即牛庄）或葫芦岛为出海之港口。于是中国方面，对于中国铁路系统上之各港口，则制定通运联络之办法。而于中国各路线及南满铁路间，则于重要之线段，拒绝为同一通运联络之协定。日方因此遂声称，因有此种差别之待遇，遂使原经由南满线——至少须经由该线之一部分——以达大连北满的货傤，横被剥夺。

运费之战争

偕同通运之争议而发生者，则为中日各线间运费之苦战。一九二九——一九三〇年间，中国于打虎山通辽吉林海龙两线通车后，低减运费，实为此项苦战之开始，彼时中国各线，似享有一天然之利益，即彼时中国银币，价格低落，各该线依据银币计算之运费，自较南满路依据日本金元计算之运费为低廉。惟日方于此，则谓中国运费过廉，实构成一不公平之竞争。中国方面答复，则称中国之目的，与南满不同，主要宗旨，不在牟利，而实在于发展乡村，使农民得以最廉之费用，远达于各大市场。

利用差别待遇以优待本国货物之双方的互诟

于运费低减之竞争中，又有一问题发生，即此方对彼方，互讧其实施差别运费，或秘密减折运费，以优待其本国人民是也。日本方面，则谓中国铁路运输，既已分等别，使中国物产，经由中国路线转运者，较外货为低廉，而对于土产，及经由中国铁路以运至中国所管海口之货傤，又复收常率以下之运费。中国方面，则谓南满铁路，曾秘密减折运费，并特别指明日本某转运经纪，对于交

---

① 编者按：kilometre 的音译，即千米。

其转运之货傤,曾收取较南满路法定率为更低之运费。

凡此种种问题,均属特别专门问题,且性质亦极为复杂。双方之互诉,究竟谁有理由,殊难断定。实则此等问题,依照通常办法,原应由铁路委员会或通常司法上之判断以解决之。[1]

港口之争议

满洲中国当局之铁路政策,原系以葫芦岛新港口之发展为焦点。营口不过为第二等港口,于葫芦岛尚未争议完全发达前,暂充主要港口。且尚有许多新路之计划,实际上可供满洲全部之用。日本方面,因谓中国实行联运及低减运费诸办法,遂使原应运至大连之大部分货物,横被剥夺,且谓此项情形,尤以一九三〇年为特著。以为由南满运至大连出口之货傤,在一九三〇年减少至一百万米突吨[2],而是年营口,较之前一年,则有实际上之增益。中国方面,则指明大连货傤减少,主要之原因,之由于一般经济之不景气,特殊之原因,则由于素为南满大宗货傤的大豆之滞销。至于营口之加增,则谓系新筑各路,通至各地,交通发达之结果。

日本方面,似系对于中国各线及葫芦岛之将来可能的争竞,特别挂虑,以为中国所以计划建筑多数新路,及发展葫芦岛港口,其目的,即在于使"大连港口及南满铁路之本身,均变为无有价值"。

今试将此种种铁路问题,综合观察,即可知其中许多问题,系具有专门性质,极能由通常公断或司法手续解决。但其余之各问题,则系由中日剧烈之竞争所造成,而此项剧烈的竞争,则又系导源于双方深固的国策之冲突。

一九三一年中日铁路交涉

一九三一年之初,凡此种种铁路问题,实际上均尚悬而未决。自一月开始,下至夏季,中日双方,曾为断断续续之努力,冀图开一会议,将双方关于此项未决各问题之政策,设法调和,顾彼所谓本村高交涉(Kimura,Kao Negotiations)者,竟未能有所成就。当一月间交涉开始之际,颇可信双方之均具诚意。乃不幸迁延复迁延,则亦应由双方负责。因有此迭次之迁延,遂使彼已为种种筹备之正式会议,直至东省事变发作时,迄尚未能开成。

---

① 原编辑者注:请参阅本报告附件专论第一号。

② 编者按:即 metric ton,公吨。

四、一九一五年中日条约暨换文及其关连之争执

"二十一条"与一九一五年之条约及换文

除铁路纠葛以外,中日间在一九三一年九月最重要之悬案,厥为由一九一五年中日条约及其换文而生之争执;一九一五年中日条约与换文,即所谓"二十一条"之结果也。此项争执,多关系南满及东内蒙古,因除汉口冶萍公司(在汉口附近)问题外,其他在一九一五年商订之协定,非经代以新协定,即经日本自动放弃。在满洲之争执系于下列规定:

(一)关东租借地之日本所有期展至九十九年(一九九七年);

(二)南满及安奉铁路之日本所有期延长九十九年(二〇〇二年与二〇〇七年);

(三)允准日本臣民在南满内地,即在根据条约或其他开放与外人居住经商之地域以外者,有商租地亩之权;

(四)允准日本臣民在南满内地有居住往来并经营工商业之权,及在东部内蒙古有参加中日合办农业之权。

上项允准与让与,日人有无法律权利享受,胥视一九一五年条约与换文之效力而定,而华人固继续否认该约与换文有束缚彼等之力。中国人民,无论其为官吏或平民,均深信"二十一条要求"一词实际上与"一九一五年条约与换文"同义,并以为中国之目的,应为解除该约之束缚;凡是种种,无论几何专门之解释或理由,不能稍移其念。在一九一九年之巴黎和会中,中国曾要求废除该约,其理由为该约系签订于"日本哀的美敦书以战争为恐吓之威胁之下"。在一九二一一二二年之华盛顿会议中,中国代表团曾提出"关于此项条约之公平与正义以及其根本效力"之问题;一九二三年三月,即中国在一八九八年租与俄国之辽东(关东)租借地原定二十五年租期行将届满之前,中国政府复照会日本声明废止一九一五年之规定,并声称"此项条约换文,本国舆论始终反对"。中国方面既坚持一九一五年之条约"根本无效",故对于该约关于满洲之规定,除情势必要外,不予履行。

对于中国人因此违犯日人条约上之权利,日人颇多怨言。日人以为一九一五年之条约与换文,曾经正式签字批准,并有效力。诚然,在日本有一部分之舆论自始即不赞成"二十一条要求";而晚近日本演说家与时论家之批评此项政策者,亦习见不鲜。但坚持该约关于满洲之各项规定为有效,日本政府与

人民,似属一致。

辽东租借地租期与南满及安奉铁路让与期之延长

一九一五年条约与换文之两项重要规定,为关东之借地之租期由二十五年展至九十九年,及南满与安奉铁路之让与同样展至九十九年。此种延长期限,为一九一五年条约之结果,而收回昔日政府租出之土地,又为反对外人利益之民族主义的"恢复利权运动"之一部,因此两种理由,关东租借地以及南满铁路时为中国人运动之对象,甚至为中国外交之对象。张学良司令之宣告满洲服从中央政府以及允许国民党传播其势力于满洲之政策,使此种争执在一九二八年后更尖锐化,虽其在实际政治常隐而不露。

与一九一五年条约及换文相关者,厥为收回南满铁路,或废除该路之政治性质使成为一纯粹的经济事业之运动。然给价收回该路之最早日期既经规定为一九三九,徒然废止一九一五年条约,并不足以将南满铁路复归中国。中国有无能力筹集资本以达此目的,亦极可怀疑之事。中国民族主义之发言人敦促收回南满铁路之言论,足与日人以刺激,盖日人之合法权利与利益因彼而感受威胁也。

对于何者为南满铁路之正当任务,日方与华方之见解,自该铁路株式会社一九○六年组织时起,即不一致。自然,就法律论,南满铁路株式会社,系在日本法律下组织之一私人合股事业,实际上为中国管辖权之所不及。尤其是自一九二七年以来,在满洲之中国人,曾有取消南满铁路株式会社之政治与行政任务,而使成为一"纯粹商务事业"之运动。但中国人似尚未提出具体计划,以完成此目的。就实际言,满铁会社确系一政治事业。彼系一日本政府之机关,政府操纵大多数之股份;其行政政策,受政府严密之管辖,以致日本一有新内阁上台,满铁会社之高级职员,几无不随之而更易。仰更有进者,在日本法律之下,满铁会社受有广泛之政治行政任务,包含警察,课税与教育。如除去满铁会社之此种任务,不啻将南满铁路株式会社之最初立意与嗣后发育滋长之"特殊使命",全部放弃。

铁路区域

关于日人在南满铁路区域以内之行政权,特别是土地取得权,课税权,设置铁道守备队权,发生多数之争执。

铁路区域除路轨道两旁之数码地除外,此带路区域包括十五个市,名为"日本铁路市",坐落于南满铁路之全线,自大连以至长春,自安东以至沈阳。

有数个铁路市,如在沈阳,长春及安东者,包含人烟稠密之中国城市之大部份。

南满铁路株式会社在铁路区域内设置实际上完全之市政府之权利,法律上系基于一八九六年中俄东省铁路公司合同之一条款,该条款称"凡该公司之地段……,由该公司一手经理"。于是直至一九二四年之中俄协定时之俄国政府,与其后为南满铁路取得中东铁路原有权利之日本政府,均将此项规定解释为让与铁路区域之政治管辖权。但中国方面始终否认此种解释,而坚谓一八九六年之合同之其他规定,足以证明该项条款之用意并非让与如此广泛之行政权,有如管理警察,课税,教育与公用事业之权者。

土地争执

关于满铁会社取得土地之争执,亦常发生。依照一八九六年原合同之条款,铁路公司有以购买或承租之方法取得"建筑经理防护铁路所必需"之民地之权利。但中国人认为日人曾将此项权利为不正当之运用,以冀取得更多之土地。结果南满铁路株式会社与中国地方当局之间,几于有不断的纠纷。

铁路区域内课税权之纠纷

对于铁路区域内课税权,双方所持之冲突的主张,引起不少之纠纷。日方之主张,系根据原合同"凡该公司之地段……由该公司一手经理"之规定;中国人之主张,系以主权国家之权利为根据。概括言之,实际情势,系满铁会社同居住满铁区域内之日本人中国人以及外人实行课税,中国官厅虽亦坚持其有此种法律权利,但并未行使。

当中国人对于运往南满路市以便由日本铁路转运大连之物产(如大豆之属)试行课税时,另种纠纷,遂因之时常发生。中国人声称此乃一致赋税,有于日本"铁路市"边境征收之必要,若非然者,将不啻特别优待南满铁路运载之物产。

关于日本在南满铁路沿线设置铁道守备队之权利问题

关于日本铁道守备队各项之争执,几于引起不断之困难。此项争执,亦足以表现前述两国政策在满洲之根本的冲突,且常为伤害不少人命之不幸事件之原因。日本所称设置此种铁道守备兵队之权利,其法律的根据,即时为世人引证之一八九六年原合同之条款,允准凡中东铁路"公司之地段……由该公司一手经理"。俄国认为——但中国否认——该条款曾给与俄国以俄兵护路之权利。在一九〇五年之朴资茅斯和约中,俄日两国,彼此保留设置护路守备兵之权利,该守备兵"每一基罗米突不得超过十五人"。但在中日两国同年于北

京签订之中日会议东三省事宜条约中,中国政府对于日俄和约中之此项规定,并未予以承认。然中日两国在一九〇五年十二月二十二日中日会议东三省事宜附约之第二款中,确曾有下列之规定:

"因中国政府声明极盼日俄两国将驻扎东三省军队暨护路兵队从速撤退,日本国政府愿副中国期望。如俄国允将护路兵撤退,或中俄两国另有商订妥善办法,日本政府允即一律照办。又如满洲地方平静,外国人生命产业中国均能保护周密,日本国亦可与俄国将护路兵同时撤退。"

日方理由

日本之条约权利,即以此条款为根据。然俄国早已将其守备队撤退,并于一九二四年之中俄协定中,放弃其设置守备队之权利。但日本以为满洲地方并未恢复安宁,中国亦无力周密保护外人,因此坚持日本仍保有设置铁道守备队之有效的条约权利。

日本辩护其使用守备队,似渐不以条约上之权利为根据,而逐渐趋重"在满洲现状下有绝对的必要"之理由。

华方理由

中国政府对于日本之申辩,始终不以为然。中国政府坚谓在南满设置日本铁道守备队,无论在法律上,或在事实上,均不能谓为正当,且损及中国之领土与行政之完整。至于业经引证之中日会议东三省事宜附约中之规定,中国政府以为仅系声明一暂时的实际情势,不能谓为给予权利,尤其是含有永久性之权利。中国政府更谓日本在法律上有撤退其守备队之义务,因俄国业已撤退其守备队,满洲地方业已恢复安宁,且只须日本守备队容许,中国当局亦能予南满铁路以充分保护,正如其保护在满洲之其他铁路。

日本铁道守备队在铁路区域之活动

因日本铁道守备队而起之纠纷,不仅限于其在铁路区以内之驻扎与活动。此种守备队系正式日本军队,时常至毗连地带行使其警察之职权,甚或已得或不得中国当局之许可,或通知或不通知中国当局,在铁路区域以外实行操演。此种行为,中国人民,无论官吏或平民,尤一致痛恶,认为不独于法律为不当,且易惹起不幸事件。

此种操演之结果,往往引起误会,并损坏中国农作物,物质的赔偿,殊不足以补救因此而生之恶感。

日本领馆警察

与日本铁道守备队问题密切关连者厥为日本领馆警察问题。此种警察附属于在满洲之日本领事馆及其分馆,不独在沿南满铁路者如是,即在哈尔滨,齐齐哈尔,满洲里,以至多数派旅满之朝鲜人居住之所谓"间岛区域"者亦莫不然。

日本在满洲设置领馆警察之理由

日本以为设置领馆警察之权利,系由领事裁判权演绎而出,且仅系推广领事法庭之司法职权,因此种警察为保护日本臣民与维持其纪律之不可少者也。实际上在中国其他各地之日本领事馆,亦曾设置较少之日本领馆警察,恰与其他有领事裁判权条约之国家之一般习惯相反。

就实际问题观察,日本政府显然相信在满洲现状之下,尤其鉴于日本在该地利益之重要,日本居民——包括朝鲜人在内——之众多,设置领馆警察,确为一种必要。

华方否认日人之主张

但中国政府对于日本在满洲设置领馆警察所持之理由,始终驳斥,并屡向日本提出关于此问题之抗议。中国政府以为在满洲任何地方均无驻扎日本警官之必要,警察问题与领事裁判权并无关系不能相提并论,领馆警察之设置,绝无条约根据,确系侵犯中国之主权。无论其为正当或非正当,领馆警察之存在,确曾屡次引起该警察人员与当地中国官厅人员之严重冲突。

日人在南满内地往来居住并经营商业之权利

一九一五年中日条约曾规定"日本国臣民得在南满任便居住,往来,并经营商工业等一切生意"。此为一重要之权利,但亦为华人所反对者;因在其他中国各地,除约开商埠而外,一切外人均不准居住及经商。盖此乃中国政府之政策,在领事裁判权取消与外人受中国法律管辖之前,不予彼等以此项特权。

然在南满之此项权利,亦有相当限制:日人在南满内地者,必须携带护照并遵守中国之法律及规则。但中国施行于日人之规则,非先"与日本领事成立谅解",不能执行。

中国官厅之行动,常有与此条约条文不相符合者,盖彼等始终不承认该条约为有效。中国代表,对于中国限制日人在南满内地居住往来与经商,及中国官吏出示禁止日人及其他外人于商埠外居住或续租房屋之事实,在其正式提交本调查团之文件内,并未加以辩驳。官厅之压力,间或辅以严厉之警厅措

置，每加于日人之上，强其由南满及东部内蒙古之市镇退出，并加于中国人管有产业者，使之不敢出租房屋于日人。日人声称中国官厅并曾拒绝发给护照与日人，重累彼等以不法之课税，且在一九三一之前数年内，未曾实行条约内之规定，即凡管理日人之规则，应先送交日本领事。

华方之解释与答辩

中国人之目标，乃在实行其限制日本在满洲特殊权利之政策，以增进其管辖东三省之力量。彼等以一九一五年条约"根本无效"为理由，证明此行为正当。彼等更进而指出日人曾企图于满洲全部居住并经商，虽条约上之规定，只限于南满。

此项纠纷为直至九一八事件以前之不断的刺戟物

中日两国之政策及目标，既各背道而驰，其因此项条约规定而起连续且剧烈之纠纷，自所难免。两国均自承认此种情势为直至一九三一年九月事件以前彼此关系中之日益恶化的刺戟物。

关于商租之争执

与在南满内地居住及营业之权利有密切之关系者，厥为租地之权利。一九一五年之条约，曾允许日人有下项租地之权："日本国臣民在南满为盖造商工业应用之房厂，或为经营农业，得商租其需用地亩。"当时两国政府之换文，曾将"商租"一词加以解释。依照中国文本，"商租"二字含有"不过三十年之长期限有无条件续租之可能"之意义。日文本则仅规定"长期租借以至三十年，并得无条件续租"。究竟日人租约，能否凭其单方面的意旨，"得无条件续租"，双方亦发生争执。

日人在满洲取得土地之欲望，无论其以承租，购买，或抵押之方法，在华人眼光中，均为日本"收买满洲"之国策之明证。故中国当局，曾设法阻碍日人之取得地亩。一九三一年八月以前之三四年为中国"收复利权运动"极盛时期，阻碍日人在满洲取得土地，亦以此时为最力。

中国官厅制定严厉条例，禁止日人购买土地，或自由保有地权，或因抵押而取得地权，显然在其合法权利之内；盖条约固仅予日人以租地之权利也。惟日人以为不准以地抵押，颇与该条约之精神不合。

然中国官吏并未承认该条约为有效，因此使尽方法，阻碍日人租地或以省政府或地方政府之命令，使租地与日人者得受刑事上处分；或向此项租约征收特税，规定先期缴纳；或训令地方官吏，如核准地亩之转让日人，必予以处分。

日人以承租购买与抵押之方法在北满与南满同样获得地方

虽有上述种种之障碍,然实际上日人不仅租得大宗土地,且竟行收买,或用其较普遍之方法取消抵押地亩之取赎权,而取得大片土地之自由保有不动产权——虽此种地权,不为中国法庭所承认。日本放债者,尤其是大资本之放债团,有专以取得地亩为目的者;故抵押之土地,泰半为彼等所得。根据日本官方报告,在全满及热河租与日人之土地,在一九二二,一九二三年至一九三一年内,由八○,○○○英亩左右增至五○○,○○○英亩以上。其中一小部份,系在北满地方——依照中国法律与国际条约,日本在该地并无租地之权。

关于商租问题之中日交涉

因此项商租问题至为重要,故中日双方在一九三一年以前之十年间,至少曾有三次之直接交涉,以冀能成立一协定,一可能之解决方法——此方法深信曾经双方予以考虑者——为以商租问题与取消领事裁判权问题,同时讨论;日本允在满洲放弃领事裁判权,中国则许日人在满洲自由租地。但数次之交涉,均归失败。

此项中日长久争执之日人租地权问题,一如与其他上述诸问题,起于两国根本冲突之政策;隐藏于此种政策后之目标,较之彼此以违反国际条约互相攻讦之辞语之本身的意义,更为重要。

五、满洲之朝鲜人问题

朝鲜人在满洲而依照日本法律有日本国籍者,为数约八十万,足使中日两国政策之冲突,益形剧烈。因此争端纷起,而朝鲜人遂成为牺牲,蒙受痛苦与苛待。①

中国方面之反对朝鲜人以购买或租赁方法获得满洲土地,引起日本人之仇视。据日本人主张,朝鲜人为日本国臣民,应享受一九一五年条约及换文赋予日本租地之权利。又日本人不承认朝鲜人归化为中国人,故复发生两重国籍之问题。至日本领馆警察对朝鲜人之监视及保护,则为中国人所深恶,中日两国警察,遂有无数之冲突。在朝鲜边界正北之间岛地方,有朝鲜居民四十万,三倍于中国。因之特殊问题,往往发生。及至一九二七年,中国人因此种种问题采取限制朝鲜人在满洲自由居住之政策,此种政策,日本人认为系无正

---

① 原编辑者注:参阅附载本报告书之专论第九号。

当理由之压迫。

关于朝鲜人在满洲地位之中日协定

朝鲜人在满洲之地位及权利,大都在三种中日协定内确定,即一九〇九年九月四日中日图们江中韩界务条款,一九一五年五月二十五日关于南满与东内蒙古之条约及换文,及一九二五年七月八日之所谓"三矢协定"。至朝鲜人两重国籍之问题,并未经中日间之协定予以规定。

迄一九二七年,在满洲之一般中国官吏渐信朝鲜人事实上已成为日本"侵略并吞满洲之先锋队",并以日本人既不承认朝鲜人取得中国国籍,而日本领馆警察复以监视朝鲜人为恒事,故朝鲜人以购买或租赁获得土地,确为一种政治上与经济上之危险,"危害在满洲中国人民之生存"。

中国方面之论点

在中国人中有一种论调,即朝鲜为日本所逼迫而自祖国移殖满洲,因日本政府熟筹之政策,在使日本人移殖朝鲜以替代朝鲜人,或使朝鲜人于政治上及经济上感受颠连困苦不得不移殖满洲,其迫朝鲜人让渡地产即为日本政府虐待朝鲜人之尤著者也。在中国人之意见,朝鲜人为"被压迫民族",且为一异族政府所统治,而所有重要官职均为日本人所独揽,故被迫而迁入满洲,以求享政治上之自由与经济上之生存。朝鲜垦民十九业农,且大约均能种稻,故初至满洲时,中国人表示欢迎,认为经济上之资产;又因其受或有之压迫,表示自然之同情。中国人以为若日本人不否认朝鲜人归化中国,且不为给予朝鲜人必要之警察保护为词施行追随朝鲜人至满洲境内之政策,则朝鲜人之移殖满洲,不至发生政治与经济上之重大问题。中国人对满洲地方当局,尤其是一九二七年以后,限制不为佃户及工人之朝鲜人在满洲自由垦殖之措施,不承认为"压迫"之事件。

日方否认中国方面之非议

日本人承认中国人之疑忌实为中国人"压迫"朝鲜人之主因,但竭力否认曾实行鼓励朝鲜人移殖满洲之政策,声言"朝鲜人之移殖满洲应视为自然趋势之结果,日本既不鼓励,亦不限制",此种现象不受政治或外交动机之影响。因此日本人声明"中国对日本以利用朝鲜人图谋并吞两区域之畏惧,实属毫无根据"。

朝鲜人问题使中日敌意增剧朝鲜人自身成为牺牲

此种不可调和之意见,使各种问题如租地,管辖权,日本领馆警察等,益形

严重。此种问题已为朝鲜人造成一极不幸之局面,而使中日关系更行恶化。①

朝鲜人与租地问题

除朝鲜人之在间岛者外,并无中日协定特别规定允许或否认朝鲜人在约开商埠外居住及从事职业,或在满洲租赁或以他法取得土地之权。但现在约有四十万朝鲜人散居间岛以外之满洲地方。此种朝鲜人分布甚广,特别在满洲东半部,而尤以朝鲜以北之区域与吉林省人数为多,并已前进至中东铁路东部一带,松花江下游流域及沿中俄边界自朝鲜东北以至乌苏里及黑河之两旁,即在毗连之苏俄境内,亦有居住垦殖之朝鲜人,且多数朝鲜人现在间岛外之满洲地方,均租有或购有农地,盖朝鲜人有因其祖先迁徙满洲在数代以前而成为满洲之土著者,又有因与日本脱离臣民关系而归化中国者。但大多数为佃户,中国人为其佃主,依照租约耕种稻田,以收获为分配之则。此种租约期限大约自一年至三年。地主得斟酌情形,继续允租。

关于朝鲜人租地权中日间协定之争执

中国人否认朝鲜人在满洲间岛地方外有购买或租赁农地之权。因涉及此问题者仅有一九〇九年之图们江中韩界务条款,而该条款之适用,限于间岛。故朝鲜人之已为中国人民者,始得在满洲内地享受购买或居住及租赁土地之权。中国否认朝鲜人在满洲自由租地之主张,其理由为一九〇九年中日图们江中韩界务条款准许朝鲜人仅在间岛一地方有居住及置地之权,并明确规定视朝鲜人应受中国之管辖。该条款为一完全之文件"意在双方让步之下解决中日间关于该处之地方悬案"。上述条款包含一交换条件,即日本放弃对于朝鲜人之管辖权,中国予以置地之特权。

中国方面之理由

自一九一〇年朝鲜归并日本后,中日两国继续履行上述条约,中国方面以为一九一五年之条约及换文,不能更易关于图们江条款之规定。且一九一五年条约内载有一条,明言"关于东三省中日现行各条约,除本条约另有规定外,一概仍旧照行",图们江条款并不除外。中国政府又谓一九一五年之条约及换文不适用于间岛区域,因间岛区域在地理上非"南满"之一部分,盖"南满"二字,地理上与政治上之定义,殊不明了。

---

① 原编辑者注:参阅附载本报告书之专论第九号。

日本方面之争点

自一九一五年以来,中国方面之论据为日本人所否认,以为一九一○年朝鲜归并日本,则朝鲜人已成为日本臣民,而一九一五年之中日条约及换文关于南满与东内蒙古之规定既予日本人在南满以居住及租地之权,并准其参加东内蒙古之合办农业,则是项规定,对于朝鲜人同样适用。日本政府又谓图们江条款因与一九一五年条约之规定抵触,已为其所废止。中国方面所谓该条款为一完全之文件,实无根据,因朝鲜人在间岛所得之权利,由于日本同意,承认间岛为中国领土之一部份。如日本不为在满洲之朝鲜人取得业已赋予其他日本人民之权利及特权,则日本不啻歧视朝鲜人。

日本赞助在满洲之朝鲜人取得土地之理由,本为遂其运米于日本之志愿。顾此种志愿未能尽偿,一九三○年产米七百万蒲式耳(Bushel)。大约一半在当地消费,余米之输出,则受限制。日本以为朝鲜佃民垦殖荒地使中国地主得蒙其利不应反遭不正当之摈斥。

双方争议对于朝鲜人状况之影响

在中国人方面,亦欲使可耕种之低田产米,但大抵雇用朝鲜人为佃农或工人以免耕地落日人之手。多数朝鲜人遂入中国国籍,借置田产。但朝鲜人有已购置田产而让与日本之押产会社者,以故日本人中对朝鲜人归化中国日本政府应否予以承认,主张颇不一致也。

在满洲朝鲜人之两重国籍问题

一九一四年中国国籍法只准外国人其本国法律有归化他国之许可者,有取得中国国籍之资格。但一九二九年二月五日修正之中国国籍法,并不规定外人须丧失其原有国籍,始能取得中国国籍。以故朝鲜人得归化中国,虽日本坚持异议,不顾也。日本国籍法从未准朝鲜人丧失日本国籍,虽一九二四年修正之国籍法载有一条,谓"自愿取得外国国籍之人,丧失日本国籍",然此法从未经过天皇特命,许其适用于朝鲜人。惟朝鲜人之在满洲各处者,自百分之五至百分之二十,已取得中国国籍,而以日本领事馆势力所不尽及之地方为尤众。亦有朝鲜人自满洲边界而至苏俄领土,遂为苏俄人民者。

朝鲜人两重国籍对于中国政策之影响

朝鲜人两重国籍之问题,引起中国国民政府及地方当局对于不限制朝鲜人归化之反感,深恐朝鲜人因暂时取得中国国籍,将成为日本取得农田政策之工具,故一九三○年九月吉林省政府颁布关于买卖该省土地之章程,规定"如

归化中国之朝鲜人购买土地时,应查明是否为永久归化人民居住之用,抑为日本人代购"。但地方官厅之态度,以游移不定,有时实行长官之命令,惟常发暂时归化证书,以替代正式证书。前项证书,须经省政府及南京司法部之核准。其与日本领事馆距离甚远之处,地方官往往愿允才予朝鲜人证书,有时亦实行强迫朝鲜人入中国籍,否则饬其离境。此种举措,系受日人政策及国籍证书费收入之影响。中国人声称日本人纵容朝鲜人归化中国,其目的在利用朝鲜人为名义地主,或以让渡方法从归化中国之朝鲜人取得土地。大概言之,日本当局不容许朝鲜人改入中国籍而尽量施行管辖之权。

关于警察管辖权中日主张冲突而发生之问题,特别严重,涉及朝鲜人

日本主张因领事裁判权而在满洲领事馆有驻扎警察之权,此种主张凡涉及朝鲜人时,即为冲突不已之原因。不问朝鲜人是否切望此种表面上为彼辈利益计之日本干涉,日本领馆警察尤其是在间岛者,不仅行使保护之职,抑且擅自行使查封朝鲜人住所之权,而对朝鲜人犯参加独立运动或共产或反日工作之嫌疑者为尤甚。中国警察当施行中国法律维持治安或遏制不良朝鲜人之动作时,往往与日本警察发生冲突。中日警察亦尝屡次通力合作,如一九二五年"三矢协定"所规定者:照此协定,双方同意中国人在奉天省东部当取缔"朝鲜人之会社",并应日本人之请求,将"品行不端之朝鲜人",送交日本人。然实际上仍有不断之争执与冲突。此种情势,其不能不发生纠纷者,势使然也。

间岛之特别问题

朝鲜人问题与由此而生之中日对于间岛之关系,其性质已变成极复杂而严重。按间岛(日本文为:Kanto,朝鲜文为:Kando)包括辽宁(奉天)省之延吉和龙兴汪清三县,且实际上征诸日本政府所持之态度,珲春亦在其内。此四县者,与朝鲜东北隅毗连,正对图们江。

日本对间岛之态度与政策

日本人论及朝鲜人对间岛之传统态度,不愿承认一九〇九年中日图们江中韩界务条款已将此区域是否属于中国或朝鲜之问题永远解决;以为此区域内太半之农地为朝鲜人所耕种,"彼等在该处已有极深之根基,故可视为朝鲜人之范围"。日本政府在间岛坚持行使管辖及监视朝鲜人之权,历年来驻在该处领事馆之警察,在四百名以上。日本领事馆与朝鲜总督所委派之日本官吏,通力合作,在该处行使有行政性质之广泛职权,包括维持日本学校;医院;及受政府资助而为朝鲜人设立之金融机关。故日人视间岛为移殖朝鲜种稻人之天

然尾闾。以言政治，间岛尤为重要，因间岛已成为提倡朝鲜独立者及共产团体与其他反日之徒之捕逃薮。一九二〇年朝鲜独立运动爆发后，朝鲜人即在珲春举事，反抗日本，故日本在间岛已有严重之政治问题，与统治朝鲜问题有密切关系。以言军事，间岛之重要，亦显而易见，盖图们江下游为中国日本苏俄三国之界线也。

中日对于图们江条款解释上之冲突

中日图们江中韩界务条款规定"中国政府仍准韩民在图们江北垦地居住"；朝鲜人居住是项垦地者，嗣后应"服从中国法权归中国地方官管辖裁判"；并与中国人受同等之待遇，所有民刑各案件，涉及朝鲜人者，应由"中国官员按照中国法律秉公审判"；但日本领事官特别关于人命案件得到庭观审，并有"请求"中国官厅按照中国特别法律程序"另派员复审"之权。

但据日方之见解，一九一五年中日条约与换文已将图们江条款涉及管辖等问题之规定予以废止，而自一九一五年以来朝鲜人已成为日本人，则按照中日现行条约，享受领事裁判权之权利与特权。此种论调，中国政府始终未尝承认，且坚持如图们江条款内关于朝鲜人有居在垦地权之规定，可以适用，则该条款内关于朝鲜人应受中国之管辖各条，亦应有效。又日本人解释允准朝鲜人居住垦地一条为购买租赁间岛之农地，而中国人之见解，则以为此条应从字面解释，享受间岛间地之权仅限于朝鲜人之已归化中国者。

朝鲜人置产实在情形之不规则

以故实在情形，极不规则，盖在间岛之朝鲜人有未曾取得中国国籍而已置地者，中国官吏亦纵容之。但大抵朝鲜人承认取得中国国籍为间岛购地必须条件。照日本官厅统计，间岛过半之耕地（包括珲春）为朝鲜人"所有"，而朝鲜人在该处者百分之十五已归化中国。朝鲜人享有农地之所有权者，是否为已归化中国之人，不得而知。此种情形，往往引起争执，而中日两国警察，且常因此而发生冲突矣。

日本对中国人压迫朝鲜人之非议

日本人称一九二七年将终，时苛待朝鲜移民之运动，爆发于满洲。此种运动系受中国官吏之指使，而为普遍反日潮流之余波。又谓自满洲各省归附南京国民政府以后，苛待朝鲜人，日益剧烈。调查团接到日方所供给关于中国政府及满洲地方当局命令之译件多种。日方以此项译件足以证明中国有确定之计划，以虐待朝鲜人，如令其归化中国，迫其出境，驱之稻田外，强其缴纳苛捐

杂税,不准其签订租赁房地契约,并施以种种虐待。此种压迫运动,对"亲日"之朝鲜人为尤烈,朝鲜居民会社受日政府之资助者,亦遭摧残。而朝鲜人所设立或为朝鲜人设立之学校,均被封闭。至于"不良之朝鲜人",则任其敲诈并凌辱朝鲜农民。又迫令朝鲜人改着中国服装,处此窘苦状况之下,并令其放弃日本之保护或协助。

对于满洲当局颁发歧视未归化中国之朝鲜人之命令,中国人未尝否认,此项命令之众多及其内容,尤其是一九二七年所颁发者,足以证明满洲当局对于朝鲜人以日本管辖权为保障而潜入内地,视为一种危机,应予抗拒。

调查团对于朝鲜人问题之特别注意

鉴于日本论调之严重,并鉴于朝鲜人在满洲之窘苦,调查团对此问题,予以特别注意。调查团并不信此种訾议尽与事实相符,亦不谓某种抑制朝鲜人之措置毫无正当之理由,但调查团可以证实者,中国对满洲某部份地方之朝鲜人之措置,确有如日方之所申述。调查团在朝鲜时曾接见许多代表团,自称为代表朝鲜民众者。

所显而易见者,朝鲜人之在满洲,足使中日对租地,管转权,及警察等问题之争执与夫经济上之竞争,愈形复杂;而此项竞争及争执,实为一九三一年九月间事件之先声也。朝鲜人虽大半俱愿安居乐业,但就中亦有如中国人或日本人或中日两国人之所称之"不良之朝鲜人",内中包含共产主义之信徒,提倡及赞助脱离日本统治而建立朝鲜独立国者,以作奸犯科为业,如私运货物,贩卖药品者;又有与中国土匪勾通专事向同种人敲诈或勒索银钱者。即朝鲜农民自身中,亦不乏因其愚昧而无远虑,并因其愿对较有智慧之地主担负债务,以致往往自取侮辱者。

中国对其待遇朝鲜人之解释

在中国方面之意见,此项涉及朝鲜人之争执实为日本对满洲政策必然之结果,许多对朝鲜人之措置,日方视为"压迫"者,实不得谓之"压迫"。且中国对朝鲜人一部份之办法,为日本当局所赞同,或默许。并谓所应注意者,朝鲜人大半痛恶日本人,对于日本割并其祖国之举,不能甘服。且朝鲜人之来满洲,非其素志,徒以感受政治上与经济上之困难,不得已而出此,故一般均愿脱离日人在满洲之监视。

一九一五年之所谓"三矢协定"

中国人承认对朝鲜人表示同情,但同时指"三矢协定"之存在,足以证明中

国当局甚愿取缔日本人视为"品行不端"之朝鲜人之行为足以危害日人在朝鲜人之地位者，并足以证明一部份之措置即为日本人所欲使他人相信中国人"压迫"朝鲜人之事件者，实得有日本官厅之许可。上述协定，外人知者殊鲜，为日本驻朝鲜总督所派之日本警察厅长与奉天省警察厅长所签订，规定中日两国警察通力合作，以遏制奉天东部之"朝鲜人会社"（大约有反日之性质），"中国当局应立即缉获并引渡朝鲜人会社之领袖，其姓名为朝鲜当局可宣布者"；又"品行不端"之朝鲜人中国警察应缉获送交日本人审讯惩处。故中国人声述："对朝鲜人某种限制办法之采取，大半为实行此项协定起见。如日方以此种办法为中国当局压迫朝鲜人之证据，则即令日方所称属实，其主要目的，实为维护日本之利益计。"中国方面又称："鉴于与本地农民经济竞争之剧烈，中国当局行使其主权，采取方法以保护本国人民之利益，实为当然之事。"

六、万宝山事件及朝鲜排华之暴动

万宝山事件对于一九三一年九月事变之关系

万宝山事件，及中村事件，恒被视为中日满洲事变爆发之近因。不过万宝山事件之真正重要性，颇觉夸张过甚。惟以对于此项并无死伤发生之事件，为震骇听闻之纪述，遂使中日双方顿生极劣之恶感，且使朝鲜方面发生鲜人肆意攻击华侨之惨剧。因有此种排华之暴动，遂又使中国对日之经济绝交复活。实则就万宝山事件之本身而论，较之过去数年间在满洲所数见之其他中日军警冲突之事件，固未必更具有较甚之严重性也。

中国经纪人与中国地主间之租地合同须得中国官宪之同意

万宝山系一小村，在长春北约十八英里（三十启罗米突），与伊通河旁之低湿区域相毗连。有一中国经纪人郝永德者，代表长农稻田公司，从中国地主手中，以一九三一年四月十六日所缔结之合同，租得广大之田地。该项合同曾规定，如该项合同之条款，县知事拒绝同意，则合同应为无效。

中国经纪人将所租之地更行转租

未几，郝永德即将彼所租得之地，全部转于若干朝鲜人。此项转租合同，并无官府同意始克有效之规定，且推定朝鲜人可以凿筑灌溉之水渠，并筑通渠之小沟。郝永德转租该地于朝鲜农民时，并未先将郝与原地主间所订之合同，取得官府正式之同意。

鲜人横贯华农地亩凿筑灌溉水渠乃当地华民反对之主要原因

转租合同缔结后,鲜人即开始凿筑长数英里之水渠,引伊通河之水,以转注于该项低湿之地域,使克适宜于种稻。此项水渠,横贯广大之田地,田地所有主之华农,则既非原约之当事人,亦非转租之约之当事人,以彼辈田地,乃系在伊通河及此项朝鲜人所租田地之中间也。又为使渠中之水,得以充分灌溉其转租之田地起见,鲜人乃又横跨伊通河,从事建筑堰壩。

华农停筑水渠之要求及鲜人之撤退

水渠大半凿成后,因凿渠而田地被穿过之中国农民,遂全体起而反对,且向万宝山当局提出抗议,请求代为干涉。结果中国当地官宪,派警前往,令鲜人停止开凿之工作,且令其离去该地。同时长春日本领事,亦派遣领馆警察前往,保护鲜人。中日代表,曾就地交涉,未克生效。未几,双方更增派警察,因而更有种种抗议,答辩,及试行之交涉。

长春中日双方当局商定共同调查

六月八日,双方同意撤回警察,进行共同调查。因共同调查,遂发现原租合同,曾有一款,载明中国县知事,如对于该合同不予同意,则全合同为无效。并发现中国县知事,始终未曾给予此项之同意。

调查无结果

不幸双方之共同调查员,未能同意于彼此之决定。盖中国方面,以为凿渠以横贯华农之田地,自不能谓为不侵犯华农之权利。日本方面,则谓应许鲜人继续凿渠,以为若以彼辈并不负责的租地手续上之错误,遂事反对,未免有欠公允。此后逾时未久,鲜人以日本领馆警察之协助,仍行继续凿渠。

七月一日事件

迨至七月一日,因凿渠而田地受害之华农四百人,遂以农具戈矛等为武器,群起驱逐鲜人,并将一大部之水渠填塞。日本领署之警察,当即开枪轰击,驱华农以保鲜人,但并无死伤情事。华农旋即撤退。日警则留驻彼地,直至水渠及横跨伊通河之洲壩,均由鲜人筑成而后已。

七月一日事件后,中国市政当局,对于日本领署警察及鲜人之行为,则继续向长春日领抗议。

朝鲜排华之暴动

远较万宝山事件为严重者,则为因此事件在朝鲜所生之反响。日本及朝鲜报纸,既对于万宝山事件,尤其对于七月一日事件,故为惊人之纪载。遂使

朝鲜全境排华之暴动,层见叠出。该项暴动,系于七月三日肇始于仁川,旋即迅速蔓地,至于各地。

在鲜华侨之生命财产受重大损失

中国方面,根据各正式报告,谓华侨惨遭杀死者为一百二十七,受伤者为三百九十三。财产之损失,达日金二百五十万元。并以为在朝鲜之日本官吏,事前既未采取适宜之步骤,从事防范,事后亦待至华侨生命财产蒙受重大损失后。始事制止,对于此项暴动之结果,应负重大部分之责任。试观日本及朝鲜之各报纸,关于七月一日事件,任意登载耸骇听闻虚伪不确之消息,即未见日方制止,而此种耸骇听闻虚伪不确之纪载,固系具有激动鲜人对华侨之愤恨之性质者也。

至于日本方面,则谓此种暴动,系属种族间感情之自然的爆发,且称日本当局,曾即时设法制止。

朝鲜暴动使中国对日经济绝交转趋激烈

此种种暴动之一重要结果,即为中国全国对日经济绝交之复活。

日本政府对于排华暴动表示遗憾并提议赔偿死者家属

朝鲜排华暴动后,万宝山事件尚未解决之时,中国政府,即因暴动事件向日本抗议,以日本未能制止,谓应由日本担负全责。日本政府,七月十五日答复,则对于暴动发生,表示遗憾,并提议予死者家属以赔偿。

关于万宝山事件中国抗议之理由

自七月二十二日起至九月十五日止,关于万宝山事件,中日双方地方及中央之官吏,曾迭有交涉,并迭有公文之往还。中国方面,则谓万宝山地方之困难,即在于鲜人在彼无权居住之地方居住,因按照一九〇九年九月四日之中日图们江中韩界务条款,鲜人居住及租地之权,原不能推延至间岛区域以外。

中国政府,对于日本领署警察之驻留中国,亦事抗议,以为七月一日事件之发生,乃适由派遣大批该项警察之所致。

日本之主张

日本方面,则坚持鲜人享有条约上之权利,以在万宝山居住并租地。以为鲜人之特权,并不以图们江条款所列举者为限,即给予一般日本臣民在南满全部居住租地之权利,亦应包括在内。以为鲜人之地位,应与其他之日本臣民一致。日本并力称鲜人,原系以善意从事种稻之计划,日本当局对于中国租地经纪人之不规则行为,不能担负责任。日本政府将日本领署之警察,自万宝山撤

回。但彼租地之鲜人，则仍居留彼地，以继续其耕种稻田之工作。

直至一九三一年之九月，万宝山事件，迄未得完全之解决。

七、中村上尉案件

中村事件之重要

中村上尉案件，据日方意见，谓系中国极端藐视日本在满权益各事件中之绝顶重大的事件。该上尉系于一九三一年之仲夏，在满洲荒僻辽远之某地方，为中国兵士所杀。

中村系负有陆军使命在满洲内部活动

上尉中村震太郎，系日本陆军现役军官。据日本政府所承认，且系奉有日本陆军之使命从事某工作。当其经过哈埠中国官吏查验其护照时，渠自称为农事专家。中国官吏当即予以警告，谓彼所游历之地方，乃群匪丛集之地，并将此项事实载入彼之护照之内。该上尉携有武器，且带有特许药品，据中国方面之所述，此项药品中，有非为医药用之麻醉品在内。

中村上尉及其旅伴为中国兵士所杀

六月九日，中村偕同译员助手等三人，自中东路西段之宜力克都车站出发。迨至行抵洮南方面之内地某地点时，中村及其旅伴遂为屯垦军第三团团长关玉衡部下之兵士所扣留，旋于数日以后，约为六月廿七日，中村及其同伴二人均为中国兵士所杀，并焚尸以灭迹。

日本方面之主张

日本方面坚称，杀死中村及其旅伴为无理由，且系对于日本陆军及日本国家之大不敬。并称中国在满之当局，迟延正式调查，推卸事件责任，即其所称正竭力确查此案之实情，亦系无有诚意。

中国方面之主张

中国方面，首称中村上尉及其旅伴，系被暂时扣留，以待查验彼等之执照，盖按照惯例，凡外人游历内地者，均须持该项执照也。并云待遇彼等甚优。至中村上尉，则系于意图潜逃时，始为哨兵枪杀。并称曾于中村身上，寻出一日本军用地图，及日记两本，足以证明中村，不为一陆军之间谍，即系一负有特殊陆军使命之军官。

调查

七月十七日，中村被杀之报告，传至驻齐齐哈尔之日本总领事。是月月

杪,在奉天之日本官吏,即告当地之查中国当局,谓已得有确实证据,以证明中村上尉已为中国兵士所杀。八月十七日,在奉天之日本陆军当局,发表中村被害之第一次报告(参阅一九三一年八月十七日《满洲日报》)。同日林久治郎总领事,及东京参谋本部派往满洲调查此案之森赳少校,即与辽宁省长臧式毅会晤,臧氏当即应允,立即从事调查。

臧氏于会晤之后,即转呈在北平医院中养疴之张学良司令,并转告南京之外交部长,且派遣中国调查员两名,即刻驰往所称之谋害地点从事调查,该两调查员,当于九月三日返奉。又代表日本参谋本部,独自进行调查之日本森赳少校,则于九月四日返奉。林久治郎总领事,即于四日访华方参谋长荣臻,当由荣告知,两调查员之调查结果,不能视为确定与满意,故尚须进行第二次调查。荣臻旋于是日前往北京,与张学良司令会商,而于九月七日返奉。

中国图求解决之努力

张学良既知满洲形势之严重,乃即训令省长臧式毅及荣臻将军,即刻就地进行第二次调查。张氏复由其日本陆军顾问处,得悉日本陆军方面,对于此事之重视,当复派遣日本少校柴山谦四郎前赴东京,声明渠愿将此案平和解决。柴山于九月十二日抵东京,按照此后报纸之报告,柴并曾声称,张学良司令系诚意欲将中村案件得一早日公平之结束。是时张学良司令业又已派遣高级官吏汤尔和氏,特往东京,会晤日外相币原,以探讨究将以何者为共同立足点,俾克将满洲之各项悬案解决。汤氏曾先后与币原外相,南陆相,及其他高级陆军官员会谈。九月十六日,张氏向新闻界发表谈话,则谓按照日方意旨。中村案件,将由省长臧式毅及满洲当局自行处置。而不由南京之外交部办理。

派遣就地为第二次调查之中国调查人员,于前往中村被害地点后,当于九月十六日晨,遄返奉天。九月十八日下午,日本领事晤见荣臻时,荣称团长关玉衡,以应负中村被害之责任,已经于十六日带至奉天,且即将由军事法庭审判。嗣后日人占领奉天,并曾由日方声称,关玉衡实系被禁于一陆军监狱。

九月十二三日间即闻奉天日本总领事林久治郎,已报告日本外部,谓荣臻将军,既已确实承认中村之死,应由中国军队负责,则"调查人员返奉后,自不难得一和平解决"。又电通社驻奉访员九月十二日,曾发一电讯,谓"外传之中国屯垦军,杀害日本参谋本部上尉中村震太郎一案,不日可望和平解决"。但许多日本军官之表示,而尤以土肥原上校为最,则以本案应负责之关团长,既已由中国当局带至奉天收押,审讯之期,乃宣称在一礼拜以内,因对于中国努

力以图本案之圆满解决,是否具诚意,仍事继续怀疑。惟是中国当局,于十八日下午正式会议之际,既对日本驻奉领事官,承认中村之死,应由中国军队负责,并表示愿即将本案以外交之途径解决,则似意图解决本案之外交交涉,直至九月十八日之夜,事实上均仍在顺利进行之中。

中村案件之结果

中村案件,较之其他之任何单独事件,实更使日人之忿恨加增,且更使日人鼓吹以强权方法解决满洲中日现存之困难。且是时中日关系,正因万宝山事件,朝鲜排华之暴动,日本陆军越过图们江国界之操演,以及青岛方面,以反抗当地日本爱国团体之行动中国暴民所为之暴行等等,特形紧张,遂以使本案自身,亦顿增其严重性。

中村系日本现役军官。日方主张采用强硬迅速之陆军动作,即以此为理由。在满洲,在日本,均迭有民众大会,冀以使舆情结晶,一致拥护此项动作。在九月之前两礼拜中,日本报纸,时时宣称,军部已决定"此事解决应用武力",因此外别无他法也。

中国方面,则谓本案之重要,颇属夸张过甚,以为此不过日本所利用之借口,冀以达其陆军占据满洲之目的。至于日方所称,中国官吏处置本案,缺乏诚意,或办理迟缓,则均予以否认。

因有本章所云之种种争议及事件,在一九三一年八月之末,中日两方,关于满洲之关系,遂致非常紧张。惟所谓两国间有三百件未决之案,又为解决各该案件,和平方法已由一方逐渐用尽等语,则均未能证实。实则此之所谓案件者,无宁谓为系由较广大之问题所发生之局势,而此所谓较广大之问题,则又系植根于根本不能相容之政策。双方互诟,中日种种协定之规定,已为彼方所违犯,所片面解释,所弃置弗顾。双方亦自各有合法之不平。

就此间所云此方或彼方意图解决各案之努力观察,即可知一部分之努力,系欲以正则的外交交涉及和平方法,解决各案。而此项和平方法,则要尚未用尽。但以长时期之迁延,日人遂不复更能忍耐。陆军方面,尤极力主张中村案件,应立即解决,且需要求满意之赔偿。各团体,如所谓帝国在乡军人会者,则尤极活跃。以从事于日本舆情之鼓荡。

九月中,日方关于中国问题之舆情,以中村案件为焦点,极为激昂。且时时有一种论调,以为容许满洲方面,有如许未决之悬案实已使中国当局,轻视日本。于是必要时应以武力解决一切悬案之语,遂为一通行之口号。凡武力

解决之参议,陆军省参谋本部等讨论武力计划之会议,以及关于必要时如何实行此项计划所发致关东军司令官及驻在奉天九月初被召至东京且主张从速以武力解决一切悬案之土肥原上校之确定的训令,均在各报中,随意引载。阅各报,关于此种种方面及其他团体之情感之记载,即可知情势日趋于危险的紧张。

第四章　九月十八日及其后事变之叙述

事变发生前之形势

中日两国在满洲利害冲突日趋严重之局势,及其影响于两国武人之态度,前章均已述及。良以日本内部各种经济政治因素,致使日本人民对于满洲要求重采"积极政策"者,由来已久。例如军人之不满,政府之经济政策;军队乡区青年及国家主义青年团所代表之新政治势力。此项势力对于一切政党均表示不满,且鄙视西方文明之协调政策,迷信旧式日本之道德,摒斥无论银行家或政治家之自私行动;又因物价低落,初级制造家咸主急进的对外政策以挽救厄运;加以商业不景气,工商界迷信采用较强之对外政策或可收事业改善之结果——凡此种种皆为放弃币原对华"亲善政策"之张本,此项政策固曾在华获有若干效果者。至在满洲之日人,因鉴于本年夏季形势日趋紧张,愈觉忍无可忍。将近九月时凡关心时事者早已料及,此种严重局势早晚必须决裂。双方报纸不特不缓和舆论,反从而鼓动之,登载日本陆相在东京之激烈演说,主张日本满洲之军队,采取直接行动。而中国官应对于中村上尉被刺事件侦查及救济之迟缓,使满洲之日本青年军官愈形忿怒。而日本军官对于不负责任之中国军官在街市酒肆及公共场所表现之不负责任举动与侮辱,更不免有神经过敏之反感。悲剧之舞台至是乃准备开幕矣。

九月十八日至十九日之夕

九月十九日星期六晨,沈阳居民睡梦方醒,惊悉全城已入日军掌握。前夜频频闻枪声,但并不以为奇,因一星期来日军于夜间举行操演,猛烈之步枪及机关枪声早已习闻之故。十八日夜诚有少数居民对于炮弹轰炸声觉察有异,惟大多数仍以为日军大规模之演战耳。

调查团认此事之发生极为重要,因其为武力占领满洲之初步,故对于是夜事变发生种种情形,不惜广为调查。其中中日双方军事长官之正式陈述,当然认为最有注意之价值。日本方面陈述者为河本中尉岛本中校及平田上校。河

本为本事件之最初证人，岛本乃率队进攻北大营北兵房之营长，平田乃占领该城之日本上校也。此外我等更从日本关东军司令本庄中将及其僚属查得真相。中国方面陈述者为驻守北大营之王以哲旅长，益以参谋长及参加战役军官之口头陈述。此外我等更从张司令长官学良及其参谋长荣臻获得若干材料。

日本方面之陈述

根据日本方面之陈述：河本中尉于九月十八夜间率部下兵士六名巡逻，并沈阳城北南满铁路路轨旁练习防御工作。彼等循沈阳方向南行，其时夜光隐约，目力所及范围甚小。彼等行至一小径与铁轨交叉处。陡闻巨大轰炸声发于其后，与彼等距离不远，乃折回行二百码地，发现下行铁轨被炸毁一段，其炸裂点在两铁轨衔处，成三十一英寸之缺段。当彼等行抵炸裂地点时，突有弹自铁路东田野间向巡哨兵飞来，河本中尉立即指挥巡哨兵展开阵线，实行回击。对方约有五六人，旋即停火北退。日本巡哨兵立尾其后，北进至二百码地，复遇大队袭击，约三四百人。河本中尉恐受大队包围之危险，乃派一兵报告第三连连长，该连亦为参加操演之伍兵，驻扎于北，约距一千五百码，同时更命一哨兵打电话（附近有电话机）至沈阳营部请援。

彼时自长春南下火车车声已辘辘可闻，日本巡哨兵深恐火车行至炸毁处出轨，乃停止射击，置爆炸物于路中，冀火车临时得一警告，但火车开足马力前进，至炸毁处竟侧驶逾越而过，并未停止。该列车于十三时分准时抵沈阳。据河本中尉云，彼最初闻炸声时当为十时也。

是时战斗重开。川岛上尉比闻炸声时率领第三连南开，中途遇河本中尉所派之信使，遂由此信使向导至肇事地点，时为十时五十分。同时营长岛本中校接得电话，立即下令留驻沈阳之第一第四两连随同向该地出发，并传令在抚顺之第二连——距离约有一小时半行程——尽速会合前进，此二连自沈阳乘车至柳条沟下车，步行至肇事地点时已逾夜半。

此二连自沈阳开到时，河本中尉之巡哨得川岛上尉之接应，正与藏匿高粱中之中国兵士开火相持。岛本中校虽明知部下仅五百人，而中国军队在北兵房者数达万人，但据彼称："进攻为最妙之防守"，故当时立即下令向北兵房冲锋。自铁路至北兵房约距二百五十码，中多水沼，大队人马不易越过；同时野田中尉率领第三连一部分兵士沿铁道而下，对于被迫后退经过此处之中国兵士拦住截击，日军抵北兵房时，该处电光璀耀，第三连即进攻占据左翼之一角，

兵房内之中国兵士亦奋勇相持,双方激战约数小时,第一连由右翼,第四连由中路同时猛攻。至晨五时二小炮弹穿出兵房南门落于中国兵士对面近邻之小屋中。至六时,全部兵房为日军占领。是役计死日本兵士二人,伤二十二人。一部分兵房在战时起火,其余为日军于十九日晨纵火焚毁。据日方宣称,是役埋葬中国兵士达三百二十人,但受伤者仅二十人。

同时在其他处所之兵事行动亦迅速而普遍。平田上校约于下午十时四十分接到岛本中校电话,谓南满铁轨道为中国军队所毁,彼(岛本)正预备追击敌军云云,平田上校准其所请,并决定亲自进攻城垣,因于十一时三十分将军队集中完毕,开始进攻。城内毫无抵抗,间有奋战,多为中国警察,计被击死者七十五人。至二时十五分已将全城包围,三时四十分即占领之。上午四时四十分接报告,知第二师将佐及第十六团一部分兵士已于三时三十分离辽阳,旋于上午五时到达。至六时许东城已占领完毕,而兵工厂及飞机场则于七时三十分克服,当即进攻东兵房,于下午一时不战垂手而得。是役共伤日兵七名,死中国兵三十名。

是日本庄中将出外检阅,至翌日(十九日)始归,于十一时许始从新闻记者电话中得悉沈阳事变情形,其参谋长则于十一时四十六分得沈阳特务机关派出所来电。对于战事有详细报告。乃飞檄驻扎辽阳营口抚顺之日军直赴沈阳,并令旅顺舰队直驶营口,一面电朝鲜驻军司令增援。本庄于上午三时三十分离旅顺,中午抵沈阳。

中国方面之陈述

根据中国方面之陈述:日军之进攻北大营兵房全系无故起衅,令人猝不及防。九月十八日夜第七旅全部兵士约一万人驻扎在北兵房。九月六日奉张学良司令命令①,谓鉴于现时局势紧张,应特别注意,避免与日军冲突。故城堞上巡哨兵步枪并无实弹。同一原因,环营土城通铁道之西门亦经严闭。日军于九月十四日起至十七日每夜在北兵房四周演操,十八日下午七时则在文官屯举行夜演操。九时据刘军官报告:有火车一列,挂车辆三四,以特种车头拖带,停留该处云云。至十时忽闻一猛烈炸声,枪击即随之而起。参谋长立以电

---

① 原编辑者注:在北平时调查团曾阅该电原文如下:"中日关系现甚严重,我军与日军相处须格外谨慎。无论如何挑衅,俱应忍耐,不准冲突,以免事端。该军长应密饬各官长士兵遵照为要。"

话报告王以哲司令,王司令是时距北兵房南约六七英里近铁道之私宅。参谋长打电话时,即据报告日兵袭击北兵房,哨兵二名已受伤,十一时日军向北兵房之西南角开始总攻击,十一时三十分日军已破城洞而入。当日军开始进攻时,参谋长立即令熄灭营中灯火,并再报告王司令,王司令覆以不抵抗。十时三十分又闻远处炮声发自西南及西北方,午夜后炮弹飞落北兵房中。第六百二十一团退至南门时日军正在该门进攻,守卫兵士均后退,乃急避藏壕沟中,俟日军入城始逃出南门,翌晨二时抵北兵房东之二台子。其余军队由东门经东城外之空营退出,清晨三时与四时间亦抵该镇。

当时与日军抵抗者仅为驻扎东北角兵舍及南部第二号兵舍之第六百二十团。据该团团长云:日军进南门时约在晨一时,中国军队即由兵舍步步撤退,任日军攻击退空之兵舍。中国大队兵士撤退后,日军转向东路攻击,占据东门,第六百二十团见出路被截,不得不谋力战夺路,五时突围七时始完全退出。北大营中仅有此一接触耳!结果死伤甚多。该团兵士为最后退抵二台子者。

中国军队会集后,于十九日破晓离镇赴通岭,复取道至近吉林省某镇,置得冬季军装。乃派王上校谒熙洽将军商准该军进驻吉林省城。该地日侨闻中国军队将至,大为惊骇,乃由长春四平街及沈阳调大批日本援军来吉。中国军队不得已折回沈阳,在离沈阳城外十三英里处下车分为九队,星夜向沈阳四郊前进。王以哲司令因避免为日军发觉起见,乔装农民轻骑过镇。次晨日军已悉中国军队近城,乃派飞机侦炸。于是中国军队日间深藏,夜间潜行,最后抵北宁路某站,得车七列,于十月四日抵山海关。

调查团之意见

他上两种事略为当事人对调查团之报告,所谓九月十八日之事变,如是而已。因环境之关系,两者内容之纷歧矛盾,故无足怪。

我人鉴于事变发生前形势之严重与人心之激昂,并深知关系人所处地位不同,所述各节自难一致,尤以是夜事变经过情形最为纷歧,因此我人在远东时尽量接见当时在沈阳或嗣后至沈阳之外人代表,包括新闻记者及最先视察战地者。暨发表日本最初正式报告者在内。调查团对于此项人士之意见及关系方面之报告详细考虑,后对于各项文件充分研究,更对于呈送或搜集之大宗证据慎重衡量后,遂得下列之结论:

中日双方军队间情绪之激昂实无容讳。本调查团曾得一种证明:日方于事前确有充分计划以应付中日间万一发生之战事。此计划于九月十八日至十

九日之夜见诸实行,迅速证确。中国方面遵守上峰之训令,既无进攻日军之准备,在彼时或在该地亦无危害日人生命财产之计划。对付日军并未集中应战,亦未奉命开火,故日军之突袭及其以后之行动,莫不认为诧异。至九月十八日下午十时至十时半在路轨上或路轨旁发生炸裂之事虽无疑义,惟铁轨纵有破坏,实际上并未阻止长春南下列车之准时到站,断不能引为军事行动之理由。故前节所述日军在是夜所采之军事行动,不能认为合法之自卫手段。虽然,本调查团之为此言,并不摒弃下列之假定,假定为何?即当时在场之军官或者系认为自卫而出此也。兹更述事变后之经过于下:

日军之行动

九月十八日夜满洲日军之防地分配如下:路警营中有四连担任进攻北兵房,平田上校率领之第二师第二十九团攻占沈阳城垣,前文已述及。此外第二师之其余部分分配于下列地点:第四团司令部设于长春,第十六团司令部设于辽阳,第三十团司令部设于旅顺。其队伍则散驻于安东营口及南满铁路之长春沈阳支线及沈阳安东支线各地。另有一营路警驻长春。各队路警及宪兵随第二师散驻上开各地。此外更有朝鲜驻军若干。

所有满洲全部日军以及若干朝鲜驻军于九月十八日夜在南满铁路自长春至旅顺一带区域内几乎同时发动,全部兵力如下:第二师凡五千四百人,野战炮十六尊。路警凡五千人,宪兵凡五百人。中国军队之在安东营口辽阳及其余各小村镇者均被击败缴械,毫无抵抗。路警及宪兵仍驻各该地。第二师各部队则遄赴沈阳集中参加大战。第十六团及第十团准时赶到,联合平田上校所部协力攻占东兵房。第二十师之第三十九混成旅(四千步兵及炮队)于十九日上午十时在朝鲜边界新义州地方集合,于二十一日渡鸭绿江,夜半抵沈阳。更从沈阳分队至郑家屯,新民,于二十二日占领之。

九月十八日至十九日占领长春,二十一日占领吉林省城

宽城子及长春南岭之中国驻军,人数约一万人,炮四十门,于九月十八日晚间遭日军第二师第四团及驻扎该地之第一铁道守备队(长谷部少将所统率者)之攻击。中国军队曾略示抵抗,战事于午夜开始。日军于十九日上午十一时将南岭兵营占领,旋于同日下午三时占领宽城子兵营。是役,日军死官佐三名,兵士六十四名,伤兵佐三名,兵士八十五名。沈阳战事甫告完毕,日军第二师各团遂集中于长春。多门司令及其干部军官,率领第三十团及野炮一营队,于二十日抵该地。天野司令所率之第十五旅则于二十二日到达,二十一日,日

军不费一弹而占领吉林省城;中国军队撤退约八英里。

据当时日本半官式之刊物《亚细亚先锋报》载称,日本政府认为一切军事行动,均已完成,将不再调动军队。但事实上军事行动仍继续进行,该报对此则归罪于中国之挑衅;如二十日间岛地方之反日示威运动,龙井村车站之被毁,及九月二十三哈尔滨所发生对于日人房屋毫无损害之炸弹事件,该报皆举为挑衅行为之例证。此外,土匪及被解散军队之活动,亦被认事件发生之原因。故日方声称,基于上述种种原因,日军终被迫而不得不违反其本意采取新军事行动云。

轰炸锦州

此种新军事行动之开始,即十月八日之轰炸锦州,因张学良将军已于九月底,将辽宁省政府迁至该地故也。据日本方面声明,此次轰炸,系以该地兵营及省府所在之交通大学为主要目标。以武力轰炸民政机关,已属不合;而轰炸区域之范围,事实上是否一如日人所称,尤不无疑问。中国政府名誉顾问美人鲁易斯君于十月十二日抵锦州,曾致函顾维钧博士,报告该地之情形。此函后经顾博土,以中国参与代表之资格,转送本调查团。据鲁易斯君言,该地兵营完全无恙,炸弹多落城内各处,即医院及大学房屋亦遭波及。其后不久,日本某报,接得日本轰炸机司令官之报告,谓已于八日晨八时三十分自长春调飞机四架至沈阳,在该地与其他飞机联合,组成一侦察机六架轰炸机五架之飞机队,满载炸弹及燃料,向锦州进驶。该机等,于下午一时抵锦州,约十分钟至十五分钟内,投弹八十枚,旋即驶回沈阳。据鲁易斯君言,中国军队绝未还击。

嫩江桥之役

其次则为嫩江桥之役。是役始于十月中旬终于十一月十九日日军之占领齐齐哈尔。据日人对此争事辩白,谓此次军事行动之发生,乃因嫩江桥被马占山将军所毁,日军在修理时,被华军攻击所致。但此事之叙述,应溯及于较早之时期,对铁桥之被毁亦有加以说明之必要。

十月初,洮南镇守使张海鹏,突沿洮昂铁路,向前推进,其用意,显系欲以武力夺取省政府;张氏以前与马占山,万福麟地位相埒,对于黑龙江长官一席,早具取而代之之心。此次攻击,实为日人所煽动;不独中国代表说帖第三号中,曾加以声明,抑且为中立方面之报告所证明。马占山将军,为阻止张军之前进,下令拆毁嫩江桥,两军遂隔河对峙。

洮昂铁路之建筑,其资本系由南满铁路所供给;该路即为借款之担保。南

满铁路当局,认为值此北满谷物运输需要特殊之时,不能任该路交通继续中断。时马占山将军已于十月二十日到齐齐哈尔,日本政府乃训令驻齐齐哈尔总领事,向马氏提出从速修复桥梁之请求,但未附有时间之限制。桥梁之中断足以帮助马氏阻止张海鹏军之前进;日本当局明知马氏必尽力迟延其修复。十月二十日,有洮昂铁路及南满铁路职工一小队,无军队之护送,企图视察该桥损害状况;事先虽曾向黑龙江省防军某军官有所说明,但终遭中国军队之枪击。如是事态,益趋严重。十月二十八日本庄繁驻齐齐哈尔代表林少校旋即提出限十一月三日正午修理完竣之要求,并宣称,如届时不克修理完竣,日本将派军队保护南满铁路工程师,担任此项工作。中国当局要求宽展时限,日本置之不理,而将军队自四平街开赴该地,以保护修理工事之实施。

直至十一月二日,交涉尚毫无进步,亦无何等决定。是日,林少校送达一最后通牒于马占山及张海鹏,要求双方均不得利用铁路,以达军事目的,并各将军队,沿河两岸,撤退十公里。此外,并暗示,如两军对南满铁路工程师之修理工作,加以妨害,日军将以敌人视之。最后通牒自十一月三日起,发生效力。十一月四日,日本所派保护修理工事之军队,奉令进驻嫩江北岸之大兴。马占山于接到通牒后,曾提出答复,谓在未奉中央训令以前,暂依其自身之职权,接受日本要求;关于此点,中国代表(第三号说帖),日本驻齐齐哈尔总领事,及第二师多数军官之声述完全一致。不过,日本方面之证人,更补充声明;彼等不信马占山有诚意,因彼显然不欲桥梁得以迅速或有效的修理完竣故也。十一月四日,双方曾合组一混合委员会,两度前赴桥梁所在地,冀免冲突之发生;参加组织者,计有林少校,日本总领事代表一人,中国军官及文官数人;中国代表要求,日本暂缓前进。日本拒绝,而步兵第十六团团长滨本上校,遂遵令率步兵一营,野炮队二连,及工程师一队进驻江桥,依照最后通牒之条款,以开始其修理工事矣。在花井上尉领导之下,该工程师等于十一月四日晨开始工作,而日步兵一连,执日本国旗二面,于当日正午进驻大兴车站。

当四日午后,前述混合委员会赴纠纷地点正再度设法使中国军队撤退之际,战事即告开始。双方开火后,滨本上校见所部所处地位,极形困难,乃将其所有可用的军队,开往增援。经过一番迅速之侦察后,彼即深信,在此低湿之地面上,正面攻击,实不可能;日军如欲脱离所处困难地位,舍向敌军左翼,采取包围之形势外,几无他法。如是,彼立即调集其预备队,向中国军队左翼所据之小山进攻。但因人数过少,且无法使大炮进至较近距离之故,直至午后八

时半始将该山占领,而是日即亦无法再向前进。

关东司令部,接得关于此项情势之报告后,立派大批军队前往增援。是日晚间,有步兵一营开到。日军得援,乃于十一月五日拂晓,重取攻势。经二小时后,到达中国军队第一道阵地;据该上校本人致调查团之报告,称中国军队在该地掘有极坚固之战壕,并有自动机枪约七十架。日军之攻势,至此完全停顿。中国军队用步兵及骑兵实行包围式之反攻,日军蒙受极大之损失,而不得不向后撤退,直迨日暮,仅足保持其原有阵地。十一月五六两日晚间,又有两营军队开到,形势为之一变;日军乃于六日晨,向华军全线猛攻,结果大兴车站,于正午入日军手。滨本上校之任务,既限于占领大兴车站,以掩护修理桥梁之工事,故对中国军队亦未追击。但日军仍占据车站附近区域。

中国代表,在第三号说帖中,声称:林少校曾于十一月六日向黑龙江省政府提出新的要求,内容为:(一)马占山应辞长官职,由张海鹏继任;(二)组织一公安委员会。该代表并将林少校提出此项要求之信函之照片一纸,提示本调查团。上述说帖更称:前项要求提出之次日,日军不待中国答复,即向当时驻扎大兴以北约二十英里三间房地方之中国军队,开始新的攻击;十一月八日,林再函马占山将军,请其辞职,以让张海鹏,限半夜以前答复。中国报告又称:十一月十一日,本庄繁本人亦电马氏,请其去职退出齐齐哈尔,并要求日军有进驻昂昂溪车站之权,亦限半夜以前答复。十一月十三日,林少校更提出第三项要求,谓日军不仅应占据昂昂溪车站,即齐齐哈尔车站亦应在占据之列。马占山对于此点,则以齐齐哈尔车站与洮昂铁路无关答复之。

十一月十四五两日,日军各部联合,用飞机四架协助,继续进攻。十六日本庄繁要求马占山退至齐齐哈尔以北,将中国军队撤至中东铁路以北,并不得以任何方法妨害洮昂铁路之工作及运输;该项要求,自十一月十五日起,限十日内履行完竣,并应将答复送达哈尔滨日本特务机关。马占山拒绝接受,多门司令乃于十八日重行总攻。马军初退齐齐哈尔。该地旋于十九日被日军占领,马军乃向海伦退却,同时将省府各机关迁移该地。

据在场指挥之日军司令所提出之证据,谓在十一月十二日以前,日军并未开始新军事行动。是时马占山将军将其部队,约二万人,集中于三间房以西,且调集黑龙江屯垦军及丁超之部队。此种强大之军力,显示一种益形威吓之形势。日军与之对抗者,仅有甫经集中之多门师,其中所包者,不过天野及长谷部分别统率之两旅而已。为欲缓和此种紧张局势,本庄繁乃于十一月十二

日要求黑龙江军队退至齐齐哈尔以北,并允许日军北进,俾保护洮昂铁路。在十一月十七日以前,日军尚未前进,而是日中国军队即以骑兵,绕过日军右侧,而施以攻击。据多门司令报告本调查团,当时彼仅有步兵三千人,野炮二十四门,军力虽薄,但仍冒险进击,卒于十一月八日将中国军队完全击败,而于十九日晨占领齐齐哈尔。一星期后,第二师开回原防。天野司令则率领步兵一团及炮兵一中队,留驻齐齐哈尔,以御马占山军。此少量之日军,后为新组成之满洲军所补充。但在一九三二年五月,吾等到齐齐哈尔时,该项新军,尚未被认为足与马占山军战。

后附军事形势图第二号,表示行政院通过第一次决议案时,双方正式军队之分布;至对溃散之军队及当时在辽河东西两岸与间岛区域骚扰特甚之土匪,则毫无纪载。中日两国,均以故意煽动土匪,指责对方——日本以此归咎于中国欲使满洲失地发生纷乱之动机,中国则疑日人欲以此,为占据该地及扩大军事行动之借口。实则此种土匪之实力及军事价值,甚为暧昧,而且变化多端,欲将其在军事形势上之重要性,确切估定,殆不可能。从此图中,吾人得知,东北军在辽宁省西南部,已组成一强有力之军队,在大凌河右岸,筑有坚固之壕沟,与日军前哨,颇为接近。此项正式军队,共有三万五千人,较当时驻满日军,几逾一倍,日本军事当局,一加估计,当感几许之焦虑也。

天津事件

十一月间,因日人为天津所发生之数项事件而采取之行动,满洲方面之局势,始告和缓。关于此项不幸事件之起源,各方报告,极不一致。该地,于十一月八日及二十六日前后,发生暴动两次,但全部事实,仍极不明了。

十一月八日之暴动;日人之说辞

关于此次事变,日本《亚细亚先锋报》所载如次:天津中国人,分拥张(学良)及反张二派。后者组织武力,于十一月八日在中国地界,向保安队,施行攻击,以造成政治示威运动。当两方争扰之时,日本驻军司令最初严守中立。但其后日本租界附近之中国卫队,向日租界胡乱开枪,日军始被迫开火。日军司令虽要求中国交战军队,退出距租界边境三百码以外,但于事实,毫无补助。十一月十一日或十二日,形势更趋严重,致外国驻军,全部出动。

中国之说辞

天津市政府之报告,则完全异趣。该报告申称,日本雇用中国暴徒及日本便衣队,在日租界内,组织别动队,谋在中国地界举事。中国警察当局,随时接

有关于此事之报告,对于此种发自日租界之乱徒,确有扑灭之力量。由被捕暴徒之供词,足以证明此种暴动,实为日人所组织,而所用枪械弹药,亦称日本所制造。该报告对于日驻军司令于九日晨宣称日军数人伤于流弹,及要求撤退三百码之事,并不否认,但谓该府虽已接受此项条件,日本正式军队反以铁甲车及大炮向中国地界进攻。

该市府报告更称,十一月十七日,双方曾成立协定,对于撤退三百码之实行,有详细之规定。但因日方对于其所负部分,未克履行,形势乃更加恶劣。

十一月二十六日,突闻一可怖之爆炸声,继以大炮声,机关枪声,及步枪声,日本租界电灯完全熄灭,便衣队自内冲出,向中国地界之警察局进攻。

十一月二十六日之暴动;矛盾的报告

关于第二次骚乱,日本方面之报告,以《亚细亚先锋报》所载者如次:二十六日形势本已极为良好,日本之义勇军亦已解散。乃中国军队,忽于黄昏时分,向日本兵营开火,虽经日军抗议,炮火迄次日正午,仍未停止。日军至此,舍接受中国之挑衅而应战外,殆无他法。战事继续至二十七日午后,而和平会议,召集成功,在和会中,日本要求立即停止抵抗行动,并要求中国军队,撤至外军驻地二十华里以外。中国对于军队之退,表示撤意,至于警察,因负有保护该地外人安全之责任,则不允撤退。但据日人言,十一月二十九日,中国忽表示愿将警察撤出租界附近区域,日本对于该项提议表示接受,中国武装警察遂于二十九日晨撤退,防御工事亦于三十日撤除焉。

天津骚乱对满洲局势之影响

因二十六日天津形势之险恶,关东军参谋官向该军司令建议,派遣军队,经锦州山海关,以增援天津方面濒于危险之少数日军。如此事系一单纯之运输问题,则取道大连由海道增援,或可较未便捷。但自战略上言之,则所拟议之路程,实较为有利,盖此举足使前进之军队得以沿途解决集中军州中国军队故也。同时,因预料中国军队之抵抗必极轻微甚至毫无抵抗之故,彼等更认定即由此路,亦不至久稽时日。此项建议,旋邀批准。十月二十七日,铁甲车一列,兵车一列,及飞机二架,渡过辽河,其中国军队最前哨之攻击,即足使中国军队自其战壕阵地,向后退却。同时,铁甲车,亦变更其地位。中国军队,稍示抵抗,日军即增派铁甲车步兵车多列及大炮多门前往增援,并连续以炸弹轰击锦州,旋天津形势改善之消息传来,该军以原有目的已失,于十一月二十九日撤回新民,中国军队,不胜惊异。

此外,寓居日租界之废帝自与土肥原一度谈话之后,于十一月十三日避难旅顺,此亦一第一次天津骚乱之结果也。

锦州之占领

日军撤退之区域,中国军队重行进据,此广被传播之事实也。斯时,中国军队,士气稍振,不规则军及土匪之活动,益见加增。加之,时值冬季,辽河各处冰冻;彼等乃越过辽河,攻入沈阳近郊。日本军事当局深觉,既欲维持彼等现有之地位,亦有增兵之必要,并望能以此援兵之力,排除集中锦州中国军队之威胁。

日本接受十二月十日行政院议决案时之保留

在日内瓦方面,满洲形势,成为继续讨论之主题。当接受十二月十日议决案时,日本代表曾声明:对于此项接受,"须了解此节(第二节)之用意,并非阻止日本军队得采取'为直接保护日本人民之生命财产,抗拒蔓延满洲各处之土匪及其他不法份子之活动计,势所必须之行动'。该项行动实系一种'例外之办法,基于东省之特殊情形',将来该地常态,一经恢复,则此种办法之必要性自亦将归于消灭。"中国代表对此提出下列之答复,即:"不得扩大情势之告诫,不得借口于满洲现在事态所造成之无纪律而予以破坏。"而当时参加讨论之行政院会员数人则承认"将来满洲或将发生足以危及日人生命财产之情形,如遭此种紧急情形,日本在邻近区域之军队采取行动,将为无法避免之事"。当日本军官在调查团面前供给证据之时,提及此事辄认为十二月十日议决案,已赋予日本在满洲之"驻军权",并课以剿除该地土匪之责任。彼等于叙述以后行动时,辄言当行使该项权利,进剿辽河附近之土匪时,彼等曾偶然与锦州附近中国残留军队发生冲突。结果,该项军队撤入长城以内。但事实之真相,为日本在日内瓦提出保留案以后,仍继续本其既定计划以对付满洲之局势。

援兵之开到

第二师,除驻防齐齐哈尔者外,均集中沈阳。援兵随即源源而来。[①] 十二月十日至十五日间,第八师第四旅开到。十二月二十七日经日皇之裁可,第二十师干部,及其他军队一旅亦自朝鲜开援。至当时长春,吉林,则仅由独立铁道守备队防守。

---

① 原编辑者注:此处关于日军单位及实力之数字,系以日本官方报告为根据。

关于中国军队之撤退谈判无结果

因日军向锦州前进,情势急迫,中国外交部长为防止继续战争计,曾建议将华军撤入关内;但须列强三四国保证日军不再进攻,并在锦州之南北画一中立区域。此项建议,并无结果。同时张学良氏又在北平与日本驻华代表,试行商洽,因有其他原因,亦无结果。据华方在其第三号说帖附件戊中所称,日代表每次来访(分别在七日,二十五日,及二十九日)必将其要求华军撤退条件提高,及将日方节制其军队行动之诺言,改以极空泛之语句。至日方则谓华方之允许撤军,并无诚意。

锦州之进攻

日军于十二月二十三日开始集中其兵力向前进攻;而华方之第十九旅遂被迫放弃其原有防地,自此以降,日军即节节进攻,几于全无抵抗,因华军司令已下总退却令也。日军旋于二月三日上午占据锦州,仍续推进,至山海关然后已,至是日军遂得与其原在该处之驻军,取得永久之联络。

张学良将军之所以将其军队完全撤出满洲,始终未事抵抗者,盖与关内政情,不无关系。中国军人,向喜从事内战,前已言之;此时吾人之所应注意者,厥维此项内战,自满洲肇事后,迄未稍戢。

哈尔滨之占据

日军之长驱直下山海关也,未遇剧战,而即告厥成功,用能将其原在该处之军队改调他处;至其第二师之主力,则因满洲战事,几盖由其担任,故不得不调回辽阳,沈阳及长春各处之总司令部,略事休养。但在另一方面,铁路各处,均须长期驻军,以防土匪之来袭,致使日军之防区延长,而战斗力亦锐减,是以日军仅留其第二十师之两旅兵力于其新占区域,而于该区域之北,另以第八师第四旅佐之。此时,日军事当局曾向吾等保证:在此保护周密之区域内,法律与秩序,不久即已恢复;而在辽河两岸,亦必能于数星期内将土匪扫数肃清。此系六月中事;但当吾等草撰本报告书时,据报纸所载,时有义勇军侵入营口及海城各处,即沈阳长春,亦皆受其威胁。

在本年春,吉黑二省府之残余军队,已退守哈尔滨之东北,其所驻防之区域,较之日方之占据区域,犹见安谧。此项北方军官,似与北平之司令部,仍有联络,且常受其接济。日方之进取哈尔滨也,其情景与其进攻齐齐哈尔时,正复相同,初以华军对华军,使之自相残杀。在本年二月初旬,熙洽将军即准备北征;而其目的,则为哈尔滨之占领。此时据城应战之军队为丁超李杜二将

军之部队,即通称反吉林军者也。当吾等草拟初步报告之时,日本参与代表曾向吾等提供材料,谓作战之双方本可成立某种妥协,后以北平当局之从中阻横,而尽成泡影。就事实而言,当熙洽之军队在二月二十五日进抵双城之时,双方谈判,确曾一度开始,但在翌晨,两军即在城南近郊,发生剧战,熙洽军队之前进,因受阻止。哈尔滨原有日侨鲜侨甚多,故日方认为此项战局,对于该项侨民,殊有危险。自中国近年之历史观之,当多数非正式军队发生混战之时,结果:败北军队往往退据城堡固守,而当地居民,因以发生恐怖,此数见不鲜者也。据日方宣称,当前项战事发生之时,该处之日侨鲜侨曾呼吁于关东军,请求保护;即华方商人,亦有参加此项举动者,盖恐其财产之或受劫夺也。

是月二十六日,日方以时机紧迫,乃派土肥原上校(现称将军)赴哈尔滨,将该处原有特务机关,收归己手。土肥原氏曾告本调查团,谓两军环绕哈尔滨作战,已有十日之久,该地日侨四千人深感生命之危险;而寄居传家屯近郊之鲜侨一千六百人,且有横被屠戮之虞。实则在此赓续不断之十日战事中,日侨鲜侨之因而遭劫者,实属少数。未几,日侨即自组义勇军,佐其同胞逃往他处。据传有日侨一人鲜侨三人因欲逃走而被杀害。此外,尚有驶往该处侦查战况之日机一架,因机件损坏而被迫降落,据传其乘驾人员均为丁超部队所戕害。

有此二事之发生,而日方军事当局遂决计对于上项战事,加以干涉。此次调往该处保侨者,仍为第二师。但长春以北之铁路,乃中俄合办之铁路,故此时日方之所最感困难者,非作战问题而为运输问题。该第二师司令,以中东路南段之车辆,已大见缺乏,故第一次只派长谷部将军及步兵二营前赴该处,彼等随即与铁路当局开始交涉;但进展极迟,而日方遂决意以武力实行输送矣。对于日方此举,铁路当局曾提抗议,及拒绝开车;但日方竟置之不顾。至二月二十八日,日方竟能组成三列车,向前开驶。该项列车驶至松花江第二桥而被迫停止,因该桥已被华方军队所毁坏也。日军在一月二十九日,从事于该桥之修理;至三十日下午,遂得到达双城。翌晨拂晓日方之一小部队与丁超军队相遇,曾有剧战;结果华军被迫后退,但在是日,并无其他进展。至是中东铁路当局已允为日方运兵;但附带提出条件两项:即所运送之日军应纯以保侨为目的;及车价应以现金给付是也。日军营二月一日起开始到达该处;至二月三日,遂得将其军队集中于双城之近。此时日军并曾由齐齐哈尔(犹忆十一月十九日以降,第二师团曾拨兵一部,留驻齐齐哈尔)调兵增援。但日方此举,亦有许多困难,因齐哈间之路线,已被华方截断;而此项华军且不时对于散驻中东

路东段之独立守备队,加以袭击也。

反吉林军于二月三日退守哈尔滨之南部边界,掘壕固守,时其兵力约有由一万三千人,至一万四千人之谱,共有大炮十六门。同日,日军即向前进;至二月三晚四晚,遂陆续开抵南城子河,约距双城二十哩。翌晨,战事开始;至二月四日薄暮,华军之阵地,遂有一部陷入日军之手;至二月五日中午,而胜败遂决。同日下午,日军进占哈尔滨;华军向三姓一带退却。

由此时迄一九三二年八月底之日方军事行动

日方第二师之胜利,使哈尔滨入其手中;但退却之华军并未采取其他行动,故于满洲之全局,影响极微。哈尔滨以东及以之铁路及松花江之重要水路,仍在反吉林军及马占山部队之手。日军迭得援军之助续向东北方进展,经六个月之战斗,遂得将其占据区域扩张,北至海伦,东至方正及海林。据日方官报,反吉林军及马占山部队已完全溃散;而据华方报告,则谓此项军队,现犹健在,至是此项军队之实力,业已锐减,故力避与日方正式作战;但仍能予日军以相当之牵掣。据各报所载,中东路之东西段由海林至哈尔滨各处,时为此项军队所毁坏。

自二月初以来,日方之行动,可节述之如左:

第二师于三月底离哈尔滨向方正进展,其目的在征服丁,李之军队。该师进至三姓,遂退回哈尔滨。至是第十师乃来接防。第十师之任有二:其一为以其驻守三姓附近之主力,向丁,李部队继续攻击;第一为以其一小部份之军队驻防于中东路东段海林一带。

至五月上旬,日方又调其第十四师,增援北满,该师之一联队曾与反吉林军作战,进至木兰河(三姓以南),将反吉林军驱向吉省之东隅。而该师之主力,则于五月下旬,在哈尔滨以北一带,与马占山将军之部队作战。该师之主力,沿呼海线向哈尔滨以北进攻;而另以一部份兵力进攻克山之东(即齐克线之原定终点)。据日方所传,马占山之军队,迄八月上旬,又已再度溃散;至马将军本人,则业经证实阵亡。但据华方消息,则谓马将军现犹健在。关于上项军事行动,新抵该处之日本步兵亦曾参加。

在八月间,双方并曾于奉天及热河之交界,发生多次小战。此次战事,大抵集中于锦州至北票之铁路(北宁铁路)支线上,盖此为由铁路入热河省之唯一路线也。华人认为此举,乃日人进占热河之先声,故深引为隐忧。考热河为中国本部与其满洲军队之唯一联络路线;而热河省又曾被"满洲国"宣言为其

领土之一部,是以此项隐忧,当非无据。对于此项紧急情形,日本报界,议论甚多。

对于上项事件,日本参与代表曾提出如左之报告:

有名石本者,系关东军司令部职员。于七月十七日,在由北票至锦州之火车上,被义勇军绑去(在热河省府辖区内)。日军步兵之一小联军队曾携轻炮往拯;但未得手,结果:遂将热河边界之一小村落占领。

在由七月底至八月间,日方曾派机侦查热境,并掷弹多枚;但所炸之处,多系"郊外无人居住之地",曾经日方审慎挑选者。八月十九日,日方派军官一人,前赴南岭(系北票及热河省境间之一小城),洽商石本释放事。在归途中,忽遭袭击,时该员率有步兵一小队,为自卫计,遂向对方还击,后以日方另有步兵一联队来援,即能占据南岭;但翌日即退出。

至中国参与代表所提出之节略,则系以热河省府主席汤玉麟之报告书为根据者。此项报告谓双方之战事颇烈,华方之参战者,为护路军一营;日军人数较多,且有铁甲车二,以供应用。至日方报告所称之飞机掷弹,大抵集中于朝阳(该区中较大之城)一带,结果被害者,计有军民三十人。至八月十九日,日方又复开始攻击,以铁甲车一向南岭进攻。

日方参与代表所提供之消息末谓:热河治安之维持,原系"'满洲国'之内政问题,但以热河之治安与满蒙之治安极有关系,热河如发生纷扰,则满蒙必且受其影响,故日本对之,遂亦不能采取旁观之态度"。

至汤玉麟氏之报告书,则在结论上曾谓:倘日方仍复向前进攻,则彼决采一切可能之手段,对之为有效之抵抗。

自上项文书观之,中日之冲突区域,殊有继续扩大之虞,吾人固应早日为之计也。

华方之抵抗性质

华军之主要部份,迄一九三一年年底,虽已撤入关内;但在满洲各处,日方尚时遭非正式之抵抗。如嫩江战役之战事,虽已绝迹;但此项非正式之战事,却广播满洲各处,始终接连不断。对于一切反日及反"满洲国"之军队,日方往往一律目之为"土匪";实此项军队,与土匪并无关系,不能混为一谈。查反日军队,共分二类,一为正式军队;一为非正式军队;至于此二项军队之人数,各有若干,则殊难核算,因本团始终未能与其躬自参战之将官相晤,故对于下述消息之可靠性,自亦不能不稍作保留也。关于此项继续抗日之军队,华方当局

自不愿宣泄其正确消息；至于日方当局所提之报告，则力图将此项军队之人数及其战斗能力减低。

原有东北军之残余势力

原有东北军之残余势力，大抵仅存于吉黑二省。至在一九三一年底锦州华军之改组，则殊乏耐久之能力，因其均已陆续入关也。原在一九三一年九月以前驻守松花江及中东路一带之华军，从未与日军热烈交绥：但时滋骚扰，俾日军及"满洲国"军疲于奔命。此项军队之领袖，如马占山，丁超，李杜三氏，以其继续抗日故，在中国颇享令名。考马丁杜[李]三氏均系北满护路军旅长，大抵张学良将军之统治权被推翻后，其部队均能对其长官效忠及对其国家效忠，用能对日抵抗。马占山之军队，因其本人曾一度变志，故欲对其实力加以估计，殊为困难。但马氏既任黑龙江省府主席，是以该省之军队扫数归其统率，据传其实力共有七旅。自四月以降，马氏曾率其军队，坚决抗日及反"满洲国"。其军队在呼兰河海伦与大黑河之间者，据日方计算，只有六团，即由七千人至八千之谱。丁李二氏有旧日张学良军队六旅，后又补充三旅。当吾等草制初步报告书之时，其实力据日方当局计算，共有三万人。自四月以来。马丁李三氏之军队在人数上当已大减，迄今恐已不满此数矣。哈尔滨被占领后，彼等之军队曾遭日军之集中攻击，损失甚大。以现情而论，此项军队已无制止日方军事行动之能力，故力避与日军正式在战场相遇。日方常用飞机，而此项军队则无之，其所以损失甚重者，盖以此也。

非正式军队义勇军

当吾人研究满洲非正式军队之时，务须将在吉林省与丁李部队合作之各种义勇军之类别认清。在一九三二年四月二十九日之初步报告书中，我等曾于第五页"义勇军"标题之下，言及义勇军共有三大队及七小队。现在有一小队，在敦化与华宝山之间，仍与李丁二氏之正式军队互相联结。因其所占区域全无铁路，而其他交通工具亦告阙如，用能固守原防，始终健在，其领袖王德林联合一切"反满洲国"之势力，而自任其司令。此项义勇军，如与日军兵力相较，自不足道；但以其现况而言，似仍能于吉省各处固守原防，以拒"满洲国"军队之征剿，盖日军之活动，始终未及敦化以东也。当"大刀队"与王德林取得联络之时，曾在间岛一带，大滋骚扰；至在最近，则消息颇沉寂，而日军对之，亦从未作任何重要处置也。

据日本官方所提交本团之报告书所载，此项义勇军分为若干路或其他组

织,每路兵力,约由二百人至四百人之谱。其活动范围包括如下各区域:沈阳左近及沈阳安东间之铁路,锦州及奉热二省交界各处,中东路西段及沈阳新民间一带。故如将此项区域与反吉林军所占区域合并计算,则其活动范围,当占满洲过半数之总面积也。

土匪

满洲之时有土匪出现,其情景亦正与中国内地相同。东三省各处,均有以匪为业之非法份子;而政府中人且有利用之以推进其政治目的者;至于此项土匪之消长则与政府实力之消长成反比例。据中国政府所提交本团之文件所载,在最近二三十年间,日本曾派人予土匪以种种披励,俾遂行其政治上之目的,此项报告书并曾引录南满铁路当局所公布之关于"一九三〇年满洲进展之第二次报告书"之一段云:专以铁路区而论,匪案在一九〇六年只有九件;至一九二九年,竟骤增至三百六十八件。该报告书又谓:土匪之所以能滋生不已者,盖由于日人自大连及关东私运军火以资其用。华方又谓:在去年十一月,日方曾以军火资助著名匪魁凌印清(译音);并有日人三,指导其组织独立自卫军,以为进攻锦州之用。此计既已失败,日方乃转而利用其他匪首;幸而其所资匪之军火,均入华军之手,以其军火均系日方所制,故深信日方有此企图也。

至于日本当局,则其对于此项土匪之观点,向与华方完全不同。据其所见,此项土匪之存在,完全由于中国政府无能。日方并谓:在相当程度之内,张作霖颇盼土匪之继续存在,因彼认为:遇有不测,此项土匪均可收归己用也。日本当局曾承认:张学良之被推翻,大足增加土匪之数目;但在另一方面,却谓日军如继续留满,则在二三年之内,主要之土匪必可扫数肃清。日方希望"满洲国"警察及各市自卫团之组织,能使土匪逐渐绝迹。彼等相信:土匪中定有不少良民,因其家财荡然,始而加入匪类。此项由良民出身之土匪倘能得有机会重事耕耘,当必乐于恢复其固有之安静生活也。

第五章 上 海

上海事件

一月底,上海战事发生,关于自战衅开始至二月二十日止其经过情形之梗概,国联所委派之领团委员会已有报告。二十九日,本调查团行抵东京时,战时仍在进行中,曾与日本政府中人,对于日本以武力干涉上海事件之起因,动

机及结果,作数次之讨论。三月十四日,我等抵上海,是时战争已息,但停战谈判,殊感困难。调查团适于此时莅止恰合时机,对于顺利空气之产生,或能有所裨助,我等了悉最近战争所造成之紧张情绪且对于有关于此次争执之困难与焦点,且能得一种更亲切与明确之印象。调查团并未奉命继续领团委员会之工作,或对于上海最近事件作一特别研究。国际联合会秘书长且曾通知本调查团谓中国政府曾表示反对,足使调查团因研究上海战事情形,而致延期前往满洲之任何建议。

我等已听得中日两国政府对于上海事件之意见,并接到由双方交来有关本题之大宗文件。我等亦曾视察为战事所毁坏之区域,并聆日本海陆军官对于战事之申述。又曾以个人名义,与上海各界代表谈话,以探察各方舆论,盖凡上海居民对于此事均有亲切详明之记忆也。但我等并未以调查团之名义,正式查究上海事件,是以对于有关系之争点,不表示意见。但为完成纪录起见,我等对自于二月二十日起至日军撤退日止之战争经过,应予以纪载。

上海事件自二月二十日以后之纪述

领团委员会之最后报告,称日军于二月二十日在江湾与吴淞区域开始新攻击,当为吾人所能回忆,此次进攻于日军并无甚大胜利,虽续攻数日,仍属徒然,但日军因此得知十九路军及中国警卫军之一部(即第八十七师与第八十八师)已与之抵抗,此项抵抗事实,及上海地方情形,所产生之困难使日本决定增加第十一与第十四两师团之生力军。

二月二十八日,日本军队占据江湾西部中国军队所退出之区域。是日又有日本海空军轰炸吴淞炮台及长江一带要塞。其掷弹飞机则参与前线之全部战争,炸毁虹桥飞机场与京沪铁路。日本所派之日军总司令白川将军,于二月二十九日抵沪。自此以后,日军司令部乃有真实进展之报告。在江湾方面,日军前进甚缓,据日本海军司令部称在闸北之对方军队,以每日受炮攻之结果,显有退让之现象。同日距沪百哩之杭州飞机场亦遭日空军之轰炸。

三月一日前线攻击渐见进展,但仍迟缓,日军司令官,为开始包抄并袭击中国军队之左翼起见,饬令第十一师团之主要部份,在长江右岸济雅口(译音)附近登陆。此种策略颇见成功,中国军队被迫后退至日军司令官于二月二十日哀的美敦书中所要求之二十公里之外。吴淞炮台因迭经日本海空军之轰击,中国军队乃于三月三日退出,同时日本军队进占该处,先一日日本空军之轰炸曾及于距京沪铁路昆山车站以东七公里之地方,其目的在制止中国之后

方军队之运往前线助战。

三月三日下午日军司令官下令停战,四日华军司令官亦发出同样号令。自停战后,日军第十四师团于三月七日至十七日之间在上海登陆,约一月之后,该师团开拔至满洲,以补充驻彼之日军,中国人民对之深为愤慨。

是时因友邦与国际联合会之协助,调停战争之努力继续进行。二月二十八日英国海军提督克莱在彼旗舰上接双方代表,当经提出一基于双方同时退兵与暂时性质之协定。旋以双方对于谈判根据之意见不同,会议遂无结果。

二月二十九日国际联合会行政院长,提出建议组织"一共同会议,在以有关系各国代表之前力谋结束战事,并确实制止战斗行为,其办法可就地商议之"。双方表示接受,惟因日本代表提出苛刻条件,致谈判无良好结果。日本代表要求:(一)中国军队应先行撤退;(二)日本军队俟中国军队确定撤退后,方始后退,惟不退至以前所声称之公共租界与越界筑路等处,而退至自上海至吴淞之一带区域。

三月四日,国联大会重提行政院之建议:(一)催促两国政府实行停止战斗行为;(二)请求其他有关系之各国以上项之执行情形通知大会;(三)建议此项谈判由其他列强予以协助,俾能缔结协定使战斗行为确定停止;又规定日本军队之撤退,并愿各国以关于该项谈判之进展情形通知国联大会。

三月九日,日本当局将节略交由英国公使转送中国当局,该节略内称日本准依据国联大会所提出各点,开始谈判。

三月十日,中国当局,送由英国公使转致答复,表示亦愿依此原则准备谈判,但以确实停止战斗行为,及完全且无条件的撤退日本军队为限。三月十三日,日方表示,对于中国方面之保留条件不认为得以变更国联议决案之意义,并不认有束缚日方之性质,日方并称双方应以议决案为会晤之根据。

三月二十四日,中日开停战会议,此时日本陆海军队,亦实行开始撤退。三月二十日其海空后备队离开上海,使所留军队之实力"不比寻常为多"。日本司令部于三月二十七日又将军队撤回,并声称此与前面所述之和会或国际联合会无关,是为日本帝国陆军司令部之单独决议,认为上海毋须多留军队故决定自动撤回。

三月三十日和会报告:在前一日关于确实停战之协定,业经决定。惟他种困难继之而起,至五月五日全部和议协定,方准备签字。该协定规定确实停止战斗行为,划定上海以西一带,为中国军队前进之暂时界限,以待恢复常态办

法之决定,又规定日本军队撤退至公共租界及越界筑路,一如一月二十八日以前之情形。又因日本军队之数量过多,租界内不能容纳,租界以外之某数地段暂时包括在日军暂驻区域之内,此类地段现在可以不必提及,因日军已早从该处撤退矣。又设一共同委员会,由英美法义四国友邦及中日双方之各代表组织之,以监视双方撤兵。该委员会并得协助布置由日军移交于中国警察接管之事宜。

中国方面对于该协定,附加二种声明:第一,声明此协定内并无对于中国军队在上海境内之行动有任何永久之限制;第二,在日本军队暂时驻扎之区域内,一切市政职务包含警察在内,仍归中国官厅办理。

该协定之条件,大体已见诸实行。日本军队退出之区域,于五月九日与三十日之间,已移交与中国特别保安队接防。然该四区域之移交已较迟于原定时间。中国房主厂主与铁路职员及其他居民等当其回至兵灾区域时,每见有抢夺劫掠,故意毁坏财产掳走什物等事,以为均须诉之于日军司令部,此殆为战后之当然情形,依照中国人之意见,全部赔偿问题,应容后再行谈判,彼等计算军民人等之伤亡,及失踪者达二万四千一百人之多,物质损失约计十五万万元。关于越界筑路区域之草案业经上海工部局代表与市政府代表签押,但工部局与市政府尚未核准,工部局已将该草案交由领袖领事转送领事团察阅矣。

上海中国军队之抵抗对于满洲情形之影响

上海事件自大有影响于满洲之情势。日军能不费力而占据满洲之大部分与中国军队之毫不抵抗,不特使日本海陆军界相信中国军队战斗力之极为薄弱,且使全中国人民亦大为沮丧。自十九路军在上海开始奋勇抵抗继以警卫军第八十七师与第八十八师之助战,一旦战情披露,举国狂热。原有之三千日本海军加以三师团与一混成旅之补充,血战六星期后,始得将中国军队击退,此足以予中国民气以一种深切之印象。于是全国均觉中国非自救不可。中日冲突之事,传布全国,各处舆论紧张,抵抗精神增加,以前所抱悲观主义忽而变为同等过甚之乐观主义。上海消息传入满洲,使其仍在抵抗中之散漫军队增加勇气。马占山亦因是而再起抵抗,并激起寰球华人爱国之心,义勇军之抵抗力亦由此而增加。日方遣军远征,亦无胜利可言,在数处,日军每反取守势,且在时受攻击之各铁路不得不加意布防。

一九三二年二月一日之南京事件

自上海战事发生后,他处事件继之以起,如南京受短时间炮击即其一端,

此事造成非常惊慌，即国外亦受其影响。此事发生于二月一日午夜，幸不到一小时即停止。该事之发生，或为误会所致，结果使中国政府，由南京暂迁洛阳。

中日两国所解释之原因与事实，相差悬殊。我等由日本方面所得之解释有二点：第一，自上海战事发生后，中国方面已将狮子山炮台扩大。沿长江之城门口及对江，掘战壕，设炮垒。以扩大军事准备，惹起江面泊有军舰之日人之注意。第二，本地报章曾宣传上海方面中国胜利之不确实消息，更使南京之华人非常紧张。据称凡日人所雇之华人亦因受恐吓而被迫离职，华商拒绝卖给食物与日人包括领事馆馆员与兵舰上之水手在内。

关于以上之烦言，中国方面并未批评，只称彼时之不安定与空气之紧张，由于日本方面在沪事发生后增加兵舰，先自二艘增至五艘，最后增至七艘（日本当局称共六舰，其中三舰为炮舰，三艘为驱逐舰）。军舰司令官派水兵若干名登陆，在日清轮船公司码头，任保卫之职，以保护避居趸船上之日本领事馆馆员与日本居民。上海之事，尚深印一般脑海，所以此种举动使已受惊之南京人民，复感同样恐慌之经验。

我等于首都警察厅致外交部之报告书中得悉对于中国人民与外国侨民安全负完全保护责任之南京地方当局，对于日本海军之登岸，深为愤激，曾向日本副领事提出抗议，据其答复，谓无力干预此事，同时又特别令饬上述日本船码头，所在地下关警察厅分局，靠近日本兵舰碇泊之地点，以阻止华人与日人在该区间内互相接触，尤其在夜间。依照日方正式报告，避难之日本人，已于一月二十九日以后之数日内登日清轮船公司之某轮船，且大部份已送往上海。日人申说在二月一日夜，其炮舰三艘，忽受炮击，其声显然为狮子山炮台所发。同时中国军队攻击江边之日本海军卫兵，致伤二人，其中一人因伤毙命。日军当即还击，但只向海军登陆之附近地点还击，至岸上停止轰击为止。此乃日本方面之说辞。中国方面，绝对否认有任何开火之事，但称狮子山炮台，下关及其他地点，遭炮轰击有八乡之多，继则以机关枪步枪扫射。是时兵舰上之探险灯直向岸上探射，使一般居民受莫大恐慌，因此均向城内奔命，幸无死伤，物质损失亦不大。

此事件之发生，最初或系起于一般兴奋之中国人民之燃放爆竹亦未可知，因彼等借燃放爆竹以庆祝上海战事之假定的胜利也。

第六章 "满洲国"

一、建设"新国家"之历程

由于日本占领沈阳所生之纷乱

由于一九三一年九月十八日事变所生之结果,如上章所述,沈阳城与辽宁省(奉天)之民政,尽行解组,即其他两省之民政,在较小范围内,亦受影响。沈阳非惟为满洲政治之中心,且除大连而外,并为南满商业最要之中心;突然袭击沈阳,对于中国民众,实引起一大恐怖。重要官员与教育界商业界之领袖分子,能走避者,大半皆仓皇携眷远离。在九月十九日之后,有十万以上之中国居民,由北宁铁路离去沈阳,其不能离者,则多潜匿;即警察与监狱看守,亦皆不见。沈阳市县省府之行政,完全推翻,公用事业公司,供给电灯饮水之类者,及公共汽车电车电话电报之类,停止其职务;银行与店铺,紧闭大门。

恢复沈阳城之秩序与民政

目前急要之事,即为组织市政府,与恢复该城之市民日常生活,此举由日人担任,进行颇为敏捷。土肥原上校任沈阳市长,在三日内,民政即恢复常态。并因该省主席臧式毅氏之助,数百警察与大半监狱看守人员,概行招回;公共事业之效用,亦回复原状。土肥原氏任职一月,设有紧急委员会,内多日人,以资赞助。迄是年十月二十日,市政府之治权,移交于有相当资格之中国团体,以赵欣伯氏为市长(赵系律师,在日本求学十一年,为东京帝国大学之法学博士)。

改组省政府(一)辽宁省

其次问题,即为改组三省之省行政。此举在辽宁,较其他两省为艰,因沈阳为该省行政之中心,重要人物,多已逃避,且一时有中国之省行政,继续在锦州进行,故经三月后,改组始完成。

臧将军拒绝组织独立省政府

中将臧式毅为当时之辽宁省政府主席;于九月二十日,首先与之接洽;请其组织离中国中央政府而独立之省政府。事为臧氏所拒,致受逮捕;迄十一月十五日释放。

九月二十五日设立自治委员会以袁金铠为主席

臧式毅将军拒绝赞助建设独立之政府后,另与其他有力之官吏袁金铠氏

接洽。袁为前任省长东北政务委员会副会长。日本军事当局邀袁及【其】他中国居民八人,组成所谓"维持治安委员会"。该会宣布于九月二十四日成立。日本报纸遂宣称该会为独立派运动之第一步;但袁金铠氏于十月五日公然否认有此种用意。据云"该会设立于旧行政组织瓦解后。借以维持地方治安秩序;并协助救济难民,恢复金融市场,及处理其他事件,专为预防过分之损害。然无意于组织省政府或宣布独立也"。

十月十九日设立财政局

十月十九日该委员会设立财政局;派日本顾问数人,协助中国职员。财政局长在实行该局决议以前,须先取得军事机关之同意。在县之收税公署,受日本宪兵队或他项机关之监督。有时须将其账簿,逐日呈请宪兵队稽查;凡支给警察司法教育等类之公用款项,须得其允许。有汇寄税款于锦州"敌党"者,须即报告于日本当局。同时组织财政整理委员会以改组课税制度为主要任务。日人代表与中国同业公会之代表,准予参加讨论课税事宜。依据一九三二年五月三十日所编由在长春"外交公署"交于本调查团之《"满洲国"独立史》所载,因该会讨议之结果,遂于一九三一年十一月十六日,废除税捐六种,税率减半者四种,改归地方政府者八种,并禁止一切无法律根据之征税。

十月二十一日设立实业局

十月二十一日,该会设立实业局;该会之名称改称为"辽宁省自治公署"。此事曾经取得日本军事当局之同意,并派有日本顾问多人。该局长欲发命令,事先须取得日本军事当局之许可。

东北交通委员会

最后辽宁省自治公署组织一新东北交通委员会;该会逐渐管辖各方铁路,不特以在辽宁省者为限,即在吉林黑龙江者亦包括在内。该会于十一月一日与辽宁自治公署分离。

十一月七日之宣言与十一月十日设立省政府

十一月七日辽宁省自治公署改为临时辽宁省政府,发表宣言,与前东北省政府及南京中央政府脱离关系。且要求辽宁各地方政府须遵守其所发布之命令,并宣称自今以后将行使省政府职权。于十一月十日公开举行成立典礼。

最高顾问部之职务

同时与辽宁省自治公署改为临时辽宁省政府而开幕者,有最高顾问部,以于冲汉为主席;于氏曾任维持治安委员会副会长。该局之目的,据于氏宣称,

在维持秩序,取消恶税,减轻税率,及改良生产贸易之组织,借以改善行政。该部并指导及监督临时省政府,与扶助地方自治之发展,适合于地方民众之习惯及现代之需要。该部内设各司,分掌总务调查文约指导监督等事,并设一自治训练所。其重要职员几全为日本人。

十一月二十日改省名为奉天十一月十五日以臧式毅为省长

十一月二十日该省之名改为奉天,即为一九二八年以前该省未归国民政府统治时之旧名;且于十二月十五日,以被禁新释之臧式毅氏,接替袁金铠为奉天省长。

(二) 吉林省

设立省政府于吉林省,为事较易。是月二十三日第二师司令多门少将与中将熙洽会晤;时张作相将军不在,由其代理该省行政长官;因邀之担任该省政府主席。会晤之后,熙洽将军召集各机关及法团于九月二十五日开会,有日本军官参加。对于建设新省政府之意思,并无反对表示,遂于九月三十日宣布成立。吉林之新省政府之组织法,旋即宣布。委员制之政府即行废止;政务由省长熙洽负责进行。数日后由其委派新政府主要官吏,并添派日本职员数人。总务处长为一日人。各县亦有行政上之改组与人员之更换。四十三县中,有十五县经改组后撤去中国官员。有十县之官员,宣示忠于将军熙洽,仍行留任。其他诸县,仍为效忠于旧政府之军事领袖所保持,或对于争斗各方超然不加干预。

(三) 中东铁路之特别行政区

特区行政长官中将张景惠,系一亲日派。虽未带领军队,而有旧势力能指挥吉林与黑龙江多数军队及特区之护路军。九月二十七日由其在哈尔滨公署召集会议讨论该特区紧急委员会之组织。该委员会以张景惠将军为主席,其余人员中,有王瑞华将军及丁超将军。丁氏嗣于一九三二年正月,成为"反吉林"军领袖,抵抗熙洽将军。十一月五日,反吉林军在张作相将军指挥之下,设立新吉林省政府于哈尔滨。张景惠将军于一九三二年正月一日,被任为黑龙江省长;一月七日即以职权宣布该省独立。一月二十九日丁超将军占据特区行政长官公署,监禁张将军于其私宅。迨日本军队向北进攻,于二月五日占领哈尔滨,击败丁超将军后,始恢复其自由。自是而后,日本在特区之势力,益见强盛。

(四) 黑龙江

在黑龙江省因有张海鹏将军与马占山将军之冲突,情形较为复杂;此层已

述于上章。十一月十九日日人占领齐齐哈尔后，一照例式之自治会随之成立，号称代表民意，邀特区张景惠将军兼充黑龙江省长官。惟时因哈尔滨附近情势未定，且与马占山将军尚未订立确定的协定，犹未妥协，延至一九三二年一月初始行就职。此际马将军之态度，一时仍无明显之表示。马氏与丁超合作，迄丁氏于二月败退后，始与日本协议取张景惠之黑龙江长官之职而代之；继与他省长官合作，参加"新国家"之建立，一月二十五日在齐齐哈尔设立自治指导部；而与其他二省同样之省政府，亦逐渐成立焉。

（五）热河

热河省向来系持超然态度，迄未参加满洲之政变。此省为内蒙古之一部，有中国居民三百万，渐将素以游牧为生部落为制之蒙古民族，向北推出。该族号称百万人，与在奉天西之蒙古诸旗，仍相联络。在奉天与热河之蒙古人，皆联为"盟"，其最有力者，为锡林盟。该盟参与独立运动，其他蒙古人如在黑龙江西部之巴加区（译音）或称呼伦贝尔者，亦尝思脱离中国而独立。此项蒙古人不易与中国人①同化，颇自骄大，常不忘成吉思汗之伟绩，与中国被蒙古战士之克服，愤中国之统治，而尤怨中国人民之移殖，渐侵占其疆土。热河之昭乌达盟及卓索图盟，与现受治于委员制之奉天诸旗，互相联络。热河省主席汤玉麟将军，闻自九月二十九日起，对于该省，负担全责，并与其在满洲之同僚之通声气。三月九日举行"满洲国"之成立典礼时，热河亦包括于"新国家"之中，实则该省政府未取确定之步骤。关于该省最近之情事，见前章末段。

创建"独立国家"

各省所设地方自治行政机关，如上所述者，随后联合而自成为一独立"国家"。欲明了此事所以成功之情形，与夫中国人赞成其事之证据分量之多寡，须先审查中国社会生活之特殊状况，该项特别状况有时成为一种力量，有时成为一种弱点。公共义务为中国人所认识者，为对于家族，对于某地或某人，较之对于国家为优，已如第一章所述。爱国主义如西方人所了解者，仅方在萌芽。举凡公会，社团，旗盟，及军队，莫不习于追随某人领袖。故若能以劝导或胁制方法，取得助某领袖之拥护，则在该领袖势力下全区域中之徒众，自亦一致拥护无疑。由是以观，可见中国之特点，被巧于利用，以组织各处省政府；且仍借此少数之人为工具，以完成其最后一局焉。

---

① 编者按：即指代汉族人民。下同。

自治指导部

造成独立之主要机具，厥为自治指导部，其总事务所设在沈阳，据本调查团所得之可靠证言，该部为日人所组织，虽有一中国人为领袖，但其中职员多为日人，其功用在为关东陆军总司令部第四部之机关，以扶助独立运动为主要目的，奉天省之各县，分设地方自治执行委员会，受中央部之指导与监督，各县遇有必要情形，中央部即由多数并富有经验之职员中派出稽查员，指导员，及演讲员等，其中多为日本人，且编辑发行报纸一种，以供利用。

一月七日沈阳发表自治指导部之布告

此项中央部所发训令之性质于一月七日所颁之一月一日布告中显然可以见。布告称东北急待发展，须有大规模之公众运动，以建设"新独立国"于满洲及蒙古，并叙述其在奉天省各县之工作，又略示进展其活动于他县，及他省之计划。且复诉请东北人民，推翻张学良将军加入自治会，协助廉洁政治之建设，改良人民之生活，而终结之词为："统一东北之组织，拥护'新国家'，拥护独立"。此项布告计分散五万份。

一月间该部长官之计划

一月间，自治指导部之部长于冲汉，即已与省长臧式毅计划建设"新国"，使于二月十日成立，第一月二十九日哈尔滨之暴变，及马占山将军与丁超冲突时，态度之不显明，似实为当时暂停进行他种步骤之要因。

迨丁超败退后，张景惠中将与马将军接洽，成立二月十四日之协议，以马将军为黑龙江之省长，二月十六日及十七日在沈阳开会，以布置"新国家"之建立，三省省长，特别区之行政长官，及担任一切重要预备工作之赵欣伯博士，均亲自出席。

在此五人会议中，决定设立"新国家"，组织东北行政院，暂握最高政权，以统辖诸省及特别区，且立即进行建立"新国家"之一切预备工作会议之第二日，有二蒙古王子到会，一系代表黑龙江西部之巴加区即呼伦贝尔，其一，为支旺（译音）王子，属于锡林盟代表诸旗，此人为诸旗所最高信仰之领袖。

二月十七日之最高行政院

最高行政院，即于是日成立。其中人员为该院主席张景惠中将，奉天，吉林，黑龙江，热河之省长及代表蒙古诸地，支旺王子与林鲜王子，该院第一次议决为："新国家"采取共和制，尊重组成"新国"各省之自治权，予行政长官以执政之名号，及发表独立宣言，由四省省长，特别区行政长官，代表诸旗之支旺王

子,与代表黑龙江呼伦贝尔居以福王子(译音)署名。是夜,关东军总司令设备公宴,以庆贺"'新国家'之领袖",祝其成功,且表示遇必要时,必为协助。

二月十八自宣布独立

独立宣言,发表于二月十八日,叙及人民之热望永久和平,并请彼所称之民选各省长,负责以应此项愿望。此项宣言,并陈述建立"新国家"之必要,并认东北行政院,即本此目的而组织,现既与国民党及南京政府脱离关系,允许人民享善良政府之利益,并曾将宣言内容,通电于满洲各地,于是马将军与熙洽省长遂分返其各人之省垣,但派定代表,往与臧式毅长官张景惠长官及赵欣伯市长接洽,以进行计划中之详细工作。嗣于二月十九日,复由诸人开会决定建立共和国,于宪法中确定分权之原则,邀废帝宣统为行政长官。此后又决议首都应设在长春,定政府之新年号,为"大同",国旗之形色,亦并经决定。

"新国家"之计划

二月二十五日,遂将此种种决议,通知诸省(包括热河)及呼伦贝尔,锡林,昭乌达,及卓索图诸盟之蒙古行政公署,上文所称诸盟,设立于热河,诸盟不能对于该省政府主席有反抗其意志之行为,已如前述。

促进"新国"成立之运动

宣布独立与通告"新国家"之计划后,自治指导部,首先领导组织民众示威运动,以为援助,并进行组织"新国成立促进会"且训令奉天各县之地方自治执行委员会尽力设法,以增进与促成独立之运动。其结果,则此种"新促进"会,如雨后春笋,环自治执行委员会而发生。

二月二十日以后,此种新立之"促进会",积极活动,预备标语,印刷口号,发行书本小册,编辑《东北文化半月刊》,并分配红纸对联且由邮局分送传单于各重要人物,请其赞助宣传,在沈阳则此种红纸对联即由商会分散以黏贴于门柱。

民众赞成独立之组织

同时自治执行委员会,则在各县当地绅士,及商会,农会,实业会与教育会之主席,及其重要分子以开民众代表会议。此外复组织民众大会,及游行大会,在各县城之大街要道游行,在各地人民及民众之集会,通过许多之决议,号称有数千人之参加,出于人民共同,或特种团体之意思。此项决议,当然呈送于沈阳之自治指导部。

二月二十八日沈阳决议赞成"新国家"

自促进会与自治执行委员会,活动于奉天各县之后,于是复在沈阳组织一

全省大会，借以具体表示民众之意系欲建立"国家"，于是在二月廿八日，因即开一会议，参加者为该省各县官吏及各阶级各团体之代表，为数约六百人。此项会议，当并发一宣言，谓推倒从前压迫人民旧军阀而开一新纪元，实足为奉天之一千六百万人民庆幸。就奉天而论，所谓民众运动者，遂即以此结局。

吉林省之独立运动

至于在吉林省之赞成"新国"之运动，亦系有组织，有指挥。当二月十六日沈阳会议之际，熙洽曾发出通电于彼所辖之各县官吏，令其呈明人民公意所趋之政策俾"新国家"有所遵循，并令各县官吏协力指导其县中各同业公会及各会社，各地响应通电群起做独立运动，二月二十日吉林省政府遂设立国家创建委员会，以指导各种组织，进行其独立运动，二月二十四日，人民协会在长春召集民众大会。据称到会者约四千人，彼等要求促进"新国家"之建立。其他各县，及哈尔滨亦召集同样之集会，二月二十五日，开全省民众大会于吉林城，据称到场者约万人，并发表正式宣言，其内容则与二月二十八日在沈阳所通过者相同。

在黑龙江省

在黑龙江省内，沈阳自治指导部负担重要部份之工作。一月七日张景惠将军就黑龙江省长职后，即宣告该省独立。

该部对于黑龙江促进运动之进行曾予协助。特派遣指导员四人，由沈阳赴齐齐哈尔，其中二人为日人，彼等既到该处二日之后，时在二月二十二日，即在省府接待室内，召集会议，公团代表出席者颇众，称为全黑龙江会议，以议定，筹备建设"国家"之方法，并决议于二月二十四日，召开民众大会。

参加民众大会者有数千人，标语旗帜，满布齐齐哈尔，以志纪念。日军炮队鸣礼炮一百零一响。日本飞机，盘旋空中，散布宣传纸片。大会随即发表宣言，赞成共和政体，行责任内阁制，以总统为"国家"元首。所有政权集中于中央政府，取消省政府，以县及市为地方政府之单位。

二月底时，奉天吉林黑龙江及特别区中省县发表宣言之一阶段，即已过去。蒙古诸旗，因知"新国"行将划出蒙古特别自治区域并保障蒙古人民之权利，对于"新国"，亦表示归服，回教徒则早于二月十五日，在沈阳集会，表示归依。少数未经同化之旗人，因悉清废帝或将出任行政官亦泰半拥护"新国"。

二月二十九日沈阳之全满大会

各县各省正式表示拥护"新国"计划之后，自治指导部即发起召集全满洲

会议。于二月二十九日,在沈阳开会,各省及奉天省各县以及蒙古各地,均有官方代表出席。此外尚有团体代表,如吉林及特别区之朝鲜人与满蒙青年同盟会各分会等,均有代表到会。总计出席者,在七百人以上。

会场上有若干人之演说,全体通过宣言及决议各一,前者指摘旧政府,后者欢迎"新国家"。复通过第二议决,推举废帝宣统,即今以其私名亨利溥仪君称者,为"新国"之临时总统。

废帝亨利溥仪出任"满洲国"元首

东北行政院,随即召集紧急会议,推举代表六人前赴旅顺,邀请废帝,盖废帝自去年十一月离津后,即住居该地,溥仪初则拒绝。三月四日,复有二十九人之代表团往邀,得其同意,但允任职以一年为限。行政院遂推举该院院长张景惠中将,及其他九人,组织迎驿委员会,于三月五日赴旅顺,当赐觐见。三月六日,废帝应彼等之请求,而离旅顺,赴通江子。八日起,受贺为"满洲国"执政。

三月九日长春举行就职典礼

三月九日就职典礼举行于新都长春,溥仪以执政名义,发出宣言,声称"新国"政策,基于"道德仁慈与博爱"。同月十日,任命政府重要官员,如内阁阁员立法院监察院院长,参议府正副参议长及参事,各省及特区之省长或长官,各省警卫军军长,及其他高级官员。并于三月十二日通电列强报告"满洲国"之成立。该通电之用意在于通告列强组织"满洲国"之基本目的,及其外交政策之主义,并请列强承认"新国"。

执政未来以前,多数法规即早已由赵欣伯博士先期预为制定,以待采用颁布。三月九日,于政府组织法施行时,此种现成法规,亦同时施行。以前适用之法律,凡不与新法律或"新国"之基本政策相抵触者,亦于同日以特别命令,暂准援用。

报告事实之来源

此项关于建立"满洲国"过程之纪载,乃由来自各方之报告集合而成。诸事件之发生,日本报纸,有较详之登载,尤以日本人主办之《满洲日报》为最详尽。至于现政府于五月三十日在长春所撰之两文,一曰《"满洲国"独立之历史——"满洲国"之外交部》,一曰《"满洲国"概要——"满洲国"外交部》,及调查团中国代表所撰之《东三省所谓独立运动之说帖》,亦经详细研讨,除此之外,凡中立者方面所可得之报告,亦均经利用。

九月十八日以来之民政

自九月十八日至"满洲国政府"成立为止,日本军事当局,关于民政方面之行动,其最显著者,如银行之监管,公用事业之行政,铁路之管理,均在在足以表现其自采取军事行动以还,其目的固不仅为暂时之军事占据。自九月十九日占沈阳之后,所有中国之银行,铁路办事处所,公用事业之局所,矿务管理局之事务所,及其他类似房屋之内外均一律有军警监守,嗣即进而调查此等事业之经济及普通状况,迨至准许其复业时,则必须聘请日人为顾问,专家,秘书等官职,且大半挟有行政权。至于东三省之前政府,及前各省所有事业,因前既被政府认为战时之敌人,其银行,矿业,农业,工商业,铁路,公用事业,凡前政府以公家或个人资格,得沾利益之一切税收事业,无一不受监视。

铁路

至于铁路方面,日本当局于军事占据开始时起所采之行动,欲在有利于日人利益状况之下,确切解决中日间久相争持之铁路问题,该项问题,业经在第三章内述及。日方曾以敏捷手段,为下列之行动:

(一)长城以北,中国所有之铁路,及其存于满洲各银行之银钱,均予以扣留。

(二)为欲求诸铁路与南满铁路和调起见,在沈阳及其附近路轨之安置,加以变更;使北宁铁路轨,在南满铁路栈桥地方之下穿过;俾辽宁中车站奉天东车站,奉天北门车站等相连接,并与通吉林之中国国有铁路之联络断绝。(嗣后另有更动)

(三)在吉林将海龙吉林路线,吉林敦化路线,及吉林长春路线,实行联络。

(四)在铁路各部份中,设置【日本】专门顾问。

(五)中国当局所采用之"特别价目"概行废止,恢复原来价额,使中国铁路之运货额,与南满铁路之价额,更相符合。自九月十八日,东北交通委员会停止工作时起,至设立"满洲国交通部"之日为止,对于铁路上之行政,日本当局负完全责任。

其他公用事业

关于沈阳及安东之公共电力之供给,日本采取与上述情形相类似的处分;该项处分,超过保护其侨民生命财产所需要之程度。自九月十八日起,至建立"满洲国"止,日本当局对于中国政府之电话电报及无线电之行政及管理,加以

变更,使与日本在满洲之电话电报事业为密切的调和。

结论

自一九三一年九月十八日以后,在日本军事当局之行动中,不论在军事或民政方面,政治意味,特为浓厚。日方逐步以武力占据东三省,使齐齐哈尔,锦州,哈尔滨,及最后满洲境内一切重要城市,脱离中国之统治,并于每次占据之后,即将该地民事行政机关改组。故独立运动,于一九三一年九月以前,在满洲从未听得;所以能有此项运动者,仅由于日本军队之在场;其为明显。

与第四章所述之日本新政治运动有密切关保之现任或已退职之日本文武官吏,曾考量,组织,并实行此项运动,认为一种解决九月十八日事变后满洲局面之方法。

该官吏等利用某种华人之名义及举动,并利用不满从前政府之少数居民,企图达到上述目的。

日本参谋本部,自始或至少在短期内,明了此项自治运动之可以利用,又毫无疑义。故该部对于独立运动之组织份子,予以援助及指导。

调查团认为满意者,即依各方所得一切证据,确信助成"满洲国"成立之原动力,虽有若干种,无其中两种,即一为日本军队之在场,一为日本文武官吏之活动;两者联合,发生之效力最大;依我等之判断,若无此两者,"新国家"不能成立。

基此理由,现在政体,不能认为由真正的及自然的独立运动所产生。

二、现在"满洲国"政府

基本法

"满洲国"依照其基本法与公民权保证法而统治之,基本法规定政府机关之基本组织。该法于"大同元年"(一九三二)三月九日,以命令第一号公布之。

执政为国家之元首,有一切行政之权,及否决立法院决议之权。执政由参议府辅佐之,以备关于重要事件之咨询。基本法之特点,为画分统治权为四部份,行政,立法,司法,及监察是也。

行政之部

行政部份之职务,由国务总理及各部总长,组织国务院或内阁,于执政指挥之下执行之。国务总理监督各部事务,并有以权力之总务厅,直接管辖各部机要事项,职员之任用,会计及供给事项。隶属于国务院者,有咨议局及立法

局等。故行政权大部集中于国务总理与执政。

立法之部

立法权属于立法院,一切法律及预算案,须得其核准。但立法院否决任何法案时,执政得令其再议,如仍否决,执政得于咨询参议府后,裁决可否。现在立法院组织法尚未制定通过,一切法律由国务院起草;经咨询参议府及经执政核准后,即生效力,故在立法院未组成前,国务总理之地位,实甚重要。

司法之部

司法机关包括许多法院。法院分三级,即最高法院,高等法院,及地方法院是也。

监察之部

监察院监察公务员之行为,并审核政府机关之收支簿记。监察官及审计官,除受刑事或惩戒处分外,不得撤职,亦不得违反其意志,停职,调任,或减俸。

各省及特区

为地方自治便利起见,"满洲国"画为五省二特区。五省即奉天,吉林,黑龙江,热河,兴安是也,兴安包括蒙古区域,故复分成三区或附省,以符旗制,及联旗为盟之制度。二特区,即前中东铁路或称哈尔滨区,及新成立之间岛或朝鲜区。依此行政区画,凡重要之少数人如蒙古人,朝鲜人,及俄人,均于可能范围予以保证,即设立特别行政机关,以应彼等之需要。调查团虽屡次索观所谓属此"满洲国"疆土之地图,但迄未获得,仅曾接得一函,内述该"国"之地界如下:

"'新国'南以长城为界,蒙古旗盟包括呼伦贝尔与锡林昭乌达卓索图及盟旗。"

各省之长官为省长。但因欲集中行政权于"中央政府",省长对于军队与财政,均无权处理。在省政府一如在"中央政府",总务厅实处监督之地位,管辖机要事宜,官员之任用,会计文书及不属于其他各厅之事宜。

县与市

省复画分为县,其行政权大半操诸县自治机关,在其指挥之下,复有若干课,尤以总务课为最显著。在沈阳哈尔滨及长春,有市政府。在哈尔滨方面,现拟建设大哈尔滨,包括俄国及中国城。特别铁路区将取消,其一部将归入大哈尔滨,其余部分之在中东铁路东西两旁者,将并入黑龙江及吉林两省。

"满洲国政府"以省为行政区域，而以县与市为财政单位。"中央政府"厘定其税额及审核其预算。地方税收，均交"中央国库"，由"国库"管理适当之支出，地方当局，不得如旧日习惯，将税收之全部或一部截留。当然，此种制度，尚未能完满的施行。

日本官员及顾问

在"满洲国政府"中，日本官员甚为显要，各部均有日本顾问。国务总理及各部总长，虽均为华人，但在"新国"组织中实际上操有最大权力之各总务厅，其厅长，则均属日人。其初命名为顾问，但最近职位之最重要者，已被实授为政府官员，一如华人。仅计"中央政府"方面，而不计地方政府，军政部军队，以及政府经营事业中之日人。日人之为"满洲国"官员者，为数已近二百。

日本人控制事实上等于国务总理衙门之总务厅，法制局，咨议局，及各部各省之总务厅，各县区之自治指导委员会，以及奉天吉林及黑龙江省之警察厅。日本顾问参议及秘书，各局大率有之。

日人在铁路局及"中央银行"者，为数亦众。监察院方面，总务局主任，监督局主任，及审计局主任之职位，均为日人所据。立法院秘书长，亦为日人。最后凡执政府中最重要官员，如内务处长，及执政禁卫军司令等，亦为日人充当。[1]

政府之目标

依据二月十八日东北行政委员会，及三月一日"满洲国政府"之宣称，政府之目的，欲以"王道"基本原则治国。英文殊乏"王道"之相同名词。"满洲国"当局之通译员，译为"博爱"，而学者则谓"王者之道"。但"王者之道"，其义广泛而不一。按中国旧时之因袭，其意为以人民幸福为怀之善良政治。中国人常以"王道"为"霸道"之反。"霸道"者，孙中山博士于"三民主义"中，指为基于武力与强制。故孙博士解释"王道"乃"强权即是公理"之反面。

自治指导会，曾为造成"新国家"之主要机关，其政策由代替该会之咨议局，继续施行之。军事当局，不准干涉行政事务。制定政府官员资格条例，凡公务员之任用，悉依本人才能而定夺。

赋税

赋税应行减低，并使之有法律根据，而按经济及行政之良好原则，予以改善，直接税收。转交县区及市政府间接赋税之所入，则由"中央政府"保管。

---

[1]　原编辑者注：较重要之任命已同时于《"满洲国"政府公报》上发表。

长春当局所供给之文件中声称,有若干税捐,业已取消,其余悉已减征。并表示希望,政府事业及政府所有财源,如重行整顿后,能增加收益,将来减缩军备后,亦能节省经费。但现时"新国"之财政情形,不能认为满意。因义勇军战事,军费浩繁。但同时对于通常税源,政府无所收入。第一年之支出,约计八千五百万元,而税收不过六千五百万元,不敷之数,达二千万元,此数拟向新设之"中央银行"借贷,下文当再说明。[①]

政府宣称,于财政情形较好时,将尽量移款充教育公益开发内地之用,包括屯垦荒地,开发林矿富源,及扩大交通方法,并声称欢迎外人投资协助,以发展其"国家",遵循机会均等门户开放之原则。

教育

政府现已恢复初高级小学校,并将训练大批能切实了解"新国"精神及政策之教育。采取新学制,编订新教科书,废除排外教育。新教育制度,注意初级小学之改善,重视职业教育,小学教员之训练,及教授关于康健生活之健全思想。中等学校,务须教授英日文,在小学校内并不强制教授日文。

司法及警察

"满洲国"当局决定,凡属司法事项,不容行政当局之干预。法官之地位,有法律为之保障,俸给从优。司法官之资格,亦行提高。领事裁判权,暂时遵守。政府正拟于现行制度实施改良后,向各国交涉废止。警察之遴选,训练,及给养,尤须妥慎适宜,与军队全然分离,不准军队僭行警权。

陆军

改组陆军,亦在筹划之中,但因现时陆军,泰半为旧时满洲军队,为避免增加不满及叛变起见,殊有审慎之必要。

一九三二年七月一日"满洲国中央银行"在长春设立总行在满洲其他城市设立分行

"满洲国中央银行",于六月十四日成立,七月一日,正式开张营业。总行设于"满洲国国都"长春。分行支行,有百七十处,分散于满洲境内之城市内。

"中央银行"之组织,为股份公司,依其特许证,得继续营业三十年。其重要职员,为中日银行家及金融家。其权力得"调节国内货币之流通,维持其稳定,管理金融服务"。银行之资本,准有三千万元(银元),并许其留存准备库至

---

① 原编辑者注:参阅本报告书所附之专论第四号。

少百分之三十,发行纸币。

"中央银行"合并旧有省立银行包括边业银行在内

旧有一切省立银行,包括边业银行在内,均合并于新设之"中央银行",各银行之全部营业,包括其附带事业在内,均行归并。并规定旧有省立银行在满洲外分行之清理办法。

除于旧银行方面所获得之余资外,"中央银行"向日人借款之数,据报有日币二千万元①及"满洲国"政府之集资七百五十万元。② 该银行曾拟统一满洲币制,依照一九三二年七月一日正式公布之价额,买回旧币,易以新纸币。

新币以银元为本位但能否换现则未明白规定

新纸币以银元为本位,须以最少足抵百分之三十之银,金,外币,或存款为准备。至于新纸币能否无限制凭票换现,官方布告中,并未明言。旧钞于通过变币法后二年内,仍得通用,过时无效。

现在满洲币制大体与一九三一年九月十八日以前者无异

"中央银行"新钞定单,已经存放于日本政府,但至今钞币及新银币,尚未见诸流通。现在满洲币制,除钞币上必须于经过各银行时,加盖荣厚(新"中央银行"行长)签署外,概与一九三一年九月十八日以前之制度无异。

"满洲国"统一计划以供给不敷之现款为基础

新"满洲国"银行,以有限之资本可供使用,如何能成就其统一及其稳固全满洲币制之伟大计划,实不明了。承袭旧有省立银行方面之财源,加之向日本银行界所借之款及募自"满洲国"政府之资本,似乎完全不足以达其目的。且银行与"满洲国"政府间之财政关系,究依何标准而设定,亦不明了,按其财政总长向调查团所提之初步"满洲国"预算表,"满洲国"于第一年内,即将短少二千万元。③ 据该总长言,"中央银行"(彼时尚未成立)将贷款,以资弥补。以一

---

① 原编辑者注:此数或系华币之元。

② 原编辑者注:按照一九三二年五月五日"满洲国"财政部长向调查团提出之初步预算表。

③ 原编辑者注:调查团某委员接见"满洲国"财政部长时,预算表内此项及以下各项均用"日圆",但于"满洲国"外交部所提《满洲国概要》之英文译本中,则又用"华元"。故调查团于指此项及预算表中以下各项时,宁用"华元"而不用"日圆"。良以中文指元之字,与日文指圆之字,写法有时相混,故于研究中日双方向调查团所提之英法文译本时,备见困难。

政府,出资七百五十万元与银行,而贷款超过二千万元之数,以使其预算表收支相等,"中央银行"及政府之预算表,均乏健全之财政基础,概可想见。

"中央银行"似能统一币制而不能兑现

除非"中央银行",能集得比诸现在似有之现款较多外,殊难希望全满洲币制之统一及稳固,而使新币能兑现。即使其能建立一币制虽统一而不能兑现,亦可谓有多少成就。但币制虽统一,如因不能兑现,而不能保持其稳固性,仍不具备健全钱币制之要件。

日人扩张其势力于中国之公用机关

关于各种公用事业及铁路,会议定办法,冀使中日两方之机关有所联络。沈阳事变前,日人极望此事能早实现,但华人始终未允所请。于是自九月十八日迄于"满洲国"成立,在此期间内日人遂立刻进行期达其目的,此中经过已于本章第一节中述之矣。自"新国"成立后,"满洲国交通部"之政策似欲与南满铁路株式会社订约,准其利用其若干主要之铁路线。

中国电话电报及无线电机关

中国在满洲之电话电报及无线电等机关以其系完全国有,各有其本国主管人员,并隶属于东北电话电报及无线电行政机关统一管辖之下。自九月十八日以后,所有此三种机关,均与在满洲之日本机关进行更密切之合作。日人与东北电报行政机关又订约办理满洲各地间,及关东租界地,日本,朝鲜,台湾,及南洋群岛各地间来往之直达通报事宜。北满各主要城市与大连,沈阳,及长春之日本邮局间,更建有直接电线以速电信之传达。

用日文字母①通电,索价特别低廉。而报局内之华员现受特别训练,以习运用日文字母之方法。在各主要城市中,拟逐渐添加日人职员,俾与华人职员一同工作。满洲与日本帝国间之电报交通,遂得各种之便利,因而两"国"间之商业关系自然益臻稳固。

盐税——日本军事当局于一九三一年九月管理盐税基金

九月十八日至十九日之事件发生后,日本当局命令保管盐税之各官署及银行;嗣后凡未经彼等允许不得动用该项税款。

关于盐税之管理权,所以坚持主张者,其理由为盐税虽名为国税,而实际上其大部之收入均被张学良将军之政府所扣留。一九三〇年盐税之收入大约

---

① 原编辑者注:一种日本注音符号。

共有银洋二五，〇〇〇，〇〇〇元，其中之二四，〇〇〇，〇〇〇元，均被扣留于满洲，汇交上海盐务稽核总所者不过一，〇〇〇，〇〇〇元而已。

张学良于一九二八年允许呈缴满洲应付之盐税

一九二八年十二月张学良将军加入国民政府后，彼曾允许按月付银八六，六〇〇满洲元以为偿还盐税抵押借款时满洲应付之部分。嗣于一九三〇年四月重订新章，满洲每月应付之总数增为二一七，八〇〇元。但张学良将军以满洲当地财政上发生困难，请求暂缓实行。沈阳事变时，彼之欠款已达五七六，二〇〇元。第一次按新章所汇之二一七，八〇〇元实为一九三一年九月二十九日所汇，经日本陆军军官允许者也。自是而后，直至一九三二年三月底为止，满洲新组织之政府，曾汇款与中央政府，其所汇非仅为每月应付之定额，即张学良将军时代所欠之应付定额，亦予汇寄。惟彼等以为盐税之盈余乃满洲的而非国家的收入，故为扣留盐余作地方之用为正当。

一九三一年十月及十一月牛庄盐税之攫夺

沈阳维持治安委员会改为临时省政府后，曾命令牛庄盐务稽核分所将所有款项交与省银行，以便财政支配。据中国官方报告：牛庄中国银行内所存之盐款，共计银洋六七二，七〇九•五六元，亦于十月三十日被迫交出，并未得原存款人之允许。由辽宁财政局出名，给与收据一纸，其上仅有该局日人顾问之签名。

新吉林省政府亦攫夺盐税

新吉林省政府对吉林及黑龙江之盐运署，亦采取相同之步骤。据中国官方报告，该省政府令将盐款转交省库。该署盐运使因拒绝其请求，被拘禁数日，旋由省长熙洽派员接替。并于十月二十二日强占该署，盐务稽核所亦由熙洽命令封闭，中国银行及交通银行所存之盐款亦为新吉省政府所索取，于十一月六日移交省银行，自此以后，盐款由地方当局随时提取使用，惟其应缴部分，仍按月汇送上海。一九三一年十月三十日至一九三二年八月二十五日之间，有中国官方报告数目可稽。盐税之被扣留于满洲者，共计银洋一四，〇〇〇，〇〇〇元。

满洲之盐务行政，虽在上述之限制及监督下，仍然继续进行。直至三月二十五日"满洲国政府"之财政总长始命令将存款，账目，文件，及其他财产之属于盐务督办者，于翌日悉数移交"满洲国"之盐务管理专员。前由中国银行经管之盐税征收事务，亦改属东三省银行。该财政总长声言：盐务职员之愿继续

在"满洲国"盐政机关服务者,须先将其姓名呈报管理盐务专员公署,若能先行脱离中华民国政府之关系,自当郑重考虑,予以录用。

"满洲国"政府取得盐税之管理权

牛庄之盐务稽核分所于四月十五日被迫解散。正副所长均被解职,官署被占,箱柜,文件及印章等均被查封。其他职员虽被请求留任,但闻彼等均拒绝不允。一部盐务人员随同所长赴天律,静候上海总所命令。自是东三省盐务稽核所之事务,遂完全属于"满洲国"之盐务管理署矣。但"新政府"曾谓关于以盐税担保之外债,仍愿继续缴付其应缴部分云。

海关

满洲之关税,一向汇寄中央政府,故日本军事当局并未干涉海关行政,亦未干涉汇往上海之款项。第一次干涉关税者却为"满洲国政府",以为彼等"国家"乃一独立之国家。

满洲之海关收入

东北政务委员会(即二月十七日成立之"满洲国临时政府")首先谕知满洲各商埠之海关监督,谓从权利上,关税虽属于"满洲国",且不久将归委员会管理,但目前各海关监督及税务司须照常工作。监督及税务司等探悉满洲之各商埠,均派有日人海关顾问一名,以监督海关之行政为目的。所称之商埠,即龙井村,安东,牛庄,及哈尔滨及其他分关,一九三一年上列各地之税收为海关两五七四,〇〇〇两,三,六八二,〇〇〇两,三,七九二,〇〇〇两,及五,二七二,〇〇〇两。爱珲商埠现仍在满洲政府管辖势力之外,故仍在中国海关管理下工作焉。至关东租界地治下之大连,则有特殊之地位,满洲各埠(大连在内)征收之关税,一九三〇年在全中国之税收为百分之十四·七,在一九三一年为百分之十三·五。于此,则可知满洲在中国关务行政上所占地位之重要矣。

"满洲国"当局夺取满洲全部海关行政之步骤,可于安东地方之行动见之,兹将总税务司描写该地之情形录之如次:

"满洲国政府"于一九三二年三月至六月取得海关之管理权及关税。三月间一日人海关顾问奉派赴安东海关公署,但并未积极工作。至六月中旬传达"满洲国"财政部命令:中国银行应停止将关税汇寄上海。六月十六日武装"满洲国"警察四人偕警察副官一人(日人),同至中国银行,通知经理,谓彼等乃为看守关税而来。六月十九日中国银行交与东三省银行银七八三,〇〇〇两,并

通知税务司谓此实乃威胁下不得不作之行为。

六月二十六及二十七日。"满洲国"之日本顾问一人要求安东之海关须交付与彼。税务司不许。"满洲国"警察（均为日人）遂强使税务司离去海关。该税务司仍图在其家中继续办理关务，盖以安东关税百分之八十，均由铁路区域内所征收，所望日本当局不准在此区域内任加干涉耳。乃"满洲国"警察竟入日本之铁路区域，捕获海关职员若干人，对其他职员施以威吓，并强迫停止中国海关工作。

大连之海关状况

在六月十七日以前，每隔三四日即将大连之海关收入汇至上海，但至六月九日，"满洲国政府"通知：不准继续汇款。停止向上海汇款，后海关监督犹以电报命大连之日本税务司照常进行。但该税务司拒绝将收据交与海关，其理由为日本租借地政府之外交处长劝彼勿再汇款，恐对日本之利益有重大之妨害也。总务税司因大连税务司故意抗命，遂于六月二十四日将其免职。

六月二十七日"满洲国政府"委派此免职之税务司及其僚属为"满洲国"官吏，仍在原职服务。设如日本当局阻止彼等管理大连海关时，彼等拟在关东租借地边境之瓦房店地方设立新关，以威胁之。租借地之日本当局并未反对将海关行政权交与新派之"满洲国"官吏。彼等认为此问题与日本无关，其症结乃在一方面之"满洲国"及另一方面之中国政府与其大连关税务司而已。

"满洲国政府"对海关之态度

"满洲国政府"之主张：为"满洲国"既为独立国，则从权利上应有全权管理其境内之关务。但该政府曾谓多数外债及赔款皆以中国之关税为担保，故愿每年交纳应付之部分以偿债务。除将此项的款储于横滨正金银行外，希望能于一九三二年至一九三三年得关余洋一九，○○○，○○○元以供地方之需。

满洲之邮政

九月十八日以后日本军事当局在满洲除检查新闻纸及信件外，对邮政并无何种极端干涉。"满洲国"成立之后，其"政府"即欲接收境内之邮政。四月十四日委派专员办理接收邮政事宜，四月二十四日请求加入万国邮政协会，但尚无加入该会之资格。

各邮政局邮务长均拒绝交代，一时只得保持现状；但"满洲国"曾在数邮局中派有监察员实行管理权。最后"满洲国政府"决定印行邮票不再通用中国之邮票，七月九日其交通部命令通知各地于八月一日即可售票卖新邮票及明信

片。中国政府于此时命令各邮政局邮务长将满洲之各邮局全体停办,邮局之职员或给薪俸三月,成调往中国他处服务,均听自择。在"满洲国"方面,对邮局职员之愿留任者仍继续聘请,并允许担保邮局职员得享有在中国邮政管理下所享之报酬及其他权利。七月二十六日"满洲国政府"遂将满洲邮政之全部接收完毕。

私有财产之待遇

"满洲国政府"曾宣称对私有财产及中国中央政府或前满洲政府所给之特许权利均将尊重,但此特许权利只以用合法手续依当时法规所给予者为限。以前行政当局之合法借款及债务亦允为偿还,并指定委员会清理债务,至于张学良将军及其他昔日重要领袖之财产将如何处置则迄无表示。据中国官方报告,张学良将军万福麟将军鲍毓麟将军及其他官员之财产均被没收。"满洲国"当局为前政府之官吏尽力搜刮金钱以饱私囊,故不能承认如此取得之财产为私有财产。前政府之产业均经详细调查。关于银行存款一项据闻业已调查完毕。

评语

吾人既已详述"满洲国"政府之组织,计划,及其表示与中国分立之行为矣,当就吾人对于其工作及其特质之结论一陈述之。

此"政府"之计划中列有若干开明之改革,其实行不仅适宜于满洲亦且适宜于中国之其他部分,而在事实上此种改革已多见于中国政府计划之中。此"政府"之代表与本调查团会晤时曾宣称:彼等有日人之辅助,足能于相当期间内恢复治安与秩序,并能使之永远如此。彼等深信若尽建设廉洁有力之政府,担保捕灭盗匪,减少军费借以减轻赋税,改革钱币制度,改良交通并实行人民政治代表制,则人民方面必肯起而拥护。

"满洲国"在此短期间虽得自由实施其计划,并对于其已施步骤,虽已予以相当注意,然仍无象征足以证明该"政府"在事实上能实施甚多改革。试举一例言之①,彼业经颁布之预算及钱币改革计划,其实施之前途似有严重之阻碍。在一九三二年之不安定及扰乱情形之下,澈底的改革计划,安定情况,及经济繁荣,决难实现。

至于该"政府"及行政机关,其各部名义上之领袖虽系居住满洲之中国人,

① 原编辑者注:参阅本报告附载之专论第四第五号。

但其重要之政治行政权，则仍操诸日本官吏及日人顾问之手。该"政府"之政治的及行政的组织，不仅予此项官吏及顾问以供[贡]献专家意见之权，抑且予以实行管理及指挥行政之机会。此辈固不受东京政府之训令，其政策亦非与日本政府或关东军司令部之政策相符合。但遇重要问题发生时，该官吏及顾问等（其中有于新组织成立之初期可以自主行动者）均渐受胁迫，遵照日本当局之意旨行事。此当局者因其军队占领满洲土地，而"满洲国政府"又依赖该军队维持其对内对外之权威，同时"满洲国"管辖下之铁路，又委托南满铁路株式会社代行管理，最后又以有日本领事驻在重要城市以通声气，是以无论遇何时机，彼日本当局者，均有运用其绝大力量之方法。"满洲国政府"与日本当局间之联络自最近派遣专使后更觉密切。此专使虽未经政府正式授权，但已驻在满洲"都城"，以关东租借地总督之名义管辖南满铁路株式会社，同时兼行外交代表，首席领事及驻军总司令之职权。

"满洲国"与日本之关系前此颇不易解说，但据调查团所得之最近消息，日本政府有不久即将此项关系加以确定之意向。今年八月二十七日日本代表曾致函调查团谓武藤专使已于八月二十日离东京赴满洲。武藤抵满后即将开始谈判以便缔结日本与"满洲"间之基本友谊条约。日本政府认此项条约之缔结为对"满洲国"之正式承认。

三、满洲居民之态度

满洲居民之态度

调查团目的之一即为欲确知满洲居民对新"国家"之态度。在当时调查团情况之下搜集此项证据颇多困难。盗匪，朝鲜共产党，及新"政府"之拥护者为恨中国代表之到满及其批评该政制之言论因而发生不利于调查团实在的或想象的危险，均成为使调查团蒙受特殊保护之理由。在此不安定之地方，实际上诚时有危险发生之可能。吾等对于沿途得力保护，表示感谢。但警戒之结果，徒使一般证人，不得接近，甚至有多数华人，不敢与调查团人员一观面者。吾人在某地接得消息谓在吾人达到之前官方布告，凡未得政府之允许者皆不得与调查团会面。以故与各界接谈殊匪易易，且须秘密行之。虽然如此，多数人尤告吾人，虽秘密会晤，亦极危险也。

调查团仍排除万难，除与"满洲国"官员及日本领事与军官作公开会晤外，仍得设法与商人银行家，教员，医师，警察贩夫各色人等作私人之谈叙。吾人

尚接到书信文件一千五百余起,其中有为亲手交来者,但大多数则由邮局展
[辗]转递到。对于所接书件中之报告均尽量与中立方面之报告比较参证。

代表团体及书面意见

本调查团曾接见各公共团体及会社之代表,彼等常以书面之陈述交阅。
各代表大都由日本或"满洲国"当局介绍而来。吾人深信彼等所交来之陈述,
均系先经日人同意者。实际上,彼给予陈述之人有时于事后来告我等谓斯项
意见系日人所作或经日人将主要部份修改者,并谓斯项意见不得视为彼等真
意之表示云。此项文件颇值注意盖以其中对日本参与"满洲国"行政权之成立
或维持一层故示疏略不加可否也。大概言之,此项意见书,皆系不满于旧时中
国行政之种种怨语,并对于新"国家"之未来表示希望及信仰而已。

书信

收到书信悉为农民,小织工,城市工人,及学生所投寄者,其中详述作者之
感想及经历。六月间本调查团返北平后,此种书信均经特选之专家加以翻译,
分析并整理,在此一千五百五十件之书信,除二件外,均对"满洲国政府"及日
人深表仇视。此种信件,皆甚诚恳,并足为民意之表现。

"满洲国"之官吏

"满洲国政府"之高级中国官吏,所以能任职者,即有甚多原因,多数官吏
为昔日之官吏,其留任或因利诱或因各种方法之威胁,其中有人写信与调查团
谓彼等系威吓而留任,所有政权均操之于日人之手,彼等忠于中国,并谓彼等
在日人监视下与调查团所谈之话,不足置信。有数官吏之留任乃为避免财产
之被充公,盖彼之逃往中国者其财产有被没收者焉。其他享有令名之人亦多
加入。彼等希望能有改良行政之权力,并希望日人能践行约言许其自由行动。
有数满洲人加入,系因希望为满洲族人谋幸福。此项人员多已失望,并诉称彼
等从未获得真实之权力。至另有一部份官吏,其留任则因彼等个人对以前政
府表示失意,并希望能借留任而获利。

下级及地方官吏

下级及地方官吏大部均在新政治下留任,或因维持生活及供给家庭之不
得不然,或因彼等深恐离去之后,继任失人。当地县官大都留职,或因对治下
人民之责任心所驱使,或因压迫所致。若请名誉超著之中国人任高级官吏殊
属困难,但使中国人任低级及地方官吏则甚容易。不过在此情形下,其服务之
忠实如何,颇属问题。

警察

"满洲国"警察,一部为旧日之中国警察,一部为新募者。在较大之城市中事实上均有日人为警察官长,在其他地方亦有日人顾问。警察中有个人来与吾人谈话者,彼辈表示对"新政府"不满,并称为索生活起见,不得不继续工作。

陆军

"满洲国陆军"之大部,亦为昔日之满洲军队,惟曾经日人指导改编。初时为此项军队以职责仅限于维持地方治安尚愿在新政制下服务。然日后调此军队与中国军队正式战争,并听从日人命令与日本军队联合攻击。"满洲国陆军"遂渐不可靠。日人方面报告"满洲国"军队时常投降中国,而中国方面则宣称"满洲国陆军"为接济军需之最可靠最有效之来源。

商人及银行家

与吾人会面之中国商人及银行家对"满洲国"均极仇视。彼等深恶日人;彼等为生命及财产而生惧心,且常称"吾等不愿变为朝鲜人",九月十八日以后到中国①之商人为数极多,但彼不甚富裕之商人现在仍复归去。概言之,较小之商家希望与日人竞争时所受损失不致如大商贾之大,因后者曾与昔日官吏常有利益关系故也。吾人前往调查时尚有多数商店未曾复业。盗匪之增加对乡间之商业颇有影响。信用制度亦大部动摇。日人预备经济侵略满洲之明白表示,及前数月内日本经济调查会之屡次来满,使中国商人顿生疑虑。惟闻此经济调查会等于回日本后亦均表示失望云。

职业阶级:医师,教员,学生

职业阶级,教员及医师对"满洲国"亦均极仇视。彼等指称常被监视并受威胁。干涉教育,停办大学及其他学校,改换学校教科书,凡此均因爱国心之激动而增加敌对之心。新闻纸,邮件及言论之检查,与中国印行之新闻纸之不得入"满洲国"境,同为一般人所愤恨。但亦有中国人在日本留学回国者,不在此一般人之列。吾人尚接到学生及青年送来之许多书信,其中均为反对"满洲国"。

农民及城市工人

关于农民及城市工人之态度其证据均甚散漫,搜集自属不易。外国人及受过教育之中国人之意见以为彼等对"满洲国"或为仇视或不过问。农民及工

---

① 编者按:即指中国关内地区。

人缺乏政治知识,寻常不甚识字,普通对政府亦漠不相关。农民对"满洲国"仇视之理由,可于下列证人所述之意见中得之。此项理由已于农工阶级所送来之信件中证实。农民深信新政治势力能使朝鲜甚至日本人之移民增加。朝鲜移民与中国人不能同化,彼等耕种之方亦异。中国农民大部分种豆,高粱及麦,而朝鲜人种稻,势必致修沟渠以灌溉田地。设有大雨,朝鲜人所造之沟渠必为冲毁,并流过中国邻地,而损其收获。彼等在昔日亦常因土地所有权及地租问题引起纠纷。自"满洲国"成立后中国人宣称朝鲜人常不付地租,并从中国人手中攫取土地,日人强迫中国人以低价售卖土地。在铁路及城市附近之农民不许于距铁路及城市五百米达内之区域种植高粱,因高粱长成时高约十尺便于盗匪之行动也。中国每季出关之移民,因经济衰落及政治紊乱关系,已逐渐减少。昔日中国移民可以领用之公地现时亦为"满洲国"所有。

自一九三一年九月十八日以来,乡间之匪祸与不法事件滋长更甚。其原因半出被裁之军队,半出受匪毁害之农民因家产毁尽不得不流而为匪以维生计。至正式有组织之战争多年来满洲已较中国各地为少,今则在东三省各部又开始有日本军队与"满洲国"军队以及其他仍效忠于中国之散漫队伍之作战。此种战争自予农民以极大之苦楚。而尤其在日人疑惑有反"满洲国"军队埋伏时,任意以飞机掷弹毁灭乡村。其一种之结果即为广漠之田亩无法耕种,次年纳税之时农民当更难应付。自此种扰乱发生,多数中国之最近迁来者又逃回关内。有此种实际上之理由重以深恶日人之心理,致多数证人俱异口同声告吾等以中国农民在"新政府"下之受苦与其不满意,并谓此辈农民系满洲居民之大多数,其态度多抱消极的仇视。

至城市居民亦当受苦于日本军队,宪兵,与警察之行动。就大体言日本军队之行为尚佳,虽我等所接信件中有诉述个人之残暴行为者,但各处尚无扩大之抢夺或残杀。在另一方面日人对于其疑有敌意之份子压制甚厉。中国人民谓有无数杀戮之事发生,且有许多囚犯在日本宪兵派出所受尽威吓与酷刑。

据吾人所知"满洲国"之开幕典礼,尝欲使各城居民作热烈表示,乃未能办到。就大体论城市居民之态度系一种消极的默认与仇视之混合性。

少数民族

吾人已知大多数之中国人民对于"满洲国"或表示敌意或漠不关念,然尚有少数在满洲之各民族对"新政府"予以赞助,如蒙古人,朝鲜人,白俄人,以及满洲人等。彼等或因以前政府之压迫,或因近数十年中国移民之增加使彼等

多少各蒙经济上之不利。彼等中虽无一能十分热忱,但颇希望由"新政府"治下能得较善之待遇,而"新政府"之政策亦以鼓励此等少数民族为能事。

蒙古人

蒙古人与中国人①显然别为一族,如上所述彼等持有坚强之民族自觉心,并保持其部落制度,贵族政治,语言,服装,以及其特殊之生活习尚,风俗宗教等。虽大都仍属游牧民族,但亦渐事耕种,并亦常用畜类或车以运输出产物。住居满洲边境之蒙古人近以中国移民而痛苦增加。中国移民占用并耕种彼辈之田地因之彼辈将渐被排挤。此足引起不能避免之恶感。吾人接见之蒙古代表曾诉述其所受昔日中国官吏及征税员蹂躏之苦楚。内蒙古人见外蒙古已受苏俄之支配,深畏其势力将侵入内蒙古。彼等愿于中国及苏俄两方侵略之下保持其民族独立之生存。虑此不安全之状态,彼等以为若图在"新政府"下保持独立之生存希望较多。但吾人须知此辈王公大都依其不动财产及特殊权利为生,故彼等对此事实上当局亦愿附和也。惟在北平时,本调查团曾接见蒙古王公代表,彼等对"新政局"则深表反对。现在住居满洲边境之蒙古人与"满洲国"之关系尚不明了,"满洲国"迄今亦尚未干涉蒙古人之行政。对于蒙古人倘能谨慎应付,则其现时之赞助当属真实,设一旦日人有危害其独立或经济利益时彼等必立即取消其赞助。

满洲人

满洲人民几已全部与中国人民同化。在吉林及黑龙江虽尚有少数政治上不甚重要之满洲人居留地,其人民虽用两种语言,而仍显然为满洲民族。自民国成立后残余之满洲民族失去其特权地位。虽民国仍继续允与津贴然均付以低价之货币。因此彼辈不得已而经营向无经验之农商事业。其他少数特殊之满洲民族仍持有无限希望以为"满洲国"之成立必能使彼等立时恢复向来之特权地位,因彼等之主使者常述及满洲之住民与其他中国人民显然有别,且谓满洲最后之帝皇当为其民族中之元首。满洲族人民之在位者均具有如是希望,惟在满洲之中国人民则谓此辈官员见日人之把持一切而彼等之建议全被忽视现已如梦初觉。虽其中仍不免有少数份子效愚忠于废帝,但绝无重要之满洲民族醒觉运动。彼等既已大多数与中国人民同化,虽经努力使登用满洲人民主持行政,努力鼓励满洲民族自觉,然此项"新政府"之援助之源,殊不足当代

---

①　编者按:中国人、中国移民、中国人民,均指代汉族人民。下同。

表人民之任何名义。

朝鲜人

在过去,朝鲜农民受日本当局之指使,与中国官吏地主及农民曾有许多冲突。当时朝鲜农民确受尽凶暴敲诈之苦。朝鲜代表在调查团前大都表示欢迎"新政府",但吾人殊不知彼等所能代表其社会者究至若何之程度。不过无论如何,此等朝鲜人系政治通逃者,既为日人专制而逃亡在外当不至再欢迎日人专制之扩张。向彼等宣传共产主义实易生效。彼等并常与朝鲜内部之革命团体相联络。[1]

白俄

在满洲最少数之居民为白色俄民,其人数至少亦在十万。近年来在哈尔滨内外之白俄受祸最烈。因彼等系最少数之居民又无政府为之保护。彼等曾受中国官吏警察之各种屈辱,又与其本国之政府有冲突,即在满洲亦时为此而有不安。在彼等居民中之比较富有而受有教育者得自谋生活,但亦常受苦楚,无论何时中国当局思从苏俄政府获得利益,即以彼等为牺牲品。彼比较穷困者又觉谋生为难,且又时受中国警察与中国法庭之苦。在此税收不依法律而可自由论价之省,俄国居民所纳之税率常较中国居民为高。而在商业或各种运动上彼等受许多限制,常以请查护照,请签合同或转卖田地均须施贿于中国官吏。此等居民其生活之苦无以复加,吾人自无怪其欲欢迎日人,以期在新政之下得以改进彼等之生活也。

当吾人在哈尔滨时曾接见一白俄代表并接有许多函件,总括其意皆愿赞助能给下列各种保障之任何政府:

(一)享受庇护之权;

(二)施行诚实而有效之警察行政;

(三)法院之公正;

(四)公平之税则制度;

(五)经商居住之权,无须用贿赂得来;

(六)教育儿童之便利:

彼等此项要求,大半关于外国语之教授须增加效率,以使彼等得以向外移殖,以及完美之专门教育使彼等得在中国营商;

---

[1]　原编辑者注:参阅本报告书第三章及专论第九号。

（七）关于土地居住及向外移民之援助。

调查团之结论

以上所述为我等在满洲旅行期间本地居民所报告之意见。细心研究各方所获得之证据，无论公私谈话或书信文件，吾人得一结论：即一般中国人对"满洲国政府"均不赞助，此所谓"满洲国政府"者在当地中国人心目中直是日人之工具而已。

第七章 日本之经济利益与中国人之经济绝交①②

中国人之抵制日货为中日冲突之重要原因

前三章以专述一九三一年九月十八日以后军事及政治事件为主旨，顾欲使中日冲突之叙述，臻于准确或完备之程度，犹须论及另一重要冲突原因，即中国人之抵制日货是。兹为了解此种抵货运动所用之方法，及此类方法及于日本商业之影响起见，对于日本之概括的经济地位，与其在中国之经济暨财政利益，及中国之对外贸易，亦应略为叙述；且为了解次章所述中国与日本在满洲所有经济利益之范围及性质计，此亦有叙述之必要。

日本人口之过剩

当一千八百六十余年明治复兴之际，日本以二世纪闭关自守之国家，崭然露其头角，不及五十年，竟一跃而为世界之一等强国。其往日几无增减之人口，乃开始为迅速之增加，当一八七二年之际，其人口之总数，不过三千三百万，及至一九三〇年，竟达六千五百万；此种人口之激增，现仍继续不断；其每年之平均率约为九十万人。

以日本之人口与其土地面积之总数相比较，每方哩约合四百三十七人；其在美国则每方哩约为四十一人，在德国为三百三十人，在意大利为三百四十九

---

① 原编辑者注：boycott一字(译者按即抵货一字)，按此字初用于爱尔兰，系自船主(Captain)Charles Cunningham Boycott(生于一八三二年，殁于一八九三年)之名而来，该船主系爱尔恩侯(Earl of Erne)管理梅由郡(County Mayo)产业之代理人。当一八八〇年时，因该船主拒绝收受租户依自定标准所缴之租金，有人欲谋害其生命，致其仆人被逼他去，蔽障被毁，函件被截，食物之来源被阻。此字不久遂通常沿用于英语之中，而迅即为多种外国语言所采用。(见一九二九年第十四版《大英百知全书》)

② 原编辑者注：关于此点之专论，见附录第八号。

人,在大不列颠为四百六十八人,在比利时为六百七十人,在中国为二百五十四人。

若以日本可耕土地每方哩可容之人口与他国相比较,则日本岛国因地理上特殊结构之关系,其人口之密度特高:

日本	二七七四	德国	八〇六
大不列颠	二一七〇	法国	四六七
比利时	一七〇九	美国	二二九
义大利①	八一九		

因农业区域内有集中甚密之人口,故每人所占之土地异常狭小,每农人耕种不满一英亩之地者,占百分之三十五,其耕种不满二英亩半者,占百分之三十四。就可耕土地之开拓及其耕植之集约而言,均已达最高之限度。总之,日本之土地,既不能希望其生产较今日更为多量之增加,亦不能望其能再行容纳多量之佣工。

土地上之困难

再者,因耕植之集约,肥料之广施,致使生产费用高涨。土地价格之高,远过于亚洲其他各部,即较诸欧洲人口最密之地方,亦有过之无不及。在此债台高筑之人民中,似有诸多不满意之表现,租户与地主之冲突,方兴未艾。尝以向外移民为可行之救济方法,但以次章所述之种种原因,直至今日尚未见其能解决此困难也。

日本于采行工业主义之初,即意在扶植都市人口之发达,以期得一销售农产品之本国市场,并利用劳力,制造货物以供国内外之用。自是以后,迭经变迁。就粮食而论,日本往昔本系自给而有余,兹则其进口货物中食料已占进口总数百分之八至百分之十五。其进口食料之所以或多或少者,乃由于国内五谷收获之情形时有变化,尤以米为最甚。夫食料既须由国外输入,而国内对于此类进口货之需要,复有继长增高之势,故不得不设法增加出口工业品,使本国已经失利之进出口贸易,得以维持平衡。

进一步发展工业之必要

日本如欲对于工业为更进一步之发展,俾其增添之人口有雇佣之机会,则出口贸易之发展,与开拓能以吸收数量增添之制造品及半制造品之国外市场,

---

① 编者按:即意大利。

益见重要。此种市场,同时亦可为供给原料及食料之渊源。

中国及日本出口贸易之市场

日本之出口贸易,就已往之发展情形而论,其主要之趋向有二:奢侈品及生丝运销于美国,而大宗以棉织物为主之制造品则销售于亚洲各国。美国所销者,占出口货物百分之四二点五。亚洲全部所销者,占百分之四二点六。销售于亚洲之货物中,其百分之二四点七,为中国关东租借地及香港所吸收,其余部分中为亚洲别部之中国人所经售者亦属不少。(按一九二九年数额之记载见一九三一年之《日本年鉴》)

一九三零年间,是年为有完全可稽字数之最近一年。日本出口货物之总额,为十四万万六千九百八十五万二千元日金;其进口货物之总额,为十五万万四千六百○七万一千元日金。而出口货物中之运往中国(关东租借地及香港除外)者,价值二万万六千零八十二万六千元日金,或合全数百分之十七点七。至其进口货物中之运自中国(关东租借地及香港除外)者,价值一万万六千一百六十六万七千元日金,或合全数百分之十点四。

兹就自日本运往中国之主要货物分析之,则知中国所销日本之流质物品占其出口流质物品百分之三二点八;炼粉占百分之八四点六;煤占百分之七五点一;棉纱占百分之三一点九;平均计算其合百分之五一点六。

兹就运自中国之进口货物加以同样之分析,则知日本进口之豆及豌豆运自中国者,占百分之二四点五;油饼占百分之五三;蔬菜干占百分之二五;平均计算共合百分之三四点五。

以上之数额,既系专指中国而言,至香港及关东租借地并不包括在内,故对于以大连为主要口岸之日本与满洲间贸易之数额,尚未予以说明。

中日贸易关系之重要

上述事实及统计足以明示中日通商对于日本之重要。顾日本在中国之利益,并不限于通商一端;其在实业,铁路,航业,银行各方面所投之资本,亦为数甚巨。且于最近三十年中,所有此类财政经济之活动,其发达之概况,已呈突飞猛进之趋势。

日本在中国之投资

一八九九年间,日人唯一重要投资,厥为在上海与华人合股经营之小轧棉机一架,约值银十万两。至一九一三年,日人国外投资之总额,计有五万三千五百万元日金之多,而其中投于中国【其他部分】及满洲者,竟达四万三千五百

万元日金。欧战告终之时,日本在中国【其他部分】及满洲之投资,较诸一九一三年增至一倍有余,而其增加之投资,大部分与著名之西原借款有关,该项借款之成立,一部分系含有政治作用。顾虽经此曲折,日本在中国及满洲之投资,于一九二九年几占其二十一万万元日金国外投资总额中之二十万万元日金。[①] 此足证日本在国外之投资,几全部集中于中国【其他部分】及满洲,而尤以满洲所吸取之资本,居极多数(尤以投于铁路者为甚)。

除上述之投资外,中国尚积欠日本各种中央及省市之借款。于一九二五年总计为二万〇四百四十五万八千元日金(大半系无担保者),另有利息一千八百〇三万七千元日金。查日本之大宗资本,虽系投于满洲,然其投于中国本部之实业,航业及银行等事业者,亦为数甚巨。当一九二九年时,中国纺织工业所用之纺锤,几有百分之五十为日本人所有者。就中国之航运业而言,日本在中国居第二位。至于日本在中国之银行,在一九三二年间,计有三十所之多,其中有少数系中日合资经营者。

中日贸易之发展对中国之利害关系

上述之总计,虽以日本为主体,然其对于中国方面关系之重要,亦属显而易见。迄一九三二年止,中国对外贸易总额中,中日贸易向居第一位。一九三〇年间,中国出口货中百分之四二点一系运往日本,而同年之进口货中,亦有百分之二四点九系运自日本。兹与日本方面之统计相对照,可见中日贸易在中国对外贸易总额中所占之百分位,高于中日贸易在日本对外贸易总额中所需之百分位。惟中国在日本并未投资,亦无银行或航业之利益。中国尤须能增加其物产之出口额,俾有款购买其所需之制成物品,并在信用方面,建立一稳固之基础,借以告贷资本,以应进一步发展工业之要求。

中日之经济及财政关系易受任何纷扰原因之影响

由前述论据观之,中日经济及财政关系之广复,因此易受任何纷扰原因之影响并易为其所紊乱,乃明显之事。就大体言之,日本所仰赖于中国者,较诸中国所仰赖于日本者为多。故遇有关系紊乱情事,日本较易受害,且损失亦较多。

由是可知自一八九五年中日战争以来,两国间所发生之种种政治纠纷,均会一一影响相互间之经济关系,且两国间商业之屡经纷扰而仍继续增进,足证

---

① 原编辑者注:依照另一统计,日本在中国投资之总额满洲包括在内约合十八万万日金。

相互间实隐伏为政治冲突所不能割断之经济关系。

经济绝交之起源

就中国商人银行家及手工匠同业公所之组织而言，中国人素习于抵制之方法，已数百年于兹矣。此类同业公所，为适应近代情形起见，虽正在改革之中，但为数仍属甚多，且于维护同业共同利益方面，对于同业人员具有伟大之势力。此种由数百年同业团体生活所养成之训练与态度，在今日之经济绝交运动中，实与国民党所代表之近代热烈民族主义相混合。

晚近抵制外货之运动

晚近利用全国抵制外货以为抵抗外国之政治武器一事（与中国商人用为职业上互相对抗之工具不同），其时期自一九〇五年始。当年因中美商约经延长及修订后，内有修款一项，规定对华人赴美之限制，较前为严，故有抵制美货事件发生。① 自是以降，以迄于今，显著之经济绝交，其范围之广遍于全国者（局部之排外运动除外），计有十次之多。十次之中，对日计有九次，而对英者仅一次而已。

此种经济绝交运动之原因

如将此种经济绝交运动，详加研究，则知每一运动之发生，与某项确定事实，事件，或事变有关。此类事件，概属政治性质，且常为中国所认为与其实质之利益有碍，或与其民族威望有损。是以一九三一之经济绝交，系直接因同年六月间万宝山事件及七月间韩人之屠杀，方始发生，而同年九月之沈阳事件一九三二年一月之上海事件，复使之变本加厉。每次经济绝交均有其本身可稽之近因，但苟非第一章所述民众心理为之背景，则该项原因之本身，无一足以引起如此大规模之经济报复。查构成此种心理之原因，厥为：不公平之感想

---

① 原编辑者注：兹将历次经济绝交之日期及其近因分别如左：

一九〇八年　二辰丸事件

一九〇九年　安奉铁路问题

一九一五年　"二十一条件"事件

一九一九年　山东问题

一九二三年　交还旅顺大连问题

一九二五年　五卅惨案

一九二七年　出兵山东事件

一九二八年　济南惨案

一九三一年　满洲事件（万宝山及沈阳事件）

（无论对与不对），中国文化优于外人之传统信仰，及西洋式之热烈民族主义。论其性质，大都以防御为目的，但亦间有攻击之趋势。

一九二五年前之经济绝交运动

为国民党先驱之兴中会，曾对于一八九三年即告成立，所有自一九○五年至一九二五年之经济绝交，虽均揭有民族主义之标题，毫无意义，然并无具体之证据，足以证明最初民族主义之团体及以后之国民党，曾经直接参与该项经济绝交运动之组织者，商会及学生联合会，因有百年来之秘密会社与职业团体之经验心理为之引导，一旦受孙中山先生新信条之感动，办理此事，极能胜任。商人则供给专门之知识，组织之方法，及进行之规则。学生则以新得之感想与坚决之精神，以赴国难，热烈从事运动，以促其实现。学生大都纯为民族情绪所驱使，至商会虽则同具此种情绪然以为参加运动，应以能操缩经济绝交之运动为目的。初期经济绝交之实施规则，原以防止购买被抵制国家之货物为目的。继而抵制之范围逐渐扩张，至拒绝将中国货物运往该国，或拒绝为该国驻华侨民服役。终至于最近之经济绝交，其明显之目的，遂进而至于欲与"敌国"完全断绝一切经济关系。

兹应表而出之者，即因此制定之规则，绝未充分予以实行，其种种理由，已详述于本报告书附录之专论。概括言之，经济绝交，在南方因有民族情绪率先依附，热烈赞同，故其触发之机，恒较北方为多。其在山东，此事绝鲜赞助。

一九二五年以来之经济绝交运动与国民党行动

自一九二五年以来，经济绝交运动之组织，确有变更。国民党自始即系赞助此种运动者，故每次经济绝交发生，国民党辄增加其控制之能力；时至今日，国民党遂为组织，促进，联络，及监督此项示威运动之真正原动力矣。

就本调查团所有之证据而言，国民党于进行此项运动时，非独未将往日于经济绝交运动负指导责任之团体，摒弃不用，抑且赞助其行动，整理统一其方法，并坦然以其强有力之党部组织所有精神与实质之力量，为该运动之后援。该党支部遍于全国，且有大规模之宣传及通讯机关，又受强烈民族情绪之激励，故能迅速组织成并激起迄当时几为空前未有之运动。自是以后，虽各抵货团体同时留有相当自由行动之权衡，而经济绝交之组织者，对于商人及一般群众之强制力，则较前为强。

使用之方法

经济绝交之规章，以地方情形之不同，经继续予以变更，乃抵货团体所用

之方法,则愈归一律,愈形严密,亦愈有效能,与其组织之益臻稳固,可称并行不背[悖]。同时国民党布发通告,禁止毁坏日人商店,或伤害日人身体,此非谓在华日人之生命,在经济绝交期间,从未遭受威吓;顾就大体而言,在最近经济绝交运动中,反抗日人之暴行,较往昔已属众减少而趋缓和耳。

兹就经济绝交所用之方法,研究其抵制之术,然后知其所采行者,要不外以一种可畏之宣传,一致遍布于全国,借精选之标语,以激发群众心理,使反抗"敌"国,予以造成群情愤激之空气;盖非此则经济绝交不能有功也。

抗日宣传

据调查团所见,现正进行之对日经济绝交,其种种有效方法均用以使人民对于不购日货之爱国义务有深切之观念。中国报纸篇幅中,充满此类宣传文字。城市房屋墙垣之上,遍贴标语,其语气,每趋于极端激烈。[①] 抗日口号,亦有印于钞币,书信,电报纸之上者,亦有以连索信,互相传授者。凡此种种,不一而足。上举各例,借示所用方法之性质而已。此项宣传方法,与一九一四年至一九一八年世界大战时,欧美某某等国所用者,大致相同,适足以证明两国间政治上之紧张状态所引致中国人对日恶感之程度。

抗日团体所通过之对日经济绝交规则

经济绝交之最后胜利,虽以政治环境为主要成分,但抗日团体之程序规则,如不能一致,此种运动断难有效。一九三一年七月十七日上海抗日会第一次会议所通过之四项原则,足以说明此项规则之主要目标。其原则如下:

(甲)凡已定日货,应即撤回定单。

(乙)凡已定日货,而尚未交货者,应即停止载运。

(丙)凡已到货栈,而尚未付款之日货,一概拒绝收受。

(丁)凡已买日货,应向抗日会登记,暂停出售。登记手续另行规定。

报告书附件内所载该会其后所通过之决议,益形详尽,且对于一切可能及或能之事件均有规定。

强制中国商人登记其所储存之日货,为实施经济绝交最有力之方法。抗日会检查员注意日货之运输,查验来路可疑之货物,以断定其是否日货,搜查

---

① 原编辑者注:凡调查团所过城市,大都已将此种标语事先除去。但据当地可靠之目睹者所言,则上述事实,已足证明;且彼等每持有此种标语之样张。标语样张,在调查团档案中亦有之。

有贮存未登记日货嫌疑之商店及栈房,并将所发见违反规则之案件,报告主事者注意。被认为确系违反规则之商人,径受经济绝交团体之罚金处分,并公布于众俾其受舆论之制裁。至其所有货物,则充分拍卖,将卖价充抗日会之经费。

经济绝交,并不限于商业。中国人并被警告勿乘日本船舶,勿与日本银行往来,不论商业家居,勿以任何名义供日人使用。不顾此等劝告者,将受各种指斥与威胁。

此项经济绝交且有另一特点,前此之经济绝交亦然,盖其愿望不独在于破坏日本之实业,同时且鼓励制造向自日本运来之某种物品,以图提借中国实业。其主要结果,为中国纺织工业之发展,上海地方之日华纱厂因之大受打击。

一九三一年至一九三二年间经济绝交运动之起伏

一九三一年之经济绝交,依上述途径而组织,继续进行。迨至同年十二月间,已见松懈。一九三二年一月,当上海市长与日本总领事,在上海进行谈判之时,中国甚至自动解散当地之抗日团体。

在上海战事期间,及日军撤退数月中,经济绝交,虽从未完全放弃,而形势趋于和缓。春末夏初时,日本商业似已能在中国各处,渐形恢复。嗣于七月终八月初,适热河边境,传闻有军事行动之说,经济绝交运动,突形复活。劝国人勿购日货之文字,重见于中国报纸之中。上海市商会,发表一函,提议恢复经济绝交。该市煤业公会决议限制日本煤之输入,减至最低限度,同时采用更激烈之手段,例如,向有销运日煤嫌疑商人之屋地上,抛掷炸弹,向店主投递恫吓信,告以如不停卖日货,即将毁灭其财产。转载于报事之信,其中有具名为"铁血团"或"血魂锄奸团"者。

作本报告书之情形,大约如此。上海日本总领事对于经济绝交之复兴,已向地方当局,提出正式抗议。

经济绝交运动物质上之影响

历次经济绝交运动,对于中日关系,在物质上,心理上,均有重要之影响,而尤以此次经济绝交为更甚。

兹就物质上之影响,即商业上之损失而言,中国方面,为欲表现经济绝交为一种精神之抵抗,并非经济上之侵害行为,所言自不免有将此项商业损失低估之趋势。至于日本方面,则对于某种商业统计,亦未免过于重视。关于此事

双方所持之理论，将于上述所附专论中加以研究。该专论内有日人商业上损失总计之详细纪载，此种损失，实属可观。

问题之另一面亦应提及者。则为中国人本身所受之损失，如借款已付因未向抗日会登记而被扣拍卖之货物；因违背经济绝交规则而缴付之罚款；中国海关所减损之税收；总而言之，贸易之衰落；此类损失，为数亦属不赀。

对于中日关系心理上之影响

经济绝交，对于中日关系心理上之影响，较诸物质上之影响，更难评断。但以其所引起日本大部份民意对于中国不幸之反响而言，其严重之程度，则不稍逊。调查团在日本时，东京及大阪商会，对于此点均极注重。

日本民情因感所蒙损害，欲抵御而无从，倍增愤慨。吾等在大阪接见之商人，对于经济绝交所用方法不当之处，如暴行恫吓等等，均有言过其实之倾向。但对于日本最近之对华政策，与中国持为对抗武器之经济绝交，两者间之密切关系，则加以忽视，或竟完全否认。此辈日本商人不认经济绝交为中国之自卫武器，反力持其为侵略行为，谓日本之军事行动系对此之报复。总之，近年来中日间关系之日趋恶劣，经济绝交为其原因之一，则要无疑义。

关于经济绝交争论之点

关于经济绝交之政策及方法，其争论之点有三。

（一）此种运动是否出于自动抑系组织而成

第一点问题所在，为此种运动是否如中国人所称，纯系出于自动，抑或如日本人所述，系国民党利用人民，有组织之运动，所用手段，有时且等于威胁。关于此点，双方各有其辞。就一方面言之，设无一坚强之民众意识为基础，欲一民族表现为支持一地区广阔时间久长之经济绝交，所必具有之牺牲与合作精神，显为不可能之事。就另一方面而言之，国民党利用中国人民旧时同业会馆及秘密团体传统之心理与方法，以指挥最近之经济绝交，尤其在现时之此项运动中，其指挥至于若何程度，已经显露无遗。他如所适用之规则，纪律，以及制裁"汉奸"之方法，在现时经济绝交中，固占主要部份，在在均可表现此项运动，无论其若何出于自动，实具有严密之组织。

一切民众运动，总须赖有一种组织，方能奏效。盖群众拥护一共同目的，其忠诚断难一致坚强，胥赖纪律以求目的与行动之一致。吾人之结论，认为中国之经济绝交，既出于民众复具有组织，虽系强烈之民族情绪所产生，为强烈之民族情绪所拥护，然操纵之指挥之者，大有能发能收之团体在。至于实施之

方法,诚有等于威吓之处。在组织方面,虽包括多数各别之团体,而重要支配之机关,厥为国民党。

(二) 经济绝交之方法是否合法

第二点之问题,为在经济绝交运动之行为中,所采用之方法,是否始终合法。调查团就所搜集证据而得之结论,除认为不法举动,常有施行,而当局与法院,本加以尽量之制止外,殊难另下其他断语。若谓此种方法,与旧时中国所运用者,大致相同,此说作一种说明则可,不能视为正当之理由。盖旧时同业公会,公议宣告经济绝交时,搜查可疑同业之房屋,将其解至同业法庭,惩处违背规则之行为,令缴罚金,并拍卖搜获之货物,此种举动,与当时习俗固属相符。且此系中国社会之内部事件,并不涉及外国人民。现时情势则异,中国业已制定新法典,其法律与中国相袭之经济绝交方法,不能两立。中国代表之说贴,为本国关于经济绝交之立场辩护,对于此点未有异说。但辩称"经济绝交……就大体而言,系依合法之方式而进行"。但调查团所得之证据,对于此说未能证实。关于此点,应将直接妨害外籍居民之非法行为,例如,对于日人者,与妨害中国人而显具侵害日人利益之目的者,划为两事。就前者而言,此项行为,非独在中国法律之下显属非法,亦且违反条约上,保护生命财产,维持贸易居住行动自由之义务。对于此点,中国人亦无异说,而排货会以及国民党,对于此种情事,虽制止有时无效,然确曾设法制止。且现在此种行为,已如上文所述,亦不若前此之屡见矣。①

关于妨害中国人之非法行为,中国代表,已于其关于经济绝交之说贴内,第十七页上,加以详论:"吾人首欲提请注意之点,为一国之国内法律问题外国无权提出。其实,吾人亦自觉遇有此项斥为非法行为之问题。但此系中国人民对中国人民之侵害行为,其制止系属中国当局之事。加害人与被害人既同属中国国籍,中国刑法对此若何适用,似非他人有权所得过问。总之,一国纯粹国内事件之治理,不论何国无干涉之权,此即所谓互相尊重主权与独立原则之真义"。

_____

① 原编辑者注:据最近日本方面之消息,自一九三一年七月至一九三一年十二月底,为日本人所有之货物,被上海抗日会会员截夺扣留之事件,共有三十五起之多,货价估计,约有二〇八万七千元之巨。截至一九三二年八月间,此类事件,止[只]有五起尚未解决。

照此说法，其理论自属颠扑不破。但其疏忽之点，在于日本人所持为称诉之论据者，并非中国人民被另一中国人民非法侵害之事，乃系因所采用之方法，害及日本人之利益，而此种方法，复违反中国法律。在此种情形之下，而不能执行其法律，则应视为中国政府，对于日本所受之损害，负有责任。

中国政府对于经济绝交所负之责任

至此，势须进而讨论关于经济绝交政策争论中最后之一点，即中国政府所负责任至何地步是也。中国官方态度，认为"购买选择之自由，为私人之权利，政府不能干涉，政府虽负有保护生命财产之责任，但未见有任何公认之规章原则，谓政府须禁止惩处每一公民基本权利之行使"。调查团所得之书面证据，该项证据，见于报告书附件专论第八号中，显示中国政府对于现时之经济绝交之参加，较上文引句中所表示者，更为直接。吾人并非暗示谓政府各部份援助经济绝交运动有何不当之处，惟所欲指明者，即官方之鼓励，不无含有政府之责任耳。于此，势须审察政府与国民党间之关系。关于后者之责任，自属毫无问题。国民党实为整个经济绝交运动后幕指挥联络之机关。国民党固可谓政府之创造者与主人翁，然而，欲决定该党责任之终点，与政府责任之起点何在，则系一宪法上之复杂问题，调查团自觉不应有所表示。

评语

中国政府宣称，经济绝交，为抵御强国武力侵略之合法武器，尤以在仲裁方法未经事先利用之事件中为然。此说引起一性质更广之问题。中国人民，在不违反国家法律之条件下，其个人拒绝购买日货，使用日本银行，乘坐日本船舶，为日本雇主作工，卖给日本人货物，与日本人发生社交关系，或以个人行动或团体行动宣传此项意见之权，无人可予否认。然而单独对于某一国家之贸易，实行有组织之抵制，是否合于睦谊，抑或与条约义务不相抵触，乃系一国际法之问题，而不在调查团调查范围之内，但为举世各国之利益计，调查团希望此项问题，应及早加以讨论，并以国际协约加以规定。

于本章中，已述明者，第一，日本为其人口问题，正在设法增加工业产量，并为此求获可靠之海外市场。其次，日本除生丝运销美国外，以中国为出口货物之主要市场，同时赖中国大宗原料与食品之供给。再者，中国吸收日本之向外投资几占其全部，虽在今日不安定不发达情形之下，仍不失为日本各种经济财政活动之沃土。最后，如将自一九〇八年迄于今日，日本在中国之利益，因屡次经济绝交，所受之损失，一加分析，则可知是类利益之易于摧残矣。

日本依赖中国市场固为日本人所完全承认。一方面,中国又为一急需发展各种经济生活之国,在一九三一年,虽有经济绝交之事,而日本仍占中国国外贸易总额之第一位,似可见日本与中国在经济方面之联络,实较他国尤密也。

以中日贸易之互相依赖,及双方之利益而言,经济接近实有必要。但两国间政治关系一日不圆满,以至于一方采取武力,一方则采取经济抵制力量以相扼持,则一日无接近之可能。

第八章　在满洲之经济利益[1]

如前章所已述及,中日两国经济上之需要,除非受政治原因之影响,当只有引至互相谅解与合作,而不至发生冲突。即就中日间在满洲经济利益互相关系之本身而研究之而不涉及近年来政治上之事变,亦可得同样之结论。盖两国在满洲之经济利益并非不可调和者;实则欲充分开发满洲现有之富源暨致力于将来经济之发展,两国经济利益之调和,甚属必要也。

关于日本,舆论所称满洲之富源,不论其为现实的与将来可能的均于日本经济命脉,极关重要一节,已于第三章中详细讨论。本章之目的在考虑此种称述,核与经济实况究竟符合至若何之程度。

投资

日本为在南满一带外人中之最大投资家,与苏俄之在北满相同。就东三省全部而论,日本所投之资本虽因无可靠之数目足资比较,不能断言其重要究至若何程度,然视苏俄所投者较为重要,盖无疑义。关于投资问题,本报告书之附件中当有详论,兹略举几项重要数目即足以表明日本苏俄及其他参与满洲经济开发各国间之相互比例矣。

依据日人方面之报告一九二八年日本在满洲之投资约计十五万万日金,此项数额如果确实,则现时当可增至十七万万日金。[2] 惟据俄人方面之调查,现时日本在满洲全部之投资包括关东租借地在内,约值十五万万日金,其中东

---

[1]　原编辑者注:关于本章各节参阅专论第二,三,六,七号。

[2]　原编辑者注:另一日本专家估计一九二九年日本在中国全境之投资总额包括满洲在内约值十五万万日金。

三省约占十三万万日金，日本资本之大部份系集中于辽宁一省。

至从各项投资之性质而论，大部分资本系用于运输事业（以铁路为主要），其次则为农业采矿及森林。依事实言，日本在南满投资大部分均集中于南满铁路；而苏俄之在北满投资，无论直接或间接，大半均与中东铁路有连带关系。

日本以外之外人投资数额更难估计，吾人虽难承有关系各方之援助，然所得之报告极少，至日方所供给之数字，大半均系一九一七年以前者，现时自不适用。关于苏俄，如上所述，亦不能得确实之估计。至于其他各国，据新近俄国方面在北满一带之调查估计，以英国为第二大投资家，计金洋一千一百十八万元，其次为日本，计金洋九百二十二万九千四百元，再次为美国，计金洋八百二十二万元，又波兰计金洋五百○二万五千元，法国计金洋一百七十六万元，德国计金洋一百二十三万五千元，此外零星投资计金洋一百十二万九千六百元，总计金洋三千七百七十八万四千四百元。但此项估计无法证实，且在南满方面欲求一类似之报告而不可得。

日本与满洲之经济关系

现应将满洲在日本经济生命中所占之地位加以分析。本报告书之附件中，对于本题有详细之研究，从此项研究中可知满洲在日本经济生命中之地位虽属重要，但同时受情势之限制，此亦不可忽视者也。

依据已往之经验满洲似非一适于日本大规模移民之区域，因近数十年来自山东直隶两省移往之农民与劳工已据有土地，现时日人之移住者均为商人官吏暨雇佣，彼等均为管理其所投资本，发展各种企业，及开发天然富源而来，此种情形恐多年后仍将如是。

农业

从满洲农产物之供给而论，日本现赖满洲之主要接济者为大豆及以大豆所制之物品，此项农产物在食品与饲料上之用途恐将日增。用为肥料在现时虽亦为主要用途之一，然嗣后恐将因日本化学工业之发达而减少其重要。但关于粮食接济问题，日本在现时并不严重。因日本既占有朝鲜及台湾，至少在最近期内可以助其解决食米问题也。如将来日本帝国对于此项物产需要孔亟时，满洲亦可成为一新来源。但在此种情形之下，恐将需巨大资本以从事于充分灌溉计划之建设。

重工业

如日本因欲利用满洲富源而兴办重工业，以期日后能脱离外国而自谋经

济独立,则所需之资本恐将更巨。现日本正在东三省设法鼓励为日本国防上不可缺少之各种原料之生产,满洲虽能以煤,油,及铁,供给日本,然该项供给在经济上之利益尚难确定,因煤之一物日本仅能利用其产额中之一较小部份。油亦只能从泥石中采获极有限之数量,至于铁之生产实属得不偿失。但日本之为此并非专在经济方面着想。实欲借满洲之富源以助其独立冶金制度之发展也。无论如何日本所需用之焦炭及不含矽酸①之矿砂必须大部份仰给于国外。东三省虽确能供给日本国防上不可缺少之几种物产,然欲达此目的,恐非有财政上之巨大牺牲不可。在本问题中有关之日本在满之军事策略,则已于本报告书中他处说明矣,再满洲似不能供给日本纺织业所必需之各种主要原料。

满洲为日本货物之市场

东三省为日本制造品之一长年市场。该市场之重要将与该处之繁荣同驱并进,惟曩昔大阪贸易赖于上海者较赖于大连者为多。满洲市场虽或较为稳固,然较之中国市场则狭小多矣。

自"经济区域"说由西欧传入日本后,日人自以为该项可能之辖区应包括日本帝国及满洲。此种论调时可于日本政治家大学教授及新闻记者之著作中见之。即日本之现任商工省大臣,在彼未就职之前,亦曾作一文,论及世界各国如美国苏俄欧洲及英国等之经济辖区,并声称日本亦应与满洲成立一类似区域。

现在尚无事实表示该项制度可以实行;日本近已有人对于此种幻想,发表言论以警告其国人。盖日本大部份商业,依赖美国,中国本部②,及英属印度者,远过于其依赖满洲也。

满洲对于人口过剩之日本,将来或可大有裨助之处,但不审明其可能性之有限,其为危险,与低估其效用之危险正复相同。

中国与满洲之经济关系

我人研究中国其他部份与东三省之经济关系,即见与前述日本在满洲情形显然不同,中国早期发展满洲之主要助力,即为遣送临时工人及永久移民徙入满洲,而满洲农业之重大发展,及出于彼辈之努力。最近尤其在近十年中,

---

① 编者按:即硅酸。
② 编者按:中国本部,指代中国关内地区。下同。

中国参预建筑铁路,开发矿产森林,扩充工业贸易银行,其进步甚为可观;惟该项进步,因缺乏确切材料,不能充分说明。以大概论之,满洲与中国其他部份间之主要结合,与其谓为属于经济的,毋宁谓属于种族的社会的。满洲人民,大都为近来移民所组成;业经在第二章提及。该项移民出于自动,大足以表示移民之举,确已满足实际之需要。移民虽在某种程度内,由于中日两方之鼓励;但实际为饥荒之一种结果也。

日本为抚顺煤矿,大连港务工程,及建筑铁路等事项,曾在数年中,招募华工;但募得之数常甚有限,招工事宜,于一九二七年遂告停止;盖斯时当地工人之供给,似尚足用故也。

满洲各省当局,亦曾屡次扶助安置中国移民;惟实际上东省当局之措施足以影响移民者,颇为有限。华北当局及慈善机关,在某时期内,亦曾努力鼓励人民移居满洲。

移民所受之主要帮助,即有南满铁路中国铁路及中东铁路之减价运送;此种给与新来者之鼓励,表示至少在一九三一年年底以前,南满铁路,满洲各省当局,及中国政府,对于此种迁徙加以赞许。虽彼等对于移殖运动之关系,未能一致;惟东省殖民,于彼等有利则同。

移殖于满洲之人民,居定之后仍保持其与中国本部原籍省分之关系。此种事实,一经考查移民汇往彼等诞生村落内家中之款项即可了然。该项汇款,或从银行及邮政局汇出,或由移民返乡时带回,其总数不能估计,大约每年寄往山东及河北两省者,计洋两千万元。一九二八年邮政局统计,表明辽宁吉林两省汇往山东之汇票,其款额与中国其他一切省分汇至山东之总数相等,此项汇款,构成满洲与中国本部间一种重要的经济连锁,殆无疑义。此项汇款,即为移民与其原籍省分家属间保持接触之标志。此种接触,亦甚容易,因长城内外情况,原无甚区别;土地出产物,大致相同,农业方法亦无差异。满洲与山东间农业状况最显著之区别,在于气候,人口多寡,及经济发展各种情形之不同。但此种异点,并不妨碍东三省农业有逐渐接近山东农业之趋势。辽宁为一久经开垦之区,其农业状况,较土地新近开放之黑龙江省,更与山东农业情形相接近。

在满洲与农人直接交易之组织,亦与中国本部情形相同。此种贸易,在东三省握于中国人手,只有中国人可自农家直接购买。在东三省此种本地交易中,挂账办法,具有重要功用;正与在中国本部者相同。更进一步言之,满洲与

中国本部商业组织之相似,不仅在当地乡村交易中可以看出,即在城市交易中,亦可见之。

事实上在满洲之中国社会的及经济的组织,等于一自关内移殖而来之社会;仍保持其家乡风俗语言及动作。其唯一的变更,仅为适合此土地较广居民较稀及外来势力开放较多之各种情形上之需要而已。

此种大队迁移,是否仅为一种偶然之事,抑将来仍得继续进行,不无疑问。当计算南满洲及南部东部诸流域如松花江辽河及牡丹江流域之面积时,即见单就农业方面观察,满洲尚能吸收多数移民,甚为明显,据中东铁路职员中最高专门家宣称:满洲人口,在四十年内,能达到七千五百万人之数。

但将来经济状况或将限制满洲人口之速迅增加,实则经济状况,能单独使将来耕种大豆事宜,入于不安稳状态。由他方面观之,新近输入满洲之种植,颇有发展希望,尤以种稻为最。日人中有希望发展种棉事业者,但种棉似受一定的限制。故经济上及技术上种种要素,或将在某种范围内限制移民入东三省。

近来政治上事变,并非为国中移民入满洲低落之唯一原因。一九三一年上半年经济恐慌,已使临时的移民减缩。世界不景气,加增不可避免而地方恐慌之影响,俟经济恐慌终了,秩序恢复时,满洲仍将为中国本部人民之出路。华人为最适宜于移殖满洲之人民,若用武断的政治手段,为不自然的移民限制,则不特妨害山东河北利益,而满洲利益亦咸受损害也。

满洲与中国其他部份主要的结合,属于种族与社会方面,同时经济联络,亦日益巩固;满洲与中国其他部份商业关系,逐渐发展。但据海关报告,日本为满洲最良顾客及最要供给者,中国本部反居第二位。

满洲输入中国其他部份之主要货物,为大豆及由大豆制成物品,煤,少量落花生,生丝,杂粮,极少量铁,玉蜀黍,羊毛,及木材等。中国本部输入满洲之主要货物,为棉织物,烟叶,丝织品,其他织物,茶叶,谷类,种子,生棉,纸,及面粉等。

故中国本部依赖于满洲者,为食品原料;其中最重要者,为大豆及由大豆制成物品,但除煤外,由满洲输入之矿物,木材,兽产,其供制造用之原料等,在过去时期内,并不重要。此外中国本部,利用满洲盈余之一部份,抵销其自身之亏短,中国所以能为此者,并非由于政治上之结合,如一般人所想象者;而实因满洲邮局海关为获利最丰之机关,又因中国移民汇交巨款于其山东及河北

之家属之故耳。

评论

满洲富源雄厚,倘尚未能完全估定。其发展有赖于人民,资本,技能,组织,及内部安定。人民几完全由中国供给;现有人民大多数生于华北数省,仍与其原籍家族,维持密切关系。至今日,资本,技能,及组织等,在南满者多由日本供给;在长春以北者多由俄国供给。其他各国在东三省各处,亦有利益,主要在大城市中,但较之日俄相差远矣。该各国代表,在近年政治紧张中,努力运用和解势力。倘掌握重要经济权力之日本,不为垄断该项活动区域之企图,彼等仍将继续其和解努力。现在最要问题,即为设立一能为人民所乐于接受之行政机关,须能供应最低限度之需要,需要维何? 即法律及秩序之维持是也。

华人占满洲人口之大部份,从事耕种土地;实际上在满洲各种企业中,供给其劳力。故任何外国,如不得华人好感及诚意的合作,不能在从事支配满洲之尝试中,开发其富源,或获取任何利益。在东三省停止为强邻野心之逐鹿场以前,中国亦将不能常免忧虑与危险。故中国须满足日本在满洲之经济利益,日本亦须承认满洲人民具有不可变易之中国特性。

门户开放之维持

如欲使有关系各国合作,发展满洲,则维持门户开放原则,似属必要,该项原则之维持,应与上述之中日谅解相辅而行,不仅在法律方面观察,应当如是;即就商业,工业,与银行业之实际情形而言,亦当如是。在满洲各国商人,除日本人外,抱持一种恐惧。即恐日本商行,利用现在政治上地位,采取自由竞争以外之方法,获取利益,若此种恐惧果属正确,则各国利益将受打击,而满洲人民首蒙其害。故在商业,投资,及金融各界中,以自由竞争方法表现真正之门户开放,于中日两国,俱属有益。①

---

① 原编辑者注:关于此节有须说明者,即大宗货物正在私运入满洲者甚多,尤以在朝鲜边境及经过大连者为最,此种私运,不特损害海关收入,抑且破坏商业组织;且引起一种揣测,谓实际管理海关行政之国家,竟实行歧视其他各国商业;该项揣测之当否,姑勿具论也。

第九章　解决之原则及条件

前章之复述

中日问题之本身,用公断方式,非无解决之可能,然因各该国政府,处理此问题,尤其满洲问题,使两国关系益臻恶化,遂致冲突,迟早不能避免,业于本报告书之前数章述明。中国乃一由政治上之纠纷,社会上之紊乱,与夫因过渡时代所不可避免之分裂趋势而进展之国家,亦经陈其梗概。日本所主张之权利与利益,如何因中国中央政府权力薄弱,致受重大之影响,及日本如何急欲使满洲与中国政府分离,亦经阐明。又对于中俄日三国政府之对满政策,为简略之考察,足以证明以前东三省地方政府对中国中央政府,曾屡次宣布独立,顾其人民大半为中国人,未尝有与中国脱离之意。最后:我等曾悉心详查一九三一年九月十八日及自是日以后所发生之真确事件,并曾发表我等对此之意见。

问题之复杂

现在我等可对于过去之感想作一结束,而集中注意点于将来。凡阅过前章者必明了现在冲突中之问题,并不如寻常所拟议者之简单。此项问题实属异常复杂,而惟深悉一切事实及其历史背景者,始足以表示一正确之意见。良以此案既非此国对于彼国不先利用国际联合会盟约所定和解之机会而遽行宣战之事件,亦非此一邻国以武力侵犯彼一邻国边界之简单案件,实因满洲具有许多特点,非世界其他各地所可确切比拟者也。

此项争议系发生于国际联合会两会员国间,涉及一领土其辽阔与法德两国相埒,双方均认有权利与利益于其间,而其权益中为国际公法所明白规定者,仅有数端耳。又该领土在法律上虽为中国不可分之一部,其地方政府实具有充分自治性质,足与日本直接谈判构成此次冲突根源之事件。

满洲情况非他地所可比拟

日本管有一条铁路,及由海口直达满洲中心之一段土地,约有一万兵力保护该地,日本并主张依照条约于必要时有增兵至一万五千之权。该国对于在满洲之日侨,行使法权,并遍设领馆警察于东三省。

解释之不同

上述各节为辩论此问题者所必须考虑之事实。日本军队未经宣战,将向

来毫无疑义属于中国领土之一大部分地面,强夺占领,使其与中国分离并宣布独立,事实具在。此事经过所采之步骤,日本谓为合于国际联合会盟约,非战公约,及华盛顿九国条约之义务,而实则各该约之意义正在防止此种行为。且此种行为开始于本案提出于国际联合会之初,而完成于嗣后之数月。乃日本政府以为此种行为与九月三十日及十二月十日其代表在日内瓦所提出之保证相符合。其为此项行动辩护之理由,谓一切军事行动为合法之自卫行为,该项自卫权利,在上述各项国际条约中既均已默认,而国联行政院各项决议亦未加以取消。至于替代中国在东三省之行政组织之新组织,则谓系当地人民之行动,盖当地人民因自愿独立,遂与中国脱离关系,另组政府。日方声称,此种真正之独立运动,自不为任何国际条约或国联行政院之任何决议所禁止。且是项事实之发生,已将九国条约之适用,予以重大之改易,并将国联正在调查之事件之性质,完全变更。

此种辩护论调实使该项冲突顿形复杂与严重。本调查团之任务,并不在就该案作辩论;但欲设法供给充分之材料,使国联能得一适合于争议国双方之荣誉,尊严,暨国家利益之解决办法。仅恃批评不足以达此目的,必须从事于调解之切实努力。我等曾力求过去满洲事件之真相,而坦白说明之;并承认此仅为一部分之工作,且非最要部分。我等在调查期间,曾迭告双方政府,愿以国联之力,助两国调解争端,且决定向国联建议,以适合于公道与和平之法,保持中日两国在满洲之永久利益。不能认为满意之解决办法:

(一)恢复原状

由上述各节观之,可以明了,如仅恢复原状,并非解决办法。因此次冲突原系发生于在去年九月前所存在之各种情形之下,故今日如将各该情形恢复原状,亦徒使纠纷重见,且有仅仅顾及全案之理论方面,而忽略其局势之真相之弊。

(二)维持"满洲国"

从前述两章观之,维持及承认满洲之现时组织,亦属同样不适当。我等认为此种解决办法与现存国际义务之与基本原则不合,并与远东和平所系之两国好感有碍,且违反中国之利益,不顾满洲人民之愿望,兼此种办法,最后是否利于日本永久之利益,至少亦属疑问。

满洲人民对于现时组织之情感如何,可无疑义;中国亦决不愿接受东三省之完全分离,作为一种最后之解决。至以远处边陲之外蒙古与满洲相比拟亦

欠切当,因外蒙古与中国并无经济上与社会上之密切关系;且人口稀少,大部分均非汉人。满洲之情形,与外蒙古大异。自各方面言之,现今在满洲耕种之数百万汉人早已使满洲成为中国领土由关内向关外之延长;且从种族文化及国民情绪各方面言之;东三省之为中国东三省,直与其大部分移民所自来之邻省河北山东无异。

且就已往之经验,可以证明从前支配满洲之当局,曾对于中国其他各部——至少华北——之事务有重大之影响,且占有毫不容疑之军事上与政治上之便利。无论在法律上事实上将该省等自中国他部割离,日后恐将造成一严重之"未收回领土"问题,使中国常存敌意,以致危及和平,且有引起继续抵制日货运动之可能。

本调查团曾接到日本政府关于该国在满洲重大利益之明晰,而有价值之声明书。关于日本对于满洲经济上之依赖,前章已经论及,本调查团不必再为之铺张;本调查团亦不主张日本因经济关系即可操纵东三省经济上乃至政治上之发展;但我等仍承认满洲在日本经济发展上之重要性。日本为谋满洲之经济发展,要求建设一能维持秩序之坚固政府;此项要求,我等亦不以为无理。但此种情况,惟有一合于当地民意而完全顺乎彼等之情感及志愿之行政机关,始能为安全的与切实的担保。抑尤有进者,惟有在一种外有信仰内有和平而与远东现有情形完全不同之空气中,为满洲经济迅速发展所必要之投资始可源源而来。

日人现虽备受激进人口过剩之压迫,然彼等尚未充分使用其现有之便利,以从事于移民,而日本政府迄今犹无大规模移民满洲之计划。但日本确欲利用再进一步之实业计划,以谋应付农业危机及人口问题,此种实业计划需要更大经济出路,而此种广大而比较可靠之市场,日本仅能在亚洲尤其中国获得之。日本不仅需要满洲市场,即全中国市场亦在需要之列,而中国之巩固与近代化自能使生活程度抬高,因而使贸易兴奋,并增加中国市场之购买力。

中日间此种经济上之接近,固于日本有重大之利益,即于中国亦有同等之利益,盖中国因与日本有经济上及技术上较为密切之合作而可获得建设国家基本工作上之助力。中国若能抑制其民族主义难堪之趋势,并俟友好关系恢复后切实担保有组织之抵货运动不再发生,则于此项经济接近大有裨助。在日本方面,若不求单独解决问题,使其脱离日本对华关系之整个问题,致令中国友谊及合作成为不可能,则此项经济接近亦当易于实现。

但日本在满洲之动作及政策,其取决于经济原因之处或较少于其自身安全之顾虑。日本政治家及军事当局常称满洲为"日本之生命线",职此故也。常人对于此种顾虑可表同情,且亦能谅解日本担负国防重任之当局所采取之行动及意旨。日本之欲谋阻止满洲被利用为攻击日本之根据地,以及如在某种情形之下满洲边境被外国军队冲过时,日本欲有采取适当军事行动之能力,吾人均可承认,但同时吾人认为置满洲于无期限之军事占领之下,势必负财政上之重担,是否确系抵制外患之最有效方法,仍不无疑问。又设遇外患侵袭之时,日本在满军队受时怀反侧之民众包围,其后又有包含敌意之中国,日本军队能否不受重大之困难,亦殊难言。为日本利益计,对于安全问题,似应考量其他可能的解决方法,使更能符合现时国际和平机关之基本原则,而与世界其他列强间所定之办法相同。日本甚或可因世界之同情与善意,不须代价而获得安全保障,较现时以巨大代价换得者为更加。

国际利益

中日两国以外,世界其余各国在中日争议中,亦有应予维持之重大利益。例如现行各种多方面条约,前已提及。又此问题之真正及最后之解决,必须适合世界和平组织所依赖之基本条约。华府会议时驱使各国代表之意旨,现仍有效。扶助中国建设,维持中国主权及领土与行政之完整为保持和平之必要条件;今日此项政策之与列强利益相吻和,亦正与一九二二年无异。各种分解中国之行为,必致立即引起国际间之竞争,此种国际竞争,如与相异的社会制度间之冲突同时发生,则将更形激烈。要之:维持和平之旨趣,举世相同。倘国联盟约与非战公约原则之实施,在世界任何部分失其信仰,则此项原则之价值及效能将无往而不受减损。

苏俄之利益

调查团对于苏俄在满洲之利益范围未能获得直接之报告,而对于苏俄政府关于满洲问题之意见亦未能确定。但虽无直接报告,而苏俄在满洲之地位,及其因领有中东【铁】路暨中国国境外北部及东北部之领土而获得之重要利益,均不容忽视。故解决满洲问题时倘忽略苏俄之重大利益,则此项解决必将引起将来和平之决裂,且不能持久,事极显然。

结论

倘中日两国政府均能承认彼此主要利益之相同性质,并愿以维持和平与夫树立睦谊为彼此利益之部分,则上述各节足以指示问题之解决途径。至恢

复一九三一年九月以前状态之不可能。前已述及之矣。由现时组织，毋须经过极端之变更或可产生一种满意之组织。我等将在次章提出若干种建议，以贯彻斯旨，兹先规定任何圆满解决所应依据之原则如下：

圆满解决之条件

（一）适合中日双方之利益。双方均为国联会员国，均有要求国联同样考虑之权利，某种解决，苟双方均不能获得利益，则他种解决必无补于和平之前途。

（二）考虑苏俄利益。倘仅促进相邻二国间之和平，而忽略第三国之利益，则匪特不公，抑且不智，更非求和平之道。

（三）遵守现行之多方面条约。任何解决必须遵守国联盟约，非战公约，及华盛顿九国条约之规定。

（四）承认日本在满洲之利益。日本在满洲之权利及利益乃不容漠视之事实，凡不承认此点或忽略日本与该地历史上关系之解决，不能认为满意。

（五）树立中日间之新条约关系。中日二国如欲防止其未来冲突，及回复其相互信赖与合作，必须另订新约，将中日两国之权利利益与责任，重加声叙。此项条约应为双方所同意之解决纠纷办法之一部份。

（六）切实规定解决将来纠纷之办法。为补充上开办法以图便利迅速解决随时发生之轻微纠纷起见，有特订办法之必要。

（七）满洲自治。满洲政府应加以变更，俾其在适合中国主权及行政完整之范围内，获得足以适应该三省地方情形与特性之高度自治权。新民政机关之组织与管理，务须满足良好政府之要件。

（八）内部之秩序与免于外来侵略之安全。满洲之内部秩序，应以有效的地方宪警维持之；至为实现其免于外来侵略之安全起见，则须将宪警以外之军队，扫数撤退，并须与关系各国，订立互不侵犯条约。

（九）奖励中日间之经济协调。为达到此目的，中日二国宜订新通商条约。此项条约之目的，须为两国间之商业关系，置于公平基础之上；并使其与两国间业经改善之政治关系相适合。

（十）以国际合作促进中国之建设。现时中国政局之不稳，既为中日友好之障碍，并为其他各国所关怀，因远东和平之维持，为国际间所关怀之事件；而上述条件，又非待中国具有强有力之中央政府时，不能满足，故其圆满解决之最终要件，厥惟依据孙中山博士之建议，以暂时的国际合作，促进中国之内部

建设。

条件满足后之结果

现在情势如能改变，至足以满足上述条件及包括上述意见之程度，则中日二国当可将其困难解决，而两国间之密切谅解及政治合作之新时代，或将由此开始。如二国间不能成立此项协调，则无论具有何种条件之解决办法，必将毫无效果可言。然则际此险象环生之时，上项新关系果真无实现之可能与？少年日本现正力主对中国采取强硬政策及在满洲采取澈底政策。凡作此项要求之人靡不对于九月十八日以前之延宕及刺激，表示厌倦。彼辈现甚急躁并亟欲求其目的之达到。但即在日本，为达到任何目的，亦有寻求适当方法之必要。经与主张积极政策最力之辈——尤其一般富于理想及个人信仰之造成"满洲国"之先锋队——接近之后，本调查团遂不得不承认，日人方面问题之核心，纯为日人对于新中国之政治发展及此种发展之未来趋势所表示之焦虑。此种焦虑，已使日人采取行动，其目的冀以支配上项发展并领导之使之趋向于日人经济利益，得以安全，及其帝国国防战略上之需要，得以满足之途径。

但日本舆论已微觉日本对满洲及对中国其他各部采取两个单独政策之不复合于实际。故日本纵以其满洲利益为目标，其对于中国民族精神之复兴，亦当表示承认与同情的欢迎；与之为友，引导其趋向，而畀之以扶助，使其不必另求他助。

中国有识之士亦已承认建设与国家之近代化为该国之重要问题，亦即该国之真正国家问题，而彼等不得不确认为完成此种业已开始且有如许成功希望之建设及近代化政策起见，必须与一切国家，尤其与其距离最近之邻国，培植友好之关系。在政治上，及经济上，中国均需要列强之合作，而日本政府之友善态度及在满洲方面之中日经济合作，尤为可贵。中国政府应将其新醒之民族主义之一切要求——纵属正当而且急切——置于此项国家内部有效的建设之最高需要之下。

第十章　考虑及对于行政院之建议

便利最后解决之建议

以解决现时纠纷之建议，向中日两国政府直接指出，非本调查团之职责。但如白里安君向行政院说明组织本调查团之决议时所言，"为便利两国间目前

纠纷原因之最后解决起见",本调查团特以我等研究之结果向国际联合会提出建议,期于联合会适当机关,因欲提交于争议两方而起草确定方案时有所裨助。此项建议,意在表明前章所设各条件,足以适用之一端,故其性质仅涉广泛原则,各项细目留待补充。如争议两方愿意接受基于此种原则之解决方法时,亦仅有修正之余地。

即使日本在日内瓦讨论本报告以前,即已正式承认"满洲国"——此为不容忽视之可能的事实——吾等工作亦不致因此而丧失其价值。吾等深信行政院如欲为满足中日两方在满洲之重大利益,而有所决定或向两国有所提议,则对于本报告书所载建议,终将认为不无裨助。

吾等悬此目标,故一方面以国联原则,及关于中国一切条约之精神及文字,以及和平之一般利益,存诸胸中,而在另一方面,并未忽视现存之事实,即对于正在演化中之东三省行政机关,亦曾加以注意。为世界和平之最高利益计,行政院之职责,应不问结局如何,毅然决定如何始能使本报告书中之建议推行并适用于现尚日在发展中之事件;以期利用现正在满洲酝酿之一切正当势力,无论为理想或人力,无论为思想或行动,借谋获得中日间持久之谅解。

请当事双方讨论解决办法

吾等首先建议国联行政院应请中国政府暨日本政府依照前章所开之纲领,讨论两国纠纷之解决。

顾问会议

此项邀请,如经接受,第二步即应及早召集一顾问会议,讨论并提出一种特殊制度之设立,以治理东三省之详密议案。

此项会议,可由中日两国政府之代表,暨代表当地人民之代表团两组组成之。该两代表团,一由中国政府规定之方法选出之,一由日本政府规定之方法选出之。如经当事双方同意,顾问会议可得中立观察人员之协助。

如该会议有任何特殊之点不克互相同意时,该会议可将此意见参差之点提出于国联行政院,行政院对此当设法觅得一同意之解决办法。

同时于顾问会议开会期中,所有中日间关于各该国权利利益所争论之事件,应另行讨论,倘经当事双方同意,亦可得中立观察人员之协助。

吾等未复提议此项讨论与谈判之结果,应包括于下列四种文件之中:

一、中国政府宣言,依照顾问会议所提办法,设立一种特殊制度治理东三省;

二、关于日本利益之中日条约；

三、中日和解公断不侵犯与互助条约；

四、中日商约。

在顾问会议集会之前，应由当事双方，以行政院之协助，对于该会议应行考量之行政制度之方式，先行协定其大纲。当事双方此际所应考议之事件如下：

顾问会议之集会地点，代表之性质，是否愿有中立观察人员；

维持中国领土行政完整之原则及准许东省有高度之自治；

以一种特殊宪警为维持内部治安唯一办法之政策；

以所拟各种条约解决所争各项事件之则；

对于所有曾经参加东省最近政治运动人员之准予特赦。

此种原则大纲，既经事前同意，关于其详细办法，当以最充分可能之审择权，留诸参加顾问会议或磋商条约之代表。至再行诉诸国联行政院之举，仅得于不能同意时行之。

此项程序之优点

此项程序各种优点之中，应称述者为此项程序既与中国主权不相违反，仍可采取实际有效之办法，以适应满洲现存之局势，同时复留以后修改之余地，此类修改将视中国内部情形之变迁而定。例如：在满洲最近已提议，或已实际施行之某种行政上与财政上之变更，如看政府之改组，"中央银行"之设立，以及外国顾问之雇用等等，皆本报告书所已注意及之者。此类特点，顾问会议或可因其利便而予以保留。又如依照吾等所提议之方法而选择满洲居民代表出席顾问会议，亦足以便利现政体之转入新政体。

此项为满洲而设之自治制度，拟仅施行于辽宁(奉天)，吉林，黑龙江三省。日本现时在热河(东内蒙古)所享有之权利，当于关系日本利益之条约中，加以规定。

兹将四项文件依次讨论如下：

一、宣言

顾问会议之最后议案，当送交中国政府，由中国政府以该项议案列入宣言之内，而以此宣言转送国际联合会及九国条约之签字各国。国联会员国，及九国条约之签字国对于此项宣言当表示知悉，而此项宣言将被认为对于中国政

府有国际协定之约束性质。

此项宣言嗣后倘须修改,其条件当依照前述之程序彼此同意后,于宣言本身中,预为规定。

此项宣言当对于中国中央政府在东三省之权限与该地方自治政府之权限,加以划分。

保留于中央政府之权限

兹提议保留于中央政府之权限应如下列;

(一)除特别规定外,有管理一般的条约及外交关系之权,但中央政府不得缔结与宣言条款相违反之国际决定。

(二)有管理海关,邮政,盐税之权,并或可有管理印花税及烟酒税行政之权。关于此类税款之纯收入,中央政府与东三省政府间如何公平分配,当由顾问会议规定之。

(三)有依照宣言所规定之程序,任命东三省政府行政长官之权,至少初步应当如此。至出缺时,当以同样方法补充,或以东三省某种选举制度行之,此则应由顾问会议合意议定,并列入宣言之内。

(四)有对于东三省行政长官颁发某种必要训令,以保证履行中国中央政府所缔结关于东三省自治政府管辖下各事项之国际协定之权。

(五)顾问会议所合意议定之其他权限。

地方政府之权限

一切其他权限均属于东三省自治政府。

地方民意之表现

应计划切实可行之制度,期使人民对于政府政策得表示其意见。或即袭用自昔相沿各机关如商会,公所,及其他各市民机关亦可。

少数民族

应订立某种规定,以保护白俄及其他少数民族之利益。

宪警

兹提议以外国教练官之协助,组织特别宪警,为东三省境内之唯一武装实力。该项宪兵之组织,或于一预定时期内完成之,或在宣言内,预定程序,规定其完成时期。该项特别队伍,既为东三省境内唯一武装实力,故一俟组织完成,其他一切武装实力,即应退出东三省境内。所谓其他一切武装实力,包括中国方面或日本方面之一切特别警队或铁路守备队。

外国顾问

自治政府行政长官得指派相当数额之外国顾问,其中日本人应占一重要之比例。至细目应依前述程序订定,并于宣言内声明之。小国人民有被选之权,与大国人民同。

行政长官得就国联行政院提名单中,指派国籍不同之外籍人员二名,监督(一)警察及(二)税收机关,该二员在"新政制"草创及试行期内,当掌有广泛之权限。顾问权限当在宣言中规定之。

行政长官当就国际清理银行董事会提出之名单中,指派一外国人为东三省"中央银行"之总顾问。

至于雇用外籍顾问及官员一节,实与中国国民党总理及现今国民政府之政策相符,东省方面实际状况,及外人在彼利益与势力之复杂。为谋和平及善良政治起见,不能不有特殊之办法,吾人希望中国舆论对此,不难予以认识。惟此间所谓外籍顾问及官员,及在新制度草创期内应有特别广泛权限之顾问,亦不能认为仅系代表一种国际合作之方式。盖此项人员之选出,必须在中国政府所能接受之状态内行之,且须与中国主权不能相抵触。经指派后,此项人员,应自视为雇用国政府之公仆,与在过去时期内关税及邮政或国联与中国合办之专门机关所雇用之外籍人员相同。

关于此节,内田伯爵于一九三二年八月二十五在日本会议演说中之一段,颇堪注意。

"我国政府自明治维新以后,雇用多数外籍人员为顾问或正式官吏;在一八七五年前后,其数目超过五百人之多。"

兹有应注意之点者,即在中日合作空气中指派较多日籍顾问,可使此项官员,贡献其特别适合于当地情形之训练与学识。在此过渡期内所应抱之目标,乃为造成一种完全中国人之吏治,终使雇用外人,不复需要。

二、关系日方利益之中日条约

中日间拟议之三种条约商订人,自应有完全审择之权,但于此处略示订约时所应议之事项,亦不为无益。

此项条约既须提及东省方面之日本利益,及热河方面之日本一部分利益,自必首要涉及日侨之某种经济利益及铁路问题。

条约目的

此项条约之目的应为：

（一）东省经济上之开发，日本得自由参加，但不得因此而取得经济上或政治上管理该地之权。

（二）日本在热河现在享有之权利，予以维持。

（三）居住及租地之权，推及于东省全境；同时对于领事裁判权之原则，酌予变更。

（四）关于铁路之使用，订一协定。

日人之居住权

在南满与北满间虽未曾订有固定界线，但日本人民之居住权向仅限于南满及热河。日本人民行使此项权利之态度，常使中国方面认为不能容受，因是而发生不断之龃龉与冲突。在纳税及司法方面，日本人民及朝鲜人民俱认为享有领事裁判权之待遇。关于鲜民方面，实另有特殊规定，不过此项规定未能厘订明确，致常为争执之焦点。就调查团所得证明，吾等相信，若不附有领事裁判权，中国或愿将现在有限制之居住权推及于东省全境。因附带领事裁判权之结果；认为可使在中国境内造成一日本民族之国家也。

居住权与领事裁判权关系密切，至为明显。而在东三省司法行政及财务行政未达到较前此更高之程度以前，日本不欲放弃领事裁判权地位，其事亦同样明显。

于是有调和方法二种：其一，现有之居住权及附带之领事裁判权地位，应予以维持，其居住权范围应加以扩大，俾在北满及热河之日本人民及朝鲜人民，均得享受，但无领事裁判权。其二，在东三省及热河之任何地方，日本人民应予以居住权及领事裁判权，而朝鲜人民则仅有居住权而无领事裁判权。是两项建议各有优点，亦各有可以严重反对之处。倘能将东北各省之行政效率增高，使领事裁判权不复需要，此则本问题最满意之解决方法也。吾等以是建议该地方之最高法院应延用外国顾问，至少二人，其一须为日本国籍。其他法院延用顾问，亦殊为有利。法院审理涉及外国人之案件时，顾问对于各条之意见，不妨公布。吾等又以为在改组期间，财务行政方面参以外人之监督，亦颇相宜。关于此节，吾人于讨论中国宣言时业已有所提议矣。

更进一步之保障，可依和解条约，设立公断法院，以处理中国政府或日本政府，以政府名义或其人民名义所提出之任何声诉。

此项复杂而困难之问题,其决定必须归诸议订条约之当事双方,自行酌夺。但现时所取之保护外国人制度,苟施于多如朝鲜人之少数民族,在朝鲜人数目继续增加,及其与中国人民密接杂处情形之下,其将发生刺激之机会,因而引致地方意外及外国干涉,殆为必然之事。为和平利益计,此项冲突之源,应予消弭。

日本人民之居住权利,如有任何推广,应在同权条件之下,适用于其他一切享有最惠国条款利益之国家之人民,只须此类享有领事裁判权人民之国家,与中国订立同样条约。

铁路

关于铁路问题,在过去期中,中国与日本之铁路建造者及当局者,缺乏合作,不知成就一广大而互利之铁路计划,此在第三章中已论之矣。将来苟欲免除冲突,则在现所拟议之条约中,必须加以规定,使已往之竞争制度,归于消灭,而代以关于各路运费及价目之共同谅解。此项问题在本报告书之附件特别研究第一号内,另有讨论。在本调查团之意以为有两种可能之解决。此两种解决可择一而行,或可视为达到最后解决之步骤。

第一种方法,范围较为限制,为中日铁路行政之一种业务协定,足以便利彼此合作者。中日两国可协议在合作原则之下管理其各在满洲所有之铁路,并设一中日铁路联合委员会,至少有外国顾问一人参加。铁路联合委员会行使之职务则类若他国现行之理事会然。至于更澈底之救济方案,莫若将中日两国之铁路利益合并。如双方能同意于此种合并办法,实为中日两国经济合作之真实标记,而中日两国经济合作,乃本报告书所靳求之目的之一也。此种合并办法一方面既可保障中国之利权,一方面又可使满洲一切铁路得利用南满铁路专门经验之利益,而将近数月来应用于满洲铁路之制度,引伸推用,当亦无甚困难。且将来可借此关一范围较广之国际协定之新途径,将中东铁路亦包含在内。此种合并方法之详细说明虽已载在附件之内,惟只能视为一种举例,其详细计划惟有当事双方直接谈判,始可产生耳。铁路问题如此解决,则南满铁路将成为纯粹的营业性质,特别宪警队一旦完全组成,铁路得有保障,则护路队可以撤退,借可节省一宗极大开支。此项办法如果实行,特别地产章程及特别市政制度,应即在铁路区域范围内,预先制定成立,俾南满铁路与日本人民之既得利益有保障。

如能依照以上大纲,议订条约,则日本在东三省与热河之权利,可有法律

根据,其有益于日本至少当与现有之条约及协定相同,而在中国方面,则当较易接受。如一九一五年等条约与协定所给予日本之一切确定让与,苟未为此项新条约所废弃或变更者,中国方面对之当不致再有承认之困难。至于日本所要求之一切较为次要之权利,其效力问题如有争执,应提出协商。如不能同意时,应照和解条约中所载之办法补救之。

三、中日和解公断不侵犯及互助条约

本条约之内容,因已有许多先例及现行成案可稽,自可不必详细叙述。

此项条约应设一和解委员会,其职务当为协助中日两方解决两政府间随时发生之任何困难。并设一公断庭,以具有法律经验及明了远东情形者组织之。凡中日两国间关于宣言或新条约解释上之争执,以及和解条约中所列举之其他争执,均应归诸公断庭办理。

最后依照约文内不侵犯及互助各规定,缔约双方应同意满洲应逐渐成为一无军备区域。以此为目的,应即规定俟宪警组织完竣后,缔约国之一方或第三者,如对无军备区域有任何侵犯,即成为一种侵略行为,其他一方,——或遇第三者攻击时,则缔约双方——有采取其所认为适当之任何办法,以防卫无军备区域之权,但并不妨碍国联行政院依照盟约而为处理之权。

倘苏联共和国政府愿意参加此种条约之不侵犯及互助部分,则此项相当之条款,可另行列入一种三方协定。

四、中日商约

商约自应以造成可以鼓励中日两国尽量交易货物,而同时并可保护他国现有条约权利之情形为目的。在此项条约内,并应由中国政府担任在其权力之内,采取一切办法以禁止并遏抑有组织之抵制日货运动,但不妨碍中国买主之个人权利。

评论

以上关于宣言,及各项条约之目的,吾等所为之建议与理由,系备提供国联行政院之考虑。无论将来协定之细目为何,最要之点,在尽早开始谈判,并应以互信之精神行之。

吾等工作现已告竣。

满洲素称天府之国,沃野万里,一年以来,叠经扰攘,当地人民,创巨痛深,

恐为前此所无。

中日关系已成变相战争，瞻念前途，可胜忧虑。

其造成此种景况之情形，吾等于本报告书中已言之矣。

国联当前问题之严重，及其解决之困难，尽人皆知。本调查团正在结束报告之际，报章适载中日两国外交部长之宣言。披阅之余，各有要旨一点，兹特为揭出：

八月二十八日罗文干先生在南京宣称：

"中国深信解决现在时局之合理办法，必以不背国联盟约，非战公约及九国条约之文字与精神，与夫中国之主权，同时又确能巩固远东永久之和平者，为必要条件。"

八月三十日据报内田伯爵在东京宣称：

"政府认中日关系问题较满蒙问题，更为重要。"

吾等以为结束报告，莫妙于重述此两项宣言所隐伏之意思。此种意思与本调查团所搜集之证据，及本调查团对本案之研究暨其判断，其确切相合，竟若符节，故敢信此种宣言所表示之政策，倘迅为有效之应用，当能使满洲问题达到圆满之解决，不特有裨于远东两大国之利益，即世界人类，亦胥受其赐焉。

国联调查团报告书（日文版）

リットン報告書[①]

緒　論

一九三一年九月二十一日の支那の正式出訴

　　一九三一年九月二十一日在「ジュネーヴ」支那政府代表は聯盟事務総長に書翰を送り九月十八日より十九日に至る夜中奉天に於て発生せる事件より起れる日支間の紛争に関し理事会の注意を喚起せんことを求め且規約第十一条に基き「国際の平和を危殆ならしむる事態の此の上の進展を阻止する為即時手段を執らんこと」を理事会に訴へたり。

九月三十日理事会は左の決議を可決せり

　　「理事会は

　　一、理事会議長が日支両国に致せる緊急通告に対する右両国の回答及概通告に従ひ為されたる措置を了承す。

　　二、日本が満州に於て何等領土的目的を有せざる旨の日本政府の声明の重要なるを認む。

　　三、日本政府は其臣民の生命の安全及其財産の保護が有効に確保せらるるに従ひ日本軍隊を鉄道附属地内に引かしむる為既に開始せられたる軍隊の撤退を出来得る限り速に続行すべく最短期間内に右の意向を実現せんことを希望する旨の日本代表の声明を了承す。

　　四、支那政府は日本軍隊撤退の続行並支那地方官憲及警察力恢復の成

　　①　編者按：《国联调查团报告书》（日文版）录自：日本外務省全訳『リットン報告書』、東治書院、昭和７年（1932年）10月６日印刷。

就に従ひ鉄道附属地外に於ける日本臣民の安全及其財産の保護の責任を負ふべき旨の支那代表の声明を了承す。

五、両国政府が両国間の平和及良好なる了解を撹乱する虞ある一切の行為を避けんことを欲すと信じ、両国政府は各自に事件を拡大し又は事態を悪化せざる為の必要なる一切に措置を執るべしとの保障を日支両国代表より与へられたる事実を了承す。

六、両当事国に対する其間の通常関係の恢復を促進し且之が為前記約定の履行を続行且速に終了する為両国が一切の手段を盡すべきことを求む。

七、両当事国に対し事態の進展に関する完全なる情報を屢々理事会に送らんことを求む。

八、緊急会合を余儀なくするが如き未知の事件発生せざる限り十月十四日（水曜日）同期日に於ける事態審査の為更に寿府に会合す。

九、理事会議長が其同僚特に両当事国代表の意見を求めたる後事態の進展に関し当事国又は他の理事会員より得たる情報に依り前記理事会招集の必要なきに至れりと決定する場合は右招集を取消すことを議長に許可す。」

右決議採択の討議中支那代表は「日本の軍隊及警官の迅速且完全なる撤退並に完全なる現状恢復を確保する為に理事会の計画すべき最良の方法は中立の委員会を満州に派遣することなり」との支那政府の見解を表明せり。

十月十三日乃至二十四日の理事会

理事会は紛争を考究する為更に十月十三日より二十四日迄会議を開催したるが日本代表の反対の結果該会議に於て提案せられたる決議に対し全会一致を得ること能はざりき。

十一月十六日乃至十二月十日の巴里に於ける理事会

理事会は再び十一月十六日「パリ」に会合し約四週間熱心に事態を研究せり。十一月二十一日日本代表は九月三十日の決議が其の精神に於て且条章に於て遵守せらるべきことを日本政府は念じ居るものなることを述べたることを述べたる後一の調査委員会を現地に送らんことを提案せり。右提案は次いで他の一切の理事会員の歓迎する所と為り、一九三一年十二月十日

左の決議を全会一致を以て採択せられたり。

十二月十日の決議

「理事会は

一、両当事国が厳粛に遵守する旨宣言し居れる一九三一年九月三十日理事会全会一致可決の決議を再び確認す依て理事会は右決議の定むる条件により日本軍の鉄道附属地内撤収が成るべく速に実行せられんが為日支両国政府に対し右決議実施を確保するに必要なる一切の手段を講ぜんことを要請す。

二、十月二十四日の理事会以来事態更に重大化したるに鑑み理事会は両当事国が此の上戦闘又は生命の喪失を惹起することあるべき一切の主動的行為を差控ふべきを約することを了承す。

三、両当事国に対し情勢の進展に付引続き理事会に通報せんことを求む。

四、其他の理事国に対し其関係地域に在る代表者より得たる情報を理事会に提供せんことを求む。

五、上記諸措置の実行とは関係なく

本件の特殊なる事情に顧み日支両国政府に依る両国間紛争問題の終局的且根本的解決に寄与せんことを希望し。

国際関係に影響を及ぼし日支両国間の平和又は平和の基礎たる良好なる了解を撹乱せむとする虞ある一切の事情に関し実地に就き調査を遂げ理事会に報告せんが為め五名より成る委員会を任命するに決す。

日支両国政府は委員会を助くる為め各一名の参与委員を指名するの権利を有し両国政府は委員会が其必要とすべき一切の情報を実地に就き入手せんがの為各般の便宜を委員会に供与す。

両当事国が何等かの交渉を開始する場合には右交渉は本委員会所定任務の範囲内に属せざるべく又何れかの当事国の軍事的施措に苟も干渉することは本委員会の権限に属せざるものと了解す。

本委員会の任命及審議は日本軍鉄道附属地外撤収に関し九月三十日の決議に於て日本政府の与へたる約束に何等影響を及ぼすものに非ず。

六、現在より一九三二年一月二十五日に開かるべき次回通常理事会期迄の間に於て本件は依然理事会に係属するものにして議長に於て本件経過

を注意し必要あらば新に会合を召集せんことを求む。」

議長の宣言

決議を採用するに当り議長「ブリアン」氏は左の宣言を為せり。

「茲に提出せられたる決議は異れる二方針に則りて措置すべきことを規定す即ち（一）平和に対する直接の脅威を終熄せしむること（二）二国間に存する紛争の原因の終局的解決を容易ならしむることなり。日支両国の関係を撹乱するが如き事情の調査は夫れ自体望ましきこととなるが、今回の会期中右調査が両当国間に対し受諾し得べきもののなることを発見したるは理事会の欣快とする所なり。依て理事会は十一月二十一日理事会に提出せられたる委員会設置案を歓迎せり。決議の末項は右委員会の任命及職能を規定す余は茲に決議に付項を逐ひて説明を加へんとす。

第一項—本項は九月三十日理事会が全会一致を以て採択せる決議を再ひ確認し、同決議中に記されたる条件の下に日本軍を成べく速に鉄道附属地内に撤退することを特に強調するものなり。理事会は此の決議を最も重要視し且両国政府が其の九月三十日に為したる約束の完全なる履行に努むべきことを確信す。

第二項—前回の理事会以来事態大に悪化し且当然の憂慮を抱かしむるに至りたる諸種の事件の発生したるは不幸なる事実なり。此の上戦闘を惹起することあるべき一切の主動的及事態を悪化せしむる虞ある他の一切行動を差控ふること最も緊要なり。

第四項—本項に於て当事国外の理事国は現地に在る自国代表者より接受する情報を引続き理事会に提供せんことを求めらる。

此の種情報は過去に於て頗る価値あるものなることを証したるを以て諸地点に斯の如き代表者を派遣し得る各国は現在の方法を継続し且之を改善する為出来得る限りのことを為すべきことに同意せり。

之が為両当事国にして希望するに於ては此等代表者を派遣すべき地点を両当事国が右各国に指示し得る様右各国は両当事国と接触を保つべし。

第五項—本項は調査委員会の設置を規定す。本委員会は純然たる諮問性質を有するものなるも其の所定任務は広汎なり。本委員会が調査の要ありと認むる問題は、苟も国際関係に影響を及ぼし、日支間の平和又は平和の基礎たる良好なる了解を撹乱せんとする虞ある事態に関するものなる限り

原則として除外せられざるべし。両国政府は何れも其の特に審査を希望する問題に付之が考慮を委員会に請求するの権利を有す。委員会は理事会に報告すべき問題を定むることに付充分なる考慮を有し且望ましき場合に於て中間報告を為すの権能を有す。

九月三十日の決議に遵ひ両当事国の為したる約束が委員会の到着の時迄に実行せられざる場合に於ては委員会は出来得る限り速に理事会に対し其の事態に付報告すべし。

「両当事国が何等かの交渉を開始する場合には右交渉は本委員会所定任務の範囲内に属せざるべく又何れかの当事国の軍事的施措に苟も干渉することは本委員会の権限に属せざる」旨特に規定せらる。此の後段の規定は何等委員会の調査権能を制限せず又委員会が其の報告に必要なる情報を得る為行動の充分なる自由を有すべきこと明白なり。

両当事国の留保及批判

日本代表は決議を受諾するに当り決議第二項に関する留保を為し「本項は満州各地に於て猖獗を極むる匪賊及不逞分子の活動に対し日本臣民の生命及財産の保護に直接備ふるに必要なるべき行動を日本軍が執ることを妨ぐるの趣旨に非ずとの了解の下に」日本政府に名に於て本項を受諾するものなる旨を述べたり。

支那代表は又決議を受諾せるも原則に関する其の或意見及留保が左の如く議事録に挿入せられんことをもとめたり。

「一、支那は規約の一切の規定、其の加入せる一切の現存条約並に国際法及国際慣例の承認せられたる原則に則き支那の有し又は有し得べき一切の権利、救済方法及法律的地位を完全に留保するを要し且之を留保す。

二、支那は理事会の決議及理事会議長の声明に依り明白ならしめられたる施措を以て必要にして且相関関係を有する左の四個の本質的にして相関関係を有する要素を包含する実際的措置と認む。

（イ）敵対行為の即時停止

（ロ）日本の満州占領の能ふ限り短期間内に於ける清算

（ハ）今後生じ得べき一切の事件に関する中立国人の観察及報告

（ニ）理事会の任命したる委員会に依る全満州の事態に関する現地の包括的調査。

　右施措は条章及精神に於て右の基本的要素に基くものなるか故に其の完全性は右要素の一たりとも予定の如く具体化せられかつ実際に現実化せられる場合には明白に破壊せらるべし。

　三、支那は決議中に現定せらるる委員会は其の現地に到着せるとき日本軍隊の撤退が完成せられざるときは右の撤退に関し調査し且勧告を載せたる報告を為すことを其の第一任務と為すべきものと了解し且希望す。

　四、支那は右協定は満州に於ける最近に於ける最近の事件より発生せる支那及支那人に対する損害賠償の問題をも直接に暗黙的にも害することなきものと想定し此の点に関し特別なる留保を為す。

　五、茲に提出せられたる決議を受諾するに当り支那は理事会が此の上戦闘を惹起することあるべき一切の主動的行為及事態を悪化せしむる恐れある他の一切の行動を避くる様日支両国に命令し以て此の上戦闘及流血の惨を阻止せらるることの付理事会の努力を謝す決議が終熄せしむることを真に目的としたる事態より生じたる無法律の状態が存在することの口実を以て右の命令を破るべからざることに之を明白に指摘せざるべからず現に満州に在る無法律の状態の多くは日本軍の侵入に依りて生じたる通常生活の中絶に因る所多きことを看過すべからず。通常の平和的生活を恢復する唯一の確実なる方法は日本軍の撤退を迅速ならしめ且支那官憲をして平和及秩序維持の責任を負はしむることに在り。支那は如何なる外国の軍隊に依りても其の地域の侵入及占領を許容することを得ず。支那官憲の警察職務を冒すことを右軍隊に許すことは一層為し得ざる所なり。

　六、支那は他の列国の代表者を通して為す中立的意見及報告の現在の方法を継続し且改善するの意向を満足を以て了承す。而して支那は斯かる代表者を派遣すること望ましと思考せらるる地方を時々必要に応じ指示すべし。

　七、日本軍の鉄道附属地内への撤収を規定する本決議を受諾するに当り支那は右鉄道附属地内に於ける軍隊維持に関し其の常に執り来れる態度を何等放棄するものに非ざること了解せらるべからず。

　八、支那は其の領土的又は行政的保全を害する如き政治的の紛議（例へば所謂独立運動を助くるが如き又は之が為に不逞分子を利用するが如き）を挑発せんとする日本側の一切の試を以て事態の此の上の悪化を避くべし

との約束の明白なる違反と看做すべし。」

調査委員会の任命

委員会委員は次で理事会議長に依り選定せられ両当事国の賛成を得たる上一九三二年一月十四日の理事会に於て左の如く最終的に承認せられたり。

エイチ、イー、アルドロヴァンディ伯爵(伊国人)

アンリ、クローデル中将(佛国人)

リットン伯爵(英国人)

フランク、ロッス、マッコイ少将(米国人)

ハー、エー、ハインリッヒ、シュネー博士(獨逸人)

委員会の構成

欧洲諸国の委員は米国委員の代表者と一月二十一日「ジュネーヴ」に於て二回の会合を催したるが右会合に於て「リットン」卿は満場一致を以て委員長に選挙せらるると共に委員会の事業の仮計画は是認せられたり。

日支両国政府は十二月十日の決議に基き委員会を補助する為夫々一人の参与員を指名する権限を有したるに付右参与員として「トルコ」駐剳特命全権大使吉田伊三郎及前総理大臣前外交部長顧維鈞を任命せり。

国際聯盟事務総長は聯盟事務局部長「ロバート、ハース」に委員会の事務総長を委嘱せり。

委員会は其の事業中「ジー、エィチ、ブレークスリー」教授(米国「クラーク」大学教授「ドクトル、オヴ、フィロソフィー」、「エル、エィチ、ディー」)、「デネリー」氏、(佛蘭西大学教授)、「ベン、ドルフマン」氏(「ビー、エー」及「エム、エー」、米国「カリフォルニア」大学「ウイリアム、ハリスン、ミルス」「フェロー」)、「エー、ディー、エー、デ、カット、アンジェリノ」博士、「ティー、エー、ハイアム」大佐(「カネーディアン、ナショナル」鉄道会社長補佐員)、威海衛駐在英国領事「ジー、エス、モッス」氏(「シー、ビー、イー」、「エイチ、ビー、エム」)、「シー、ウォルター、ヤング」博士(「エム、エー」、「ドクトル、オヴ、フィロソフー」在「ニュー、ヨーク」世界時事問題協会の極東代表者)の専門的進言に依り補助せらるる所ありたり。

(注)事務総長は委員会書記局員として左記諸氏を配置せり

「ベルト」氏(情報部員)、「フォン、コッツエ」氏(国際事務局に関する事務

担任の事務次長補助員）、「バスチュホーフ」氏（政治部員）、「タブリユー、アスター」氏（臨時事務局員にして委員長の秘書役）、「シャーレル」氏（情報部員）

「ビー、ジューヴレー」少佐（佛国軍医「クローデル」将軍の随員）「ビッドル、中尉（「マッコイ」将軍の随員にして又事務局の一般事務にも協力せり）

「ドベイール」氏（在横濱佛国副領事にして日本語通訳者）

青木氏及呉秀峯氏（情報部員にして委員会書記局と協力せり）

委員会の欧洲諸国委員は二月三日「ル、アーヴル」及「ブリマス」を出帆し二月九日「ニュー、ヨーク」に於て米国委員の参加を得たり。

聯盟規約第十条、第十一条及第十五条に基く支那の聯盟出訴

斯る間に於て極東の形勢の発展は支那政府をして一月二十九日聯盟規約第十条、第十一条及第十五条に基き聯盟に対し新なる出訴を為さしめたり。一九三二年二月十二日支那代表者は理事会に対し聯盟規約第十五条第九項に基き紛争を総会に附託することを要請せり。

然れとも委員会は理事会より何等の新なる指令をも受領せざりしに付十二月十日の理事会よりの命令を解釈し行けり右の中には左記のものを含む。

一、理事会に付議せられたる日支間の紛争の調査、但し紛争の原因其の発展の状態及調査当時の情況を含む。

二、両国間の根本的利益を調整すべき日支紛争の解決策に対する考慮。委員会の使命に関する此の概念は事業の計画を決定せり。

一九三二年二月二十九日委員会東京到着

紛争の本舞台たる満州に到着せざる以前に両国の利害関係を確むる為に日支両国政府及各方面の意見を代表する人士と接触を保ちたり。即ち委員会は二月二十九日東京に到着し同地に於て日本参与員の参加を受けたり。尚委員は日本国皇帝陛下より謁見の光栄を賜りたり東京には九日間の滞在を為したる処右期間中は日日閣員（及其の他）との会見を為したるが右の中には犬養総理大臣、芳澤外務大臣、陸軍大臣荒木中将、海軍大臣大角大将を含みたり。右の外有力銀行家、実業家及種々の団体の代表者等とも会見を遂げたり。吾人は右等人士より満州に於ける日本の権益及日満の歴史的関係に関する情報を受領せり。上海事件に関しても議する所ありたり。東京出発後吾人は京都に於て「満州国」なる国名の下に満州に建国ありたる

次第を知りたり。大阪に於ては実業界の代表者との会見の手筈を定めたり。

上海(三月十四日―二十六日)

委員会は三月十四日上海に到着し支那参与員の参加を得たり。同地滞在二週間を一般調査の外吾人が曩に東京滞在中芳澤外相と議したる最近の戦闘に関する事実及休戦の可能性に関しても成るべく知らんことを努むるに用ひたり。吾人は荒廃地域を訪ひ最近の戦闘動作に関する日本の陸海軍当局の陳述を聴取せり。吾人は又若干の支那政府閣員及広東をも含む実業、教育界其他の主脳者とも会見せり。

南京(三月二十六日―四月一日)

三月二十六日委員会は南京に赴きたるが其の一部途中杭州に立寄たり。翌週中委員会は国民政府主席に面謁するの栄を得たり。行政院長汪精衛氏、軍事委員長蒋介石将軍、外交部長羅文幹氏、財政部長宋子文氏、交通部長陳銘枢氏、教育部長朱兆華氏[1]其他の政府要員とも会見せり。

揚子江沿岸(四月一日―七日)

吾人は更に充分代表的与論及支那各地の現状を知らんか為途中九江に立寄りたる上四月一日漢口に赴きたり。委員会の代表者は湖北四川省の宜昌、萬県及重慶を視察せり。

北平(四月九日―十九日)

四月五日委員会は北平(北京の現称)に到着したるか同地に於ては張学良及九月十八日夜奉天兵営の指揮官たりし支那将軍より証拠の提出ありたり。吾人の北平滞在は支那参与員顧維鈞博士の入満困難の為延引せり。

入満に当りて委員会は二団に分れたり。即ち一行中の或者は山海関を経由して鉄道に依り奉天に赴きたるが顧博士を含む他の者は海路大連を経由し日本の鉄道附属地内に止まることと為れり。

顧博士に対する「満州国」の領域入国の反対は委員会が日本の鉄道附属地の北方に於ける終点たる長春到着の際終に撤回せられたり。

満州(四月二十日―六月四日)

吾人は満州内に六週間止まりたるが其の間奉天、長春、吉林、哈爾賓、大

---

① 编者按：原文如此，应是朱家骅氏。

連、旅順、鞍山撫順及錦州を視察したり。吾人は又齊々哈爾にも赴かんと欲
したるも哈爾賓滞在中附近に間断なき戦闘あり且当時日本の軍当局より東
支鉄道の西部線の旅行に関し委員会の安全を保障し得ざる旨を告げられた
るに鑑み随員の一部のみ航空機に依り齊々哈爾に赴きたり。

　彼等は同地より洮昂鉄道及四洮鉄道に依る旅行に依り奉天に於て委員
会の一行に合せり。

　満州滞在中吾人は予備報告を起草し四月二十九日之を「ジュネーヴ」に
送付せり（附属書参照）。

　吾人は関東軍司令官本荘中将、其他の陸軍将校及日本の領事官憲と数
次の会談を為したり長春に於ては「満州国」執政即目下は其の「ヘンリー」溥
儀なる名に依り知らるる前皇帝宣統帝を訪問せり。吾人は又日本の国籍を
有する官吏、顧問を含む「満州国」政府要員及各省長とも会見を重ねたり。
各地方住民代表をも接見したりが右は概ね日本人又は「満州国」当局に依り
引合はされたり。公の会見の外に吾人は支那人及外国人の多数と会見を遂
ぐるを得たり。

北平（六月五日―二十八日）

　委員会は六月五日北平に帰着したるが同地に於て蒐集したる膨大なる
資料の吟味開始せられたり。行政院長汪精衛氏外交部長羅文幹氏、及財政
部長宋子文氏とは更に二回の会見を遂げたり。

東京（七月四日―十五日）

　六月二十八日委員会は朝鮮経由東京に向へり。委員会の日本への出発
は海軍大将齋藤子爵の内閣に於ける外務大臣の任命を見ざりし為遅延せ
り。七月四日東京到着後総理大臣海軍大将齋藤子爵、外務大臣内田伯爵及
陸軍大臣荒木中将を含む新内閣の首脳と会見したるが之に依り吾人は満州
の情況の発展並に日支関係に関する政府の現在の見解及政策を知りたり。

北平（七月二十日）

　斯の如くにして日支両国政府と重ねて接触を遂げたるに付委員会は北
平に帰着し報告書の起草に着手せり。

参与員

　委員会の事業に対して終始多大の盡力を惜まざりし両参与員は数多の
貴重なる証拠書類を提出せり。一参与員より受領せる材料は之を他の参与

員に提示し以て之に対する批判を為すの機会を与へたり。是等の書類は発表せらるべし。

　附属書に表示せられたる如く会見せる人物及団体の数の多きことは以て吾人の審査したる証拠の如何に多数に上りたるかを知るに足るべし。更に吾人の旅行中吾人は多量の印刷物請願、要請及書翰を受領せり。単に満州に於てのみにても英文、佛文及日本文のものを除き約千五百五十通の漢文の書翰及四百通の露文書翰を受領せり。是等の書類の整理、翻訳及研究は多大の労力を必見としたるが一地より他地への間断なき移動にも拘らず之を遂行し七月北平に帰着後日本への最終訪問に出発前完成することを得たり。

十二月十日の決議に基く使命の概念は委員会の報告書の構想を定めたり

　委員会の事業の計画及旅程を決定したる委員会の使命に関する概念は又同様に報告書の構想を指導せり。

　吾人は先づ第一に紛争の根本的原因を成す満州に於ける両国の権益を記述して歴史的背景を明ならしめんと試みたり。

　次で現在の事変勃発直前に於ける個々の案件を審議し更に一九三一年九月十八日以来の事件を記述せり。終始問題の考察に当りては吾人は過去の行為に対する責任よりも寧ろ将来に於て之を繰返すことを避くる方法を発見せることの必要を強調せんとするものなり。最後に報告書は委員会の直面したる種々の問題に関し理事会に附議せんことを欲する若干の省察及考察並に紛争の永続的解決を計り且日支両国間の良好なる了解の再建を成就する為吾人の可能なりと認むる方針に基く若干の提言を以て結ばれ居れり。

第一章　支那に於ける近時の発展の概要

現在の紛争の完全なる了解に必要なる事前の状態に関する知識

　現在の紛争が初めて国際聯盟に持ち出されるに至れる1931年9月18日の事件は、日支間の関係緊張を加え来れるを示せる長期のより重要ならざる軋轢の連鎖の結果に他ならず、現在の紛争を完全に理解せんが為には

右２国間の最近の関係の主要なる要素に関する知識を必要とす。従って問題の研究を満州事態以外に及ぼし且現在の日支関係を決定するあらゆる要素を最も広範なる局面に付観察する必要ありたり。例えば支那共和国の国民的翹望、日本帝国及旧露西亜帝国の膨張政策、現時「ソ」連邦よりの共産主義宣布及右３国の経済的及軍略的必要等の如きは如何なる満州問題の研究にあたりても根本的に重要視せらるべき要素なり。

　　支那の此の部分は地理的に日露両国の領域の間に介在するを以て満州は政治的に紛争の中心となり右三国間の戦争は此の土地に於いて行われたり。実に満州は相衝突する要求及政策の遭遇点にして現在の紛争の具体的事実を十分に正解するに先ち先ず之等の相衝突する要求及政策を考察するを要す。故に吾人は先ず右根本的要素を順じ検討せんとす。

1. 近代支那の発展

支那は進展しつつある国家なり

　　支那に於ける主導的要素は徐々に行われつつある国民自体の近代化なり。現代支那は其国民生活のあらゆる方面に於いて過渡的証跡を示しつつ進展しつつある国家なり。政治的撹乱内乱、社会的及経済的不安は中央政府の衰微をもたらすとともに1911年の革命以来支那の特徴となりたり。之等の状態は支那の接触し来れるあらゆる国家に不利なる影響を及ぼし来れるものにして、匡救せらるるに至る迄は常に世界平和に対する脅威たるべく又世界経済不況の一原因たるべし。

一八四二年支那始めて外国人に開放せらる

　　現在の状態に至る迄の諸段階に就きては本報告に於いては詳細なる歴史を記載するを得ず。単に簡単なる概要を述ぶるに止むべし。支那は個々の西洋人と交際したる最初の数世紀中は、歴史よりの影響の関する限り限りに於いては実際上孤立せる国家たりき。此孤立状態は、第19世紀の初にあたり近代的交通機関の改良が距離を狭め極東を他の諸国より容易に到達し得るに至らしむるに及びて当然終了すべき運命にありたり。然れども此時にあたりても支那が此新なる接触に応ぜんとする用意無かりき。1842年の戦争の終末を告げたる南京条約の結果として支那の数港は外国人の貿易及居住の為に開かれたり。外国の影響は之を採り入るる何等の準備をも

為し居らざる政府を有する国に導入せられたり。外国の商人は政府が外国人の行政的、法律的、司法的、知識的及衛生的必要に対する設備を為し得ざる以前に其諸港に居住し始めたり。外国商人等は自己の慣れたる状態及標準をもたらしたり。諸条約港には外国都市建設せられ組織、行政及商業の外国方法採用せられたり。外国と支那との此の対照を緩和し得べかりし両方よりの努力も効果なく軋轢と誤解との長年月之より継続するに至れり。

度々の武力衝突に於いて外国武器の大なる効力を見たる支那は兵器廠を建て西洋式方法に依りて軍隊を教練し力を以て力に対抗せんとしたり。範囲に於いて限られたる支那の此方行への努力は結局失敗すべき運命にありたりき。支那が外国人に対抗し得んが為には更に根本的なる改革を必要としたつも支那は斯かる改革を望まざりき。寧ろ反対に支那は外国人に対し支那の文化と主権を護らんと保したりき。

日本との比較

日本も初めて西洋の影響に対し国を開きたる当時同様なる諸問題、即撹乱的なる諸思想との新なる接触、相異なる標準の衝突、其結果たる外国居留地の設定、一方的関税協定及治外法権要求等の諸問題に面せざるを得ざりき。然れども日本は内政上の改革に依り、自己の近代的要求の標準を西洋の標準迄高むる事に依り及外交交渉に依り之等の諸問題を解決せり。日本に依る西洋諸思想の同化は未だ完全ならざるやも知れず、又相異なる時代の新旧思想間の軋轢は時に之を見ることもあるやも知れず。然れども日本が自己の古き伝統の価値を減ずることなく西洋の科学と技術を同化し西洋の標準を採用したる速度と完全性は遍く賞嘆せられたり。

支那の問題は更に頗る困難なり

日本の同化改革の問題が如何に困難なりしにもせよ支那が直面せる諸問題は、支那の領土の広大なること、支那の人民に国家的統一の欠如せること及徴収せられたる収入の全体が中央国庫に到達せざる伝統的財政組織を有することに依り、更に頗る困難なり。支那が解決することを要する問題は日本が直面したる問題に比し更に頗る複雑にして二者を比較するは不正当なりとするも而も支那の必要とする解決は結局日本の採用せる如き方針に依らざるを得ず。支那の外国人を接受することに対する嫌悪及支那在住外国人に対する支那の態度は当然重大なる結果を生むべきものなり。此の

態度は其当事者の注意を外国人の勢力に対する反抗及其制限に集中せしめ、支那が外国居留地に於ける進歩せる諸状態の経験に依り利益することを妨げたり。其結果として支那をして新しき諸状態に対抗し得しむる為に必要なる建設的改革は殆ど全く着手せられざりき。

諸外国と衝突に依る支那の損害

各自の権利及国際関係に関する相容れざる二思想の不可避的衝突は戦争及論争となり其結果は次第に主権の割譲及一時的又は永久的の領土喪失となれり。支那は黒龍江の北岸に於ける大地域及沿海州、琉球諸島、香港、ビルマ、安南、東京、ラオス、交趾支那(印度支那の諸地方)、台湾、朝鮮其他数個の朝貢国を失い、又其他の領土を長期にわたり租貸したり、又外国法廷、行政、警察及軍事施設を支那の領土に於いて許容せり。自国の輸出入関税を自由に規定する権利は一時喪失せられたり。支那は外国人の生命及財産に対する危害に対する賠償を支払い又戦敗しては巨額の償金を支払いたるが之等は其後常に支那財政の重荷たるに至れり。支那領土の諸外国の勢力範囲への分割に依り国家としての存在さえも脅かさるるに至れり。

一九〇〇年団匪撹乱後改革運動起る

1894〜95 年の日支戦争に於ける敗北及 1900 年団匪反乱の惨憺たる結果は支那主導者中の心ある者の眼を開き根本的改革の必要を感ぜしめたり。改革運動は当初は満州朝廷の指揮を甘んじて受くる意ありしも其目的及指導者が西太后の手に欺き取られて後は同王朝より離反し光緒帝は其百日の改革の代償として1908 年崩御に至る迄事実上の牢獄生活を送りたりき。

満州王朝の崩壊

満州王朝は支那を250 年間統治したりき。同王朝は其後年に至りては太平乱(1850—65 年)、雲南に於ける回教徒の乱(1856—73 年)及支那「ターキスタン」に於ける反乱(1864—77 年)等度々の反乱により力を失いたりき。殊に太平乱は同帝国の基礎を揺るがし王朝は其威厳上遂に回復する事を得ざる大なる打撃を受けたり。而して1908 年西太后の崩御後、其内部の虚弱よりして遂に倒壊せり。

革命主義者は幾度か反乱の小計画を試みたる後南支那に於いて成功せり。斯くて短期間の間革命の指導者孫逸仙博士を臨時大統領とする共和政府南京に樹立せられたりき。1912 年 2 月 12 日当時の皇太后は幼児たる皇

帝の名に於いて退位の勅書に署名し次て袁世凱を大統領とする臨時立憲政治開始せられたり。皇帝の退位と共に各省、県及地方に於ける皇帝の代表者は皇帝の権威に基づきて彼等が有し来れる勢力及道徳的威厳を失えり。彼らは普通の人間となり其決定を強制し得る限りに於てのみ人民は彼らに服従することとなれり。斯くて各省に於いて文官都督か武官たる都督に依りて代らるるに至りたるは当然の結果なり。中央主権者の地位も亦同様に最も強大なる軍隊を有する軍閥首領又は省又は地方の有力軍閥の最も強力なる一団に依り支持せられたる軍閥首領によりてのみ保持せられ得るに至れり。

北方に於ける軍閥専制の傾向

南方よりも北方に於いて顕著なりし軍閥独裁の傾向は、軍隊が革命に対してしばしば与えたる援助に依りて人気好かりし事実に依りて容易となりたりき。首領軍人は革命を成功せしめたる功労に対し報酬を要求するに躊躇せざりき。彼等の大部分は北方の首領にしてある程度まで所謂北洋軍閥―日支戦争後袁世凱に依りて訓練せられたる模範軍隊に於いて低き身分より高き地位に上りたる人々―として一群を為したりき。之等の軍人は袁世凱にとりては、西洋に於ける組織の特徴たる団体に対する忠実の観念未だ発達せざる支那に於いては最も重要なる個人的忠誠の絆に依り結ばれ居るを以て比較的信頼し得るものなりき。之等の軍人は袁世凱に依り其支配下にある諸省の督軍に任命せられたり。之等の諸省に於いて権力は彼等の手中に止まり、従って省の収入は彼等が自由に取りて以て自己の個人的軍隊及部下の為に使用し得るに至れり。

南方に於ける状態

南方諸省に於いては一には諸外国との交際の結果として又一には人民の異なれる社会的慣習のために事態を異にしたり。南支那の人民は常に軍閥の独裁政治及外部よりの公務干渉を好まざりき。孫逸仙博士其他南方の指導者は立憲主義の理想に忠実なりき。然れども揚子江の南方の諸省に於いては軍隊の改造は未だ余り進歩し居らず又設備整える造兵廠を有せざりし為、彼らは其背後に有力なる軍隊を有せざりき。

一九一三年に於ける袁世凱に対する叛乱

遷延に遷延を重ねたる後、1913 年第一の議会が北京に於いて開催せら

れたる時には、袁世凱は既に其軍事的地位を確立し只缺くるところは各省軍隊の忠誠を確保するに足る財源のみなりき。世に善後借款と云わるる大外債は彼に必要なる財力を供給せり。然れども彼が右借款を議会の同意を得ずして締結したる行為に依り国民党に属する彼の政治的反対者は孫博士の指導の下に結合し、公然彼に背反するに至れり。軍事的の意味に於いては南方は北方よりも弱かりしが、北方の勝ち誇れる督軍連が南方の数省を征略し之を北方の将軍の下に置くに至りて更に其弱きを加えたり。

一九一四年より一九二八年に至る内乱及政治的不安

其後袁世凱に解散せられたる1913年の議会を回復せしめ又は偽国会を開かんとする数次の企画、王政を樹立せんとする2度の計画、大統領及内閣の幾度となき変更、軍隊首領間に於ける服属関係の不断の変化及一省又は数省の一時的独立の多くの宣言を見たりき。広東に於いては孫博士を首班とする国民党政府は1917年以来時に活動を止めたることあるも兎も角存続するに成功せり。此十数年間に於いて支那は各軍閥間の戦争に依り荒廃せられいたる所に存在する匪賊は零落せる農夫、飢饉に襲われたる諸地方の絶望せる住民及給料不渡の兵士を加えて癒其数を増し有力なる軍隊を成すに至れり。南方に於いて戦いつつありし立憲主義の人々さえも幾度となく彼ら自身の中に発生する軍事的確執の危険に曝されたり。

国民党の改組

1923年、自己の主義の勝利を得るの為には確定せる「プログラム」厳重なる党規及組織的宣伝の必要なる事を露国革命に依りて確信するに至れる孫逸仙博士は彼の「綱領」及「三民主義」（民族、民権、民政）の中に略述せる「プログラム」を以て国民党を改造せり。系統的組織は党の規律及中央執行委員会の仲介に依る行動の統一を確保せり。政治訓練処は宣伝者及地方党支部の組織者を教育すると共に他方黄埔に於ける軍官学校は露国士官の援助の下に党の理想を抱懐せる指導者を有する能率ある軍隊を党の為に作り上げたり。斯くして地方党支部は党と連絡せる農夫工人組合に組織せられたり。斯くして先ず民衆の心を獲ち得たる国民党は1925年孫博士の死後国民党軍の北伐に成功し1928年の末には多年存せざりし名目上の統一に成功し暫時は実際上の統一をもある程度迄実現せり。孫博士の「プログラム」の第一段即ち軍事的段階は斯くして成功するに至れり。

党独裁の下に於ける訓政の第二期開始せられ得ることとなれり。

右時期は民衆の自治政治の技術上の教育及国家の再建に捧げられるべき時期なりき。

中央政府の樹立

1927 年、南京に中央政府樹立せられたり。同政府は党に依りて統制せられたり。―実際に於いて政府は党の一重要機関に過ぎず。政府は五院（行政、立法、司法、監督、考試の諸院）より成れり。人民が一部は直接に又一部は其選挙せる代表者を通じて自ら政府を指揮すべき最後の段階即位立憲政治の段階への推移を容易ならしむる為に、政府は能う限り孫博士の「五院憲法」―「モンテスキュー」の三権分立に支那の古来の 2 制度たる監察院と考試院とを加えたるものの方針に依りて構成せられたり。

各省に於いても同様に省政府の組織に付きて委員制度採用せられたるが他方村落、都市及地方に於いては人民は地方自治政治実行上の教育を受くることとなれり。党は今や其政治的及経済的再建の計画を実行するの用意なりたるも、内部の不和私的軍隊を有する諸将軍の定期的反乱及共産主義の脅威の為に実行し得ざりき。実際に於いて中央政府は幾度となく其生存の為に戦うこと必要なりき。

中央政府の権威は外部より否認せられ内部の不和により弱められたり

暫時は統一は表面に於いては保持せられたり。然れども有力なる軍閥が相互に同盟を結びて南京に向かいて進軍せる場合には統一の外観さえも保持すること不可能なりき。此等軍閥は一度も目的を達せざりしも彼らは敗戦の後に於いても軽視せられ得ざる潜勢力たりき。加ふるに彼等は決して中央政府に対する戦争は叛逆行為なりとの態度を採らざりき。彼らの眼中に於いては此戦争は単に彼等の党派と単に国都に在住し諸外国に依り中央政府として承認せられたる他の党派との間の争覇の戦闘に過ぎざりき。此上下関係の突如は、党そのものの中の重大なる付和に依り中央政府が孫博士の疑うべからざる後継者たるの資格弱めらるる為癒々以て危険なり。此新たなる分裂の結果として南方の有力なる諸首領は離反し広東に退きたるが同地方の地方官憲及国民党の地方支部はしばしば中央政府と独立に行動し来れり。右概要の叙述より見るに支那の分裂的諸勢力は今尚強きものの如し。此の結合の欠如の原因は国民の大衆が支那と諸外国との間の関係

緊張せる時期を除きては国家を基礎とせず家族及地方を基礎として考える傾向にあり。現今に於いては自己独立主義的感情を超越せる指導者もありといえども、真の国家統一がもたらさるるが為には先ず更に多数の市民が国家的見地を有するに至らんことを必要なるは明瞭なり。

現時の支那と華府会議当時の支那との比較

避くること得ざる政治的、社会的、知識的及道徳的乱雑を示しつつある支那の過渡期の状況は支那の性急なる友人を失望せしむるものにして平和に対する危険となりたる不和怨恨を作りたるも、而も種々の困難、遷延及失敗にも拘らず事実に於いて相当の進歩が遂げられたるは事実なり。現在の紛争を論議する際に於いて常に聞く一議論は支那は「組織ある国家に非ず」又は「完全なる混沌及意想外の無政府の状態にあり」而して支那の今日の状態は当然支那より聯盟の一員たる資格を失わしめ支那より規約に基づく保護要求権を奪うものなりとの言説なり。

之に関しては華府（ワシントン）会議に際し参加各国が全く異なりたる態度を取りたることを記憶すること必要なるべし。而も当時に於いても支那は北京及広東に於いて二箇の全然異なる政府を有し又奥地の交通通信をしばしば妨害する多数の匪賊に依る撹乱を受けたる一方に於いて支那全体を其の渦中に投ずべき内乱の準備行われつつありたり。1922年1月13日、即ち華府会議の尚開催中にありたるとき中央政府に発送せられたる最後通牒に続き開始せられたる右内乱の結果として中央政府は同年5月転覆し右政府に代わり北京に樹立せられたる政府に対する満州の独立は同年7月張作霖に依り宣言せられたり。此の如く独立を主張する政府は実に3個ありたり。而も実際上独立せる省又は省の部分若干存在せり。現在に於いては中央政府の権威は尚若干省に於いて薄弱なりといえども中央の権力は少なくとも否認せらるることなく若し中央政府が現在のままに維持せらるるに於ては地方行政、軍隊及財政は漸次国家的性質を帯びるに至るべきものと期待することを得べし。叙上の諸理由は他の諸理由と共に聯盟総会をして去年9月支那を理事国として選挙せしむるに至りたるものなること疑いを容れず。

支那の復興に対する努力

現政府は其の歳出及歳入の均衡並びに健全なる財政的原則の遵守に努

め来れり。諸種の課税は統一せられ且簡単化せられたり。正当なる予算の
制度なき場合には財政部は毎年度の歳出及歳入の説明書を発表し来れり。
中央銀行は設立を見たり。国家財政委員会任命せられ其の委員には銀行及
商業界の有力者包含せらる。財政部は又徴税の方法未だ甚だ満足ならざる
地方の財政を監督するに努めつつあり。総て此等の新たなる措置は政府の
功に帰せらるべきものなるも而も政府は間断亡き内乱の為に其の内債を
1929年以来約10億ドル（銀）増加することを余儀なくせられたり。政府は
資金の欠乏に妨げられ其の野心に満ちたる復興の諸計画を実行することを
得ず又国内の殆ど総ての問題の解決に欠くべからざる交通通信の改良を完
成することを得ざりき。政府は数多の事項に付失敗したること疑いなきも
而も既遂の業績多々あり。

国民主義

近代支那の国民主義は支那が今や過渡しつつある政治推移の時期に於
ける一つの通常なる事象にして之と同様なる国民的感情及翹望は同様の状
態に置かれたる如何なる国に於いても見ることを得べし。然れども国民的
統一を意識するに至れる人民が外的制肘を離脱せんと欲する自然的欲望に
加うるに国民党の勢力は一切の外部的勢力に益反感を抱かんとする異常な
る色彩を支那の国民主義に注入し来り其の目的を拡大して尚「帝国主義的
圧迫」の下にある一切のアジア民族の解放を包含せしむるに至れり。今日
の支那の国民主義には其の再現を希う過去の偉大さに対する記憶も亦多分
に盛られあり。右主義は租借地、鉄道付属地に於いて外国の手に依り行使
せらるる行政上及他の純粋に商業的ならざる諸権利、租界に於ける行政権、
並びに外国人が支那の法律、法廷及課税に服従せざることを意味する治外
法権の返還を要求す。世論は国民的屈辱と看做さるる此等の権利の存続に
強く反対なり。

治外法権問題に対する諸外国の態度

諸外国は概して此等の要望に対し同情ある態度を取り来れり。1921—
22年の華府会議に於いては右要望の妥当なること原則として容認せられ
たるも只之を満足せしむべき最善の時期及方法に付ては意見の相違存し
たり。

此等の権利を直ちに放棄するに於ては財政上其の他の内面的困難に基

づき支那が今直に達成することを得ざるが如き程度の行政、警察及司法を樹立する責任を支那に負担せしむるに至るべしとすること当時の感想なりき。当時単一に取扱はれたる治外法権の問題は若し之を尚早に撤廃するに於いては諸外国との間に他の別個なる諸問題を誘発したるなるべし。又若し外国人が支那の多数の地方に於いて支那国民の蒙りつつありたると同様の不公平なる待遇及苛酷なる課税を受くることと為るに於ては国際関係は改善せられず、却って悪化すべしとすること亦当時の感想なりき。此等の留保に拘らず特に華府会議に於いて又同会議の結果として達成せられたるもの多々ありたり。即ち支那は五箇所の租借地中の二、多くの租界東支鉄道付属地の行政権、関税自主権及郵政権を回収し均等の基礎に立つ多くの条約も亦商議せられたり。

支那は華府会議を機とし其の困難を解決する為の国際的協調の道程に上りたるを以て若し右道程に従い進みたるに於ては爾後の10年間に於いて更に顕著なる進歩を遂ぐることを得たるなるべし。只支那は其の毒々しき排外宣伝の遂行に依り妨害せられたり。右宣伝は特に2方面に於いて実行せられ其の結果現在の紛争を惹起せる雰囲気の醸成を誘導せり。即ち第七章に記述せる経済的「ボイコット」の利用及諸学校に対する排外宣伝の注入之なり。

諸学校に於ける国民主義

1931年6月1日発布せられたる支那の臨時約法には「三民主義は中華民国に於ける教育の基本的原則たるべし」との規定あり（「人民の教育」の章、第47条）。孫逸仙の思想は恰も従来古典の有したる権威を持つが如きものとして今や諸学校に於いて教授せられ孫先生の遺訓は革命以前に於いて孔子の教訓が受けたると同様の尊敬を受けつつあり。然れども不幸にして青少年の教育にあたり注意は国民主義の建設的方面に対するよりも寧ろ其の否定的方面に注がれたり。諸学校の教科書を熟読する者は其の着者が愛国心を燃やすに憎悪の焔を以てし男性的精神の養成を虐待を受け居れりとの意識の上に置くことに努めたりとの印象を得。此の結果として学校に於いて植付けられ且社会生活のあらゆる方面を通して実行せられたる毒々しき排外宣伝は学生を駆って政治運動に従事せしむることと為り時には国務大臣其の他の官憲の身体、居宅又は官庁の襲撃又政府の転覆を図るが如

き事態に立至らしめたり。斯くの如き態度は有効なる内部的改革又は国民的素質の改善を伴はざりし為諸外国を驚愕せしめ現在諸外国の唯一の保障たる諸権利の放棄を益々躊躇せしむるに至れり。

法律及秩序の諸問題。適当なる交通通信の必要

法律及秩序の維持の問題に関連し現在支那に於いて交通通信の手段の見るべきものなきは重大なる障害なり。国家の軍隊を迅速に輸送すべき交通及通信の便が充分に備わるに非ざれば法律及秩序の維持は仮令全部に非ずとするも其の大部分は地方官庁の手に委せられざるべからず。而して地方官憲は中央政府の遠隔なる為地方的問題の処理にあたり自らの裁量に依ることを許されざるべからず。斯くの如き状態にありては独立せる考慮及行動は容易に法律の規矩を逸脱し其の結果地方は漸次私有の領地なるが如き貌を呈するに至る。

地方軍隊

地方の軍隊は其の指揮官に与するも国民に与せず。中央政府の命を以て一軍の指揮官を他の軍に転任せしむることは多くの場合に於いて不可能なり。中央政府が全国に互り其の威令を敏速且永久に行う為の物理的手段を有せざる限り内乱の危険は存続せざるを得ず。

匪賊

支那の全歴史を通じ存在し且今日も支那のあらゆる地方に存在する匪賊の問題に対しても右と同様の考察を加えることを得。匪賊は支那に於いてかつて絶えたることなく政権は未だかつて之を掃滅することを得ざりき。適当なる交通及通信の便を欠きたることは政権が四囲の状況に伴い増減する此の害悪を芟除することを得ざりし理由の一なり。之に加はる他の理由は特に悪政の結果として支那に頻発せる地方的騒擾及叛乱に之を求むることを得べし。仮令斯くの如き叛乱が無事鎮圧せられたる後に於いても叛民の投合したる匪賊団は支那の諸地方に於いて活動を継続せり。右は太平乱(1850—65 年)の鎮圧後に於いて特に顕著なりき。近時に於いては給料不渡にして他に生活の途を樹つることを得ず且内乱に従事して掠奪に慣れたる兵卒も亦匪賊の源と為りたり。

支那の各地に於いて匪賊を増加せしむるに至れる他の原因は洪水及旱魃なり。此等は寧ろ常規的に発生し常に飢饉及匪賊を随伴せり。問題は急

速に増加する人口の圧迫に依り悪化せられたり。人口周密なる地域に於いては通常の経済的困難は更に増加し僅かに生命を支ふるのみにして不時の災厄に備ふるの余裕なき人民の間にありては其の生活状態の極めて些少なる悪化も多数の者を生活不能ならしむに至れり。従って匪賊は当時の一般的経済状態の影響を蒙ること大なりしなり。一賊は富裕なる時代又は地方に於いては減少せるも上記何れかの理由に依り生存競争深刻と為り又は政治的状態が撹乱せられたる場合に於いては必ず増加したり。

匪賊が一旦ある地域に於いて其の勢力を確立するに至れる時は内地に於ける交通及通信の便欠如したるに依り之を実力を以て鎮圧すること困難と為れり。接近困難にして数哩を行くにも幾日かを要するが如き地方に於いて武装せる多数の賊団は自由に行動し出没を恣にし、其の居所及行動を知ることを得ざらしめたり。

匪賊の討伐を永く放置し、しばしばありしが如く兵士も之と内応するときは水陸の路に依る交通は妨害せらるるに至る。此の如き事態の発生は只適当なる警察力に依りれのみ之を阻止することを得。奥地に於ては必然的に出没戦を惹起するが故に匪賊の討伐益困難なり。

共産主義①は中央政府に対する挑戦なること

地方軍閥の私兵及全国に瀰漫する匪賊の集団は支那の内部的平和を撹乱するものなりと雖も此等は其れ自体として今や中央政権の権力に対する脅威たらざるに至れり。然れども此処に他の原因よりする此の種の脅威あり、即ち共産主義之なり。

一九二一年支那の共産主義の渕源

支那の共産主義運動は其の発生の初期に於いては知識及労働の2階級に限られ、1919年乃至1924年の期間に相当の勢力を得るに至れり。当時支那の農村地方は殆ど此の運動の影響を蒙らざりき。1919年7月25日の「ソビエト」政府の宣言は旧帝政政府が支那より「奪取」せる一切の特権を喜んで放棄すべきことを宣言せるものとして支那全国、殊に知識階級の間に好感を以て迎えられたり。1921年5月「中国共産党」正式に組織せられ宣

① 编者按：《国联调查团报告书》（日文版）中对共产主义、中国共产党及其革命事业存在错误描述。请读者鉴别。下同。

伝は特に上海の労働階級の間に行われ、同地に赤色「シンジケート」組織せられたり。1922 年 6 月の第 2 回大会に於いて当時党員三百を超えざりし共産党は国民党との合作を決議せり。孫逸仙は共産主義には反対なりしも支那共産党員を個人として入党せしむることには反対せず。1922 年の秋「ソビエト」政府は「ヨッフェ」を首班とする一団を支那に派遣し孫「ヨ」両者の間に行われたる重要会談の結果、1923 年 1 月 26 日の共同宣言と為り、右宣言に依り「ソビエト」政府は支那の統一及独立の為に其の同情と援助とを与ふべき旨の保障を与えたり。一方、共産党の組織及「ソビエト」式統治組織は当時の支那に於ける状態の下に於いてはこれを輸入すること不可能なる旨明瞭に声明せられたり。右協定に基づき1923 年末迄に若干の軍事及政治顧問「モスクワ」より派遣せられ「孫逸仙の監督の下に国民党の内面的構成及広東軍の改革に従事したり」。

1924 年 3 月召集せられたる国民党第 1 回全国代表大会に於いて支那共産党は国民党に加入することを正式に承認せられたるが只之に対しては斯くの如き党員は以後「プロレタリア」革命の準備に参加すべからざる旨の条件附せられたり。斯くして容共時代開始せらるるに至れり。

容共時代　一九二四―二七

右時期は1924 年より27 年に及ぶ。1924 年初期に於いて共産党員は2千名又赤色「シンジケート」は6 万の会員を擁したり。然れども共産党員はまもなく国民党内部に於いて勢力を扶植し旧来の国民党員をして之に対し不安を感ぜしむるに至れり。右共産主義員に属するものを除く一切の不動産の国有、国民党の改組、共産主義に反対する一切の軍閥頭目の艾除、共産党員 2 万並びに労働者及農民 5 万の武装の如きもの迄も包含せられたり。然れども右提案は否決せられ為に共産党員は従前国民群の編成に最努力したるに拘らず国民党の企図する北方軍閥の討伐に対し援助を許与することを中止するに至れり。然るに後に至り右討伐に加わり北伐が中央支那に及び1927 年武漢に於いて国民党政府樹立せらるや国民党要人がその軍隊の南京及上海占領に至る迄合作を肯せざるに乗じ同政府内の実権を把握するに成功せり。武漢政府は湖南及湖北の両省に於いて幾多の純然たる共産主義的施政を実行し国民革命は将に共産革命に転化せしめられんとするに至りたり。

国民党及共産党の分裂、一九二七年

国民党要人は遂に共産党の脅威重大にして最早之を寛容し得ざることを決断し、自己の勢力が南京に確立せられ1927年4月10日、別個の国民政府、同地に組織せらるるや布告を発して南京政府は直ちに軍隊及行政部より共産主義を駆逐すべき旨命令せり。7月15日、従来在南京国民党要人との合作を肯せざりし在武漢国民党中央執行委員の大多数も国民党より共産党員を除去し「ソビエト」顧問の支那退去を命ずる決議を採択せり右決定の結果国民党は其の統一を回復し南京政府は広く同党の承認を受くるに至れり。

南昌及広東事件

容共時代に於いて数箇の軍隊共産主義に加担するに至れり。此等軍隊は国民党軍の北伐に際しては大部分江西地方に遺留せられたるが右軍隊を連絡し且国民政府に対し事を挙げんことを説得する為共産党員派遣せられたり。1927年7月30日、江西省首府南昌の駐屯軍は他の部隊と共に叛乱し人民に対し幾多の暴虐を行いたるも8月5日、政府軍の撃破する所と為り、南方に退去せり。12月11日、広東に共産主義者の暴動あり。同市は二日間其の手中に帰したり。南京政府は右二叛乱には「ソビエト」政府代表者の活発なる干与ありたるものと認め1927年12月14日の命令を以て一切の支那駐在「ソビエト」連邦領事の許可状を撤回せり。

共産党軍との武力紛争の継続

内乱の再発は1928年乃至1931年の時期に於いて共産党の勢力に伸張に幸いせり。赤衛軍は編成せられ江西、福建両省に於ける広大なる地域は「ソビエト」化せられたり。中央政府が共産主義の鎮圧に力を用いることを得るに至りしは漸く1930年11月、即ち北方軍閥の強力なる連合を撃破したる稍後の事なり。共産軍は江西、湖南両省の各地に策動し当時二、三ヶ月の間に20万人の死者と約10億ドルに上る物的損害とを惹起したる旨報ぜられたり。此等軍隊は今や其の勢力強大と為り政府の第1回討伐軍を撃破し第2回の討伐軍を粉砕するに至れり。第3回討伐軍は総司令官蒋介石軍の指揮の下に数度の会戦に於いて共産軍を撃破し、1931年7月半に至る迄に共産軍の最も重要なる根拠地を陥れ共産軍は福建方面に総退却を行えり。蒋介石軍は共匪の蹂躙したる地方の再興を目的とする政治委員会を組織する一方、赤軍を追撃して之を江西省南西の山岳地帯に撃退せり。

斯くの如く南京政府は将に主要なる赤軍をして活動の余地なからしめんとし居たる処、遇々支那の各地に各種の事件発生し政府をして其の攻撃を中止し、軍隊の大部分を撤退するの余儀なきに至らしめたり。即ち北方に於いては石友三将軍叛乱を起こし一方広東軍湖南省に侵入して右石軍に策応するあり之と時を同じくして奉天に於いては9月18日事件発生せり。此等の情勢に乗じ赤軍は再び攻撃を開始し討伐の戦勝に依り収められたる成果は幾何もなくして殆ど完全に失われたり。

現在に於ける共産党組織の範囲

福建、江西両省の大部分及広東の若干部分は信頼すべき報道に拠れば、完全に「ソビエト」化せられ居れり。共産党の勢力範囲は更に広大にして揚子江以南の支那の大部分並びに揚子江以北の湖北、安徽及江蘇各省の諸地方に跨れり。

上海は共産主義宣伝の中心と為れり。共産主義の個人的同情者は恐らく支那の各都市に発見せられ得べし。現在は二箇の共産主義地方政府が江西及福建に於いて組織せられたるに止まると雖も比較的小なる「ソビエト」組織は数百に達す。共産主義政府自体は地方の労働者及農民の会議に依り選挙せられたる委員会に依り組織せらる。右共産主義政府は実際は支那共産党の代表者に依り支配せられ居り支那共産党は其の目的の為に訓練せられたる人員を派遣し而も其の派遣人員の大多数は曩に「ソビエト」連邦に於いて訓練せられたるものなり。

支那共産党中央委員会の支配下にある地方委員会は先ず省委員会を支配し、省委員会は更に県委員会を支配す。斯くして工場、学校、兵営等、内に組織せられたる共産主義細胞に及ぶ。

共産主義者に用ひられる方法

一県が赤軍に依り占領せられ其の占領が多少なりとも永久的性質を有すと認めらるるに於ては其の県が「ソビエト」化する為努力す。如何なる民衆の反対も恐怖主義に依り弾圧せらる。共産主義政府は上記の如くして建設せらるるなり。斯くの如き政府の完全なる組織は左記の組織即ち内政局、反革命主義者に対する争闘の為の局（「ゲー・ペー・ウー」）、財政局、農業経済局、教育局、衛生局、郵便及電信局、交通局並びに軍事委員会及労働者及農民取締委員会を包含す。斯くの如き精細なる政府組織は完全に「ソビ

エト」化せられたる県に於いてのみ存在す。他処に於いては比較的微温的なる組織なり。行動綱領は債務を放棄し並びに私の大地主又は寺院、僧院、及教会の如き宗教団体より強力を以て接収せる土地を「プロレタリア」及小農に分配するにあり。課税は簡単化せられ農民は其の土地の生産高の一定部分を納付せざるべからず。農業改良の為灌漑、農村信用制度及組合を発達せしむる手段が講ぜらる。小学校、病院及調剤所も建設せらるることあり。

斯くの如く最貧困なり農民は共産主義に依り驚くべき利益を得るに反し富裕及中産階級の地主、商人並びに地方紳士は即時没収又は徴収及罰金の何れかに依り完全に没落せしめらる。而して此の農業綱領を適用することに於いて共産党は群集の支持を得ることを期待す。此の点に関し其の宣伝と行動とは共産主義原理が支那の社会組織と衝突するの事実にも拘らず非常なる成功を勝ち得たり。圧制的課税より生ずる怨嗟の存在するを以て不法徴発、横領及兵卒又は匪賊に依る掠奪は極度に行わる。特殊なる「スローガン」が農民、労働者、兵卒及知識階級の為に特に婦人に適する様工夫せられて使用せらる。

支那に於ける共産主義の特質

支那における共産主義は「ソビエト」連邦以外の多数の国に於けるが如く既存の政党員に依りて支持せらるる政治上の主義にも非ず。又他の政党と権力を争う特別の党組織にも非ず。支那共産主義は国民政府の事実上の競争相手と為れり。支那共産主義は其の独自の法律、軍隊及政府並びに其の行動の特別の地域的分野を有す。此等の事態に関しては他の如何なる国に於いても比較すべきものなし。加之支那に於いては共産主義の戦闘に依り生ぜる混乱は、国家が国内改造の重大時期を経過しつつある事実に依り一層重大化せられ更に最近の11月間の例外的重大性を有する対外危機に依り一段と複雑化せられたり。国民政府は共産主義の勢力を利用し各県の支配を再び得て一度此等の各県に於いて其の権力を回復したる暁には経済的更生の政策を遂行せんと決心したるものと認めらる。然れども既述の国民政府の地位を弱めたる内外の困難を別とするも軍事行動に於いて国民政府は資本の欠乏と不完全なる交通とに依り悩まされたり。支那に於ける共産主義の問題は斯くの如く国民的改造の大問題と関連する所あり。1932年夏、南京政府は重要なる軍事行動は赤色抵抗の徹底的鎮圧を其の目的と

する旨声明せり。軍事行動は開始せられ上記の如く再獲得地方の全般的社会的及行政的再組織を伴うべき筈なりしが現在に至る迄何等の重要なる結果も公表せらるるに至らず。

此等事態の日支関係に及ぼせる影響

日本は支那の最近接せる隣国に於いて且最大なる顧客なるを以て日本は本章に於いて既述せられたるむ法律状態に依り他の何れの国よりも苦しみたり。支那に於ける居留外人の三分の二以上は日本人にして満州における朝鮮人の数は約80万を算す。故に現在の状態に於いて支那の法律、裁判及課税に服従せざるべからずとせば之に依り苦しむ国民を最多く有する国は即ち日本なり。日本は其の条約上の権利に代わるべき満足なる保護が期待し得られざるに於ては到底支那側の願望を満足せしむること不可能なるを感じたり。日本の支那に於ける利益は特に満州に於いて著しきものある処他の大多数の国の利益が撤回せらるるの時機に際し更に顕著に主張せらるるに至れり。日本の支那に於ける其の臣民の生命及財産の保証に対する不安は内乱又は地方的混乱に際ししばしば干渉を行わしめたり。斯くの如き行動は痛く支那の憤激を買い特に1928年済南に於いて起これる武力衝突に依り行われたる時に於いて然り。近年日本の主張は支那に於いては他の列国の総ての権利以上に国民的願望に対する重大なる挑戦なりと認めらるるに至れり。

支那改造問題に対する外国の関心

本問題の日本に及ぼせる影響は列国以上に大なりと雖も日支間のみの問題には非ず。支那は例外的権力及特権は其の国民的栄誉及主権を侵害するものなりと感ずるの故を以て此等の特権を直ちに還付することを要求す。諸外国は支那に於ける状態が此等諸外国の国民の保護に充分なるに至らざる限り右支那側の希望に応ずることを躊躇せり。蓋し此等外国人の利益は特別の条約上の権利に依り獲得せらるればなり。

本章が記述せんと試みたる過渡期に於いて不可避なる撹乱過程は世論の力を発達せしむるに至り此の世論の力は恐らく中央政府が国家の統一と改造とを安成するに失敗して弱められ居る限り其の外交政策の遂行にあたり中央政府を困却せしむるものなるべし。外国関係に於ける支那の国民的願望の実現は内政の分野に於いて近代的政府の機能を発揮する能力の如何

に基づくものなり。而して此等の機能の齟齬が除去せられざる限り国際的軋轢及事件の発生の危険「ボイコット」並びに武力干渉は継続せらるべし。

国際協力は解決の最善の希望を興ふ、

現在の国際的軋轢の極端なる事例は再び支那をして国際聯盟の干渉を求むるの余儀なきに至らしめたるか若し満足なる解決が達成せらるるに於いては支那をして1922年華府に於いて有益なる結果を持って着手せられたる国際協力の政策の利益を覚知せしむることを得べし。現在支那は其の国民的改造を援助を籍らずして完成するに必要なる資本をも、訓練せられたる専門家をも有せず。孫逸仙博士自身も此の事実を認め現に同国の経済的発展に対する国際的参加の計画を作成せり。国民政府も亦近年其の諸問題の解決に於いては1930年以来財政問題に於て、1931年国民経済委員会の組織以来国際聯盟技術委員会と連絡して経済的計画及発展に関する問題において並びに同年の大洪水に依り蒙れる被害救済に於いて国際援助を求め且之を受諾せり。国際協力の此の行路に従い支那は其の国民的理想の達成に向て最確実にして最速なる進歩を為すべく而して斯くの如き政策は諸外国にとり中央政府の求むる所のものを与えて世界列国との平和的関係を危殆ならすむるの処ある軋轢のあらゆる原因を能う限り速やかに且有効に除去することに於て援助を与えることを一層容易ならしむべし。

第二章　満　州

記述　支那の他の部分及露西亜との関係[1]

1. 記述

序論

満州は支那に於いては東三省として知らるる広汎且豊穣なる地域にして僅々四十年以前にはほとんど開発せられ居らず現在に於いてすら猶人口稀薄なるを以て支那及日本の過剰人口問題解決に益々重大なる役割を演ずるに至れり。数百万の窮乏せる農民は山東省及河北省より満州に流入せる

---

[1]　編者按：原文如此。

一方、製品及資本は日本より同地方に輸出せられ食糧及原料と交換せられたり。斯くの如く満州は支那及日本の各自の必要に応ずることに依りて日支双方の有力なる伴侶たる実を挙げたり。即ち日本の活動なくんば満州は斯くの如き大なる人口を誘致且収容し得さりしなるへく又支那農民及労働者の移住なくんば満州は斯くも急速に発展し以て日本に対し市場並食糧肥料及原料を供給すること能はさりなるべし。

満州は先ず軍略上の要地として続て農業及鉱業上の資源として垂涎せられたる地域なり

然れども他国の協力に依倚すること多大なる満州は上述の理由に依り先ず日露の間に於いて次いで支那及其の二強隣邦間に於ける紛争の地域となるの運命を有したり。当初満州は之等政策の大衝突の地域たるに止まり満州の占拠に依り極東政治を支配し得るものと考えられたるか其の後満州の農業、鉱業及林業上の資源発見せらるるに及び満州其のものを垂涎せらるるに至れり。先ずロシアは支那の犠牲に於いて特殊の条約上の権利を獲得したるが其の南満州に関するものは後日日本に譲渡せられ而も斯くの如くにして獲得せられたる特権は其後南満州の経済的開発を促進する手段として行使せられたり。軍略上の理由は依然として重要なるものあるもロシア及日本は夫々満州開発に積極的に従事し広汎なる経済的利益を得たる為其の外交政策を固持すること益々甚だしきに至れり。

支那農民の土地占拠

支那は当初開発の方面に活動することなく殆ど満州を其の支配よりロシアの手に移さむとせり。而して満州における支那の主権を再び確認せる「ポーツマス」条約後に於いても同地方開発にあたれるロシア及日本の経済的活動は支那の夫れに比しより顕著に世界の目に映じたり。此の間数百万の支那農民移住したるが右は将来に於ける土地所有の根拠をなせるものにして事実平和的にして目立たざるも実質的なものなりき。ロシア及日本が北満及南満に於ける各自の勢力範囲の設定に従事せる間に支那農民は土地を所有するに至り今や満州は正しく支那のものなり。斯かる状態に於いて支那は再び其の主権を主張するの好機会を待望することを得たるが1917年のロシア革命は北満に於いて支那に此の機会を与えたり。支那は過去久きに亙り等閑に附し居たる地方の開発及当地に一層積極的活動を開始し近

年に於いては南満州に於ける日本の勢力を減少せしむと試みたるが右政策の結果軋轢高まり遂に1931年9月18日其の頂点に達せり。

人口

全人口は約三千万と算せられ其の中二千八百万は支那人及同化せる満州人なりと称せらる。朝鮮人の数は八十万にして其の大部分は朝鮮国境の所謂間島地方に集合し爾余の者は満州に広く分布す。蒙古種族は内蒙古に接する牧地に居住し其の数少なし。満州に於けるロシア人は約十五万ある模様なるが其の大部分は東支鉄道沿線地方特に哈爾賓に在り。約二十三万の日本人は南満州鉄道沿線の居留地及関東州租借地(遼東半島)に主として集中し居れり。満州に於ける日本人ロシア人及其の他の外国人(朝鮮人を除く)は四十万を超過せず。

面積

満州は佛蘭西及獨逸を合したる大きさの面積を存する広大なる地域にして約三十八万平方哩と算せらる。支那に於いては之を常に「東三省」と称す蓋し其の行政区劃は南部に遼寧(奉天)、東部に吉林、北部に黒龍江の三省に分たるるを以てなり。遼寧は面積七万平方哩、吉林は十万平方哩、黒龍江は二十万平方哩以上と算せらる。

地理

満州は其の特性大陸的なり而して東南部に長白山脈、西北部に大興安山脈の二山脈あり。右両山脈間に満州大平原横はり其の北部は松花江盆地に南部は遼河盆地に属す。右両盆地の分水界は歴史的に争闘重要なるものなるが満州平原を南北に分かつ一つの山脈なり。満州は西は河北省及内外蒙古に境を接す。内蒙古は以前三個の特別行政地域即熱河察哈爾及綏遠に分かれ何れも1928年国民政府に依り省としての完全なる地位を賦与せられたり。内蒙古特に熱河は常に満州と関係を保ち満州問題に多少の影響を与え居れり。満州は其の西北、東北、及東に於いては「ソ」連邦の西伯利亜に、東南に於いては朝鮮に境し南に於いては黄海に臨む。遼東半島の南端は1905年以来日本に保有せられ其の面積千三百平方哩を超え日本の租借地として統治せらる。加之日本は租借地外に互り南満州鉄道を敷設せる狭き地帯に対し或種の権利を行使す。右地帯の全面積は僅々百八平方哩なるも線路の長さは六百九十里に達す。

経済的資源

満州の地味は一般に豊穣なるも其の開発は交通の利便に左右せられ多数の重要都市は河川及鉄道に沿いて繁栄す。過去に於ける開発は大体河川系統に頼りしものなるが右河川系統は鉄道が交通機関として第一位を占むるに至れる今日に於いても依然として甚だ重要なり。大豆、高粱、小麦、粟、大麦、米、燕麦の如き重要穀物産額は十五年間に倍加し1929年此の種穀産物は八億七千六百万「ブッシェル」以上と算せられたり。1931年の満州年鑑所掲の算定に依れば1929年には全面積の28.4％は耕作し得るに拘らず僅々12.6％開墾せられ居るに過ぎず従って経済状態改善せらるるに於いては将来生産額の着しき増大を期待し得べきが如し。1928年度に於ける満州の農産物の全価格は一億三千万金ポンド以上と算せられ其の大部分は輸出せらる。絹紬又は柞蚕亦満州の他の重要輸出品なり。

木材及鉱物

山岳地方は木材及鉱物殊に石炭豊富なる。鉄及金の鉱床も存在すとせられ他方良質の油頁岩、白雲石、菱苦土石、耐火粘土、滑石珪土も多量に発見せられたり。従って鉱業は極めて有望なりと期待せらる。（第八章並びに本報告書付属の特別研究第二及第三参照）

2. 支那の他の部分との関係

清朝没落に至る迄の歴史

満州は有史以来各種「ツングース」族居住し蒙古韃靼人と自由に雑居したるが優越せる文明を有する支那移住民の影響を受け団結心に目覚め数個の王国を建設し此等王国は時に満州の大部分並びに支那及朝鮮の北部地方を支配せり。殊に遼、金及清朝は支那の大部分又は全部を征服し数世紀間之を支配したり。一方支那は有力なる皇帝の下に北方の侵入を防止し之に代わりて自ら満州の大部分に其の主権を樹立するを得たり。移住支那人の植民は古代より行われ周囲の地方に支那文化の影響に及ぼしたる支那人の都邑は同じく古代より存在せり。即ち二千年間永久的の拠所維持せられ支那文化は満州の極南部に於いて常に行われたるが右文化の影響は事実上満州全体に其の権力を振へる明朝(1368—1644)の統治中極めて強大となりたり。満州人が1616年満州における明朝の施政を覆し1628年万里の長城を

越えて支那を征服せる以前既に満州人の間には支那文化普及し著しく支那
人に同化せられたり。満州軍中には多数の支那人ありて旗として知らるる
別個の部隊に編成せられたり。

　右征服後清朝は支那の重要都市に守備兵を置き満州人の一定職業に従
事するを禁じ満州人支那人間の結婚を禁止し支那人の満州及蒙古移住を制
限せり。右の措置は人種的差別よりは寧ろ政治的差別に基づき清朝の永久
的支配を擁護するの目的に出でたるものなり。而して右措置は多数の支那
旗人には及ばず彼等は事実上満州人同様の特権的地位を享有せり。

　満州人及其の味方たる支那人の出境は満州の人口を著しく減少せしめ
たるも南部に於いては支那人の部落は依然として存在し右部落より少数の
移住者は奉天省の中央部を横断して分散せり。而して其の数は排斥法を潜
るに成功し又は時々同法の変改を利して支那より絶えず移住民入込める為
増加したり。満州人及支那人は益々同化し支那語は実質上満州語に代わる
に至れり。尤も蒙古人は同化せられず之等移住民の為奥地に後退せしめら
れたり。最後に北方よりするロシア人の南下を阻止する為清朝政府は支那
移住民を奨励するに決し1878年満州各地を開放し且移住民に各種の奨励
を与えたる結果1911年の支那革命当時満州の人口は千八百万と算せられ
たり。

　1907年即退位の数年前清朝は満州に於ける施政を改革することに決
定せり。満州各省は従前独自の政体を有する関外領域として統治せられ、
省行政を考試も及第せる学者の手に委する支那の慣例は満州に於いては行
われずして純粋なる軍政施れ、右軍政の下に満州官吏及慣習維持せられた
り。支那に於いては官吏は其の出生せる省に於いては官職に就くを許され
ざりき。満州各省には督軍ありて軍事のみならず一切の施政に付き完全な
る権力を行使したるが後に至り文武政の分離試みられたるもその結果は満
足ならざりき。依て1907年右の試は放棄せられ特に外交政策の方面に於
ける権力集中の目的を以て三名の督軍に代ふるに全満州に対する総督を必
くこととし総督の監督の下に省長省行政を掌りたり。右改組は支那の省政
府組織を招来せる後日の行政改革の為路を開きたるものなり。清朝の右最
後の措置は1907年以後満州の政治を掌れる有能なる為政家に依り大なる
効果を収めたり。

清朝没落後

1911 年革命起こるや共和政体に賛せざる満州官憲は後日満州及北支の独裁官となるに至りたる張作霖に対し革命軍の前進阻止を命じ以て内乱の騒擾より此等の省を救うに成功したり。共和国建設せらるるや満州官憲は既成事実を受諾し進んで共和国第 1 大統領に選任せられたる袁世凱の統率に従いたり。各省には省長及督軍任命せられたるが満州に於いては支那の他の部分と同様督軍は忽ち同僚たる省長を無力の者たらしめたり。

一九一六年、張作霖の奉天省軍任命

1916 年張作霖奉天省督軍に任命せられ同時に省長の職を執りたるが其の実力の及ぶ所は遥かに大なりき。対獨宣戦の問題起こるや彼は支那将領と共に之に反対せる会議の解散を要求せり。而して右要求大統領に依り拒絶せらるるや彼は奉天省は北京中央政府に対する功績に依り東三省巡撫使に任せられたり。斯くして満州は再び特別の制度を有する一つの行政単位となりたり。

一九二二年、張の北京中央政府に対する忠誓断絶

張作霖は中央政府の与えたる顕職を受領したるも其の態度は変転常なき中央政府の支配者たる軍閥との個人的関係の如何に依り変化せり。彼は自己と政府との関係を視るに個人的同盟の意味を以てしたるものの如し。1922 年 7 月其の権力を長城以内に樹立するに失敗し其の政敵北京政府を支配したる際彼は中央政府に対する忠誠を廃棄し満州において行動の完全なる独立を維持し遂には其の権力を長城以南に及ぼし北京の支配者となりたり。彼は外国の権利を尊重するの意あるを表明し支那の義務を承認したるも外国に対し満州に関する一切の事項に付いては今後自己の政府と直接交渉せむることを要求せり。

一九二四年「ソ」連邦との奉天協定

依て彼は1924 年 5 月 31 日露支協定が支那に有利なるに拘らず之を廃棄し1924 年 9 月ソ連邦を説き之と別個の協定を締結せるが右は1924 年 5 月 31 日の中央政府との協定と実質的に同一なり。右の事実は張作霖が内外政策に関し完全なる行動の自由を固持せることを明証するものなり。

張作霖元帥呉佩孚将軍を破る

1924 年彼は再び支那に侵入したるが馮玉祥将軍(クリスチャン将軍)

が其の上官呉佩孚将軍（現在元帥）を戦闘の最も重要なる時期に裏切りたる為成功せり。其の結果中央政府は忽（タチマ）ち転覆し南方上海に至る迄張元帥の勢力拡大せり。

1925年張元帥は又々武力に訴え其の同盟者たる馮将軍に対抗せり。此の戦闘に於いて彼の部下の将軍の一人郭松齢は最も重要なる時機に際し彼を裏切り馮将軍に味方せり。

郭松齢の反逆

1925年11月の郭松齢の叛逆はソ連邦及日本にも関係し前者の行動は間接に馮将軍に有利して後者の夫れは張元帥に有利なりしを以て単に一時的の問題たるに止まらざりき。郭松齢は元帥の部下たりしに拘らず社会改革に関し馮将軍と見解を同じくし上官の没落が内乱終息に必要なりとの信念より彼に対し鋒を逆にせるものなり。右叛逆は元帥を甚だしく危機に陥れたり。郭松齢は鉄道の西方の地域を占領し居り元帥は着しく減少せる兵力を擁し奉天に在りたるが此の時日本は南満州に於ける自己の利益より南満州鉄道の両側に各20支里（7哩）の中立地帯を宣言し軍隊の之を通過することを禁止したり。右は郭松齢の元帥に対し進軍するを妨げ黒龍江より援軍到着の余裕を与えたり。援軍は現金を以て運賃を支払はざる限り鉄道輸送の許可を拒否せる「ソビエト」鉄道吏員の行動に依り遅延したるも他の行路に依り進むことを得たり。右援軍の到着及多少とも日本の与えたる公然の援助は戦闘を元帥に有利に導き郭松齢は敗北し馮将軍は後退を余儀なくせられ北京を張元帥の為遺棄したり。張元帥は右の際に於ける東支鉄道吏員の行動を憤り該鉄道の権利を絶えず侵犯し以て報復余す所なかりき。右事件の与えたる経験は彼をして満州三省の首都を連絡する独立の鉄道綱を建設せしめたる重要なる要因たるの観あり。

満州独立の意識

張作霖元帥が時を異にし宣言せる独立なるものは彼又は満州の人民が支那との分離を希望せることを意味せるものには非ず。彼の軍隊は支那が恰も外国なるかの如く之を侵略したるに非ずして単に内戦に参加したるに過ぎず。他省の軍閥と同様元帥は或は援助し或は攻撃し又は其の領域を中央政府より独立せるものと宣言したるも右は支那を個々の国家に分割するに至るが如き遣方にて為されたるに非す之に反し支那の内乱の多くは真に

強力なる政府の下に同国を統一せむとする何等かの大計画に直接又は間接関係あるものなりて従って一切の戦争及「独立」の期間を通し満州は終始支那の完全なる一部たりしなり。

張作霖及国民党

呉佩孚に対する戦争に於いて張作霖及国民党は同盟せるに拘らず前者自身は国民党の主義を承認せざりき彼は孫博士の希望せる如き憲法は支那人民の精神と調和するものとは見受けられざりしを以て之を是認せざりき。

然れ共張は支那の統一を希望せり。而して満州に於けるソ連邦及日本の利益範囲に対する張の政策は出来得べくんば両者を一層せんと欲したるを示せり。ソ連邦の範囲に関しては張は右政策の実行に殆ど成功し又南満州鉄道を同鉄道の培養地域の或部分より切断する結果を生ずべき上述の鉄道建設政策に着手したり。張が満州に於ける日ソ両国の利益に対し斯かる態度に出でたるは一は張が其の日ソ両国との関係に於ける自己の権威の制限を堪え難しとせると、他は張が支那における外国人の特権的地位に関し各種の支那世論と共に感じたる憤怨に因るべし。事実 1924 年 11 月張は孫博士を改革会議に招請したる処同博士は会議議題中に生活標準の改善、国民会議支召集及不平等条約の廃棄を包含せしめんことを求めたり。右会議は博士の重患に陥りたる結果開催を見ずして止みたるが、右孫博士の提議は孫張と元帥との間に一脈の諒解の相通ずるものあり、且両者の間に支那外交政策に関し合意の基礎を求め得べかりしを想はしむ。

張作霖の晩年

張作霖元帥は其の晩年に於いては日本に対し日本が各種の条約及取極に依り取得せる特権の利益を漸次容認せざる意向を示すに至れり。日本との関係は特に稍緊張したり支那における党派的闘争に関係せず専ら力を満州の開発に用ふべしとの日本の忠告に対し張は憤怨を感じ之を無視したるが、其の子張学良亦彼に倣へり。馮将軍敗北後張作霖は大元帥の称号の下に北方軍閥同盟の盟主と成れり。

1928 年張は第一章に説述せる北伐に際し国民党軍の為敗られ、日本より早きに及んで其の軍隊を満州に引揚ぐべき旨勧告せられたり。日本の目的は当時言明したる如く戦捷軍に追撃せられたる敗残兵の遁入に依り満州が内乱の災禍に投ぜらるることを防止せんとするに在りたる。

一九二八年六月四日張作霖元帥の死

右勧告に対し元帥は憤慨したるも結局之に従うの他なかりき。張は 1928 年 6 月 3 日北平（先の北京）より奉天に向け出発したる処翌日奉天市外即京奉線が南満州鉄道線の鉄橋下を通過する地点に於いて爆裂の為其の搭乗せる列車破壊せられ死亡せり。

右殺害の責任は今日迄確定せられず。惨事は神秘の幕に蔽われ居れるも当時右事件に日本が共謀したるやの嫌疑起こり既に緊張し居たる日支関係に一段の緊張を加ふる原因となれり。

後継者張学良

張作霖の死後其の子張学良は満州の支配者と為れり。学良は新時代の国民的要望を多分に有したるを以て内乱を中止し国民党の統一政策を援助せんと欲したるが既に国民党の政策及傾向に付多少の経験を有したる日本は斯かる勢力が満州に浸透せんとする形勢は之を歓迎せざりき。日本は若き元帥に対し右の趣旨を勧告する所ありたるが彼は父と同じく斯かる勧告を不快とし自己の判断に従うべく決心せり。

若き元帥中央政府への忠順を宣す

斯くて彼と国民党及南京との関係は緊密を加え1928 年 12 月彼は易幟を行い中央政府に対する忠順を宣言し東北辺防軍総司令に任ぜらるると共に内蒙古の一部約六万平方哩の面積を有する熱河を加えたる満州政権の長官たることを確認せられたり。

国民党との聯繋資質上よりも名義上のものなり

満州が国民党支那と合体せる結果満州の行政組織は中央政府の夫れに近似する様多少の変更を必要とするに至り委員会制度採用せられ民党の各級支部設立せられたるが事実は従来の通旧制度の下に旧人物活動せり。支那に於いて不断に行われたる如き国民党支部の地方行政に対する干渉は満州に於いては容認せられず総ての主要文武官憲は国民党員たるべしとの規定は単なる形式として取扱われ軍事、政務、財務、外交等総ての問題に付中央政府との関係は満州側の自発的協力を必要とせり。無条件服従を要求するが如き命令又は訓令は容認せられざりしなるべく満州官憲の意に反したる任免の如きは想像し得られざりき。政府及党の問題に関する右の如き行動の独立は支那の其の他の各地方に於いても存したるが斯かる場合総ての

重要なる任命は地方官憲に依りて行われ中央政府は単に之を確認するに止まれり。

国民政府との合体が満州に置ける外交政策に及ぼしたる影響

外交政策の範囲に於いては地方官憲は依然多大の行動の自由を有したるに相違なきも然も満州と国民政府との合体は相当重要なる結果を招来せり。東支鉄道の満州に於ける地位に対する張作霖元帥の執拗なる攻撃及日本の要求せる或る種の権利に対する無視は満州に於いては既に国民党との合体以前より「進取政策」の採用せられ居たることを示すものなるが国民党との合体後は満州は同党の良く組織せられたる且系統的なる宣伝に解放せられたり。同党は其の公式の印刷物に於いて又同党と関係深き多数の機関紙において常に喪失主権回復の極めて重要なること、不平等条約の廃棄、帝国主義の邪悪を強調するを止めざりき。支那の領土上に於ける外国の利益、裁判所、警察、警備兵又は軍隊の実体が明白なる満州に於いて斯かる宣伝が深き印象を与えたるは必然なり。国民党の宣伝は同党の教科書に依り学校に侵入し又遼寧人民外交協会の如き協会出現して国民主義的感情を鼓舞強調すると共に抗日煽動を実行し又支那人家主及地主に対しては日本人及朝鮮人たる借人への賃貸料の引上げ又は賃貸契約の更新拒絶を強要したり(本報告書付属の特別研究第九号参照)。日本人は当委員会に対し多数の此の種事件を訴え来れり。朝鮮人移民は組織的迫害を蒙れり。諸種の抗日的命令及訓令発せられ軋轢の機会は重なる緊張加れり。1931年3月各省首都に国民党省党部設立せられ続いて其の他の都市及地方に支部の設立を見たり。党の宣伝員にして支那より北上し来る者は次第に其の数を加え日本人は抗日運動の日に激化するのを嘆きたり。

1931年4月、奉天に於いて人民外交協会後援の下に5日間の会議開催せられ満州各地よりの代表者三百余名之に参加し満州に於ける日本の地位一掃の可能性に付討議せられたるか其の決議の中には南満州鉄道回復の一項を含めり。当時ソ連邦及其の市民亦右同様の傾向に悩まされたるか一方白露人は何等返還すべき主権又は例外的特権を有せざるに係らず屈辱的虐待を蒙れり。

内政に及ぼせる影響

内政問題に関しては満州官憲はその欲する権力をことごとく保持した

り。而して其の権力の根本に触れざる限り彼等は中央政府の採用せる行政
規則及方法に異議なかりき。

東北政務委員会

国民政府との合体後間もなく奉天に東北政務委員会設立せられたるが
右は中央政府の名目的監督の下にある東北諸省の最高行政官憲なりき。同
委員会は13名より成り其の中1名を委員長に選べり。同委員会は遼寧、吉
林、黒龍江及熱河の4省並びに1922年以来東支鉄道の行政管轄下に帰せる
所謂特別区の政府の活動を指揮監督する責に任したり。同委員会は特に中
央政府に留保せられたる以外のあらゆる事項を処理し且中央政府の法律規
則に抵触せざる如何なる措置をも執り得るの権限を有し省及特別区の政府
は右委員会の決定を実施するの義務ありたり。

各省の行政組織は支那の其の他の地方に於いて採用せられたる組織と
根本的には相異する所なきも満州を一行政単位として維持せんが為に特権
を保持せること最も重要なる差異なり。尤も右特権無かりせば満州側の自
発的合体は恐らく行われざりしなるべし。事実満州に於いては外部的変更
に係らず旧事態引続き存在せり。満州当局は従来の如く其の権力が南京よ
り来るよりも遥かに多く彼等の軍隊より来るものなることを認識せり。

軍隊。全経費の80％を占むる軍費

右事実は約25万に上る大常備軍維持せられ又2億ドル（銀）以上を費
やしたりと伝えらるる大兵工廠の保持せられ居ることを説明するものな
り。軍事費は全経費の80％に達したりと推計せられ其の残額を以て行政、
警察、司法及教育の費用を支弁するに足らぬ又国庫は官憲に対し適当なる
俸給を支給する能はざりき。而してあらゆる権力は少数軍人の手に帰した
るを以て官職は彼等の手を通してのみ得られ斯かる事態の避け難き結果と
して親戚特寵、腐敗、悪政は跡を断たざりき。当委員会は右悪政に対する甚
大の不平が広く各地に存するを認めたり。尤も右事態は満州に特有のもの
には非ざりしものにして支那の其の他の地方にも同様乃至更に悪化せる事
態存在せり。

軍隊給養の為には重税を課するの要ありたるが通常収入にてはなお不
足せるを以て当局は省政府不換紙幣の価値を着々下落せしむることに依り
更に人民に課税せり（本報告書付属の特別研究第四号及第五号参照）。右政

策は殊に最近に於いて既に1930年頃に殆ど独占的となり居たる「豆類公買」に関連して行われたり。満州重要産物の管理権を取得することに依り当局は外国の豆類買入業者就中日本人に対し高値買入を強い以って其の収入を増大せんと欲したるが斯かる取引は当局が如何なる程度に銀行及商業を管理したるやを示すものなり。官吏は又同様にあらゆる私的企業に自由に従事し其の権力を利用して自己及その寵愛者の為に富を蒐めたり。

満州に於ける支那政権の建設的努力

1931年9月の事件以前の満州に於ける行政が不完全なりしは事実とするも同地方の或る部分に於ては行政改善の努力行われ殊に教育の進歩、都市行政及公共事業の方面に於いて若干の効果挙がりたることは之を認めざるべからず。此の時代において張作霖元帥及張学良元帥の行政の下に満州の経済資源の開発及組織に関し支那人民及支那の利益が従来よりも遥かに大なる役割を演ずるに至りたる事実は特にここに強調するの要あり（第八章及本報告書付属の特別研究第三号参照）。

既述せる如く支那移民の増加は満州と支那の其の他の地方との経済的及社会的関係の発展に貢献したり。然れ共右殖民以外に此の時代に於いて日本の資本に関係なき支那鉄道殊に奉天海龍鉄道、打通鉄道（京奉線支線）「チチハル」克山鉄道、呼蘭海倫鉄道建設せられ又葫蘆島築港計画、遼河改修事業及諸河川に於ける航行事業の開始を見たり。支那官民の多数は此等企業に参加するに至り鉱山業に於いては本渓湖、ボクリョウ、札賓及老頭溝炭鉱に関係を持ち其の他諸鉱山の開発に付単独責任を有したるが此等鉱山の多くは官立東北鉱業公司の指揮の下に採掘せられたり。支那人は猶黒龍江省の採金事業にも利益を有したり。森林業に関しては支那人は鴨緑江採木公司に於いて日本人との共同の利益を有し猶黒龍江省及吉林省に於いて伐木事業に従事せり。満州各地に農事試験場開設せられ農業組合及灌漑計画奨励せられたり。最後に支那人の資本は製粉及織物工業、ハルピンに於ける豆、油及小麦製粉事業。繭綢及柞蚕絹、木綿及羊毛の紡績及製織工場に投ぜられたり。

支那他地方との貿易

満州と支那の其の他の各地方との間の貿易亦増大せり（第八章及本報告書付属の特別研究第六号参照）。右貿易は一部分支那の銀行就中満州の

主要都市に支店を設けたる中国銀行に依りて金融を受けたり。支那汽船及「ジャンク」は支那本部と大連、営口（牛荘）及安東との間を往復したるが其の運輸貨物量漸増し満州海運業界に於ては日本のトン数に次第二位を占めたり。支那保険業も漸次増加の趨勢に在り又支那海関対満が貿易に依り取得する収入は増加しつつありたり。斯くの如く日支衝突以前に於いては満州と支那の其の他の各地方との政治的及経済的連繋は漸次強固を加えつつありたり右漸増しつつありたる相互依存関係は満州及南京に於ける支那人指導者をしてロシア及日本の取得せる権益排除を目的とせる国民主義的政策を益々実行せしむるに与て力ありたり。

3. 対露関係

対露関係

1894—95年の日清戦争は其の後の事件の立証せる如くロシアをして表面上は支那の為に而して事実上は自己の利益の為に支那に対し干渉を為すの機会を与えたり。日本は1895年、下関条約に依りて日本に譲渡せられたる南満州に於ける遼東半島を外交上の圧迫に依り支那に返還するの余儀なきに至りたるかロシアは日本が支那に課したる戦争償金の支払に付支那を援助したり。

東支鉄道

1896年、露支両国間に防守同盟密約締結せられ同年ロシアは上述の対支援助の報償として満州を横断して「チタ」よりウラジオストックに至る直通線をシベリア横断鉄道の支線として建設する権利を獲得したり。同線は日本が再び支那を攻撃したる場合にロシア軍隊を東部に輸送するの必要に出でたりと称せられたるが露清銀行（後の露亜銀行）は本計画の官的色彩を多少隠蔽せんが為に設立せられたり。同銀行は本件鉄道の建設及運輸の為に東支鉄道会社を設立したり。

一八九六年九月八日の契約

1896年9月8日、露清銀行と支那政府との間に締結せられたる契約の条項に依れば東支鉄道会社は本件鉄道を建設し80年間之を運転すべきものにして其の期間満了後は無償にて支那の所有に帰すべきものなるが支那は30年後に於いて協定せらるべき価格を以って之を買収するの権利を有

したり。契約期間中は鉄道会社は其の土地に対し絶対的排他的の行政権を有すべきものなりしが本条項はロシアに依りて契約の其の他の諸条項が許与せりと認めらるるより遥かに広義に解釈せられたり。支那はロシアが契約の範囲を常に拡大せんと試みつつあるに対し抗議したるも之を阻止する能はざりきロシアは東支鉄道の地域内に於いて其の鉄道都市の急激なる発達に伴い主権にも等しき権利を行使するに漸次成功したり。猶支那は鉄道の必要とする総ての政府所有地を無償にて引渡すに同意したるが私有地は時価を以って買上げ得ることとしたり。鉄道会社は更に同社に必要なる電信線を建設運用することをも許与せられたり。

一八九八年露西亜の遼東半島租借

ロシアは1898年、かつて日本が1895年放棄を余儀なからしめたる遼東半島の南部に対し25ヶ年間の租借権を得ると共に東支鉄道を哈爾賓より、租借地内の旅順及「ダルニー」(現在の大連)に連結するの権利をも取得したり。右支線の通過地方に於いて鉄道会社は列車用として伐木採炭の権利を認められ又1896年9月8日の契約の各条項は新支線にも適用せられたる。ロシアは租借地内においては自由に関税を取極むることを許され1899年ダルニーは自由港たるべき旨声明せられ外国の船舶及貿易に開放せられたり。右支線の通貨地域内に於いては如何なる鉄道特権も他国臣民には許与せらるるを得ず且租借地北方の中立地帯に於いては如何なる港も外国貿易に開かるることなく又ロシアの同意なくしては如何なる特許特権をも許与せらるべからざりき。

一九〇〇年露国の満州占領

1900年露国は団匪の蜂起が露国臣民を危殆ならしめたることを理由として満州を占領せり。他の諸国は之に抗議し且露国軍隊の撤退を要求したるも、露国は右の措置を執ることを遷延せり。1901年2月露支秘密条約案「セント・ピータースブルグ」に於て討議せられたるが、其の条項に依れば支那は、満州に於ける其の行政権を回収し、之が代償として、露国が1896年の基礎契約第6条に基づき樹立せる鉄道守備隊の維持を承認すること及他の諸国又は其の臣民に対し露国の同意なくして満州、蒙古及新疆に於ける鉱山又は他の利益を譲渡せざることを約することとせり。該条約案の右条項及他の数条項周知せらるるに及び、支那及他の諸国に於いて世論の反

対を惹起し、1901 年 4 月 3 日露国政府は右計画は撤回せられたる旨の回章を発したり。

一九〇四年二月十日日本は露国に対しかいさんせり

日本は右策動を注視し来りたり。1902 年 1 月 30 日、日本は日英同盟条約を締結したるを以て一層自国の安固なるを覚えたり。然れども日本は依然露国が朝鮮及満州に侵略し来ることあるべきを懸念したり。従って日本は他の諸国と共に満州に於ける露国軍隊の撤退を要求せり。露国は自国のものに非る企業に対し事実上満州及蒙古を閉鎖するに至るべき条件の下に撤退に異存なきことを宣言せり。露国の圧迫は朝鮮に於いても亦増大せり。1902 年 7 月露国軍隊は鴨緑江の河口に現れたり。其の他数多の行為は日本をして露国が日本の生存に対する脅威に非ずとするも日本の利益に対する脅威たる政策を執るに決したりと信ぜしめたり。1903 年 7 月、日本は門戸開放主義の維持及支那の領土保全に関し露国と商議を開始したるが何等成功を見ざりしを以て1904 年 2 月 10 日開戦せり。支那は中立を保ちたり。

「ポーツマス」条約

露国は敗退せり。1905 年 9 月 3 日、露国は「ポーツマス」条約を締結し之に依り日本の為に南満州に於ける其の特殊権益を放棄せり。租借地及租借に関係せる一切の権利は日本に譲渡せられ同時に旅順口長春間の鉄道及其の支線並びに右鉄道に附し又は右鉄道の利益の為に経営せらるる右地域内の一切の炭鉱も亦日本に譲渡せられたり。両当事国は租借地を除き、各自の軍隊に於いて占領し又は其の管理の下に在る満州全部を挙げて全然支那専属の行政に還付することに同意せり。両国は満州に於ける各自の鉄道線路を保護せんが為(特定条件に基づき)守備兵を維持するの権利を留保し、右守備兵の数は一「キロメートル」毎に十五名を超過することを得ずとせり。

露国の勢力北満に制限せらる

露国は其の勢力範囲の半ばを失い爾来其の範囲は北満州に限定せらることとなれり。露国は同地方に其の地位を保持し爾後其の勢力を増大したるが、1917 年、露国革命勃発するに及び支那は右地域における其の主権を再び主張する決心をなせり。

西伯利亜出兵

初め支那の行動は連合国の干渉(1918—20 年)参加に限定せられ居た

るが、右干渉は露国革命後シベリア及北満州に於いて迅速に拡大しつつありたる混乱状態に関連し、浦塩斯徳に集積貯蔵せられたる莫大なる兵器軍需品の保護及東部戦線より西伯利亜経て退却中なりし「チェコ・スロバキア」軍約五万の撤退援助の両目的の為北米合衆国に依り提議されたるものなりき。右提議は受諾せられ且各国はシベリア横断鉄道の各自の特定部分を担任すべき七千名の遠征軍を派遣すべく、東支鉄道は支那軍の単独の責任に委することに協定せられたり。連合国軍隊と協力し鉄道の運行を確保する為一の特別の連合国鉄道委員会は1919年組織せられ右委員会の下に技術部及輸送部を配せり。1920年右干渉終了し連合国軍隊は日本軍を除きシベリアを撤退したるが、日本軍は既に過激派と公然敵対状態に入り居りたり。右戦闘は殆ど二ヶ年に亘り続行せり。1922年「ワシントン」会議後、日本軍亦撤退し同時に連合国委員会は其の技術部と共に消滅せり。

一九一七年露国革命勃発後支那は一八九六年露国に許容せる特権を廃止す

其の間支那は、東支鉄道の首脳者ホルヴァト将軍が鉄道地帯に一独立政権を樹立せんとする企図に失敗したる後、右地帯に於ける秩序維持の責任を引き受けたり(1920年)。同年支那は改造後の露亜銀行と一協定を締結し、且新ロシア政府と協定の締結ある迄暫時鉄道の最高支配権を執るの意向を表明したり。支那は又1896年の契約及会社の原定款に依り会社に許与せられたる諸便益を回収するの意向を表明せり。爾来会社督弁及董事四名並びに稽察局員二名は支那政府之を指名することとなれり。ロシアの優勢は又其後行われたる他の多くの措置に依り衰えたり。鉄道地帯に於けるロシアの武装兵は武装を解除せられ支那兵に代われりと。ロシア人の治外法権は廃止せられたり。其の法廷は侵入せられ且閉鎖せられたり。ロシア人は支那の法律、裁判及課税に服せしめられたり。ロシア人は支那警察が大なる権力を有し且統制不充分なりし為右警察に依り逮捕せられ且無期限に拘禁せらるべきこととなれり。

特別行政区域の形成

1922年、従来会社の行政に服し来たる鉄道付属地は奉天に対し直接責任を負う一行政長官の支配する東三省の特別区に改編せられたり。鉄道に付属する土地の行政にも亦干渉を受けたり。張作霖元帥はロシア新政府が

承認せらるるに先ち事実上ロシアの勢力範囲を清算し了りたるか私人の利益は右経過中に於いて甚だしき侵害を受けたり。ソビエト連邦政府が其の前政府の満州に於ける遺産を継承せる時には同鉄道は既に其の特権の大半を失い居たり。

一九一九――一九二〇年の「ソ」支協定

1919 年及 1920 年ソ連邦政府が為したる支那に関する政策の宣言は帝政政府が支那に於いて獲得したる特権殊に北満州に於いて獲得したる特権の完全なる放棄を包含せり。

一九二四年の協定

右政策に従い、ソ連邦政府は新協定に依りて既成事実の調整を行うことに同意せり。1924 年 5 月 31 日のソ支協定に依り東支鉄道は共同管理下の純商業的企業と成り支那も亦右企業に財政上の利益を獲得せり。然れどもソ連邦政府は広大にして範囲確定せざる権力を行使する総支配人の任命権を有し且右協定に依りソ連邦政府鉄道業務に優越せる勢力を振い又北満州に於ける其の経済利益の重要部分を保持し得たり。上述の如く北京に於いて支那政府と締結せられたる1924 年 5 月の協定は張作霖之を承認せん、自ら別個の協定を締結することを主張したり。1924 年 9 月調印せられたる右協定は其の条項殆ど同一なりしも之に依り鉄道の租借は80 年より60 年に短縮せられたり。右協定はソ連邦及満州に於ける張作霖政府間の友好関係の一期間を招来せざりき。

「ソ」連邦権益張作霖の侵略政策

1924 年の2 協定に於いて未解決に残されたる多くの問題を処理すべき会議の開催は各種の口実に依り延期せられたり。1925 年及 1926 年に於いて両度に亘り東支鉄道総支配人は張作霖軍隊の鉄道輸送を拒絶せり。右第2 次の拒絶事件に依り総支配人逮捕せられソ連邦は最後通牒を発するに至れり（1926 年 1 月 23 日）。而して此等は孤立せる事件には非ざりき。然るに支那官憲はロシアの利益に反し且ソ連邦政府及白系露人に依り均しく遺憾とせられたる政策を固執せり。

一九二九年満州に於ける「ソ」連邦勢力を清算せんとする支那最後の努力

満州が南京政府に服属したる後、国民主義精神は力を増し、且鉄道に対

し優越なる支配を維持せんとするソ連邦の努力は従前に比し一層反感を以て迎えられたり。1929 年 5 月、ロシアの利益範囲の残存せるものを清算し終らんとする企図行われたり。攻撃は各地に於ける支那警察のソ連邦領事館襲撃に依り開始せられたるが、支那警察は多数を逮捕し且ソ連邦政府及東支鉄道の雇用者が共産主義革命を陰謀し居たることを証する証拠を発見したりと主張せり。7 月、鉄道の電信電話機関は押収せられ且多数の重要なるソ連邦機関及企業は強制的に閉鎖せられたり。最後に、東支鉄道ソ連邦支配人は支那側任命の者に事務を引継ぐべき旨要請せられたるも同人は之を拒絶したる為其の任務遂行を禁止せられたり。支那官憲は自由にソ連邦幹部を免職して自己の指名者を以て之に代え、且多数のソ連邦民を逮捕し其の一部を追放せり。支那側はソ連邦政府が支那の政治社会制度に反対する宣伝を行わざる旨の誓約に背きたりとの理由に基づき右強力好意を正当なりとせり。ソ連邦政府は其の 5 月 30 日付公文に於いて右非難を否認せり。

「ソ」連邦の措置

残存せるロシア利権が強制に依り清算せられたる結果、ソ連邦政府は行動に出づべく決意したり。数度の公文交換を行いたる後、ソ連邦政府は支那より其の外交官及商務代表並びに東支鉄道に於ける其の職員全部を召還し且其の領土と支那との間の一切の鉄道交通を断絶せり。支那も亦同様にソ連邦との関係を断絶し一切の支那外交官をソ連邦領土より召還せり。ソ連邦軍隊は満州国境を越えて侵攻を開始し、1929 年 11 月には武力侵入となるに至れり。南京政府が紛争の解決を託せる満州官憲は敗戦し且甚だしく威信を失墜したる後、ソ連邦の要求を承認するの止むなきに至りたり。

一九二九年十二月二十二日「ハバロウスク」議定書

1929 年 11 月 22 日、ハバロウスクに於いて議定書調印せられ之に依り原状回復行われたり。右紛争中ソ連邦政府は不戦条約の締約国たる第三国よりの数多の覚書に対する解答に於いて常にソ連邦の措置は正当なる自己防衛の発動にして何等右条約違反として解釈し得ずとの態度を取りたり。

一九〇五年以後満州に関する日露関係

満州に於ける日本の利益は次章に於いて詳説せらるべきも之に先ち今満州に於けるロシアの地位を叙述するにあたり、1905 年以後の日露両国関

係に付略説するの必要あり。

一九〇七――一七年の協調政策

日露戦争の殆ど直後に於いて両国間に密接なる協調政策行われたることは興味ある事実にして、講和成るに及両国は北満州及南満州に於ける各自の利益範囲に関し満足なる合意に到達することを得たり。残存したる抗争の痕跡は満州の発展に活発に従事せんと欲したる他の諸国との論争に依り間もなく拭い去られたり。他の競争者に対する憂慎は二国融和の過程を促進したり。1907年、1910年、1912年及1916年の諸条約は二国を益々親密ならしめたり。

露西亜革命の日本に及ぼせる影響

1917年のロシア革命、次て為されたる支那国民に対する政策に関する1919年7月25日付及1920年10月27日付ソ連邦政府宣言並びに1924年5月31日付及1924年9月20日付ソ支協定は満州に於ける日露の了解及協調の基礎を粉砕せり。政策の此の根本的変更は極東に於ける三国の関係を全く改編せり。更に連合国干渉（1918―20年）は之に伴えるシベリアに於ける日本及ソ連邦軍隊の確執と共に日露関係の変更を大ならしめたり。ソ連邦政府の態度は支那の国民主義的願望に強き刺激を与えたり。ソ連邦政府及第三「インターナショナル」は現行条約を基礎として対支関係を維持せる一切の帝国主義諸国に反対する政策を採用したるを以て右両者が主権回収の闘争に於いて支那を援助することはあり得べきことなりとせられたり。此の形勢の発展は日本が隣邦ロシアに対して嘗て抱きたる一切の懸念及疑惑を復活せり。嘗て日本と戦争したる露国は其の戦争後数年の間に友邦及同盟国と成りたり。然るに今や右関係は変化し、北満国境を越え来る危険の可能性は再び日本の関心事となれり。

北部に於ける共産主義者の教義と南部に於ける国民党の排日宣伝との提携の有り得べきことを想像し、日本は益々日露両国の間に共産主義及排日宣伝に染まざる満州を介在せしめんとする希望を感ずるに至れり。日本の疑惧はソ連邦が外蒙古に於いて獲得せる優越なる勢力及支那に於ける共産主義の発達に依り最近数年間に於いて更に増大したり。

1925年1月、日本及ソ連邦間に締結せられたる協定は正規の関係を樹立せるも革命前に於ける密接なる協調を復活するに至らざりき。

第三章　日支両国間の満州に関する諸問題

1. 支那に於ける日本の利益

1931 年 9 月に至る四半世紀間に於いて満州と支那の他の部分との結合は追々強固となりつつあり夫れと同時に満州における日本の利益は増加しつつありたり。満州は明らかに支那の一部たりしも同地方に於いて日本は支那の主権行使を制限するが如き特殊の権利を獲得若しくは主張し両国間の衝突は其の当然の帰結なりき。

一九〇五年の条約に依る日本の権利

1905 年 12 月の北京条約に依り支那は従来ロシアの租借し居たる関東州租借地及ロシアの管理し居たる東支鉄道南部線中長春以南の鉄道の日本への譲渡を承認し尚追加協定に依り支那は安東奉天間の軍用鉄道を改良し之を十五ヵ年間経営する権利を日本へ譲与したり。

一九〇六年八月南満州鉄道株式会社創立せらる

1906 年 8 月、勅令に依り従前のロシア鉄道を安奉鉄道と共に引受け且管理する為南満州鉄道会社設立せられたるが、日本政府は鉄道、其の付属財産並びに撫順及煙台の価値ある炭鉱を提供する代償として同会社の株式の半額を其の有とし同会社を統制する地位を得たり。同会社は鉄道地帯に於ける行政を委任せられ徴税を許され且鉱業、電気事業、倉庫業其の他の諸事業経営の権限を与えられたり。

朝鮮の併合

1910 年、日本は朝鮮を併合したるか是に依り朝鮮人移住民は日本国民となり日本官吏は之等鮮人に対し法権を行使することとなりたる為、満州に於ける日本の権利は間接に増大したり。

一九一五年の条約及交換公文

1915 年一般に二十一ヶ条要求として知らるる日本の異常なる要求の結果、同年 5 月 25 日、日支両国間に南満州及東部蒙古に関する条約の調印及公文の交換行われたり。右協定に依り旅順及大連を含む関東州の元来二十五ヵ年間に租借期限、並びに南満州及安奉両鉄道に関する期限は総て九

十九ヵ年に延長せられ、日本臣民は南満州において旅行及居住し、各種の営業に従事し、且商業、工業及農業の為め土地を商租する権利を得、尚日本は南満州及東部内蒙古における鉄道及其の他或種借款に対する優先権並びに南満州における顧問任命に関する優先権を獲得したり。然れども1921—22年のワシントン会議において日本は右諸権利の中借款及顧問に関する権利を放棄したり。

　上記各条約中及其の他の諸協定は満州において重要にして且特殊なる地位を日本に与えたり。即ち日本は関東州租借地を事実上完全なる主権を以て統治し、南満州鉄道会社を通じて鉄道付属地の施政に当れるが、右鉄道付属地は数箇の都市並びに奉天及長春の如き人口大なる都会の広大なる部分を含み、此等地域において日本は警察徴税、教育及公共事業を管理したり。又日本は租借地に関東軍を置き、鉄道地帯に鉄道守備隊を駐屯せしめ、各地方に領事館警察官を配する等満州諸地方に武装部隊を存置し来れり。

満州に於ける日支両国間の政治、経済及法律関係の特殊性

　上記満州において日本の有する数多の権利の概説に依り満州における日支両国の政治、経済及法律関係の特殊性は明瞭にして、此の如き事態は恐らく世界の何処にも其の例なかるべく、又隣邦人の領土内に此の如き広汎なる経済上及行政上の特権を有する国は他に比類を身ざるべし。若し此の如き事態にして双方が自由に希望し又は受諾し、且経済的及政治的領域に於ける緊密なる協力に関する熟策の表現及具体化なりとせば、不断の紛争を醸すことなく之を持続し得べきも、斯かる条件を欠くにおいては右は軋轢及衝突を惹起するのみ。

2. 満州に於ける日支両国間の根本的利害関係の衝突

満州に対する支那の態度

　支那人は満州を以て支那の構成部分と見做し同地方を支那の他の部分より分離せしめんとする一切の企てに対して憤慨す。従来東三省は常に支那及諸列国が共に支那の一部と認むる所にして、同地方に於ける支那政府の法律上の権限に付異議の称えられたることなし。右は多数の日支間諸条約及協定並びに他の諸国際条約により明らかなる所にして又日本を含む諸国の外務省より正式に公表せられたる多数「ステートメント」に繰返され

居る所なり。

日支国防の第一線としての満州

支那人は満州を以て其の「国防の第一線」と考え居れり。支那の領土として満州は之と接壌する日本及ロシアの勢力が之等の地域より支那の他の地方に侵入するを防ぐ為の前哨とせられ居れり。北京を含む長城以南の支那へ満州より侵入することの容易なるは歴史上の経験に依り支那人の熟知する所なるが、右東北よりの外国の侵略を虞るる念は鉄道の発達に依り近年一層増大し且前年の事件中一層激化せられたり。

満州に於ける支那の経済的利益

支那人は又経済的理由によるも満州の彼等の為に重要なるを認むるものにして、数十年来彼等は満州を「支那の穀倉」と呼び更に近年に至りては之を近隣諸省の支那農民及労働者の季節的勤労地と認むるに至れり。

支那は全体として人口過剰なりと謂い得べきやは疑問なるも、或地方又は或省例えば山東省の如きが住民を他地方に移出する要ある程度に人口過剰なることは此の問題に関する権威者の一般に認むる所なり(付属書第三号の特別研究参照)。従って支那人は満州を以て現在及び将来に於ける支那の他地方の人口問題を緩和し得る辺境地方と認め居れり。

支那人は満州の経済的開発が主として日本人の力に依るとの主張を否定し、其論駁の根拠として特に1925年以降に於ける支那人の植民事業、彼等の鉄道建設及其の他の事業を挙げ居れり。

満州に於ける日本の利益、日露戦争より生せる感情

満州における日本の利益は諸外国の夫れと其の性質及程度に於いて全く異なるものあり。1904—5年、奉天及遼陽南満州鉄道沿線、鴨緑江、並びに遼東半島等、満州の野に於いて戦はれたる日本のロシアに対する大戦争の記憶は総ての日本人の脳裏に深く印せらるる所なる。日本人にとりては対露戦争はロシアの侵略の脅威に対する自衛の為生死を賭したる戦として永久に記憶せらるべく此の一戦に十万の将士を失い且二十億円の国費を消費したる事実は日本人をして此の犠牲を決して無益に終らしめざらんことを決心せしめたり。

然れども満州における日本の利益は其の源泉を日露戦役より十年以前に発す。1894—5年の主として朝鮮問題に関する日清戦争は大部分旅順及

満州の野に於いて戦われたるか、下関に於いて調印せられたる講和条約に依り遼東半島は完全に日本に割譲せられたり。日本人にとりてはロシア、フランス及ドイツが此の獲得したる領土の放棄を強制したる事実は日本が戦勝の結果満州の此の部分を獲得し之に依りて日本は同地方に対する道徳的権利を得、其権利は今尚存続するものなりとの確信に何等の変更を及ぼすものに非ず。

満州に於ける日本の戦略上の利益

満州はしばしば日本の「生命線」なりと称せられ、満州は現在日本の領土たる朝鮮に境を接す。支那四億の民衆が一度統一せられ強力となり且日本に敵意を有し満州及東部アジアに幡踞するの日を想像することは多数日本人の平静を撹乱するものなり。然れども彼らが国家的生存の脅威及自衛の必要を語る時多くの場合彼等の意中に存するのは寧ろロシアにして支那に非ず。従って満州における日本の利益中根本的なるものは同地方の戦略的重要性なり。

日本人中には日本はソ連邦よりの攻撃の場合に備える為満州に於いて堅き防禦線を築く要ありと考え居るものあり。彼等は朝鮮人の不平分子が隣接せる沿海州のロシア共産主義者と連携して将来北方よりの軍事的侵入を誘致し、又はこれと協力することあるべきを常に懼れ居れり。彼等は満州を以てソ連邦及支那の他の部分に対する緩衝地帯と認め居れり。殊に日本の陸軍軍人はロシア及支那との協定に依り、南満州鉄道沿線に数千の守備兵を駐屯せしむる権利を得たるは日露戦争に於ける日本の莫大なる犠牲に対する代償としては尠（スクナ）きに失し、同方面よりの攻撃の可能性に対する安全保障としては貧弱に過ぐると考え居れり。

満州に於ける日本の「特殊地位」

愛国心、国防の絶対的必要及特殊なる条約上の権利等の総てが合体して満州に於ける「特殊地位」の要求を形成し居れり。乍併日本人の懐く特殊地位の観念は支那又は他の諸国との間の条約及協定中に法律的に規定せられ居る所に局限せられ居るものに非ず。日露戦役の遺産たる感情及歴史的聯想並に最近四半世紀間に於ける在満州日本企業の成果に対する誇は「特殊地位」の要求の現実なる――捕捉し難きも――部分を為すものなり。従て特殊地位なる語を日本政府が外交用語として使用する時其の意味は不明瞭

にして、他の諸国が国際文書により之を認むることは不可能に非ずとするも困難なると蓋し当然なり。

　　日本政府は日露戦争以来随時ロシア、フランス、英国及米国より満州における日本の「特殊地位」、「特殊勢力及利益」又は「最高の利益」の承認を得んことを試みたるが、其の努力は単に部分的に成功したるに止まり斯かる要求が稍々明確に認められたる場合にも右承認を含む国際協定及了解の多くは時の経過と共に正式なる廃棄又は其他の方法に依り消滅するに至れり。旧ロシア帝政政府と結ばれたる1907年、1910年、1912年及1916年の日露秘密協約、日英同盟協約、1917年の石井・ランシング協定は其の例なり。

　　ワシントン会議に於ける1922年2月6日の九国条約の調印国（米、白、英、支、佛、伊、日、蘭、葡の九ヶ国）は、「支那に於いて一切の国民の商業及工業に対する機会均等」を維持する為、支那の「主権、独立並びに其の領土的及行政的保全を尊重すること」を約定することに依り、支那に於いて「特別の権利又は特権を求むる為」支那に於ける情勢を利用することを差控えることに依り、また「支那自ら有力且安固なる政府を確立維持する為、最も完全にして且最障害なき機会」を之に供与することに依り、満州を含む支那の各地方に於ける調印国の「特殊地位」又は「特別の権利及利益」の要求を広き範囲において非とせり。

　　然れども九国条約の規定及廃棄其の他の方法に依る前記諸規定の失効は日本人の態度に何等の変更を生ぜしめざりき。石井子爵が其の最近の「メモリアル」（外交余録）中に左記の如く述べ居るは良く同国人一般の意見を表明し居るものと謂うべし。

　　「石井・ランシング協定は廃棄せられたりと雖も日本の特殊利益は何等変化を受くることなく存在す。支那に於いて日本の有する特殊利益は国際協定に依り生じたるものに非ず。又廃止の目的物と為り得るものにも非ず」

　　満州に於ける日本の「特殊地位」の要求は支那の主権及政策に抵触す

　　上記満州に関する日本の要求は支那の主権に抵触し又国民政府の翹望と両立し得ざるものなり。蓋し同政府は支那領土を通じて今尚諸外国の有する特別の権利及特権を減殺し、且将来之等の特別の権利及特権の拡張を阻

止せんことを企図するものなるを以てなり。日支両国が夫々満州において
行い政策を考察せば此の衝突が益々拡大すべきこと自ら明らかとなるべし。

満州に於ける日本の一般的政策

1931 年 9 月の事件に至る迄 1905 年以来日本の諸内閣は満州において
同一の一般的目的を有したるものの如く為るもその目的は成就する為最も
適当なりとする方法に関して見解を異にし、又治安維持に対して日本の取
るべき責任の範囲に付稍意見の相違ありたり。

満州における彼等の一般的目的は日本の既存利益を維持発展し、日本
の企業の拡張を助成し且日本人の生命財産の充分なる保護を得るに在りた
り。以上の目的を実現する為に採られたる諸政策の総てに共通する一つの
主要なる特徴は満州及東部内蒙古を支那の他の部分と明瞭に区別せんとす
る傾向にして、右は満州における日本の「特殊地位」に関する日本人の観念
より生ずる自然の結果なり。日本の諸内閣の主張したる各特別なる政策、
例えば幣原男爵の所謂「友好政策」と故田中男爵の所謂「積極政策」との間に
如何なる相違ありたるとするも前記の特徴は常に共通のものなりき。「友
好政策」はワシントン会議の頃より始まり1927 年 4 月迄継続せられ、「積極
政策」之に代わり1929 年 7 月に至り更に「友好政策」に戻り1931 年 9 月迄外
務省の正式の政策として継続せられたり。右両政策の原動力たる精神には
着しき相違あり。「友好政策」は幣原男爵の言を以てせば「好意と善隣の誼
を基礎」とし、「積極政策」は武力を基礎とするものなり。然れども満州にお
いて採るべき具体的方策に関する両政策の相違は大部分満州における治安
維持及日本の利益保護の為為すべき行動の程度の如何に在りたり。

田中内閣の「積極政策」は満州を支那の他の部分より区別することを強
調し、其の積極的性質は「若し動乱満州及蒙古に波及しその結果として治安
乱れ、同地方に於ける日本の特殊地位及権利利益の脅威を受くる場合、其の
脅威の如何なる方面より来るを問わず日本は敢然其の権益を擁護すべき」
旨の腹蔵なき宣言に依って明らかにせられたり。田中政策は其以前の諸政
策が其の目的を満州における日本の利益の擁護に限定せるに反し満州にお
ける治安維持の責を日本国がとるべき旨を明らかにしたり。

日本政府は満州において有する特殊なる権益を維持発展せしむる為満
州においては概して支那の他の地方に於けるより一層強硬なる政策を行え

り。或内閣は武力に依る威嚇を伴う干渉政策に傾けり。右は1915年支那に対する二十一ヶ条要求の際に於いて殊に然るものありしが、二十一ヶ条要求並びに他の干渉及武力政策の得失に関しては日本国内に常に着しき意見の相違ありたり。

華盛頓会議の満州に於ける日本の地位及ひ政策に対する影響

ワシントン会議は支那の他の地方の事態に着しき影響を及ぼしたるも満州においては実際殆ど変化の見るべきものなかりき。1922年2月6日の九国条約は支那の領土保全及門戸開放に関する規定あり又同条約の効力は条文上満州にも及ぶべきものなるに拘らず、満州に付いては日本の既存利益の性質及範囲に鑑み単に其制限的適用ありたるのみ。前述の如く日本は1915年の条約に依り許与せられたる借款及顧問に関する特別の権利を正式に放棄したるも、九国条約は満州に於ける既存利益に基づく日本の要求を実質上何等縮小することなりき。

日本国の張作霖との関係

ワシントン会議より1928年の張作霖将軍の死に至る期間、満州に於ける日本の政策は東三省の事実上の支配者との関係に関するものなりき。日本は彼に或る程度の支持を与えたるか、特に前章記載の郭松齢謀叛の際に於て然りとす。張作霖将軍は日本の要求中の多数に反対したりと雖も、右支持の報償として、日本の希望に対し適度の承認を与えることを必要なりと感じたり。右希望は優越せる兵力に依り何時にても強要せられ得えるものなりを以てなり。張作霖は又時に北方に於けるロシアの敵対に対し、日本よりの支持を得られんことを希望せり。

換言すれば、日本の張作霖将軍との関係は日本の見地よりして相当に満足なるものなりき。

尤も彼の晩年には、彼が日本側主張の約束及協定の一部を履行せざりし結果右関係は次第に不穏を加えるに至れり。1928年6月における彼の敗北及奉天への最後の退却前の数ヶ月前に於いては、日本側の感情が張作霖に反対に激変せむとする徴さえ顕然たるに至れり。

日本国の満州に於ける平和及秩序維持の主張

1928年春、支那国民軍が張作霖軍を駆逐せんが為、北京に進軍中なりし時、田中男爵を首相とせる日本国政府は、日本国の満州に於ける「特殊地

位」に鑑み右地方に於ける平和及秩序を維持すべき旨の声明を発せり。国民軍が内乱を長城以北に及ぼさんとする惧れあるに至るや日本国政府は5月28日、指導者たる支那将軍に左の通告を送れり。

「満州の治安維持は、日本国政府の最も重視する所にして、苟も同地方の治安を紊し、若しくは之を紊すの原因を為すが如き事態の発生は、日本国政府の極力阻止せむする所なるが、既に戦乱京津地方に進展し其の禍乱、満州に及ぼさんとする場合には日本国は満州治安維持の為適当にして且有効なる措置を執らざるを得ざることあるべし。」

右と同時に、田中男爵は日本政府は「敗退軍又は其の追撃軍」が満州に入るを防止すべしとの一層確然たる「ステートメント」を発せり。

右遠大なる政策の宣明は、北京及南京の両政府よりの抗議を招致したるが、南京政府の「ノート」は日本の提議するが如き措置は、唯に「支那国内事項の干渉たるに止まらず、又領土主権相互尊重の原則の甚だしき侵犯」なりと陳述せり。

日本においても、田中内閣の右「積極政策」は一党より強き支持を受けたる一方、他の一党特に幣原派に依り全満州における治安維持は日本の責任に非ずとの理由を以て、非議せられたり。

日本国及張学良間の緊張せる関係

1928年、亡父の後を承けたる張学良と日本との関係は、当初より次第に緊張を加える所ありき。日本は、満州が南京に新に樹立せられたる国民政府より分立し居らむことを希望したるが、張学良将軍は南京政府の政権を承認せんことに傾き居たり。日本官憲より張学良に与えられたる中央政府に忠順を誓うべからずとの緊忽の忠言に付いては、既に記述する所ありき。然れども奉天政府が1928年12月、奉天における政府諸官所に国民党旗を掲揚したるとき日本政府は干渉を試むることなかりき。

日本と張学良将軍との関係は、緊張を継続し1931年9月直前の数ヶ月に於いては険悪なる軋轢の進展を見たり。

3. 満州に於ける日支鉄道問題

満州の国際的政策は主として鉄道政策

四分の一世紀間、満州に於ける国際政戦は、主として鉄道政戦なりき。

純粋なる経済上及鉄道運輸上の性質に付いての考量は国策の命ずるがままに無視せられ満州諸鉄道は、同地方の経済的発展の為、其の全能力を発揮したりと云うこと能わざるの結果を来せり。吾人の満州鉄道問題研究が示す所に依れば満州においては包括的にして相互に有益なる鉄道計画を達成せんとする協力は支那及日本の鉄道建設当事者及官憲間には殆ど皆無なりき。鉄道の拡張が主として経済的考量に依り決定せられたる西部カナダ及アルゼンチンの如き地方に於ける鉄道の発達に反し、満州に於ける鉄道の発達の歴史は主として日支両国間の拮抗問題に終始せり。従来満州に建設せられたる重要なる鉄道にして支那及日本は他の利害関係を有する外国間の公文交換を伴わざるものなし。

南満州鉄道は満州に於ける日本の「特殊使命」を遂行せり

満州に於ける鉄道の建設は、ロシアが投資及支配下に在りたる東支鉄道を以て始まり、日露戦争後南部に於いては日本の管理する組織即ち南満州鉄道之に代わり斯くして支那日本間の将来の対抗を必然ならしむるに至れり。南満州鉄道会社は名義上私営会社なりと雖、事実上においては日本政府の企業なり。其の職能は、単なる鉄道の経営のみに非ずして、政治的行政の特殊権能をも包含す。会社設立の当時より、日本人は同鉄道を純なる経済的企業として見たることなし。同社の初代社長たりし故後藤子爵は、南満州鉄道は満州に於ける日本の「特殊使命」を果さざるべからずとの基本的原則を定めたり。南満州鉄道網は発達して、能率高き良く管理されたる鉄道企業と成り、満州の経済的発展に大に貢献すると共に、支那人に対し学校、研究所、図書館及農事試験所の如き鉄道以外の諸施設に付模範を示す所ありき。然れども会社は其の政治的性質、日本における政党政治との連繋及何等相応せる財政的利益を期待し得ざる或種の大なる支出の為に生ずる制限及積極的障害を免れざりき。右鉄道会社の組織以来、其の政策は其の鉄道線に連絡せらるるが如き支那鉄道の建設に対してのみ資本を供給し、斯くして直通運輸協定の手段に依り、貨物の大部分を租借地内大連に於ける海運輸出の為南満州鉄道に転向せしめんとするにありき。此の種鉄道の投資に巨額の支出ありたるが、其の建設は或る場合においては、純粋の経済的根拠に照らし妥当なりと為し得べきやは疑問なり。殊に与えられたる大なる資本の前貸及包含せられたる貸付条件に鑑み然りとす。

**満州の南京に対する忠順宣誓に先つ支那の自国鉄道を建設せんとする
努力**

支那国土に南満州鉄道の如き外国管理の施設存在することは、自然支
那官憲に依り嫌悪せられ、条約及協定による権利及特権に関する問題は、日
露戦争以来常に発生せり。特に1924年満州に於ける支那官憲が、鉄道発達
の重要なるを認むるに至り、日本の資本より独立せる自身の鉄道を発達せ
しめんとことを企図したる後においては右問題は一層危機を孕むに至れ
り。本問題には経済的及軍事的考慮の両者包含せられたり。例えば打虎
山・通遼線は、新地域を開発し且北京・奉天鉄道の収入を増加せんが為、計
画せられたる次第なるが一方1925年12月の郭松齢謀叛は、独立に所有せ
られ運用せれるる支那鉄道の有することあるべき軍事的政治的価値を示す
所ありき。日本の独占を覆し其の将来の発達を妨害せんとする支那の試み
は、南京政府の政治的勢力が満州に及ぶの時期以前より存せしところにし
て例えば打虎山—通遼、奉天—海龍城及呼蘭—海倫の諸鉄道は、張作霖将軍
の時代に建設せられたるものなり。中央政府及国民党の助成に依り蔓延せ
る「利権回復」運動に依り強硬を加えたる1928年政権獲得後における張学
良の政策は、恰も当時南満州鉄道を中心とし集中せられたる日本の独占的
膨張的の政策と衝突を来たせり。

併行線に関する紛争

1931年9月18日及其の以後満州に於いて兵力に訴えたることを正当
なりとする日本側の主張に於いて、日本は其の「条約上の権利」の侵害せら
れたることを挙げ且1905年11月—12月、北京に於いて開催せられたる日
支会議中支那国政府の為せる左記趣旨の約束を支那が履行せざりしことを
強調せり。

「清国政府は南満州鉄道の利益を保護するの目的を以て該鉄道を未だ
回収せざる以前に於いては該鉄道付近に之と併行する幹線又は該鉄道の利
益を害すべき枝線を建設せざることを承諾す。」

満州に於ける所謂併行線問題に関する紛争は久しきに亘る重要なるも
のなり。同問題は1907-08年、日本国政府が右権利を主張し、支那が英国商
会との契約の下に新民屯—法庫門鉄道を建設せんとするを防止したる時、
初めて発生せり。1924年満州に於ける支那人が更新の意気を以て日本の

財政的関係より独立せる自身の鉄道を発達せしめんことを企図してより以来、日本政府は支那側の打虎山—通遼及吉林—海龍城鉄道建設に抗議したり。尤も右両鉄道は日本側の抗議にも拘らず完成開通せり。

「条約上の権利」又は「秘密会議録」の存在に関する問題

調査委員の極東到着以前にありては日本の主張するが如き約束が現に存在するやに付大いに疑問ありき。右紛争は久しきに亘る重要なるものに鑑み、委員は緊要なる事実に関する情報を得る為特別の苦心を払えり。東京、南京及北京に於いて一切の関係文書を審査せり。而して今や吾人は彼の所謂「併行線」に関する1905年11—12月の北京会議における支那全権の約束なるものは何れの正式条約中にも包含せられあらざること、彼の問題の約束は1905年12月4日の北京会議の第11日目の会議録中に存することを陳述し得。御仁は右北京会議録中に記載ある他彼の約束を包含する文書はほかに存せざることに付日本国及支那国参与員よりの同意を得たり。

論点たる真の問題

故に論点たる真の問題は、支那側に依り満州に於いて或る鉄道が右の如き約束に違反して建設せられたることを日本が主張するに足る「条約上の権利」ありや否やには非ずして、1905年の北京会議録中の前記記載辞句が「プロトコール」と称せらるると否とを問わず正式約定の効力を有し、其の適用において期間又は事情の制限なく支那側を拘束するの言質なりや否やの点にあり。

北京会議録中の右記載辞句が、国際法上の見地よりして拘束力ある約定なりや、若し然りとすれば、右に与えらるるべき妥当なる解釈は唯一なりやの問題の決定はまさに公正なる司法的裁判所に依り判定せらるるべき事項なり。

会議録中の右記載辞句の支那側及日本側の正式訳文に依れば「併行線」に関する右問題の辞句が支那側全権の意図も宣言又は声明なることに付いては疑いの余地なし。

右の如き意図の声明を為したることに付いては支那側においても之を否認せざりき。然れども論争を通し表明せられたる意図の性質に付、両国間に意見の相違ありき。日本は右使用せられたる辞句は南満州鉄道会社が同鉄道と競争線なりと認むる如何なる鉄道をも、支那が之を建設し又は建

設することを許可することを禁止するものなりと主張せり。他方支那側が
論争の辞句に包含せらるる唯一の意思表示は南満州鉄道の商業上の効用及
価値を不当に侵害するの故意の目的を以て鉄道を建設することなしとの意
図の陳述なりきと主張す。新民屯―法庫門鉄道計画に関する1907年の公
文の交換に際し、慶親王は支那政府を代表して日本公使林男爵宛1907年4
月7日付の通告中北京会議において日本全権は南満州鉄道よりの特定哩数
に依り「併行線」なる語の定義を定むることには同意を拒否したるも「日本
は満州の開発の為支那国の将来執ることあるべき措置を妨ぐるものに非
ず」と宣言することを述べたり。故に支那政府は日本が南満州に於いて鉄
道建設を独占する権利ありとする正当なる主張権を有したりとすることに
付いては常に之を否認し来れりと雖も右期間中事実上南満州鉄道の利益を
明白且不当に害する鉄道を建設すべからざるの義務あることは之を承認し
たるものの如し。

　支那側において何が併行線なりやに関する定義を希望したるも、右定
義は未だ定められたることなし。日本政府が1906-08年新民屯―法庫門鉄
道の建設に反対したるとき日本は「併行線」とは南満州鉄道より略35哩以
内に在る鉄道なりと思考したりとの印象を生ぜしめたるが1926年日本は
計画鉄道と南満州鉄道との間の距離は平均70哩以内なることを指摘し「競
争併行線」として打虎山―通遼鉄道の建設に抗議したり。充分満足なる定
義を作成することは困難なるべし。

斯くの如く広く且非専門的に表示せられたる字句の解釈に於ける困難

　鉄道運用の見地より言えば「併行線」とは「競争線」を云うものにして即
ち他の鉄道より其の吸集し得べかりし貨物の一部を奪う線なりと云うこと
を得べし。競争的運輸は、地方的運輸及直通運輸の両者を包含す。而して
特に後者を考慮するときは、「併行線」の建設に反対する規定は如何に甚だ
広き解釈となり得べきやを知ること困難ならず。尚又何が「幹線」又は「枝
線」なりやに付ても支那および日本間に何等の意見の一致なし。此等の語
は、鉄道引用の見地よりすれば変化するものなり。打虎山より北方に延長
する北京支奉天鉄道は、当初其の鉄道当局に依り枝線と見做されたり。然
るに同線が打虎山より通遼迄完成せられたる後においては、之を幹線と見
ることを得。

並行線に関する約束の解釈が、支那及日本間の激しき論争に至らしめたるは素より自然の数なりき。支那側は南満州に於いて自己の鉄道を建設せむることを企てたるが、殆ど総ての場合において、日本よりの抗議を惹起せり。

満州に於ける支那鉄道建設に対する日本借款より起る諸問題

客年9月の事件発生以前、日支間の緊張を加えしめたる鉄道問題の第二類は、満州に於ける支那国政府の諸鉄道建設の為、日本側が資金を貸付けたる契約より生ぜるものなり。遅延金及利子をも含み、1億5千万円の現在価格に達する日本資本は、左記支那鉄道即ち吉林—長春、吉林—敦化、四平街—洮南及洮南—昂々渓鉄道並びに或る狭軌鉄道の建設に支出せられたり。

日本側は支那側が右債務の支払を為さんとせず、又債務に対し適当なる準備を為さんとせず、尚又日本人鉄道顧問の任命に関するが如き契約中の諸条項を実行せんとせざることを訴えたり。日本側に於いては日本側財団が吉林—会寧鉄道の建設に参与することを許さるべしとの支那政府に依り為されたる約束を、支那側が履行せんことを繰返し要求したり。右計画線は吉林—敦化鉄道を朝鮮国境まで延長し、日本の為其の海港より満州の中心に至る新たなる海陸路の利用を可能ならしめ、他の鉄道と連結して内地との交通を短縮すべし。

支那側の弁疏

支那側は債務支払履行を弁疏し、右は正常なる貸借行為に非ることを指摘せり。支那側は貸付は主として南満州に於おける鉄道建設を独占せんが為、南満州鉄道に依り為されたること、其の目的は元来軍事的及政治的なること及何はともあれ新線は甚だしく過剰に資本を投下せられたるものなるを以て少なくとも当分は建設費及債務の償還に必要なる金銭を収得することの財政上不可能なることを主張したり。支那側は債務不履行の何れに付いても、公正なる審査を為すにおいては、其の行為の正当なることを証すべしと抗議せり。

吉会鉄道については日本側の主張せる協定の道徳的及法的効力をも排除せり。

南満州鉄道株式会社は支線綱設定を要望せり

借款論争を自然惹起せしむる此等鉄道協定に関連し存在せる一定の事

態ありき。南満州鉄道は事実上何等支線を有せず。而して貨物及旅客運輸を増加する為栄養線綱を発達せしむることを欲せり。仍て会社は仮令借款が近き将来において償還せられ得るの望少なき場合と雖も新線の建設に出資することを乱せざりき。又初期の借款が行悩める場合にもより以上の出資を継続することを乱せざりしなり。

斯かる状態に於いて、而して新規に建設せられたる支那線が南満州鉄道の栄養線たるの役目をなし且或程度迄右南満州鉄道の勢力下に運営せられたる限り、南満州鉄道は借款の償還を強制する為何等の特別の努力を為さざりしものの如く、支那線は常に増大する借款義務を負いて運用せられたり。然れども此等鉄道線の或るものが新規の支那鉄道綱に連結せられ且1930年乃至1931年に南満州鉄道と激烈なる競争を起こすに及んで借款の不償還は直に苦情の目的となりたり。

西原借款

此等借款協定の或る場合に於ける他の紛議を生じ易き要素は其の政治的性質なり。吉長鉄道が南満州鉄道会社の支配下に置かれ、同線未済の負債が1947年に満期となる長期借款に借換えられたるは所謂「二十一ヶ条要求」の結果なり。所謂「満蒙四鉄道協定」の結果として1918年に出資せられたる前渡金二千万円は其の使用の目的に付何等の制限なく「安福派」軍閥政府に対し為されたる所謂「西原借款」の一なり。吉会鉄道建設を目的とする1918年の借款呼び契約に関連して安福派に一千万円を前渡せるも西原借款の結果なり。支那国民の感情は「西原借款」に関し其の交渉以来激発せるにも拘らず支那政府は右借款を拒絶せざりき。斯かる状態に於いて支那国民は借款契約の条件を履行すべき道徳的義務を殆ど感ぜざりき。

吉会鉄道計画

日支関係に於いて特に重要なるは吉会鉄道計画に関する問題なり。最初の問題は1928年建設完成せる吉林より敦化に至る線の一部に関連す。爾来日本側は支那側が建設を目的とする日本前渡金を鉄道収益に依り保障せらるる正規の借換せざるを理由とし不平をならし又支那側が同線の為日本人会計吏の任命方を拒絶し契約に違反したる旨を主張せり。

一方支那側は建設費が日本人技師の見積高より遥かに大なるのみならず、憑証提出せられたる金額をも超ゆること大なる旨を主張し、建設費の決

済せらるる迄正式に同線を引受くることを拒絶し且右決済に至る迄日本人会計吏を任命すべき何等の義務をも負わざる旨を抗議せり。

　何等の主権または政策の問題を包含せるかかる特定の技術的問題は明らかに仲裁又は司法的解決に付するを適当とするも、本問題は未解決のまま残され日支人相互の憤怨を助長せしめたり。

敦会線計画

　一層重大且複雑なるは敦化より会寧に至る鉄道の建設に関する問題なりき。同線は長春より朝鮮国境に至る鉄道を完成すべく右国境に於いて付近の朝鮮港に通ずる日本鉄道と連絡すべし。中部満州に直接開通し且木材及鉱物資源の豊富なる地方を開拓すべき本線は経済的価値あると共に日本にとりて大なる戦略的重要性を有すべし。

　日本側は本線は必ず建設せらるべく且右資金供給に与からざるべからず旨を固執し又支那側は既に右の為の条約上の保障を与へたる旨を主張せり。又日本側は支那政府が1909年9月4日の間島協定に於いて「日本政府と商議の上」同線を建設すべきことを約せる旨指摘せるが右約束は満州の間島地方に対する朝鮮従来の要求を日本が放棄する代償として与えられたるものなり。後年1918年に於いて支那政府及日本諸銀行は本線建設の為の借款に対する予備的協定に署名し右協定に依り銀行側は支那政府に一千万円の金額を前渡せるが右は支那側より見れば協定の効力を阻害する事実たる西原借款の一なり。

　然れども此等契約は孰れも無条件に且特定期日前に支那側をして日本資本家の右鉄道建設参加を認めしむべき確定的借款契約協定には非ざりき。

一九二八年五月の契約

　本線建設の為の正式且確定的締約は1928年5月、北京に於いて署名せられたる旨主張せられたるも、其の効力に関しては幾多の疑義あり。斯かる契約は5月13日乃至15日に非常的状態の下に張作霖元帥当時の北京政府の交通部代表者に依り確かに調印せられたり。然れども支那側は当時国民軍に依り強抗に圧迫せられ且将に北京を撤退せんとせる張元帥は若し彼にして本契約を承認せざれば奉天への退去は危殆に瀕すべしとの日本側の威嚇に因る「強迫の束縛」の下に、其の代表者をして署名せしむることを承諾せるものなる旨を主張す。又張作霖元帥自身も果たして契約に署名せ

りや否やは論争の点なりき。張元帥の歿後奉天東北政治委員会及張学良元帥は共に本契約は形式に欠陥あり且束縛の下に締結せられ北京内閣又は東北政治委員会に依り未だ嘗て批准せられたることなしとの理由に依り契約を承認することを拒絶せり。

敦会線建設に対する支那側反対の理由は日本の軍事的及戦略的目的を恐れ且国家の権利及利益は日本海より満州への日本の新たなる接近に依り威嚇せらるべしと信じたることに在りたり。

此の特殊の鉄道問題は元来財政的又は商業的問題に非ずして日本及支那の国家的政策の衝突を包含するものなりき。

運輸連絡に関する紛争

又支那及日本線間の運輸連絡措置、運賃率問題及大連港と営口(牛荘)の如きは支那港との間の競争に関する問題もありき。

1931年9月迄に支那政府は独力にて全長約千基米の鉄道を布設し所有し、且運用せり。其の最も主なるものは奉天海龍間、海龍吉林間、齊々哈爾克山間、呼蘭海倫間及打虎山通遼間(京奉綱支線)鉄道にして、支那政府は京奉鉄道及日本資本の投ぜられたる線即吉長線、四洮線及洮昂線を所有せり。現在の紛争勃発前二年間支那側は此等諸線を一大支那鉄道綱として運用せんとし且支那港たる営口(牛荘)可能の場合には胡蘆島において海口を有する支那側運用線路のみを使用して能う限りの一切の貨物を運輸すべく努力せり。其の結果支那側は其の全鉄道綱に亙り運輸連絡の措置をなすと共に重要線区に於いて支那線と南満州鉄道との間に同様なる運輸連絡協定をなすことを拒絶せり。日本側は右差別は普通少なくとも満鉄線の一部を通過し大連に出口を求むべき北満よりの多大の貨物を南満州鉄道より奪取するものなる旨主張せり。

鉄道運賃競争

此等運輸連絡紛争と併行して激烈なる運賃率問題日支両線間に勃発せり。右は支那側が打通線及吉海線の開設後賃率を低減したる1929年乃至1930年に始まれり。支那線は当時支那銀貨幣価値の暴落し従って此等諸線に於ける銀貨による賃率が南満州鉄道における金円による賃率より低廉となりし結果自然的利益を得たるもののごとし。日本側が支那の賃率の余りに低廉なる為右は不正競争を構成するものなる旨を主張せしも、之に対

し支那側は其の目的は南満州鉄道の場合の如く元来収益を獲得するに非ずして国土を発展せしめ地方住民をして能う限り低廉に市場に到達せしむるに在る旨答え居れり。

国産製造品の利益を計る為の国家的差別の主張

将又運賃率引下げの競争に偶然随伴して双方より夫々他方は其国民の利益の為賃率の差別を又は秘密なる割戻金の支払をなす旨主張せり。日本側は支那側が支那産品を外国品より低廉に支那線上を運搬せしめ得るが如き鉄道等級の区分をなし居るを非難し且支那管理の諸港に向け支那線を通じ仕向けらるる自国産品及貨物に対し普通よりも低廉なる賃率を与えるを難詰せり。又支那側においては之に対し南満州鉄道は秘密の払戻をなすを非難し特に日本の運送業者が其の取扱に係る貨物に対し南満州鉄道の正規表定賃率より低廉なる運賃率を掲げ居ることを指摘せり。

此等問題は全く技術的にして複雑なるものなりき。而して日支双方が夫々相手方に対して為せる非難は何れが妥当なるやを決定するは困難なりき。本問題の如きは鉄道委員会又は司法的決定(本報告諸付属特別研究第一参照)に依り通常解決せらるべきものは明らかなり。

港湾に関する紛争

満州に於ける支那官憲の鉄道政策は胡蘆島に於ける新たなる港湾発展に集中せられたり。牛荘は第二次港たる唯だ胡蘆島の完成に至る迄主港たるものなり。事実満州のあらゆる部分に至るべき数多の新規の鉄道が計画せられたり。日本側は支那側に依り実施せられたる運輸連絡の施設及低廉なる賃率の為通常大連に向けて運輸せらるべき多くの貨物を大連より奪取し右状態は1930年に特に顕著なりし旨主張せり。日本側は南満州鉄道に依り大連に向け輸出せらるる輸出貨物は1930年に於いて百万米噸以上の減少を見たるに牛荘港は現実に前年より増加を示したる旨指摘せり。然れども支那側は大連に於ける貨物の減少は主として一般不況及普通南満州鉄道に依り輸送せらるる貨物の大部分を占むる大豆の着しき暴落に起因せるものなる旨を指摘せり。支那側は又牛荘に於ける貨物の増加は新規の支那鉄道線に依り最近開拓せられたる地方よりの貨物運送の結果なりと主張せり。

是等数多の鉄道問題を全般的に考察するに其の問題の多くは其の性質

技術的にして且通常の仲裁又は司法手続に依り解決し得らるるものなること明白なれ共或るものは国家的政策に深き根拠を有する紛争より来れる日支両国間の激甚なる競争に因れるものなり。

一九三一年の日支鉄道交渉

事実上一切の此等鉄道問題は尚 1931 年の当初に於いて未解決なりき。此等懸案たる鉄道問題に付政策を調和せしむるを目的とする会議の開催方に付日支双方に依り為されたる最後的且友好的努力は1月より夏迄断続的に継続せられたり。所謂木村・高間の商議は何等の効果を齎さざりき。交渉が1月に開始せられたる際には双方に誠意の証跡ありたり。然れども種々の遅延あり(右に対して日支双方に責任あり)結局周到なる準備をなせる正式会議は現今の扮装の起これる時には尚行われ居らざりき。

4. 1915 年の日支条約及交換公文並びに関係問題

二十一ヶ条要求並に一九一五年の条約及交換公文

鉄道紛争を除き1931 年 9 月に起これる重大なる日支問題所謂二十一ヶ条要求の結果たる1915 年の日支条約及交換公文より勃発せるものなり。漢冶萍鉱山(漢口付近)問題を除き1915 年に締結せられたる他の協定は或る新たなるものに替えられ又は日本国に依り自発的に放棄せられたるものあるを以て此等論争は左記諸規定に関するものなりき。

(一) 関東州租借地の日本所属期限を九十九年(1997 年)に延長すること。

(二) 南満州鉄道及安奉鉄道の日本所属期限を九十九年(夫々2002 年及 2007 年)に延長すること。

(三)「南満州」の内部に於いて即ち条約に依り或は外国人の居住及商業の為に開放せられたる地域外に土地を賃借するの権利を日本臣民に許与すること。

(四) 南満州の内部に於いて旅行し、居住し及営業をなすの権利並びに東部内蒙古に於いて日支合弁に依り農業の経営をなすの権利を日本臣民に許与すること。

日本人の是等特権及特典享有の適法なる権利は全然 1915 年の条約及交換公文の支那政府を拘束することを否認し来れる。如何に技術的説明又

は議論をなすとも「二十一ヵ条要求」なる語は事実 1915 年の条約及交換公文と同意語なること並びに支那国の目的は此等より自由となることに在りとする信念を支那国国民、管理の心情より奪うことを得ず。1919 年のパリ会議において支那は是等の条約は「日本国の開戦強迫の最後通牒の強迫に基づき」締結せられたものなりとの理由に依り其の廃棄を要求せり。1921 年乃至 1922 年のワシントン会議においては支那代表は「此等諸協定の公平及公正に付及従って其の根本的効力に付」問題を提示せり。而して支那が 1898 年ロシアに許与せる関東州の二十五年租借期限の満了に先立つ少し以前即ち1923 年 3 月に支那政府は日本に対し1915 年の諸条項の廃棄要求の通告を発し且「1915 年の条約及交換公文は支那に於ける世論に依り頑強に非難せられ来れる旨」を述べたり。支那は1915 年の条約は「根本的効力」を欠如せる旨を主張せるに依り情勢に依り実行するを便宜なりとせる場合を除き満州に関する諸条項の実施を怠れり。

日本は痛烈に支那に依る屢次の条約上の権利侵害を非難せり。日本は 1915 年の条約及交換公文は正当に署名せられ完全なる効力を有するものなる旨を主張せり。確かに日本国における世論の相当部分は当初より「二十一ヵ条要求」に同意せざりき。次いで日本の言論界は本政策を非難すること普通となれり。然れども日本政府及国民は満州に関する此等条項の有効なることを固執するに一致し居るものの如くなり。

関東州租借期限及南満州及安奉鉄道特権の延長

1915 年の条約及交換公文の二大重要規定は関東州租借期限を二十五年より九十九年に並びに南満州及安奉鉄道の特許を同じく九十九年の期限に延長せるの規定なり。此等延長は1915 年の条約の結果なること並びに以前の政府の租借せる地域の回復は支那に於ける外国の利益に反対せる国民党の「国権回復」運動中に含まれ居ることの二つの理由に依り関東州租借地及南満州鉄道はしばしば煽動の目的となり又時には支那外交部の抗議の目的となれり。

斯かる問題は実際政策の背後に隠れ居りたるも、中央政府に対する満州の忠順を宣言し満州に国民党の勢力の伝播を許容したる張学良将軍の政策に依り此等問題は1928 年以後深刻性を加え来れり。

又 1915 年の条約及交換公文に関連して南満州鉄道の回収或は之を純

粋なる経済的企業と為す為に其の組織より政治的性質を剝奪せんとする運動ありたり。之が資本金及利子を払戻たる上此の鉄道を回収し得べく定められたる最も早き時期は1939年なりしを以て、単に1915年の諸条約を廃棄することに依りては支那は南満州鉄道を回収すること能はざりしなるべし。何れにせよ、支那が此の目的のために必要なる資金を調達し得べかりしや否やは極めて疑問とすべき所なり。支那国民党「スポークスマン」等が折に触れ南満州鉄道の回収を唱えたることは、日本人にとりては一の刺激となり彼らの合法的権益は之に依りて脅威を感ぜしめられたり。

　元来南満州鉄道の妥当なる機能の範囲如何に関する日支間の紛議は、1906年、同鉄道会社組織当時より存続し居れり。もちろん技術的には同鉄道会社は日本の法律の下に株式組織の民間企業として成立し居るものにして、実際上全然支那の管轄県外に在り。特に1927年以来、在満支那人諸団体の間には南満州鉄道よりその政治的行政的権能を剝奪して之を「純粋なる商業的企業」たらしめんとする運動ありたるが、此の目的貫徹の為の具体案は何等支那に依りて提議せられざりしものの如し。

　事実上該鉄道会社は一つの政治的企業たりき。日本政府は其の株の過半数を掌握し居り該会社は同政府の代理者たり。即其の業務上の方針は密接に同政府に依りて左右せられたるが故に、日本において新内閣成立の際は該会社の高級社員は殆ど常に更迭せられたり。更に又、該会社に常に、日本の法律の下に警察、徴税及教育を含む広汎なる政治的行政的機能を付与せられ居れり。従って該会社より此等の権能を剝奪することは、当初考案せられ其後拡大せしめられたる南満州鉄道の「特別使命」全部を放棄せしむることを意味したりしならむ。

鉄道付属地

　南満州鉄道付属地内における日本の行政権に関し、特に土地の取得、徴税、鉄道守備隊の駐屯に関しては無数の問題を生じたり。

　鉄道付属地は鉄道線路の両側数ヤード以外に、大連より長春並びに奉天に至る南満州鉄道全系統の沿線に於ける日本の「鉄道市街」と称せらるる十五市邑を含む。右鉄道市街の中、奉天、長春及安東市街の如きは人口稠密なる支那人町の大地域を包含し居れり。

　鉄道付属地内において南満州鉄道が実際上完全なる市政を施行する権

利を有する法律的根拠は、1896年露清鉄道原約、当該鉄道会社に対し「其の土地に対する絶対的且排他的行政権」を付与せる一条項に存す。露国政府は1924年の蘇支協定にいたる迄、又南満州鉄道に関する限り東支鉄道の本来の権利を継承する日本政府はその後に於いても共に此の規定を以て鉄道付属地の政治的支配権を許与するものと解釈せり。然しながら支那側においては、1896年の原約中の他の条項は該規定が警察、徴税、教育及公共工事の管理等の如き広汎なる行政権を許与することを意味したるものに非ることを明瞭にし居る旨を主張して前記解釈を絶えず否定し来れり。

土地に関せる紛争

又鉄道会社の土地取得に関する紛争はしばしば繰り返されたる所なり。1896年の原約中の一条項に基づき、鉄道会社は「鉄道線路の建設、経営及之が保護の為実際上必要なり」私有地を買入又は賃借する権利を有せり。然れども支那側においては日本側より多くの土地を獲得せんが為に此の権利を乱用せんとしてる旨主張せり。其の結果、南満州鉄道会社と支那地方官憲との間には殆ど紛争の絶ゆることなかりき。

鉄道付属地内に於ける課税権に関する紛争

鉄道付属地内における課税権に関する主張の相違はしばしば紛議を醸したり。日本側は元来鉄道会社が「其の土地に対する絶対的且排他的行政権」を許与せられ居ることに其の主張の根拠を置けるに反し支那側は主権国の権利を以て其の論拠とせり。

要するに実際の事態としては該鉄道会社は其の鉄道付属地に居住する日本人及外国人に対し租税を賦課徴収せるも、支那官憲はかかる権力を行使せずに単に法律上徴税権を有することを主張せるに止まれり。累次発生せる紛議の好例としては、日本側鉄道に依りて大連に輸送する為南満州鉄道市街迄列車にて運搬せらるる大豆の如き産物に対し支那側が課税せんとした場合に起これるものを挙げ得べし。支那側の主張は、該課税をなさざるにおいては南満州鉄道に依りて輸送せらるる産物に特恵を与えることとなるべきが故に、右は日本「鉄道市街」の境界に於いて当然統税として徴収すべしと云うに在り。

日本の南満州鉄道沿線に鉄道守備隊駐屯権に関する問題

日本の鉄道守備兵に関する問題は、間断なく紛争を惹起せり。此等の

問題は、既に言及せる満州に於ける国是の根本的衝突を示すものにして、夥しき人命を犠牲にしたる数多の事変の原因を成せり。日本が此等守備隊駐屯権を有すと主張する法律的根拠は、既にしばしば引用せる如く1896年の原約中存在する東支鉄道に対し「其の土地に対する絶対的且排他的行政権」を許与せる条項に在り。露国は、右条項に依り露国軍隊の該鉄道を守備する権利が認められたるものと主張し支那は之を否定せり。1905年の「ポーツマス」条約中に、日露両国は該両国間に於いて一km毎に二十五人を超過せざる鉄道守備隊を保有する権利を留保せり。然るに其の後同年中、日支間に締結せられたる北京条約に於いては、支那政府は日露間に協定せられたる右の特別条項に同意を与えざりき。然れども日支両国は、1905年12月22日の北京条約付属協定第二条中に左の如く規定せり。

「清国政府は満州に於ける日露両国軍隊並びに鉄道守備隊の成るべく速やかに撤退せられむことを切望する旨を言明したるに因り日本国政府は清国政府の希望に応せむことを欲し若し露国に於いて其の鉄道守備隊の撤退を承認するか或は清露両国間に別に適当の方法を協定したる時は日本国政府も同様に照弁すべきことを承諾す若し満州地方平静に帰し外国人の生命財産を清国自ら完全に保護したるに至りたる時は日本国も亦露国と同時に鉄道守備兵を撤退すべし」

日本側の主張

本条は日本の条約上の権利の根拠をなすものなり。然れども露国は1924年の蘇支協定に依り其の守備兵を撤去し右駐兵権を放棄せり。然るに日本は、未だ満州には平静確立せず且支那は外国人を完全に保護する能力を有せざるを以て尚鉄道守備隊を駐屯せしむべき有効なる条約上の権利を有する旨を主張せり。

支那側の主張

日本は右鉄道守備隊の使用を弁護するに当り、条約上の権利を根拠とするよりも寧ろ「満州の現存事態の下における絶対的必要」を根拠として論することに漸次傾き来れり。

支那政府は日本の主張を絶えず論駁し、日本鉄道守備隊の満州駐屯は法律上においても事実上においても正当ならず、支那の領土及行政的保全を害するものなる旨を主張せり。前掲北京条約の規定に関しては支那政府

は右は単に一時的性質なる事実上の事態を声明したるものにして、一ッ権利殊に永続的性質を有する権利を付与したるものと言う能わざる旨を主張せり。更に、露国は既に其の守備兵を撤去し満州の平静は回復せられ、且支那官憲に於いて日本の守備隊の妨害なき限り他の在満諸鉄道に対して為しつつあるが如く南満州鉄道に対しても適当の保護を与え得きが故に、日本は其の守備隊を撤退せしむる法律上の義務を負うものなる旨主張せり。

日本の鉄道守備隊の鉄道附属地外に於ける活動

日本の鉄道守備隊に関し発生したる紛争は鉄道付属地内における駐屯及活動に限られたるものに非ず。右守備隊は日本の正規兵にして、彼らはしばしば其の警察職権を持続地域に及ぼし又或は支那官憲より許可を得ず或は之に通告をなすことなく、鉄道付属地外において演習を挙行することしばしばなりき。

此等の行動は、官辺民間を問わず支那人一般に特に嫌悪せられ、不法なるのみならず不幸なる事変を挑発するものと見做されたり。右演習は屡次誤解を生ぜしめ且支那人の農作物に夥しき損害を与え之に対し物質的賠償を為すも其の醸されたる反感を緩和し得ざりしなり。

日本領事館警察

日本の鉄道守備隊問題に密接に関連したるものに日本領事館警察の問題あり。右警察は単に南満州鉄道沿線のみならず哈爾賓、齊々哈爾及満州里の如き都市並びに多数の在満鮮人の居住する地域たる所謂間島地方等在満各日本領事館管轄地域に存する日本領事館及同分館に所属せり。

領事館警察の満州駐在に対する日本側の主張

日本側は領事館警察存置の権利は治外法権に当然付属するものなり即此等警察官は日本臣民を保護し懲罰する上に必要なるを以て右は領事館裁判所の司法的権能の延長に過ぎずと主張せり。事実日本の領事館警察官は、其の数は満州に於けるよりも少なきも、満州以外の支那諸地方に在る同国領事館にも所属し居るものにして右は治外法権条約を有する他の諸国の一般に実行し居らざる所なり。

実際問題として日本政府は同地方の現状に於いて特に日本の重大なる利益存在し多数日鮮人の居住し得る点を顧慮せば、満州に於ける領事館警察の存置は必要事なりと信じ居るものの如し。

日本の主張に対する支那側の否定

然れども支那政府は日本が満州に於ける領事館警察存置の理由として提示せる右論旨を常に反駁し、屡本問題に関し日本に抗議し満州の如何なる地方にも日本の警察官を駐在せしむる必要なきこと、警察官問題は治外法権と関連せしめ得ざること、並びに斯かる警察官の存在は何等条約上の根拠を有せず支那主権の侵害なることを主張せり。事の当否は姑らく措き、領事館警察の存在は多くの場合に於いて右警察官と支那地方官憲との間に重大なる紛争を誘発せり。

日本人の南満州内地に於ける往来、居住及営業の権利

1915年の日支条約は「日本国臣民は南満州に於いて自由に居住し各種の商工業其の他の業務に従事することを得」と規定せり。右は一つの重要なる権利なるが、支那の他の地方に於いては外国人は一律開市場を除く他、居住及営業を許容せられ居らざるに付。右規定は支那側にとりては好ましからざるものなりき。支那政府は治外法権撤廃せられ外国人が支那の法律及司法権に服するに至る迄は右特権を許さるることを以て其の政策となし居れり。尤も南満州に於ては右権利には一定の制限を付せられたり。即日本人は南満州の内地を旅行中旅券を携帯し且支那の法規を遵守することを要せり。然れども日本人適用せらるべき支那の法規は先ず支那官憲に於いて「日本領事館と協議の上」に非されば施行し得ざるものとせり而して多数の場合に於いて支那官憲の行動は該条約の規定に合致せざりき。尤も右条約の有効性に関しては支那側は常に争い来れり。南満州の内地に於ける日本国臣民の居住、往来及営業に対して制限の存したる事実並びに日本人又は他の外国人の開市場外居住或は建物賃借契約の更新を禁止したる命令及規則が諸種の支那人官吏に依りて発せられたる事実に関しては、支那参与員が本調査委員会に提出したる公文書中に何等論及せられ居らず。然れども日本人を南満州及東部内蒙古の多数の市邑より退去せしむる為又は支那側家主が日本人に家屋を貸付くることを阻止する為しばしば苛酷なる警察手段に依り支持せられたる官憲の圧迫が加えられたるは事実なり。又日本側の声明したる所に依れば、支那官憲は日本人に旅券を発給することを拒み不当課税に依り彼らを悩まし又1931年9月以前数年間は日本人を拘束すべき規則は先ず日本領事に提出すべきことを約せる前記条約中の規定を

遵守せざりし趣なり。

支那側の弁解及説明

支那側の目的は満州に於ける日本人の例外的特権を制限し以て東三省に対する支那の支配を強固ならしなんとする其の国策の実行に在りたり。彼らは1915年の条約を以て「根本的効力なきものと看做し其の理由の下に彼等の行動を正当なりとなし、更に条約の規定には南満州と局限しあるに拘らず日本人は満州全地域に亘り居住営業を為さんと試みるものなることを指摘せり。

右論争は一九三一年九月の事件に至る迄絶えず両国を刺激せり

日支両国の相反する国家的政策及目的に鑑みれば、右条約規定に関し絶えず痛烈なる論争の生ずるは殆ど避け得ざりし所なり。両国は共に斯かる形勢が1931年9月の事件に至る迄の彼等の相互関係に漸次刺激を加重し来れることを認容するものなり。

商租権問題

南満州内地に於ける居住並びに営業の権利と商租権とは密接なる関係を有す。右商租権は1915年日支条約に基づき日本人に許与せられたるものにして関係条文左の如し。

「日本国臣民は南満州において各種商工業の建物を建設する為又は農業を経営する為必要なる土地を商租することを得」

右条約締結の際の両国政府間に於ける交換公文は「商租」とは支那文に依る「三十箇年より長からざる期限付きにて更新するの可能性ある租借」(不過三十年之長期限及無条件而得続租)を含むものなりと定義せり。

日本文は単に「三十箇年迄の長き期限付きにて且無条件にて更新し得べき租借」となり居れり。其結果日本側商租は日本側の選択に依り「無条件に更新せらるるものなりや否や」の問題に関し争論発生せるは蓋し自然なり。

支那人側は日本人が満州に於て土地を獲得せむとする願望は其の租借に依ると、買入に依ると将又抵当権に依るの如何を問わず、之を以て「満州を買収せむとする」日本の国策の証左なりと解釈せり。従って支那官憲は挙つて右目的を達せむとする日本人の努力を妨害せんと試みたり。而も右は1931年9月直前三四年間、支那の「国権回復運動」が最も猖獗を極みたる

時、其の勢益々旺んとなれり。

支那官憲が日本人の土地買収、其の完全なる所有権に依る保有、又は抵当に依る之が留置権の獲得に対し、峻厳なる規則を制定せるは元来前記条約が単に商租権を許与せるに過ぎざりしことに鑑み、其の正当なる権利に基づきたるものと見るを得べし。然れども日本人側は土地に対する抵当権の設定を禁止するは条約の精神に悖る旨苦情を述べたり。

北満州並に南満州に於ける日本人の土地租借抵当権設定及買収

然るに支那官吏は条約の効力を認めず、日本人が土地を租借せむとするに当りては省令又は地方庁の命令を以て極力之を妨害し、日本人に土地を租借せしむる時は之を刑法を以て罰すべしとなし、或は其の租借にあたり事前に特別手数料及税を課し、或は地方官吏に訓令し日本人への土地譲渡の許可を禁止せんか為刑罰の脅威を以てせり。前記の如き各種の障害ありしにも拘らず、事実日本人は広大なる地域に亘る土地を端に租借せるのみならず、売買又は一層普通に行われ居る抵当流の方法に依り実際其の所有権を取得せり。但し之等地権が支那の法廷に於いて其の効力を認められしや否やは別なり。

之等土地に対する抵当権は日本の金融業者、殊に大規模なる金融会社にして其の中の或るものの如きは特に土地の取得を目的として組織せられたるものの手に落ちたり。今日本の官庁よりの資料によれば、全満州並びに熱河に於ける日本人租借地の全面積は1922—25年に於ける約80,000エーカーより1931年における500,000エーカー以上に増加せり。——右の内日本人が支那法又は国際条約の何れによるも商租権を有せざる北満州に於いて僅少なり。

日本人の土地獲得は其の売買によると租借によるとを問わず「満州に於ける支那人の生存を脅かす」経済的及政治的脅威たるべきなり。

支那側の点

支那人間に広まれる見解に従えば、朝鮮人は日本よりの移住民をして朝鮮人にに代らしめ又は政治的は経済的は殊に所有土地の処分を余儀なくせしむることにより朝鮮人の生活を窮乏化し自然満州への移住を招来せんとする日本政府の深謀より出たる政策の結果其母国を追われたるものなりとす。即ち支那側の見解に依れば、朝鮮人は其の母国に於いて外国人の政

府に依りて統治せらるる一切の重要なる官職を日本人に専有せらるる「被圧迫民族」たるを以て彼らは政治的自由及経済生活の途を求めんが為、満州に移住するの止む無きに至れるなりと云う。朝鮮移民の九割は農民にして、其の殆ど全部は米の耕作に従事す。然して彼らは当初支那人により経済的に有用なるものとして歓迎せられ、其の所謂圧迫に対し自然に流露せる同情よりして大いに好意を寄せられたり支那側をして言わしむれば若し日本にして朝鮮人が帰化して支那臣民たることを拒まず、且彼らに必要なる警察の保護を与うと称する口実の下に、彼らを満州内に追躡することなかりせば、朝鮮人の満州植民は重大なる政治的乃至経済的問題を惹起するに至らざりしなるべしと謂う。支那側においては特に1927年以後満州の支那官吏が単なる小作人若は労役者以外の朝鮮人の満州定住を制限せんと努めたることを以て直ちに「虐待」の例証と看做さるることを拒絶せり。

支那側の非議に対する日本側の否認

日本側に於いては支那側の右の如き猜疑心が支那側の鮮人虐待の主たる原因なるべく認むるも、朝鮮人の満州移住を奨励する為に確定的政策を採りつつありとの非難は力強く之を否定し、「日本としては之に対し特に奨励し又は制限を加え居らず、朝鮮人の満州移住は自然の大勢の然らしむる所にして何等政治的乃至外交的動機に基かざる一現象と見る他なし」と述べたり。従って彼等は「日本は朝鮮移民を利用して之等二地方を併合せむと企画しつつありとの支那側の危惧は全然其の根拠なし」と声明せり。

朝鮮人問題による日支関係激化並に朝鮮人の犠牲

之等の相互に妥協し難き両者の見解は商租権、法権及日本の領事館警察に関する諸問題を先鋭化するの結果を招来し之等は朝鮮人にとり最も不幸なる情勢を齎し、日支関係をして益々悪化せしめたり（報告書付属書第九章参照）。

朝鮮人と商租権問題

現在日支両国間には特に朝鮮人に対し開港場以外の地において定住、居住又は営業を為すの権利、又は所謂間島地方以外の満州各地において租借又はその他方法に依り土地を取得するの権利を許与又は拒否せる何等の協定存せず。

土地商租問題に関する日支交渉

然りと雖も間島以外の満州各地に居住する右商租権問題の重要性に鑑み、1931年に至る十年間において、少なくとも三回に亘り日支直接交渉に依り何等かの協定に到達せんとの企図行われたり。而して商租権と治外法権撤廃の両問題を共に取上げ、即ち満州に於て日本人は治外法権を廃棄し、支那人は日本人に土地の自由なる租借を許すの建前による解決案か、両者において考究せられつつありしものと信ずべき理由あるも、右商議は遂に不成立に終われり。

右日本人の土地商租権に関する日支間の長期に亘る紛争は記述の他の諸問題と等しく、其の依りて来る源は相反する両国の政策に於ける根本的の不一致にありて、国際協定の侵犯呼り又は之が反駁の如きは右両国政策の根本的目的に比すれば左まで重要なるものに非ず。

5. 満州に於ける朝鮮人問題

日本の法律に依り日本の国籍を有する八十万朝鮮人の満州内居住は日支間の諸政策の衝突の先鋭化を促進せり。右自体の結果諸種の紛争惹起せられ為に朝鮮人自身犠牲となり厄災と惨禍とを蒙りたり（本報告付属書第九章参照）。

朝鮮人が売買又は租借に依り満州において土地を取得するに対し支那の反対ある処、日本側は朝鮮人も等しく日本臣民として1915年の条約並交換公文によりて獲得せる商租権に均霑すべきものなりと主張して之に反対せり。而して日本人は朝鮮人が帰化によりて支那臣民たることを否認せるが為茲に亦二重国籍の問題発生せり。朝鮮人の関し及保護の為日本領事館警察の使用は支那側の忿満を招き屢日支警察の衝突を惹起せり。殊に朝鮮の北境に接する間島地方の如く朝鮮人の居住者四十万人に及び同地支那人をして1927年に至るに及満州に於ける朝鮮人の自由居住を禁止するの政策を採るに至らしめたり。右政策は日本人側より許すべからざる弾圧の一例として目せられたり。

満州に於ける朝鮮人の地位に関する日支協定

満州に於ける朝鮮人の地位及権利は主として日支間に於ける左記三協定に依りて決定せらる。即ち1919年9月4日の間島協約、1915年5月25

日の南満州及東部内蒙古に関する条約及交換公文並びに1925 年 7 月 8 日の所謂「三矢協定」之なり。而して朝鮮人の場合に起こり来る二重国籍に関する機微なる問題に関しては日支間に何等の協定なし。1927 年に至るに及び支那官憲は一般に事実朝鮮人は満州に対する「日本の侵略並びに併合の前衛」なりと信ずるに至れり。斯かる見解よりすれば日本が朝鮮人の帰化して支那臣民たることを認めず殊に日本の領事館警察が常に朝鮮人に対する監視を怠らざる以上、朝鮮人の数も恐らく四十万人を超過すべく而して彼等は各処に広く分布し特に満州の東半部に拓れり。彼等は吉林省中朝鮮の北境に近き地方に多く居住し。又東支鉄道の東部線地方、松花江下流地方及朝鮮の東北部より烏蘇里、黒龍両江の流域地方に及ぶ露支国境方面に迄浸潤し、彼等の居住並びに定住は隣接ソ連邦の領域内迄溢れ出たり。加之其の祖先が数代以前に移住して満州民族となり終せる朝鮮人の群れ夥多ある一方、朝鮮人中には日本の羈絆を脱し帰化支那臣民となれるものがある為、朝鮮人中事実間島以外の満州各地において所有権又は租借権により農地を取得せるもの多数に上れり。然れども彼等の大部分は支那人地主との間に収穫分配の基礎の上に結ばれたる租借契約に依り、単なる小作人として米作に従事するに過ぎず。而してその契約は概ね一年乃至三年の期限に限られ、且其の更新も地主の自由に委せらるるを常とす。

朝鮮人の商租権に関する日支協定に付いての紛争

支那側は朝鮮人が間島地方以外の満州各地において土地を買収し、又は租借する権利を否認す。何となれば本件に関する日支間の唯一の協定は1909 年の間島協約あるのみにして右は其の適用を此の地方に局限し居ればなり。故に唯支那臣民たる朝鮮人のみか満州内地において土地を売買し又は居住並びに土地租借の権利を有す。支那政府は朝鮮人の満州に於ける土地の自由租借の権利に関する要求を否認し間島地方に限り朝鮮人に対し土地取得の特殊なる権利を伴う居住権を与え之等朝鮮人が支那の法権に服すべき旨を取極めたる1909 年の間島協約は、夫自身「当時日支間において懸案となり居たる地方的諸問題を互譲によりて解決せんとせる」独立せる取極めなりしなりと称せり。即ち間島協約は支那が朝鮮人に農地を所有すべき特殊権利を与える代償として、日本が之等朝鮮人に対する法権を放棄すべき筋合いのものたりしなりと謂う。

支那側の主張

斯て日支両国は1910年日本が朝鮮を併合したる後も、同協約を遵守し来りし処、支那側においては1915年の条約並びに交換公文は、右間島協約の規定に変更を加えること能わず。何となれば特に新条約はその一条項中において「満州に関する日支現行各条約は本条約に別に規定するものを除くの他一切従前の通実行すべし」と規定すればなりと謂う。而して間島協約に関し、何等の例外規定は設けられざりき。尚支那政府は1915年の条約並びに交換公文は間島地方には適用せられず、何となれば右地方は地理的に云えば南満州——由来本語は地理的並びに政治的に誤用せられたり一部には属せざればなりと謂う。

日本側の主張

右支那側の見解に対しては1915年以来は絶えず論争し来れり。彼等は曰く、1910年朝鮮併合に依り朝鮮人は日本臣民となりたるを以て日本臣民に対し南満州に於ける居住権並びに東部内蒙古における合弁農業企業参加を許与したる南満州並びに東部内蒙古に関する1915年の条約並びに交換公文の規定は等しく朝鮮人に対しても適用せらるべきものなりと。即ち日本政府の主張に依れば、間島協約の条項中1915年の協約の条項と矛盾するものは後者よりて廃棄せらるべく（間島において朝鮮人の獲得せる権利は実に日本が右地方を支那の一地方なりと承認せる結果に基づくものなるを以て）支那側が間島協約を目して全然独立なる取極めなりと主張するは全然誤れるものと謂うべし。日本側においては若し満州に於ける朝鮮人に対し他の日本臣民の許与せられたると同様の権利及特権を要求せざらんか、右は朝鮮人に対し差別を設くることとなるべしと主張す。

日本側が満州に於ける朝鮮人の土地獲得を奨励せる理由の一つは日本のために米穀の輸出を得んとする願望による処右願望は今迄の処一部分達成せられたるのみなり。何となれば恐らく1930年産出の700万ブッシェル以上の米の中約半分が地方的に消費せられ、残部の輸出は制限せられたればればなり。日本側は朝鮮人小作人は支那人地主の為に荒蕪地を開墾して利益あるものと為したる後不法に追放せられたりと主張す。

両国主張の相異の朝鮮人の地位に及ぼす影響

一方支那側は可耕低地が米を産出することを等しく希望するも彼等は

土地其のものが日本人の手に入ることを防がんが為に概ね朝鮮人を小作人又は労働者として雇用せり茲に於て多数の朝鮮人は土地を所有せんが為に、帰化支那臣民と為りたるが、其の中の或者は地権を獲得すると共に、之を日本人の土地抵当会社に譲渡せり。右は即ち日本人自身の内に於ても日本政府が朝鮮人の帰化して、支那臣民たるを認むべきや否やに関し議論の分かれたる一理由を暗示し居るものと云うべし。

満州に於ける朝鮮人の二重国籍問題

1914 年制定の支那国籍法によれば外国人にして支那に帰化し得べきものは其の本国法によりて他国に帰化することを認められ居る者に限れり。然るに1929 年 2 月 5 日の修正支那国籍法は支那の国籍を取得するが為には、外国人が其の原国籍を喪失することを要する旨の規定を包含す。従って朝鮮人は日本の法律の下においては其の帰化を認めざる旨の日本側主張に関係なく支那に帰化せり。日本の国籍法は未だ嘗て朝鮮人がその日本国籍を喪失することを認めず。而して1924 年の改正国籍法は「自己の死亡によりて外国の国籍を取得したる者は日本の国籍を失う」との趣旨の条項を有すれども未だ右一般的法律を朝鮮に適用すべき旨の勅令の発布を見ず。然るにも拘らず満州に於ける朝鮮人の多数は支那に帰化し、或地方殊に比較的日本の領事官憲の手の及ばざる地方に在りては其の数全朝鮮人人口の5％乃至 20％に達せり。又偶々満州の国境を越えソ連邦の領域に移住したるものにして同国の市民と成りたるものもあり。

朝鮮人の二重国籍問題が支那の政策に及ぼせる影響

右朝鮮人の二重国籍問題は支那の国民政府及満州の地方官憲をして挙げて朝鮮人の無差別的帰化を喜ばず、彼らが仮に支那国籍を取得したる後将来農地獲得に関する日本の政策の手先となるべきことを恐れしむるに至れり。1930 年 9 月、吉林省政府の公布せる同省内の土地売買に関する規則中には「帰化朝鮮人が土地を買収せんとするときは右朝鮮人は永久に帰化市民として居住する手段として右土地を買収せんと欲するものなりや、将又日本人の為に買収せんと欲するものなりやを審査するを要す」との規定あり。然れども地方官吏は時に上級官庁の命令を励行することあるも屢省政府及南京内政部の認可を擁する正式証明書の代わりに、仮帰化証を発給する等其の態度一貫せざるものあり。之等地方官吏中特に日本領事館より

遠隔の地にある者は朝鮮人よりの出願ありし場合は、直ちに斯の種証明書の発給を承諾せることしばしばなり。而して彼等は時に実際朝鮮人に帰化を強制し、或は之を国外に追放せるが、右は日本側の政策及帰化手数料より得る収入の影響を受けたるものなり。更に支那人側の主張する所によれば日本人中には之を傀儡地主として使用し又は之等帰化朝鮮人よりの譲渡により土地を獲得せんが為にしばしば自ら通謀して朝鮮人帰化の企みを為すものある由なり。然れども概括的に言えば、日本官憲は朝鮮人の帰化を排し出来得る限り其の法権を彼らに及ぼしたり。

朝鮮人の関係する警察権の主張の衝突問題

日本が治外法権を有する結果としての満州に於ける領事館警察維持の権利の主張はこれに朝鮮人の関連する場合絶えざる紛争の原因を形成せり。朝鮮人が彼等の為にする表立ちたる日本の干渉を欲すると否とに拘らず、日本の領事館警察は特に間島地方においては啻に保護的任務に当りたるのみならず、朝鮮人居宅の捜索及差押を行うの権利を欲しいままに支那側、右は独立運動者又は共産若は反日運動に関係ありとの嫌疑ある朝鮮人に対し特に甚だしかりき。又支那警察は支那の国法を実施し、治安を維持し又は「不逞」鮮人の活動を抑圧せんと努るにあたり、しばしば日本警察と衝突せり。東部奉天省において支那側が「不逞鮮人団」を弾圧し、且日本側の要求に応じ「不逞鮮人」を引渡すべきことを協定せる1925年所謂「三矢協定」に規定せる如く、日支両国の警察は幾多の場合において協力の実を挙げたるも、実情は寔（マコト）に不断の紛争軋轢に他ならず、斯くの如き形勢が紛擾を惹起すべきは当然のことなりき。

間島の特殊問題

朝鮮人問題並びに之に基づく間島地方に関する日支関係は特に複雑且重大なる性質を帯びるに至れり。間島（日本語にては「カントウ」朝鮮語にては「カンドウ」と呼ばる）は遼寧奉天省の延吉、和龍、汪清の三県より成り、且慣習上は日本政府の態度により明らかなるが如く、琿春県をも包含し、之等四県は図們江を隔てて朝鮮の東北隅に隣接す。

日本の間島に対する態度

日本側は間島地方に対する鮮人の伝統的態度を叙説し、1909年の間島協約により該地方が支那又は朝鮮の孰れに帰属すべきやの問題が、永久に

終結を告げたりと認むることを欲せず。蓋し右は、同地方に於ける朝鮮人住民数は圧倒的多数を占め、耕作地の過半は朝鮮人の耕作する所に係り、「同地方は事実上一鮮人地域と看做し得る程度に朝鮮人は牢固たる地歩を樹立したり」と云うに在り。日本政府は間島において他の満州各地に比し一層朝鮮人に対し法権並びに監視を励行せんことを主張し四百名以上の領事館警察官を多年同地に配置したり。又日本領事館は朝鮮総督府の任命せる日本人官吏と協力し同地方において行政的性質を有する広汎なる権力を行使し、其の職能は日本人学校、病院及政府の補助する朝鮮人に対する金融機関の維持を包含せり。該地方は米田を耕作する朝鮮移民の自然的捌口と看做さるる一方、永く朝鮮独立主義者共産団体及其の他不逞反日徒輩避難の地なるを以て政治上においても特殊の重要性を有す。而して又間島は1920年琿春における鮮人の反日暴動により明らかにせられたる如く朝鮮における独立運動勃発後日本が朝鮮統治の全般的問題と密接なる政治的諸問題を有したる地方なり。

この地域の軍事的重要性は即図們江の下流が日本、支那及ソ連邦領土の境界を為すものなるにより明白なり。

間島協約に関する日支解釈の抵触

間島協約は「従来の通り図們江北の農耕地における朝鮮人の居住」は支那国より許容せらるべき旨、右地域に居住する朝鮮人は以後支那国地方官憲の管轄裁判に服すべき」旨、右朝鮮民と支那人と同等の待遇を許与せらるべき旨、及右朝鮮人に関する民事及刑事一切の事件は「支那国官憲に依り審問及判決せらる」べしと雖も一命の日本国領事官は法廷に出席するを許さるべく特に人命に関する重要事件において然り。而して特別の支那司法手続きの下に「支那国官憲に対し再審を要求する」の権利を有すべき旨を規定せり。

然れども日本側は司法問題に関する限り1915年の日支条約及各処は間島協約を超えて適用あるものにして1915年以後は朝鮮人は日本国臣民として日支諸条約の下に治外法権に関する一切の権利及特権を認められるべきものとなす立場を取来れり。此の議論は支那国政府に依り認められたることなく、支那側は若し朝鮮人の農耕地居住権に関し間島協約の適用あるものとせば、朝鮮人は支那の管轄裁判に服すべしと規定する同条約の諸

条項も亦適用あるものなる旨を固執せり。日本側は朝鮮人の農耕地居住を認むる条項は間島において右土地を購入及商租するの権利を意味するものと解し、支那側は右解釈に反対して、同条項は字句通りに解せらるべきものにして只帰化に依り支那国臣民と為れる朝鮮人のみ同地において土地購入権を有すと為す立場をとり居れり。

朝鮮人土地所有の現状は変態なり

故に現状は変態を呈す。何となれば間島には支那に帰化せざる朝鮮人にして支那国地方官憲の黙認に依り土地所有権を獲得せる者あり。尤も朝鮮人自身は通例間島において土地購入権を得る為には支那国籍を取得すること必要条件なりと認め居れり。日本側当局の統計に依れば間島（琿春を含む）の可耕地の半以上は朝鮮人の「所有」と為り居る処、同時に同統計は同地の朝鮮人の15％強が帰化して支那国臣民となり居れることを認め居れり。右土地「所有」者か之等帰化朝鮮人なりや否やは茲に確言することを得ず。斯かる状態は自然幾多の不規則及不断の紛争を惹起し、日支警察官憲間の公然たる衝突となりたること一再ならず。

支那の朝鮮人圧迫に対する日本の主張

日本側は1927年末頃より一般的排日運動に伴い、支那国官憲の煽動に依り満州に於て朝鮮人迫害運動起これることを主張し又此の圧迫は満州諸省が南京国民政府に忠誠を宣言せる後更に熾烈を加えたることを陳へ居れり。或は朝鮮人を強制して支那に帰化せしめ、或は米田より彼らを駆逐し、或は彼らに移住を強制し、或は彼らに不当の納金及法外なる租税を課し、或は彼らをして家屋及土地の商租または貸借契約を結ぶことを禁じ、或は彼らに幾多の暴力を加えるなど、朝鮮人に対する支那の徹底的圧迫政策の証拠として満州に於ける中央及地方の支那官憲の発したる多数の命令の翻訳委員会に提供せられなり。日本の主張に依れば右惨虐なる運動は特に「親日」朝鮮人に対して行われ、日本政府より補助金を受ける朝鮮人居留民会は迫害の的となり、朝鮮人により又は朝鮮人の為に設立せられたる支那学校に非る学校は閉鎖せられ、「不逞鮮人」は朝鮮人農民より脅迫に依り金銭を徴収し又之に暴行加害を為すことを許され、又朝鮮人は支那服を着用することを強制せらるると共に其の悲惨する状態に対し日本の保護又は補助に依頼する一切の権利を放棄するのやむなかりし趣なり。

満州官憲が帰化せざる朝鮮人に対し差別的命令を発せる事実は、支那側之を否定することなし。此種命令の数及性質特に1927年以後のものを見るに満州の支那官憲は一般に日本の司法管轄を伴う限り朝鮮人の侵入は一つの脅威にして反対すべきものと認めたること明白なり。

朝鮮人問題に対し委員会の払ひたる特別の注意

日本の主張の重大なるに鑑み、又満州に於ける朝鮮人の哀れむべき状態に鑑み、委員会は本問題に対し特別の注意を払えり。而して本委員会は必ずしも右非難の全部が事実を適当に叙述せるものとは認めず又朝鮮人に適用せられたる右抑圧手段の或ものか全然不正なりしものと断ずることなしと雖も、只満州の或地方における朝鮮人に対する支那の行動に関する右一般的記述を確認するものなり。委員会は其の満州滞在中朝鮮人団体の陳情委員と称する多数の代表者を引見せり。

満州に於ける此の大なる少数民族なる朝鮮人の存在が土地商租、司法管轄権及警察、並びに1931年9月事件の序幕を為せる経済的抗争に関する日支紛争を複雑ならしめたることは明白なり。大部分の朝鮮人の欲する所は只自由は其の生計を稼がすとするに在るも、其の中には支那人又は日本人より又は其の両者より「不逞鮮人」と呼ばるる団体ありて、右は日本の統治より朝鮮を独立せしめんと主張する者及其の同志、共産主義者、職業的犯罪人密輸入者及売薬業者を含む職業的犯罪人、並びに支那人匪賊と結託して其の同胞より恐喝取財を行い又は金銭を強制する者を包含し居れり。朝鮮人農民自身も其の無智、無用心により又彼らより更に狡猾なる家主又は地主より借財せる為、しばしば自ら圧迫を招来せり。

朝鮮人待遇に関する支那側説明

朝鮮人が支那側見解よりすれば日本の満州に対する一般政策の不可避的結果たる争論の渦中に不識々々巻き込まれることは別とし、支那側は所謂朝鮮人「圧迫」なるものの多くは之を圧迫と称すること正当らず、又朝鮮人に対し支那の執れる方法の或ものは日本国官憲より現に是認せられ又は黙過せられたりと述べ居れり。支那側は朝鮮人の大部分は極めて反日的なること、日本が彼等の故国を併合せることに終始反対なること及朝鮮人移民は決して其の故国を去るを欲せるものに非ず政治的及経済的困難に基づく苦痛の為に故国を去れるに他ならずして一般に満州に於て日本の監視よ

り免るるを欲するものなることを忘るべからずと主張し居れり。

所謂一九二五年「三矢協定」

支那人は朝鮮人に対し或程度の同情を示すも、1925 年 6—7 月の「三矢協定」の存在に付注意を喚起し、之を以て日本国民が「不良分子」と目し又朝鮮における日本の地位に対する脅威と目する朝鮮人の行動は支那側官憲においても進んで之を抑圧したることの証拠となし、又日本側において支那側の朝鮮人「圧迫」の実例として挙げんとするが如き右記行為の或ものに対し日本自身公式の承認を与えたる証拠なりと為す。外間には未だ広く知悉せらるるに至らざる本協定は朝鮮総督府警務局長と支那奉天省警察長官との間に商議せられたるものなり。同協定は東部奉天における「朝鮮人結社」（反日的のものと推定せらる）の禁遏に関する日支警察官の協力を目的とするものにして「支那官憲は朝鮮官憲の指名せる朝鮮人結社の首領を直ちに逮捕し之を引渡すべき」こと、及「不良分子」たる朝鮮人は支那警察官之を逮捕し裁判所及処罰の為め日本警察官に引渡すべきことを規定す。故に支那側は「朝鮮人に待遇に関し或種の禁遏的手段を執れるは主として此の協定に実際的効果を与えるを目的とす。若し右手段が支那国官憲の朝鮮人圧迫を示す証拠として考えらるるにおいてはかかる圧迫手段は仮令事実なりとするも是れ主地して日本国の利益の為に行われたるものなり」と主張す。更に支那側は「自国農民との激烈なる経済競争に鑑み、支那官憲が其の同胞の利益を保護する手段を講ずる固有の権利を執行すべきは実に当然なり」と主張す。

6. 萬寶山事件に於ける反支暴動

萬寶山事件の一九三一年九月事件に対する関係

萬寶山事件は中村大尉事件と共に満州に於ける日支間の危機を齎せる直接原因として広く認めらる。然れども前者の真重要性は大に誇張せられたり。何等死傷者を出さざりし萬寶山事件の誇大なる報道は日支両国民間に強き反感を起こさしめ、朝鮮に於いては支那在留民襲撃の大事を惹起したり。此の反支暴動は次いで支那における排日ボイコットを復活せしめたり。事件其者としては萬寶山事件は過去数年間満州に発生せる日支両国軍又は警察隊の衝突を誘発せる他の数事件よりも重大なりしものには非ず。

支那人地主及支那人仲介人間の水田商租契約は支那国官憲の正式承認を要せり

萬寶山は長春の南約十八哩に位する一小村にして伊通河に沿う低湿地なり。此の地において支那人仲介業者赫永徳なる者 1931 年 4 月 16 日付契約を以て長農水田公司の為め支那人地主より広大なる一画の地を商租せり。契約中には県長其の条項の承認を肯せざる場合には契約は無効なるべき旨規定せられたり。

此の土地は支那人仲介人より朝鮮小作人に対し再商租せられたり

此後暫時にして右商租者は此の土地全部を朝鮮人の一団に再商租せり。此の第二契約は其の実施に付官憲の承認を必要とする規定を含まず、又朝鮮人が灌漑用水溝及付属の小溝を構築することを当然のことと看做し居たり。赫永徳は先ず支那人地主との原商租契約に対する支那側の正式承認を取付くることなくして朝鮮人農民に対し此の土地を再商租せる次第なり。

朝鮮人が支那人所有土地を横切りて灌漑水道を開発したること同地方の支那側反対を惹起したる主因なり

第二契約締結直後朝鮮人は数哩に亙り灌漑溝又は水道の開穿を開始し、伊通河の水を引きて此の低湿地に之を分かち此の土地を水田耕作に適せしめんとせり。然るに何れの商租契約の当事者にも非る支那人の大面積の耕地伊通河と朝鮮人の右商租地との間に介在したるを以て、右水道は該耕地を横断せり。朝鮮人は灌漑溝に依り其の土地に充分の水を引き来る為伊通河に堰を築かんとせり。

支那農民は灌漑溝工事の停止及朝鮮人の退去を要求せり

既に相当の長さの灌漑溝完成せる後水道に依り其の土地を横切られたる支那農民は群れをなして放棄し萬寶山当局に抗議し彼らの為め干渉せんことを請願せり。其の結果、支那地方官憲は現場に警察官を派し朝鮮人に対し即時開穿を停止し同地より退去せんことを命じたり。之と同時に在長春日本領事館は朝鮮人保護の為め領事館警察官を派遣せり。日支代表間の地方的交渉は問題の解決に成功せざりき。其後暫時にして両国側共増援警察官を派して互いに抗議、反駁すると共に交渉を試みたり。

長春に於ける支那及日本官憲は共同調査を行ふことに意見一致せり

6月8日、両国側は其の警察隊を撤去し萬寶山に於ける事情の共同調査を行うことに意見一致せり。此の共同調査の結果、原商租契約は若し支那県長の承認なきときは全契約「無効」となるべき旨の規定を有したること並びに県長の承認は未だ与えられたることなきこと明らかとなれり。

要領を得ざる調査

然るに共同調査員は其の調査の結果に付何等意見の一致を見るを得ざりき。即ち支那側においては灌漑溝の開穿は之に依り其の土地を横切られたる支那農民の権利を侵害せること明白なりと主張し、日本側においては朝鮮人は其の商租手続の誤謬に付何等責任無かりしも不拘、右誤謬の故に排斥せらるることは公正ならず故に其の工事継続を許容せらるべきなりと主張せり。其後幾何もなく朝鮮人は日本領事館警察官の援助を得て水道開穿を続行せり。

七月一日事件

7月1日の事件は斯かる事態より惹起されたり。同日、灌漑溝に依り其の土地を切断せられたる四百名の支那農民の一隊は農具及矛槍を携えて朝鮮人を駆逐し灌漑溝の大部分を埋立てたり。茲に於て日本領事館警察官は右暴徒を散逸せしめ朝鮮人を保護する為め発砲したるも何等被害はなかりき。支那農民は撤退し日本警察官は朝鮮人が水溝及伊通河の堰を完成する迄現場に屯留せり。

7月1日事件以後支那地方官憲は在長春日本領事に対し日本領事館警察官及朝鮮人の行動に付抗議を継続せり。

朝鮮に於ける反動暴動

萬寶山事件よりもはるかに重大なりしは朝鮮に於ける本事件に対する反動なりき。日本語及朝鮮語新聞に記載せられたる萬寶山における事態、殊に7月1日事件の誇大なる報道の結果は朝鮮全道に互り激烈なる反支暴動の続発を見たり。右暴動は7月3日、仁川に始まり急速に他市に伝播せり。

支那居留民の受ける生命財産の重大な損害

支那側は其の広報に基づき、支那人百二十七名虐殺せられ、三百九十三名負傷し、二百五十万円に達する支那人財産は破壊せられたりと称す。

朝鮮に於ける日本官憲の所謂責任

尚支那側は日本官憲が暴動阻止に付適当の手段を講ぜず且之を鎮圧せず遂に支那人の生命財産に多大の損失を与えたりとの理由の下に在鮮日本官憲は右暴動の結果に対し責任ありと主張す。日本及朝鮮の新聞は7月1日の萬寶山事件に付、支那在留民に対する朝鮮民衆の憎悪の念を起さしむるが如き性質の煽動的且不正確なる記事の掲載禁止を受けざりき。

然るに日本側は右暴動は民族的感情の自然的爆発に依るものにして日本官憲は右暴動を出来得る限り速やかに鎮圧せりと主張す。

朝鮮に於ける暴動は支那に於ける排日「ボイコット」を激成せり

此の重要なる一結果とも云う可きは朝鮮に於ける右暴動が直ちに支那全国を通じ排日ボイコットを復活せしむるに至れることなり。朝鮮における排支暴動直後萬寶山事件の未だ解決せられざるに先ち支那政府は日本に対し暴動の廉に依り抗議を為し暴動鎮圧失敗に対する全責任を負わしめたり。日本政府は7月15日、回答を発し、右暴動の発生に対し遺憾の見を表し且死者の家族に対し賠償金を提供せり。

日本政府は排支的暴動に対し遺憾の意を表し且つ死者の家族に対する賠償金を提供せり

7月22日より9月15日に至る迄日支地方及中央官憲の間に萬寶山事件に関する交渉及覚書の交換ありたり。支那側は1909年9月4日の間島協約に依れば朝鮮人の居住及借地の特権は間島地方以外に及ばざるを以て萬寶山に於ける紛議は朝鮮人が斯かる居住の権利なき場所に居住せし事実に基づくことを主張す。

萬寶事件に関する支那側抗議の根拠

支那政府は日本領事館警察に駐在することを抗議し、且萬寶山に多数の警察官を派遣せることは7月1日事件の誘因を為せる旨主張せり。

日本側の主張

他方日本側は朝鮮人の居住及借地の特権は間島協約に依り限定せられずして南満州を通じ一般日本臣民に許与せられたる居住及商租に関する権利に包含せらるるが故に朝鮮人は萬寶山において居住及商租に関する条約上の権利ありと主張せり。尚其の主張に拠れば朝鮮人の地位は他の日本臣民の地位と同一なり又日本側は朝鮮人は善意を以て米の耕作計画を為せる

のみならず、日本官憲は租借契約を取扱たる支那人仲介人の不始末に対し責任を負うことを得ずと主張せり。

　日本政府は萬寶山より領事館警察撤退に同意せるが朝鮮人小作人は依然同地に留まり其の米作地の耕作を継続せり。

7. 中村大尉事件

中村事件の重要性

　中村大尉事件日本側の見解に依れば満州に於ける日本の権益に対し支那側が全然之を無視せる幾多の事件が遂に其の極点に達せるものなり。中村大尉は1931年盛夏の候、満州の僻遠なる一地方において支那兵に殺害せられたり。

中村大尉は満州奥地に於けて軍事的使命を有せり

　中村震太郎大尉は日本現役陸軍将校にして日本政府の認めたるが如く日本陸軍の命令による使命を有したり。哈爾賓通過の際、支那官憲は同大尉の護照を検査せるが同大尉は農業技師と自称せり。其の際、同大尉は其の旅行地域は匪賊横行地域なる旨警告せられ右事情は同大尉の護照に記載せられたり。同大尉は武器を携帯し且売薬を所持し居たるが支那側に拠れば売薬中には薬用に非る痺薬ありたり。

中村大尉及従者支那兵に殺害せらる

　6月9日、中村大尉は三名の通訳者及助手を伴い東支鉄道西部の伊勤克特駅を出発せり。同大尉が洮南の方向において奥地へ相当の距離にある一地点に到達せる際、一行は屯懇軍第三団長関玉の指揮する支那兵に監禁せられたり。数日後、6月27日頃、同大尉及一行は、支那兵の為に射殺せられ死体は右行為の証拠隠滅の為、焼棄せられたり。

日本側の主張

　日本側は中村大尉及其の一行の殺害は不正にして日本軍隊及国民に対する侮辱なりと主張し又在満支那官憲は事件の公式調査を遅延し事件の責任を回避し且支那官憲は事件の真相を確むる為あらゆる努力を為しつつありと称するも何等誠意なかりしと主張せり。

支那側の主張

　支那側は当初中村大尉及一行は慣習上内地旅行の際外国人が所持すべ

き許可証を検査する期間中監禁せられたること、同大尉一行は厚遇せられたること及中村大尉は逃走を企てつつある際一歩哨に射殺せられたることを主張せり。支那側に拠れば中村大尉は身辺に日本軍事地図一葉及日記帳二冊を含む書類を携帯せることを発見せられたるが、右は同大尉が軍事偵察若しくは特別の軍事的使命を帯びたる将校なりしことを証するものなり。

調査

7月17日、中村大尉死去の報が在齊々哈爾日本総領事の許に到達せるが同月末在奉天日本官憲はは支那地方官憲に対し中村大尉が支那兵に依り殺害せられたる確実なる証拠を有する旨を通告せり。8月17日在奉天日本軍当局は中村大尉死去の最初の報道を公表せり(1931年8月17日「マンチュリア・デイリー・ニュース」参照)。同日林総領事及事件調査の為東京日本陸軍参謀本部より満州へ派遣せられたる森陸軍少佐は遼寧省主席臧式毅と会見せるが臧主席は即時同事件を調査す可きことを約せり。

臧式毅主席は其の後直ちに北平の一病院に病臥中なる張学良元帥及在南京外交部長に之を通告し、又二名の支那人調査員を任命し直ちに所謂殺害の現場へ赴きたり。右二名の調査員は9月3日、又日本陸軍参謀本部の為独立に調査を為しつつありし森少佐は9月4日、奉天に帰還せり。同日、林総領事は支那参謀長栄臻将軍を訪問し同将軍より支那調査員の判定は不確実且不満足なりしを以て再度調査の必要ある可き旨の通告に接せり。栄臻将軍は満州事態の新たなる進展に関し張学良元帥と協議の為、9月4日、奉天に帰還せり。

解決の為の支那の努力

張学良元帥は満州に於ける事態の重大なるを知り、臧式毅主席及栄臻将軍に対し遅滞なく中村事件の現地再調査を訓令せり。張学良元帥は本事件に対し日本陸軍が多大なる関心を有することを其の日本人軍事顧問より知りたるを以て事件を有効的に解決せんと欲する意思を明らかならしむる為、柴山少佐を東京に派遣せり。柴山少佐は9月12日、東京に到着したるが其の後の新聞報道に拠れば張学良元帥は中村事件の速急且公平なる結末を得んことを切望し居る旨述べたり。其の間張元帥は満州に関する諸種の日支係争問題解決のため両国にとり何等共通点ありやを確めしむる目的を

以て高級官吏湯爾和を外務大臣幣原男爵と協議せしむる為特別の使命の下に東京に派遣せり。

湯爾和氏は幣原男爵、南大将及他の陸軍高級武官と会談せり。9月16日、張学良元帥は新聞記者と会見せるが新聞は張学良元帥が中村事件は日本側の希望に基づき臧式毅主席及満州官憲に依り処理せられ南京政府は与からざる可き旨述べたりと報道せり。

第二回支那調査団は中村大尉殺害の現場を視察せる後、9月16日朝帰奉せり。18日午後、日本領事は栄臻将軍を訪問せるが其の際同将軍は関玉団長は9月16日、中村大尉殺害の責により奉天に召還せられ即時軍法会議において裁判せらる可き旨述べたり。日本側は奉天占領後関団長が支那側により陸軍監獄に監禁せられ居る旨発表せり。

在奉天林総領事は9月12日及13日、日本外務省に対し「調査員の奉天帰還後恐らく友好的解決を見る可きこと」殊に栄臻将軍は遂に支那兵が中村大尉殺害に対し責任あることを認めたることを報告せる旨報道せられたり。日本電報通信社奉天通信員は「支那兵墾軍団の兵隊による日本陸軍参謀本部中村震太郎大尉の所謂殺害事件の有効的解決は近きにあり」と9月12日電報せり。然れども幾多の日本陸軍将校、殊に土肥原大佐は中村大尉の死去に対し責任ありと称さるる関団長は奉天において監禁せられ其の軍法会議の日取りが一週間以内なる可きものとして発表せられたる事実に鑑み、中村事件の満足なる解決を図らむとする支那側努力の誠意如何に付引続き疑惑を表明せり。支那官憲は9月18日午後開催せられたる正式会議において、在奉天日本領事官憲に対し支那兵は中村大尉の死に対し責任あることを認め又速やかに事件が外交的に解決せらる可き希望を表示せるにより中村事件解決の為の外交交渉は9月18日夜迄は好都合に進展しつつありしが如し。

中村事件の結果

中村事件は多の如何なる事件よりも一層日本人を憤慨せしめ遂に満州に関する日支懸案解決の為実力行使を可とするの激論を聞くに至れり。本事件自体の重大性は当時萬寶山事件、朝鮮に於ける排支運動、日本陸軍の満州国境図們江渡河演習並びに青島における日本愛国団体の活動に対し行われたる支那人の暴行等に依り日支関係が緊張し居たる際なるを以て一層増

大せられたり。

中村大尉は現役陸軍将校なりしが此の事実は強硬迅速なる軍事行動の理由として日本側により指摘せられかかる軍事行動に好都合なる国民的感情を純化する為満州及日本国において国民大会行われたり。9月最初の二週間中日本新聞は陸軍において問題解決の為他に方法無きを以て武力に訴えるばきことに決定せりと繰り返し述べたり。

支那側事件の重大性は甚だしく誇張され居る旨並びに右は満州の軍事占領に対する口実とせられたる旨主張し支那側において事件処理上不誠意または遅延ありたりとの日本側主張を否認せり。

斯て1931年8月末頃までに満州に関する日支関係は本章に記述せるが如き幾多の紛議及事件の結果着しく緊張し来れり。両国間に三百の懸案あり且此等事件を処理すべき平和的手段が当事国の一方に依り利用し尽くされたりとの主張については充分なる実証あり得ず。此等所謂「懸案」は根本的に調和し得ざる政策に基づく一層広汎なる問題より派生せる事態なりき。両国は各地方が日支協定の規定を侵害し一方的に解釈し又は無視せりと責むるも両者何れも他方に対し正当なる言分を有したり。

両国間の此等紛争解決の為一方又は他方に依り為されたる努力に付与えられたる説明に依れば外交交渉及平和的手段の正当なる手続きに依り処理する為多少の努力が為されたることを立証せられ居るも而も右手続は未だ十分用い尽くされざりき。然るに長期に亘る支那側の調査遅延は日本側をして之を隠忍し得ざる事態に立至らしめたり。特に軍部は中村事件の即時解決を主張し十分なる賠償金を要求せり。就中帝国在郷軍人会は世論喚起に与て力ありたり。

9月中支那問題に関する一般的感情は中村事件を焦点として強大となり満州に於ける幾多問題を未解決のまま放置するの政策は支那官憲をして日本を軽視せしむるに至らしめたりとの意見しばしば表示せられたり。あらゆる係争問題の解決が実力に依るを必要とする場合には軍力に訴う可しとの決議は民衆の標語となれり。右目的を以てする計画を実行せしむ可き関東軍司令官に対する確定的訓令及9月上旬、東京に招致され且必要なる場合には実力に依り成る可く速やかにあらゆる懸案を解決す可しとする主張者として新聞に引用せられたる奉天駐在武官土肥原陸軍大佐等に関する

記事が新聞紙上に遠慮なく掲げられたり。此等及他の団体に依り述べられたる所感に付いての新聞報道は漸増しつつありし時局の危険なる緊張を支持せり。

第四章　1931年9月18日当日及其後に於ける満州に於いて発生せる事件の概要

事件突発直前の事態

　前章において満州に於ける日支両国利益の関係漸次緊張し来れるを述べ之が両国軍部の態度に及ぼす影響を述べ置きたり。既に相当期間或種の内部的、経済的及政治的要因が日本国民の満州に於て再び「積極政策」に出づるに備えつつありしことは疑いなきところなり。軍部の不満、政府の財政策、全て政党に対して不満の意を表明し、西洋文明の妥協的方法を蔑視して古代日本の道徳に依存することを主張し又財界及政界の利己的方法をも非とする軍部、農村落及国家主義的青年の間より醸成せられたる新政治勢力の出現、物価下落が主要生産者をして其の境遇を緩和せんが為に冒険的外交政策に望みを嘱するの傾あらしむるに至れること、事業界の不況が工業及商業界をして一層強硬なる外交政策により取引改善すべしと信ぜしむるに至れること、之等の事情は何れも何等実績を挙げ得ざりし対支幣原「妥協政策」放棄への道を開きつつありたるものなり。而して日本国内におけるかかる焦燥の念は在満日本人の間にありて一層甚だしく夏期を通じて通じ同地方の不安漸次加はりたり。9月に入るに及び右不安の遠からずして破裂点に達すべきことは慎重なる観察者の均しく認め得る点に達したり。而して両国の新聞は世論を沈静せしむるよりは寧ろ之を煽動するに傾けり。東京に於いて陸軍大臣が在満陸軍に直接行動に出でんことを勧告して激越なる演説を為せる旨報道せられたり。就中支那当局が中村大尉殺害事件につき満足なる調査及救済をなすを遷延せるは在満日本軍少壮将校を激昂せしめ彼らは同様無責任なる支那将校が道路、料理店其の他相接触せる場所において無責任なる言辞及誹謗を弄するに対して明らかに敏感となり居たり。斯くして次いで来るべく事件の舞台の準備整いたる次第なり。

九月十八日—夜十九日

9月19日土曜日朝、奉天市民の醒むるや同市日本軍の手中に帰したるを発見せり。夜中砲声を聞きたるも之は別に異とするに足らず日本軍は小銃及機関銃の猛射を含む夜間演習をなし来れることとて右の如きことは其週間連夜のことなりき。9月18日当夜は大砲の轟き及び砲弾の音の為之を識別し得たる少数のものが恐慌を感じたるは事実なるも市民の大部分は砲声を以て単に日本軍演習の再開に過ぎずとし恐らく、平常よりやや騒々し位に考えたり。

後述の如く殆全満州の軍事的占領に導きたる運動の第一歩として本事件の頗る重大なるを認め調査団は同夜の事件につき広汎なる調査を遂げたり。日支両軍関係指揮官公式陳述の頗る重要且興味あるは勿論なり。日本側は本事件を最初に目撃せる河本中尉北大営攻撃に当れる大隊の指揮官島本中佐及城内を占領せる平田大佐により説明せられたり。吾等は又関東軍司令官本荘中将及若干参謀将校の証言を聴取せり。支那側主張は北大営支那軍指揮官王以哲之を説明し之が補足として彼の参謀長並軍事行動中現場にありたる其の他の将校の個人的談話ありたり。吾等は又張学良元帥並参謀長栄臻将軍の証言を聴取せり。

日本側の説明

日本側説明によれば河本中尉は兵卒六名を率い9月18日夜、警戒任務を受け奉天北方の南満州鉄道線路に沿いて防禦演習を行いつつありたり。彼等は奉天の方向に南進しつつありたるが同夜は天晴れたるも暗夜にして視界広からず。彼等が小道が線路を横断せる地点に達せる時やや後方に当りて爆発の大音響を耳にせるを以て方向を転じて走り還えりたる処、約200ヤード行きたる地点にて下り線軌道片方側の一部分が爆破され居るを発見せり。右爆発は二軌道接合点に起これるものにして両軌道の尖端は全く引き離され之が為め線路に31インチの間隙を生じたり。爆破点に達するや歩哨隊は線路両側の畠地より砲撃されたるを以て河本中尉は直ちに部下に対し展開応戦すべきを命じたり。此処に於て約五、六名と覚ひしき攻撃隊は射撃を止め北方に退却せり。日本歩哨隊は直ちに追撃を開始したるが約200ヤード前進せる処にて約三、四百名に達する一層有力なる部隊の為め再び射撃せられたり。河本中尉は此の有勢なる部隊に包囲せらるるの危

険あるを認め部下の一名をして約1500ヤード北方に於て同様夜間演習中の第三中隊長に報告せしめ同時に他の一名をして（現状付近にある電話筒により）在奉天大隊本部に救援を求めしめたり。

此の時長春発南下列車の接近しつつあるを聞きたるが列車が破損線路に到達して破壊すべきを恐れ日本歩哨隊は交戦を停止し列車に警告を与えんが為め線路上に音響信号を設置せり。而るに列車は全速力にて通過し去りたり。列車は十時半奉天着の筈にて定刻どおり到着せるより見れば河本中尉の初めて爆発を聞きたるは十時過ぎなるべしと同中尉は語りたり。

次いで戦闘再開せられたるが第三中隊を揮ゆる川島大尉は既に爆発を聞きて南下の途中河本中尉の使者と遭遇し之が案内にて現場に向かい約十時五十分到着せり。一方大隊長島本中佐は電話に接するや直ちに奉天にありたる第一及第四中隊に現場に向かうべきを命じ又一時間半の距離にある撫順駐在の第二中隊に対し出来得る限り速やかに之に加わるべきを命じたり。右の二中隊は奉天より汽車にて柳条溝に至り次いで徒歩にて現場に向かい夜半到着せり。

河島中隊の援助を受けたる河本歩哨隊が繁茂せる高粱の葉陰に潜む支那軍の射撃を受けつつある際右の二中隊奉天より到着せり。

島本中佐は其兵力五百に過ぎず而して北大営支那軍一万に及ぶと信じたるに拘らず彼の吾人に語りたつところによれば彼は「攻撃は最大の防禦」なりと信じ直ちに営舎の攻撃を命じたり。線路、営舎間約250ヤードの地面は水溜りの為め集団にて横断すること困難なりしが支那軍が右地面を越え撃退されつつある際、野田中尉は第三中隊の一部を以て彼等の退路を断つ為に鉄道に沿いて進出することを命ぜられたり。日本軍が煌々と点燈しつつありたりと伝えらるる北大営舎に到達するや第三中隊は攻撃を行い左翼隅占領に成功せり。右攻撃に対し営内支那軍は頑強に抵抗し激戦数時間に亘れり。第一中隊は右翼を第四中隊は中央部を攻撃す。午前五時、営舎南門は其の直前にある付属家屋内に支那軍の支那軍の放置せる大砲よりの二弾に依りて破壊せられ同六時、全兵舎占領せられたるが日本側兵卒死者二名傷者二十二名を出せり。兵舎建物中には交戦中火災を発したるものありたるが残余は19日朝、日本軍により焼き払われたり。日本側にては支那兵三百二十名を埋葬せるが負傷者は二十名を発見せるに過ぎずと陳述

せり。

一方、他の地点においても同様に迅速且徹底的に軍事行動実施せられたり。平田大佐は午後十時四十分頃、島本中佐より南満州鉄道線路支那軍の為め破壊せられたるを以て将に敵軍攻撃に向はんとする旨の電話を受けたるが、同大佐は島本中佐の行動を是認し自ら城内攻撃に当るべきを決定し、午後十一時三十分までに軍隊の集合を完了し攻撃を開始せり。而して何等の抵抗も受けず時々市街上に戦闘ありたるも主として支那警察隊との間に行われたるものにて之が為め支那側巡警の間に死者七十五名を生じたり。午前二時十五分、市の城壁を乗越し三時四十分迄之を占領せり。午前四時五十分、彼は第二師団本部及第十六連隊一部午後三十分遼陽を出発せる旨の情報に接したるが右軍隊は午前五時直後到着せり。而して午前六時、東部城壁の占領を完了し兵工廠及飛行場は七時半占領せられ、次いで東大営を攻撃し午後一時戦闘を見ずして之を占領せり。之等の行動による死傷数は、日本側傷者七名、支那側死者三十名なり。

当日宛も検閲より帰来せる本荘中将は午後十一時頃新聞記者よりの電話にて初めて奉天に起こりつつある事件の報道を接受せり。参謀長は奉天特務機関より午後十一時四十六分電話にて攻撃の状況につき仔細の報告を受け次いで遼陽、営口、鳳城にある軍隊に対し直ちに奉天出動を命令せり。艦隊は旅順を出発して営口に赴くことを命ぜられ在朝鮮日本軍司令官は援軍派遣を求められたり。本荘中将は午前三時半旅順を出発し正午奉天に到着せり。

支那側の説明

支那側の説明によれば、日本軍北大営攻撃は何等挑発によるものに非ずして全然奇襲に出たるものなり。9月18日夜、第七旅全軍約一万北大営にありたり。9月6日、張学良元帥より当時の緊張せる状態において日本軍との衝突は一切之を避けんがため特別の注意を為すべき旨の訓令(北平において調査団に示されたる電文下の如し。「日本との関係頗る機微なるものあるを以て彼等に接する際には特に慎重なるを要す。如何に彼等に於いて挑戦するも吾人は特に隠忍し断じて武力に訴うることなく以て一切の紛争を避くべし。貴官は秘密且即時全将校に命令を発し右の点につき彼等の注意を喚起すべし。」)を接受せるを以て兵営城門の衛兵は木小銃を携

帯したるのみにて任務に服したり。而して同様の理由に依り兵営周囲土壁内の鉄道線路に導く西門は閉鎖せられ居たり。9月14、15、16、17日夜、日本軍は兵営付近において夜間演習を行い、18日夜午後七時には文官屯なる一村落にて演習しつつありたり。午後九時、将校劉某は通常の型の機関車を有せざる三、四輛の客車よりなる列車が同地に停車せる旨を報告せるが、午後十時爆発の大音響あり之に続いて銃声を聞きたり。依りて直ちに電話により参謀長より之を兵営南方六、七哩鉄道線路近くの私宅にあるたる司令官王以哲に報告せるが参謀長が尚電話中日本軍の兵営を攻撃しつつある旨並衛兵二名負傷せる旨の報道あり。十一時頃より兵営西南隅に対する総攻撃開始せられ十一時半、日本軍は城壁の隅より侵入し来れり。攻撃開始せらるるや参謀長消燈を命じ再度王以哲に電話にて報告せる処、王は抵抗すべからざる旨を答えたり。十一時半、南西及半西方向遠方よりの大砲の音を聞きたるが夜半に至り兵営内に砲弾落下し始めたり。退却中の第六百二十一団軍南門に達するや日本軍が同門を攻撃し居り守備兵撤退中なりを以て同軍は日本軍の内部に侵入する迄塹壕内に逃避し、然る後南門を経て逃るることを得約午前二時頃、営舎東方の二台子村落に到着せり。他軍は東門及東門外直前の空舎を経て逃れ遂に三時より四時迄の間に同村落に達するを得たり。

　唯一の抵抗は北東隅建物及其の南方第二位建物内にありたる第六百二十団の試みたるものなり。同団長は日本軍が午前七時南門より侵入し来るや支那軍は建物より建物へと逃れ日本軍をして空虚なる建物を攻撃せしめたる旨述べ居れり。支那軍主力撤退後日本軍は東方に向かい東方出口を占領せり。斯くして第六百二十団は連絡を絶たれたるを以て自ら戦いて活路を開くの他なきに至れり。彼等は午前五時に至り突破を試みたるが全然脱出し得たるは午前七時なりき。之れ営舎内に起これる唯一の実戦にして死傷の大部分も之が為めなり。本団が最後に二台子村落に到着せる部隊なり。

　支那軍は全部集合するや19日早朝、直ちに同村落出発、東陵に向かい次いで同地より吉林近傍の一村落に至りて冬衣の支給を受け又王大佐を派し熙洽将軍より軍隊の吉林入市を求めたり。在吉林日本土向林日本土留民は支那兵の接近に恐れを抱きたるを以て即刻長春四平街及奉天より吉林に

援軍派遣せられたるが之が為め支那軍は再び奉天方面に向かうこととなれり。彼等は奉天外十三哩の地点に下車し九隊に分かれ、夜間奉天を込回行軍せり。日本軍の発見を免れんが為め王以哲自ら農民に仮装し市中を乗馬にて通過せり。朝に至り日本軍は彼等存在の報に接し飛行機を発して之を爆撃せるを以て彼等は昼間隠遁するの己むなかりしも夜間は進軍を続行し遂に京奉線の一駅に達し此処にて七列車を命じ之により10月4日山海関に達したり。

調査団の意見

以上は所謂9月18日事件につき両国当事者の調査団に語れるところなり。二者相異なり矛盾しをるは明らかなるが之れ其の事情に鑑み別に異とするに足らざるところなり。

事件直前の不安状態並興奮を考え又利害関係者の特に夜間に起これる事件に関する陳述には必ずや相異するところあるべきを認め吾等は極東滞在中事件発生当時又は其直後奉天にありたる代表的外国人に出来得る限り多数会見せるが其の内には事件直後現地を観察し又先ず日本側の正式説明を与えられたる新聞通信員其他の人々あり。利害関係者の陳述と共に斯かる意見を充分に考慮し多数の文書資料を熟読し又接受若しくは収集せる幾多の証績を慎重研究せる結果調査団は左の結論に達したり。

日支両軍の間に不安気分の存在したることに付いては疑うの余地なし。証拠につき調査団に説明せられたるが如く日本軍が支那軍との間に於ける敵対行為起こり得べきことを予想して慎重準備せられたる計画を有し居たるが9月18—19日夜、本計画は迅速且正確に実施せられたり。支那軍は一八七頁①に言及せる訓令に基づき、日本軍に攻撃を加え又は特に右の時及場所において日本人の生命或は財産を危険ならしむるが如き計画を有したるものに非ず。彼等は日本軍に対し連繋ある又は命令を受けたる攻撃を行いたるものに非ずして日本軍の攻撃及其の後の行動に狼狽せるものなり。9月18日午後十時より十時半の間に鉄道線路上若しくは其付近において爆発ありしは疑いなきも鉄道に対する損傷は若しありとするも事実長春よりの南行き列車の定刻到着を妨げざりしものにて其れのみにては軍事

---

① 编者按：即指本册文献集第526页的训令。

行動を正当とするものに非ず。同夜における叙上日本軍の軍事行動は正当なる自衛手段と認むることを得ず尤も之により調査団は現地に在りたる日本将校が自衛の為め行動しつつありと信じつつありたるなるべしとの仮説を排除せんとするものには非ず。尚爾後の事件につき述べざる可からず。

日本軍隊の移動

9月18日夜、在満日本軍は左の如く分布せられ居たり。上述の如く北大営の攻撃に参加せる鉄道守備大隊四中隊及奉天城市を占領せる平田大佐部下の第二師団第二十九連隊の他、第二師団残部は各地に分散され居り第四連隊本部は長春、第十六連隊本部は遼陽、第三十連隊本部は旅順にあり。而して之等を各連隊に関する他部隊は安東、営口、南満州鉄道の長春—奉天線及奉天—安東線沿線幾多小都市に駐屯せり。又鉄道守備隊一個大隊は長春にあり又鉄道守備隊は上記各小都市に第二師団と共に分布され居れり。最後に朝鮮警備軍ありたり。

在満全軍及朝鮮軍幾分は9月18日夜、長春より旅順に至る南満州鉄道全域に亘り殆ど同時に行動を開始せり。其全勢力左の如し。

第二師団	5400	野砲 16 門
鉄道守備隊	約 5000	
憲兵	約 500	

安東、営口、遼陽其他の小都市にある支那軍は為す所を知らず無抵抗に武装を解除せられたり。鉄道守備隊及憲兵は之等の場所に留まり第二師団部隊は直ちに奉天に終結してより重要なる行動に加われり。第十六及三十連隊は早く到着して平田大佐に合して東大営の占領を援助せり。第二十師団所属三十九混成旅団(兵四千及砲兵)は19日午前十時、朝鮮国境新義州に終結。21日鴨緑江を越え夜半奉天に到着し同地より分遣隊は鄭家屯及新民に派遣せられ22日之を占領せり。

九月十八—十九日長春占領九月二十一日吉林占領

兵約一万、大砲四十門を有する長春に於ける寛城子及南嶺支那兵営は9月18日夜、同地駐屯の第二師団第四連隊及第一鉄道守備大隊(長谷部少将指揮下にあり)により攻撃せられたるが同地にては多少支那軍の抵抗ありたり。夜半戦闘開始され南嶺兵営は19日午前十一時、寛城子兵営は同日午後三時占領さる。之による日本側全死傷は死者将校三名及兵卒六十四名、

傷者将校三名、兵卒八十五名なり。奉天の戦闘終了と共に第二師団の各連隊は長春に集結せられ、多門中将及参謀部。第二十連隊及野砲兵一大隊は20日又天野少将指揮下の第十五旅団は22日到着せり。吉林は21日発砲を見ずして占領され支那軍は約八十哩外に移されたり。

当時日本の半官出版物たりし「ヘラルド・オブ・エシア」は軍事行動は之にて完了せるものと思考せられ之以上軍隊を移動することは予期せられ居らざる旨述べ居れり。爾後に於ける軍事行動は支那の挑発によるものとせられ20日、間島に於ける反日遊行、龍井村における停車場爆破及9月23日哈爾賓において数個の爆弾破裂したるも日本側建物には損傷なかりし事件等が斯かる挑発の例として挙げられ居れり。且馬賊の漸次跳梁しつつあること及敗残兵の活動等につきても抗議せられ居れり。而して之等の事情により日本軍は其の意に反して新たなる軍事行動を起こすに至れるものなりと主張せられ居れり。

錦州爆発

之等行動の第一は、10月8日の錦州爆撃なるが同地は9月末、張学良が遼寧省政府を移転せる処なり。日本側の云うところによれば爆撃は主として政庁事務所の設置されたる兵営及交通大学を目標とせる由なるが兵力に依り政庁を爆撃するは正当とすることを得ず且又爆撃区域が事実日本側主張の如く制限せられたりや否や疑問の余地あり。支那政府の名誉顧問米国人ルウイス氏は、10月12日、錦州に到着し其見聞せるところを顧博士に申送り顧博士は後に参与人の資格において其情報を調査団に伝達せるがルウイス氏の云うところによれば兵営には全然異常なく爆弾の大部分は市内至るところに落下し病院及大学建物にも落下せる由なり。爆撃機指揮官はその直後新聞記者に対し長春よりの四機は八日午前八時三十分、奉天に向かう旨命令せられたる由を告げたるが、同地にて右四機は他機と合流し、偵察機六機爆撃機五機の一隊は爆弾及燃料を満載して直ちに錦州に派遣せられ、午後一時到着十分乃至十五分以内に爆弾八十個を投じ直ちに奉天に帰還せり。ルウイス氏の談によれば支那軍は応戦せざりし由なり。

嫩江橋頭戦闘

次の行動は橋頭において行われたるものにして10月中旬開始せられ、11月19日、日本軍の齊々哈爾占領に了れるものなり。之に対し日本側の

理由として挙ぐるところは馬占山により破壊せられたる橋梁の修理中、日本軍が攻撃せられたりと云うにあり。然れども之れ以上に遡りて陳述し橋梁破壊につき説明するの要あり。

10月初め、嘗て馬占山、萬福麟と同地位を保有し彼等に代わりて黒龍江主席たらんとせしことある洮南守備隊長張海鵬は明らかに強力により省政府を奪取するの目的を以て洮南―昂々渓鉄道に沿い進出を開始せり。支那側参与員提出文書第三号には、進出が日本側の煽動によるものとなし居れるが中立の方面より得たる情報もこの見解を支持し居れり張海鵬軍の進出を防止せんがため馬占山は嫩江橋梁の破壊を命じ両軍は広大且沼沢地たる同河流域を隔てて相対峙せり。

洮昂線は南満州鉄道提供の資本により建設せられ右線路は借款の担保とされ居るを以て南満州鉄道当局は北満よりの農産物運搬の特に必要なる時に当り同線の運輸妨害を続くることは許す可からずと感じたり。在齊々哈爾日本総領事は政府の訓令により10月20日齊々哈爾に到着せる馬占山に対し成るべく早く橋梁の修理をなすべきを求めたるが、右請求には期限は付せざりき。日本当局は交通途絶により張海鵬軍を一定距離外に止め得べきを以て馬占山としては出来得る限り橋梁の修理を遷延するものと信じ居りたり。10月20日、洮昂線及南満州鉄道使用人の一隊は軍の護衛によらず橋梁破損の観察をなさんとしたることろ、予め黒龍江省軍将校に説明し置きたるに係らず射撃せられたり。之が為め事態悪化したるにより10月28日、在齊々哈爾本荘中将代表者林少佐は11月3日迄に橋梁修理の完成を要求し若し同日迄に実行されざるにおいては南満州鉄道修理員が日本軍保護の下に之に当るべき旨を述べたり。支那当局は期限の延長を求めたるも右要求には何等の回答なく、右修理事業遂行保護の目的をもって日本軍四平街より派遣せられたり。

11月2日迄交渉は進捗せず何等の決定を見ざりき其の日林少佐は馬占山将軍及張海鵬将軍に対して両軍何れも鉄道を作戦上の目的に使用すべからざること及各自の軍隊を河の両側より10kmの地点に撤退せしむべき旨の通牒を手交せり。

右通牒は若し右両将軍の何れかが南満州鉄道会社の技術員の鉄橋修理を妨害するときは日本軍は之を敵軍と見做すべき旨を表明し11月3日よ

り効力を発生することとなり居りたり。而して日本救援隊は其の峡谷の北側なる大興に11月4日迄に到着すべき命令を受け居りたり。中国参与員（第三号文書）在齊々哈爾日本総領事及第二師団の将校は何れも馬占山将軍は中央政府の訓令有る迄彼の独断を以て仮日本軍の要求に応ずべき旨回答越せりとの意見に一致せり。然れども一方日本側の証人は馬将軍が破壊されたる橋梁を迅速に又は有効に修理することを許す意無きことを明白なりしを以て其の誠意を信ぜざりざきと付言したり。11月4日に於いて日本総領事館代表者林少佐中国将校及官吏を含む共同委員会は二度も敵対行為の開始を防止するため橋梁に赴き且中国代表者は日本軍の前進を延期方依頼せり。右要求は容れられず歩兵第十六連隊長濱本大佐は彼の命令通り其の連隊中の一個大隊、野砲兵二個中隊及一個中隊の技術員を率い日本軍の最後通牒条項に従い修理作業開始のため橋梁に前進せり。技術員は花井大尉の指揮の下に11月4日の朝作業を開始し歩兵一個小隊は同日正午迄に二箇の日本国旗を押し立てて大興駅に向かい前進を開始せり。

　　戦闘は実際においては前記共同委員会が再度努力をなし居りたる最中、即ち11月4日の昼過ぎ中国軍を撤退せしむべく最後の努力を試みたるため再度現場に赴きたる際開始せられたり。発砲の開始せらるるや濱本大佐は彼の部下の頗る苦戦の状況に在るを曉り其の用うべき全兵力を率いて之が救援に赴けり。彼は直ちに全面は沼地なる為め正面攻撃は不可能にして此の苦境を脱するには敵の左翼を包囲攻撃するより他に方法なしと信じたり。仍て彼は其の補充中隊を分派して敵の左翼の占拠せる丘陵を攻撃せしめたるも兵力の寡少なると砲の有効射撃距離迄充分接近せしむることを得ざりしたる黄昏迄には右地点を占領するを得ざりき。丘陵は午後八時三十分に占領せられたるも同日は夫れ以上の前進不可能なりき。

　　関東軍司令部は状況の報告を受くるや直ちに強力なる増援部隊を派遣し歩兵一個大隊はその夜の裡に到着したるを以て同大佐は11月5日未明攻撃を再開するを得たり。数時間後支那軍の第一線に到着せる時においても依然として約七十余挺の自動機関銃及機関銃を以て防禦せる塹壕に拠る頑強なる敵兵に遭遇せることは同大佐自身の委員会に対して陳述せる所なり。彼の攻撃は阻止され中国軍の歩兵、騎兵の包囲逆襲に遭い彼の部隊は多大の損害を蒙りたり。日本軍は己む無く退却し夜に入る迄その陣地を支

えるほかなかりき。11 月 5 日より 6 日に亘る夜間において新に二個大隊到
着せるを以て日本軍は苦境を脱するを得、6 日中国軍の全線に亘り攻撃を
再び開始し、同日正午迄に大興停車場は日本軍の掌中に帰したり。

　　濱本大佐の使命は橋梁修理援護の為大興駅を占領するに在りたるを以
て退却する中国軍を追撃せざりしも日本軍は停車場付近に留まれり。中国
参与員は前記第三号文書中に林少佐は 11 月 6 日黒龍江省政府に対して新
に(1)馬占山将軍は張海鵬将軍のために省主席を辞職すること(2)治安維持
委員会を組織すべきことを要求せる旨を主張し居れり。林少佐の是等要求
を含める書簡の真贋は聯盟調査委員に呈示せられたり尚右文書は 11 月 7
日、日本軍は黒龍江省の回答を待たずして当時大興の北方約二十哩の三軒
房に駐屯せる同省軍に対して新に攻撃を開始せること及 11 月 8 日、林少佐
は再応書簡を送り馬占山は張海鵬に代わるため黒龍江省政府主席を辞職す
べく之に対しては同日夜半迄に回答すべき旨の要求を繰り返したることを
述べ居れり。更に中国側の報告に依れば 11 月 11 日、本荘将軍自ら電報を
以て馬占山将軍は辞職の上齊々哈爾を撤退すべきこと、日本軍の昂々渓前
進の権利有ることを要求し、之に対する回答も同様同日迄に回答すべき旨
を要求したり。11 月 13 日、林少佐は第三回要求中に日本軍は昂々渓のみ
ならず齊々哈爾停車場をも占領すべしとの一項を増加せり。馬占山将軍は
其の回答中に齊々哈爾停車場は洮昂鉄道と何等無関係なる旨を指摘せり。

　　11 月 14 日及 15 日、日本混成部隊は飛行機四機の援護の下に攻撃を再
開せり。11 月 16 日、本荘将軍は馬占山将軍は齊々哈爾の北方に退却する
こと、中国軍隊は東支鉄道以北に撤退すること、如何なる方法に依るを問わ
ず洮昂鉄道の交通運輸を阻害せざることを保証すること、是等の要求は同
月 15 日より十日間に実行せらるべきこと、右に対する回答は在哈爾賓日本
特務機関に送付すべきことを要求せり。馬占山将軍が右要求を容るるを拒
むや多門将軍は 11 月 18 日、新に総攻撃を開始せり。馬占山将軍は最初齊
々哈爾に退却せるが同地は省政府行政官署を移転せり。現場において指揮
せる日本軍諸将の証言に拠れば、右新軍事行動は 11 月 12 日以前に於いて
は開始せられたること無しとの趣なり。当時馬占山将軍は既に麾下軍隊二
万を三軒房の西方に集中し黒龍江省屯墾軍及丁超将軍の軍隊も集めたり。
益々威嚇的態度を示せる之等大部隊に対して日本軍は天野、長谷部両将軍

麾下の二個旅団より成る近々漸く集中せる多門師団のみを以て対抗し得るのみなりき。此の緊張せる事態を救う為11月12日、本荘将軍は全黒龍江省軍は齊々哈爾の北方へ撤退し日本軍をして北進し洮昂鉄道を守備するを得せしむべき旨を要求せり。11月17日、支那軍が其の騎兵部隊をして日本軍の右側を包囲攻撃せしむるまで日本軍は前進を開始せざりき。多門将軍は委員会に対し彼の部隊は歩兵三千、野砲二十四門より成る小部隊に過ぎざりしも敢えて支那軍を攻撃し11月18日、完全に之を撃滅したる結果、同19日朝、齊々哈爾を占領したりと述べたり。一週間後第二師団は馬占山軍に対抗し齊々哈爾を防守せしむる為天野将軍を歩兵一個連隊、砲兵一個大隊と共に同地に残し原駐地に帰還せり。此の小部隊は後に新に編成せられたる「満州国」軍隊の増援を得たるも吾人が1932年5月、齊々哈爾を訪問せる当時は未だ馬占山将軍の軍隊に対抗し得と認むるを得ざりき。

項中の付属軍事状況地図第三号は、聯盟理事会第一回決議当時に於ける双方の正規軍の配置を示す。当時特に遼河東西及間島地方に出没せる武装解除兵及匪賊に関し叙述せられ居らず双方互いに匪賊を使嗾せる旨を非難し合い居れり。即ち日本側は支那側において満州の失地の秩序を撹乱せんとする動機より之を使嗾すと言い支那側が支那の国土を占領し益々其の軍事行動を拡大すべき口実を発見せんため之を使嗾せりと言う。是等無頼の徒の勢力及其の軍事的価値は頗る漠然活不定なるを以て右軍事状況図解の中に其の重要性の正確なる評価を記入することは不可能なるべし。同地図は東北軍の指揮官が遼寧省の東西地方において着しく強力なる部隊を組織したるを示し居れり。此の部隊は日本軍の最前線に間近き大凌河の右岸に強力なる塹壕陣地を建設するを得たり。斯かる形勢が日本軍当局をして右部隊の正規軍の全兵力は三万五千人或は当時日本が満州に於て有すと認められたる兵力の約二倍なりと評価し、相当の不安を感ぜしめたるは無理からざることならん。

天津事変

本事変は11月中、天津に於いて惹起せる或事件の結果執られたる行動に依り発生せるなり。紛争の発端に関する報告は非常に相異なり居れり。

十一月八日の擾乱日本側の所見

11月8日及同26日の再度の撹乱ありたるが事件全体が極めて曖昧な

り。「ヘラルド・オフ・エシヤ」所載の日本側の説明に拠れば天津の支那住民が張学良元帥の支持者及其の反対者に分れ後者が11月8日、支那街において武装団体を組織し公安保持当局を攻撃し、政治的示威運動を為したりとの趣なり。右支那人両派間の紛争において日本軍司令官は最初より厳密に中立を守りたるも日本租界付近の支那警衛隊が日本租界に向けて矢鱈に発砲するに至るや己む無く日本側も砲火を開始せり。同司令官は交戦中の支那軍に対し日本租界より300ヤード外に離るべき旨要求せるが事態は緩和せず極度に緊張したるを以て11月11日又は12日、一切の外国軍隊警備を整うに至れり。

支那側の見解

天津市政府の陳述は右と頗る異なれり。彼らは日本側が支那人無頼漢及便衣隊を傭いたるものにして是等は支那街に於いて事件を惹起せしむるため日本租界内において軍事行動を為す暴力団に編成せられたりと主張し居り幸いにして警察当局が其の諜報者より此の形勢の報告を受けたるを以て右無秩序なる暴徒が日本租界より闖入するを撃退せるが右暴徒中逮捕されたるものの自白により暴徒は日本租界において編成せられ日本製の銃器及弾薬を以て武装せることを証明するを得と述べ居れり。彼らは9日朝、日本軍司令官が其の部下数名流弾に依り負傷せるに対し抗議し300ヤード外に撤退すべき旨要求せることは認めたるも支那側において右諸条件を受諾せるにも拘らず日本正規軍隊は支那街を装甲自動車を以て攻撃し且砲撃を加えたりと主張し居れり。天津市政府側は11月17日、300ヤード外に撤退することに関する詳細なる付則を有する協定成立せる旨を述べ日本側は協定による義務を履行せざりしため事態は益々悪化せりと主張し居れり。

11月26日、凄まじき爆破聞こえ次いで直ちに大砲機関銃及小銃の発射起こりたり。日本租界の電燈は消され、同租界より便衣隊現れ付近の公安局を襲撃せり。

十一月二十六日の事件の発端、相異せる報告

其の後起こりたる本撹乱に関する「ヘラルド・オブ・エシア」所載の日本側の報告によれば、26日事態頗る好転せるを以て日本義勇隊を解散したる処、同日夕刻支那側は日本兵営に向けて発砲を開始し抗議せるにも拘らず27日正午に至るも発砲を中止せざりしが故に挑戦に応じ支那軍と戦う

より他無かりきとあり。戦闘は27日の午後和平交渉開催迄継続せり。其の際、日本側は戦闘の即時停止及支那軍隊並びに警察隊をして外国軍隊の駐屯する凡ての地点より二十華里外に撤退すべきことを要求せり。支那側は、その軍隊の撤退に同意するも同地方の外国人の安全に対する唯一の責任者たる警察隊の撤退には肯ぜざりき。日本側の言によれば11月29日、支那軍側より日本租界付近より警察隊を撤退すべき旨申越したるを以て之を容れたるが、支那武装巡警に29日朝撤退し30日防禦工事を除去せる由なり。

天津事件の満州の事態に及ぼせる影響

26日の天津における緊張せる状態は関東軍参謀をして司令官に対し危機に瀕する天津の小部隊に対して錦州及山海関を経て直ちに増援部隊を派遣すべしと提議せしむるに至れり。単に輸送上の問題としては増援隊を大連を経て海路派遣する方、一層容易且迅速なりしならん。然れども戦略上より考慮せんに右経路によれば前進部隊をして途中錦州付近に集中せる邪魔になる支那軍隊を片付けるを得せしむる利益ありたり。此の経路を執るも支那軍の抵抗は皆無又は殆ど無しと想像し得るを以て左程延着すとは思われざりき。右定義は容れられ、11月27日、一連の装甲列車、二機の飛行機遼河を越え支那国軍の前線を攻撃せるのみにて塹壕に拠る支那軍の撤退を開始せしむるに充分なりき。

装甲自動車隊も亦陣地を変更せり。日本軍は抵抗のために装甲列車、歩兵列車及砲兵列車の数を増し兵力増強を為すに至れり。又日本軍はしばしば錦州に爆弾を投下せるも天津の事態好転せる報道達するや直ちに出動は本来の目的を失い、11月29日、日本軍隊は新民屯へ撤退し、支那軍をして大いに驚異せしめたり。

当省の天津事件の他の結果は日本租界に居住し居りし前清皇帝が土肥原大佐と会談の後、1月13日旅順より安全なる避難所を求められたることなり。

錦州占領

日本国の撤退せる地方は支那軍に依り再び占領せられ此の事実は広く宣伝せられたり。支那軍の士気稍々昇り、不正規兵及匪賊活動増大せり。彼等は冬期を利用し氷結せる遼河の諸所を渡り奉天付近地方を襲いたり。日本軍当局は現在の位置を維持するにさえも増援軍必要なることを語り是等

援軍を以て錦州に支那軍の集合する危険を除かんことを希望するに至れり。

十二月十日の理事会決議承認に際する日本の留保

其の間、満州に於ける事態はジュネーブにおいても猶も論争の議題なりき。12月10日の決議を承認したるとき日本代表は「本項第二は日本軍が日本臣民の生命財産を満州各地において跳梁し居れる匪賊及無法なる徒輩の活動に対して直接保護を為すに必要なる行動を執ることを妨ぐる意図に出でたるに非ずとの了解」に基づき受諾するものにして斯かる行動は明らかに「満州に於て頻発し居れる特殊の事態のため必要なる例外的手段」にして同地方が「常態に復す時は不必要となるならん」と声明せり。之に対し支那代表は「紛争当事国に対して事態を拡大すべからずとの命令は満州に於ける現状に依り惹起せる無秩序状態の存在を口実として違反すべからず」と応答し、右討論に列席し居りたる数名の理事は「日本臣民の生命財産に危険を及ぼすが如き事態発生すること有り得べく斯かる緊急の場合には其の付近の日本軍が行動するは己むを得ざるべきこと」を容認したり。

日本将校が本問題に関して委員に対し証言を提供したる際、該将校は常に12月10日の決議は「日本に対し」満州に於て「其の軍隊を維持するの権利を賦与し」若は日本軍をして同地方に於ける馬賊討伐の責に任ぜしめたりと主張せり。爾後の軍事行動を説述するに当り、日本将校は遼河付近において土匪軍に対し叙上権利を行使するに際し同時に錦州付近に残留せる支那軍隊と衝突し其の結果支那軍隊は関内に撤退せられたりと主張す。即ちジュネーブにおいて保留を為したる後日本が其の計画に拠り引続き満州の形勢を処理せんとしたるは事実存す。

援軍の到着

齊々哈爾守備隊を除き第二師団は奉天西方に集中せられたり。援軍は相次いで速やかに来着し第八師団の第四旅団は（茲に記載せる日本軍の部隊の番号及兵力は総て日本側の公報に依る）12月10日より15日の間に到着せり。更に12月27日朝鮮より第二十師団司令部並びに一個旅団派遣の御裁可を得たり。又長春並びに吉林は差当り独立鉄道守備隊に依りてのみ保護せられたり。

支那軍隊撤退に関する交渉の失敗

錦州に対する日本軍進撃が切迫せる為め支那外交部長は、三乃至四個

師団が錦州北方及南方に中立地帯維持を保障するの意あるに於いては支那軍隊の関内撤退を提議し以て戦争の進展を阻止せんことを企図したるも、この提議は何等効果を収めざりき。一方北平において張学良と日本代理公使との間に交渉行われたるも之亦諸般の理由に依り失敗に終われり。支那側は其の調書第三号付属書「ホ」中に12月7日、25日、及29日に於ける訪問の度毎に日本代理公使は支那軍隊の退却に関する其の要求を増大し且つ日本軍の抑制に関する其の約束は益曖昧となれりと主張し居れるに対し、他方日本は支那の撤退に関する約束は決して真摯なるものに非ざりしと論難す。

錦州攻撃

　日本軍の集団的攻撃は12月23日を以て開始せられ而して支那第十九旅団は其の陣地を放棄するの己む無しに至れり。支那軍司令官は総退却の命令を発したるに依り、其の日より日本軍の進撃は整然として行われ殆ど何等抵抗を受けざりき。斯くて錦州は1月3日朝占領せられ、日本軍は山海関即ち長城直下に至るまで進撃を続け、同地に於ける日本守備隊と恒久的接触を遂げたり。

　張学良軍の完全なる満州撤退殊に相手に対し殆ど一撃をも加えずして撤退せるは長城以南の内部的情態と関係なかりしものに非ず。相拮抗する諸将領間に幡まれる確執に就きては前章に記述せる所なるが此の確執が当時終息せざりしことを記憶するを要す。

哈爾賓占領

　山海関に至る進撃が比較的容易に遂行せられたることは日本をして其の軍隊を原駐地より移動し之を他方面の進撃に使用するを得せしめたり。乃ち従来殆ど戦闘の全局を担当せる第二師団の主力は休養の為め遼陽、奉天並びに長春の駐屯地に復帰したり。一方随所において受くる虞ある馬賊の襲撃に対し保護を加うべき鉄道線路の延長は多数の軍隊使用を必要とせるが、該軍隊は斯くの如き広範なる地域に分駐せしむる為め其の戦闘力は殺減せられたり。第二十師団司令部の隷下に在る二個旅団は此の目的に対し新占領地帯に残留せしめられ、而して第八師団の第四旅団は更に北方に於いて両旅団と連結したり。日本軍憲は此等の守備完全なる地域内においては安寧秩序は速やかに確立せられ而して爾後数週間に馬賊は遼河の両岸

において殆ど其の影を潜むるに至れりと確言せり。此の声明は6月に余等
に対し為されたるが而も本報告書を記述しつつある際に当り余等は義勇軍
が営口並びに海城を盛んに侵攻し奉天及錦州をさえ襲撃せんと威嚇しつつ
ある報道に接したり。

　本年初頭に於いて最も紛乱を来たせるは哈爾賓の北方並びに東北地方
にして該地方に於いては予て旧吉林及黒龍江政府当局の残存せる追従者が
移動したり。該北方地域に於ける支那将領等は北平の本拠と若干の接触を
保持し居たりしものの如く、北平より随時或る支援を受けたり。曩に齊々
哈爾に対し行われたる如く、哈爾賓進撃は支那両軍間の遭遇戦を以て開始
せられたり。1月初旬、熙洽将軍は哈爾賓占領を目的とし北方に遠征軍派
遣の準備を為せり。当時、吉林と哈爾賓間には反吉林軍と称せられたる軍
隊を率いる丁超、李杜両将軍幡距したり。我々の仮報告書が討議に付せら
れつつありし際、日本参余員より北平当局の声援だに莫かりせば両当事者
間の交渉に依り満足なる条件を設定し得べしとの情報を与えられたり。事
実交渉は開始され而して交渉進行中熙洽将軍は麾下の軍隊を率いて双城子
に進撃し1月25日、同市を占領せるも翌朝同市南方隣接郊外において激戦
を交えるに及んで右進撃は忽ち阻止せられたり。斯くして発生せる形勢は
在哈爾賓多数日本居留民並びに鮮人にとり大いに危険なるものと日本人を
して思惟せしめたり。蓋し同市隣接地域における多少とも不正規なる二個
の支那軍隊の間の戦闘は敗退せる軍隊が同市に向け退却するの結果となり
しならん。而して其の結果幾多の惨事を惹起したるべきは支那近世史上多
くの実例を見るなり。故に至急救援の要請は関東軍に向け発せられ、日本
人の確言する所に拠れば支那証人等すら其の財産の劫掠せらるべきを恐れ
此の要請に賛同したりと言う。

　此の危急時に当り日本特務機関事務局管理引継ぎの為め26日哈爾賓
に派遣せられたる土肥原大佐（現時少将）は委員会に対し同市付近に於ける
支那両軍の戦闘は約十日間継続し、而して脅威せららたる地区に主として
居住せる四千の日本居留民及哈市郊外普家甸の支那街にありて虐殺の危険
に曝され居りたる一千六百の鮮人に付多大の脅威存したりと述べたり。尤
も反吉林軍は戦争の続行せられたる十日間、同市を保持せるも日鮮居留民
の死傷数は比較的僅少なりき。其の際日本居留民は義勇隊を組織し、同胞

の郊外支那街より脱出し来ることを助けたり。同所を脱出せんとするに当り日本人一名、鮮人三名が虐殺されたりと云う。加之此の危急なる形勢偵察の為め派遣せられたる日本軍飛行機中の一機は、機関の故障の為め着陸を余儀なくせられ而して搭乗者は丁超軍の為めに虐殺せられたりと云う。叙上の事件は日本軍憲をして戦闘に干渉するの決意を為さしめるに至り、第二師団は再び危険に瀕せる同胞救助の任務を帯ぶることとなれり。然るに其の際長春以北の鉄道が露支合併たる関係上如何にして軍隊を輸送すべきか、戦闘よりも重要なる問題なりしなり。東支鉄道の南部線における車輌は大いに減少し居たるを以て第二師団司令官は第一着手として僅かに長谷部将軍の率いる歩兵二個大隊を派遣するに決し鉄道当局と交渉を開始せるも該交渉遷延すべしと見るや日本将校は軍隊輸送を強行するに決したり。鉄道当局は之に対し抗議し列車の運転を拒絶したるも、其の反対に拘らず1月28日夜、日本軍憲は三個の軍用列車の仕立てに成功せり。右列車は松花江の第二鉄橋迄北上し、同所において同鉄橋が支那軍により破壊せられたるを発見したり。其の修理は翌29日に行われたるを以て日本軍は30日双城子に達したり。翌払暁、天末だ明けざる時、此の少数の日本軍隊は闇に乗じて来襲せる丁超軍の攻撃する所となり、激戦の結果、支那軍隊は撃退せられたるも、其の日は前進すること能わざりき。此の間、露支鉄道当局は日本軍隊が単に在哈爾賓日本居留民保護の目的を以て前進しつつありとの諒解の下に、東支鉄道に依る日本軍隊輸送を許可する同意したり。是に於いて其の乗車賃は現金を以て支払われ、2月1日、日本軍隊は続々到着し第二師団の主力は2月3日朝、双城子付近に集結せられたり。更に援軍は既説の如く11月19日以来第二師団の一部が駐屯せる齊々哈爾よりも亦招致せられたり。而も哈爾賓齊々哈爾間の鉄道は支那軍の為に破壊せられたるが故に猶幾多の困難を克服せるを要せり。支那軍は又同時に各処に於いて東支鉄道南部線沿線の独立鉄道守備隊を攻撃したり。是れより先、2月3日、今や砲十六門を有し其の総兵力一万三千乃至一万四千と算せられたる友吉林軍は同市南方境界に沿いて塹壕陣地を構築したり。同日、第二師団は此の陣地に対し前進を開始し3日夜より4日に至る間に双城子の北方約二十哩の南城子河に達し、翌朝戦闘は開始せられたり。4日夕、支那軍陣地の一部は日本軍の占領する所となり越えて5日正午迄に最後の始末を

告げたり。哈爾賓は同日正午占領され、支那軍は三姓に向け退却したり。

一九三二年八月末迄の日本軍隊行動の進展

第二師団の攻撃成功に依り哈爾賓市は日本軍憲の手に帰したるも右攻撃に次ぐに直ちに敗退支那軍の以て追撃を以てせざりし為め全局的には北支の形勢には何等し変化を齎さざりき。哈爾賓北方及東方の鉄道並びに松花江の重要なる水路は依然反吉林軍及馬占山軍の支配に委せられたり。故に占領地域が北に於いては海倫、東に於いては方正、海林地方に拡大せらるる迄援軍の増派、当方並びに北方に向けての遠征軍の反復的派遣及六箇月に亙る戦闘は行われたり。日本側の公表に依れば馬占山軍と合わせる反吉林軍は全く撃破せられたりと伝えらるるも支那側の公報に依れば同軍は今猶存在すと云う。其の戦闘力は減殺せられたりと雖も反吉林軍は絶えず日本軍の行動を妨げ同時に戦場に於ける実際的会戦を回避しつつあり。新聞報道に拠れば東支鉄道東部、西部両支線依然哈爾賓海林間の各所に於いて襲撃を受け破壊せらるるの現状なり。

2月初頭以来の日本軍の行動は次の如く略説するを得べし。

3月末頃第二師団の主力は丁超及李杜の反吉林軍討伐の為め方正方面に向け哈爾賓を出発せり。同師団は三姓地方迄前進したる後4月初旬哈爾賓に帰還せり。此の部隊は約一ヶ月間その主力を以て三姓付近において又その小支隊を以て海林方面に於いて東支鉄道東部線に沿い反吉林軍と不断の戦闘に従いたり。

5月初旬、北満の日本軍は更に第十四師団の増援を受けたり。同師団の一支隊は反吉林軍との戦闘に参加し三姓の南方牡丹江渓谷に進出し敵対軍をして吉林省の最北方隅に退却するの余儀なきに至らしめたり。而も5月下旬に開始されたる第十四師団の主要行動は哈爾賓の東方地方に行われ馬占山軍攻撃を目的としたり。同師団は呼蘭―海倫鉄道に沿いて哈爾賓の北方まで主要なる攻撃を遂行し又小部隊を以て斉々哈爾―克山鉄道の終点たるべき克山より東方に向かいて攻撃をなせり。日本側は8月初旬、馬占山軍は再び有効に撃破せられ且つ馬占山が死亡せる確証を有すと主張するも、支那側は馬占山は今猶生存せりと確言す。此の戦闘に於いては日本より新に到着せる騎兵部隊も亦参加したり。

8月中、数回の小規模なる戦闘は奉天熱河両省の境界主として鉄道に

依り熱河に至る唯一の途たる(京奉鉄道の)錦州―北票支線付近に於いて行われたり。支那に於いては此等の戦闘は単に日本分の熱河占領を目的とする一層大規模なる軍事行動の序幕に過ぎずとの危惧広く行なわる。今も猶支那本部と満州に於ける支那軍との間に存する主要交通路は熱河を貫通するを以て、既に「満州国」領土の一部と主張せらるる熱河省に対する日本軍攻撃の危惧は強ち兵稽の事に非ず。右攻撃の切迫せるは日本新聞の公然論議する所なり。

最近の事件に関し日本参与員が委員会に提出したる日本側の説明は左の如し。

石本と呼ぶ関東軍付官吏は7月17日、支那「義勇軍」の為め熱河省内に於いて北票錦州間に運転せらるる一列車より拉致せられたり。軽砲を有する日本軍の歩兵小部隊は直ちに同氏救出を企てたるも其の目的を達する能わず。其の結果、日本軍は熱河省境の一村落を占領せり。

7月下旬並びに8月中、日本軍の飛行機は熱河の同地方上空を数回飛行し数個の爆弾を投下したるも而も慎重に「諸村落外の無住地域」をば選びたり。次いで8月19日、日本参謀将校一名石本氏釈放交渉のため北票と省境間に位する小都邑南嶺に派遣されたるが少数の歩兵部隊を随へて帰還の途中、同将校は射撃されたるを以て自衛上応戦し他の歩兵部隊の到着と共に南嶺を占領せるが翌日同地を撤退せり。支那参与員は熱河省長湯玉麟の報告中より摘録せるものを委員会に提出せるが右報告は叙上戦闘は遥かに大規模に行われ而して鉄道守備隊の支那兵一個大隊は装甲列車に支持せられたる優秀の日本軍歩兵部隊と交戦したること並びに日本側の謂う所の爆撃は同地方大都邑の一つたる朝陽を目標とせること並びに其の結果、軍隊及住民間に三十名の死傷を出せることを主張す。8月19日、日本軍の攻撃は一装甲列車の南嶺攻撃と共に再び開始されたり。

日本参与員の提供せる情報の末尾に於いて熱河に於ける秩序の維持は「満州国国内政策の一事項たりと雖も日本は満蒙に於ける平和と秩序の維持に関し其の重要なる責務を有するに鑑み同地方の形勢に無関心なる能わず、且つ熱河に於ける如何なる紛乱も直ちに満蒙全体に重大なる反響を惹起すべき」ことを説叙す。

一方、湯玉麟は其の報告の末尾に於いて日本軍の攻撃再開せらるる場

合は有効なる抵抗を為すべく、あらゆる可能的方法を採用しつつありと
述ぶ。

此等の報告に顧みれば此の地方に於ける戦闘地域の拡大は正に考慮せ
ざるべからざる事項なり。

支那側の抵抗の性質

支那軍の主要部隊は、1931 年末、関内に撤退せられたるも日本軍は満
州各地において絶えず不規則的なる抵抗に遭遇せり。会て嫩江に於て行わ
れしが如き戦闘は最早起らざりしも戦闘は不断にして且広汎なる地方に亘
りて諸所に之を見たり。日本人は現今自己に反抗するあらゆる部隊をば無
差別に「匪賊」と称するを常とせり。事実に於いては匪賊の他日本軍隊若し
くは「満州国」軍隊に対する組織ある抵抗をなすものに截然たる二種別あ
り。即ち支那正規軍隊並不正規軍隊是なり。

右両軍隊の兵数を概算するは至難にして、委員一行は依然戦闘に従事
しつつある何れの支那将領とも会見するを得ざりしを以て下記情報の確実
性に就き留保を為すの必要あり。支那当局は満州に於て今猶日本軍に対す
る抵抗を持続しつつある軍隊に関する正確なる情報を与えるを欲せざるは
当然なり。他方日本当局は自己に抵抗を続けるある軍隊の戦闘価値を最小
限度に局量せんとする傾向あり。

旧東北軍の残党

旧東北軍の残党は全く吉林黒龍江両省においてのみ之を看る。1931
年末、錦州を繞りて行われし軍隊の改編は是等の全ての部隊が其の後関内
に撤退せられたるを以て永続せざりき。而も 1931 年 9 月以前松花江地方
並びに東支鉄道沿線に駐屯せられたる支那正規軍隊は未だ嘗て日本軍と激
戦を交えたることなく、従来日本軍隊並に「満州国」軍隊に対し多大の困惑
を与え今猶与えつつある奇襲戦を継続す。馬占山、丁超、李杜の三将領は此
等軍隊の指揮者として支那全土を通して盛名を博したり。右三将領は曩に
北満に於ける護路軍若は駐屯軍の司令たりし旅長なり。恐らく其の麾下に
在りし軍隊の大半は各其の指揮者及張学良政府破壊後の支那の主張に忠誠
を尽くしたるならん。馬占山の勢力は同将軍が其の忠誠を改変せるを以て
容易に測定するを得ず。黒龍江省長として馬占山は省軍隊全部を統率した
るが余等に提示せられたる兵数は合計 7 個旅団を算せり。4 月以降彼は日

本並びに「満州国」に対し明らかに反対の立場を執れり。呼蘭河、海倫、大平河間に在りて馬占山の有せし兵力は日本当局の概算に依れば六個連隊即ち七千乃至八千なり。丁超並びに李杜は旧張学良軍の六個旅団を支配し且爾来同地方に於いて更に三個旅団を徴募し、仮報告作成当時は其の総兵力を約三万と概算したり。然れども馬占山軍及丁超、李杜軍は4月以来着しく其の兵数を減じ、現今叙上概算数以下に在りと看るは恐らく妥当ならん。

下段に記す如く此等両軍は哈爾賓占領以来日本正規軍の集中攻撃に依り大損害を被れり。現在両軍は日本軍の如何なる行動をも阻む能わずして努めて公然日本軍と会戦するを回避す。日本軍の飛行機を使用するに反し支那軍が全然此の武器を欠如せることは従来支那軍の被りたる損害の大半の原因をなすものなり。

不正規軍を考慮するに当りては丁超李杜軍と協力したる吉林省各種義勇軍を区別すること必要なり。1932年4月29日の調査団仮報告に於いては調査団は第五項に義勇軍なる題下に三種義勇軍及七種の小集団を掲げたるが後者の一つは敦化及萬寶山間にありて丁超李杜軍隊と連絡を保ちつつあるものなり。右集団は之等地域における鉄道及其他交通機関の欠如に依り今尚其地位を保持しつつあり。其の長たる王徳林は各種反「満州国」軍を集め之を堅く其の支配下に置き居れり。本集団は日本軍（日本軍は敦化以東においては何等活動を示し居らざるが）に比し其の重要さ僅少なるやも知らざるも「満州国」軍には対抗し得るが如く見え、吉林省の広き地域において其の地位を維保し居れり。

王徳林と連絡を有し間島地方において相当妨害をなせる大刀会の現在の活動については何等確証を得られず。他方、日本軍は大刀会に対し何等重要なる軍事行動を執らざりき。

多数の所謂路軍及他の支那軍を掲記せる日本側の一公式文書、調査団に提出せられたり。右路軍及支那軍は各々二百乃至四百名より成り。右は義勇軍の小単位をなすものなり。之等支那軍の活動区域は奉天及安奉線付近の地区、錦州、奉天、熱河省境、東支鉄道西部線及新民屯奉天間の地方に及ぶ。斯くの如く義勇軍及反吉林軍連合の占拠し居る地域は満州の大部分を含む。

8月中旬奉天近郊、南満州鉄道の南段各地殊に海城及営口において交

戦行われたり。数度日本軍は苦戦せるが義勇軍は何れの地においても何等重要なる勝利を得る能わざりき。満州の一般状態が近き将来に於いて何等か変更を見ること予想せらるべきや否やは疑わしきが如きも本報告完成の際には交戦は広汎なる地域に亙り継続せられ居れり。

匪賊

支那に於けると同様満州に於ても匪賊は常に存在したりき。職業的匪賊は政府の強弱に応じ其数或は大となり或は小となりて東三省の凡ゆる地域に存し、政治的目的の為め各党派に依り用いられたり。支那政府は調査団に対し最近二十年又は三十年の間に日本側の手先が其の政治的目的を遂ぐる為め非常に匪賊を使嗾せる旨述べたる書類を提出せり。右書類には南満州鉄道出版の「1930年に於ける満州開発に関する第二回報告」の一節引用せられあるが右に依れば付属地内においてすら匪賊の数は1906年の九件より1929年の三百六十八件に増加したる由なり。上述支那側書類に依れば匪賊は大連及関東州よりの大規模の武器密輸に依り奨励せられたる由。例えば有名なる馬賊頭目凌印清は去年11月所謂独立自衛軍組織の為武器弾薬其他供給せられたる旨述べられあり。右自衛軍は三人の日本側手先の助力に依り組織せられ且錦州攻撃を目的とせるものなり。右企てが失敗せる後他の匪賊頭目が同様の目的の為日本側の助力を得たるが日本製品の材料と共に支那軍の手に捕われたり。

勿論日本官憲は満州匪賊に関し別種の見方をなし居れり。日本官憲に依れば匪賊の存在は全然支那政府の無能に基づくものなり。日本官憲は又張作霖は或程度迄其領土内に匪賊の存するを支持したりと称す。何となれば張作霖は非常時には匪賊は容易に兵卒に改編せられ得べしと思考したればなり。日本官憲は張学良政府及其の軍の完全なる打倒が大いに満州匪賊数を増加せしめたる事実を肯定する一方日本軍が満州に在る結果二、三年間に主要匪賊団は掃討せられ得べき旨主張す。日本官憲は「満州国」警察及各部族に於ける自衛団の組織が匪賊を消滅せしむるに役立つべきことを望み居れり。現在の匪賊の多くは元来良民にして其の財産を凡て失いたる為め現在の職業に投ずるに至れるものと信ぜられ居れり。農工の業を再び営む機会あらば之等匪賊は従前の平和的生活に復帰すべきこと望まれ居れり。

第五章　上　海

上海事件

　　1月末上海に於いて戦闘発生せり。2月20日迄の本事件の経過概要は聯盟の任命せる領事国委員会に依り既に報告せられたり。領事国が2月29日、東京に到着せる時、戦闘は猶進行中にして、上海に於ける日本政府の武力干渉の起因、動機、及結果に関し調査団は同政府当局と数度討議を行いたり。調査団が3月14日、上海に到着せる時は戦闘は終了し居たるも停戦交渉は難関に在りたる次第にて恰も此の時に当り調査団が到着したることは機を得たるものにして良好なる空気を助成せしやも知れず。調査団は最近の敵対行為に基づく緊張せる感情を諒解し且又本紛議に関連する困難及問題の双方につき直接且明確なる印象を得たり。調査団は領事国委員会の事業を引継ぎ又は上海に発生せる最近の出来事に付特に研究すべき旨の訓令を受けたることなく却って調査団は支那政府においては調査団が上海に於ける事態調査の為其の満州に赴くことを延引すべしとの如何なる案にも反対の意向を表示したる旨聯盟事務総長より通報に接し居たり。

　　調査団は上海事件に関する日支両国政府の意見を聴取し又本問題に関する多数の文献を日支双方より接受せり。尚調査団は戦火を蒙れる地域を視察し日本陸海軍将校より最近の軍事行動に関する陳述を聴取したり。又個人の資格に於いて調査団は上海在住の何人の記憶にも新しき事実に関し各種の意見を代表する人士と会談せり。然れども調査団としては正式に上海事件を調査することなく従って之に関連する争点に関し何等意見を表示せざりき。然れども調査団は記録の為2月20日以降日本軍の最後の撤収に至る迄の軍事行動の叙述を完成すべし。

二月二十日以降上海事件の記述

　　領事国委員会の最終報告は2月20日、日本側が江湾及呉淞地方に於いて新たなる攻撃を開始したる旨の記述にて筆を止めたり。右攻撃は其の後引続き行われたるに拘らず日本軍にとりて何等顕著なる成功を齎さざりしが日本軍は其の結果、所謂支那警衛師第八十七師及第八十八師の一部が今や第十九路軍と同様日本軍と戦いつつあるを知るを得たり。此事実及地勢

に基づく困難ありし為日本側は二個師団即第十一師団及第十四師団を増派することを決定せり。

2月28日、日本軍は支那側の撤去せる江湾西部を占領せり。同日、呉淞要塞及揚子江上の諸砲台は再び空中及海上より爆撃せられ爆撃機は虹橋飛行場及滬寧鉄道を含む全戦線に亘り活動せり。日本軍司令官に任命せられたる白川大将は2月29日上海に到着せり。同日以後、日本軍司令部は着々と前進の旨報ぜり。江湾地方にては日本軍は徐々に前進せるが海軍司令部は連日砲撃の結果、閘北に於ける支那軍は退却の兆しある旨報ぜり。同日上海より百哩隔たれる杭州飛行場に対する空中爆撃行われたり。

3月1日、前線の攻撃の進捗遅々たりしを以て日本軍司令官は七了口付近の揚子江右岸に第十一師団主力を上陸せしめ支那軍左翼を奇襲せむが為広汎なる包囲運動を開始せり。本軍事行動は成功し支那軍は日本軍司令官の2月20日付最後通牒中に要求せる20km線外に直ちに退却するの己む無きに至れり。3月3日、日本軍が空中及海上よりの爆撃後呉淞要塞に入りたるときは支那軍は既に撤去し居たり。其の前日、滬寧鉄道の崑山停車場の東7kmの地点迄爆撃行われたるが右は支那軍前線への援軍輸送阻止の為めなりと称せられる。

3月3日午後、日本軍司令官は停戦命令を下したり。支那軍司令官は3月4日、同様の命令を発せり。支那側は日本軍第十四師団が戦闘行為停止後3月7日より3月14日の間に上陸し約一ヵ月後、在満日本軍救援の為満州に輸送せられたることを強硬に抗議せり。其間友好国及聯盟の幹旋に依り停戦確保に対する試続けられ居たり。2月28日、英国提督サー・ホワード・ケリーは旗艦に日支代表を接受し、相互且同時撤退の基礎とする暫行的協定を提議せられたるが右会議は交渉に基礎に関する意見相違の為に成功を見るに至らざりき。

2月29日、聯盟理事会議長は特に「地方的取極めを為すことを条件とし戦闘の終局的終了及決定的停戦の為他の関係国参加の下に共同会議」の開催方を勧告せり。両当事国は之を受諾せるも日本代表が(1) 支那側が最初に撤退すべく(2) 其撤退実行を確かめたる後日本側は撤退すべし但し右は以前も述べられ居たるが如く共同租界及拡張道路への撤収にあらずして、上海より呉淞に及ぶ地域への撤収なりとの条件を出せる為交渉は成功

を見ること能わざりき。3月4日、聯盟総会は理事会の提案に言及し(1) 日支両国政府に戦闘行為停止を確実ならしめんことを求め(2) 関係国に対し前項の実行に関し情報提出方を求め(3) 戦闘行為停止を確実ならしめ且日本軍の撤退を定むる取極締結の為め列国援助の下に交渉を開始せむことを勧告すると共に右交渉の進行に付列国より情報を受けんことを希望せり。

3月9日、日本側は英国公使を通じ聯盟総会の定めたる基礎に依り商議する用意ある旨述べたる覚書を支那側に送付せり。

3月10日、支那側は同様英国公使を通し右基礎に依り交渉するの用意あるも会議が戦闘行為の決定的停止及日本軍の完全且無条件の撤退に関する事項に限らるることを条件とする旨回答せり。3月13日、日本側は支那側の留保は聯盟の諸決議を変更し又は如何なる意味に於いても日本側を拘束するものと認めざる旨を通報せり。日本側は日支双方は聯盟決議の基礎の上に会合すべきものなりと思考せり、

3月24日、日支停戦会議開かれたり。其間日本陸海軍の撤収は現実に開始せられたり。

3月8日、海軍及航空部隊は上海を去り其結果残留日本兵力は「常数を超過すること遠からざるもの」となれり。日本軍司令部は3月27日、更に撤収を行うに際し、右撤収は上述会議又は聯盟とは何等関係なく単に上海に最早必要ならざる部隊を帰還せしめむとする日本陸軍司令部の独自の決定に過ぎざる旨声明せり。

3月30日、停戦会議は前日戦闘行為の決定的停止に関する協定成立せる旨発表せるも更に難問題発生し5月5日に至り漸く完全なる停戦協定を調印し得るの運びを見るに至れり右協定は戦闘行為の決定的停止を定め、正常状態快復したる後更に取極あるまで上海の西方に支那軍の進出を一時制限すべき線を画定し又1月28日の事件以前におけるが如く共同租界及租界外拡張道路上へ日本軍の撤収を定めたり。但し日本軍の数は共同租界内にのみ駐屯せしむるには多きに過ぎたるを以て共同租界外の若干地域は当分の間包含せらるべきものとなりたるが其後日本軍撤収せるを以て此等の地域に付いては記述の要なし。米英佛伊友好国並びに両当事国の参加せる共同委員会を設置し双方の撤退を確むることとし本委員会は亦日本軍より支那警察への引継ぎにも協力することとなれり。

　　支那側は停戦協定に二個の留保を付加せり。第一の留保は、協定中の如何なる規定も支那領土内における支那軍の行動を永久的に制限することを意味せざる旨の声明にして第二の留保は、日本軍駐屯の為暫時設けられたる地域に於いても警察を含む一切の地方行政は支那官憲の手に存すべきむねの声明なり。

　　停戦協定の条項は大体主要部分において履行せられたり。撤退地域は5月9日、同月30日の間に支那特別警察に引渡されたり。但し之等四地域の引継ぎは多少延引を見たり。家屋及工場を所有する支那人、鉄道会社の役員及其他の者が撤収地域に復帰し始めたるとき掠奪、故意の破壊及財産喪失に関し多数の苦情が日本軍当局に提起せられたるは蓋し自然のことなり。支那側に於いては賠償に関する全問題は将来商議せらるべきものなりとし死傷及行方不明の将卒及人民の数二万二千四百、物質的損害全額は略々十五億墨弗に達すと推定し居れり。租界外拡張道路地域に関する協定草案は上海工部局及支那大上海市政府代表に依り署名せられたり。然れども本案は未だ上海工部局又は市政府の何れよりも承認を得ず。工部局は領事国の意見を求むる為主席領事に本案を移牒せり。

上海に於ける支那側抵抗の満州の事態に及ぼせる影響

　　上海事件は疑いもなく満州に於ける事態に着しき影響を及ぼせり。日本側が容易に満州の大部分を占領し得たること及支那軍より何等抵抗を受けざりしことは単に日本陸海軍をして支那軍の戦闘力が無視し得べき程のものなりと信ずるに至らしめたるのみならず全支那をして大いに意気喪失せしめたり。然るに第十九路軍が最初より第八十七師及八十八師の援助の下に試みたる強硬なる抵抗は全支那に於いて熱狂的歓呼を受けたるが当初の三千の日本陸戦隊に三個師団及一混成旅団の応援加わり六週間の戦闘の後漸く支那軍敗退駆逐せられたるの事実は支那側士気に多大の印象を与え支那は其自身の努力に依りて救われざるべからずとの感情拡まれり。日支紛争は支那全民の念頭に入り支那各地何れにおいても支那人の意見強硬となり抵抗心増加して従前の消極主義は消去り誇張せる楽観主義行わるるに至れり。満州に於ては上海よりの報道は当時尚日本軍と戦いつつありし各地支那軍に新たなる勇気を与えたり。右報道は馬占山其後の抵抗を強むることとなり又世界各地に在る支那人の愛国心を刺激せり。義勇軍の抵抗も

増大あるが為之等支那軍討伐は捗しき成功を収めず、或地方に於いては日本軍は鉄道沿線に陣地を占め守勢を執り居たるが右鉄道もしばしば支那側の攻撃を受けたり。

一九三二年二月一日の南京事件

上海に於ける交戦に伴い数個の事件発生せるが其の一つは南京砲撃なり。本事件は支那以外においても多大の興奮と驚愕とを生ぜしめたるが右は2月1日の深更発生せるも一時間以上は継続せざりき。本件は多分誤解に基づくものならんか、支那政府の南京より洛陽への臨時遷都なる重大なる結果を招来せり。

南京事件の原因及事実に関する日支双方の解釈には非常なる懸隔あり。日本側より調査団に提出せる主張二ありしか。第一は上海の戦闘発生後支那側は獅子山砲台を拡張し塹壕を築き、江畔の城門及江の反対側に砲兵陣地を設け江に軍艦を碇泊せしめ居たる日本側に心配を生ぜしむるに足るが如き規模の軍事施設をなせりと云うに在り。第二は支那新聞は上海支那軍の勝利の虚報を拡め南京支那人を大いに昂奮せしめ其の結果日本側の云う所に依れば日本人雇用の支那人は其の職を去る様強迫せられ支那商人は領事館員及軍艦乗組員外日本在留民に食糧品供給を拒絶するに至れりと云うにあり。

支那側は之等の主張に対し何等批評を加えず。支那側は当時一般の不安及緊張せる空気は日本側が上海事件発生後碇泊軍艦数を二隻より五隻に増加し次いで七隻（日本側当局は右数を六隻なりとし三老齢砲艦及三駆逐艦なりとす）に増加したるに基づくものなる旨又日本海軍司令官は水兵若干を上陸せしめ之を日本領事館員及全日本居留民が「ハルク」に避難せる日清汽船埠頭の前に歩哨として配置せるが上海事件の記憶尚新たなる際斯かる措置は既に南京の昂奮せる人民をして同様事件発生せざるやとの恐怖の念を生ぜしめたるならんと称す。

調査団は南京警察署長が外交部長に提出せる報告に依り南京の支那住民及外国人の保護に全責任を有する南京当局が日本水兵の上陸に対し忿懣を抱き居たる旨を知れり。南京当局は日本副領事に対し数度抗議をなせるが同副領事は右上陸に関し何等の処置を執り得ざる旨答えたり当時軍艦碇泊し居り上記埠頭の存する下関の地方警察署に対し出来得るならば同方面

に於ける日支接触殊に夜間に於ける如何なる接触をも阻止する様特別の訓令発せられたり。日本側公報に依れば日本人避難民は2月29日以後日清汽船会社の一汽船船内に収容せられ其の多数は上海に送られたる由なり。日本側は2月1日深更三発の砲弾突如発せられたるが右は獅子山砲台よりなされたるものと認めらるる旨述べ居たり。右と同時に支那軍正規兵は河畔にありし日本海軍歩哨に向かい発砲し二名を負傷せしめたるか其の中一名は死亡せり。右攻撃に対し反撃加えられたるが右は歩哨上陸地点直近の箇所にのみ向けられ岸より発砲止むや直ちに停止せられたり。以上は日本側の述べる所なるが支那側は之に対し発砲の事実を否定すると共に日本側より砲台、下関停車場及其他の場所に合計八発の砲弾発せられ且機関銃及小銃射撃行われたる旨並びに右の間サーチライトが岸に向けられたる旨主張す。右は住民に多大の恐怖を生ぜしめ住民は南京市内部に急遽引移れるが死傷者はなく物質的損害も大ならざりき。

　南京事件が昂奮せる支那人民が上海支那軍勝利の虚報を祝いて鳴らしたる爆竹に端を発したりと云うことも亦有り得べきことなり。

第六章　「満州国」

1.「新国家」建設の階段

日本軍の奉天占領の結果招来せる混乱状態

　前章に於いて説述せる如く1931年9月18日事件の結果、奉天市の市行政及奉天省の省行政は完全に破壊せられ延いて其他の二省の省行政に至る迄程度は少きも影響を蒙りたる。奉天に対する攻撃余りに急速なりし為め全満州の政治的中心なるのみならず大連に次いで南満州の最も重要なる商業的中心たる同市は支那人民の間に恐慌を惹起するに至れり。著名の官公吏並びに教育界及商業界の主要人物の大多数は直ちに家族と共に逃亡せり。9月19日後の数日間に亘り十一万人以上の支那人住民は京奉鉄道に依り奉天を去りたるが逃亡し得ざるものは多く潜匿せり。警官及監獄看守人に至る迄失踪せり。奉天市、奉天県及奉天省の行政は完全に崩壊し電燈、水等供給の公共事業会社、乗合自動車、市街電車並びに電話及電信業務は一

切停止するに至れり。銀行及商会は閉鎖せり。

奉天市の秩序及び市政の復活

至急を要するは市政府の組織及市の正常生活の復活にありたるが之は日本人に依り着手せられ迅速且有効に取り運ばれたり。土肥原大佐は奉天市長に就任し三日以内に正常市政は復活せられたり。数百の警官及監獄看守人の大部分は臧式毅将軍(省長)の援助に依り復帰せしめられ公共業務は回復せり。非常時委員会の大部分は日本人より成れるが土肥原大佐を援助し同大佐は一ヶ月間其の職に留まれり。10月20日、市政府の施政は趙欣伯博士(11年間日本に留学し東京帝国大学の法学博士の称号を有する法律家)を市長とする一定の資格ある支那人団体に復帰せられたり。

省政府の再組織(一)奉天省

次の問題は三省の各省政を再建するに在りたり。右事業中奉天省は他の二省に比し一層困難なりき。何となれば奉天は同省行政の中心にして有力者の多くは逃亡し、暫時支那人による省行政は錦州において依然として継続せられたればなり。故に省政の再組織が完全に成就せるは三ヵ月後なりき。

臧式毅将軍の独立省政府組織の拒絶

遼寧省省長たりし臧式毅中将は最初9月20日支那中央政府より独立せる省政府組織に関し交渉を受け勧誘せられたるが之を拒絶せり。次いで同中将は逮捕せられ、12月15日釈放せられたり。

九月二十五日袁金凱を委員長とする「治安維持委員会」の設置

臧式毅将軍が独立政府樹立に関する援助を拒絶したる後、支那人有力者の一人たる袁金凱氏が交渉を受けたるが同氏は元の省長にして東北政治委員会の副委員長なりき。日本軍事当局は袁金凱氏及其他八人の支那人住民をして治安維持委員会を組織せしめんことを勧誘せり。同委員会は9月24日組織せられたる旨声明せられたり。日本側新聞は直ちに之を以て分離運動に対する第一歩として称賛せるが10月5日、袁金凱氏は斯かる意思無きことを公然声明せり。袁氏曰く同委員会は「旧施政崩壊後平和及秩序保持の為め実現せられたるものにして逃亡者救出及金融市場回復を援助し且其他の事務に当れるが右は全く単に不必要なる困難を避けしめんが為なりき。然れども同委員会は省政府を組織し又は独立宣言の意思無かりき」

云々。

十月十九日財政部の開設

10月19日、治安維持委員会は財政部を開設し支那人官吏を補佐する為め日本人顧問任命せられたり。財政部長は同部の決定に対し効力を発せしむるに先ち軍事当局の承認を得るを要したり。各県内における収税吏は日本人憲兵隊又は其他の代理人に依り支配せられたり。場所に依りては右収税吏は毎日憲兵隊の検閲に供する為め帳簿を提出するを要し、憲兵隊の承認は警官、裁判、教育等公共の目的に要する一切の費用の支出に対し必要なりき。錦州に於ける「敵対者」に向かっての税金送達は直ちに日本当局に報告せられたり。之と同時に財政整理委員会組織せられ其の主要事務は租税制度を建直すに在りたり。日本人代表者及支那人組合代表者は税制に関する論議に参加するを許されたり。長春に於ける「外交部」より調査委員に対し送付せられたる1932年5月30日付「満州国独立史」中における声明に拠れば前述税制審議の結果1931年11月16日付を以て六税の廃止、其他四税の半減、尚其他八税の地方政府への移譲並びに法律的根拠無き一切の課税を禁止することを決定せり。

十月二十一日実業部の設立

10月21日、治安維持委員会「遼寧省自治委員会」改名せらるに依り実業部開設せられたり。日本軍当局の承認を求め且右承認を得たり而して多数の日本人顧問任命せられたり。凡て命令を発するに先ち同部長は日本軍事当局の承認を得るを要求せられたり。

東北交通委員会

最後に遼寧自治委員会は新に東北交通委員会を組織したるが同委員会は漸次遼寧省のみならず吉林省及黒龍江両省における許多の鉄道に関する管理を掌握するに至れり。同委員会は11月1日遼寧自治委員会より分離せり。

十一月七日の声明及び十一月十日省政府の樹立

11月7日、遼寧省自治委員会は臨時遼寧省政府成る形体に転化し声明書を発表して旧東北政府及南京中央政府より分離せり。臨時遼寧省政府は同省内の各地方政府に対しその発布せる命令を遵守すべきことを要求し、爾後省政府として権限を行使すべき旨発表せり。

11 月 10 日公開式挙行せられたり。

最高諮議委員長の任命

自治委員会が臨時遼寧省政府に改造さるると同時に最高諮議委員会なるもの于沖漢氏の委員長の下に創設せられたり。于沖漢氏は従来治安維持委員会の副議長なりしなり。于沖漢氏は最高諮議委員会の目的を左の如く発表せり。即ち秩序の維持、悪税の廃止による施政改善、租税軽減並びに生産及販売組合の改善是なり。同委員会は更に臨時省政府を指揮監督し各地の伝統及近代的要求に準拠し省自治政府の発展を助成するに在りき。同委員会は総務課、調査課、儀礼課、指導課、監査課及自治指導部の各課より成る。主要吏員の多くは日本人なり。

十一月二十日奉天省の改名及び十二月十五日臧式毅の省長就任

11 月 20 日、省名は奉天省と改正せられたるが右は1928 年国民党支配下の支那との合同以前の名称なり。亦 12 月 15 日、袁金凱氏は臧式毅将軍に依り代られたり。彼は監禁より釈放せられ奉天省長に就任せるなり。

(二) 吉林省

吉林省に省政府を樹立する事業は遥かに容易なりき。23 日第二師団多門少将は張作相将軍の不在中省長代理たる熙洽中将と会見し省長たらんことを勧誘せり。右会見後 9 月 25 日熙洽将軍は許多の政府当局者及公共団体を召集会合せしめたるが多数の日本人士官も亦参加せり。新省政府樹立の思案に対し何等反対の表明無く 9 月 30 日右趣旨の布告書発表せられたり。次いで吉林省政府に関する組織法公布せられたり。政府の委員制度廃止せられ熙洽省長は省政府の行為に対し全責任を負えり。数日後熙洽氏に依り新政府の主要官吏任命せられ其後若干の日本人吏員追加せられたり。総務長官は日本人なりき。県政においても亦行政改革せられ且人員の変動ありたり。四十三県の中十五県は改革せられたるが其中支那人県吏の解任も含めり。其他十県における県吏はき毫将軍に忠誠を宣明したる後其侭就職を持続せり。其他は依然として旧政権に忠実なる支那人軍閥の下に留まるか又は闘争各派に対し中立を保てり。

(三) 東支鉄道の特別区

特別区行政長官張景恵将軍は日本人に対し友好関係に在りき。旧政権は特別区内における鉄道守備隊及吉林、黒龍江両省における相当多数の軍

隊を尚有し得たるに対し張景恵氏は何等軍隊の背景を有せざりき。9月27
日、張景恵はハルピンに於ける事務所において会合を催し特別区の非常時
委員会の組織を論議せり。同委員会は張将軍を委員長として其他八人の委
員より成り其中王瑞花将軍及1932年1月熙洽将軍に敵対せる「反吉林軍」
の指揮官となれる丁超将軍を含めり。11月5日、張作相下の将官の指揮に
依り反吉林軍はハルピンにおいて新に吉林省政府を樹立せり。1932年1
月1日張景恵将軍黒龍江省長に任命せらるるや省長の資格において1月7
日同省の独立を宣言せり。1月29日丁超将軍行政長官の官庁を占領する
や張将軍を其屋内に幽閉せり。張将軍は日本軍が北上し丁超将軍撃退後2
月5日ハルピンを占領するや再び自由となれり。爾来日本の勢力は特別区
内に益々拡大するに至れり。

(四) 黒龍江省

黒龍江省に於いて説述せる如く張海鵬及馬占山両将軍の抗争に因り一
層複雑せる形勢を生ぜり。11月19日、日本軍のチチハル占領後常例の形
式の自治協会なるもの設立せられたるが人民の意思を代表すと称せらるる
該協会は特別区の張景恵将軍に対し黒龍江省長を兼任せむことを勧誘せ
り。然れどもハルピン付近の形勢尚依然として不安定にして馬占山将軍と
の間に確定協定成立せざりしに因り右勧誘は1932年1月に至る迄受諾せ
られざりき。1月に至りてさえも馬占山将軍の態度は暫く曖昧なりき。馬
占山将軍は2月丁超将軍が敗北する迄之と相提携し然る後日本軍と和睦し
張将軍の掌中より黒龍江省長の職を受取りたるが次いで左の省長と共に新
「国家」の建設に協力せり。1月25日チチハルにおいて自治指導委員会設
立せられ他の省と同一形式の省政府の形態漸次成立するに至れり。

(五) 熱河省

熱河省は従来満州に於ける政治的変動に対し中立を維持し来れり。熱
河省は内蒙古の一部分なり。目下三百万以上の支那人移民同省内に住居し
漸次遊牧蒙古人を北方に追放しつつあるが蒙古人は依然として伝統的部族
又は旗人組織の下に生活す。約百万を数ふる斯種蒙古人は奉天省の西部に
居住する蒙古旗人と若干程度の関係を保持し来れり。

奉天省及熱河省の蒙古人は「盟」を組織したるが其の中最も有力なるも
のを「チェリム」盟と為す。チェリム盟は独立運動に参加せるが従来しばし

ば支那の支配より免れんと試み来れる「バルガ」地方即ち黒龍江省西部の
「コロンバイル」の蒙古人も亦同運動に参加せり。

　　　蒙古人は容易に支那人と同化せず。彼等は自尊心強き人種にして皆
「チンギス」汗の偉業及蒙古武人の支那制服を記憶し居れり。彼等は支那人
の支配を受くることを悪み殊に支那移民の来住を好まず。蓋し右移住に因
り蒙古人は漸次自己の領土より駆逐せられ居ればなり。熱河省のチチハル
及チョサツの両盟は奉天省の各旗と連絡を取り居れるか後者は今や委員会
に依り支配せられ居れり。熱河省の主席湯玉麟は9月29日同省に対する
全責任を執り満州に於ける同僚と連絡を取り来りたる由なり。3月9日の
「満州国」建国に当り熱河省は「新国家」に包容せられたるか、実際に於いて
は同省政府は何等決定的措置を執ることなかりき。同省に於ける最近の出
来事に付いては前章の末尾において言及するところありたり。

　　「独立国家」の創立

　　　以上の如くにして各省に設立せられたる地方自治政府機関は次いで分
離独立せる「国家」として相結合せられたり。「新国家」が容易に成立したる
こと及「新国家」が成立の後支那人之に対して与えたる支持に関して提出せ
られたる多くの証拠を理解する為には、或場合には強みとなり他の場合に
は弱点となる支那社会生活の一特徴を考慮すること必要なり。既に第一章
に於いて述べたるが如く、支那人の認むる共同生活上の義務は国家に対す
るよりは寧ろ家族、地方または個人に対するものなり。西洋に所謂愛国心
は支那にては今日漸く感得せられ始めたるに過ぎず。職業組合、協会、盟及
軍隊等皆或個人的指導者に従うを例とす。斯かるが故に説得または強制に
依りて或特定の指揮者の支持を得るときは右指揮者の全勢力範囲内の追従
者の支持も亦自ら得ころろなるなり。前掲の如き事件の記述は支那人の
斯かる特徴が各省政府の組織に如何に巧みに利用せられたるかを示すもの
にして、同一の之等少数の有力者の働きは最終の階梯を完成する為に用い
られたり。

　　自治指導部

　　　独立を達成する主要なる手段となりしは奉天に中央事務所を有したる
自治指導部なり。信憑すべき証人が委員会に対して陳述したる所に依れば
右自治指導部は日本人に依り組織せられ且首長は支那人なるも大部分の職

員は日本人に依り充たされ関東軍司令部第四部の機関として活動したる趣なり。而して同部の主たる目的は独立運動を作興するに在りたり。右中央部の指揮監督の下に奉天省各県に地方自治執行委員会組織せられたり。之等各県に対し中央部は其の有する監督員、指導者及講師より成る多数且経験に富める人員中より必要に応じ部員を派したるが其の多くは日本人なりき。尚中央部は其の編集発行せる新聞を利用したり。

一月七日の在奉天自治指導部の布告

右中央部より発せられたる訓令の性質は同部が1月1日付を以て同月7日発布したる布告を見れば明らかなり。同布告は東北は今や満州及蒙古に於いて新「独立」国家の建設の為一大民衆運動を遅滞なく起こすの必要に直面せりと告げ居れり。同布告は尚奉天省各県に於ける其の事業の発展の状を叙し且奉天省の爾余の各県、更に進んでは奉天以外の各省に対し其の活動を拡張する為の計画を概説したり。而して更に布告は東北民衆に対し張学良を打倒し、自治協会に加入し、清廉なる政府を設立し、人民の生活状態を改善するが為に協力すべしと訴え次の語を以て結べり「北部及東部の組織よ団結せよ。新国家へ。独立へ。」右布告は五万枚頒布せられたり。

一月中に於ける部長の計案

尚1月中には早くも自治指導部部長于沖漢は省長臧式毅と共に「新国家」に対する計案を作りつつありたるが右「新国家」は2月10日樹立せらるべき旨報ぜられたり。然るに1月29日哈爾賓に於いて兵変勃発したること及丁超との戦闘中馬将軍の態度不明なりしことは当時右準備の進行を一時延期せる主なる理由なりしが如し。

二月十六日―十七日の奉天会議

其の後丁超敗退後張景恵中将と馬将軍との間の商議の結果、2月14日協定成り之に依り馬将軍は黒龍江省省長に就任することとなれり。「新国家」の基礎を協定すべき会議は2月16日及17日、奉天に於いて開かれたり。東三省または省長及特別区長官並びに従来の一切の準備事業において重要なる役割を演じ来れる趙欣伯博士自ら出席せり。

右五人の会合において「新国家」を建設すべきこと、一時東三省及特別区に対する最高権力を行使すべき東北行政委員会組織すべきこと、及最後に右最高委員会は遅滞無く「新国家」の建設の為必要なる一切の準備をなす

べきこと決議せられたり。会議の第二日には二人の蒙古王族出席したるが其の一は黒龍江省西部のバルガ地方へコロンバイルを代表し、他即ちチェリム盟のチワン親王は同親王を他の如何なる指導者よりも尊敬し居る殆ど凡ての旗を代表したり。

二月十七日の最高行政委員会

同日、最高行政委員会組織せられたり。其の委員は委員張景恵中将、奉天、吉林、黒龍江及熱河の四省長並びに蒙古地方代表チワン親王及リン・シェン親王なり。同委員会最初の諸決議は次の如し、即ち、「新国家」に共和制を採用すること、構成各省の自治を尊重すること、執政に「摂政」の称号を与えること、四省及特別区長官、全旗体表チワン親王及黒龍江省コロンバイル代表クエイフの署名すべき独立宣言を発すること。関東軍司令官は同夜「新国家の幹部」の為公式の晩餐会を催したるが、同司令官は右幹部に対し其の成功を祝すと共に必要の際には援助を与うべき旨確言するところありたり。

二月十八日の独立宣言

独立の宣言は2月18日発布せられたり。右宣言は永遠の平和を享受せんとする人民の熱烈なる願望及人民に依り選定せられたりと称せらる各施政者が右人民の願望を充たすべき義務に言及せり。宣言は「新国家」樹立の必要に言及し且東北行政委員会は此の目的の為設置せられたる旨述べたり。今や国民党及南京政府との関係破棄せられたるを以て、人民は善政を享受すべしと約束したり。同宣言は通電を以て満州各地に発送せられたり。馬省長及熙洽省長は夫々其の省首都に帰還せるが、代表を任命して臧式毅省長、張景恵長官及趙欣伯市長と会合し以て細目を決定せしめたり。

「新国家」に対する計案

此の団体に依り次いで開かれたる2月19日の会合において共和国を建立すること、憲法中に於いて権力分立主義を規定すること、及前宣統皇帝に執政たらんことを謂うべきことを決議せり。次の数日中において首都は長春とすること、年号は「大同」(大調和を意味す)とすることを決議し尚国旗の図案も決定せられたり。2月25日、右諸決議は熱河省を含む各省政府並びにコロンバイル及チェムリ、チャタオ、チョサツ諸盟の蒙古行政諸官署に通告せられたり。右の中最後に掲げたる三盟は熱河省に設立せられたる

ものにして、従って既述の如く熱河省省長の意に反する何等の措置を執ること能わざりき。

国家建立促進運動

独立宣言及「新国家」建設諸計画発表後、自治指導部は民衆を組織して之に対する支持を表明せしむる上において指導的役割を演じたり。同部は「新国家建設促進」の為の諸協会設立に与って力ありたり。同部は其の奉天省各県に於ける支部、即ち自治執行委員会に訓令して一切の手段を尽くして独立運動を強化促進せしめたり。此の結果、新たなる促進協会は、自治執行委員会を中心として続々設立せられたり。2月20日以後此等の新に組織せられたる促進協会は活動を開始せり。ポスターは準備せられ、スローガンは印刷せられ書籍及パンフレットは発行せられ「東北文化半月刊」は発行せられ亦配布せられたり。リーフレットは郵便に依りて多数の名士に発送せられ宣伝事業に対する助力を求めたり。

独立に対する民衆の賛意の組織化

奉天に於いては支那商業会議所は聯を配布して戸口に貼付せしめたり。同時に各県の自治執行委員会は地方紳士並びに商業、農業、工業及教育団体の会長又は着名会員等の如き人民代表の会議を招集せり。加えるに民衆大会は組織せられ行列又は遊行県首都の主要街路に行われたり。一般人民又は特殊の団体の希望を表明せる決議は地方有力者会議又は幾千人の出席者ありたりと称せらるる民衆大会に於いて通過したり。此等決議は勿論在奉天自治指導部に送達せられたり。

「新国家」に賛成する二月二十日奉天決議

促進協会及自治執行委員会が奉天省の各県に於いて活動を続けたる後「新国家」建設に対する民衆の一般的希望を具体的に表示する為奉天に於いて省大会組織せられたり。斯くて2月28日、会合は開催せられたるが、右会合には同省の一宣言署を発して旧圧制軍閥の没落及新時代の黎明に対する奉天省一千六百万住民の喜悦の情を表明せり。奉天省に関する限りに於いては右運動は斯くして終結を告げたり。

吉林省に於ける独立運動

吉林省に於ける「新国家」賛助運動も亦組織せられ且指導せられたるものなりき。奉天における2月16日の会議に出席中、熙洽省長は同省各県官

吏に対し通電を発して「新国家」が行うべき政策に付いての世論に関し情報を与えられんことを求めたり。之等各県官吏は各自の県に於ける諸職業組合及協会に対し十分の指導を与うべき旨命ぜられたり。右通電に対する直接の反響として独立運動は各地に台頭せり。2月20日、吉林省政府は、国家創立委員会を組織したるが、其の目的は各種団体の独立運動を指導するに在りたり。2月24日、在長春人民協会は民衆大会を開催せるが、約四千名の出席有りたる旨報ぜられたり。彼等は「新国家」建立の促進を要求せり。同様なる会議は其の他の地方及哈爾賓に於いても亦開催せられたり。2月25日、全省民衆大会吉林市に於いて開催せられたり。約一万人の出席者ありたる旨報ぜられたり。2月28日、奉天に於いて通過せられたると同様の宣言然るべく発せられたり。

黒龍江省に於ける

黒龍江省に於いては奉天自治指導部が重要なる役割を演じたり。1月7日、張景恵将軍は黒龍江省長の職責を引受けるや同省の独立を宣言せり。

前記奉天自治指導部は、黒龍江省に於ける右加速度的運動を指導援助せり。四名の将校(内二名は日本将校)奉天より齊々哈爾に急行したり。此等将校が齊々哈爾到着後二日を経て即ち2月22日省政府庁舎内の大広間に会合を催したるが右会合には各団体より多数の参加者ありたり。右会合は全黒龍江省大会にして建国準備の方法を決定せむがためのものなりが右大会は2月24日、大示威運動をなすべき旨の決議を可決したり。

齊々哈爾に於ける右示威運動には数千の群衆参加し行列はポスター、巻旗、旗を以て覆われ此事件を祝賀したり。日本の砲兵隊は当日を祝福して101発の礼砲を発し、日本飛行機上空を旋回し印刷物を投下したり。直ちに宣言発せられたるが此れに拠り責任内閣制とし且元首に大統領を推戴する共和政体建設せられたり。総ての権力は中央政府に集中せられ省政府はこれを廃止することとし県及市町村は地方行政の単位として存置したり。

2月末に至るまでに奉天、吉林、黒龍江及特別区は既に夫々宣言を発し、蒙古旗族も亦特別自治区を形成し地方蒙古族の権利を保障し得ること或は可能ならしむること判明したるを以て其の忠誠を「新国家」に対し誓うに至れり。回教徒は奉天における2月15日の会合に於いて既に彼等の忠

誠を誓いたり。其他未だ帰属せざる少数の満州人の大部分は「新国家」の執政として多分前皇帝が推挙せらるべしとのことを知るや「新国家」を歓迎したり。

二月廿九日奉天に於ける全満大会

各省区が「新国家」建設計画に対し正式の賛同を与えたる後自治指導部は2月29日、奉天に全満州大会を召集したり。右大会には各省並びに奉天省及蒙古地方の各郡等より正式代表其他多数参列し、又吉林及特別区の朝鮮人並蒙古の青年同盟支部等諸種の団体の代表者会合し其の総数7百名以上に達したり。

諸種の演説為され、満場一致を以て宣言及決議可決せられたるが前者は旧制度を攻撃し、後者は「新国家」を歓迎したり。又「新国家」の臨時的元首として前皇帝の宣統帝（帝はヘンリー溥儀氏として知らる）を推挙するの第二決議も採択せられたり。

前皇帝「ヘンリー」溥儀氏「満州国」元首を承諾す

東北行政執行委員会は直ちに緊急会議を開き六名の代表者を選び之を旅順に派遣し去年11月、天津出発以来同地に滞在中の前皇帝を招ぜしめたり。溥儀氏は最初之を拒絶したるも3月4日、第二回目の29名より成る代表者は遂に僅か一年を期限として氏の承諾を取り付け得たり。於此前記執行委員会は陸軍中将張景恵を委員長とし他に九名の委員を選出して歓迎委員会を組織したるが右委員会は3月5日、旅順に赴き謁見を賜りたり。前皇帝は委員の懇請を容れて3月6日、旅順を出発し湯崗子に至りたるが2日の後、即ち3月8日には既に「満州国」の執政としての礼遇を受けたり。

三月九日長春に於ける就任式

3月9日、新都長春に於いて就任式行われたり。溥儀氏は執政として「新国家」の政策は「道義、仁慈、愛撫」を基礎とすべきことを約する旨の宣言を発したり。10日には新政府の幹部即ち内閣の閣僚、立法院長監察院長、参議院総裁及副総裁、各省庁及特別区長、各省防備司令其他の高官の任命を見たり。「満州国」建設に関する通告は3月12日諸外国に発せられたるが、右通告の目的は諸外国に対し「満州国」建設の根本目的、対外政策の主義を通告し、「新国家」としての承認を要求するにありとせられたり。

執政の到着前、既に相当数の法規は制定せられ公布せらるる迄になり

居たるが(右法規の制定には趙欣伯博士も時々参加し来りたり)此等法規は
3月9日、新政府組織法と同時に実施せられ、其れ迄有効なりし諸法規は新
法規又は「新国家」の根本方針と抵触せざる限り同日付の特別命令に依り暫
定的に採用せられたり。

情報の出所

「満州国」創設に至る経過に関する此の既述はあらゆる出所より得たる
情報に依り編転せられたるものなり。諸種の事件は其の都度詳細に日本の
新聞に報ぜられたるが日本人の編転する「マンチュリア・デイリー・ニュ
ース」には多分最も豊富に報ぜられたり。5月30日、長春に於いて現政府
により準備せられたる「満州国独立史—満州国外交部編」「満州国概観—満
州国外交部編」の二冊支那参与員に依り準備せられたる「東三省に於ける所
謂独立運動に関する覚書」は夫々注意深く研究せられたり。加之能う限り
第三者より得たる情報利用せられたり。

九月十八日以来の民事行政

9月18日より「満州国政府」建設に至る迄の間に於ける日本軍憲の民
事行政、特に銀行の監督、公共事業の経営及鉄道の運用に関する措置は軍事
行動開始の時以来、一時的軍事占拠の必要以上の永続的なる諸種の目的が
遂行せられたることを示したり。9月19日、奉天占拠の直後、支那銀行、鉄
道事務所、公共事業事務所、鉱山管理事務所等の内部又は門前に護衛を置き
然る後此等事業の財政的又は一般的情況の調査行われたり。此等の事務所
再開せらるるに及び日本人は顧問、専門家又は秘書に任命せられ執行権限
を有したり。多くの企業は前東三省政府又は各省政府の所有したるものな
るが此等の政府は戦時においては敵国政府と看做さるるを以て何れの銀行
も、鉱山も、農工施設も、鉄道事務所も公益営造物も実際此等政府が嘗て公
的に又私的に利害関係を有したる収入の唯一の源と雖も管理を受けざるも
のなかりき。

鉄道

鉄道に関し軍事行動の当初以来、日本官憲に依り執られたる措置は日
支間の鉄道に付永年係争中なる諸問題の或もの(本問題に関しては第三章
に既述せらる)に関し日本のために有利に決定することにありたり即ち急
速に左の如き措置執られたり。

（1）長城以北の総ての支那所有鉄道及在満州諸銀行に在る此等鉄道関係預金は没収せられたり。

（2）満鉄と協調せしむる為奉天の内外に於いて線路の変更を為したり。即ち満鉄橋下において京奉線を切断し遼寧中央停車場、奉天東駅、奉天北門駅を閉鎖し且吉林行支那政府鉄道（後に復旧せらる）との連絡を断ちたり。

（3）吉林に於いては海倫吉林線、吉林敦化線及吉林長春線の間に有機的連絡を設定したり。

（4）日本の技術的顧問は各鉄道に配置せられたり。

（5）支那官憲に依り採用せられたる「特別運賃率」は廃止せられ旧運賃率採用せられたり即ち満鉄の運賃率と一致する運賃率の採用を見たり。

9月18日即ち東北交通委員会が機能を停止して以来、「満州国」交通部の開設に至るまでは日本官憲が諸鉄道の管理に付全責任を負いたり。

其他の公共事業

在留民の生命及財産の保護の為め必要なる程度を超えて行われたる此種の措置は奉天及安東における電気供給の場合に於いても日本官憲に依りて行われたり又9月18日より「満州国」建設までの期間、日本官憲は支那政府の電話、電信及無電の管理及運用に関し変更を加えたるが右は満州に於ける日本の電話及電信事業と共同し得べし。

結論

1931年9月18日以来、日本軍憲の軍事上及民政上の活動は本質的に政治的考慮に依りて為されたり。東三省の前進的軍事占拠は支那官憲の手より順次齊々哈爾、錦州及哈爾賓を奪い遂には満州に於ける総ての重要なる都市に及びたり。而して軍事占領の後には常に民政が快復せられたり。1931年9月以前に於いて聞かざりし独立運動が日本軍の入満により可能となりたることは明らかなり。

日本における新政治運動に密接なる接触を保ち居たる（第四章参照）日本の文官及将校の一団は其の現職にあると否とを問わず9月18日の事件後に於ける満州の事態の解決策として此の独立運動を計画し組織し、且遂行したり。

彼等は右目的を以て支那人の生命及行動を利用して前政権に対し不平を抱く住民中少数民族を利用したり。

日本の参謀本部が当初より又は少なくとも暫時を経て斯くの如き自治運動を利用することを覚えたること亦明らかなり。其結果彼等は此運動の組織者に対し援助及指導を与えたり。各方面より得たる証拠に依り本委員会は「満州国」の創設に寄与したる要素は多々あるも相俟って最も有効にして然も吾人の見る所を以てせば其れなきにおいては「新国家」は形成せられざりしなるべしと思考せらるる二つの要素ある其れは日本軍隊の存在と日本の文武官憲の活動なりと確信するものなり。

右の理由に依り現在の政権は純粋且自発的なる独立運動に依りて出現したるものと思考することを得ず。

2.「満州国」の現政府

政府組織法

「満州国」は組織法及人権保障法に依りて統治せらる。政府組織法は、政府諸機関の根本的組織を規定したるものにして大同元年(1932年)3月9日付教令第一号に依りて公布せられたり。

執政は国家の元首にして総ての行政権は執政に属し執政は又立法院を統制するの権能あり。執政は重要国務に関し助言を与える参議府に依り補佐せらる。

政府組織法の特質は政府の権力を国務、立法司法及監察の四院に分かつ点にあり。

国務院

国務院の任務は執政統御の下に総理及各総長に依りて遂行せられ総理及此等総長は相合し国務院即ち内閣を組織するものとす。総理は各総長の事務を監督し強力なる総務長を通じて機密事項、人事、主計、需要の事務を直裁す。国務院に付属して諸種の事務局あり就中資政院及法制局は重要なり行政権は斯くの如く主として執政及総理の手に集中せられ居れり。

立法院

立法権は立法院にあり総ての法律及予算は立法院の翼算を経るを要す。然れども立法院が或法案を否決したる場合には執政は立法院に其の再議を要求することを得。而して尚再び其の法案が否決せられたる場合には執政は参議府に諮りて其の可否を裁決することを得。然れども現在に於い

ては立法院の組織に関する法律は制定せられ居らず。従って諸法律は国務院に依り起草せられ参議府に諮問せられ且執政の承認あらば効力を発生す。従って立法院が組織せられざる限り総理の地位は最も有力なり。

司法院

司法院は数多の法院を包含し此等の法院は最高法院、高等法院及地方法院の三階級に分たる。

監察院

監察院は管理の業績を監察し会計を検査す。監察院の職員は犯罪行為又は懲戒処分によるの外免職せらるることなく且其の意思に反して停職、転任又は減俸せらるることなかるべし。

省及特別区

地方行政のため「満州国」は五省及二特別区に分たる省は奉天、吉林、黒龍江、熱河及興安なり。最後に掲げたる興安省は蒙古地方を包含し旧来の旗制度及諸旗聯盟の連合に適合する如く三地方即ち県に分たる特別区は、旧東支鉄道即ち哈爾賓地方及新に制定せられたる間島即ち朝鮮人地方なり。此の行政的区画に依り主要少数民族なる蒙古人、朝鮮人及ロシア人は彼等の需要に適合する特別の行政を出来得る限り保障せらるべきものとす。委員会は「満州国」に包含せらるることを要求せらるる地方の地図を示されんことをしばしば要求したれども右地図は与えられずして「満州国」の境界を左の如く示す一の書簡を受領したり。

「新国家は南は長城に依り界せられ同国に於ける蒙古諸盟及諸旗はコロンバイル並びに哲里木、昭烏達、卓索図の諸旗盟を包含す。」

各省の長官には省長あり。然れども行政権を中央政府に集中せんとするに依り省長は軍隊又は財政の何れに対しても何等の権限も与えらるるを得ず。省に於いても中央政府に於いても総務部が支配的地位を保持す総務部は機密事項、人事、会計、文書及他の管轄に属せざる事項を管理す。

県及市町村

省は県に分たる。県は一般に県自治機関に依り治められ右機関は其の指揮下に各部特に総務部を有す。市政府は奉天、哈爾賓及長春に存す。尤も哈爾賓に於いてはロシア市街及支那市街の双方を包含すべき大哈爾賓を建設せんとする計画あり。鉄道特区は廃止せらるべし同区の一部は大哈爾

賓に包含せらるべく、又、東支鉄道沿線の残部は黒龍江省及吉林省に加えらるべし。

　「満州国政府」は省を目して行政区画と為し、県及市町村を目して財政上の単位と為す。同政府は省、県及市町村の租税の額を決定し予算を裁決す。一切の地方的収入は中央の国庫に払込まるべく、国庫は然る後適当なる支出を管理す。此等の収入は旧制度の下において普通行われたる如く地方官憲に依り全部又は一部保留せらるることを得ず。自然本制度は未だ満足なる運用を見るに至らず。

　「満州国政府」においては日本人官吏は枢要の地位を占め且日本人顧問は総ての重要なる部局に付属す国務総理及其の大臣は総て支那人と雖も「新国家」の組織に於いて最大の実権を行使する各総務部の長は日本人なり。最初日本人は顧問として任命させれたれども最近に至り最も重要なる地位を占むる日本人は支那人と同一の地位に於いて完全なる官吏と為されたり。地方政府若しくは軍政部及軍隊又は政府の企業に於ける者を除き中央政府のみにおいて約二百名の日本人は「満州国」官吏なり。

日本人官吏及顧問

　日本人は総務庁並びに法制局及諮問局(右は実際上国務総理の官房を構成す)、各院及省政府に於ける総務部及県に於ける自治指導委員会並びに奉天、吉林及黒龍江各省における警察部を管理す。加之大多数の局課には日本人の顧問、書記官及事務官あり。

　尚鉄道事務所及中央銀行にも多数の日本人あり。監察院においては日本人は総務部長、管理部長及審計部長の地位を占む。立法院に於いて書記長は日本人なり。最後に執政の最も重要なる官吏は宮務局長及執政護衛隊司令官を含み日本人なり(重要なる任命は「満州国政府公報」に発表せられたり)。

政府の目的

　政府の目的は2月19日の東北行政委員会の宣言及3月1日の「満州国政府」の宣言に表明せられたるが如く「王道」の根本原則に従って統治するに在り。此の語に対する英語の正確なる同意語を発見するは困難なり。「満州国」当局に依り提供せられたる通訳者は之を「愛」と訳したれども、学者は多数の意味合いを有し得べき「王者の道」(キングリー・ウェー)なる意義を

之に与う。而して右は支那の伝統に依れば往時より誠心誠意民の安泰を念としたる善政の基礎たりしものなり伝統的に支那人は「王道」なる表現を「覇道」に正反対なるものとして使用したり。右「覇道」なる表現は孫逸仙博士に依り其の著「三民主義」中に論ぜられたる如く力と強制とに依頼することを意味す。孫逸仙は依て「王道」は「力是正義」の正反対なりと説明したり。

新政府創設の主たる立役者たる自治指導部の政策は該部に代わりたる諮問局に依り継続せられたり。軍事官憲は行政事項に干与することを許されざりき。官職勤務の資格を規律する規則は制定せらるべく且任命は候補者の能力を基礎として為されるべきものなるとせらる。

課税

課税は之を軽減し且法律的基礎の上に置かるべく、又経済及行政の健全なる原則に従い改革せらるべし。直接税は県及市町村の政府に移譲せらるべく、中央政府は間接税より得らるる収入を確保すべし。長春当局より供せられたる書類は若干の租税が既に廃止せられ同時に他の租税が軽減せられたる旨を述べ居れり。政府の企業及政府の所有する財源の調整が収入を増加せんこと及将来に於ける軍隊の縮小が支出を減少せんことを希望する旨表明せられたり。然れども目下の所「新国家」の財政的地位は不満足のものなり。不正規兵との戦争は軍費を大ならしめ他方同時に政府は正規の諸財源より収入を受領し居らず。第一年度の支出は現在大約六千五百万ドルの収入に対し八千五百万ドルの支出と見積もられ二千万ドルの不足を示せり。而て右付則はの地に説明するが如く（本報告諸付属の特別研究第四号参照）新に設置せられたる中央銀行よりの借入金を以て補充せらるる予定なり。

政府は財政的状態の改善するに従い其の収入の出来得る限り多額を教育、公安及国の発展（荒蕪地の開墾、鉱物及森林資源の開発並びに交通制度の拡張を含む）に使用すべき旨の意向を表明したり。政府は国の発展に付外国の財政的援助を歓迎すべきこと並びに機会均等及門戸開放の主義を固守すべきことを述べたり。

教育

政府は既に初等学校及中等学校を再開したり。而して政府は「新国家」の精神及政策を完全に了解すべき極めて多数の教員を訓令するの意向を有

す。新課程は採用せらるべく、新教科書は編纂せらるべく、而して一切の排外教育は廃止せらるべし。新教育制度は初等学校を改善すること及職業教育、初等学校教員の訓令及衛生的生活に関する健全なる思想の教授を強調することを目的と為すべし。英語及日本語の教授は中等学校に於いて義務的たるべく、又日本語の教授は初等学校において随意たるべし。

司法及警察

「満州国」当局は司法に対し行政官憲の干渉の許容せられざるべきことを決定したり。司法官の地位は法律に依りて保障せられ且其の俸給は充分なるものたるべし。司法官の地位に対する資格は高めらるべし。治外法権は当分の間尊重せらるべきも政府は現制度に対する適当なる改革の遂行せられたるとき治外法権の撤廃の為直ちに諸外国と交渉を開始するの意向なり。警察官は適当に選択、訓練、給与せられ且完全に軍隊(軍隊は警察職務を簒奪することを許されざるべし)より分離せしめらるべきものとす。

軍隊

軍隊の改変は計画せられ居るも現在のところ軍隊は大多数旧満州軍より成るを以て増大する不満と謀叛とを避くる為警戒を怠らざること必要なりと感ぜられ居れり。

「満州国」中央銀行は千九百三十二年七月一日長春に其の本店を及他の多くの満州都市に支店を開きたり

「満州国」中央銀行は6月14日設置せられ7月1日に正式に営業を開始せり。同銀行は「満州国」の首都長春に其の本店を並びに満州の都市の大部分に百七十の数に達する支店及出張所を有す。同銀行は三十年間有効の特許状を有する株式会社として組織せられたり。其の最初の行員は支那人及日本人たる銀行家及財政家なりき。同銀行は「内国通貨の流通を規律し、其の安定を保持し及金融を管理する」の権限を付与せられたり。同銀行の資本は三千万ドル(銀)として許可せられ且少なくとも30%の正貨準備を条件として紙幣を発行するの許可を与えられたり。

中央銀行は一切の旧省銀行(邊業銀行を含む)を併呑したり

旧省銀行(邊業銀行を含む)は新中央銀行と合併せられ其の前業務(傍系事業を含む)は新中央銀行に引渡されたり。尚旧省銀行の満州以外の支店を清算する為に措置を講ずる所ありたり。

新通貨は銀弗を基礎とするも兌換し得るや否やは不明なり

中央銀行は其の建設資金として旧銀行より救出し得べきものに加える
に二千万円(之が「元」の意味なることあり得べし)と報ぜらるる日本の貸付
金及其の資本に対する「満州国政府」の七百五十万ドル(銀)の応募とを有す
(1932年5月5日「満州国」財政部長より委員会に与えられたる仮予算に依
る)同銀行は一切の満州通貨を1932年7月1日より公式に定められたる率
を以て新紙幣に代えて買戻すことに依り之を統一せんと計画したり。此等
の紙幣は銀弗を基礎とし且少なくとも30％迄銀、金、外国通貨又は預金を以
て保証せれるるを要す。新通貨が要求に応じ且無制限に硬貨に代えらるべ
きや否やは公式の発表には明らかにせられ居らず旧紙幣は兌換法の通過よ
り二年間流通することを許さるべきも夫れ以後は有効ならざるべし。

現満州通貨は実質的に一九三一年九月十八日前に在りしものと同じ

新中央銀行紙幣の注文は日本国政府に発せられたるも今日迄のところ
右紙幣も新硬貨も未だ流通し居らず。満州の現通貨は紙幣が各銀行を通過
するとき栄厚(新中央銀行総裁)の署名を追加せられ居り外依然1931年9
月18日前に存したるものなり。

硬貨の不充分なる供給に基礎を置く「満州国」の統一政策

新「満州国」銀行が如何にして其の自由に処分し得る制限せられたる資
本を以て一切の満州通貨を統一し安定せんとする熱心なる計画の完成を所
期し得るやは明らかならず。旧省諸金融施設より受け継ぎたる財源は日本
の諸銀行よりの借入金及其の資本に対する「満州国政府」の応募と共に右目
的の為全然不充分と思考せられ。加之如何なる基礎に於いて同銀行の「満
州国政府」との関係が設定せらるべきや明らかならず。財政部長より委員
会に与えられたる「満州国」仮予算に依れば、「満州国」は其の成立の第一年
度中に二千万元①の不足に直面せんことを予期す。部長の意見に依れば右

---

①　予算中本事項及之に続く諸項は「満州国」財政部長の一委員との会見に於いて
「円」として与えられたるも「満州国」外交部より提出せられたる「満州国概観」の英訳に
於いては右は「元」なる用語を以て表示せらる従って委員会は本項及之に続く予算項目
に言及するに際し「円」よりも寧ろ「元」を使用することとす。「元」に対する支那人の記
号は日本人が「円」に対し使用する記号と同一なる為、支那側及日本側双方より委員会
に提供せられたる英訳及佛訳を取扱うに当り絶えざる困難ありたり。

は中央銀行(当時は存在せざりき)よりの借入金によ補充せらるべきものなりき。其の銀行に七千五百万元応募し、然る後右銀行より其の予算均衡を保つ為二千万元以上を借入れんとする政府は其の中央銀行又は其の予算を健全なる財政的基礎の上に建つるものに非ず。

中央銀行は通貨を兌換可能ならしむるより寧ろ之を統一せんとするが如し

中央銀行は現に有すと認めらるる以上に多額の現実の硬貨を獲得し得るに非ざれば、一切の満州通貨を兌換可能の銀弗を基礎として統一することを殆ど庶幾し得ざるべし。仮令同銀行が通貨の統一(兌換可能ならすとするも)を創成するに於ては同銀行は何等か成就したりと云うべけんも、統一的通貨にして其の安定性が兌換に依りて保証せられざるにおいては健全なる通貨制度の要件を充たしたるものに非るなり。

日本人の支配は公共事業に及ぶ

各種の公共造営物及鉄道に関し支那側系統と日本側系統とを連結せんことをもくてきとしたる諸取極作成せられたり。奉天事変勃発前日本側は之が実現を熱望したりしも、支那側は絶えず同意を与えることを拒絶したり。尤も9月18日と「満州国」の成立との間に於いて既に本章第1節中に説述したる如く日本側の希望を実現すべき措置直ちに執られたり。「新国家」の成立以来「満州国」交通部の政策は其の権力下に在る主要鉄道線路の少なくとも若干の開発に付き南満州鉄道会社と協定を為さんとするものの如し。

支那電話電信及ラジオ制度

満州に於ける支那電話、電信及ラジオ制度は全然官有なるを以て政府自身の経営者を有し、東北電話、電信及ラジオ政庁の統一的管理下に置かる。9月18日以来、右制度の3者何れも全満州に於ける日本側制度と更に密接なる共同作業を為したり。加之満州に於ける各地より来り又は各地に至る中継電報並びに関東州租借地、日本、朝鮮、台湾及南洋諸島における各地に至り又は各地より来る中継電報に付き日本電信官庁と東北電信政庁との間に取極作成せられたり。北満州に於ける主要中心地と大連、奉天及長春に於ける日本郵便局との間に通信の迅速なる伝達を確保する為直通線建設せられたり。

日本語仮名の通信は殊に低率とせられたり。日本語信名の取扱を学ぶ為支那人の書記に対し特別なる訓練を与え、又日本人の書記をして主要中心地に於いて漸次支那人電務従業員に加わらしむる様計画せられ居れり。斯くして満州及全日本帝国間の電信交通を便利ならしむる為あらゆる便宜を供与せられたり。之に依りて自然両国間の通商関係着しく強固となれり。

塩税　日本軍憲は一九三一年九月塩税収入を管理せり

9 月 18、19 日事件の後、日本官憲は塩税収入を留保し居る官衙及銀行に対し日本官憲の同意無くして此等の保管金より何等の支出を為すべからざる旨の命令を発したり。

右塩税の監理は此の財源よりする収入の大部分が名義上は国家のものなりと雖事実張学良元帥の政府に保留せられ居りたる事実を根拠として主張せられたるものなり。

此の財源よりの収入は1930 年に於いては約銀二千五百万ドルに上り右の中二千四百万ドルは満州に於て保留せられ単に百万ドルが在上海塩務稽核総弁に送金せられたり。

張学良元帥は一九二八年満州分担額の支払に同意せり

張学良元帥は1928 年 12 月、国民政府に参加後、塩税を担保としたる借入金に対し満州より支払うべき定額即ち銀八万六千六百万ドルの月割分担額の支払に同意せり。其の後 1930 年 4 月改正発表せられ之に依り満州の月割分担額は銀二十一万七千八百ドルに増額せられたり。然れども満州財政の地方的逼迫のために張元帥は新割当の支払延期を要求せり。奉天事件の際に於ける彼の滞納額は五十七万六千二百ドルに上れり。新率に依る二十一万七千八百ドルの最初の送金は日本陸軍将校の同意を得て1931 年 9 月 29 日に実行せられたり。満州に樹立せられたる新政権は右以後、1932 年 3 月迄に（3 月を含む）中央政府に対し啻に之等のつき割り分担額を送金したるのみならず張学良元帥が未払いのまま残したる滞納額をも送金せり。然れども彼等は塩税剰余金を以て国家の収入と認めず之を満州の収入と認め従って之を地方的目的の為に留保することを正当と思考したり。

一九三一年十月及十一月牛荘に於ける塩税の差押

奉天治安維持委員会が省政府に合流せし後、財政庁の支払に充つる為

在牛荘塩務稽核署に対し其の総ての保管金を省銀行に移管すべき旨命じたり。支那の公報に依れば在牛荘中国銀行も又原預金者の承諾無くして10月30日、銀六十七万二千七百九弗五十六仙に上る塩税収入保管金の提供を強要せられ遼寧省財政庁の名に於いて同庁日本人顧問のみが署名したる一葉の領収書を交付せられたり。

新吉林省政府亦監税収入を差押へたり

新吉林省政府は吉林及黒龍江の監運署に関し同様の措置を採れり。支那の公報に依れば、新吉林省政府は塩税収入を省金庫に移管すべき旨要求したり。署長が之を拒絶するや彼は数日間拘留せられ且熙洽省長は署長を更迭し後任者を任命したるが同後任者は11月22日同署を強制占領し又監査署は熙洽省長の命令に依り閉鎖せられたり。此の場合に於いても亦中国銀行及交通銀行に保管せられ居りたる塩税収入は新吉林官憲に依り要求せられ11月6日省銀行に移管せられたり。爾来月割分担額は規則正しく上海に送金せられたりと雖も塩税収入は地方官憲に依り随時引き出し費消せられたり。1931年10月30日より1932年8月25日迄の期間に対しては支那政府の計数を入手し得らるる処、右期間に於いて銀一千四百万ドルに上る塩税収入は満州に於て保留せられたり。

全満州に於ける塩務行政は既述の如き制限及監督の下に在りと雖も尚3月28日迄は引続き行われたるが同日「満州国政府」の財政総長は稽核署に属する預金、勘定、書類其他の財産を「満州国」塩税務司に翌日引継ぐべく又元来中国銀行の扱いたる塩税の徴収は東三省銀行に移管すべき旨の命令を発したり。財政総長は引続き「満州国」の塩務行政に勤務を希望する官吏は塩税務司事務所に其の氏名を申出すべき旨を声明すると共に彼等が先ず支那共和国政府に対する忠順を放棄するにおいては其の出願を十分考慮すべき旨を約せり。

「満州国」政府塩税行政を押収す

4月15日、牛荘稽核署は強力を以て解散せられ所長及副所長は署より免職せられ構内は占領せられ金庫、書類及印章は押収せられたり。其の他の官吏は引続き勤務方要求せられたるが彼等は何れも之を拒絶したりと報ぜられ居れり。多数の署員は署長に随い天津に赴き上海よりの訓令を待ちたり。斯くて東三省における旧塩務稽核署の職務は「満州国」の新塩税務司

事務所に依り完全に引継がれたり。尤も新政府は塩税を担保とする外債の為に必要なる金額の衡平なる分担額を引続き支払う用意ある旨を声明せり。

税関

満州に於て徴収せられたる関税収入は常時中央政府に送金せられ居たるを以て日本軍憲は関税行政又は上海への送金に干渉する所なかりき。此の収入に対する干渉は先ず「満州国政府」に依り彼等の「国」は独立国なりとの理由を以て行われたり。

満州に於ける関税収入

「満州国」の省政府として2月17日設立せられたる東北行政委員会が最初に為したる行動の一は在満開市場における税関監督に対し関税収入は当然の権利として「満州国」に属すべきものにして将来該委員会の監理の下に置かるべきものなるが当分税関監督及税務司は平常通り職務を執行すべき旨を訓令するに在りたり。彼等は一般税関行政を監督する為満州各港に夫々一名の日本人税関顧問が任命せられたり旨通報を受けたり。右と関係あるは龍井村、安東、牛荘及哈爾賓並びに其の支署にして右各港において1931年に徴収せられたる収入は夫々五十七万四千海関両、三百六十八万二千海関両、三百七十九万二千海関両及五百二十七万二千海関両なり。現在尚「満州国政府」の統治外にある愛琿港は支那関税行政の下に活動しつつあり。関東州租借地に在る大連港は特殊の地位を有し居れり。大連を含む満州諸港に於いて徴収せらるる関税収入は全支那の総関税収入に対し1930年に於いては其の14.7％に上り、又1931年に於いては其の13.5％に上るの事実は支那関税行政における満州の重要さを示すものなり。

「満州国」官憲が満州に於ける全関税行政を押収したる手続は安東に於ける措置に依りよく例証せらる。右手続は総税務司に依り次の如く記述せられたり。

「満州国政府」は一九三二年三月より六月迄に関税行政及収入を押収せり

3月任命せられたる安東税関日本人顧問は6月中旬迄は何等積極的行動を執る所無かりしが、同月彼は中国銀行に対し関税収入は爾今上海に送金すべからざる旨の「満州国」財政部の確定的命令を送達せり。6月16日、四名の「満州国」武装警察官は一名の日本人警部に伴われ中国銀行に赴き、同銀

行支配人に対し彼等は関税収入を警備する為来れる旨を告げたり。6月19
日、中国銀行は東三省銀行に対し七十八万三千両を交付すると共に税務司に
対し右措置は不可抗力の結果として執られたるものなる旨を通報したり。

6月26日及27日、「満州国」政府の一日本人顧問は在安東税関を彼に
引渡すことを要求したるに対し、税務司が之を拒否したる処「満州国」警官
(総て日本人)の為同税務司は税関より退去せしめられたり。然るに税務司
は安東税関収入の80％は鉄道付属地において徴収せらるるものなるを以て
日本官憲が此の地帯内における干渉を許さざるべきことを希望し、其の官
舎に於いて尚、税関の事務を執らんとしたる処、「満州国」警官は鉄道付属地
に入り、多数の税関吏員を逮捕し残余の吏員を脅威し税務司をして支那の
税関行政を停止するの余儀なきに至らしめたり。

大連税関の地位

6月7日迄は大連の関税収入は3日、又は4日おきに上海に送金せられ
たるが「満州国政府」は6月9日付を以て爾今此等の送金を為すべからざる
旨の通牒を発したり。上海に収入の送金途絶えたるに及総税務司は在大連
日本人税務司に対し本件に対し電報する所ありたるが右に対し税務司は日
本租借地政府の外事課長より関税収入の送金を続くることは日本の利益に
影響する所大なるべき旨勧告ありたるの理由を以て関税収入の送金継続を
拒絶したり。依りて総税務司は6月24日、大連税務司を命令不服従の廉を
以て罷免したり。

「満州国政府」は6月27日、右罷免税務司及職員を「満州国」の官吏に任
命し従前の職務に従事せしめたり。「満州国政府」は若し日本官憲が同政府
をして大連税関の監理を為さしめざるにおいては租借地境瓦房店に新税関
を設置すべしと威嚇的態度を示せり。租借地の日本官憲は関税行政が新任
「満州国」官吏の手に移ることに反対せず。本問題は日本に関係なく単に
「満州国」を一方とし支那政府及大連税務司を他方とする両者間に於ける係
争問題なりと主張したる。

関税に関する「満州国」政府の見解

「満州国政府」は「満州国」は独立国成るを以て権利として其の領域内に
おける関税行政に対し完全なる管轄権を行使すと主張す。然れども同政府
は各種外債及賠償金は支那の関税収入を基礎となし居るの事実に鑑み、此

等債務を果たす為必要なる年額の衡平なる分担額を支払うの用意ある旨を声明したり。同政府は右分担額を横浜正金銀行に預金したる後、地方的使途に流用し得る関税余剰金は1932年より1955年迄においては約一千九百ドルあるべきことを期待し居れり。

満州に於ける郵務行政

9月18日後、在満日本軍憲は新聞及封書に対し検閲を為す以外は郵便局に対し甚だしき干渉を加えざりき。「満州国」の建国後、「同国政府」は其の領域内の郵便行政を押収せんことを欲し、4月14日、郵務行政の移管を実行する為、特別の官吏を任命せり。4月24日、「同国政府」は未だ加盟の資格を有せざりし萬国郵便連合に之が加盟許可方を申込めり。

郵務司が郵便局の引渡しを拒否したる為、暫次現状維持せられたるも官吏手段を行使する為、或る事務所には「満州国」の監督官配置せられたり。尤も、「満州国政府」は遂に「同国」の印紙を発行し支那の印紙使用を停止することに決定したり。7月9日付の交通部令を以て「同国政府」は新印紙及新葉書を8月1日より発売すべき旨を布告せり。茲において支那政府は郵務司に対し在満郵便局の閉鎖を命じると共に、職員に対し三ヵ月分の給与を受くるか又は他の地において勤務する為支那における指定地に帰還するかの選択を許したり。「満州国」官憲は残留を希望する全郵務使用人に対し、順次就職を勧誘し、且支那行政の下に於いて彼等の獲得したる財政上の其の他の権利を保障することを約したり。7月26日、「満州国政府」は全満州を通し完全に郵務行政を押収せり。

私有財産の取扱

「満州国政府」は私有財産並びに支那の中央政府又は満州旧政権の何れかに依り与えられたる総ての免許にして右免許が従前施行中の法令及規則に従い合法的に与えられたるものなる限り之を尊重すべき旨を声明せり。同政府は亦旧政権が負える適法の負債及債務を支払うことを約し、且負債に対する請求を裁決する為に委員を任命せり。張学良元帥其の他前政権の要人に属する財産に対し如何なる措置が採らるべきやを記述することは未だ尚早なり。支那の公報に依れば張学良元帥、萬福麟将軍、鮑毓麟将軍、其の他若干の者の私有財産は没収せられたり。尤も「満州国」官憲は旧政府の官吏は其の権力を行使して彼等自身のために蓄財したるものなるを以て斯

くの如き方法に依り得られたる財産は之を以て当然私有財産として承認するの用意なしとの見解を持し居れり。旧官吏の所有物に関しては慎重なる調査行われつつあり但し銀行預金に関する限り右調査は既に終了したりと報ぜらる。

批判

吾人は斯くして「満州国政府」の組織、其の政綱及同政府が支那よりの独立を確認する為執りたる手段の若干を叙述したるを以て、次に該「政府」の行動及其の主たる特質に関する吾人の結論を述べざる可からず。此の「政府」の政綱は数多の自由主義的改革案を包含し、此等の実施は単に満州に於てのみならず支那の他の部分に於いても亦望ましきものなるべし。事実此等改革案の多数は支那政府の政綱中にも亦顕はれ居れり。本委員会との会見の際、右「政府」の代表者は、日本人の援助により彼等は相当期間中に平和と秩序を確立することを得べく、而して聽ては其れを永遠に維持することを得べしと主張せり。彼等は、人民に対し公正にして且効果的なる行政、匪賊の略奪に対する保障、軍費削減の結果たる租税の軽減、通貨の改革、改善せられたる交通機関及一般人民の政治参与権等を与えることに依り、人民の援助を獲得するを得べしとの信念を述べたり。

しかれども現在迄「満州国政府」がその政策を遂行する為費やしたる時日の短きことを充分酌量し、且既に講ぜられたる手段に対し篤と斟酌を加えるも猶此の「政府」が事実上其の改革案の多数を遂行し得べきことを示す何等の徴候存せず。単に一例を挙げんに(報告書付属書特殊調査第四及第五参照)彼らの予算制度及貨幣制度の改革案実現の前途には幾多重大なる障礙存するが如し。諸改革、秩序ある状態及経済的繁栄等に関する根本的な政綱は1932年に於いて存在したる不安及撹乱の状態の下に於いては到底実現せらるるを得ざるべし。

「政府」及公共事務に関しては、仮令各省の名義の上の長は満州に於ける支那人たる在住民なりと雖も、主たる政治的及行政的権力は日本人の役人及顧問の掌中に在り。「政府」の政治的及行政的組織は、此等役人及顧問に対し単に技術的意見のみならず、事実上行政を支配し指揮するを得しむるが如き仕組みなり。彼等が常に必ずしも日本政府又は関東軍司令部の公の政策と合致せざりしことあり。然れどもあらゆる重大問題の場合には此

等の役人及顧問は新組織の初期に於いては若干の者は多少独自の見解に依り行動することを得たるも、爾後漸次ますます日本の公の権力の指揮に従うを要するに至れり。実際に於いて此の権力は其の軍隊による同地方占拠の理由により「満州国政府」が内的にも外的にも其の権力の維持の為日本の軍隊に依存することに依り、且「満州国政府」の管轄下に在る諸鉄道の管理に関し南満州鉄道会社に益々重要となれる任務が委託せられたる結果として、更に最も重要なる地方的諸中心地に於いて連絡機関として日本領事の存在することにより如何なる緊急の場合に於いても抵抗すべからざる圧迫を加える手段を有するなり。

　「満州国政府」と日本の公の権力との間の連絡は最近の特派使節の任命に依り更に一層緊密となりたり。右特派大使は信任状の交付に依り公式に派遣せられたるものに非ずして満州の首都に駐在し、関東長官の資格に於いて南満州鉄道会社に対する支配権を行使し且同官職に外交代表者、領事事務の首長及占拠軍の総指揮官たる権能を集中す。

　「満州国」と日本国との関係は従来之を明らかにすること若干困難なりき。然れども本委員会の有する最近の情報に依れば日本政府に於いて近く此の関係を明らかにする意思ありとのことなり。1932 年 8 月 27 日付本委員会宛日本参与員の書簡に特派使節武藤大将は「8 月 20 日、満州に向け東京を出発せり。到着後同大将は日本と満州との間の友好関係の樹立に関する基本条約締結のため交渉を開始すべし。日本国政府は右条約の締結を以て「満州国」の正式承認と看做すべし」との旨の記載しありたり。

3. 満州居住民の意見

満州居住の態度

　満州居住民の「新国家」に対する態度を確かむることは本委員会の目的の一なりき。然れども調査を行いたる現地の状況に依り証拠を蒐集することに付若干の困難に遭遇せり。匪賊、朝鮮人共産主義者及支那側参与員の新政権批評の為同人の同伴を憤慨すべき新政府の擁護者等よりの本委員会に対する実際の又は予想せられたる危険は、委員会保護の為の例外的手段を執ることとなりたる一理由と成れり。同地方の同様せる状態に於いては確かに実際の危険がしばしば存せり。而して吾人は吾人の旅行中与えられた

る効果的なる保護に対し感謝するものなり。然れども斯くて執られたる警察的手段の結果は承認を近づかしめざりしことなり。而して多数の支那人は吾人の部員と会見することすら率直に恐怖し居たり。吾人は或場所において、何人と雖も官の許可なくして本委員会と会見するを許されざる旨吾人の到着前に通達せれたることを聞きたり。依て会見は常に甚だしき困難と且秘密裡に準備せられたり。然も斯かる方法に依りてすら吾人と会見することは彼等にとり余りに危険なりし旨を吾人に知らせたる人多かりき。

斯かる困難にも拘らず吾人は「満州国」の役人及日本国の領事官及陸軍将校との公の会見の他実業家、銀行家、教育家、医師、警察官、商人及其の他との私的会見を行うことを得たり。吾人は又 1500 通以上の書面を接受したるが、其の中若干は手交せられ大多数は各宛先に郵送せられたり。斯くして得られたる情報は之を中立的方向により出来得る限り真偽を照合せり。

代表団及用意せられたる陳述書

公の団体又は協会を代表する多数の代表団を接受せるが彼等は通例吾人に陳述書を提出せり。代表団の多くは日本国又は「満州国」の官憲により紹介せられたり。而して吾人は彼等が吾人に手交せる陳述書があらかじめ日本側の同意を得たるものなりと信ずべき強き理由を有せり。実際若干の場合に於いては陳述書を手交したる人々が後に至り右陳述書は日本人により書かれ又は甚だしく修正せられたるものにして彼等の真の感情を表せるものと看做しきれざるものなることを吾人に告げたり。此等の陳述書の顕著なる特質は「満州国」政権の樹立又は維持に対する日本の参加に対しては有利にも又反対にも批評することを故意に避けたる点なり。大体に於いて此等の陳述書は従前の支那政権に対する不平の叙述に関するものにして且「新国家」の将来に対する希望と信頼を表明せる文句を包含せり。

信書

接受したり信書は農民、小商人、都市労働者及学生より発せられたるものにして、筆者の感情及体験を述べ居れり。本委員会が6月、北平に帰還せる後、此の手紙の山は特に其の為に選任したる専門委員をして翻訳、分析及配列を為せしめたり。此等千五百五十通の手紙に二通を除き他は凡て新「満州国政府」及日本人に対し痛烈に敵意を示せり。此等は真摯且自発的に意見を表明したるものの如く思われたり。

「満州国」官吏

「満州国政府」の支那人の高級官吏は種々の理由の為に其の地位に在る なり。彼等の多数はかつて旧政権の官吏たりしが誘惑又は種々の脅迫によ り引留られたるものなり。彼等の或者は脅迫により其の地位に留まること を強制せられたること、一切の権力は日本人の手中にあること、彼等は支那 に忠誠なること及彼等が日本人立会いの下に行われたる本委員会との会見 に於いて述べたることは必ずしも信を置くべきものに非ざること等の趣旨 の通報を吾人に為したり。若干の官吏は彼等の財産の没収を禦ぐ為その地 位に留まりたり。而して斯かる没収は支那本部に遁入せる官吏中若干人の 場合に事実として起こりたり。他の評判良き人々は、彼等が行政を改善す る権力を有するに至るべしとの希望と、彼等が自由行動権を有すべしとの 日本人との約束の下に参加したり。若干の満州人は満州種に属する人々の 為に利益を得るの希望の下に参加したり。彼等の或者は失望し且新の権力 が彼らに与えられざることを訴えたり。尚少数の者は旧政権に対し個人的 不平を有せし為或は利得せるが為其の地位に在るなり。

下級及地方官吏

下級及地方の官吏は大体に於いて一部分生計を得て彼等の家族を扶養 せんが為又一部分は若し彼等が去らばより悪しき人間が彼等の地位に代わ るべしとの理由により彼等の地位を維持したり。地方県知事の多数も亦一 部は彼等の責任下に在る人民に対する義務観念より、又一部は圧迫の下に 其の地位に留まれり。高級の地位を評判良き支那人を以て充たすことは困 難なりしも、下級の地位及地方官庁に入るべき支那人を得ることは容易なり き。尤も斯かる事情の下に為されたる執務の忠実性は少なくとも疑問なり。

警察

「満州国」警察は一部分は旧支那警察の部員により又一部は新募集者に より構成せらる。大都市に於いては警察中に実際日本将校あり。又他の多 くの場所に於いては日本人の顧問あり。吾人と談話せる若干の個々の警察 官は新政府に対する彼等の反感を表明し唯彼等は生計を営む為引続き奉職 せざるべからずと云えり。

軍隊

「満州国」軍隊なるものも亦主として日本側の監督の下に改編せられた

る旧満州の軍人より成る。斯かる軍隊は最初彼等は単に地方の秩序を維持するのみにて足ることを条件として新政府の下に勤務することに甘んじたり。然れども爾来彼等はしばしば支那軍に対する真剣なる戦争に従事し且日本側の指揮の下に日本軍隊と相並んで戦うことを要求せられて以来、「満州国」軍隊は益々信頼し得ざるものとなりつつあり。日本側より出たる情報は「満州国」軍隊の頻発する支那側への内応を報ずるに対し、支那側は彼等の最も信頼に足る且効果大なる軍需品の源泉の一つは「満州国」軍隊なりと主張す。

実業家及銀行家

吾人と会見したる支那実業家及銀行家は「満州国」に対し敵意を抱けり。彼等は日本人を嫌悪せり。彼等は彼等の生命及財産に対し恐怖を有し且しばしば次の如く述べたり。「吾人は朝鮮人の如く成ることを欲せず」と。9月18日以後、実業家の支那へ脱出するもの多数ありたり。然れども比較的富裕ならざる若干の者は今や帰還しつつあり。一般的に言えば、比較的小なる商人は日本人の競争に苦しむこと旧政権の役人との間に有利なる関係を有したる大商人及製造業者の場合に比し、より少なかるべしと期待す。多数の商人は吾人の到着の時に於いて尚閉店し居りたり。匪賊の増加は辺境地方における商売に不利なる影響を与え、信用機構は大いに破壊せられたり。満州を経済的に開発すべしとの日本側の意思の発表及過去二、三ヶ月において日本経済使節の夥しき満州訪問は、此等使節の多くが失望して日本に帰えれりと報ぜらるる事実に拘らず支那実業家の間に不安の念を惹起しつつあり。

自由職業隊級即医師、教師、学生

自由職業階級たる教師及医師は「満州国」に対し敵意を有す。彼等は其行動を探偵せられ脅迫を受けたりと主張す。教育に対する干渉、大学其の他の学校の閉鎖及教科書の改訂等は愛国的理由に基づき燃え上がりつつありし彼等の敵愾心に油を注ぎたる観あり。新聞、郵便及言論の検閲並びに支那において発行せらるる新聞紙の「満州国」への搬入禁止に対しては反感を抱き居れり。もちろん日本において教育を受けたる支那人にして前記の一般的叙述の例外を成すものあり。「満州国」に反対する学生及青年より多くの書面を接受せり。

農夫及都会労働者

　　農夫及都会労働者の態度に関する証拠は多種多様にして勿論之を蒐ること困難なり。外国人及教育ある支那人間の意見を徴するに彼等は「満州国」に敵意あるか然らざれば無関心なり。農夫及労働者は政治的に教育せられ居らず、一般に文盲にして普通政治に興味を有すること少なし。農民が「満州国」に敵意を抱くべきことに対し次の理由を述べたるものあるが右は其の後此の階級に属する者より受けたる手紙の内或ものによりて確認せられたり。農夫は新制度が朝鮮人の及恐らく日本人の移民を増加せしむるに至るべしと信ずるの理由を充分有す。朝鮮人の移民は支那人と同化せず而して支那人の農夫は主として豆、高粱及小麦を栽培するも朝鮮人の農夫は米の耕作に従事し両者は農業方法を異にせり。水田の耕作は溝渠を掘り田野を灌漑することを伴い若し豪雨あれば朝鮮人により造られたる溝渠は溢れ付近の支那人の土地に氾濫し其の収穫を皆無ならしむるが如きこともあり得べく又彼等は過去において土地所有権及地代等の問題につき朝鮮人と絶えず争い来れり。「満州国」の建設以来支那人は朝鮮人がしばしば地代を支払うことを停止せること。彼等が支那人より土地を押収せること及日本人が支那人を強制して其の土地を低廉なる値にして売らしめたることを主張す。鉄道及都市の付近の農夫は鉄道及都市より五百米以内に高粱―高さ十呎（フイート）に成長し匪賊の作動を助くる穀物―の栽培を行うことを禁ずる命令により苦しみつつあり。支那本土より来る労働者の季節的移住は経済的不況を主とし政治的撹乱を例とする原因により減少しつつあるが右の傾向は尚継続の勢いに在り。支那より来る移民にとり比較的容易なる条件にて常に利用し得たる公有地は今や「満州国」に移管せられたり。1931年9月18日以降、農村には従来に其例を見ざる匪賊及不逞の徒の跳梁を見たるが是れ一部分敗残兵によるものか一部分は匪賊により零落せしめられたる末生活の為却って自ら匪賊に投じたる農夫によるものなる。支那の他の部分と比較し満州は多年組織的戦闘の為苦しめらるること稀なりしやに今や日本軍及「満州国」軍と支那に尚忠誠なる散軍との間に東三省の各部分に互り此の如き戦闘行われつつあり。此の如き戦闘は自然農夫に大なる困難を蒙らしむるものにして殊に日本飛行機は反「満州国」軍庇護の疑いある村落を爆破せしことあるにおいては特に然りとす。其結果広大なる地面に

作付せざりし事例あるが此の如き農夫は次年度において地代を支払うに困難を感ずるに至るべし。

支那より最近来りたる移民の大多数は事変の勃発以来長城内に逃げ帰れり。是等の実際的理由は日本人に対する或根底深き憎悪心と結合するときは多くの証人をして吾人に対して満州在在住民の圧倒的多数を形成する支那人農夫は新制度の為苦しみ且之を嫌悪し彼等の態度は受動的敵意のそれなることを吾人に告げしむるに至れり。

都会住民については、彼等は所によりては日本の兵士、憲兵及警察官の態度の為苦しみたり。一般的に謂えば日本兵の行状に善良にて個人的蛮行を訴えたる投書に接し居るも一般的略奪又は虐殺の事例なし。他方において日本人は敵意ありと信じたるものに対しては強硬なる手段を執り来たれり支那人は多くの処刑が行われたる事及捕虜が日本憲兵部において脅迫及拷問せられたる事を主張す。

「満州国」の建国式に際し民衆を刺激して之に対する熱心を現わさしむること不可能なりしと聞けり。一般的に謂えば都会人の態度は受動的黙従と敵意の混合なり。

少数民族

吾人は支那人の大多数が「満州国」に対し敵意あるか然らざれば無関心なることを発見すると同時に新政府は満州に於ける少数民族団体—蒙古人、朝鮮人、白系ロシア人及満州人の如き—より或支援を受け居れり。彼等は程度は異なれるも孰れも旧政権の為圧迫を受け又は過去数十年間における多数の支那移民の為経済的不利益を蒙りたり而して何れの部族も新政権に全く傾倒せるものと云い能わざるも新政権より従来に優れる待遇を受くべきことを予期し新政権亦之等少数民族を支援す。

蒙古人

蒙古人は漢人より別個なる人種として残存せり而して既に述べし如く強き民族意識並びに其の部族制度、貴族政治、言語、服装、特別の生活様式、習慣及宗教を保存せり。彼等は尚主として牧畜の民なりと雖も漸次農作に従事し又荷車及動物による農作物の運搬に従事す。満州に接壌する蒙古人は彼等の土地を獲得し耕作し彼等を漸次追い出しつつある漢人移民の為益々苦しみ来たり為に慢性的不可避の反感を有するに至れり。内蒙古人は外

蒙古がソ連邦の労力に下に帰するを見たるが彼等はソ連邦の内蒙古への進出し来ることを恐れつつあり。彼等は一方において支那代、他方においてソ連邦が侵略し来るに対抗して別個の国家的存在を維持せんと欲す。彼等は従来叙上の如き不安定なる地位に置かれたるを以て新制度の下においても其の別個の存在せんとするの大なる希望を繋ぎ居れり。加之、王族は其の富の維持の為め主として不動産及其の特権に依倚するのなるを以て自然彼等は事実上の権威者に対し従順たるの傾向ある事を注目するを要す。然れども吾人は北平において或蒙古王族の代表者接したるが彼等は新制度に対し反対なる事を述べたり。現在満州に接する蒙古人と「満州国政府」との間の関係は明確ならず。而して「満州国政府」亦今日迄彼等の施政に干渉する事を抑制せり。現在における是等蒙古人の或ものの新政権に対する支援は多少の不安を交え乍も兎も角本心よりなるも彼等は若し日本が或将来において彼等の独立または経済上の利益に対する脅威となること明らかなるに至らば此の如き支援は忽之を撤去するに至るべし。

満州人

満州人は漢人と殆ど完全に同化せられたり尤も吉林及黒龍江においては尚少数の重要ならざる満州人の植民地ありて二国語を話すも明らかに満州人として残存す。民国成立以来満州民族は其の特権的地位を失いたり。即ち民国は彼等の補助金の支払いを継続すべきことを約したるも減価せる通貨を以て支払われたるが故に彼等に余儀なく経験なき農耕及商売を始むるに至れり。「満州国」に好意を寄せるものはしばしば満州の住民を以て支那の他の住民と人種を異にすと為し、最後の満州皇帝は現執政なりとなすが現存の明らかなる満州人は「新国家」の成立とともに再び特権的待遇を得べしとの希望を懐くものあるべし。満州人は斯かる希望を以て「政府」に入りたるも満州に於ける漢人の証人の言うところによれば彼等は全くの権力は日本人の手に握られ彼等の提議は顧みられざるを見て失望を感じつつある由なり。満州人の血を有する者の間には先帝に対する或精神的忠誠の念尚存すべしと雖も何等顕著なる民族意識ある満州人運動存在せず。彼等の殆ど全く漢人と同化したるを以て今更満州人を官吏に登用して以て民族意識の振興に資せんとの企みあるも此の方面よりの新政府に対する支援は民意代表の名を冒すに足る実を具ふるものにあらず。

朝鮮人

過去において一方において日本官憲の庇護を受くる朝鮮農夫と地方において支那の官吏、地主及農夫との間に多くの軋轢ありたり。過去において朝鮮農夫は暴行及搾取により苦しみたりこと疑いなし。本委員会に陳情を齎したる朝鮮代表は一般に新制度を歓迎す然れども吾人は如何なる範囲迄彼等が其の問題の代表なりしやを確むるを得ず。兎も角政治的避難民たる朝鮮人は日本の統治を遁れるため移住せるものなるを持って更に日本の統治の拡張を歓迎するものとは想像せられず。是等の避難民は共産主義宣伝の善き目的と成り又朝鮮内における革命団体と接触を維持し居れり（第三章及特殊調査第八を参照）。

白系露人

満州に於ける一切の少数民族の団体の内哈爾賓及其の付近における少なくも其の数10万人を算する白系露人の小植民地は近年最も迫害を蒙りたり。彼等は庇護すべき国民政府なき少数民族団体なるの故を以て支那の官吏及警官により各種の屈辱を蒙りたり。彼等は故国の政権と不和の関係に在りて満州に在りてさえ此の故に絶えざる不安の裡に在るものなり。彼らの内裕福にして教育ある者は生計を立て得るも支那官憲が彼等を犠牲にし供して或種の利益をソ連邦より得らるると考えるときは之が為に苦しめらるるを常とす。より貧困なる者は生活を営むこと甚だ困難を見又絶えず警察の手及支那法廷において苦を嘗めつつあり。請負制度により租税が賦課徴収せらるる地方においては彼等は其の支那人たる隣人よりも餘き割合の課税を支払うを要したり。彼等は其の取引及行動に関し多くの制限を経験せり而して彼等の旅券が検査せられ、其の契約が認証せられ又は其の土地が譲渡せらるるには官吏に対し賄賂を贈ることを要したり。彼等の多くにとりては現在よりも劣れる条件を想像し能わざるを以て日本人を歓迎したるは尤もことにして今や彼等の運命は新政権の下に開け行くべしとの希望を抱懐することは怪しむべきに非ず。

吾人は哈爾賓をに在りしとき白系露人の代表並びに多くの書面に接したり而して吾人は之により彼等は左記事項を彼等に保障する如何なる制度をも支持すべしとの結論を得たり。

1. 庇護権
2. 公正にして有効なる警察行政
3. 法廷における正義
4. 衡平なる課税の制度
5. 賄賂の支払いに依らざる取引及定住の権利
6. 児童の教育に対する便宜　彼等の此点における要求は主として彼等をして移民せしむるに役立つ外国語の習得及彼等をして支那において職を得せしむる為の技術教育。
7. 土地、定住及移住に関する或援助

結論

以上は満州に於ける吾人の旅行中吾人に伝達せられたる地方人民の意見なり。公私の会見書面及声明書等の形を以て吾人に提供せられたる証拠を注意して研究したる後、吾人は「満州国政府」なるものは地方の支那人により日本の手先と見られ支那人一般に之に何らかの支援を与え居るものに非ずとの結論に達したり。

第七章　日本の経済的利益及支那の「ボイコット」[1][2]

日支紛争に於ける重要なる要素たる日本貨物に対する支那の「ボイコット」

前三章は主に1931年9月18日以来の軍事及政治上の事件の記述に止

---

[1]　「ボイコット」此語は最初愛蘭土（アイルランド）において使用せられ「マヨ」県におけるアーヌ伯領の差配チャーレス・カニンガム・ボイコット大尉（1832—97）の名に起因す。借地人によりて定められたる地代を1880年受領することを拒絶せるが為め「ボイコット」大尉の生命は脅かされ、彼の召使は離別を余儀なくせられ垣根は破壊され、手紙は奪取せられ又食料の供給が阻害せられたり。此語は直ちに英語として使用せられ且迅速に多数外国語に採用せらるるに至れり。「エンサイク・ペディア・ブリタニカ」1929年第十四版。

[2]　本問題に関する特別の研究に付き付属第八参照。

めたり。日支間紛争の討究は紛争に於ける他の重要なる要素、即ち日本貨物に対する支那のボイコットを説明せざる限り正確または完全ならざる可し。

右ボイコット運動において使用せられたる方法及其の日本の通商に及ぼしたる影響を諒解せんが為には日本の一般経済的地位、其の支那における経済的財政利益及支那の外国貿易に付記述するの要あり。尚満州に於ける日本及支那の経済的利益の範囲及性質を諒解すること必要にして右は次章において討究す可し。

日本の人口過剰

前世紀の六十年代における明治維新の頃、日本は二世紀以上に亘る孤立より脱却し而して五十年を俟たずして世界の第一等強国にまで発展せり。以前殆ど停滞し居りし人口は急速に増加し始め1872年に三千三百万なりしものが、1930年には六千五百万に達せり。而して此の驚くべき増加は一年に約九十万の割合を以て尚継続す。

可耕地一平方哩におけり日本の人口を他の国の夫れに比せんに日本の割合は例外的に高し。右は島帝国の特殊の地理的構成に起因す。即ち、

日本	2774
イギリス	2170
ベルギー	1709
イタリア	819
ドイツ	806
フランス	467
アメリカ	229

農業地に高度に人口が集中し居るため各自の保有地面積は頗る狭小にして農夫の35%は一エーカー未満を34%は二エーカー半未満を耕作す。可耕地は其の及ぶべき限度に到達し居り又集約農法の限度に達す。約言すれば日本の土地は今日以上に生産することを期待する能わず。又就業に機会を今日以上に多く供給すること能わず。

農業の困難

尚集約農法及肥料の普及的使用の結果として生産高は高まり、土地の価格はアジアの如何なる地方よりも、否欧羅巴の人口過剰の地方よりも遥

かに高し。財政的負担を痛く課せられ居る人民の間に不満存し居るものの如く、借地人と地主との間における争議は増加しつつあり。移民は救済の見込みある方法として考慮せられたるも次章において述ぶるが如き理由を以て現在迄の処解決手段とならざりき。

日本の最初都会の人口増加を支ふる為産業主義に転向せるが右は農産物の為国内市場を提供し且内地及外国において使用さる可き物資の生産に労働を向はしむべきものなり爾后幾多の変化を生ぜり。以前日本は食料品供給の見地より観て自足以上の状態にありしが近年は全輸入の8％乃至15％は食料品の輸入及此の輸入必要の恐らく増加すべきことは既に逆となれる貿易感情を工業品輸出の増加によりて補うことを要す。

工業化の必要

若し日本が増加しつつある人口に対する職業を是以上の工業化の行程において見出すの要ありとせば輸出貿易の発展並びに増加しつつある製造品及半製品を吸収し得る外国市場の開拓が益々緊要なり。而して如斯市場は同時に原料品及食料品の供給地たり得べし。

日本の輸出貿易市場たる支那

今日迄発展したる日本の輸出貿易は二つの主なる方面を有す。即ち贅沢品たる生絲は合衆国に主要製造品（主として綿製品）はアジアの諸国に向かい、合衆国は輸出の42.5％、アジアにおける市場は総括して42.6％を占む。而して後者の中支那、関東租借地及香港は24.7％にして残余の大部分はアジアの他の地方において支那商人によりて取扱わる（1929年の数字にして「ジャパン・イヤーブック」1931年版に依る）。

1930年即ち完全なる数字の判明し居る最近の年において日本の輸出総額は十四億六千九百八十五万円即ち17.7％は支那（関東租借地及香港を除く）に向かい右輸入中一億六千百六十六万円即ち0.4％は支那（関東租借地及香港を除く）より来れり。

日本より支那に輸出さるる重なる商品を細別するときは支那は日本より輸出さるる一切の水産物の32.8％、精糖の84.6％、石炭の75.1％、綿織物の31.9％、平均51.6％を占むることを見る可し。

尚支那より輸入さるる物品を細別するときは日本が輸入する大豆及豌豆の総額の24.5％、油糟の53％、植物性繊維の25％、平均34.5％は支那より

来るものなることを示す。

以上の数字は香港及関東租借地を除きたる支那のみに関するものなるを以て重に大連港を経由して行われつつある日本の対満貿易の範囲を示し居らず。

日支貿易関係の重要性

叙上の事実及び数字は明らかに日本にとり対支貿易の重要なる事を示せり。尚日本の支那における利益は単に貿易に止まらず即ち日本は巨額の資本を工業的企業並びに鉄道、船舶及銀行に投じ此の方面の財政活動において発展の一般的傾向は最近三十年間に顕著なるものありしなり。

支那に於ける日本の投資

1898年に於いて挙ぐるに足るべき日本の唯一の投資は支那人との合弁に係り約十万両の価格を有する在上海の小製綿工場に過ぎざりき。1913年迄に支那及満州における日本の投資見積総額は日本の海外投資見積総額三千五百万円の内四億三千万円を占め世界大戦の終期迄に日本は支那及満州における1913年の投資額に比し其の投資を倍以上となせり。右増加の相当部分は有名なる西原借款に基づくものにして右借款は政治的考慮をも加味せられたるものなり。此の故障ありしに拘らず日本の支那及満州に於ける投資額は1929年に於いて海外投資二十一億円の内約二十億円に上れり（他の見積によれば支那[満州を含む]における日本の投資は総額約十八億円なり）右は日本の海外投資は殆ど全く支那及満州に限定せられ而も後者が此の投資の大部分（特に鉄道）を吸収したるものなることを示す。

右投資以外に支那は日本に対し諸種の国債省債及市債として債務を負い其の額は1925年に於いては三億四百四十五万円（其大部分に無担保）及利息千八百零三万円なり。日本の投資の大部分は満州に於いてなるが支那本部に於いて工業、船舶業及銀行業に投ぜられたる金額亦尠からず。1929年に於いて支那の紡績及紡織工場において運転せる紡錘の総数の約50％は日本人によりて所有せられ、又日本は支那における通運業において第二位を占め、支那における日本の銀行の数は1932年に三十に達し内若干は日支合弁なり。

支那の対日貿易発展に於ける利益

叙上の数字は日本側より観察したものなる処支那側より見るも其相対

的重要性を容易に知ることを得。日本との外国貿易は1932年迄において支那の外国貿易の首位を占めたり。1930年に輸出の24.1％は日本に向かい、同年輸入の24.9％は日本より来れり。右を日本側見地よりする数字に比較せんに支那の外国貿易において日本との貿易は日本の貿易総額に於いて対支貿易が占むるパーセンテージよりも多きことを知り得。然るに支那は日本に於いて何等の投資をも銀行業または船舶業の利益をも有せず。支那は多数の製造品に対する支払いを可能ならしめ且堅実なる信用の基礎を築き以て将来の発展に必要なる資本を借入れんが為其の製産物の輸出増加を可能ならしむることを要す。

日支経済財政関係は紛争によりて容易に影響を受く

依是観之日支経済財政関係は広汎且多岐にして従って紛争要因によりて容易に影響され且混乱せしめらるるものなること明らかなり。尚概言せんに日本の支那に依存することは支那の日本に依存することよりも大なるものの如し。由て日本は支那との関係混乱する場合に於いては支那に比較し一層害せられ易く且失う所も多し。

尚1895年の日清戦争以来両国の間に起こりたる幾多の政治的紛争が順次に相互の経済的関係に影響したることも明らかなり。而して右紛争に拘らず両国の貿易が絶えず報加したる事実は政治的敵愾心も割くこと能わざる基本的経済的連鎖の存することを示すものなり。

「ボイコット」の起源

数世紀にわたる支那人は商人、銀行家の団体及同業組合に於いてボイコットを慣用し、右組合は近代の情勢に合致する様変形せられたるも尚多数に存在し、其の共通の職業的利益擁護の為組合員に対し絶大なる勢力を振るいつつあるなり。右数世紀の歴史を有する組合生活に於いて得られたる訓練及態度は現代のボイコット運動に於いて近年の熾烈なる国民主義と結合せり。而して国民党は右国民主義の組織的表現なり。

近代の排外「ボイコット」

国民的基礎において外国に対する政治的武器（右は支那商人相互間に行われたる職業的方便たるボイコットより区別し）として使用せらるる近代の排外ボイコットは時代は1905年米国に対して為されたるボイコットにより始まりたりと云うを得べし。右ボイコットは同年改訂せられたる米支

通商条約の規定が従前よりも一層厳重に支那人の渡米を制限せるに起こりたり。この時以来今日に至る迄規模に於いて国民的と称せらるべきボイコットが判然と十回も行われたり（此の他に地方的性質の排外運動ありたり）右の内九回は対日①にして一は対英なり。

此等「ボイコット」運動の諸原因

若し此等ボイコットを仔細に研究せば、何れも或る一定の事実、事故又は事件にして概して政治的性質を有し、支那が同国の重大利益に反して行われ又は同国の国家的対面を毀損すと解するものに其縁由を繹ね得ることを発見しべし。斯くして1931年のボイコットは同年6月の萬寶山事件に続いて発生せる7月の鮮人の虐殺の直接の結果として開始せられ9月の奉天事件及1932年1月の上海事件に促進せられたるものなり。各ボイコットは各直接に繹ね得る原因あるも其の原因事体は第一章に述べたる群集心理無かりせば斯くの如き広汎なる経済的報復を生起せざりしなるべし。此の心理の創生に寄与せる要素は不正の確信（不正と考えることが正しくとも或は誤れるとも）外国人に比し支那の文化が優越なりとする相伝的信条。及西洋式の熾烈なる国民主義（目的に於いて主として守勢的なるも其の間攻撃的傾向を欠如せず）なり。

一九二五年以前の「ボイコット」運動

国民党の前身とも見らるる興中会は遠く1893年に創設せられ又1905年より1925年に至る総てのボイコットは疑いもなく国民主義の矢叫を以

---

① 之等ボイコットの年度及直接原因は次の如し。

1908年	辰丸事件
1909年	安奉線問題
1915年	二十一ヵ条
1919年	山東問題
1923年	旅大回収問題
1925年	5・30問題
1927年	山東出兵
1928年	済南事件
1931年	満州問題（萬寶山及奉天事件）

て開始せられたるものなりと雖も最初の国民主義者の団体及後の国民党が此等ボイコットの組織に直接関与せるの確証なし。商会及学生同盟は孫逸仙博士の新綱領に鼓舞せられ又実際に於いては世紀を経たる秘密結社、同業組合の経験及心理に導かれ斯かる仕事に充分の能力を有せり。商人は専門的知識、組織方法及手続き方法を供し一方学生は新たに獲得せる確信及国家的目的に対する決意の精神を以て其の運動を鼓舞し以て之が実行を助成せり。学生は概して国民主義的感情のみに動かされたるものなるか商会は其の感情は同じふするもボイコットの実行を支配せむとするの欲望より之に参加するを賢明と思考せり。初期ボイコットの実際の方式を排除せらるる国の商品の購買防止にありしが其の活動の範囲は漸時該国に対する支那商品の輸出拒絶又は支那における該国人に対する有償無償の奉仕拒絶せられ終に最近のボイコットの確定せる目的は「仇国」との間の総ての経済的関係を完全に断絶することに存するに至れり。

　斯く樹立せられたる方式は本報告書に付属する特別研究において詳述せられたる理由に因り未だ充分に徹底的には実行せられたることなきを指摘せざる可らず。概説するにボイコットは北方（特に山東は之に対する支援を差控えたり）に於けるよりも国民主義的感情が最初の且最も熾烈なる信者を発見せし南方に於いてより激烈性を有せり。

一九二五年以後の「ボイコット」運動、国民党の活動

　1925年より此の方ボイコット組織に確定的変化起これり。国民党は其の創設以来同運動を支援し順次のボイコットに其の支配権を増加し、遂に今日に於いては其の実際の組織的、原始的、調整的及監督的要素たるに至れり。

　之を為すにあたり国民党は委員所有の証拠に示さるる如く従前ボイコット運動指導に与り居たる各団体を除外せざりき。同党は寧ろ右団体の努力を調整し、其の方法を組織化及統一し、其の運動の背後に強力なる党組織の精神的及物質的の重みを充分に付与せり。同党は全国に支部を有し広汎なる宣伝及情報機関を所有し強き国民主義感情に刺激せられ居るものにして当時迄稍散在的なりし運動に組織及刺激を与えることに急速に成功せり。その結果として商人及一般民衆に対するボイコット組織者の強制的権力は以前よりは一層強きを加えたり尤も同時に個々のボイコット団体に対

し多少の自治権及発案権残し置かれたり。

使用せられたる方法

ボイコット方式は地方状況に従い改編を続けたるが右は組織の強力化と平行して為されボイコット団体により使用せられたる方法は一層統一的に、一層厳格且効果的となれり。同時に国民党部は命令を発して日本人に属する商業家屋の破壊又は日本人に対する肉体的加害を禁止せり。右はボイコット中において在支日本人の生命が決して脅かされたることなきを意味せざるも、概括的には最近のボイコットにおいては日本人民に対する暴行は従前に比し少なく且甚しからざりしと言うを得べし。

使用せられたる方法の技巧を検討するにボイコットの成功に必須なる民衆感情の雰囲気は「仇」国に対する民心を刺激する為技巧妙に選ばれたる標語を用い、全国に亘り統一的に実行せられたる猛烈なる宣伝により創生せられ居るを見る。

反日宣伝

委員会の実見せるに現在の対日ボイコットに於いては民衆に対し日貨の不買が愛国的義務印るなを象あらゆる手段が使用せられ居たり。例えば支那新聞紙の紙面は此の種宣伝に充たされ、又市内の建築物の壁はポスターを以て蔽われ居りたるが、此の種ポスターにはしばしば極端に激烈なる性質ものあり①。反日標語は紙幣、書信及電報用にも印刷せられ、「チェーン・レターズ」は転々と発せられたり此等事例は決して茲に全部を尽くし居るものにはあらざるも使用せられたる方法の性質を示すに足るべし。此の種宣伝が1914—18年の世界大戦中欧米の或る国々において用いられたるものと本質的に異ならざるの事実は日支両国間の政治的緊張として支那人が日本に対して感ずるに至れる敵意の程度を証するのみ。

反日会に依り採用せられたる「ボイコット」方式

ボイコットの政治的雰囲気は其の最後の成功に欠くべからざるものなれど、斯かる運動は若しボイコット団体が其の手続きの方式に於いてある

---

① 委員会の訪問せる多くの都市に於いては此の種ポスターは予め撤去せられありたるもしばしば此の種ポスターの見本を所有せる信頼すべき地方の証人よりの言明ありたるにより上記の事実を確認せり。尚又右見本は委員会の記録中に保有しあり。

種の統一性を得るにあらざれば決して効果的なる能わず。1931 年 7 月 17
日に開催せられたる上海反日会の第一回会議において採用せられたる四原
則は此の種規則の主要目的を例証するに足るべし。

　　イ、既約日貨の注文を取消すこと。

　　ロ、既約日貨にして積込未了のものは船積を停止せしむること。

　　ハ、既に倉庫に在るも支払い未了の日貨は受領を拒絶すること。

　　ニ、既購入日貨を反日会に登記し其の売却を一時停止すること。登記
の手続きは別に決定す。

　　同会により採用せられ本報告書付属書に採録せられたる其の後の決議
は一層詳細にしてあらゆる場合に対する規定を包含す。

　　ボイコットを励行する強力なる手段は支那証人の手持ち日貨の強制登
記なり。反日会の検査員は日貨の動きを監視し出所疑わしきものは日貨な
りや否やを確かむる為之を検査し、未登記日貨の存在の嫌疑ある商店及倉
庫は手入れを行い、規制違反発見の場合は其の首領の注意を喚起す。斯か
る規則違反を犯せるを発見せられたる証人はボイコット団体により罰金を
課せられ、公然民衆の非難に曝され、一方其の所有商品は没収の上公売に付
せられ其の売上金は反日団体の資金となる。

　　ボイコットは商売のみに限らるるにあらず。支那人は日本船にて旅行
をなし、日本の銀行を利用し、又は業務上家事上を問わず如何なる資格に於
いても日本人に仕えざる様警告せらる。此等命令を無視する者は各種の非
難及脅迫を蒙る。

　　此のボイコットの今一つの特徴は前例の如く単に日本の工業を害する
のみならず従前日本より輸入せる或る種貨物の生産を刺激し、支那の工業
を促進せんとする希望なり。其の主なる結果は上海に於ける日本人所有の
工場を犠牲とせる支那の紡績工業の拡張となれり。

一九三一―三二年に於ける「ボイコット」運動の消長

　　上述のラインに於いて組織せられたる1931 年のボイコットは同年 12
月、ある種の弛緩の顕れたる迄継続せり。1932 年 1 月には当時進行中の大
上海市長と同地日本総領事との間の交渉中において支那側は地方反日組織
を自発的に解散することさえ約せり。上海に於ける敵対行為中及日本軍撤
退直後の数ヶ月間に於いてはボイコットは決して完全に放棄せられざりし

も緩和せられ、晩春及初夏に於いては支那各地方に於ける日本との貿易再び興るやにさえ見受けられたり其の時極めて突然に7月下旬より8月上旬に亘れる熱河境における日本軍の行動の報と時を同じうしてボイコット運動の顕著なる復活を見たり。民衆に対し日貨不買を強調する記事は支那各新聞に新たに掲載せられ、上海商会はボイコット再開始を慫憑する公開状を発し、同市に於ける石炭商同業組合は日本炭の輸入を最小限度に制限するに決せり。同時に日本炭取扱の嫌疑ある石炭商の構内に爆弾を投入し、又は商店主に対し手紙を送り日貨を売るを止めざれば其の財産を破壊すべしと脅迫する等の一層激烈なる方法用いらるるに至れり。新聞に掲載せられたる此の種脅迫状は「鉄血団」又は「血魂除奸団」と署名せられ居りたり。

斯の如きが本報告書起草中の状況なり。ボイコット活動のこの再発は在上海日本総領事をして官憲に対し正式抗議を提出せしめたり。

「ボイコット」運動の物質的影響

各種のボイコット運動及特に現在のボイコット運動は物質的及心理的意味において共に日支関係に重大なる影響を及ぼせり。

物質的影響に関する限り即ち貿易業の損失に於いては支那人はボイコットを経済的加害行為としてよりも寧ろ道徳的抗議を示さんとする望みを以て之を内輪に表示するの傾向あり。然るに日本人は或る種の〇貿易上の統計に余りに絶対的の価値を付し居れり。之に関連して両者に用いられたる議論は前述の付属研究に検討せられあり。同研究に於いては正に相当多額に達する実害の程度に付詳細の記述を為しあり。

本問題の他の一面も亦之を述ぶるを要す。支那側自身は既に支払いを了せる商品にしてボイコット団体に登記せず為に公売の為押収せられたるにより、またボイコット規則違反に対し同団体に支払いたる罰金により、将又支那海関が其の収入を得ざることにより損失を蒙り居り、而して全般的に言えば取引を失いたるにより損失を蒙り居り、此等損失は相当の額に達す。

日支関係に及ぼせる心理の影響

ボイコットの日支関係に及ぼせる心理的影響は物質的影響よりも算定に困難なれども、広範囲の日本世論の対支感情上に惨憺たる反響を起こしたる点において確かに物質的影響に劣らず重大なり。委員会の日本訪問中

東京、大阪の両商工会議所はこの点を力説せり。

日本の世論は日本が其の蒙りつつある損害に対し自らを保護すること能わざるを以て憤激せり。委員会が大阪において会見せる商人等は乱暴狼藉及恐喝の如きボイコット手段の或る種乱用を過大視し、日本の最近の対支政策と右政策に対する防御的武器としてのボイコットの実行との間に存する密接なる関係を過小に見積り又は全然之を否定する傾向あり。反対に之等商人はボイコットを支那の防御武器とは見ずボイコットを以て侵略行為と為し之が報復として日本が軍事行動を執りたるなりと主張せり。兎に角ボイコットは近年日支間系を深く悪化せる諸原因の一たりしことは疑いの余地なし。

ボイコットに関する論争点

ボイコットの政策及手段に関し三箇の論争点あり。

（一）運動は自発的なりや又は組織せられたるものなりや

第一は、該運動は支那人自身主張するが如く純粋に自発的なりや、又は日本の主張するが如く国民党がしばしば恐怖政治に均しき方法に依り人民に強制する組織的運動なりや否やの問題なり。この点については双方に多くの言い分あるべし。一方に於いては民衆の強き感情の基礎なかりしならば重大なる地域に互り且長期間継続するボイコットを持続するに伴う此程度の協力及犠牲を示すこと一の国民にとりて不可能なりと認めらるる。他方支那人が其の古き同業公会及秘密結社より継承せる心理状態と方法とを国民党が利用し如何なる程度迄近時のボイコット特に現在のボイコットを支配するに至れるかは明らかに示されたり居ることは該運動がいかに自発的なりとはいえ確かに強固に組織せられ居ることを示すものなり。

あらゆる民衆運動は或程度の有効なる組織を必要とす。凡ての同志が共同目的に対して有する忠実さは決して画一的に強固なるものに非ず。故に目的及行動の統一を貫徹する為には規律を設くるの要あり。本委員会は支那のボイコットは民衆運動たると同時に組織せられたるものにして又右ボイコットは強き国民的感情に胚胎し之により支持せらるると雖も之を開始又は終息せしめ得る団体により支配せられ又命名せらるるものにして且確かに脅迫に等しき方法に依り強行せらるるものなりと結論す。ボイコットの組織中には多くの別々の団体ありと雖も主たる支配的権力は国民党に

あり。

　（二）ボイコットの方法の適法性又は不法性

　　第二の論点は、ボイコット運動の実行に際し用いられたる方法は常に適法なりしや否やに在り。委員会の蒐集せる証拠に依れば不法行為は常に行われ而も此等不法行為は官憲及法廷により充分に禦壓せられざりしところなりと云う以外に何等かの結論を為すこと困難なり。此等の方法が往時支那に於いて用いられたるものと大体に於いて同一なりとの事実は一の説明となるべしと雖も弁明とはならず。昔時支那の同業公会がボイコットを宣言し被疑者たる之会員の家宅を捜索し、彼等を公開裁判所に引出し、反則の廉により罰し、科料を課し、押収品を売却したりしも公会は当時の慣習に従い行動したるなり。加之右は支那社会の内部問題たりしものにして外国人の関係なかりし所なり。現在の状態は右と異なる。支那は近代的法典を採用したるが此等の近代的法律は支那におけるボイコットの伝統的手段と両立せざる所なり。支那参与員がボイコットに関する支那側の意見を弁護せる覚書は以上の記述を駁せず、単に「ボイコットは一般的に言わば合法的手段により行わるる……」と論ずるのみ。委員会の有する証拠は右の主張を支持せず。

　　右に関して不法行為にして直接に在支外国人即ち今の場合日本人に対して行われたるものと、支那人に対して行われたるも其の目的たるや明瞭に日本人の利益を害するに在りたるものとを区別せざるべからず。前者に関する限り此等の行為は支那法律により明らかに不法なるのみならず、生命財産を保護し並びに通商、居住、往来及行動の自由を保持するの条約上の義務に違反す。之は支那人も意義なき所にしてボイコット団体も国民党の当事者も此の種の犯行を予防するに努めたりしも必ずしも成功せざりしものの如し。既に述べたるが如く現在のボイコットに於いては此の種の行為は既往に於けるよりも少なかりき。[1]

---

　　[1]　最近日本より得たる情報に依れば上海に於いて1931年7月より同年12月末迄の間、排日諸団体員により日本商人の商品が捕獲抑留せられたる事件は三十五件なり。右商品の価格は約二八七〇〇〇ドルと評価せらるる。右事件の中、1932年8月に於いて未解決のまま残されたるものは五件なり。

支那人に対して行われたる不法行為に関しては支那参与員は其のボイコットに関する覚書第十七項に於いて曰く。

「吾人はまず外国は国内法上の問題を提起することを許されざることを述べんとす。実際吾人の直面せる行為は不法なりと摘発せらるるも支那人が他の支那人に損害を加えたるものなり。此等の行為の抑圧は支那官憲の関係事項にして支那の刑法が加害者も被害者も同じく支那国籍を有する事件に如何に適用せらるるかに対し何人も容喙する権なきやに認めらるる。如何なる国家と雖も他の国家の依然たる国内問題の処理に干渉する権利なし。主権及独立の相互尊重なる原則の意味するところ即ち之なり」と。

右の如く叙述せらるるときは右の議論は反駁の余地なしと雖も日本側の苦情は一の支那人が他の支那人により不法に損害を蒙りたりと云う点に根拠を有するには在らずして支那法律により不法なる方法に依り日本の利益が侵害せられ而して右の如き事情の下において法律を励行せざることが日本国に対して為されたる損害に対する支那政府の責任問題を惹起するものなりとの点に根拠を有するの事実を無視するものなり。

（三）ボイコットに対する支那政府の責任

茲に於いて吾人はボイコット政策の包含する最後の論争点即ち支那政府の責任の範囲の考察に逢着す。支那政府の態度は「物を買うにあたり自由に選択を為すことは個人の権利にして如何なる政府と雖も干渉し得る所に非ず政府は生命財産の保護に対しては責任を有するも一般に認められたる如何なる規則も原則も政府に対し各市民の基本的権利の行使を禁止し処罰すべしとは要求せず」と云うに在り。委員会は本報告書付属第8号に採録せられたる証拠資料を提供せられたり。

該証拠資料は現在のボイコットに於いて支那政府が上記引用支那側覚書の指示するように認めらるる所よりも一層直接的なる関与を為したることを示す。委員会は政府各部がボイコット運動を支持するの事実に何等か不適当なるものありと諷示せんとするには非ず。委員会は単に政府の奨励は其の責任問題を惹起することを指摘せんと欲す。此の点に関し政府と国民党の関係の問題を考慮するを要す。後者の責任に関しては問題なし。国民党は全ボイコット背後に存する支配的且調整的機関なり。国民党は政府を作るものにして又其の主人なるやも知れざるも如何なる点迄が党部の責

任にして如何なる点より政府の責任が開始するやを決定することは憲法上の一の複雑なる問題にして本委員会はこの点に関し断案を下すは適当に非ずと感ず。

批判

ボイコットは強国の軍事的侵略に対抗する防衛なる合法的の武器にして特に仲裁裁判の方法が前以て利用せらざりし場合に於いて然りと為すとの支那政府の主張は一層広汎なる性質の問題を提起す。個々の支那人が日本品を買うこと、日本の銀行若しくは船舶を利用すること、日本人たる使用者の為に働くこと、日本人の物品を売ること又は日本人と交際することを拒絶するの権利あるいは何人も否定することを得ざるべし。又支那人が個人的に又は組織せられたる団体としても上述の如き思想の宣伝をなすことを否定するを得ず。尤も此の場合常に其の方法が国法に違反せざることを要すること勿論なり。然れども一つの特定の国家の商業に対しボイコットを組織的に行うことが友好的関係と両立するや又は条約上の義務と合致するや否やは委員会の調査会の題目なりと言わんよりは寧ろ国際法上の問題なり。然れども委員会は一切の諸国の利益の為に本問題は近き将来において考慮せられ、国際約定により規律せられんことを希望す。本章中において、第一に、日本は其の人口問題に関連し其の産業能力を増加せんとし、此の目的の為に頼り得べき海外市場を求めつつあること、第二に、対米生絲輸出を除きては支那は日本の輸出の主たる市場にして同時に日本帝国に多くの原料品及食料品を供することを示せり。加之支那は日本の海外投資の殆ど全部を護し従って現時の如き混乱と未開の状態を以てすら支那は日本の諸種の経済的乃至財政的活動に対し有利なる天地を供す。最後に、1908年より今日に至る迄陸続として起これる種々のボイコットが支那における日本の権益に加えたる損害の検討は、此等の権益は毀損せられ易きものなることに付注意を喚起せり。

日本が支那市場に依存することは日本人自身も充分之を認むる所なり。他方支那は経済生活の各方面に於ける発展を最も焦眉の急とする国なり。而して1931年に於いてボイコットにも不拘其の全貿易額に於いて首位を占めたる日本は、他の如何なる外国よりも支那の経済的に支那の友邦たるべきものと思料せらる。

此等二箇の隣邦の貿易上の相互依存と両国の利益との為には其の経済的近接必要なり。然れども両者の政治的関係が然く険悪にして一方が兵力を、他方がボイコットなる経済的武器を用いる間は此の如き接近不可能なり。

第八章　満州に於ける経済上の利益[①]

前章に於いて日本及支那の経済上の要求は政治的理由により妨害せられざる限り紛争を齎さずして両国相互の了解及協調を齎すべきことを示せり。満州に於ける日本及支那の経済上の利益の相互関係を近年の政治上の出来事と切離し考究するに亦同様の結論に到達す。満州に於ける両国の経済上の利益は融和し難きものにあらず、満州に於ける現在の富源及将来の経済的可能性を其の最高限度迄充分に発展せしめんとせば、両者の融和は洵に必要なりと謂うべし。

満州に於ける富源は其の現実のものたると未開のものなるとを問わず日本の経済生活に必須なりとの日本世論の主張は第三章において充分検討せられたるが、本章の目的は右主張が如何なる程度迄経済的事実と合致し居るやを考察するに在り。

投資

南満州に於て日本は最大の外国側投資者なることは事実にして又北満州に於てはソ連邦に付同様なりと謂い得べし。三省を総括して之を見るに日本の投資はソ連邦の夫れよりも重要なり。尤も如何なる程度に重要なりやは信憑するに足る比較数字を得ること不可能なるを以て之を明らかにすること困難なり。投資の問題は本報告書の付属書中において詳細検討しあるを以て、茲には満州の経済的開発の参与分子として日本、ソ連邦及其の他の諸国の相対的重要性を説明する為少数の根本的数字を挙ぐるを以て足るべし。

日本側より得たる報道によれば日本の投資額は1928年において約十五億円なりし趣なるを以て、右の数字にして正確なりとせば今日において

---

① 本章に関しては特別研究第二、第三、第六及第七参照。

は約十五億円①に増加したるべきなり。露国側より出でたる報道は日本の現時の投資額を関東租借地を含む満州全体にて十五億円、東三省に対し約十三億円なりとし日本資本の大部分は遼寧省に投下せられ居れりと称す。

是等投資の性質に関し述べんに資本の過半は運輸企業（主として鉄道）に向けられ、農業、鉱業及林業之に次ぐ。

事実南満州に於ける日本の投資は主として南満州鉄道を中心として集中せられ居り、又北方に於けるソ連邦の投資も亦多くは直接又は間接に投資鉄道と関連せるものなり。

日本以外の外国の投資は之を算定することに困難多く、直接関係者の有益なる援助ありしにも拘らず委員会の得たる知識は貧弱なり。日本側より与えられたる数字の大部分は1917年以前のものにして時勢遅れなり。ソ連邦に関しては既述の如く確実なる計算可能ならず。他の諸国については北満州のみに関する露国側の最近の計算あり。右計算は之を検証すること能わざりしも、是に依れば英国は第二の最大投資者にして千百十八万五千金ドル、日本之に次ぎ九百二十二万九千金ドル、米国八百二十二万金ドル、波蘭五百二万金ドル、佛国百七十六万金ドル、獨国百二十三万金ドルにして、其の他百二十万九千金ドルの投資を合わせ総計三千七百七十八万四千四百金ドルなり。同様の計算は南満州については之を得難し。

日本と満州との経済的関係

満州が日本の経済生活において演ずる役割を茲に分析すること必要なり。本問題に関する詳細の研究は本報告書の付属書中に採録しあり。右付属書に依れば該役割は重要なるものなるも同時に周囲の事情により制限を受けることを知るべく、この点は看過を許さず。

過去の経験より推して満州は大規模の日本移民に適当ならざる地方なるものの如し。第二章において既に述べたるが如く山東省及直隷省よりの農民及苦力は最近数十年間に満州の地を取得せり。日本人の移住者は大部分資本の投下各種企業の発展及天然資源の開発事業を管理する為に来れる実業家、官吏及俸給生活者にして将来も多年の間然るべし。

---

① 別個の日本側数字は1929年に於ける日本の満州を含む対支全投資額を約十五億円なりとす。

農業

日本は其の供給を受くる農業中満州に倚頼し居るは主として大豆及其の副産物なり。食料及飼料としての大豆等の使用は将来更に増加すべきも、今日其の主要用途たる肥料としての重要性は日本に於ける化学工業の発達と共に減少すべきやに認めらる。然れども朝鮮及台湾の獲得が日本の米の問題の解決を少なくとも当分の間援助したるにより、食糧問題は日本にとりて現在の処緊急ならず。将来或る時日において米の必要が日本帝国にとり緊急をつげたる場合においては満州は別個の補給地を供給し得べし。然れども斯かる場合においては充分なる灌漑組織を発達せしむるが為多額の投資を必要とす可し。

重工業

満州富源の利用の結果、同地方に於ける日本の重工業が外国より独立すべき運命をゆうするものなりと仮定せんに、是等重工業の創設には更に巨額の資本を要すべきやに認めらる、日本は東三省において何よりもまず日本の国防に必須なる原料の生産を発達せしめんことを求め居れり。満州は日本に対し石炭、油及鉄を供給することを得れども右供給が経済上有利なりや否やは確実ならず。石炭について謂えば生産高の比較的小部分が日本により利用せられ居るのみにして石油も亦油母頁岩より極めて制限せられたる量が搾出せられ居るのみなり。又鉄は明らかに損失の下に生産せられ居るものの如く見受けらる。然れども経済的考慮は日本政府を左右する唯一の点に非ず。独立の鉱産物供給組織の発達を助くる為に満州の富源を以て之に充てんとするものなり。何れにするも日本は其の必要とするコークス及或種の珪土不含有原鉱の大部分の供給を海外に仰がざるを得ず。東三省は日本の国防に欠くべからざる数種の鉱産物の供給につき大なる保障を与うべきも、是等鉱産物を得んが為には大なる財政的犠牲を払うを要すべし。此の問題中に関連せる日本の満州に於ける戦略上の利害関係は別章に述ぶる所ありたり。尚満州は日本が其の紡織工業に最も必要とする原料を供給すること能わざるやに認めらる。

日本生産品の市場としての満州

東三省は日本の生産する加工品に対する常市場にして此の市場の重要性は東三省の繁栄の増加と共に更に増大すべし。尤も大阪は過去に於いて

常に大連よりも上海に倚頼するところ多かりき。

満州市場は安全性に於いて支那市場に優るべきも、支那市場に比し其の範囲に制限あり。経済ブロックの観念は西洋より日本に迄浸透せり。日本帝国及満州を包括するブロックの可能性に関しては日本の政治家、学者及操觚者の文書中にしばしば之を見受く。現商工大臣は其の就任の暫く前に執筆せる論説中に於いて世界に於ける米国、ソ連邦、欧州及英帝国の経済ブロックの成立を指摘し、日本も満州と共に斯くの如きブロックを創設すべきことを述べたり。

右の如き組織が実現し得べきや否や現在のところ示すべきものなし。最近日本に於いては其の同胞に対し幻想の危険につき警告の声を挙ぐる者ありたり。日本が其の貿易に付満州に倚頼する所は其の米国、支那本部及英領印度に依頼する所に比し遥かに少なし。

満州は将来に於いて人口過剰の日本に対し大なる援助となることあるべきも其の可能性の限度を弁識せざることは其の可能性の価値を軽視することと同様に危険なり。

支那の満州との経済的関係

東三省と東三省を除く支那との経済的関係を研究するときは、日本の場合に於けると異なり、支那の満州開発に対する初期の主なる貢献は満州の農業上の大発展に寄与せる季節的労働者及永住移民を送りたることに在ること明瞭なるべし。

然るに近年、殊に最近十年間に於いては支那の鉄道建設、鉱物及林産の開発並びに工業、商業及銀行業に対する参与は着しき進歩を示せるものある処、其の範囲は材料無き為適当に之を示す能わず。大体に於いて満州と爾余の支那との主要なる連鎖は経済的よりも寧ろ民族的及社会的ものなりと謂うを得べし。

第二章に於いて満州現在の住民は大部分近時の移民より成れるものなることを述べたるが、是等移民運動が自発的に行われたるに見るもの其の如何に実際の必要に基づきたるものなるかを知るを得べし。即ち右移民は飢饉の結果なり。尤も或程度において日本人側及支那人側双方により奨励せられたり。

日本人は多年撫順炭鉱、大連築港工事及鉄道建設のため支那人労働者

を募れるが、右の如くして募集せられたる支那人の数は極めて限りあるものなりき。而して右募集は1927年に至り地方的の労働供給を以て充分なりと認められたる結果中止せられたり。

　満州の地方官憲も数次支那移民の来往を助けたることあるが、実際に於いては東三省官憲の活動が移民数に対し及ぼしたる影響は極めて小なり。北支官憲及慈善団体も亦或時期に於いて満州に対する家族移民を奨励せり。

　移民の受けたる主なる補助は南満州鉄道、支那鉄道及投資鉄道の与えたる割引運賃なり。新来者に提供せられたる右奨励方法は南満州鉄道、満州各省官憲及支那政府に於いて少なくとも1931年末迄は移住に対し好感を以て迎えたることを示すものなり。彼等は何れも東三省植民により利益を得たり。尤も前記移住に対し彼等の有したる利害関係は常に同一なりしとは云い難し。

　満州に定着せる移民は支那本部における彼らの原住地との関係を維持す。右は移民が彼らが生まれ故郷に残したる家族に対する送金を研究すれば最も明瞭なり。銀行及び郵便局を通じて並びに帰還移民に託送して為さるる彼らの送金の総額を算測することは不可能なるが前記の方法により山東河北両省に送らるる金は毎年二千万間に達するものと信ぜられ、又1928年の郵政統計は遼寧吉林両省より山東省に対し郵便為替により送金せられたる額が支那の他の全部の省より山東に送金せられたる額と同額に達せることを示し居れり。是等送金が満州支那本部間の重要なる経済的連鎖を形成し居ることは疑いを容れず。右は移民と原住地に在る其の家族との間に維持せらるる接触のインデックスなり。右の接触は長城の両側における状況が大差なきため尚容易なり。農作物は大体同種にして、耕作法も亦同一なり。満州と山東における農業状況の最も顕著なる相違は気候、人口の密度及経済的開発の差異なるが、是等の要因は東三省の農業が益々山東における農業状況に近似することを妨げず。近年定住者を有する遼寧省に於ける農村の状況は山東のそれに酷似するも、近年開発せられたる黒龍江省においては左程迄山東に酷似せず。

　満州における農業者との直接取引組織もまた支那本部の状況と酷似す。東三省においては右の如き取引は農民のみより直接購入する支那人の

手にあり。又東三省においては支那本部におけると同様信用が右の如き地方的取引に重要なる職能を行う。満州及支那本部における商業組織の酷似は単に地方的取引においてのみならず市街地における取引においても亦之を見ることを得ると云うも過言にあらず。

　実際において満州における支那人の社会的及経済的組織は其の故国の習慣、方言及行事をそのまま移植せる社会組織にして唯本国に比し広汎にして人口少なく且外部より影響を蒙り易き満州の状況に適合せしむるに必要なる変改を要するのみなり。

　茲に前記大量移民は単なる一時的事件なりや或は将来も継続するものなりやの問題あり。南満州の地域並びに松花江、遼河及牡丹江流域の如き南部及東部に於ける数個の流域地方を考慮に入るるときは純然たる農業的見地より見るも満州は尚多数の植民を収容し得べきこと明らかなり。東支鉄道幹部の最も優秀なる専門家の意見によれば満州の人口は四十年間に七千五百万に達し得べしとのことなり。

　然れども満州に於ける人口の急激なる増加の将来は経済的条件に依り制限せらるることあるべし。事実経済的条件のみが大豆栽培の将来を不確実にするものなり。一方、最近満州に移入せられたる作物、殊に米の栽培は同地方に於いて発達すべきやに認めらる。日本人中望みを嘱したるものある棉花栽培の発達は或程度の制限を免ぜざるものの如し。故に東三省における今後の移住は経済的及技術的要因に依り或程度迄制限せらるることあるべし。

　満州に対する支那移民の減少は最近に於ける政治上の出来事のみが其の唯一の理由に非ず。経済上の危機は既に1931年の最初の六ヶ月間に於いて季節的移民の重要性を減殺せるが世界的不況は避くべからざりし地方的危機の惨禍を大ならしめたり。此の経済上の危機が去り秩序が再び回復せられたる暁には満州は又支那本部の人口の捌け口として役立つことあるべし。支那人は満州移民に最も適合せる人民なり無定見なる政治上の手段に依り此の移民を人工的に制限することは満州の利益並びに山東省及河北省の利益を毀損するものなり。

　満州と支那の他の部分との連鎖は民族的及社会的なるが、同時に経済的連鎖も不断に強固となりつつあり。右は満州と支那の他の部分との間に

於ける貿易上の関係の増進に依り示さる。然れども海関統計によれば日本は満州の最大顧客にして且第1の供給者なり。支那本部は次位を占む。

満州より支那の他の部分に対する主要輸入品は大豆及其の副産物、石炭及少量の落花生、生絲、雑穀及極少量の鉄、玉蜀黍、羊毛並びに木材なり。支那本部より満州に対する主要輸出品は綿織物、煙草類絹其他の織物、茶、穀類及種子、棉花、紙並びに小麦粉なり。斯くの如く支那本部は或種の食糧につき満州に倚頼し居り、就中最も重要なるものは大豆及其の副産物なるが、其の鉱産物輸入は石炭を除き、又其の木材、動物産品及加工のための原料の輸入は過去に於いて僅少なりき。更に支那本部は自身の入超を相殺するがため満州の出超利益金の一部分を利用し得るのみなり。右利用は一般に想像せられ居るが如く政治上の連合に依るに非ずして主として満州の郵政機関及海関が利益多きこと及支那移民の山東及河北両省にある其の家族に対する多額の送金によるものなり。

批判

満州の富源は豊富なれども未だ充分に実測せられ居らず。之が開発の為には人口、資本、技術、組織及国内の安寧を必要とする住民は殆ど全部支那より送らる。現在住民の多数は北支諸省の産にして其の故郷との家族的連絡は今尚密接なるものあり。資本、技術及組織は今日迄の所主として南満州においては日本に依り又長春以北に於いては露国により供給せられ来れり。其の他の外国も程度少なきも東三省を通じ主として大都会に於いて利益を有せり。是等諸外国の代表者は近年の政治的危急に際し調停的の役割を演じたるが経済的に最も優勢なる日本が市場独占を企てざる限り今後も右役割を行うこととなるべし。現在最も重要なる問題は住民が受諾し得べく且窮極的の要件を充たし得べき法と秩序の維持し得べき政権の樹立なり。

如何なる外国と雖も人口の大半をなし且満州の土地を耕し国内の殆ど総ての企業に対し労力を供給しつつある支那民衆の好意及満腔の強力なくしては満州を開発し又は之を管理せんとするの企てより利益を獲得すること能わず。一方支那も是等北方諸省が接壌諸国の相反する野心の戦場となること熄まざる限り永久に憂惧と危険とより解放せられざるべし。故に支那としては満州に於ける日本の経済上の利益を満足せしむること、又日本

としては満州に住民の変改すべからざる支那人的色彩を容認することが共に必要なり。

門戸開放の維持

上記の如き了解と併行し、且満州の開発に対する総ての関係国の協力を許容するが為には門戸開放の原則を単に法律的見地よりのみならず貿易、工業及銀行業の実際的運用に付維持すること必要なりと認めらる。日本人以外の外国実業家の間には日本商会が現在の政治状況を利用して自由競争以外の方法に依りて利益を獲得すべしとの危惧を懐くものあり。若し右の危惧にして理由あるに至らば外国側利害関係者を失望せしめ先ず其の損失を蒙るものは満州住民なるやも計られず。貿易、投資及財政上の自由競争に依りて表現せらるる真実の門戸開放の維持は日本及支那双方の利益なるべし①。

第九章　解決の原則及条件

前各章の再検討

本報告書の前各章において日支間の諸懸案は夫れ自体において仲裁的方法に依り解決し得ざりしに非ざりしも之等諸懸案特に満州問題に関する懸案を日支政府において取扱たる結果は両国関係を甚だしく悪化せしめ早晩衝突の免れ難きものたりしことを明らかにせり。支那が過渡時期に必然伴わるべきあらゆる政治的紛糾、社会的混乱及分裂的傾向を有する発達途上にある国家なることについても略述せり。又日本の要求する権利及利益が支那中央政府の無力なる為如何に甚だしく影響を受けたるが又日本が満州を支那の他の部分における政府より引離し置くことを如何に切望し来れるかをも述べたり。尚支那、露国及日本政府の満州に於ける政策を簡単に吟味したる結果満州各省政権は其の統治者に依り一再ならず支那中央政府よ

---

①　此の点に関し特に鮮満国境及大連を通じて為さるる満州への密輸入が非常なる範囲に亘り居ることを指摘すること必要なり。斯かる行為は単に海関収入に損失を与えるのみならず貿易を破壊し実際上海関行政を支配し居る国が他国の貿易に対して差別的待遇を為すこととなるべしとの信念を其の当否は別として起さしむべし。

り独立せることを声明せられたるも而も支那人が絶対多数を占むる之等各省人民は未だ嘗て支那の他の部分より分離することを欲する旨表明したることなきことをも明らかにせり。最後に吾人は9月18日及其の以後に起これる事態を注意深く且十分に検討し之に対する吾人の意見を表明せり。

問題の複雑性

今や吾人は将来に注意を集中する時期に達したるを以て本章の考察を最後とし此上過去には言及せざるべし。前掲各章の読者にとりては本件紛争に包含せらるる諸問題は往々称せらるるが如く簡単なるものに非ること正に明らかなるべし。即ち問題は寧ろ極度に複雑なるを以て一再の事実及其の歴史的背景に関し十分なる知識あるもののみ之に関する決定的意見を表明する資格ありというべし。本紛争は一国が国際聯盟規約の提供する調停の機会を予め十分に利用し尽くすことなくして他の一国に宣戦を布告せるが如き事件にあらず。又一国の国境が隣接国の武装軍隊に依り侵略せらるるが如き簡単なる事件にもあらず。何となれば満州に於ては世界の他の部分に於いて正確なる類例の存せざる幾多の特殊事態あるを以てなり。

本紛争は双方とも聯盟の一員たる二国間に於いてフランスとドイツを合したる面積ある地域に関し発生せるものにして右地域に関しては日支双方に於いて各々諸種の権益を有することを主張し而も此等権益は其の一部のみ国際法に依り明瞭に定義せられ居れり。右地域は法律的には完全に支那の一部なるも其の地方政権は本紛争の根底をなす事項に関し日本と直接交渉をなす程度の広汎なる自治的性質のものなりき。

満州の事態は他に類例なし

日本は海岸より満州の中心に達する鉄道及一地帯を支配し且該財産保護の為約一万の兵力を維持し且必要の場合には条約上之を一万五千に増加する権利ありと主張す。又日本は総ての在満日本人に対し法権を行使し且満州全土に亙り領事館警察を維持す。

解釈の多岐性

問題を討議するものはより叙上の事実を考慮せざるべからず。宣戦を布告することなくして疑いもなく支那の領土たる広大なる地域が日本軍隊に依り強力を以て押収、占領せられ且右行動の結果として該地域が支那の他の部分より分離せられ独立を宣言するに至れるは事実なり。日本は右事

実完了に至らしめたる手段はこの種行動の防止を目的とする国際聯盟規約、不戦条約及華府九国条約の義務に合致するものなりと主張す。更に本問題に付初めて聯盟の注意が喚起せられたる際漸く開始せられたる行動は其の後数ヶ月間に完結せられ且日本は右行動を以て9月30日及12月10日寿府に於いて其の代表の与えたる保証と合致するものなりと主張す。日本の説明に依れば其一切の軍事行為は正当なる自衛行為にして右権利は叙上の多辺的条約中に包含せられ又国際聯盟理事会の何れの決議に於いても奪われたることなし。将又東参照に於いて支那の旧政権に代われる新政権は其の成立が地方人民の行為にして彼等は自発的に其の独立を宣言し支那との一切の関係を断ち自己の政府を樹立したものなるを以て正当視せらるるものなりとせり。尚の本の主張に依れば斯くの如き真正なる独立運動は如何なる国際条約若しくは国際聯盟理事会の決議に依りても禁ぜられず、且斯かる運動の既に行われたりと云う事実は九国条約の適用を着しく改編し聯盟に依り調査せられつつある問題の全性質を根本的に変更せるものなりとせり。

本紛争を特に複雑化且重大化するものは叙上の如き合法性に関する主張なり。本件に付論議することは本委員会の機能に非るも本委員会は聯盟をして紛争国の名誉、威厳及国家的利益を損せずして紛争を解決せしむるが為十分なる材料を供給することに努め来れり。単に批評することのみにては解決を期し難し。両者の調停に資する為実際的努力なかるべからず。吾人は満州に於ける過去の事件に関し真相を捕捉するため苦心し来れるが率直に言えば右は吾人の仕事の僅か一部分にして而も決して重要部分に非ることを認む。吾人は使命を行うに当り終始両国政府に対し紛争を調停するため国際聯盟の援助の提供方を申し入れたるが今や本委員会は其の使命を終わらむとするに当り正義と平和とに合致する方法に依り満州に於ける日支の永遠の利益を確保する為吾人の定義を聯盟に提出せむとす。

解決に関する不満足なる提議

（一）原状回復

単なる原状回復が問題の解決たり得ざることは如上吾人の述べたる所に依り明らかなるべし。蓋し本紛争が去る9月以前における状態より発生せるに鑑み同状態の回復は紛糾を繰り返す結果を招来すべく斯くの如きは

全問題を単に論理的に取扱い現実の情勢をむしするものなり。

　（二）「満州国」の維持

　　前二章に述べたる所に鑑み満州に於ける現政権の維持及承認も均しく不満足なるべし。斯かる解決は現行国際義務の根本的原則若しくは極東平和の基礎たるべき両国間の良好なる諒解と両立するものと認められず。右は又支那の利益に違反し又満州人民の希望を無視するのみならず結局に於いて日本の永遠の利益となるべきや否やに付少なくとも疑いあり。

　　現政権に対する満州人民の感情については何等疑問なし。而して支那は東三省の完全なる分離を以て永久的解決なりとなして進んで之を承諾するが如きことなかるべし。

　　満州と遠隔なる外蒙古地方との類似性を論ずるは其の当を得ざるものなり。蓋し外蒙古と支那との間に何等強固なる経済的若しくは社会的紐帯なく且人口稀薄にして而も其の大部分は支那人あらざるを以てなり。満州に於ける事態と外蒙古における夫れとは極端なる差異あり。満州に定着せる数百万の支那農民は各般の関係において満州をして「長城」以南の支那の延長たらしめたり。東三省は其の人種、文化的及国民的感情に於いて支那化し其の移住者の大部分の来れる隣省河北山東省と殆ど変わることなし。

　　然しながら過去の経験に依れば満州の支配者は支那の他の部分—少なくとも北支那に於いて相当なる程度の勢力を行使し来り且明白なる各種軍事上及政治上の利益を有せり。東三省を支那の他の部分より法律的に若しくは実際的に分離するは招来に向て重大なるイルリデンデスト問題を発生し其の結果常に支那の敵愾心を盛んならしめ且恐らく日本商品のボイコットを永続的ならしめ以て平和を危殆に陥るるものと云うべし。

　　本委員会は日本政府より満州に於ける其の重大利益に関する明確且貴重なるステートメントを受領せり。前章に記述せる程度以上に日本の満州に対する経済的依拠を誇張することなく且経済的関係は日本に対し東三省の政治的は勿論経済的発達を支配するの資格を与うるものなりと提言することなく、日本の経済的開発の為満州が甚だ重大なる事を認むるものなり。将又日本が満州の経済的開発の為必要なる治安を維持し得べき安定せる政府の樹立を要求することも不合理なりと考えるものに非ず。然るに斯くの如き状態は人民の願望に合致し且彼等の感情及要望を十分に考慮する政権

に依り初めて確実且有効に保障せらるべし。尚右満州の急速なる経済的開発に必要なる資本の集中は現在極東に見られざる外部の信頼と内部の平和の雰囲気とに於て初めて可能なり。

過剰人口増加の圧迫あるに拘らず日本国民は移民に関する現在の便宜を従来十分に利用することなく、且日本政府は満州に其の国民の大移住を計画したることなし。而るに日本国民は農業的危機及人口問題に善処する方法として更に其の工業化に希望を懸けつつあり。斯くの如き工業化は新たなる経済的市場を要求すべき処日本唯一の広大且比較的確実なる市場はアジア殊に支那に於いて見出さるべし。日本は単に満州市場のみならず全支那市場を必要とする処支那が統一し近代化する結果は当然其の生活程度向上するに至り、貿易を促進し支那市場の購買力を増加すべし。

日本にとり重大利益ある右日支の経済的提携は同時に支那の利益問題なり。何となれば支那が更に日本と経済的及技術的に合作することは其の国家改造の第一事業を助成するものなるを発見すべければなり。支那は其の国民主義の狭量なる傾向を抑圧することに依り又友誼関係復活するや否や組織的ボイコットの再現することなき旨の有効なる保障を与えることに依り右提携を助成し得べし。一方日本としては満州問題を支那関係の一般的問題より切り離し、支那との友好及合作を不可能ならしむる方法にて支那問題を解決するが如きあらゆる試みを放棄することに依り右提携を容易ならしむるを得べし。

然るに満州に於ける日本の行動及方針を決定せしものは経済的考慮よりは寧ろ日本自体の安全に対する懸念なるべし。日本の政治家及軍部が満州は「日本の生命線」なることを常に口にするは特に此の関係に於てなりとす。世人は右の如き懸念に同情し且あらゆる事態に於いて日本の国防を確保する為重大責任を負わざるを得ざる右政治家及軍部の行動及動機を了解するに努むべし。日本の領土に対する敵対行動の根拠地として満州を利用するを防止せむとする日本の関心及或情勢の下に外国の軍隊が満州の国境を越え来る場合あらゆる必要の軍事的手段を執ることを可能ならしむるとする日本の希望を仮に認むるとするも果たして満州を無期限に占領し又之が為当然必要なるべき巨額の財政的負担をなすことが真に外部よりする危険に対する最も友好なる保障の方法なりや。将又右の如き方法に依り侵略

に対抗する場合、日本軍隊が若し敵意を持つ支那の後援の下に不従順若しくは反抗的なる民衆に依り包囲せらるる場合には甚だしく困難を感ずることなきや否やは尚疑問とすべき所なるべし。従って現存の世界平和機関の基礎をなす原則と、より善く合致し且世界の各地における他の強国に依り締結せられたる手続に類似せる方法に依り安全問題の他の可能なる解決方法を考慮することは確かに日本のため利益なり。日本は亦世界の他の国家の同情と好意とに依り而も日本自身は何等の負担をなすことなくして日本が目下執りつつある高価なる手段により得らるるも更に確実なる安全を得る可能性もあり得べし。

国際的利益

日支両国を別とし世界の他の強国も此の日支紛争に関し防衛すべき重大利益を有す。吾人は先に現行の他辺的条約に言及せり。苟も合意による真正且永続的解決は世界平和機関の根底を為す之等原則的協定の条項と両立するものたるを要る華府会議に於ける強国の代表者を動かしたる諸種の考慮は今日尚有効なり。平和維持のため必要不可欠なる条件として支那の改造に協力し其の主権並びに其の領土的行政的統一を保全することは今日に於いても1922年に於けるが如き列国の利益なり。支那の分裂は恐らく急速に重大なる国際競争を招来すべき処右競争が若し相異なれる社会組織の間に於ける競争と同時に起こる場合は更に激烈を加うべし。最後に平和の利益は全世界を通じ同様なるべき処聯盟規約及不戦条約の原則の適用に関し世界の如何なる方面に於いても減少すべし。

ソ連邦の利益

本委員会は満州に於けるソ連邦の利益の範囲に関し直接に情報を入手するを得ず。又満州問題に関するソ連邦政府の監察を確かむるを得ざりき。尤も仮令直接情報を入手せざりしと雖も本委員は満州に於てロシアの演じたる役割若しくはソ連邦が東支鉄道の所有者として将又支那の北方に於ける領土の所有者として該地域におけるソ連邦の有する重大なる利益を看過するを得ず。ソ連邦の重大利益を無視せる解決方法は反って将来に於ける平和を撹乱する危険あり。従って永久性なかるべきは明らかなり。

結論

若し日支両国政府が双方の主要利益の一致せることを承認し且平和の

維持及相互間に於ける友誼関係の樹立をも右利益の中に包含せしむる意思あるに於ては両国間紛争解決の基礎的大綱は叙上の考案に依り十分明示せらるべし。既述の如く1931年9月以前の状態への復帰は問題にあらず。将来に於ける満足すべき政権は過激なる変更なくして現政権より進展せしめ得べし。次章に於いて吾人は之が為或る提議すべきも吾人は先ず満足なる解決方法として準拠するを要する一般的原則を明らかにせんと欲す。此等原則は次の如し。

満足なる解決の条件

（一）日支双方の利益と両立すること。

両国は聯盟国なるを以て各々聯盟より同一の考慮を払わるることを要求する権利を有す。両国が利益を獲得せざる解決は平和の為の収得とならざるべし。

（二）ソ連邦の利益に対する考慮。

第三国の利益を考慮することなく両隣国間に於いて平和を講ずるは公正若しくは賢明ならざるべく亦平和に資する所以に非るべし。

（三）現存多辺的条約との一致。

如何なる解決と雖も聯盟規約、不戦条約及華府九国条約の規定に合致するを要す。

（四）満州に於ける日本の利益の承認。

満州に於ける日本の権益は無視するを得ざる事実にして如何なる解決方法も右を承認し且日本と満州との歴史的関連を考慮に入れざるものは満足なるものに非るべし。

（五）日支両国間に於ける新条約関係の成立。

満州に於ける両国各自の権利、利益及責任を新条約中に再び声明することは合意による解決の一部にして将来紛糾を避け相互的信頼及協力を回復するために望ましきことなり。

（六）将来に於ける紛争解決に対する有効なる規定。

叙上に付随的なるものとして比較的重要ならざる紛争の迅速なる解決を容易ならしむる為規定を設くる要あり。

（七）満州の自治。

満州に於ける政府は支那の主権及行政的保全と一致し東三省の地方的

状況及特徴に応ずる工夫せられたる広汎なる範囲の自治を確保する様改め
らるべし。新文治制度は善良なる政治の本質的要求を満足する様構成運用
せらるるを要す。

（八）内部的秩序及外部的侵略に対する保障。

満州の内部的秩序は有効なる地方的憲兵隊に依り確保せらるべく、外
部的侵略に対する安全は憲兵隊以外の一切の武装隊の撤退及関係国間に於
ける不侵略条約の締結に依り与えらるべし。

（九）日支両国間に於ける経済的提携の促進。

本目的の為両国間に於ける新通商条約の締結望まし。斯かる条約は両
国間に於ける通商関係を公正なる基礎の上に置き双方の政治関係の改善と
一致せしむることを目的とすべし。

（十）支那の改造に関する国際的協力。

支那に於ける現今の政治的不安定が日本との友好関係に対する障害に
して且極東に於ける平和の維持が国際的関心事項たる関係上世界の他の部
分に対する危惧はると共に叙上に挙げたる条件は支那に於いて強固なる中
央政府なくしては実行する能わざる所なるを以て満足なる解決に対する最
終的要件は故孫逸仙博士が提議せる如く支那の内部的改造に対する一時的
国際協力なり。

叙上の条件の実行より来るべき結果

若し現時の事態が叙上の条件を満たし叙上の観念を包含する如き方法
において緩和せられえるにおいては日支両国は其の紛争の解決を達成し以
て両国間に於ける密接なる了解及政治的協力の新時代の出発点となすを得
べし。若し斯かる提携が確保せられざるに於いてはその条件が如何にもあ
れ如何なる解決方法も真の効果なかるべし。斯かる新関係を企画すること
は現下の危機に際しても真に不可能なりや。青年日本は支那に於ける強硬
政策、満州に於ける徹底的政策を叫び居れり。右の如き要求をなすものは9
月18日以前の時期に於ける遷延策及小細工に厭き果て居れり。彼等はそ
の目的に達成する為性急なり。

然れども日本においてもあらゆる目的を達成するため適当なる手段を
見出さざるべからず。右「積極」政策の更に熱心なる代表者の若干並びに明
白なる理想主義及大なる個人的熱誠を以て「満州国」政権に於ける微妙なる

企画の先駆者となれる人士と相識れる後日本の有する問題の核心に近代支那の政治的発展及其進みつつある将来の傾向に関する危惧の存することを認識せざるを得ず。此の危惧は右支那の発展を制御し且其の進路を日本の経済的利益を確保すると共に同帝国の防衛に対する軍略的要求を満足せしむる方向に向けしむる目的を有する行動に導きたり。然れども日本の世論も朧げながら満州に対するものと支那本部に対するものと二つの別個の政策を有することが最早実行し得ざることを知覚しつつあり。故に其の満州に於ける利益を目標とする場合に於いても日本は支那の国民的感情の再興を認め同情を以て之を歓迎するやも知れず。而して日本は支那が他の何れに対しても支持を求めざることを確保する目的のみよりする同国と提携し之を誘導扶液するやも知れず。

支那に於いても亦該国家に対する死活問題、真の国家的問題は国家の改造及近代化なることを認むるに至れる処彼らは右改造の近代化の政策は既に開始せられ政綱の望多きも其の実現には一切の国家特に其の最も近隣者なる大国との友好的関係の涵養を必要とすることを認めざるを得ざるなり。支那は政治的及経済的事項に於いて一切の主要国の協力を必要とする特に支那にとり有益なるは日本政府の友好的態度及満州に於ける日本の経済的協力なり。新に目覚めたる国家主義の他の一切の要求は如何に正当にして且緊急なりとも右国家の有効なる内部改造に対する重大なる必要の前には之を従とせざるべからず。

第十章　理事会に対する考察及提議

終局的解決を容易ならしむる為の提議

現在の紛争解決のため直接支那及日本政府に勧告を提出するは本委員会の職務に非ず。然れどもブリアン氏が本委員会創設に関する決議の案文を理事会に説明するに当り使用せる字句を借りて云えば、「両国間に現存する紛争原因の終局的解決を容易ならしむる」為、吾人は茲に国際聯盟に対し、聯盟の適当なる機関が紛争当事国に与うべき確定的提案を起草することを助けんことを目的とせる諸決議を吾人の研究の成果として提出せんとす。此等の提議は吾人が前章において定めたる前条件を満足せしむべき一

方法を例示するの目的をもって為されたるものと諒解せらるべし。此等提議は主として広汎なる原則に関するものにして、多数の細目挿入の余地を残し、且紛争当事国が何等其の趣旨に副える解決を受諾するの意あるにおいては当事国によって多大の変更を加えわれ得べきものとす。

　仮令日本の「満州国」正式承認が寿府における本報告書の審議以前に行わるることありとするも―右は吾人の看過するを得ざる事態なるが―吾人は吾人の仕事が徒労に帰すべしとは思考せず。吾人は孰れにせよ理事会は本報告が満州に於ける関係両大国の死活的利益を満足せしむるの目的を以てせる理事会の決議又は右両大国に対する勧告に役立つべき諸提議を包含せることを見出すべしと信じ。吾人が国際聯盟の諸原則、支那に関する諸条約の精神及字句並びに平和の一般的利益を念頭に置きつつ、他方現実の事態を看過せず、且東三省に現存し目下発展の過程にある行政機関を考慮に入れたるは一に此の目的に出づるものなり。世界平和の至高なる利益の為、事態が如何に帰着するとも、目下満州に於て醸成せられつつある健全なる力を―理想たると人物たると将又思想たると行為たると総て之を利用し以て日支両国間の永続的了解を確保せんとする目的を以て本報告書中の諸提議が今尚日々に進展しつつある事態に如何に拡張し適用せらるべきかを決定するは理事会の職務なるべし。

解決を議せんが為の当事国の招請

　吾人は第一に、理事会が前章に示されたる大綱に依り其の紛争の解決を議せんが為支那及日本両国政府を招請すべきことを提議す。若し右招請受諾せらるるに於ては次の措置は東三省統治の為特別なる制度の構成に関し審議し且詳細なる提案を為す為可及的速やかに建言会議を招集することにあり。

建言会議

　右会議は支那及日本両国政府の代表者、並びに支那政府により指定せられたる方法により選択せられたる者一名、日本政府により指定せられたる方法により選択せられたる者一名、計二名の地方民を代表する委員を以て構成せらるべきことを提議す。当事国の同意あるに於ては、中立国オブザーバーの援助を受くることを得べし。若し右会議が何等特殊の点に付協定に達し得ざる場合には会議は意見相違の点を理事会に提出し而して理事

会は此等の点に付円満なる解決を得んことを試むべし。

最後に吾人は此等審議及交渉の結果は四個の異なりたる文書に具現せらるべきことを提議す。

一、建言会議の勧告せる条件に基づき東三省に対し特別なる行政組織を構成すべき旨の支那政府の宣言。

二、日本の利益に関する日支条約。

三、調停、仲裁裁判、不侵略及相互援助に関する日支条約。

四、日支通商条約。

建言会議会合前右決議の考慮すべき行政組織の概要は理事会援助の下に当事国間に協定せらるべきものなることを提議す。此の際考慮せられるべき事項中には左の如きものあるべし。

建言会議会合の場所、代表の性質、及中立国オブザーバーが希望せらるるや否や。

支那の領土的及行政的保全維持の原則と満州に対する広汎なる自治の付与。

提議せられたるが如き別個の条約によって各般の懸案を解決するの原則。

満州に於ける最近の政治的発展に参加せる者全部に対する大赦。

一度此等広汎なる原則にして予め協定せられんか、細目に付いては建言会議に於いて又は条約締結交渉の際、当事国代表者に対し能う限り充分なる裁量の余地を残すべし。更に国際聯盟理事会に付議することは協定失敗の場合に於いてのみ行わるべきものとす。

本手続の有利なりと主張せらるる諸点

本手続の利益在る諸点中吾人は本手続が支那の主権と抵触することなくして今日現存する満州の事態に適合せんが為有効且実際的なる手段を執ることを可能ならしむると同時に、今後支那に於ける国内事態の変化に伴い当然なりと認めらるるが如き変革を斟酌するものなることを主張す。例えば本報告においては地方政府の改組、中央銀行の創立、外国人顧問の備聘の如き提案せられたるか又は現に居る若干行政及財政上の変革に注意したり。此等事項は建言会議に於いても依然之を維持すること有利なるやも知れず。吾人の提議せるが如き方法により選択せられたる満州住民代表者の

本会議出席も亦現在の制度より新制度への転換を容易ならしむるべし。

満州に対して企図せられ居る自治制度は遼寧（奉天）、吉林及黒龍江の三省にのみ施行するを目的とす。現に日本が熱河（東部内蒙古）において享有する権利は日本の利益に関する条約中において処理せらるべし。

一、宣言

建言会議の最終提案は支那政府に提出せらるべし。而して支那政府は国際聯盟及九国条約調印国に送付せらるべき宣言中において之を具現すべし。聯盟国及九国条約調印国は右宣言を了承し、右宣言は支那政府に対し国際約定の拘束的性質を有するものなること明らかならしめらるべし。

爾後必要により本宣言を改正する場合の条件は上に定義せられたる手続に遵い協定せられたる所により宣言自体中に規定せらるべし。宣言は東三省に於ける支那中央政府の権力と自治地方政府の権力とを区分すべし。

中央政府に保留せらるべき権力

中央政府に保留せらるべき権力は左の如くなるべきことを提議す。

一、別に規定なき限り一般条約及外交関係の管理。但し中央政府は宣言の規定に抵触する国際約定を為さざるものと了解せらる。

二、税関、郵便局及監税並びに能う限り印花税及煙酒税の事務の管理。中央政府東三省間の此等収入よりの純収入の衡平なる配分は建言会議によって決定せらるべし。

三、宣言中に規定せらるべき手続による東三省政府執政の少なくとも第一次の任命権。欠員は同様の方法又は建言会議によって同意せられ且宣言中に挿入せられたる東三省に於ける或種の選任制度によって充たさるべし。

四、東三省執政に対し、東三省自治政府の管轄下にある事項に付中央政府が結べる国際約定の履行を確保するに必要なるべき命令を為すの権。

五、本会議によって同意せられたる其他の権力。

地方政府の権力

他の権力は総て東三省自治政府に帰属す。

地方世論の表現

能う限り商会、同業公会及其他の民間団体等の伝統的機関を通して政府の政策に関する民意の発現を得せしむる為何等実際的制度を案出し得

べし。

少数民族

白系露人及其他の少数民族の利益を保全する為にも亦何等規定を設くるの要あるべし。

憲兵隊

外国人教官の協力を以て特別憲兵隊を組織すべきことを提議す。右憲兵隊は東三省における唯一の武装隊たるべし。

特別憲兵隊の組織は予め決定せられたる期間内に完成せらるるか、又は完了の時期は宣言中に規定せらるべき手続に従い決定せらるることを要す。該特別憲兵隊は東三省領域に於ける唯一の武装隊なるべきを以て之が組織完成の暁には該領域より日支双方の何れに属するを問わずあらゆる特別警察隊又は鉄道守備兵を含む他の総ての武装隊の撤収行わるべし。

外国人顧問

自治政府の執政は適当数の外国人顧問を任命すべくそのうち日本人が充分なる割合を占むることを要す。之が細目は前掲の手続に依りて決定せらるべく且宣言中に陳述せらるべきものとす。小国の国民も大国の国民と同様に選定せらるることを得べし。

執政は聯盟理事会より提出すべき人名簿中より2名の異なれる国籍に属する外国人を任命し(1)警察(2)財務行政を監督せしむべし。右の二名の官吏は新制度の組織期間及試験期間中広汎なる権限を有すべく其の権限は宣言中に明定せらるべし。

執政は国際決済銀行理事会より提出すべき人名簿より一名の外国人を東三省中央銀行の総顧問に任命すべし。

外国人顧問及官吏の任用は支那国民党の創立者の政策及現国民政府の政策に合致するものなり。吾人は東三省における現下の状態並びに同地方に於ける外国の権益及勢力の複雑性が平和及良好なる施政の為に特別なる措置を必要ならしむることは支那の世論が之を認識するに難からざるべきことを期待す。然れども茲に提議せる外国人顧問及官吏(新制度組織の期間に於いて例外的に広汎なる権限を行使しべき外国人を含む)の存在は単に国際協力の形式を表現するに過ぎざるものなることは吾人の特に強調せんと欲する所なり。之等外国人顧問及官吏は支那政府の受諾し得べき形式

に依り又支那の主権に合致せる方法に於いて選任せられざるべからず。彼等は従来海関及郵政の組織に傭聘せられたる外国人又は支那人と協力せる国際聯盟の技術的期間の場合に於けると同様、任命せられたる暁には任命せる政府の雇用人なりと自覚せざるべからず。此の点に関し内田伯が1932年 8 月 25 日、日本会議に於いて為したる演説中の左の一節は興味あるものなり。

「……現に我国の如きも明治維新後多数の外国人を官吏又は顧問として傭聘して居たのでありまして、例えば明治八年頃に於ける是等外国人の総数は五百名を超過して居たのであります……」

尚日支協力の雰囲気の中に比較的多数の日本人顧問が任命せらるることは彼等をして特に地方的状況に適合せる訓練及知識を供与せしめ得べき点に於いても亦之を強調するを要す。過渡期を通じて目標とすべきは結局に於いて外国人の傭聘を不必要ならしむべき支那人のみに依りて組織せられたる文官制度の創立なり。

二、日本の利益に関する日支条約

本報告書中に提議せる日支間の三条約締結の交渉に当るべき者に対して完全なる自由裁量を残すべきことは勿論なるも、彼等が処理すべき事項を指示することは有用なるべし。

条約の目的

東三省における日本の利益及熱河に於ける或種の日本の利益に関する日支条約は主として日本人の特定の経済的権利及鉄道問題を取扱うべきものとす。即ち該条約の目的は左の如くなるを要す。

一、満州の経済的開発に対する日本の自由なる参加。尤も右は同地方を経済的または政治的に支配する権利を伴わざるものとす。

二、熱河に於いて現に日本が享有しつつある権利の存続。

三、居住権及商租権を全満州地域に拡張すること及之に伴いて治外法権の原則を多少修正すること。

四、鉄道運行に関する協定。

日本人の居住権

今日迄の所日本人の居住権は南満州及熱河に限定せられ居りたり尤も南満州の間には何等確定的境界存せず。而して之等権利は支那が受諾し得

ずと認めたる条件に下に行使せられ其の結果絶えず軋轢紛争を醸したり。課税及司法に関する治外法権的地位は日本人及朝鮮人の双方に為に主張せられ、後者に付いては不明確にして且論争の原因を為せる特別規定存せり。本委員会に提出せられたる証拠より見て支那は治外法権的地位が伴わざるに於ては現在の限定的居住権を全満州に拡張するに同意を与えるものと信ずべき理由あり。治外法権的地位が之に伴うに於ては支那領域内に日本人国家を創立するの結果を招来すべしと主張せられたり。

居住権と治外法権とは密接なる関係を有すること明らかなり。然れども司法及税制制度が従来満州に於けるよりも遥かに高き程度に到達する時期迄は日本人は治外法権的地位の放棄に同意せざるべきことも同様に明らかなり。

茲に二種の妥協方法あり。一は治外法権的地位を伴う現行の居住権は之を維持し、治外法権的地位を伴わざる居住権を日本人及朝鮮人双方の為に北満州及熱河に拡張すべしと云うにあり。他は日本人は満州及熱河の何処に於いても治外法権的地位の下に居住する権利を与えらるべく、朝鮮人は治外法権的地位を伴わざる同様の権利を与えらるべしとするにあり。右二種の提議は何れも或程度の長所を有するも同時に比較的重大なる故障あり。本問題の最も満足なる解決方法は之等地方の行政を治外法権的地位を必要とせざる程度に有能ならしむるにあること明らかなり。此の見地よりして吾人は少なくとも二名の外国人顧問(内一名は日本国籍を有することを要す)が最高法院に配属せられんこと及他の顧問が他の法院に配属せらるることの有利なることを勧告す。之等法院が外国人関係事項に関し判決することを求められたるあらゆる事件に付之等顧問の意見は公開せらるべし。吾人は右の他改組期間中において外国人が財務行教に関し或種の監督を有することを望ましいと思考し宣言に関し右の趣旨の提議を存し置きたる次第なり。

尚右の他日支何れかの政府が其の名に於いて又は人民に代わりて提起すべき苦情を処理すべき仲裁裁判所を調停条約中に於て設立することは更に一段の保障をとり付ける所以なり。

複雑にして困難なる本問題の決定は条約締結交渉の当事国側に残されるべきものなるも、朝鮮人の如く多数にして現に人口増加の途にあり且支

那住民と斯く迄も密接なる関係の下に居住する少数民族に対して現在の如き外国による保護を為すことは必然的に感情の衝突を頻発せしめ延いては地方的事件の発生及外国の干渉を招くものなり本件の如き軋轢の源泉が除去せらるることは平和の見地よりして望まし。

　　日本人に対して与えられるべきあらゆる居住権の拡張は「最恵国」条項の利益を享有する他のあらゆる列国の国民に対して同様の条件にしてに適用せらるべきものとす。但し右は治外法権国が支那との間に同様の条約を締結せる場合に限る。

鉄道

　　鉄道に関しては第三章に於いて日支双方鉄道建設者及鉄道当局の間に広汎にして相互に利益を齎す如き鉄道計画を目標とする協力は過去に於いて皆無又は殆ど無かりしことを指摘せり。若し将来に於ける軋轢を避けんとせば過去に於ける競争制度を終息せしめ之に代わるに諸線における貨客運賃に関する共通の了解を以てするの規定を本条約中に設くること必要なり。本問題は本報告に付属する特別研究第一に於いて検討せられ居れり。吾人の意見に依れば二つの解決方法あり。右二方法は何れか一つを選択すると得ると共に一個の終局的解決の段階とも見ることを得べし。

　　其の一は其の範囲において稍制限せられたるものにして日支両国鉄道当局の協力を容易ならしむべき右両当局間の業務協定なり。日支両国は協力の原則の上に満州に於ける各自の鉄道系統を経営することに同意すべく且日支混合鉄道委員会は少なくとも一名の外国人顧問を加え或る他国に存する理事会の職能に類似せる職能を行使すべし。更に徹底的なる解決は日支両国の鉄道の利益を合同することにより与えられるべし。而して斯かる合同は若し協定せられ得るに於て実に本報告が確保せんとする目的の一たる真の日支両国の経済的共同の標徴となるべし。右は支那の利益を保証しつつ満州に於ける凡ての鉄道に対して南満州鉄道の偉大なる技術的経験の利益を提供するを得しむべく且過去数ヶ月間に於いて満州に於ける諸鉄道に適用せられたる制度より容易に進展せられ得べきものなり。右は将来に於て東支鉄道を含む更に広汎なる国際協定の成立に至るの途を開くに至るやも知れず。斯くの如き合同に関する詳細なる記述は実行の可能性ある事項として付属書に之を掲載せるも詳細なる計画は当事国間に於ける直接交

渉に依りてのみ進展せらるべし。鉄道問題の斯くの如き解決は南満州鉄道をして純然たる商業的企業となすべく且一度特別憲兵隊が完全に組織せらるるにおいては右憲兵隊により与えらるる安全は鉄道守備隊の撤退を可能ならしめ相当莫大なる費用を節約し得べし。若し右にして為し得べくんば予め鉄道付属地内に特別土地章程及特別市政を施行し南満州鉄道及日本国民の既得権益を保障すべきなり。

叙上の大綱による条約にして協定し得べくむば東三省及熱河に於ける日本人の権利に対する法律的根拠は認められ且右根拠は少なくとも現行条約及協定同様日本に有利なると共に支那にはより以上に受諾し得べきものなるを以て支那は1915年の条約の如き条約及協定に依り日本に為したる一切の確定的譲与を新条約に依り廃棄又は修正せられざる限り承認するに困難を有せざるべし。日本の要求する一切の比較的重要ならざる権利にして其の効力に付争あるもには協定の題目たるべし。若し協定成立せざるに於ては調停協約に掲げたる手続に訴うべし。

三、調停、仲裁裁判、不侵略及相互援助に関する日支条約

本条約の題目に付いて多くの先例及現存実例存するを以て詳細に記述するの必要なし。

斯かる条約は日支両国政府間に発生するが如き一切の紛争の解決を援助する機能を有する調停委員会に付規定すべく又法律的経験及極東に関する必要なる知識を有する人士を以て構成する仲裁裁判所を設置すべし。右裁判所は宣言又は新条約の解釈に関する日支両国政府間に於ける一切の紛争及調停条約中に特に規定せらるるが如き他の範疇に属する紛争を処理すべし。

最後に本条約に挿入せられたる不侵略及相互援助に関する規定に基づき当事国は満州が漸次非武装地帯となることに同意すべし。右の目的を以て憲兵隊の組織が実行せられたる後において両当事国の一方又は第三国による非武装地帯の侵犯は侵略行為を構成するものとなし他の当事国又は第三者の攻撃の場合には両当事国が聯盟規約の下に行動すべき聯盟理事会の権利を害することなく非武装地帯を防禦するに適当なりと思考する一切の措置を執るの権利を有すべし。

若もソ連邦政府にして斯かる条約中の不侵略及相互援助に関する条章

に参加せむと欲するに於ては別個の三国協定中に適当なる条項を包含せしめ得べし。

四、日支通商条約

通商条約は当然他国の現存条約上の権利を保障しつつ能う限り日支両国間に於ける交易を増進し得べき条件の設定を目的とするものなるべし。本条約は支那人消費者の個人的権利を害することなく日本人の商業に対する組織的ボイコット運動を禁圧する為其の権限内に於ける一切の措置を講ずべき旨の支那政府による約定を包含すべし。

批判

前掲宣言及条約の対象に関する叙上の提議及考察は聯盟理事会に提出し其の考慮に供せらるべし。将来における協定の細目の如何に拘らず最も重きを置くべき点は交渉が与う限り速やかに開始せられ且相互信頼の精神によって行われるべきことなり。

吾人の任務は終了せり。

満州は過去一年間争闘及混乱に委せられたり。

広大、肥沃且豊穣なる満州の人民は恐らく嘗て経験したることなき悲惨なる状態に遭遇せり。

日支両国間の関係は仮装せる戦争関係にて将来に付いては憂慮に堪えざるものあり。

吾人は右の如き状態を創造せる事情に関し報告せり。

何人と雖も聯盟の遭遇せる問題の重要性及其の解決の困難に付充分了知する所なり。

吾人は其の報告を完了せんとする際新聞紙上において日支両国外務大臣の二個の声明を閲読せるが其の双方に付最も重大なる一転を抜粋すべし。

8月28日羅文幹は南京に於いて左の如く声明せり。

「支那は現事態の解決に対する如何なる合理的なる提案も聯盟規約、不戦条約及九国条約の条章及精神並びに支那の主権と両立すべきものたるを要し又極東に於ける永続的平和を有効に確保するものたるを要すと信ず。」

8月30日内田伯は東京に於いて左の如く声明せりと伝えらる。

「帝国政府は日支両国関係の問題は満蒙問題より更に重要なりと思

惟す。」

　吾人は本報告書を終了するに当り右両声明の基調を為す思想を再録するを以て最も適当と思考するものなり。右思想は吾人の蒐集せる証拠、問題に関する吾人の研究、従って吾人の確信と正確に対応するものにして吾人は右声明により表示せられたる政策が迅速且有効に実行せらるるに於ては必ずや極東に於ける二大国及人類一般の最善の利益に於て満州問題の満足なる解決を遂げ得べきを信ずるものなり。

索　引

图书在版编目(CIP)数据

国联调查团报告书 / 张生，陈海懿，杨骏编. —— 南
京：南京大学出版社，2019.12
(李顿调查团档案文献集 / 张生主编)
ISBN 978 - 7 - 305 - 08606 - 9

Ⅰ. ①国… Ⅱ. ①张… ②陈… ③杨… Ⅲ. ①李顿调
查团－九·一八事变－调查报告 Ⅳ. ①K264.2

中国版本图书馆 CIP 数据核字(2019)第 232099 号

项目统筹	杨金荣
装帧设计	清　早
印制监督	郭　欣

出版发行　南京大学出版社
社　　址　南京市汉口路 22 号　　　　　邮　编　210093
出 版 人　金鑫荣
丛 书 名　李顿调查团档案文献集
丛书主编　张　生
书　　名　国联调查团报告书
编　　者　张　生　陈海懿　杨　骏
责任编辑　张淑文　沈清清
照　　排　南京南琳图文制作有限公司
印　　刷　南京爱德印刷有限公司
开　　本　718×1000　1/16　印张 40.75　字数 667 千
版　　次　2019 年 12 月第 1 版　2019 年 12 月第 1 次印刷
ISBN 978 - 7 - 305 - 08606 - 9
定　　价　180.00 元

网址：http://www.njupco.com
官方微博：http://weibo.com/njupco
官方微信号：njupress
销售咨询热线：025 - 83594756

ISBN 978-7-305-08606-9

9 787305 086069 >

定价:180.00元